D0843183

A COMMENTARY ON I PETER

A Commentary on I Peter

Leonhard Goppelt

Edited by
Ferdinand Hahn

Translated and augmented by
John E. Alsup

WILLIAM B. EERDMANS PUBLISHING COMPANY
GRAND RAPIDS, MICHIGAN

First published as *Der erste Petrusbrief*
by Vandenhoeck & Ruprecht, Göttingen, Germany
Copyright © 1978 by Vandenhoeck & Ruprecht, Göttingen

First English edition copyright © 1993 by Wm. B. Eerdmans Publishing Co.
255 Jefferson Ave. S.E., Grand Rapids, Michigan 49503

Printed in the United States of America

Library of Congress Cataloging-in-Publication Data

Goppelt, Leonhard, 1911-1973.
[Erste Petrusbrief. English]
A commentary on I Peter / Leonhard Goppelt; edited by Ferdinand Hahn;
translated and augmented by John E. Alsup. — 1st English ed.
p.   cm.
Includes bibliographical references and indexes.
ISBN 0-8028-3719-0
1. Bible. N.T. Peter, 1st — Commentaries.   I. Hahn, Ferdinand, 1926-
II. Alsup, John E., 1941-   .   III. Title.   IV. Title: Commentary on First Peter.
BS2795.3.G6813   1993
227'.92077 — dc20
93-10865
CIP

Contents

TRANSLATION AND COMMENTARY

Translator's Preface

It has been over a decade now since Leonhard Goppelt's *Der Erste Petrusbrief* was published in the renowned Kritisch-exegetischer Kommentar (KEK) of Vandenhoeck and Ruprecht publishing house in Göttingen, Germany. As the eighth edition of this volume in that series it represented the overdue complete reworking of the material (R. Knopf's seventh edition was published in 1912) and for the first time allowed for a separation of this epistle from II Peter and Jude. The result was a methodologically up-to-date and theologically focused treatment of the subject matter. The general editor of the KEK and successor to Goppelt at the University of Munich, Ferdinand Hahn, was responsible for the posthumous publication of the volume and a bibliographical update to the year 1976 (with assistance from Jürgen Roloff and others).

Goppelt gave ample indication to those of us who studied with him that he believed I Peter to be of particular value to the world situation of the Christian community of our time. The minority position of Christian belief and life-style among the forces shaping our existence in today's world has many points of contact with the compositional situation of the epistle. This has perhaps become an even greater fact of life for us now in the '90s than it was at the time of Goppelt's unexpected death in 1973.

In some ways this volume is Goppelt's most mature work. As regards the text itself, it is the last monograph he was able to complete before he died (see Hahn's comments in the Foreword). In terms of its content one is struck by the author's sensitivity to the complex introductory questions and their far-reaching consequences, his broad grasp of comparative sources among the Church Fathers and in the history of religion, and his perspicacious integration of exegetical gleanings with practical and needful theological insights into the enduring substantive content of the epistle. For the reader it will become a truly helpful companion volume to his five other volumes now available in English (*Jesus, Paul, and Judaism in the First Three Centuries; Apostolic and Post-Apostolic Times; Typos: The Typological Interpretation of the Old Testament in the New; Theology of the New Testament* I and II; only his volume of collected essays, *Christologie und Ethik,* remains untranslated).

To assist the reader this English edition has been augmented in several ways. First, the bibliography has been updated to cover the last decade and a half of major studies on I Peter. In this connection mention should be made here of several essay volumes: *Études sur la Première Lettre de Pierre: Congrès de l'ACFEB,* ed. C. Perrot (Paris, 1980), represents a collection of articles presented in the context of a congress on I Peter held in Paris, 1979. While not an essay volume in the strict sense, *La première épître de Pierre: Analyse sémiotique,* by J. Calloud and F. Genuyt (Lectio Divina 109; Paris, 1982), represents the fruit of a structuralist approach to biblical interpretation coming from the 1978/79 I Peter seminar held at the Centre d'Analyse du Discours Religieux in Lyons. Volume 13 of *Theological Educator* (New Orleans, 1982) and volume 79 of *Review and Expositor* (Louisville, 1982) were devoted to I Peter. Most recently, the important collection of essays, *Perspectives on First Peter,* ed. C. H. Talbert (Macon, GA, 1986), was published with the contributors' hope that it might "serve alongside a commentary to facilitate the renewed investigation of this early Christian writing" (p. 2). The bibliographical contribution in this volume by Sylva (pp. 17-36) is very helpful. P. J. Achtemeier's essay ("Newborn Babes and Living Stones: Literal and Figurative in 1 Peter") in the Fitzmyer Festschrift *To Touch the Text* (New York, 1989), pp. 207-236 provides an excellent overview of the major areas of contemporary discussion in I Peter studies. Such works as these and articles from other sources have been integrated into the bibliography and footnotes. English-language resources and translations have been cited wherever possible both for major reference works (e.g., Kittel's *TDNT*) and ancient primary texts (e.g., the Loeb Classical Library). Wherever Goppelt referred to or cited a publication in German for which a published English translation exists the latter has been cited in this edition. And finally, my assessment of the life and works of L. Goppelt entitled "Leonhard Goppelt (1911-1973)" is offered — along with the dedication to his 1972 celebration volume — as an orientation for the reader unfamiliar with the author.

And yet, Goppelt on I Peter is to be discovered firsthand. Toward that end every effort has been made to help the reader come to his or her own appreciation of the stature of Goppelt as exegete and theologian and for I Peter as a timely word for our day. This book is, of course, a scholarly volume of the first order, but it is full of promise and is "user-friendly" for the beginning theological student as well. It offers a fresh translation of the text throughout, footnotes that offer basic bibliographical assistance on numerous points and fields of inquiry, references to ancient extrabiblical works in accessible (and where possible English language) editions, and informative, theologically thought-provoking special notes and excursuses.

In this translation I have followed the conventions of gender-inclusive language that best allow for readability. A special problem is the use of the masculine personal pronoun referring to God. I understand the function of the pronoun in this instance to be that of personalization to avoid abstraction and not of associating God with one sexual gender. Some choose — because of the latter association — to drop the pronoun altogether and to accept the possibility of abstraction; others adopt the cipher "Godself" in the hopes of retaining personalization. My choice has been to reduce the number of masculine personal pronouns and to substitute in these cases the name of God. Hopefully the reader will understand charitably that when the pronoun does occur it is a reference to the person of God and not to sexual gender.

Another difficult problem in this regard is I Peter's and Goppelt's use of the terms "brothers," "brotherhood," "brotherly love," etc. Neither use these terms in an exclusive sense — as though women were excluded from the Christian community. Adding "sister" or the like would be fine if we were not dealing with a technical term in the context of the eschatological community of God's new creation ("brotherly love" is contrasted with "neighborly love" and with the perspectives at Qumran). Since Goppelt himself makes it clear that in this community we have to do with "all baptized persons" of both genders (p. 84, n.22; pp. 120-121; p. 193 (#4); pp. 216ff.; cf. further remarks at p. 177 (#2); p. 189, n.53; pp. 225ff.; p. 230, n.3; pp. 232ff.; pp. 363-364; pp. 377-378, n.44), I have chosen not to diminish the technical term status of these words by further supplementation.

I gladly acknowledge the debt of thanks I owe to Abingdon Press and to John Hayes for permission to reprint my article on Goppelt in the appendix to this book. Special thanks is also expressed to Austin Presbyterian Theological Seminary for a generous sabbatical leave to work on this and other writing projects, to Ph.D. candidate Ms. Donna Key for incalculable assistance in searching the footnotes and text for English-language versions of the many references, and to my assistants Rev. Mike Wakeland, Ph.D. candidate Rev. Arch Baker, and Mark Love for preparation of the bibliographical update and the index and for their invaluable knowledge of computer use.

Georgetown, Texas   JOHN ALSUP

Foreword

In the last years of his life, Leonhard Goppelt focused his attention on two major works: his *Theology of the New Testament* and this *Commentary on I Peter.* In both cases he was not able to complete his work and deliver the manuscripts for publication. His *Theology of the New Testament* was edited by Jürgen Roloff from material that Goppelt left behind, while, as editor of the Kritisch-exegetischer Kommentar über das Neue Testament and successor to Goppelt's professorship at the University of Munich, I have prepared the commentary on I Peter for publication.

About one year before his death, Goppelt sent me an almost complete manuscript and requested a critical response. Because of his work on the New Testament theology and my own work load it was unfortunately impossible for us to discuss the commentary thoroughly before his unexpected death on December 21, 1973, after which it became my task to present the manuscript for publication on behalf of the author. I determined not to make any changes in content. Nevertheless, it was necessary to fit together parts that had been written at different times, to remove occasional repetitions, and to alter certain stylistic peculiarities which came about from the presentation of some of the material in lectures. Indeed, most of the sections in this book grew out of Goppelt's activity as teacher and were drawn together from notes into an initial version of the work, on which he had intended to make his own final revisions. The text of the interpretive commentary was complete. The Introduction had been written last, and only the two paragraphs on the canon history and text history of I Peter were missing. A much more arduous task was the completion of the footnotes. Here, to a great extent, the material had to be reexamined thoroughly, and above all much supplementation was necessary, since at numerous locations the references had not been filled out completely. Furthermore, important literature from 1973 or earlier to 1976 had to be added. It was necessary, moreover, for the entire manuscript to be tailored to the formal requirements of the commentary series.

In reworking the material I have received much assistance, without which the completion of the task simply would not have been possible. First, I thank Dora Goppelt of Tutzing for her advice and her willingness to read carefully the entire manuscript subsequent to my reworking of it. In a large number of instances she was able to clarify for me her husband's intention, which was often of considerable significance for the final formulation of a sentence. To my colleague Jürgen Roloff of the University of Erlangen, himself a student of Goppelt, I express thanks for the composition of the two missing sections in the Introduction and for assistance in compiling secondary literature on I Peter. I also owe special thanks to the three assistants in the Institute for New Testament Theology of the Ludwig Maximilian University of Munich, Dr. Hans Bald, Kurt Eschert, and Günter Unger, who worked through the entire manuscript with me, accepted the quite tedious assignment of supplementing the footnotes, saw to the supplemental bibliography and list of abbreviations, and shared in proofreading. Finally, several contract student assistant and secretaries of our Institute lent their assistance in matters of technical production; to all of them is expressed here hearty thanks.

May this book receive the recognition it is due as the legacy of an author who unfortunately died too soon. The theme dealt with programatically here, the conduct of Christians within the institutions of society, represents a fundamental concern of the life work of Leonhard Goppelt. In refining our understanding of the social-ethical views of primitive Christianity, he carried out a decisive contribution of the exegetical discipline to the theological problems of the present.

Munich, June 1, 1977   FERDINAND HAHN

Abbreviations

AAWLM.G	Abhandlungen der Akademie der Wissenschaften und der Literatur in Mainz. Geistes- und sozialwissenschaftliche Klasse
ABD	*Anchor Bible Dictionary* (ed. D. N. Freedman, et al.; New York, 1992)
ABR	*Australian Biblical Review*
AF	Apostolic Fathers
AnalBibl	Analecta Biblica
ANF	*The Ante-Nicene Fathers* (ed. A. Roberts, et al.; New York, 1885-1897)
AnglThR	*Anglican Theological Review*
AnnJapanBibInst	*Annual of the Japanese Biblical Institute*
Asc. Isa.	*Ascension of Isaiah*
ASNU	Acta Seminarii Neotestamentici Uppsaliensis
ASTI	*Annual of the Swedish Theological Institute in Jerusalem*
AThANT	Abhandlungen zur Theologie des Alten und Neuen Testaments
b.	Babylonian Talmud
BAGD	W. Bauer, W. F. Arndt, F. W. Gingrich, and F. Danker, *A Greek-English Lexicon of the New Testament and Other Early Christian Literature* (second ed., Chicago, 1979)
II, III Bar.	*II* (Syriac), *III* (Greek) *Baruch*
Barn.	*Epistle of Barnabas*
BBB	Bonner Biblische Beiträge
BDF	F. Blass, A. Debrunner, and R. W. Funk, *A Greek Grammar of the New Testament and Other Early Christian Literature* (Chicago, 1961)
BEvTh	Beiträge zur evangelischen Theologie

BFChrTh	Beiträge zur Förderung christlicher Theologie
BHH	*Biblisch-historisches Handwörterbuch* (ed. B. Reicke and L. Rost; Göttingen, 1962-1966)
BHTh	Beiträge zur historischen Theologie
Bibl	*Biblica*
BiblEphTheol-Lov	Bibliotheca Ephemeridum Theologicarum Lovaniensium
BibLiturg	*Bibel und Liturgie*
BiblSac	*Bibliotheca Sacra*
BibT	*The Bible Today*
BibThBull	*Biblical Theology Bulletin*
BibZeit	*Biblische Zeitschrift*
BiLe	*Bibel und Leben*
BT	*Bible Translator*
BWANT	Beiträge zur Wissenschaft vom Alten und Neuen Testament
BZ (NF)	*Biblische Zeitschrift* (Neue Folge)
BZNW	Beihefte zur Zeitschrift für die Neutestamentliche Wissenschaft
CBQ	*Catholic Biblical Quarterly*
CGT	Cambridge Greek Testament
CivCatt	*Civiltà Cattolica*
I, II Clem.	*I, II Clement*
CollTheol	*Collectanea Theologica*
ConcJ	*Concordia Journal*
CorpGlossLat	*Corpus Glossariorum Latinorum* (ed. G. Goetz, et al.; 1888-)
DBSuppl	*Dictionnaire de la Bible Supplément* (ed. L. Pirot, A. Robert, H. Cazelles, and A. Feuillet; Paris, 1929-)
Did.	*Didache*
Diogn.	*Epistle to Diognetus*
EcumRev	*Ecumenical Review*
EKK	Evangelisch-Katholischer Kommentar
I, II En.	*I* (Ethiopic), *II* (Slavonic) *Enoch*
Ep. Arist.	*Epistle of Aristeas*
ÉtudThéolRel	*Études Théologiques et Religieuses*
EuA	*Erbe und Auftrag*
EvTh	*Evangelische Theologie*
Exp	*Expositor*
ExpT	*The Expository Times*
FRLANT	Forschungen zur Religion und Literatur des Alten und Neuen Testaments

FrThSt	Frankfurter Theologische Studien
FS	Festschrift
GCS	Die griechischen christlichen Schriftsteller
Greg	*Gregorianum*
HarvThRev	*Harvard Theological Review*
HE	Eusebius, *Historia Ecclesiastica*
Herm.	*Shepherd of Hermas*
Mand.	*Mandates*
Sim.	*Similitudes*
Vis.	*Visions*
HeythJ	*Heythrop Journal*
HNT	Handbuch zum Neuen Testament
HThK	Herders Theologischer Kommentar
HUTh	Hermeneutische Untersuchungen zur Theologie
ICC	International Critical Commentary
Ignatius	
Eph.	*Ephesians*
Magn.	*Magnesians*
Phld.	*Philadelphians*
Pol.	*Polycarp*
Rom.	*Romans*
Smyr.	*Smyrnaeans*
Trall.	*Trallians*
Interp	*Interpretation*
JAC	*Jahrbuch für Antike und Christentum*
JBL	*Journal of Biblical Literature*
JEvThSoc	*Journal of the Evangelical Theological Society*
JStNT	*Journal for the Study of the New Testament*
JThC	*Journal for Theology and the Church*
JThSt (NS)	*Journal of Theological Studies* (New Series)
Jub.	*Jubilees*
KEK	Kritisch-exegetischer Kommentar über das Neue Testament
KuD	*Kerygma und Dogma*
LCL	Loeb Classical Library
LSJ	H. G. Liddell, R. Scott, H. S. Jones, and R. McKenzie, *A Greek-English Lexicon* (ninth ed., Cambridge, 1940)
LThK	*Lexikon für Theologie und Kirche* (ed. J. Höfer and K. Rahner; second ed., Freiburg, 1957-1967)
LXX	Septuagint (Greek Old Testament)
m.	Mishnah
Mart. Pol.	*Martyrdom of Polycarp*

MbThSt	Marburger theologische Studien
MélSciRel	*Mélanges de science religieuse*
MGWJ	*Monatsschrift für Geschichte und Wissenschaft des Judentums*
MPG	J.-P. Migne, *Patrologiae cursus completus. Series Graeca* (Paris, 1857-1868)
MPL	J.-P. Migne, *Patrologiae cursus completus. Series Latina* (Paris, 1844-1855, 1958-1975)
MüThSt	Münchener Theologische Studien
NF	Neue Folge (new series)
NovTest	*Novum Testamentum*
NPNF	*A Select Library of the Nicene and Post-Nicene Fathers of the Christian Church* (ed. P. Schaff, et al., New York, 1886-1900)
NRTh	*Nouvelle revue théologique*
NT	New Testament, Neues Testament
NTA	Neutestamentliche Abhandlungen
NT Apoc.	*New Testament Apocrypha* (ed. E. Hennecke and W. Schneemelcher, translation ed. R. McL. Wilson; 1965 [vol. II], 1991 [revised vol. I])
NTD	Neues Testament Deutsch
NTS	*New Testament Studies*
OCD	*The Oxford Classical Dictionary* (ed. H. G. L. Hammond and H. H. Scullard; second ed., Oxford, 1970)
Odes Sol.	*Odes of Solomon*
OT	Old Testament
OT Pseudep.	*The Old Testament Pseudepigrapha* (ed. J. H. Charlesworth; Garden City, NY, 1983, 1985)
Polycarp *Phil.*	*Philippians*
PRS	Perspectives in Religious Studies
Pss. Sol.	*Psalms of Solomon*
PSTJ	*Perkins School of Theology Journal*
PW	*Paulys Realencyklopädie der klassischen Altertumswissenschaft* (ed. G. Wissowa and W. Kroll; Stuttgart, 1893-)
RAC	*Reallexikon für Antike und Christentum* (ed. T. Klauser; Stuttgart, 1941-)
RE	*Realencyclopädie für Protestantische Theologie und Kirche* (third ed., Leipzig, 1896-1913)
RefTheolRev	*Reformed Theological Review*
RelStRev	*Religious Studies Review*

RestQ	*Restoration Quarterly*
RevBibl	*Revue Biblique*
RevExp	*Review and Expositor*
RevistBíb	*Revista Bíblica*
RevistCatTeol	*Revista Catalana de Teología*
RevRel	*Review for Religious*
RevThéolLouv	*Revue Théologique de Louvain*
RevThéolPhil	*Revue de Théologie et de Philosophie*
RGG	*Die Religion in Geschichte und Gegenwart* (ed. K. Galling, et al.; third ed., Tübingen, 1957-1962)
RHPhR	*Revue d'histoire et de philosophie religieuse*
RivistBib	*Rivista Biblica*
RoczTeolKan	*Roczniki Teologiczno-Kanoniczne*
RSV	Revised Standard Version
RVV	Religionsgeschichtliche Versuche und Vorarbeiten
SBLMS	Society of Biblical Literature Monograph Series
SBS	Stuttgarter Bibelstudien
SBT	Studies in Biblical Theology
ScienEcclés	*Sciences ecclésiastiques*
Script	*Scriptura*
Sib. Or.	*Sibylline Oracles*
SNTS Mon. Ser.	Studiorum Novi Testamenti Societas Monograph Series
StANT	Studien zum Alten und Neuen Testament
Str.-Bill.	(H. L. Strack and) P. Billerbeck, *Kommentar zum Neuen Testament aus Talmud und Midrasch* (Munich, 1922-1928)
StTh	*Studia Theologica*
StUNT	Studien zur Umwelt des Neuen Testaments
suppl.	supplement
SvExÅ	*Svensk Exegetisk Årsbok*
SWJTh	*Southwestern Journal of Theology*
t.	Tosefta
TDNT	*Theological Dictionary of the New Testament* (ed. G. Kittel and G. Friedrich, tr. G. Bromiley; Grand Rapids, 1964-1976)
Test. Ash.	*Testament of Asher*
Test. Benj.	*Testament of Benjamin*
Test. Gad	*Testament of Gad*
Test. Iss.	*Testament of Issachar*
Test. Jos.	*Testament of Joseph*
Test. Jud.	*Testament of Judah*
Test. Lev.	*Testament of Levi*

Test. Mos.	*Testament of Moses*
Test. Naph.	*Testament of Naphtali*
Test. Sim.	*Testament of Simeon*
Test. Zeb.	*Testament of Zebulun*
ThArb	Theologische Arbeiten
ThB	Theologische Bücherei
Them	*Themelios*
TheolEd	*Theological Educator*
TheolViat	*Theologia Viatorum*
ThLZ	*Theologische Literaturzeitung*
ThQ	*Theologische Quartralschrift*
ThR (NF)	*Theologische Rundschau* (Neue Folge)
ThSt	Theologische Studien
ThZ	*Theologische Zeitschrift*
TidsTeolKirk	*Tidskrift for teologi og kirke*
TrinJourn	*Trinity Journal*
TrThZ	*Trierer Theologische Zeitschrift*
TU	Texte und Untersuchungen zur Geschichte der altkirchlichen Literatur
TyndBull	*Tyndale Bulletin*
UnSemQuarRev	*Union Seminary Quarterly Review*
UNT	Untersuchungen zum Neuen Testament
VD	*Verbum Domini*
VetChrist	*Vetera Christianorum*
v.l.	varia lectio (variant reading)
VoxEv	*Vox evangelica*
VoxRef	*Vox Reformata*
VS	*Vie spirituelle*
WdF	Wege der Forschung
WestTheolJourn	*Westminster Theological Journal*
WMANT	Wissenschaftliche Monographien zum Alten und Neuen Testament
WUNT	Wissenschaftliche Untersuchungen zum Neuen Testament
ZKG	*Zeitschrift für Kirchengeschichte*
ZNW	*Zeitschrfit für die Neutestamentliche Wissenschaft und die Kunde der älteren Kirche*
ZsystTh	*Zeitschrift für systematische Theologie*
ZThK	*Zeitschrift für Theologie und Kirche*

Bibliography

Commentaries (in Chronological Order)

Ancient Church

Clement of Alexandria, "Adumbrationes in epistolas canonicas I. In epistola Petri prima," *GCS* 3, 203-206.

Ammonius of Alexandria, "Fragmentum in Primam S. Petri Epistolam," *MPG* 85, cols. 1607-1610.

Hesychius, "Fragmentum in epistolam I. S. Petri," *MPG* 93, cols. 1389-1390.

Ps.-Euthalius, "Elenchus capitum septem Epistolarum Catholicarum," *MPG* 85, cols. 679-682.

Didymus of Alexandria, "Enarratio in epistolas catholicas," *MPG 39,* cols. 1755-1772.

John Chrysostom, "Fragmenta in epistolas catholicas," *MPG* 64, cols. 1053-1058.

Jerome, "Divina Bibliotheca," *MPL* 29, cols. 877-882.

Cyril of Alexandria, "Fragmenta in epistolas catholicas," *MPG* 74, cols. 1011-1016.

Cassiodorus, "Complexiones in epistulis apostolorum," *MPL* 70, cols. 1361-1368.

Paterius, "Liber de expositione Veteris ac Novi Testamenti," *MPL* 79, cols. 1097-1100.

Luculentius, "In aliquot Novi Testamenti partes commentarii," *MPL* 72, cols. 857-860.

Ps.-Oecumenius, "Commentarii in epistolas catholicas," *MPG* 119, cols. 509-578.

Middle Ages

Ps.-Hilarius Arelatensis, "Expositio in epistolas catholicas," *MPL* Suppl. III, cols. 83-106.

Bede, the Venerable, "Super epistolas catholicas expositio," *MPL* 93, cols. 41-68.

Isho͑dad of Merv, *The Commentaries of Isho͑dad of Merv* (ed. and tr. M. D. Gibson). *Vol. IV: Acts of the Apostles and three Catholic Epistles in Syriac and English* (Horae Semiticae 10; Cambridge, 1913), 38f., 51-53.

Walafridus Strabo, "Glossa Ordinaria," *MPL* 114, cols. 679-688.

Ps.-Theophylact, "Expositio in Epistolam Primam S. Petri," *MPL* 125, cols. 1189-1252.

Alulfus, "De expositione Novi Testamenti," *MPL* 79, cols. 1385-1388.

Euthymius Zigabenus, *Commentarius in XIV Epistolas S. Pauli et VII Catholicas* II (ed. N. Kalogeras; Athens, 1887), 519-566.

Dionysius Bar Salibi, "In Apocalypsim, Actus et Epistulas catholicas," *Corpus scriptorum Christianorum orientalium. Scriptores Syri* II/101 (ed. I. Sedlaček; Paris, 1909-10), 134-147 (text), 103-113 (Latin translation).

Martinus Legionensis, "Expositio in epistolam I. B. Petri apostoli," *MPL* 209, cols. 217-252.

Gregorius Barhebraeus, *In Actus apostolorum et Epistulas catholicas adnotationes Syriace e recognitione M. Klamroth* (Göttingen, 1878), 27-29.

Pseudo-Thomas, *In septem epistolas canonicas* (Paris 1873-1882) XXXI, 368-398 (according to P. J. Perrier this was written by Nicolas de Gorran; cf. C. Spicq, *Esquisse d'une histoire de l'exégèse latine au moyen âge* [Paris, 1944], 299, n.6).

16th to 18th Centuries

Erasmus, D., *Paraphrases in N. Testamentum* (1516), *Opera Omnia* VII (Leiden, 1706), cols. 1081-1100.

Luther, M., *Epistel Sanct Petri gepredigt und ausgelegt* (Wittenberg, 1523), *D. Martin Luthers Werke. Kritische Gesamtausgabe* XII (Weimar, 1966), 259-399 = "Sermons on the First Epistle of St. Peter," tr. M. H. Bertram, *Luther's Works* XXX: *The Catholic Epistles* (ed. J. Pelikan and W. A. Hansen; St. Louis, 1967), 1-145. The 1523 sermons are combined with Luther's 1539 commentary in M. Luther, *The Epistles of St. Peter and St. Jude* (tr. and ed. J. N. Lenker; Minneapolis, 1904).

Butzer, M., tr., *Enarrationes Martini Lutheri in Epistolas D. Petri duas et Judae unam in quibus quidquid omnino ad Christianismum pertinet consumatissime digestum leges* (Strassburg, 1524).

Bullinger, H., "In D. Petri Apostoli Episolam Vtranque," *Heinrychi Bullingeri Commentarius* (Zurich, 1534).

Bibliander, T., *Richtige Harmonie der heiligen Schrifft Alten und Neuen Testamentes in 4 Theilen* (Güorlitz, 1705).

Calvin, J., "Commentarius in Epistolas Catholicas" (1551), *Joannis Calvini*

Opera Quae Supersunt Omnia LV (Corpus Reformatorum 83; Braunschweig, 1896), cols. 205-292 = *Calvin's New Testament Commentaries* XII (tr. W. B. Johnston, Grand Rapids, 1963), 227-323.

Coglerus, J., *In Epistolas Petri Commentarius* (Wittenberg, 1564).

Hessels, J., *In priorem B. Pauli apostoli ad Timotheum epistolam commentarius. . . . Alter item eiusdem authoris Commentarius in priorem B. Petri apostoli canonicam epistolam* (2 vols., Louvain, 1568).

Hemmingius, N., *Commentaria in omnes Epistolas Apostolorum . . . scripta, recognita, emendata et alicubi aucta* (Frankfurt, 1579), 667-708.

Aretius, B., *Commentarii in Domini nostri Jesu Christi Novum Testamentum* (Bern, 1607), 487-507.

Winckelmann, J., *Commentarii in utramque Epistolam Petri* (Wittenberg, 1608).

Serarius, N., *Prolegomena Bibliaca et Commentaria in omnes Epistolas Canonicas* (Paris, 1612).

Laurentius, J., *S. Apostoli Petri Epistola catholica prior, perpetuo commentario explicata . . .* (Campis, 1640).

Gerhard, J., *Commentarius super priorem . . . D. Petri Epistolam* (ed. J. E. Gerhard; Jena, 1641).

Parëus, D., *Commentarii in epistolas canonicas Jacobi, Petri et Judae* (ed. P. Parëus; Geneva, 1641), 180-237.

Schotanus, M., *Conciones in I. Epistolam Petri* (Franeker, 1644).

Amyraut, M., *Paraphrase sur les épîtres catholiques de saint Jacques, Pierre, Jean et Jude . . .* (Saumur, 1646).

Grotius, H., *Annotationum in Novum Testamentum pars tertia ac ultima* (Paris, 1650), 1-37.

Horneius, C., *In epistolam catholicam Sancti Apostoli Petri priorem expositio litteralis* (ed. J. Horneius; Braunschweig, 1654).

Crellius Francus, J., "Commentarius in I. epistolae Petri duo priora capita," *idem, Opera omnia exegetica, didactica et polemica* II (Freiburg, 1656), 269-284.

Gomarus, F., "In Priorem S. Petri Epistolam Explicatio," *idem, Opera Theologica Omnia* (Amsterdam, 1664), 679-705.

Estius, W., *In omnes beati Pauli et aliorum Apostolorum Epistolas commentaria* II (Paris, 1658), 1149-1201.

Calov, A., *Biblia Novi Testamenti illustrata* II (Dresden/Leipzig, 1673), 1463-1531.

Goltzius, D., *Schriftmatige verklaringe en toepassinge tot geestelijck gebrunyck, van de eerste (en tweede) algemeyne Sendbrief des apostels Petri* (Amsterdam, 1689-1691).

Antonides, T., *Schriftmässige Erklärung über den ersten allgemeinen Brieff des Heils. Apostels Simonis Petri . . . zu mehrer Erbauung ins Hochdeutsche übersetzet durch A. Plesken* (Bremen, 1700).

Alexandre, N., *Commentarius litteralis et moralis in omnes epistolas Sancti Pauli Apostoli et in VII epistolas catholicas* II (Rouen, 1710).

Laurentius, G. M., *Kurtze Erklärung des Ersten (u. andern) Briefs St. Petri. In Tabellen verfasset . . . Sammt angehängter kurtzen Paraphrasi* (Halle, 1716).

Streson, C., *Meditationes in I et II Epistolas Petri* (Amsterdam, 1717).

Calmeth, A., *Commentaire litteral sur tous les livres de l'Ancien et du Nouveau Testament* VIII (Paris, 1726), 794-831.

Lange, J., *Urim ac Thummim . . . seu exegesis epistolarum Petri ac Joannis* (Halle, 1712, 1734).

Alphen, H. S. van, *De eerste Algemeene sendbrief van den apostel Petrus, ontleedender wyse verklaard, en tot syn oogmerk toegepast* (Utrecht, 1734).

Bengel, J. A., *Gnomon of the New Testament* V (Philadelphia, 1860), 43-83 (Latin original 1742).

Benson, G., *A Paraphrase and Notes on the Seven (Commonly Called) Catholic Epistles* (London, 1749).

Wolf, J. C., *Curae philologicae et criticae in sanctorum apostolorum Jacobi, Petri, Judae et Joannis epistolas, hujusque Apocalypsin* (Amsterdam, 1752, reprinted 1962), 681-697.

Matthaei, C. F. von, *SS. Apostolorum septem Epistolae catholicae* (Riga, 1782).

Semler, J. S., *Paraphrasis in Epistolam I. Petri, cum latinae translationis varietate et multis notis* (Halle, 1783).

Pott, D. J., *Epistolae catholicae graece perpetua annotatione illustrate* (Göttingen, 1786).

Morus, S. F. N., *Praeletiones in Jacobi et Petri epistolas* (ed. C. A. Donat; Leipzig, 1794), 98-186.

19th Century

Augusti, J. C. W., *Die katholischen Briefe, neu übersetzt und erklärt mit Excursen und einleitenden Abhandlungen herausgegeben* (Lemgo, 1801-1808).

Hensler, C. G., *Der erste Brief des Apostels Petrus übersetzt und mit einem Kommentar versehen* (Sulzbach, 1813).

Hottinger, J. I., *Epistolae Jacobi atque Petri cum versione germanica et commentario latino* (Leipzig, 1815).

Eisenschmid, G. B., *Die Briefe des Apostels Petrus übersetzt, erläutert und mit erbaulichen Betrachtungen begleitet* (Ronneberg, 1824).

Steiger, W., *Der Erste Brief Petri mit Berücksichtigung des ganzen biblischen Lehrbegriffes ausgelegt* (Berlin, 1832).

Mayerhoff, E. T., *Historisch-critische Einleitung in die petrinischen Schriften* (Hamburg, 1835).

Jachmann, K. R., *Commentar über die Katholischen Briefe mit genauer Berücksichtigung der neuesten Auslegungen* (Leipzig, 1838).

Cramer, J. A., *Catenae graecorum patrum in Novum Testamentum* VIII (Oxford, 1844), 41-83.

de Wette, W. M. L., "Kurze Erklärung der Briefe des Petrus, Judas und Jakobus," idem, *Kurzgefaßtes exegetisches Handbuch zum Neuen Testament* III/1 (Leipzig, 1847; third ed., 1885).

Alford, H., *The Greek Testament* IV/1: *The Epistle to the Hebrews, the Catholic Epistles of St. James and St. Peter* (London, 1849).

Huther, J. E., *Critical and Exegetical Handbook to the General Epistles of James, Peter, John and Jude* (tr. P. J. Gloag and C. H. Irvin; New York, 1887; German original, 1851; fourth ed., 1877).

Wiesinger, A., *Der Erste Brief des Apostels Petrus* (Olshausens Commentar über sämtliche Schriften des Neuen Testaments 6/2; Königsberg, 1856).

Fronmüller, G. F. C., *Die Briefe Petri und der Brief Judä* (J. P. Lange's Theologisch-homiletisches Bibelwerk 14; Bielefeld, 1859; fourth ed., 1890); translated and augmented by J. I. Mombert in *Commentary on the Holy Scriptures, Critical, Doctrinal, and Homiletical* (ed. P. Schaff; reprinted Grand Rapids, 1960) IX/1.

Schott, T., *Der Erste Brief Petri erklärt* (Erlangen, 1861).

Ewald, J., *Sieben Sendschreiben des neuen Bundes übersetzt und erklärt* (Göttingen, 1870).

Bisping, A., "Erklärung der sieben katholischen Briefe," idem, *Exegetisches Handbuch zum Neuen Testament* VIII (Münster, 1871).

Hofmann, J. C. K. von, "Der erste Brief Petri," idem, *Die Heilige Schrift Neuen Testaments zusammenhängend untersucht* VII/1 (Nördlingen, 1875).

Camerlynck, A., *Commentarius in Epistolas catholicas* (Brügge, 1876; fifth ed., 1909).

Keil, C. F., *Kommentar über die Briefe des Petrus und Judas* (Leipzig, 1883).

Usteri, J. M., *Wissenschaftlicher und praktischer Commentar über den ersten Petrusbrief* (Zurich, 1887).

Johnstons, R., *The First Epistle of Peter* (Edinburgh, 1888).

Burger, K., *Der erste Brief Petri* (Strack-Zöcklers kurzgefaßter Kommentar über das NT 4; Nördlingen, 1888).

Goebel, S., *Die Briefe des Petrus, griechisch, mit kurzer Erklärung* (Gotha, 1893).

Beck, J. T., *Erklärung der Briefe Petri* (ed. J. Lindenmeyer; Gütersloh, 1896).

Kühl, R., *Die Briefe Petri und Judä* (KEK 12; fifth ed., Göttingen, 1887; sixth ed., 1897).

von Soden, H., *Hebräerbrief, Briefe des Petrus, Jakobus, Judas* (Hand-Commentar zum NT 3/2; Freiburg/Leipzig, 1890; third ed., 1899).

Hort, F. J. A., *The First Epistle of St. Peter I.1–II.17* (London, 1898).

20th Century

Monnier, J., *La première épître de l'Apôtre Pierre* (Macon, 1900).

Bennett, W. H., *The General Epistles* (Century Bible; Edinburgh/New York, 1901).

Bigg, C. A., *The Epistles of St. Peter and St. Jude* (ICC; Edinburgh, 1901; second ed., 1902).

Kelly, W., *The Epistles of Peter* (London, 1904/06; second ed., 1923).

Calmes, T., *Les épîtres catholiques, L'Apocalypse* (Paris, 1905).

Gunkel, H., *Der erste Brief des Petrus* (Die Schriften des Neuen Testament 2, ed. J. Weiss; Göttingen, 1906; third ed., 1917 [vol. 3]).

Windisch, H., *Die katholischen Briefe* (HNT 15; Tübingen, 1911, second ed., 1930; third ed., reworked by H. Preisker, 1951).

Knopf, R., *Die Briefe Petri und Judä* (KEK 12; seventh ed., Göttingen, 1912).

Blenkin, G. W., *The First Epistle General of Peter* (CGT; Cambridge, 1914).

Vrede, W., "Der erste Petrusbrief," M. Meinertz and W. Vrede, *Die katholischen Briefe* (Die heilige Schrift des Neuen Testaments, Bonner NT 9; Bonn, 1915; fifth ed. 1932).

Wohlenberg, G., *Der erste und zweite Petrusbrief und der Judasbrief* (Kommentar zum NT 15, ed. T. Zahn; Leipzig/Erlangen, 1915; third ed., 1923).

Schlatter, A., "Die Briefe des Petrus, Judas, Jakobus, der Brief an die Hebräer, die Briefe und die Offenbarung des Johannes," *idem, Erläuterungen zum NT* III (Stuttgart, 1921; fourth ed., 1928).

Holtzmann, O., "Die Petrusbriefe," *idem, Das Neue Testament* II (Giessen, 1926).

Moffatt, J., *The General Epistles: James, Peter, and Jude* (The Moffatt New Testament Commentary; London, 1928; eighth ed., 1963).

Felten, J., *Die zwei Briefe des hl. Petrus und der Judasbrief* (Regensburg, 1929).

Rendtorff, H., *Getrostes Wandern. Eine Einführung in den ersten Brief des Petrus* (Die urchristliche Botschaft 20; Berlin, 1929; seventh ed., Hamburg, 1951).

Beelen, J. T., and A. van der Heeren, *De Katholieke Brieven* (Brügge, 1932).

Greijdanus, S., *Petrus, Johan en Judas* (Commentaar op het Nieuwe Testament 13; Amsterdam, 1933).

Wand, J. W. C., *The General Epistles of St. Peter and St. Jude* (Westminster Commentaries; London, 1934).

Hauck, F., *Die Briefe des Jakobus, Petrus, Judas und Johannes* (NTD 10: *Die Kirchenbriefe*; Göttingen, 1936; eighth ed., 1957).

Holzmeister, U., *Epistula prima S. Petri Apostoli* (Cursus Scripturae Sacrae; Paris, 1937).

Charue, A., *Les épîtres catholiques* (La Sainte Bible 12; Paris, 1938; third ed., 1951).

Lenski, R. C. H., *The Interpretation of the Epistles of St. Peter, St. John and St. Jude* (Columbus, 1938).

Lilje, H., *Die Petrusbriefe und der Judasbrief* (Bibelhilfe für die Gemeinde, Neutestamentliche Reihe 14; Leipzig, 1938).

Staffelbach, G., *Die Briefe der Apostel Jakobus, Judas, Petrus und Johannes* (Lucerne, 1941).

Schweizer, E., *Der erste Petrusbriefe* (Zürcher Bibelkommentare [Prophezei]; Zurich, 1942; third ed., 1972).

Pury, R. de, *Ein Petrusbrief in der Gefängniszelle* (tr. V. D. M. H. Roth; Zollikon-Zurich, 1944).

Keulers, J., *De Katholieke Brieven en het Boek der Openbaring* (De boeken van het Nieuwe Testament 7; Roermond, 1946).

Selwyn, E. G., *The First Epistle of St. Peter* (London, 1946; second ed., 1947).

Ambroggi, P. de, *Le Epistole cattoliche* (La Sacra Bibbia 14/1; Turin/Rome, 1947; second ed., 1949).

Brun, L., *Forste Peters-Brev* (Oslo, 1949).

Ketter, P., *Hebräerbrief, Jakobusbrief, Petrusbriefe, Judasbrief* (Die Heilige Schrift für das Leben erklärt 16/1; Freiburg, 1950).

Preisker, H., appendix in H. Windisch, *Die Katholischen Briefe* (HNT 15; third ed., Tübingen, 1951), 152-162.

Leconte, R., *Les épîtres catholiques* (La Sainte Bible de Jerusalem; Paris, 1953).

Michl, J., *Die katholischen Briefe* (Regensburger Neues Testament 8/2; Regensburg, 1953; third ed., 1968).

Stöger, A., *Bauleute Gottes. Der 1. Petrusbrief als Grundlegung des Laienapostolats* (Lebendiges Wort 3; Munich, 1954).

ΤΡΕΜΠΕΛΑ, Π. Ν., Ὑπόμνημα εἰς τὰς ἐπίστολας τῆς καινῆς διαθήκης, III: Ἡ πρὸς Ἐβραίους καὶ αἱ ἑπτὰ καθολικαί (Athens, 1956).

Hunter, A. M., and E. G. Homrighausen, "The First Epistle of Peter," *Interpreter's Bible* (ed. G. A. Buttrick, et al.; New York/Nashville, 1957) XII, 75-159.

Beare, F. W., *The First Epistle of Peter* (first ed., Chicago, 1945; third ed., Oxford, 1970 [cited]).

Diaz, R. M., *Epistoles Católiques* (Montserrat, 1958).

Vaccari, A., *Le Lettere cattoliche* (La Sacra Bibbia 9; Rome, 1958).

Reuss, J., *Die Katholischen Briefe* (Die Heilige Schrift in deutscher übersetzung, Echter Bibel, Neutestamentliche Reihe; Würzburg, 1959).

Stibbs, A. M., and A. F. Walls, *The First Epistle General of Peter* (Tyndale New Testament Commentaries; London, 1959).

Cranfield, C. E. B., *I and II Peter and Jude* (Torch Bible Commentaries; London, 1960/New York, 1961; cf. *idem, The First Epistle of Peter* [London, 1950]).

Margot, J. C., *Les épîtres de Pierre* (Geneva, 1960).

Schelke, K. H., *Die Petrusbriefe. Der Judasbrief* (HThK 13/2; Freiburg/ Basel/Vienna, 1961; third ed., 1970).

Schneider, J., *Die Briefe des Jakobus, Petrus, Judas und Johannes* (NTD 9/10; Göttingen, 1961; second ed., 1967).

Gourbillon, J. G., and F. M. Buit, *La première épître de S. Pierre* (Paris, 1963).

Reicke, B., *The Epistles of James, Peter and Jude* (Anchor Bible; Garden City, NY, 1964).

Salguero, J., *Epistolas Catolicas* (Madrid, 1965).

Spicq, C., *Les épîtres de Saint Pierre* (Sources bibliques; Paris, 1966).

Leaney, A. R. C., *The Letters of Peter and Jude* (Cambridge Bible Commentary; Cambridge, 1967).

Kelly, J. N. D., *A Commentary on the Epistles of Peter and of Jude* (Black's/Harper's New Testament Commentaries; London/New York, 1969).

Schiwy, G., *Weg ins NT. Kommentar und Material* IV: *Nachpaulinen* (Würzburg, 1970).

Best, E., *I Peter* (New Century Bible; London, 1971).

Schrage, W., "Der erste Petrusbrief," H. Balz and W. Schrage, *Die katholischen Briefe* (NTD 11/10; Göttingen, 1973), 59-117.

Brox, N., *Der Erste Petrusbrief* (Evangelisch-Katholischer Kommentar zum Neuen Testament 21; Zurich-Einsiedeln-Cologne, 1979).

Elliott, J. H., *I-II Peter/Jude (with James* by R. A. Martin; Augsburg Commentaries on the New Testament; Minneapolis, 1982).

Bénétreaux, S., *La première épître de Pierre* (Commentaire Evangélique de la Bible 1; Vaux-sur-Seine, 1984).

Frankemölle, H., *1. Petrusbrief. 2. Petrusbrief. Judasbrief* (Würzburg, 1987).

Grudem, W. A., *The First Epistle of Peter: An Introduction and Commentary* (Tyndale New Testament Commentaries 17; Grand Rapids, 1988).

Michaels, J. R., *1 Peter* (Word Biblical Commentaries 49; Waco, 1988).

Davids, P. H., *The First Epistle of Peter* (New International Commentary on the New Testament; Grand Rapids, 1990).

SPECIAL STUDIES

Aalen, S., "Oversettelsen av ordet ἐπερώτημα i dapstedet 1 Pet 3, 21," *TidsTeolKirk* 43 (1972), 161-175.

Achtemeier, P. J., "Newborn Babes and Living Stones: Literal and Figurative in 1 Peter," *To Touch the Text* (FS J. A. Fitzmyer, ed. M. P. Horgan and P. J. Kobelski; New York, 1989), 207-236.

Adinolfi, M., *La prima lettera di Pietro nel mondo greco-romano* (Rome, 1988).

Agnew, F. H., "I Peter 1:2 — An Alternative Translation," *CBQ* 45 (1983), 68-73.

Andrianopoli, L., *Il mistero di Gesù nelle lettere di San Pietro* (Turin, 1935).

Applegate, J. K., "The Co-Elect Woman of I Peter," *NTS* 38 (1992), 587-604.

Arvedson, T., "Syneideseos agathes eperotema (1 Petr 3,21)," *SvExÅ* 15 (1950), 55-61.

Ashcraft, M., "Theological Themes in I Peter," *TheolEd* 13 (1982), 55-62.

Balch, D. L., *Let Wives Be Submissive: The Domestic Code in I Peter*. (SBLMS 26; Chico, CA, 1981). (Cf. review by A. C. Wire, *RelStRev* 10 [1984], 209-216).

————, "Early Christian Criticism of Patriarchal Authority: I Peter 2:11–3:12," *UnSemQuartRev* 39 (1984), 161-173.

————, "Hellenization/Acculturation in 1 Peter," *Perspectives on First Peter* (ed. C. Talbert; Macon, 1986), 79-101.

Baltensweiler, H., *Die Ehe im Neuen Testament. Exegetische Untersuchungen über Ehe, Ehelosigkeit und Ehescheidung* (AThANT 52; Zurich/Stuttgart, 1967).

Bammel, E., "The Commands in I Peter ii.17," *NTS* 11 (1964/65), 279-281.

Barrow, R. H., *Slavery in the Roman Empire* (New York, 1968).

Bauer, J., "Aut maleficus aut alieni speculator (1 Petr 4,15)," *BibZeit* 22 (1978), 109-115.

Beare, F. W., "The Teaching of First Peter," *AnglThR* 26 (1944/45), 284-296.

Beasley-Murray, G. R., *Baptism in the New Testament* (London, 1962).

Best, E., "Spiritual Sacrifice. General Priesthood in the New Testament," *Interp* 14 (1960), 273-299.

————, "I Peter II,4-10 — a Reconsideration," *NovTest* 11 (1969), 270-293.

————, "I Peter and the Gospel Tradition," *NTS* 16 (1969/70), 95-113.

Betz, O., "Felsenmann und Felsengemeinde (Parallelen zu Mt 16,17-19 in den Qumranpsalmen)," *ZNW* 48 (1957), 49-77.

Bieder, W., *Die Vorstellung von der Höllenfahrt Jesu Christi. Beitrag zur Entstehungsgeschichte der Vorstellung vom sog. Descensus ad inferos* (AThANT 19; Zurich, 1949).

————, *Grund und Kraft der Mission nach dem 1. Petrusbrief* (ThSt 29; Zurich, 1950).

Bishop, E. F., "Oligoi in 1 Peter 3:20," *CBQ* 13 (1951), 44-45.

Blevins, J. L., "Introduction to 1 Peter," *RevExp* 79 (1982), 401-413.

Blinzler, J., "IEPATEYMA. Zur Exegese von 1 Petr 2,5 u. 9," *Episcopus* (FS M. Kardinal v. Faulhaber; Regensburg, 1949), 49-65.

Boismard, M.-É. "Une liturgie baptismale dans la Prima Petri," *RevBibl* 63 (1956), 182-208; 64 (1957), 161-183.

————, *Quatre hymnes baptismales dans la première épître de Pierre* (Lectio Divina 30; Paris, 1961).

————, "Pierre (Première épître de)," *DBSuppl* 7 (1966), cols. 1415-1455.

Bolkestein, M. H., "De Kerk in haar vreemdelingschap volgens de eerste brief van Petrus," *Nieuwe Theologische Studien* 25 (1942), 181-194.

Bonnard, P., *Jesus Christ édifiant son église. Le concept d'édification dans le Nouveau Testament* (third ed., Paris, 1948).

Borchert, G. L., "The Conduct of Christians in the Face of the 'Fiery Ordeal' (4:12–5:11)," *RevExp* 79 (1982), 451-462.

Bornemann, W., "Der erste Petrusbrief — eine Taufrede des Silvanus?" *ZNW* 19 (1919/20), 143-165.

Botha, J., "Christian and Society in 1 Peter: Critical Solidarity," *Script* 24 (1988), 27-37.

Bousset, W., "Zur Hadesfahrt Christi," *ZNW* 19 (1919/20), 50-66.

Bovon, F., "Foi chrétienne et religion populaire dans la première Épître de Pierre," *ÉtudThéolRel* 53 (1978), 25-41.

Brandt, W., "Wandel als Zeugnis nach dem 1. Petrusbrief," *Verbum Dei manet in aeternum* (FS O. Schmitz; Witten, 1953), 10-25.

Brooks, O. S., "I Peter 3,21 — The Clue to the Literary Structure of the Epistle," *NovTest* 16 (1974), 290-305.

Brown, J. P., "Synoptic Parallels in the Epistles and Form-History," *NTS* (1963/64), 27-48.

Brown, R. E., K. P. Donfried, and J. Reumann, ed., *Peter in the New Testament: A Collaborative Assessment by Protestant and Roman Catholic Scholars* (Minneapolis, 1973).

Brox, N., *Zeuge und Märtyrer. Untersuchungen zur frühchristlichen Zeugnis-Terminologie* (StANT 5; Munich, 1961).

————, "Zur pseudepigraphischen Rahmung des ersten Petrusbriefes," *BZ* 19 (1975), 78-96.

————, "Situation und Sprache der Minderheit im ersten Petrusbrief," *Kairos* 19 (1977), 1-13.

————, "Tendenz und Pseudepigraphie im ersten Petrusbrief," *Kairos* 20 (1978), 110-120.

————, "Der erste Petrusbrief in der literarischen Tradition des Urchristentums," *Kairos* 20 (1978), 182-192.

Bultmann, R., "Bekenntnis- und Liedfragmente im ersten Petrusbrief," *idem, Exegetica* (Tübingen, 1967), 285-297.

Calloud, J., and F. Genuyt, *La première épître de Pierre: Analyse sémiotique* (Lectio Divina 109; Paris, 1982).

Carrington, P., "Saint Peter's Epistle," *The Joy of Study* (FS F. C. Grant, ed. S. E. Johnson; New York, 1951), 57-63.

Cerfaux, L., "Regale sacerdotium," *Recueil Lucien Cerfaux II* (BiblEphThLov 7; Gembloux, 1954), 283-315.

Chevallier, M.-A., "I Pierre 1,1 à 2,10. Structure littéraire et conséquences exégétiques," *RHPhR* 51 (1971), 129-142.

Clark, S. D., "Persecution and the Christian Faith," *TheolEd* 13 (1982), 72-82.

Colecchia, L. F., "Rilievi su 1 Piet. 2,4-10," *RevistBíb* 25 (1977), 179-194.

Cook, D., "I Peter iii.20: An Unnecessary Problem," *JThSt* 31 (1980), 72-78.

Coppens, J., "Le sacerdoce royal des fidèles: Un commentaire de I Petri II,4-10," *Au service de la parole de Dieu* (FS A. M. Charue; Gembloux, 1969), 61-75.

Cothenet, É., "Liturgie et vie chrétienne d'après I Pierre," *Conférences Sain-Serge* (Rome), 25 (1979), 97-113.

————, "Le réalisme de l'espérance chrétienne selon I Pierre," *NTS* 27 (1981), 564-572.

Coutts, J., "Ephesians I.3-14 and I Peter I.3-12," *NTS* 3 (1956/57), 115-127.

Cranfield, C. E. B., "The Interpretation of I Peter 3,19 and 4,6," *ExpT* 62 (1957/58), 369-372 (= *idem, The Bible and Christian Life* [Edinburgh, 1985], 176-186).

Crouch, J. E., *The Origin and Intention of the Colossian Haustafel* (FRLANT 109; Göttingen, 1972).

Cross, F. L., *I Peter. A Paschal Liturgy* (second ed., London, 1957).

Cullmann, O., *Peter: Disciple, Apostle, Martyr: A Historical and Theological Study* (tr. F. Filson; London, 1953).

————, *The State in the NT* (tr. S. Currie; New York, 1956).

Dalton, W. J., *Christ's Proclamation to the Spirits. A Study of 1 Peter 3:18–4:6* (AnalBibl 23; second ed., Rome, 1989).

————, "Interpretation and Tradition: An Example from I Peter," *Greg* 49 (1968), 11-37.

————, "The Interpretation of I Peter 3:19 and 4:6: Light from II Peter," *Bibl* 60 (1979), 547-555.

————, "The Church in 1 Peter," *Tantur Yearbook* (Jerusalem, 1981/82), 79-91.

————, "1 Peter 3:19 Reconsidered," *The New Testament Age,* Vol. I (FS Bo Reicke, ed. W. C. Weinrich; Macon, GA, 1984), 95-105.

Daniélou, J., *Sacramentum Futuri. Études sur les origines de la typologie biblique* (Paris, 1950).

Danker, F. W., "I Peter 1,24–2,17 — A Consolatory Pericope," *ZNW* 58 (1967), 93-102.

Daube, D., "Κεϱδαίνω as a Missionary Term," *HarvThRev* 40 (1947), 109-120.

————, "Participle and Imperative in I Peter," in E. G. Selwyn, *The First Epistle of St. Peter* (second ed., London, 1947), 467-488.

Dautzenberg, G., "Σωτηρία ψυχῶν (1 Petr 1,9)," *BZ* 8 (1964), 262-276.

Davies, P. E., "Primitive Christology in I Peter," *Festschrift to Honor F. W. Gingrich* (ed. E. H. Barth and R. E. Cocraft; Leiden, 1972), 115-122.

Deichgräber, R., *Gotteshymnus und Christushymnus in der frühen Christenheit* (StUNT 6; Göttingen, 1967).

Delling, G., *Römer 13,1-7 innerhalb der Briefe des Neuen Testaments* (Berlin, 1962).

————, *Die Taufe im Neuen Testament* (Berlin, 1963), 82-89.

————, "Der Bezug der christlichen Existenz auf das Heilshandeln Gottes nach dem ersten Petrusbrief," *Neues Testament und christliche Existenz* (FS H. Braun; Tübingen, 1973), 95-113.

Deterding, P. E., "Exodus Motifs in First Peter," *ConcJ* 7 (1981), 58-65.

Dey, J., ΠΑΛΙΓΓΕΝΕΣΙΑ. *Ein Beitrag zur Klärung der religionsgeschichtlichen Deutung von Tit 3,5* (NTA 17/5; Münster, 1937).

Dibelius, M., "Rom und die Christen im ersten Jahrhundert," *idem, Botschaft und Geschichte* II (Tübingen, 1956), 177-228.

Dieterich, A., *Nekyia. Beiträge zur Klärung der neuentdeckten Petrusapokalypse* (second ed., Leipzig/Berlin, 1913).

Dijkman, J. H. L., "1 Peter: A Later Pastoral Stratum?" *NTS* 33 (1987), 265-271.

Dinkler, E., "Die Petrus-Rom-Frage. Ein Forschungsbericht" I-IV, *ThR* NF 25 (1959), 189-230, 289-335; 27 (1961), 33-64; 31 (1965/66), 232-253.

————, "Die Taufaussagen des Neuen Testaments," *Zu Karl Barths Lehre von der Taufe* (ed. F. Viering; Gütersloh, 1971), 60-153.

Downing, F. G., "Pliny's Prosecutions of Christians: Revelation and I Peter," *JStNT* 34 (1988), 105-123.

Dunn, J. D. G., *Baptism in the Holy Spirit* (StBiblTh 2/15; London, 1970).

Elliott, J. H., *The Elect and the Holy. An Exegetical Examination of I Peter 2:4-10 and the Phrase Βασίλειον ἱεράτευμα* (NovTest Suppl. 12; Leiden, 1966).

————, "Ministry and Church Order in the New Testament: A Traditio-Historical Analysis (1 Pt 5,1-5 & plls.)," *CBQ* 32 (1970), 367-391.

————, "The Rehabilitation of an Exegetical Step-Child: 1 Peter in Recent Research," *JBL* 95 (1976), 243-254 (= *Perspectives on First Peter* [ed. C. Talbert; Macon, 1986], 3-16).

————, *1 Peter. Estrangement and Community* (Herald Biblical Booklets; Chicago, 1979).

————, *A Home for the Homeless: A Sociological Exegesis of I Peter, Its Situation and Strategy* (Philadelphia, 1981). (Cf. reviews by B. Olsson, *SvExÅ* 49 [1984], 89-108; A. C. Wire, *RelStRev* 10 [1984], 209-216).

————, "Salutation and Exhortation to Christian Behavior on the Basis of God's Blessings (1:1–2:10)," *RevExp* 79 (1982), 415-425.

————, "Backward and Forward 'In His Steps': Following Jesus from Rome to Raymond and Beyond. The Tradition, Redaction, and Reception of 1 Peter 2:18-25," *Discipleship in the New Testament* (ed. F. F. Segovia; Philadelphia, 1985), 184-208.

————, "1 Peter, Its Situation and Strategy: A Discussion with David Balch," *Perspectives on First Peter* (ed. C. Talbert; Macon, 1986), 61-78.

————, "First Epistle of Peter," *ABD* V, 269-278.

Ellul, D., "Un Exemple de Cheminement Rhétorique: 1 Pierre," *RHPhR* 70 (1990), 17-34.

Evang, M., "'Εκ καρδίας ἀλλήλους ἀγαπήσατε ἐκτενῶς. Zum Verständnis der Aufforderung und ihrer Begründung in 1 Petr 1,22f," *ZNW* 80 (1989), 111-123.

Fascher, E., "Petrus," *Sokrates und Christus. Beiträge zur Religionsgeschichte* (Leipzig, 1959), 175-244 (= PW XXXVIII [1938], cols. 1335-1361).

Feinberg, J. S., "1 Peter 3:18-20, Ancient Mythology, and the Intermediate State," *WestTheolJourn* 48 (1986), 303-336.

Feuillet, A., "Les 'sacrifices spirituelles' du sacerdoce royal des baptisés (1 P 2,5), et leur préparation dans l'Ancien Testament," *NRTh* 96 (1974), 704-728.

Filson, F. V., "Partakers with Christ. Suffering in First Peter," *Interp* 9 (1955), 400-412.

Finley, M. I., *Slavery in Classical Antiquity* (Cambridge, 1960).

Fridrichsen, A., "I Peter 3,7," *SvExÅ* 12 (1947), 143-147.

Furnish, V. P., "Elect Sojourners in Christ: An Approach to the Theology of I Peter," *PSTJ* 28 (1975), 1-11.

Galot, J., "La vittoria di Cristo sulla morte," *CivCatt* 138 (1987), 118-131.

Gamba, G. G., "L'Evangelista Marco Segretario-'Interprete' della prima lettera di Pietro?" *Salesianum* 44 (1982), 61-70.

Gärtner, B., *The Temple and the Community in Qumran and the New Testament* (SNTS Mon. Ser. 1; Cambridge, 1965).

Gewalt, D., *Petrus* (dissertation, Heidelberg, 1966); cf. *ThLZ* 94 (1969), cols. 628f.

Ghiberti, G., "Le 'sante donne' di una volta (1 Pt 3,5)," *RevistBíb* 36 (1988), 287-297.

Glaze, R. E., "Introduction to 1 Peter," *TheolEd* 13 (1982), 23-34.

Goldstein, H., "Die politischen Paränesen in 1 Petr 2 und Röm 13," *BiLe* 14 (1973), 88-104.

Goppelt, L., "Wiedergeburt II," *RGG* VI (1962), cols. 1697-1699.

————, *Apostolic and Post-Apostolic Times* (tr. R. A. Guelich; Grand Rapids, 1970).

————, "Die Freiheit zur Kaisersteuer. Zu Mk 12,17 und Röm 13,1-7," *idem, Christologie und Ethik* (Göttingen, 1968), 208-219.

————, "Der Staat in der Sicht des Neuen Testaments," *idem, Christologie und Ethik* (Göttingen, 1968), 190-207.

————, "Prinzipien neutestamentlicher Sozialethik nach dem 1. Petrusbrief," *Neues Testament und Geschichte* (FS O. Cullmann; Zurich/Tübingen 1972), 285-296.

————, "Jesus und die 'Haustafel' Tradition," *Orientierung an Jesus* (FS J. Schmid; Freiburg, 1973), 93-106.

————, *Theology of the New Testament* (tr. J. E. Alsup; Grand Rapids, 1981-1982).

————, *Typos. The Typological Interpretation of the Old Testament in the New* (tr. D. Madvig; Grand Rapids, 1981).

Green, G. L., "The Use of the Old Testament for Christian Ethics in I Peter," *TyndBull* 41 (1990), 276-289.

Grillmeier, A., "Der Gottessohn im Totenreich. Soteriologische und christologische Motivierung der Descensuslehre in der älteren christlichen Überlieferung," *idem, Mit ihm und in ihm. Christologische Forschungen und Perspektiven* (Freiburg, 1975), 76-174.

Gross, C. D., "Are the Wives of I Peter 3:7 Christians?" *JStNT* 35 (1989), 89-96.

Grudem, W., "Christ Preaching Through Noah: 1 Peter 3:19-20 in the Light of Dominant Themes in Jewish Literature," *TrinJourn* 7 (1986), 3-31.

Gschnitzer, F., *Studien zur griechischen Terminologie der Sklaverei* (AAWLM.G; Wiesbaden, 1964).

Gschwind, K., *Die Niederfahrt Christi in die Unterwelt. Ein Beitrag zur Exegese des Neuen Testaments und zur Geschichte des Taufsymbols* (NTA 2/3-5; Münster, 1911).

Gülzow, H., *Christentum und Sklaverei in den ersten drei Jahrhunderten* (Bonn, 1969).

Gundry, R. H., " 'Verba Christi' in I Peter: Their Implications concerning the Authorship of I Peter and the Authenticity of the Gospel Tradition," *NTS* 13 (1966/67), 336-350.

————, "Further Verba on *Verba Christi* in First Peter," *Bibl* 55 (1974), 211-232.

Hagner, D. A., *The Use of the Old and New Testaments in Clement of Rome* (Leiden, 1973).

Hanson, A. T., "Salvation Proclaimed: I. 1 Peter 3:18-22," *ExpT* 93 (1982), 100-105.

Hahn, F., *The Titles of Jesus in Christology: Their History in Early Christianity* (tr. H. Knight and G. Ogg; London, 1969).

Harnack, A. von, *Beiträge zur Einleitung in das Neue Testament VII: Zur Revision der Prinzipien der neutestamentlichen Textkritik. Die Be-*

deutung der Vulgata für den Text der katholischen Briefe und der Anteil des Hieronymus an dem Übersetzungswerk (Leipzig, 1916).

Hemer, C. J., "The Address of I Peter," *ExpT* 89 (1978), 239-243.

Heussi, K., *Die römische Petrustradition in kritischer Sicht* (Tübingen, 1955).

Hiebert, D. E., "Designation of the Readers in 1 Peter 1:1-2," *BiblSac* 137 (1980), 64-75.

Hill, D., "On Suffering and Baptism in I Peter," *NovTest* 18 (1976), 181-189.

————, " 'To Offer Spiritual Sacrifices . . .' (1 Peter 2:5): Liturgical Formulations and Christian Paraenesis in 1 Peter," *JStNT* 16 (1982), 45-63.

Hillyer, N., " 'Rock-Stone' Imagery in I Peter," *TyndBull* 22 (1971), 58-81.

Hunzinger, C.-H., "Babylon als Deckname für Rom und die Datierung des 1. Petrusbriefes," *Gottes Wort und Gottes Land* (FS H.-W. Hertzberg; Göttingen 1965), 67-77.

————, "Zur Struktur der Christus-Hymnen in Phil 2 und 1 Petr 3," *Der Ruf Jesu und die Antwort der Gemeinde* (FS J. Jeremias; Göttingen, 1970), 142-156.

Jeremias, J., "Zwischen Karfreitag und Ostern. Descensus und Ascensus in der Karfreitagstheologie des Neuen Testaments," *idem, Abba* (Göttingen, 1966), 323-331.

Johnson, D. E., "Fire in God's House: Imagery from Malachi 3 in Peter's Theology of Suffering (1 Peter 4:12-19)," *JEvThSoc* 29 (1986), 285-294.

Johnson, S. E., "The Preaching to the Dead," *JBL* 79 (1960), 48-51.

Jonsen, A. R., "The Moral Theology of the First Epistle of St. Peter," *ScienEcclés* 16 (1964), 93-107.

Jost, W., ΠΟΙΜΗΝ. *Das Bild vom Hirten in der biblischen Überlieferung und seine christologische Bedeutung* (dissertation, Gießen, 1939).

Kähler, E., *Die Frau in den paulinischen Briefen. Unter besonderer Berücksichtigung des Begriffes der Unterordnung* (Zurich, 1960).

Kamlah, E., " 'Υποτάσσεσθαι in den neutestamentlichen 'Haustafeln,' " *Verborum Veritas* (FS G. Stählin; Wuppertal, 1970), 237-243.

Kendall, D. W., "The Literary and Theological Function of 1 Peter 1:3-12," *Perspectives on First Peter* (ed. C. Talbert; Macon, 1986), 103-120.

Ketter, P., "Das allgemeine Priestertum der Gläubigen nach dem 1. Petrusbrief," *TrThZ* 56 (1947), 43-51.

Kiley, M., "Like Sara: The Tale of Terror Behind 1 Peter 3:6," *JBL* 106 (1987), 689-692.

Kilpatrick, G. D., "1 Peter 1:11 tina e poion kairon," *NovTest* 28 (1986), 91f.

Kirkpatrick, W. D., "The Theology of First Peter," *SWJTh* 25 (1982), 58-81.

Klassen, W., "The Sacred Kiss in the New Testament: An Example of Social Boundary Lines," *NTS* 39 (1993), 122-135.

Klinzing, G., *Die Umdeutung des Kultes in der Qumrangemeinde und im Neuen Testament* (UNT 7; Göttingen, 1971).

Knox, J., "Pliny and I Peter: A Note on I Peter 4,14-16 and 3,15," *JBL* 72 (1953), 187-189.

Kohler, M. E., "La communauté des chrétiens selon la première épître de Pierre," *RevThéolPhil* 114 (1982), 1-21.

Krafft, E., "Christologie und Anthropologie im 1. Petrusbrief," *EvTh* 10 (1950/51), 120-126.

Kroll, J., *Gott und Hölle. Der Mythos vom Descensuskampfe* (Studien der Bibliothek Warburg 20; Leipzig/Berlin, 1932).

Kühschelm, R., " 'Lebendige Hoffnung' (1 Petr 1,3-12)," *BibLiturg* 56 (1983), 202-206.

Kuss, O., "Zur paulinischen und nachpaulinischen Tauflehre im Neuen Testament," *idem, Auslegung und Verkündigung* I (Regensburg, 1963), 121-150.

Kvanvig, H. S., "Bruken av Noahtradisjonene i 1 Pet 3:20f," *TidsTeolKirk* 56 (1985), 81-98.

Lamau, M.-L., "Exhortation aux esclaves et hymne au Christ souffrant dans la 'Première épître de Pierre,' " *MélSciRel* 43 (1986), 121-143.

Langkammer, H., "Jes 53 und 1 Petr 2,21-25. Zur christologischen Interpretation der Leidenstheologie von Jes 53," *BibLiturg* 60 (1987), 90-98.

Leaney, A. R. C., "I Peter and the Passover: An Interpretation," *NTS* 10 (1963/64), 238-251.

Légasse, S., "La soumission aux Autorités d'après I Pierre 2.13-17: Version Spécifique d'une Parénèse Traditionelle," *NTS* 34 (1988), 378-396.

Lindars, B., "Enoch and Christology," *ExpT* 92 (1981), 295-299.

Lippert, P., "Leben als Zeugnis. Ein Beitrag des ersten Petrusbriefes zur pastoraltheologischen Problematik der Gegenwart," *Studia Moralia* III (Pontificia Univ. Lateranensis Academia Alfonsiana; Rome, 1965), 226-268.

Lohse, E., "Parenesis and Kerygma in 1 Peter" (tr. J. Steely), *Perspectives on First Peter* (ed. C. Talbert; Macon, 1986), 37-59.

Losada, D., "Sufrir por el nombre de Cristiano en la Primera Carta de Pedro," *RevistBíb* 42 (1980), 85-101.

Love, J. P., "The First Epistle of Peter," *Interp* 8 (1954), 63-87.

Lundberg, P., *La typologie baptismale dans l'ancienne Eglise* (ASNU 10; Leipzig/Uppsala, 1942).

Maier, G., "Jesustradition im 1. Petrusbrief?" *Gospel Perspectives* V: *The Jesus Tradition outside the Gospels* (ed. D. Wenham; Sheffield, 1985), 85-128.

MacKelvey, R. J., "Christ the Cornerstone," *NTS* 8 (1961/62), 352-359.

Manson, T. W., "Review of E. G. Selwyn, The First Epistle of St. Peter," *JThSt* 47 (1946), 218-227.

Martin, R. P., "The Composition of I Peter in Recent Study," *VoxEv* 1 (1962), 29-42.

Martin, T., "The Present Indicative in the Eschatological Statements of 1 Peter 1:6, 8," *JBL* 111 (1992), 307-312.

McCaughey, J. D., "Three 'Persecution Documents' of the New Testament," *ABR* 17 (1969), 27-40.

―――, "On Re-Reading I Peter," *ABR* 31 (1983), 33-44.

Michaels, J. R., "Eschatology in I Peter III.17," *NTS* 13 (1966/67), 394-401.

Millauer, H., *Leiden als Gnade. Eine traditionsgeschichtliche Untersuchung zur Leidenstheologie des 1. Petrusbriefs* (Europäische Hochschulschriften 23/56; Frankfurt, 1976).

Miller, D. G., "Deliverance and Destiny. Salvation in First Peter," *Interp* 9 (1955), 413-425.

Minear, P. S., "The House of Living Stones. A Study of I Peter 2:4-12," *EcumRev* 34 (1982), 238-248.

Mitton, C. L., "The Relationship between I Peter and Ephesians," *JThST* NS 1 (1950), 67-73.

Moreau, J., *Die Christenverfolgung im römischen Reich* (Aus der Welt der Religion NF 2; second ed., Berlin, 1971).

Motyer, S., "The Relationship between Paul's Gospel of 'All One in Christ Jesus' (Galatians 3:28) and the Household Codes," *VoxEv* 19 (1989), 33-48.

Moule, C. F. D., "Some Reflections on the 'Stone' Testimonia in Relation to the Name of Peter," *NTS* 2 (1955/56), 56-58.

―――, "The Nature and Purpose of I Peter," *NTS* 3 (1956/57), 1-11.

Munro, W., *Authority in Paul and Peter. The Identification of a Pastoral Stratum in the Pauline Corpus and 1 Peter* (SNTS Mon. Ser. 45; Cambridge, 1983) (cf. response by J. H. L. Dijkman, above).

―――, "Interpolation in the Epistles: Weighing Probability," *NTS* 36 (1990), 431-443.

Nauck, W., "Freude im Leiden. Zum Problem einer urchristlichen Verfolgungstradition," *ZNW* 46 (1955), 68-80.

―――, "Probleme des frühchristlichen Amtsverständnisses (1 Petr 5,2f)," *ZNW* 48 (1957), 200-220.

Neugebauer, F., "Zur Deutung und Bedeutung des 1. Petrusbriefes," *NTS* 26 (1979), 61-86.

Neyrey, J. H., "First Peter and Converts," *BibT* 22 (1984), 13-18.

Niederwimmer, K., *Askese und Mysterium. Über Ehe, Ehescheidung und Eheverzicht in den Anfängen des christlichen Glaubens* (FRLANT 113; Göttingen, 1975).

Nixon, R. E., "The Meaning of 'Baptism' in I Peter 3,21," *Studia Evangelica IV* (TU 102; Berlin, 1968), 437-441.

Olsson, B. "Ett hem för hemlösa. Om sociologisk exeges av NT" (review of J. H. Elliott, *A Home for the Homeless*), *SvExÅ* 49 (1984), 89-108.

Omanson, R., "Suffering for Righteousness' Sake (I Peter 3:13–4:11)," *RevExp* 79 (1982), 439-450.

Osborne, T. P., "L'utilisation des citations de l'Ancien Testament dans la première épître de Pierre," *RevThéolLouv* 12 (1981), 64-77.

————, "Guide Lines for Christian Suffering: A Source-Critical and Theological Study of I Peter 2,21-25," *Bibl* 64 (1983), 381-408.

Oss, D. A., "The Interpretation of the 'Stone' Passages by Peter and Paul: A Comparative Study," *JEvThS* 32 (1989), 181-200.

Patsch, H., "Zum alttestamentlichen Hintergrund von Röm 4,25 und I. Petrus 2,24," *ZNW* 60 (1969), 273-279.

Patterson, D. K., "Roles in Marriage: A Study in Submission: 1 Peter 3:1-7," *TheolEd* 13 (1983), 70-79.

Perdelwitz, R., *Die Mysterienreligion und das Problem des I. Petrusbriefes* (RVV 11/3; Giessen, 1911).

Perkins, D. W., "Simon Rock: An Appraisal of Peter in the New Testament Witness," *TheolEd* 13 (1982), 42-54.

Perrot, C., ed., *Études sur la Première Lettre de Pierre. Congrés de l'ACFEB* (Paris, 1980).

Pesch, W., "Zu Texten des Neuen Testaments über das Priestertum der Getauften," *Verborum Veritas* (FS G. Stählin; Wuppertal, 1970), 303-315.

Peters, T., "What is the Gospel?" *PRS* 13 (1986), 21-43.

Philipps, K., *Kirche in der Gesellschaft nach dem 1. Petrusbrief* (Gütersloh, 1971).

Piper, J., "Hope as the Motivation of Love: I Peter 3:9-12," *NTS* 26 (1980), 212-231.

Prete, B., "L'espressione he en Babyloni syneklekte di 1 Pt 5, 13," *VetChrist* 21 (1984), 335-352.

Prigent, P., "1 Pierre 2,4-10," *RHPhR* 72 (1992), 53-60.

Pryor, J. W., "First Peter and the New Covenant," *RefTheolRev* 45 (1986), 1-4, 44-51.

Radermacher, L., "Der erste Petrusbrief und Silvanus," *ZNW* 25 (1926), 287-299.

Refoulé, F., "Bible et éthique sociale. Lire aujourd'hui 1 Pierre," *Supplément* (Paris) 131 (1979), 457-482.

Reicke, B., *The Disobedient Spirits and Christian Baptism. A Study of 1 Pet. III.19 and its Context* (ASNU 13; Copenhagen, 1946).

————, "Die Gnosis der Männer nach I. Ptr 3,7," *Neutestamentliche Studien für R. Bultmann* (BZNW 21; Berlin, 1954), 296-304.

Rengstorf, K. H., "Die neutestamentlichen Mahnungen an die Frau, sich dem Manne unterzuordnen," *Verbum Dei Manet in aeternum* (FS O. Schmitz; Witten, 1953), 131-145.

Richard, E., "The Functional Christology of First Peter," *Perspectives on First Peter* (ed. C. Talbert; Macon, 1986), 121-139.

Rigato, M. L. "Quali i profeti di cui nella 1 Pt. 1,10?" *RevistBíb* 38 (1990), 73-90.

Robertson, P. E., "Is I Peter a Sermon?" *TheolEd* 13 (1982), 35-41.

Rödding, G., "Descendit ad inferna," *Kerygma und Melos* (FS C. Mahrenholz; Berlin/Hamburg, 1970), 95-102.

Rodgers, P. R., "The Longer Reading of 1 Peter 4:14," *CBQ* 43 (1981), 93-95.

Rubinkiewicz, R., " 'Duchy zamknięte w wiezięniu.' Interpretacja 1 P 3,19 w świetle Hen 10,4.12 ('Die Geister im Gefängnis.' Interpretation von 1 Petr. 3,19 im Lichte von Hen. 10,4.12)," *RoczTeolKan* 28 (1981), 77-86.

Sander, E. T., *ΠΥΡΩΣΙΣ and the First Epistle of Peter 4:12* (dissertation, Harvard, 1966/67) (cf. author's summary, *HarvThRev* 60 [1967], 501).

Sanders, J. T., *The New Testament Christological Hymns: Their Historical Background* (SNTS Mon. Ser. 15; Cambridge, 1971).

Scharlemann, M. H., " 'He Descended into Hell': An Interpretation of I Peter 3:18-20," *ConcJ* 15 (1989), 311-322 (repr. 1956).

Schelkle, K. H., "Spätapostolische Schriften als frühkatholisches Zeugnis," *Neutestamentliche Aufsätze* (FS J. Schmid; Regensburg, 1963), 225-232.

Schenke, H. M., "Das Weiterwirken des Paulus und die Pflege seines Erbes durch die Paulus-Schule," *NTS* 21 (1975), 505-518.

Schille, G., *Frühchristliche Hymnen* (Berlin, 1965).

Schlatter, A., *Petrus und Paulus nach dem ersten Petrusbrief* (Stuttgart, 1937).

Schlosser, J., "1 Pierre 3,5b-6," *Bibl* 64 (1983), 409f.

Schmid, J., "Petrus der 'Fels' und die Petrusgestalt der Urgemeinde," *Begegnung der Christen* (ed. M. Roesle und O. Cullmann; Stuttgart/Frankfurt, 1959), 347-359.

Schmidt, D. H., *The Peter Writings: Their Redactors and their Relationship* (dissertation, Northwestern University, 1972).

Schnackenburg, R., "Episkopos und Hirtenamt," *idem, Schriften zum Neuen Testament* (Munich, 1971), 247-267.

Schrage, W., *Die Christen und der Staat nach dem Neuen Testament* (Gütersloh, 1971).

―――, "Zur Ethik der neutestamentlichen Haustafeln," *NTS* 21 (1974/75), 1-22.

Schroeder, D., *Die Haustafeln des Neuen Testaments. Ihre Herkunft und ihr theologischer Sinn* (dissertation, Hamburg, 1959).

―――, "Once You Were No People," *The Church as Theological Community* (ed. H. Huebner, 1990), 37-65.

Schröger, F., "Die Verfassung der Gemeinde des ersten Petrusbriefes," *Kirche im Werden* (ed. J. Hainz; Munich/Paderborn/Wien, 1976), 239-252.

―――, "Lasst Euch Erbauen Zu Einem Geisterfüllten Haus (1 Petr 2,4-5). Eine Überlegung zu dem Verhältnis von Ratio und Pneuma," *Theologie-Gemeinde-Seelsorge* (ed. W. Friedberger and F. Schnider; Munich, 1979), 138-145.

Schutter, W. L., *Hermeneutic and Composition in I Peter* (Tübingen, 1989).

Schwank, B., "Wie Freie — aber als Sklaven Gottes (1 Petr 2,16). Das Verhältnis der Christen zur Staatsmacht nach dem ersten Petrusbrief," *EuA* 36 (1960), 5-12.

———, "Diabolus tamquam leo rugiens (1 Petr 5,8)," *EuA* 38 (1962), 15-20.

Schweizer, E., "1. Petrus 4,6," *ThZ* 8 (1952), 152-154.

Selwyn, E. G., "The Persecutions in I Peter," *Bulletin of the Studiorum Novi Testamenti Societas* 1 (1950), 39-50.

———, "Eschatology in I Peter," *The Background of the New Testament and its Eschatology* (FS C. H. Dodd; Cambridge, 1956), 394-401.

Senior, D., "The Conduct of Christians in the World (2:11–3:12)," *RevExp* 79 (1982), 427-438.

———, "The First Letter of Peter," *BibT* 22 (1984), 5-12.

Shimada, K., *The Formulary Material in First Peter* (dissertation, Union Theological Seminary, New York, 1966).

———, "The Christological Creedal Formula in 1 Peter 3,18-22 — Reconsidered," *AnnJapanBibInst* 5 (1979), 154-176.

———, "A Critical Note on 1 Peter 1,12," *AnnJapanBibInst* 7 (1981), 146-150.

———, "Is I Peter a Compositive Writing? — A Stylistic Approach to the Two-Document Hypotheses," *AnnJapanBibInst* 11 (1985), 95-114.

Sleeper, F. H., "Political Responsibility According to 1 Peter," *NovTest* 10 (1968), 270-286.

Sly, D., "I Peter 3:6b in the Light of Philo and Josephus," *JBL* 110 (1991), 126-129.

Snodgrass, K. R., "I Peter II.1-10: Its Formation and Literary Affinities," *NTS* 24 (1977), 97-106.

Souček, J. B., "Das Gegenüber von Gemeinde und Welt nach dem ersten Petrusbrief," *Communion viatorum* 3 (1960), 5-13 (= *Stimmen aus der Kirche der ČSSR/Dokumente und Zeugnisse* [ed. B. Ruys and J. Smolik; Munich, 1968], 56-69).

Spicq, C., "La I Petri et le témoignage évangélique de Saint Pierre," *StTh* 20 (1966), 37-61.

———, "La place ou le rôle des jeunes dans certains communautés néotestamentaires," *RevBibl* 76 (1969), 508-527.

Spitta, F., *Die Predigt an die Geister (1 Petr 3,19)* (Göttingen, 1890).

Spörri, T., *Der Gemeindegedanke im ersten Petrusbrief. Ein Beitrag zur Struktur des urchristlichen Kirchenbegriffs* (Neutestamentliche Forschung 2/2; Gütersloh, 1925).

Stevick, D. B., "A Matter of Taste: 1 Peter 2:3," *RevRel* 47 (1988), 707-717.

Strathmann, H., "Die Stellung des Petrus in der Urkirche," *ZsystTh* 20 (1943), 223-282.

Strobel, A., "Macht Leiden von Sünde frei? Zur Problematik von 1. Petr. 4,1f.," *ThZ* 19 (1963), 412-425.

Strynkowski, J. J., *The Descent of Christ among the Dead* (Dissertation, Gregorian University, Rome, 1972).

Sylva, D., "I Peter Studies: The State of the Discipline," *BibThBull* 10 (1980), 155-163.

————, Translating and Interpreting 1 Peter 3:2," *BT* 34:1 (1983), 144-147.

————, "The Critical Exploration of I Peter" (bibliography), *Perspectives on First Peter* (ed. C. Talbert; Macon, 1986), 17-36.

Talbert, C. H., ed., *Perspectives on First Peter* (National Association of Baptist Professors of Religion Special Studies Series 9; Macon, 1986).

————, "Once Again: The Plan of 1 Peter," *Perspectives on First Peter* (ed. C. Talbert; Macon, 1986), 141-151.

Tarrech, A. P., "Le milieu de la première épître de Pierre," *RevistCatTeol* 5 (1980), 95-129, 331-402.

Terrien, S., *Till the Heart Sings: A Biblical Theology of Manhood and Womanhood* (Philadelphia, 1985).

Thiede, C. P., "Babylon, der andere Ort: Anmerkungen zu 1 Petr 5,13 und Apg 12,17," *Bibl* 67 (1986), 532-538.

Thompson, J. W., "'Be Submissive to Your Masters': A Study of I Peter 2:18-25," *RestQ* 9 (1966), 66-78.

Thornton, T. C. G., "I Peter, a Paschal Liturgy?" *JThSt* 12 (1961), 14-26.

Tiede, D. L., "An Easter Catechesis: The Lessons of 1 Peter," *Word and World* 4 (1984), 192-201.

Tripp, D. H., "Eperōtēma (I Peter 3:21). A Liturgist's Note," *ExpT* 92 (1981), 267-270.

Tuni, J. O., "Jesus of Nazareth in the Christology of 1 Peter," *HeythJ* 28 (1987), 292-304.

Unnik, W. C. van, "De verlossing 1 Petrus 1:18-19 en het probleem van den eersten Petrusbrief," *Mededeelingen der Nederlandsche Akademie van Wetenschappen*, Afdeeling Letterkunde NS 5 (1942), 1-106.

————, "The Teaching of Good Works in I Peter," *NTS* 1 (1954/55), 92-110.

————, "A Classical Parallel to I Peter ii.14 and 20," *NTS* 2 (1955/56), 198-202.

————, "Christianity according to I Peter," *ExpT* 68 (1956/57), 79-83.

————, "Die Rücksicht auf die Reaktion der Nicht-Christen als Motiv in der altchristlichen Paränese," *Judentum-Urchristentum-Kirche* (FS J. Jeremias, BZNW 26; Berlin, 1960), 221-234.

————, "The Critique of Paganism in 1 Peter 1:18," *Neotestamentica et Semitica* (FS M. Black; Edinburgh, 1969), 129-142.

la Verdiere, E. A., "A Grammatical Ambiguity in 1 Pet 1:23," *CBQ* 36 (1974), 89-94.

Vitti, A., "Eschatologia in Petri epistula prima," *VD* 11 (1931), 298-306.

Vogels, H. J., *Christi Abstieg ins Totenreich und das Läuterungsgericht an den Toten* (Freiburger Theologische Studien 102; Freiburg, 1976).

Vogt, J., *Sklaverei und Humanität. Studien zur antiken Sklaverei und ihrer Erforschung* (Historia 8; Wiesbaden, 1965).

Voorwinde, S., "Old Testament Quotations in Peter's Epistles," *VoxRef* 49 (1987), 3-16.

Wand, J. W. C., "The Lessons of First Peter. A Survey of Recent Interpretation," *Interp* 9 (1959), 387-399.

Warden, D., "The Prophets of I Peter 1:10-12," *RestQ* 31 (1989), 1-12.

———, "Imperial Persecution and the Dating of I Peter and Revelation," *JEvThS* 34 (1991), 203-212.

Weidinger, K., *Die Haustafeln. Ein Stück urchristlicher Paränese* (UNT 14; Leipzig, 1928).

Wendland, H. D., "Zur sozialethischen Bedeutung des neutestamentlichen Haustafeln," *idem, Die Botschaft an die soziale Welt. Beiträge zur christlichen Sozialethik der Gegenwart* (Hamburg, 1959), 104-114.

Wengst, K., *Christologische Formeln und Lieder des Urchristentums* (second ed., Gütersloh, 1974).

Wenschkewitz, H., "Die Spiritualisierung der Kultusbegriffe Tempel, Priester und Opfer im Neuen Testament," *Archiv für neutestamentliche Zeitgeschichte und Kulturkunde* (Angelos 4; Leipzig, 1932), 70-230.

Westermann, W. L., "Sklaverei," PW Suppl. VI (1935), 894-1068.

———, *The Slave System of Greek and Roman Antiquity* (Philadelphia, 1955).

Wifstrand, A., "Stylistic Problems in the Epistles of James and Peter," *StTh* 1 (1948), 170-182.

Winbery, C. L., "Ethical Issues in I Peter," *TheolEd* 13 (1982), 63-71.

Winter, B., " 'Seek the Welfare of the City': Social Ethics according to 1 Peter," *Them* 13 (1988), 91-94.

———, "The Public Honouring of Christian Benefactors: Romans 13:3-4 and I Peter 2:14-15," *JStNT* 34 (1988), 87-103.

Wire, A., review of D. L. Balch, *Let Wives Be Submissive, RelStRev* 10 (1984), 209-216.

Wrede, W., "Miscellen, 3: Bemerkungen zu Harnacks Hypothese über die Adresse des 1. Petrusbriefs," *ZNW* 1 (1900), 75-85.

Załęski, J., "Posłuszeństwo władzy świeckiej według 1 Pt 2,13-17," *CollTheol* 54 (1984), 39-50 = "L'obbedienza al potere civile in 1 Pt 2,13-17," *CollTheol* 55 (special issue, 1985), 153-162.

Introduction

THE DATA OF THE LETTER
REGARDING ADDRESSEES AND AUTHOR

To a degree unparalleled by the other Catholic Epistles, with which this letter has been transmitted in the NT, I Peter gives precise information about its origin and its address: With regard to its opening (1:1f.) and conclusion (5:12-14) it is really more like the Pauline Epistles. The letter presents itself as written at the commission of the Apostle Peter by Silvanus from Rome to the Christians in all Asia Minor.

In order to clarify this claim and examine it critically we will first bring it into contact with the geographical and historical framework that is provided through other traditions. Then we will take what can be concluded about the letter's origin from its content and put this into conversation with these other traditions.

The Location of the Addressees

a. The letter is directed "to the elect foreigners in the Diaspora of Pontus, Galatia, Cappadocia, Asia, and Bithynia," i.e., to Christians living like the Jewish Diaspora as a widely dispersed minority in these regions.[1] The names Πόντος, Γαλατία, Καππαδοκία, Ἀσία, and Βιθυνία were basically designations for geographical regions of Asia Minor; here, however, they stand for Roman provinces:[2] No geographical name is

---

1. What is known concerning the geographical and provincial divisions of Asia Minor has been assembled in J. Weiss, "Kleinasien," *RE*[3] X, 535-563; V. Schultze, *Altchristliche Städte und Landschaften* II/1, 2 (Gütersloh, 1922/26); D. Magie, *Roman Rule in Asia Minor,* I, II (second ed., Princeton, 1966); A. Goetze, *Kleinasien* (second ed., Munich, 1957); cf. also the articles in PW, BAGD, *RAC,* and *OCD.*

2. So most modern commentaries (Knopf; Windisch-Preisker, 51; Selwyn, 51f.; Beare, 38-43; Schelkle, 1f.; Spicq, 12; Kelly, 3f.). Among those who regard them as geographical regions are earlier interpreters mentioned by Schelkle, 2 n.1; A. Wikenhauser, *NT Introduction* (tr. J. Cunningham; New York, 1958), 500, with the rationale that "Pontus and Bithynia were not two separate Roman provinces, there was only one Provincia

3

included here that was not the name of a province. This would be natural
for a letter from the distant capital city of the Roman Empire. Furthermore, it is only when the names are understood to refer to provinces
that they can represent a cohesive geographical area; otherwise, the
geographical regions of Phrygia, Pisidia, and Lycaonia with their main
cities of Antioch, Iconium, and Lystra, in which churches were founded
during Paul's first "missionary journey" (Acts 13:14; 14:1, 6), would
be arbitrarily left out.[3]

The region thus described encompasses, therefore, all of Asia
Minor. The province of Cilicia in the region beyond the Taurus mountains constituted a cultural unity with Syria. The small double province
of Lycia-Pamphylia was finally established under the rule of Vespasian
and consisted only of a narrow tongue of land on the southern coast.[4]

The sequence of the names is difficult to explain. Pontus and
Bithynia, at the beginning and end of the list, constituted together a
double province, though each of the two had its own local government.[5]
It has been suggested that the sequence corresponds to the route followed by the bearer of the letter.[6] From Rome eastern Asia Minor could
be reached most quickly by sea along the north coast of Pontus. The
letter carrier coming from Rome would, then, set foot on Asia Minor
at Sinope or more probably at Amisus, travel on the well-known north-
south artery to Ancyra in Galatia, and then follow the commercial route
to the southeast to Caesarea in Cappadocia. The southern east-west
artery would then bring him through Iconia and Antioch to Ephesus in
Asia, and the coastal route through Smyrna north to Nicomedia in
Bithynia.[7]

Usually, however, it has been thought that this circular letter was

---

Bithynia-Pontus." Judging to the contrary is J. Schmid in the revised German edition of
Wikenhauser's *Introduction, Einleitung in das NT* (sixth ed., Freiburg, 1973), 593: "It
appears that a differentiation between geographical areas and provinces is not feasible."

3. Weiss, "Kleinasien," 558-560.

4. *Ibid.,* 560-562.

5. *Ibid.,* 553.

6. Selwyn, 119, with the support of Hort, Note III; so also Ewald, 2f. Cf. more recently,
C. J. Hemer, "Address"; Hiebert, "Designation."

7. In contrast, the explanation given by Bengel at 1:1 (p. 45) contradicts the geographical situation: "He mentions five provinces in the order in which they presented
themselves to him, writing from the East: ch. V. 13." But this route did not offer itself to
the person who looked from Babylon to the north (so already J. J. Wettstein, *Novum Testamentum Graecum editionis receptae vol. II, continens Epistolas Pauli, Acta Apostolorum,
Epistolas Canonicas et Apocalypsim* [Amsterdam, 1752], 698).

not carried by a single courier but, in accord with the directive in Col. 4:16, passed from one Christian community to another. Nonetheless, the intended route of passage and, therefore, the sequence of the regions to be reached might have been thought of in terms of the routes of the great commercial highways. It is also possible that the questions addressed in this letter were especially critical in the double province named at the beginning and end of the list:[8] It was the region in Asia Minor reached last by the Christian mission, so that, as in fact transpires in the letter, those written to there could be addressed while they were still undergoing the transition from paganism to Christianity.

b. The letter presupposes in any case that Christianity had spread through all Asia Minor. What was the earliest date that this stage of development had been reached?

Even before A.D. 50 Christianity had been carried, above all by Paul, into the geographical center of Asia Minor, the highland region of the extended province of Galatia. During the 50s Ephesus became, through Paul, the centerpoint of missionary activity and theological concentration in Asia. We may suppose that if Christianity was able to develop as vigorously from Galatia along the commercial highways as it was from Ephesus, e.g., into the valley of the Lycus (Col. 4:12-16), then churches could have been established in Bithynia, Pontus, and Cappadocia by the 60s. The first direct information available about Christians in Bithynia and Pontus is the letter written to Emperor Trajan by Pliny the younger, who was governor of the double province in A.D. 111-113. During his time of service "this superstition" had already spread across the flatlands, resulting in a noticeable decline in attendance at the temples. Even some twenty years earlier there had been cases of Christians who had renounced their faith, probably under pressure from the civil authorities.[9] It is reasonable, therefore, to believe that probably around A.D. 90 churches existed already in most of the

---

8. Beare, 38ff., finds here a starting point for his hypothesis concerning the emergence of the letter (cf. 25ff.): Pontus and Bithynia are emphasized because in these provinces any new group taking shape was seen as a source of political unrest because of the constant social and political tensions. Therefore, Christians were suppressed by the Roman administration whenever possible. This occurred particularly — Beare thinks — after the exchange of correspondence between Pliny and Trajan, because the wave of persecution set in motion by Pliny began here for all of Asia Minor, for which the letter was written, so that the double province was emphasized among the addressees (41ff.). For a critique of this view see below, pp. 42-45.

9. Pliny, *Epistulae* 10.96.6 (LCL II, 401ff.).

large areas of the double province. This is documented directly for Asia by the letters in Revelation and by the letters of Ignatius. On the basis of all this, it is reasonable to assume that Christianity was noticeably present in the northern and eastern provinces beyond Galatia and Asia referred to in I Pet. 1:1 by the mid-60s and certainly by A.D. 80.[10]

Such rapid growth can be explained not only on the basis of the strong impetus provided above all by Paul, but also on the basis of generally favorable conditions, which could be matched in no other region of the Roman Empire. In Asia Minor numerous ethnic groups and cultures experienced mutual assimilation. Therefore, this region became the classical land of Hellenism, and cross-regional migrant peoples of the time found a home there.[11] From the second century B.C. on Asia Minor had a relatively strong Jewish Diaspora, which had considerable religious impact on its environment[12] and in many respects prepared the way for Christianity. For this reason Asia Minor, along with northern Egypt and Rome, was the focal point of missionary activity in the Empire during the second century A.D.

This rapid and intensive spread of Christianity was responsible for the early outbreak of conflicts with non-Christians (cf. Acts 19:23-40). This was especially so because the Jews in the region distanced themselves pointedly from the Christians after brief encounters of debate and, accordingly, the official sanction and tolerance accorded the Jewish religion was denied to Christians.[13] These conditions resulted from the very beginning in Jewish and Gentile Christians uniting themselves in Christian communities and in Gentile Christians soon becoming numerically dominant in these communities. I Peter clearly presupposes a predominantly Gentile Christian circle of readers.[14] Problems

---

10. Cf. A. von Harnack, *The Mission and Expansion of Christianity in the First Three Centuries* (tr. J. Moffatt; Freeport, NY, 1972) II, 326-332.

11. Selwyn, 47-52; Goetze, *Kleinasien*, 210f.

12. Cf. the data in Philo, *Legatio ad Gaium* 245, 281 (LCL X, 127, 143). Cf. H. Graetz, "Die Stellung der kleinasiatischen Juden unter der Römerherrschaft," *MGWJ* 35 (1886), 329-346; W. M. Ramsay, "The Jews in Graeco-Asiatic Cities," *Exp* 5 (1902), 19-33; G. Kittel, "Das kleinasiatische Judentum in der hellenistisch-römischen Zeit," *ThLZ* 69 (1944), cols. 9-20.

13. L. Goppelt, *Christentum und Judentum im ersten und zweiten Jahrhundert* (Gütersloh, 1954), 246-248; cf. Acts 13:50; 20:19; 21:27f.; Rev. 2:9; 3:9; *Mart. Pol.* 12:2 (LCL AF II, 328f.).

14. So the more recent commentaries (Selwyn, 42-47; Schelkle, 2; Spicq, 12f.; Kelly, 4); earlier discussion in Knopf, 2f.; see the comments below at 1:1; 1:14; 2:10; 4:3.

between Jewish and Gentile Christians are touched on nowhere in the letter; they were simply no longer of current interest in this region after the conclusion of the Pauline period.[15]

The body of Christians in this area are now being addressed, according to the letter, by Peter from Rome through Silvanus.

The Author

From the prescript of the letter the question arises: What brought Peter to address the body of Christians of Asia Minor in this way? The question concerns first of all his position and recognition in the early Church.

a. The letter presupposes that Peter was authorized to speak to the Christians of Asia Minor in terms of admonition and testimony (5:12) although, according to all indications, he had no personal connections to them. Such authorization, which Paul carefully delineates in Romans (1:5f., 8-10; 15:14-24) in relation to a church not personally known to him, is apparently here taken for granted regarding Peter. Was this already accepted during his lifetime or does this reflect a later expansion of his apostolic office for the Church as a whole? In view of this question what can be determined about the course of his life and his position in the early Church?[16]

According to a tradition that persisted from the oldest kerygma (I Cor. 15:3) up to the Lukan documents (Luke 24:34; Acts 10:41) and is by all indications historical, Peter was the first to be witness a resurrection appearance of Jesus. For this reason as well he became the leader of the early church in Jerusalem as speaker for the group of twelve disciples (Gal. 1:18; Acts 1:15–5:42). Later he became one of this church's "three pillars" (Gal. 2:9), until he left Jerusalem around the year 42 and James, the brother of the Lord, took over its leadership (Acts 12:17; Gal. 2:12).

---

15. L. Goppelt, *Jesus, Paul, and Judaism* (tr. and ed. E. Schroeder; New York, 1964), 127-131; see also n.20 below.

16. Among the more recent literature, see Fascher, "Petrus"; Cullmann, *Peter; idem,* "Πέτρος," *TDNT* VI, 100-112; Dinkler, "Petrus-Rom-Frage" I; A. Vögtle, "Petrus," *LThK* VIII, cols. 334-340; W. C. van Unnik, "Petrus," *BHH* III, cols. 1430f.; W. Trilling, "Zum Petrusamt im NT," *ThQ* 151 (1971), 110-133; Wikenhauser-Schmid, *Einleitung* (n.2 above), 585-589; R. E. Brown, et al., *Peter in the NT.* Cf. also Elliott, "Rehabilitation"; Sylva, "I Peter Studies"; Blevins, "Introduction"; Perkins, "Simon Rock"; McCaughey, "Re-Reading."

Reliable tradition says concerning Peter's life prior to Easter that he was originally called Symeon (Acts 15:14; cf. II Pet. 1:1) or in Greek Simon (Lk. 5:3) and that he belonged to the inner circle of Jesus' disciples (Mk. 5:37; 9:2; 14:33 par.). Some recent doubts notwithstanding, he was given by Jesus the Aramaic surname retained in Greek transliteration as Κηφᾶ(ς), "Rock"; out of the Greek translation of this surname (Jn. 1:42) came the name Πέτρος, Latin *Petrus*.[17] Even this surname indicates that he was singled out especially by Jesus from the circle of his trusted companions, a note that the tradition reinforces but did not invent (Mk. 1:36; 9:5; 16:7; Mt. 14:28). For his part he emerged again and again as spokesman for the circle of disciples; according to a tradition debated regarding its intent as well as its historicity, he was the first to recognize Jesus as the "Messiah," the eschatological mediator of salvation, though he misunderstood greatly the nature of this messiahship (Mk. 8:29, 32f. par.).[18] At the Passion he denied Jesus (Mk. 14:66-72 par.) and then received the first Easter appearance as renewed and forgiving acceptance.

This man, whose personal history with Jesus was matched by none other, was a fisherman on the Sea of Galilee prior to his calling (Mk. 1:16 par. Matthew; Lk. 5:2; Jn. 21:3); he was also a Galilean in terms of speech (Mk. 14:70 par.; Acts 2:7) and lived with his wife in a house in Capernaum (Mk. 1:21, 29 par.). She accompanied him on his travels as a missionary outside Palestine after he departed from Jerusalem (I Cor. 9:5).[19] His apostolic service was to establish the Church among the people of Israel and, thereby, to bring about its foundational moment

---

17. The occasion for the giving of the surname is handed on as tradition in Mt. 16:17-19; Mk. 3:16; and in the Johannine form of the disciple tradition in Jn. 1:42. Mt. 16:17-19, in its present state, is a statement of the primitive Church of Palestine. But the surname did not first come about in the post-Easter community (with Cullmann, *Peter*, 25-29, 62f., contra Dinkler, "Petrus-Rom-Frage" I, 196f.). Cf. F. Hahn, "Die Petrusverheißung Mt 16,18f. Eine exegetische Skizze" (1970), K. Kertelge, ed., *Das kirchliche Amt im NT* (WdF 439; Darmstadt, 1977), 543-561, which cites further literature.

18. Cf. O. Cullmann, *The Christology of the NT* (tr. S. C. Guthrie and C. A. M. Hall; revised ed., Philadelphia, 1963), 122ff.; Hahn, *Titles*, 199ff.; E. Dinkler, "Petrusbekenntnis und Satanswort — Das Problem der Messianität Jesu" (1964), *idem, Signum Crucis* (Tübingen, 1967), 283-312.

19. That he was a cofounder with Paul of the churches in Corinth and Rome (Dionysius of Corinth, ca. A.D. 170, according to *HE* 2.25.8 [LCL I, 183]) and that he was a missionary to Diaspora Jews in the provinces of Asia Minor named in I Pet. 1:1 (*HE* 3.1.2 [LCL I, 191], perhaps citing Origen) is concluded from I Cor. 1:12ff.; I Pet. 1:1; 5:13 (cf. Cullmann, *Peter*, 60f.).

altogether; after that is accomplished he disappears from the account in Acts, which is oriented to the emergence of the Church, not to the biographies of individuals.[20]

Paul presupposes in his letters that Peter was recognized also in the Pauline churches as an authoritative apostle; Paul was, therefore, always being played off against Peter's apostolic office by opponents (I Cor. 1:12; 9:5; Gal. 1:18f.; 2:8f., 11). About A.D. 80 Matthew highlighted the early Palestinian church's saying about Peter, Mt. 16:18f., in its validity for the whole Church. Luke portrayed the emergence of the Church as beginning with the early Jerusalem church, represented by Peter, and then leading on to Rome through the work of Paul. Around A.D. 90, Peter is contrasted in Jn. 21:15-24 with the "beloved disciple," the witness for the credibility of the Fourth Gospel, probably because Peter is regarded as the representative of the older Jesus tradition; Papias understood him to be the authority behind the Gospel of Mark.[21] Around A.D. 100 I Clement in the West and Ignatius in the East named Peter and Paul as the authoritative apostles.[22]

Thus, at a very early date Peter enjoyed the position of authority in the earliest Church which the letter claims for him. If Peter stands *in persona* behind the letter it remains, nevertheless, conspicuous that he is not more personally involved in this communique to churches not directly known to him than he is in the brief remark in 5:1.

b. Can the special personal circumstances of a period of residence for Peter in Rome be verified, a residence presupposed by our letter?[23]

---

20. The fundamental acknowledgment at the Apostolic Council that to Peter belonged "the apostolic work among the circumcised" (Gal. 2:8; in v. 9 it is extended to the others in Jerusalem) was hardly intended to depict the later region of his ministry in such a way that one could refer to him as the "leader of the Jerusalem mission" (contra Cullmann, *Peter,* 119 and passim). In the Hellenistic Church from Antioch to Rome the distinction between Gentile and Jewish Christians was already becoming blurred in the 50s, and nowhere did special Jewish-Christian communities arise alongside the churches of both Jews and Gentiles (Acts 21:21; I Cor. 8–10; Rom. 14:1–15:13; cf. Goppelt, *Apostolic,* 77-81, 119f.

21. *HE* 2.39.15 (LCL I, 297).

22. In second-century Palestinian Jewish Christian literature Peter is regarded as the true bearer of tradition over against Paul, the representative of Gentile Christianity. The pseudo-Petrine literature and the list of Roman bishops each in their own way claim Peter as the guarantor of tradition. The sources and traditions are gathered in *NT Apoc.* I, 216ff.; II, 40ff., 94ff., 102ff., 259ff., 663ff.

23. See H. Lietzmann, *Petrus und Paulus in Rom* (Berlin, 1915; second ed., 1927); Heussi, *Römische Petrustradition;* K. Aland, "Der Tod des Petrus in Rom," *idem, Kirchengeschichtliche Entwürfe* (Gütersloh, 1960), 35-104; Cullmann, *Peter,* 74ff.; E. Kirschbaum,

That Peter ever resided in Rome is mentioned in the NT only in I Pet. 5:13. The lists of greeting in the Pauline letters to and from Rome are silent about such a residence. Since Peter is not mentioned in Romans, which seeks to establish contact with the church there, then it is unlikely that Peter had any personal contact with the Roman church up to that time, i.e., 55/56. This is the case regardless of whether the chapter of greetings, Romans 16, was directed to Rome or not. Even the Prison Epistles do not name Peter (Philippians, Philemon, Colossians, Ephesians, II Timothy); Rome is still the most probable location for their composition whether they come directly or indirectly from Paul.[24] Hence, Peter can hardly have come to Rome prior to the conclusion of the two-year imprisonment of Paul in Rome, i.e., prior to 60-62.

There is only one reference to the end of Peter's life in the NT: In Jn. 21:18f., 22, with no reference to the place, it is announced that he will follow his Lord in a martyr's death. II Peter came on the scene quite late chronologically and was written as a kind of "testament" of Peter, written in view of the death he was about to experience.[25]

Among the writings of the Apostolic Fathers, only two mention the end of Peter's life. From *I Clement,* written about the year 96 in Rome, we learn about Peter's death as a martyr, but Rome as the location is mentioned only indirectly:

> Because of jealousy and envy the greatest and most righteous pillars were persecuted, and they fought to the death. Let us set before our eyes the good apostles: Peter, who because of unrighteous jealousy bore not one or two but many trials and, having thus given his testimony, went to the place of glory due to him. (*I Clem.* 5:2-4 [LCL AF I, 17])

Die Gräber der Apostelfürsten (Lucerne, 1959); Dinkler, "Petrus-Rom-Frage" II-IV; M. Guarducci, "Die Ausgrabungen unter St. Peter," R. Klein, ed., *Das frühe Christentum im römischen Staat* (WdF 267; Darmstadt, 1971), 364-414.

24. Goppelt, *Apostolic,* 102ff.

25. II Pet. 1:14 gives that document the character of a testament of the apostle before the martyrdom announced to him by Jesus and perhaps appropriates the tradition in Jn. 21:18-19a, 22. Cf. O. Knoch, *Die "Testamente" des Petrus und Paulus* (SBS 62; Stuttgart, 1973), 65ff.; W. G. Kümmel, *Introduction to the NT* (tr. H. C. Kee; Nashville, 1975), 429ff.

The two witnesses in Rev. 11:3, who succumb to the world power, represent the Church's witness and not that of Peter and Paul (contra Cullmann, *Peter,* 93-95). In I Peter 5:1 ("witness of the sufferings of Christ") martyrdom is not spoken of directly, but is at best only implied.

After a longer description of Paul's career and sufferings, the victims of the Neronian persecution are referred to:

> To these men who lived holy lives was gathered a great number of the elect, who suffered because of jealousy and became the best example among us by enduring many indignities and tortures. (6:1 [LCL AF I, 19])

In accord with the style and circumstances of I Clement, the statement about Peter is written in language more masked than those about Paul and the other victims of the Neronian persecution. But it clearly does refer to Peter's martyrdom.[26] That this martyrdom took place in Rome, like the events mentioned in 6:1 as occurring "among us" (ἐν ἡμῖν), is to be concluded on the basis of "associated with" (συναθροίζειν) in 6:1 and on the basis of the inclination of this list written in Rome.[27]

Even more veiled is what Ignatius says about the apostle's destiny when he asks the church in Rome not to hinder the execution that he expects there:

> I do not order you like Peter and Paul: They were apostles, I am a convict; they were free, I am still a slave. But if I suffer, then I will be Jesus Christ's freedman and in him will rise free. (4:3 [LCL AF I, 231])

Nothing is said here about the martyrdom of the apostle, nor is anything specific said about Rome. Yet, the reference only makes sense if Ignatius sees his own destiny in Rome as parallel to that of both apostles: This is exactly what he does in the concluding sentence in comparing their freedom with his own becoming free through martyrdom.

Until the end of the second century there are only two other references to the end of Peter's life. In the *Ascension of Isaiah* it is prophesied in apocalyptic imagery that one of the twelve will be handed over to Nero (for execution):

---

26. The key words μαρτυρεῖν and δόξα are technical terms in the theology of suffering and martyrdom (see the comments on 5:1).

27. So also the thorough exegesis in Cullmann, *Peter,* 95-113. His hypothesis (following R. Knopf, *Die Lehre der zwölf Apostel/Die zwei Clemensbriefe* [HNT supplement 1; Tübingen, 1920], 50ff.) that the "jealousy and envy" that caused the martyrdom were hostility against Peter on the part of extreme Jewish Christians and not the displeasure of non-Christians is very improbable.

Beliar . . . , the king of the world . . . , will come down from his firmament in the form of a man, a lawless king, who murders his mother, who himself, this king, will persecute the plant that the twelve apostles of the Beloved have planted. And one of the twelve will be delivered into his hand. (4:2f.)[28]

Eusebius passes on from Papias, an elder in Asia, the tradition connecting Mark with Peter:

Mark became Peter's interpreter and wrote accurately, though not in order, what he remembered of things said or done by the Christ. For he had neither heard nor followed the Lord, but later on, as I said, he followed Peter. Peter would shape his teaching to what was needed, not giving an ordered account of the Lord's sayings. Therefore, Mark did no wrong in thus writing down individual details as he remembered them. He was careful about one thing: to omit nothing of the things that he had heard and to make no false statements in them. (*HE* 3.39.15 [LCL I, 297])

Elsewhere Eusebius passes on a legendary embellishment of this account, placing the locale in Rome, claiming Clement of Alexandria and Papias for support of it, and referring to I Pet. 5:13 as a proof text:

The light of religion greatly illumined the minds of Peter's hearers, so that they were not satisfied with a single hearing or with the unwritten teaching of the divine proclamation. But with every entreaty they begged Mark, whose Gospel is extant, since he was Peter's follower, to leave them a written record of the teaching they had received verbally. And they did not cease until they had persuaded him and so came to be the cause of the writing called the Gospel according to Mark. They say that the apostle, knowing by the revelation of the Spirit to him what had been done, was pleased by their earnestness, and sanctioned the document for study in the churches. Clement cites this story in the sixth book of his *Hypotyposes,* and the bishop of Hierapolis, named Papias, agrees with him. He also says that Peter mentions Mark in his first letter and that he wrote it in Rome itself, which they say that he himself indicates, referring to the city figuratively as Babylon. (*HE* 2.15.15 [LCL I, 144f.])

---

28. *NT Apoc.* II, 642-653.

Of course it is uncertain here just how far the localization in Rome goes back to Papias and to what extent he has availed himself of I Pet. 5:13 not only as a proof text but also as a source.

That Peter and Paul worked in Rome and suffered martyrdom there can be based on general notices concerning the apostolic origin of the Roman church, even apart from special traditions, of the second half of the second century. Eusebius quotes from the letter of Dionysius of Corinth to the church in Rome (about 170):

> You also, by such an admonition, have bound together the planting of the Romans and Corinthians by Peter and Paul, for both of them also planted and taught us in our Corinth and also taught and suffered martyrdom in Italy at the same time. (*HE* 2.25.8 [LCL I, 183])

In accord with this Tertullian explains:

> How happy is its [Rome's] church! On it apostles poured all their doctrine along with their blood. There Peter endured a passion like his Lord's. There Paul won his crown in a death like that of John [the Baptist]. (*De Praescriptione Haereticorum* 36 [*ANF* III, 260])[29]

Porphyry wrote as a critical opponent and reversed the meaning of this understanding of Peter's end: Peter "was crucified after feeding the lambs not even for a few months," i.e., without accomplishing anything of significance.[30]

For additional proofs Eusebius refers to the apostle's burial chambers, quoting a document from the Roman elder Gaius from the beginning of the third century:

> But I can point out the trophies of the apostles. For if you go to the Vatican or to the road to Ostia you will find the trophies of those who founded this church. (*HE* 2.25.7 [LCL I, 183])

The "trophies" (τρόπαια) could be either where the apostles were buried or where they were executed,[31] though Eusebius regards them as the

---

29. Cf. the discussion of this statement in Cullmann, *Peter*, 119f. Similar are Tertullian, *Scorpiace* 15 (*ANF* III, 648); *Adversus Marcionem* 4.5 (*ANF* III, 349-351); Irenaeus, *Adversus Haereses* 3.1-3 (*ANF* I, 414-416).

30. Macarius Magnes, *Apocriticus* 3.22 (*The Apocriticus of Macarius Magnes* [tr. T. Crafer; London, 1919], 97f.); cf. Harnack, *Mission* I, 70-71 n.2.

31. On the meaning of τρόπαια see Dinkler, "Petrus-Rom-Frage" II, 220ff.

former. Around the year 200, therefore, people in Rome were pointing out the burial or execution places of both apostles. Archaeological research, especially the excavations beneath St. Peter's in the last decade, have produced, however, no compelling support for these traditions.[32]

Thus it has remained firm since the second half of the second century in ecclesiastical tradition that Peter suffered a martyr's death during the Neronian persecution in Rome. But before that time only unclear statements can be found about the apostle's death. It is therefore understandable that from time to time in historical research a residence of Peter in Rome has been denied altogether. The argument of a recent representative of this thesis, Karl Heussi — not just his quite inadequate treatment of I Pet. 5:13 — lends support to the opposite conclusion.[33] With a high degree of probability we can conclude from the sparse early traditions that Peter was a martyr in the Neronian persecution. From the silence of Paul's letters it is apparent that Peter first came to Rome at the time of their composition or yet later.

On the basis of our inquiry thus far we can conclude the following about the composition of our letter: If it was, as it claims, written by Peter through the mediation of Silvanus in Rome, then it would have to have been written prior to the Neronian persecution in the year 64.

c. The thoroughly formulaic naming of Peter as the author is specified more clearly at the conclusion of the letter, not only in local but also in personal terms. Adding their voices to the letter as senders of greetings are "Mark" and the church in Rome. Mark does so as a man of the earliest church and coworker with the apostles, one who, as we have seen, was recognized early as a transmitter of tradition from Peter and as the author of the Second Gospel. The Roman church does so as the especially prominent and threatened church in the capital city, the first martyr community in the Church among all those suffering within broader society.

Above all, however, the letter indicates it was "written through Silvanus," i.e., that it was drawn up by him at the commission of Peter.[34] Thereby, a man personally known from the beginning to the Christians

---

32. Cf. Cullmann, *Peter,* 120-165, and the literature listed in n.23 above.

33. K. Heussi, *War Petrus in Rom?* (Gotha, 1936), 36-39 on I Pet. 5:13. See Cullmann's report on the status of research in *Peter,* 76-83.

34. See the comments on 5:12.

of Asia Minor takes his place between them and Peter. He, like Peter, had begun his work in the earliest church in Palestine, but then had become a participant in the nurturing of the Hellenistic Church, which was influenced by Paul. He augmented the traditions of the former with those of the latter, especially since he himself had come from Hellenistic Judaism.[35] According to all that is known about both Mark and Silvanus, they could have been in Rome during the time in question.

Thus the letter's own statements about its origin provide a well-rounded picture. Now we must determine to what degree they are in agreement with what can be determined from the content of the letter about its origin and the circumstances being addressed. Are the letter's claims and its contents mutually supportive or do they exclude one another?

CONTENTS AND STRUCTURE

History of the Discussion

a. As scholars began to seek the letter's origin from its content there arose for many the embarrassment expressed by Adolf Jülicher: "A predetermined plan [from the author] cannot be found because one never existed."[36] It appears impossible to decipher from the letter a rational construction in which a thematic unity has been developed.

b. This perspective together with other observations led to the literary-critical hypothesis of Richard Perdelwitz (1911): A copyist added to the "letter" two further pieces, both from the same author. The "brief" "word of comfort" mentioned in 5:12 comprised only 1:1f. and 4:12–5:14 and was a short work of admonition and comfort dealing with severe persecution of the Church and dissensions among elders. 1:3–4:11 reflects "an address given to baptismal candidates on the occasion of a baptismal celebration."[37] The two parts must have arisen

---

35. See the concordance s.v. Σίλας, Σιλουανός. See also W.-H. Ollrog, *Paulus und seine Mitarbeiter* (WMANT 50; Neukirchen, 1977), passim, especially section 2.2.

36. A. Jülicher, *Einleitung in das NT* (fifth and sixth eds., Tübingen, 1906), 176; so also A. Jülicher and E. Fascher, *Einleitung in das NT* (seventh ed., Tübingen, 1931), 190. Cf. more recently Talbert, "Once Again."

37. Perdelwitz, *Mysterienreligion,* 19.

successively since their statements about persecution presuppose "two entirely different situations."[38] According to 4:12ff., where the text begins with a new address, the persecution is fully in progress, while it is possibly a matter of something in the future according to the statements in the earlier portion (1:6; 3:13f., 17). In 1:3–4:11 there is recurrent emphasis on the break with the past and the meaning of the "present" (1:3, 6, 8, 12; 2:2, 10, 25; 3:21). This parenesis is "in tune with the fundamental sound of joy"; it puts in sharp relief "the duties of the baptismal candidates which are expected of them in their new vocation as Christians."[39] In contrast, 4:12f. repeats in summary fashion those clarifications about suffering already given earlier.[40] Into the remarkable commentaries of Hans Windisch (1930)[41] and Francis Wright Beare (1945; third edition, 1970),[42] this literary critical explanation of the origin of the "letter" is adopted[43] with minor alterations, since it appeared to be so illuminating.

c. Within the contours of the general development of research this literary-critical hypothesis was developed further in the direction of a form-critical hypothesis. When Herbert Preisker revised Windisch's commentary (1951), he objected to the one-sided literary-critical explanation because it did not include the observation "that the writing was made up of individual and isolated fragments linked to one another without transition, each having its own stylistic peculiarities." This observation would be explained, according to Preisker, in the hypothesis that "the worship service of a group gathered for baptism (1:3–4:11) had found its literary fixation, an act that ended with the concluding worship service of the entire church (4:12–5:11)."[44] The worship service

---

38. *Ibid.,* 14.

39. *Ibid.,* 26.

40. *Ibid.,* 12-16.

41. Windisch, 76f., 82.

42. Beare, 25-28, 56 (6-9 in the 1945 first ed.).

43. B. H. Streeter, *The Primitive Church* (New York, 1929), 129ff.; Hauck (fifth ed., 1949), 35. Also, apparently without knowledge of Perdelwitz's study, Bornemann, "Erster Petrusbrief," developed the thesis "that I Pet. 1:3–5:11 was originally a baptismal address and that it was given about the year A.D. 90 by Silvanus in connection with Ps. 34 while he was in a city of Asia Minor" (p. 146). Bornemann maintains that it was not until the middle of the second century that the epistolary framework (1:1f.; 5:12-14) was added (163-165); already A. von Harnack (*Die Chronologie der altchristlichen Litteratur bis Eusebius* I [Leipzig, 1897], 451-465) had identified the epistolary framework as secondary and Wrede ("Harnacks Hypothese") had objected to this presupposition.

44. Windisch-Preisker, 156-162 (quotations from 157).

began with a psalm of prayer (1:3-12), followed by a word of instruction (1:13-21) and then, between 1:21 and 22, the baptismal act (which is not mentioned for reasons of the discipline of silence?). 1:22-25 continued then with a brief baptismal expression and 2:1-10 with a three-stage hymn of celebration. The parenesis (2:11–3:12) and a revelatory address (3:13–4:7a) concluded the baptismal service together with interwoven hymns to Christ (2:21-24; 3:18f., 22), the substitute for the concluding prayer that one would expect in a letter (4:7b-11c), and the concluding doxology (4:11). The concluding service of the entire church began thereafter and comprised an eschatological revelatory address (4:12-19), a word of caution to the elders (5:1-9), a word of blessing (5:10), and a concluding doxology (5:11). This presentation, then, was bracketed with introductory and concluding greetings (1:1f.; 5:12-14) and was sent to the churches of Asia Minor.[45]

This speculative hypothesis of Preisker, along with the commentary by Selwyn, which appeared slightly earlier but was not available to Preisker, was the first attempt to apply form criticism to I Peter. The hypothesis was then appropriated and developed further by F. L. Cross, who linked it with the idea that a paschal-baptismal-eucharistic service is preserved in the letter. According to Cross I Peter, which except in 1:1f. and 5:12-14 does not exhibit the character of a letter, offers not the entire liturgy, but only carefully worked-out pieces that the celebrant has added to the Easter service.[46] That this formulary was intended particularly for an Easter service is suggested by the following indicators: Πάσχα, "Passover," is derived from πάσχω, "suffer," in the paschal homily of Melito and by Hippolytus, and precisely this verb is a key term in I Peter as in no other writing of the NT. Moreover, Cross sees the letter's content as marked by the Easter assurance (1:3-5), exodus typology (1:13; 2:9, 11), and Passover typology (1:18f.). Other parts of the letter also contain references to the Passover worship, as that service is to be derived from the church order of Hippolytus.[47]

---

45. *Ibid.,* 157-160.

46. Cross, *I Peter,* 38.

47. The references to Easter (1:3) and to the exodus (1:13) do not exceed that which is found elsewhere in NT letters, and the conclusions drawn from the verb and from 1:18f. are not supported by the text. Therefore, these and other arguments in favor of a connection between I Peter and the Christian Passover celebration are rejected justifiably in Moule, "Nature and Purpose"; Thornton, "I Peter"; W. Huber, *Passa und Ostern, Untersuchungen zur Osterfeier der alten Kirche* (BZNW 35; Berlin, 1969), 109 n.10. Referring instead to an Easter catechesis is Tiede, "Easter Catechesis."

While M.-É. Boismard appropriated Cross's thesis with some reservations,[48] A. R. C. Leaney attempted to support the connection of
I Peter to the celebration of Passover by drawing on the Passover
Haggadah, to which, he maintains, the passages mentioned by Cross,
such as 1:18f.; 2:9f., 11, are even closer.[49] Yet, at the key location ("the
clue"), 1:19, the lamb is not the Passover lamb, even if the Passover
Haggadah is reflected in 1:18b. The connection, moreover, between
1:18b, "you were ransomed from your worthless way of life passed
down from your ancestors," and the Haggadah's introduction to Josh.
24:2-4 ("Formerly your fathers served foreign gods, but now the om-
nipotent One has made us into his servants, as it is said . . .") is so slight
that it could not be in the background, either as a connection in tradition
or as a current recollection for the author or the readers.

An examination of the discussion leads to the conclusion that these
form-critical hypotheses, which find in the letter a chain of liturgical
elements, are no more convincing than the literary-critical hypotheses
that the letter grew together out of a baptismal sermon and a letter of
comfort.[50] Both proceed from the presupposition that a rational development of thought is not to be found in the letter. But if such a development of thought can be demonstrated, then such hypotheses are no
longer necessary. They become rather preliminary investigations leading toward a substantively accurate form- critical and tradition-historical
analysis of the letter.

The Letter's Thematic Focus

The theme of the letter is characterized most often as an exhortation to
the churches in view of "affliction that is beginning and will increase
in the future."[51] The problem of the suffering of Christians is woven
like a golden thread throughout the letter, but the letter really only deals
with this theme intensively beginning at 3:13. Before that point such

---

48. Boismard, "Liturgie baptismale." Cf. below, pp. 114-121.
49. Leaney, "I Peter and the Passover," 246-248.
50. Opposing them rightly are also Selwyn, 17-24; Kelly, 15-20; Kümmel, *Introduction,* 420f. Still differently yet, but not convincingly: N. Hillyer, "First Peter and the Feast
of Tabernacles," *TyndBull* 21 (1970), 39-70. Cf. also, among others, Robertson, "Is I Peter
a Sermon?"; Shimada, "Is I Peter a Compositive Writing?"
51. E.g., Schelkle, 3.

thematic references are isolated (1:6f.; 2:19-21, 25). The theme of suffering almost appears to have grown in an unmotivated way out of general parenesis. But a closer look shows that suffering functions as an analogy in the parenesis that builds the first sections of the letter. The readers are addressed not as those who are persecuted, but, both in the address (1:1) and at the beginning of the second part (2:11), as "foreigners." Their situation in society is like that of Israel in Egypt. The parenesis instructs them in their existence as foreigners[52] and leads them to questions about suffering in society. Suffering is the counterpoint of existence in society.

Accordingly, the letter develops a unified thematic focus: the existence of Christians in a non-Christian society and overcoming that society by being prepared to bear oppression, i.e., to "suffer."

This thematic focus, i.e., the question of how to live in society — the fundamental problem of every social ethic — was for Jesus' disciples from the very beginning an acute problem. It was the earthly Jesus who had occasioned this question through his summons to discipleship. It separated from occupation and family. It was Jesus who established the interpretive direction in his sayings concerning possessions, marriage, and paying taxes to Caesar.[53] This thematic focus then became the concern for the earliest Church within the people of Israel in a different form than it did later for Christians living in the Hellenistic world. For the latter it was especially focussed as the eschatological character of Christian existence was misunderstood as pneumatic withdrawal from the world, since in this way the opinion took shape that married women or slaves who became members of the Christian community were no longer bound to their non-Christian partners. Paul answered this point of view with the important principle of early Christian social ethics: "Everyone should remain in the state in which he was called" (I Cor. 7:20; cf. vv. 17, 24).[54] Unlike the Essenes, Christians are not to abandon society but to invest themselves in a responsible way within its institutions. It is to this principle that the social-ethical instructions in Rom. 13:1-7 and the "household codes" (Col. 3:18–4:1; Eph. 5:22–6:9) address themselves.[55]

---

52. Cf. the discussion below, pp. 68-70, and the comments on 2:11.
53. Cf. Goppelt, *Theology* I, 110f.
54. Cf. the discussion of this passage in P. Stuhlmacher, *Der Brief an Philemon* (EKK; Zurich and Neukirchen, 1975), 43ff.
55. Cf. Goppelt, *Theology* II, 167ff., and the excursus below, pp. 162-179.

For I Peter the fundamental problem is eschatological existence in the context of living as foreigners and accepting duties within the institutions of society. It is the only writing in the NT to thematically appropriate this problem in view of the generally resultant conflict situation. In its further development it goes beyond Paul by incorporating the conflict: One encounters in the institutions of society not only the will of the Lord of history (cf. Rom. 13:1f.), but also human caprice and injustice (cf. I Pet. 2:18). Hence, it corresponds to the scope of its thematic focus when the letter in 2:13f. requires the subjection of oneself to Caesar and at the same time characterizes Rome in 5:13 as "Babylon."

For a long time studies of I Peter had no appreciation for this kind of developing thematic focus because such studies, operating under traditional Western rational presuppositions, were able to conceive of persecution of Christians only as the result of state-sanctioned police action. They did not see that existence in the institutions of society as such was problematic for Christians and that discrimination on the part of society as such amounted to "suffering." As soon as this thematic focus becomes apparent the rational arrangement of the letter becomes accessible.

Structure

The first major part, 1:(1f.)3–2:10, lays the foundation for the social situation of Christians in society, namely, that they are foreigners. This it does on the basis of the nature of Christian existence: Those who are baptized are called into a new existence "through the resurrection of Jesus Christ" (1:3), an existence that expresses itself in hope, faith, and brotherly love (1:13, 21, 22f.), into membership in God's eschatological people (2:9f.).

The second part, 2:11–4:11, constitutes the center and focus of the letter. This section develops out of the first part of the letter the apparently paradoxical deduction that being a foreigner in relation to society is to be confirmed precisely through responsible investment of oneself in the institutions of society, an investment that becomes a witness of faith (2:11-13). This confirmation requires that one be prepared to "suffer on behalf of righteousness" (3:14).

These fundamental developments are then made concrete in the concluding part, 4:12–5:11(-14). Pressures arising from society are unavoidable, as the worldwide experience of Christians teaches (5:9). But they are in no way surprising, but are an expression of participation in "Christ's sufferings" (4:13; 5:1).

The development of thought in the letter thus follows two key ideas, which are related to one another in polar fashion. These are the relationship of Christians to society and discipleship as suffering. At the beginning the first theme is treated broadly, then it gradually retreats while the second theme becomes more prominent. We must, however, raise the question: If the development is progressive, do not seams exist that led to the hypotheses of multiple sources?

Continuity of Thought

The concluding part, 4:12–5:11(-14), distinguishes itself from what precedes not only, as has often been observed, in its statements about the suffering of Christians, but also in two additional themes. We must examine whether these differences point to a different situation of origin or are to be understood as a further development of preceding material.

a. If the concluding part, as is generally thought,[56] speaks of persecution that is actually taking place, while the preceding part of the letter mentions only the possibility of future persecutions, then the two must come from distinctive situations. Closer examination shows that the concluding part requires submission under unavoidable present suffering, while the previous parts require preparedness for suffering that is possible at any time. It is true that the type of suffering is also described in different ways: According to 4:15f. one can be condemned to death in court just for the sake of Christ's name; earlier, the text (3:16; 4:4) speaks only of discrimination through "slanders."

But it would be quite naive to divide these different kinds of pressure into two situations, one following chronologically after the other, since one might be brought before the official courts (according to the concluding part of the letter) because of the "slanders" previously addressed. The concluding part, therefore, does not presuppose a different situation, but provides an intensification in its portrayal that corresponds to the development of the issue from the Pauline to the post-Pauline period.[57] This

---

56. Cf. below, pp. 310-312.
57. Cf. Goppelt, *Theology* II, 154ff.

often conventional intensification of a portrayal toward the conclusion has already been seen in this letter. The second part points more vigorously toward suffering than the first, which is content with the passing comment in 2:6f. To be sure, this step to the last part is considerably greater. The point behind this arrangement of the letter becomes all the more clear in the second difference between the two parts.

b. In I Pet. 2:13-17, as in Rom. 13:1-7, readers are challenged to subject themselves to Caesar and his official representatives. But in I Pet. 5:13 Rome is characterized as "Babylon," as the capital city that opposes God and his people. This difference does not reflect a development through time; rather, from the time of Nero's police action against Christians in Rome, both views existed together in the first-century Church, though they do not otherwise appear together in one document (cf. Rev. 13, 17; I Tim. 2:1f.; *I Clem.* 60:4–61:2 [LCL AF I, 114f.]). But I Peter takes up first the traditional parenesis seen also in Rom. 13 and then only at the end speaks of "Babylon." It seeks, it would seem, to integrate gradually the new situation in relation to society into the older parenesis. This also occurs in the words about suffering. This perspective is confirmed by a third difference.

c. What is said about the Church's internal situation also corresponds sequentially to the chronological movement from a Pauline to a post-Pauline situation: In 4:10-11a all are called to "stewardship" on the basis of their gifts of grace, much as in the Pauline orientation toward *charismata,* while in 5:5 subjection to the elders is required. At the time of the letter leadership by elders already overlapped with charismatic service performed by all in the churches of Asia Minor. But the two were not mutually exclusive in the forms in which I Peter speaks of them.[58]

It is, therefore, characteristic of our letter that diverse traditions are bound together in a progressive development of thought in the manner typical in addressing churches in the post-Pauline period. This uniqueness of the letter and its situation would be destroyed if one were to resolve these substantive tensions by a theory of literary-critical partitioning. The tensions compel us, rather, to make a precise analysis of the letter on the basis of its form and tradition.

---

58. Cf. below, pp. 337-339.

Epistolary Form

a. I Peter was composed from its inception as a letter, since the address "elect foreigners in the Diaspora" in the introduction (1:1f.) and the greeting from "Babylon" in the epistolary conclusion (5:12-14) belong to the tension of the entire document. The epistolary introduction is so arranged in its entirety that it leads to the specific content of the letter and the conclusion sums up the developments corresponding to the content and to the situation.

Thus it becomes all the more striking when in the thematic developments epistolary features are missing such as those characteristic of the Pauline congregational letters: The person of the author appears, except for the formal mention in the introduction (1:1) and the individuals named in the conclusion (5:12), in only one sentence, namely in 5:1, with an "I." Only in the first sentence of the thanksgiving that begins the letter do we find in addition to this a "we" (1:3-5). Otherwise, to its very end, the letter is shaped uniformly by the "you," referring to the recipients. Nowhere do the statements go into matters of personal contact or even into special situations or inquiries of the churches.

This impersonal character is due in part to the fact that this is a circular letter, though the letters in Revelation, for example, do go quite directly into particular situations. Above all, however, the impersonal character of I Peter is conditioned by the manner of presentation: The letter's words are not formulated for the moment; rather, the letter reworks ecclesiastical tradition in order to shape it in a generalized manner to produce a fundamental position on the situation as a whole. The writer does not, like Paul in I Corinthians 15, apply tradition in immediate fashion to the particular circumstance.

b. The literary form of the circular letter used in I Peter was generally and perhaps even in a specific manner prescribed. The form is seen in early Christianity also in the Apostolic Decree (Acts 15:23-29) and in Revelation (1:4, 11), while the letter that, though occasioned by actual circumstances, is also meant to be passed on (I Thess. 5:27; Col. 4:16; cf. I Cor. 1:2) belongs to another type.[59]

The form of the circular letter was well known in the ancient

---

59. On primitive Christian epistolary form see Kümmel, *Introduction*, 247-249, 416f.; D. E. Aune, *The NT in Its Literary Environment* (Philadelphia, 1987), 158-225 (bibliography in both) and the comments below on 1:1.

world[60] and especially in the OT and Jewish literature: In II Macc. 1:1-9 and 1:10–2:18 we find letters from "the Jews of Jerusalem" to "the Jews in Egypt" urging them to share in the celebration of the temple dedication festival. In terms of situation and content the two letters to the exiles in Babylon in Jer. 29:4-23 and *Syr. (II) Bar.* 78–86 come closest to I Peter. The first of these admonishes the exiles to settle in the foreign land. The latter, like I Peter, refers to "those who are dispersed" (78:7) and to the solidarity of all Israelites under suffering (78:4) and shows closer contact with I Peter's interpretation of suffering than any other Jewish document.[61] Perhaps the author of I Peter aligned himself, even if only unconsciously, with this tradition of letters written to the Diaspora in Babylon. In any case, the form of the circular letter was already known to him. In that form he developed a document with a unified and original style.

Style

The style of the letter is surprisingly unified and precise, even though it continuously appropriates very diverse traditions.[62]

First of all one notices the letter's good Greek. It utilizes fewer Semitisms than Paul.[63] Unlike many NT writings it follows more the literary than the colloquial language. On occasion in the use of particular words[64] or verbal forms, like the rarely used optative mood (3:14, 17),

---

60. Examples in M. T. Lenger, *Corpus des Ordonnances des Ptolémées* (Brussels, 1964), no. 47; P. Colomb, "La lettre à plusieurs destinataires," *Atti del Congresso internazionale de papirologia* (Milan, 1936), 202. On I Peter as a circular letter see also Aune, *NT in Its Literary Environment,* 180, 221f.; similar is Michaels, xlvi-li ("apocalyptic diaspora letter").

61. Cf. *II Bar.* 78:3, 5f.; I Pet. 2:19; 4:12ff., 16. This structural similarity is also emphasized by Spicq, 13f.

62. See P. Wendland, *Die urchristlichen Literaturformen* (HNT 1/3; Tübingen, 1912), 367f.; E. Jacquier, *Histoire des Livres du Nouveau Testament* III (Paris, 1908), 272-276; L. Radermacher, "Erster Petrusbrief und Silvanus," 287-292; Schlatter, *Petrus und Paulus,* 175f.; Selwyn, 25-27; D. Daube in Selwyn, 467-488; Spicq, 21; A. Wifstrand, "Stylistic Problems."

63. I Peter often uses the imperatival participle, which occurs frequently in Hebrew in the rabbinic literature and among the Qumran documents. But it is not original there but is taken over as a stylistic feature of Christian parenesis (see D. Daube in Selwyn, 467-488). The same is true of causal ἐν (1:2, 5, 6; 2:2; 4:16) and similar peculiarities of early Christian Greek usage, to which Schlatter, *Petrus und Paulus,* 176, points.

64. See Selwyn, 499-501, for the evidence in a list of parallels from classical and Hellenistic literature.

it comes very close to classical Greek. It has command of a considerable vocabulary so that it can vary and tailor its formulations. Whenever it lines up sentences and does not collapse them together this is not to be evaluated as "primitive";[65] rather, it serves the purpose of a more efficient appropriation of statements that were transmitted originally through public reading.

The command of language enables the author to utilize rhetorical devices of expression and to develop a sophisticated and memorable language form. He takes the reader through chains of synonyms[66] or similar-sounding words[67] and impresses his ideas on the reader with metaphors and images,[68] which are introduced by the frequently recurring ὡς. The author often formulates the same subject matter in antithetical parallels of negative and positive expressions.[69]

Repeatedly rhetorical formulations flow into a poetic-rhythmical stylization of the entire statement. As in other early Christian writings the writer does not use the poetic devices found in the Western world, meter and rhyme, but those of the Semitic world, rhythm and parallelism.[70] Thus, antithetical parallelism is found in 2:14; 3:18; 4:6 and synthetic parallelism in 2:22f.; 4:11; 5:2f.

Inasmuch as a sophisticated formulation otherwise is produced only through the rhythm of elevation and declination it is difficult to determine to what extent particular parts should be read as strophes. Windisch wants to read strophes almost throughout, but this has not been sufficiently established.[71] Even in the "Christ hymns," except in individual sentences it is impossible to make a singularly clear arrangement into rhythmically organized strophes.[72] The translation in the present commentary is arranged, therefore, into sense-lines that are generally apparent from the author's characteristic arrangement of sentences, but which do not represent regular strophes.

Within this independently shaped style, traditional materials are incorporated with more care than in nearly any other early Christian letter.

---

65. Radermacher, "Erster Petrusbrief und Silvanus," 288.

66. E.g., 1:10 (ἐξεζήτησαν καὶ ἐξηρεύνησαν); 2:9.

67. E.g., 1:4, 19: ἀμώμου καὶ ἀσπίλου.

68. 2:2, 25; 5:8.

69. E.g., 1:14f., 18f., 23; 2:16; 5:2f.: μὴ ἀναγκαστῶς ἀλλὰ ἑκουσίως.

70. Cf. O. Eissfeldt, *The OT: An Introduction* (tr. P. Ackroyd; New York, 1965), 57ff.

71. Windisch, 52, on 1:3: "In almost the entire letter it is possible to recognize a division into strophes and measured lines."

72. Cf. the discussion below, pp. 207-210.

THE LETTER'S PLACE IN EARLY CHRISTIAN
TRADITION AND LITERATURE

History of the Discussion

When one asks about I Peter's contacts with the rest of early Christian
literature, the impression arises for the literary-critical approach that,
as Heinrich Julius Holtzmann put it in 1885, the author must have known
just about the whole NT![73] This explanation of the data was altered by
the form-critical and traditional-historical perspective, which was applied critically to I Peter in 1946 by Edward Gordon Selwyn in the
commentary that has been the standard in interpretive literature on the
letter. In his introduction, Selwyn provides an overview to his procedure
and carries it out in detail in "Essay II: On the Inter-Relation of I Peter
and other N.T. Epistles."[74]

From the perspective of the form-critical approach Selwyn distinguishes four types of traditional material in the letter: (1) liturgical
traditions, (2) a "persecution-Torah," (3) several groupings of catechetical tradition, and (4) words of Christ. Alongside these traditions the
letter appropriates directly or indirectly numerous OT passages. In terms
of method, therefore, Selwyn presupposes a traditional connection with
other examples of early Christian literature wherever related concepts
are present and in cases where they are expressed or linked by the same
or similar key words. To a large extent, Selwyn follows here Philipp
Carrington's study of the earliest Christian catechism.[75] Selwyn's goal
is to reconstruct an (actual) early Christian catechism that stands behind
I Peter; moreover, he is especially concerned about proving I Peter's
connection to Silvanus and through him to the person of Peter.[76] Those
stated goals as well as the method applied make this first attempt at
determining the traditions appropriated by I Peter quite inadequate in
detail.

In the meantime, a methodological principle has come to be established that states that one can justifiably talk about a context in
tradition only if connections between statements are present not just in

---

73. H. J. Holtzmann, *Einleitung in das NT* (Freiburg, 1885), 313-315.
74. Selwyn, 17-24, 365-466.
75. P. Carrington, *The Primitive Christian Catechism* (Cambridge, 1940).
76. Selwyn, 368, 374f., 383, 389, and passim.

terminology and concepts, but also with respect to analogous structural arrangement of the statements. With the aid of these more precise categories and a more exact analysis tradition-historical study of I Peter since Selwyn has advanced through a series of articles but not yet through an overview study of monograph length. In regard to liturgical traditions, the article by Rudolf Bultmann on hymnic fragments furnished the on-going discussion with a major contribution;[77] correspondingly of value for the interpretation of suffering has been an article by Wolfgang Nauck,[78] and for parenesis one by Eduard Lohse.[79] Only Nauck has pursued in programmatic scope the pre-Christian antecedents of these traditions. And regarding the relationship between I Peter and the Synoptic tradition, the research of which has been encumbered by the complexities of Synoptic studies, Ernest Best concludes that the connections were through oral tradition available for catechetical usage, not through knowledge of one of our written Gospels on the part of the author of I Peter.[80]

Such studies have made it clear that I Peter is, in the words of Ceslaus Spicq, an "Épître de la Tradition";[81] for this reason the special character of its statements comes into relief only when the traditions standing behind them are clarified. In this commentary the exegesis of individual sections will be supplemented, therefore, with form-critical and tradition-historical analysis. The starting point for such analysis remains the conspicuous connections between I Peter and other early Christian literature that led many to the tradition-historical approach in the first place. But questions about literary familiarity and dependence have still by no means disappeared from the interpretive discussion; thus, prior to the exegetical examination of the tradition history of the different segments a survey of the most important connections will be given. Thereby attention is given to the older methodological perspectives out of which the present discussion has developed.

---

77. Bultmann, "Bekenntnis- und Liedfragmente."
78. Nauck, "Freude im Leiden."
79. Lohse, "Parenesis and Kerygma."
80. Best, "I Peter and the Gospel Tradition," especially p. 113.
81. Spicq, 15. Cf. also Bovon, "Foi chrétienne"; Brox, "Erster Petrusbrief."

Relationship to the Pauline Corpus

a. In the literary-critical stage of research it was normally assumed that the author of I Peter must have known Romans and Ephesians,[82] since it showed the following points of contact with those letters:

I Peter	Romans	Ephesians
1:3f.		1:3, 14
1:14	12:2	
1:14-18; 4:2f.		4:17f.; 5:8
1:22	12:9	
2:1		4:25, 31
2:(2)5	12:1	
2:4-6		2:20-22
2:4-10	9:25, 32f.	
2:13-17	13:1, 3f., 7	
3:1		5:22
3:9	12:17	
3:22		1:20f.
4:1	6:7	
4:10f.	12:6	
4:13; 5:1	8:17	
5:8f.		6:11-13

When one pays attention to the type of contacts, especially to matters of genre for the passages cited, it becomes plain that none of them — except for OT citations — is entirely verbatim in such a way as to make necessary the conclusion of literary citation. Of the about nine points of contact with Romans, six, including the conspicuous ones in I Pet. 2:13-17 and 3:9, are found in the parenetic portion of Romans, chs. 12 and 13. Once, in I Pet. 2:4-10 and Rom. 9:25, 32f., OT quota-

---

82. So Knopf, 8, and more confidently T. Zahn, *Introduction to the NT* II (tr. M. W. Jacobus, et al.; Edinburgh/New York, 1909), 186-188, n.4; more recently, Beare, 219f. According to Selwyn, 19, the author of I Peter might have been familiar with Romans and Ephesians, and the author of James might have been familiar with I Peter. Selwyn attempts to show, moreover, direct connections between I Peter and I and II Thessalonians (pp. 369-384), arguing thereby for the reworking of I Peter by Silvanus (383f.). But the points of correspondence are no more than a few related concepts and key words (so Kelly, 12; Schelkle, 6; Knopf, 9).

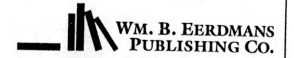
WM. B. EERDMANS
PUBLISHING CO.

COMMENTARY ON 1 PETER

by Leonhard Goppelt

translated and augmented by John E. Alsup

$34.99, hardcover
440 pages
ISBN 0-8028-3719-0
October 1993

Please send a copy of any notice you give this
book to Jeanne Elders DeWaard, Publicity Dept.

255 JEFFERSON AVE. S.E. / GRAND RAPIDS, MICHIGAN 49503
1-800-633-9326 / IN MICHIGAN CALL COLLECT 616-459-4591 / FAX 616-459-6540

tions are used in the same combination. Both parenesis and OT testimonia circulated, however, as oral tradition in early Christian communities.[83] Thus, the type of agreement as well as other usage of this material in early Christianity suggests that the contacts rest on common oral tradition. In the two remaining places (I Pet. 4:1; 4:13 and 5:1) the letters are similar only with respect to particular terms or the overall concept.

Of the seven points of correspondence given in support of a literary familiarity with Ephesians, four are a matter of standard parenetic phrases (I Pet. 1:14-18; 4:2f.; 2:1; 3:1; 5:8f.). Of the remaining three, one is a familiar ecclesiological image (2:4-6), another is a christological formula (3:22), and the other is a formula for the opening of a letter (1:3f.). Hence, it is not possible to speak here of literary dependence.[84]

The same conclusion is all the more necessary with regard to the Pastoral Epistles since here the points of contact are much fewer in number. They are as follows:

I Peter	Titus	I Timothy
1:3-5	3:4-7	
2:1	3:3	
2:9	2:14	
3:1-6		2:9-11

In sum, the points of contact with Romans are by far the most numerous, but neither with it nor with any other Pauline or deutero-Pauline writing is a literary connection probable. All the more important for an understanding of our letter, therefore, is the relationship of I Peter to the Pauline tradition *as a whole*.

b. On the basis of terminology and theology I Peter has often been characterized as a "variant of Paulinism."[85] This suggestion arises primarily from the observation that I Peter uses a series of terms typical

---

83. See the comments on 2:6f.

84. So Kelly, 11; Selwyn, 462; E. Percy, *Die Probleme der Kolosser- und Epheserbriefe* (Lund, 1946), 433-440; and essentially already Usteri, 283-290. A different conclusion is reached by Knopf, 7f.; Mitton, "Relationship"; Beare, 219f.

85. So Knopf, 8; similarly R. Bultmann, *Theology of the NT* II (tr. K. Grobel; New York, 1955), 142f. According to E. Lohse, *Formation of the NT* (tr. E. Boring; Nashville, 1981), 213, I Peter belongs within the realm of the "Pauline school tradition." Cf. also Schenke, "Weiterwirken."

of Paul. It is the only NT document outside the Pauline corpus to use ἐν Χριστῷ, which was beyond doubt introduced by Paul (I Pet. 3:16; 5:10, 14). I Peter also uses ἀποκάλυψις (1:7, 13; 4:13), καλεῖν (1:15; 2:9, 21; 3:9; 5:10), συνείδησις (2:19), and διακονεῖν (1:12; 4:10) in connection with the χαρίσματα (4:10) in the sense developed by Paul. The following concepts also remind one of Paul: dying to sin in order to live for righteousness (2:24) and participation in the sufferings of Christ followed by participation in his glory (4:13; 5:1). Therefore, the letter undoubtedly arose in a Church tradition influenced by the terminology and concepts of Paul.

But though this tradition has been influenced by Paul, it was not determined by him. It contained Pauline components, but it did not derive from him directly. Even those terms and concepts that originated with him are used, in different degrees, in divergent senses, and the terms that carry the kerygma of the letter are alien to him. When I Peter speaks of the suffering of Christ and of Christians it does so, not in terms customary for Paul, i.e., σταυρός and σταυροῦν, but with a term alien for him, πάσχω. I Peter never speaks of the Church as ἐκκλησία, but uses metaphorical images of OT origin.

Can we determine the origin of the terminology typical for I Peter? The letter occasionally formulates the same statements in Pauline terms and in Synoptic terms (2:24f.; 4:13f.). But by no means does it simply link up Pauline and Synoptic formulations, as was done later, for example, in Polycarp's letter to the Philippians. On the whole, I Peter speaks the language of a Church tradition that came from Palestine with the Synoptic tradition and that often shows connections in its present shape with Luke and *I Clement*. The language is colored, moreover, by the traditions variously appropriated. This thesis finds preliminary confirmation from the points of contact with other early Christian writings.

Relationship to Other Early
Christian Epistolary Literature

When one compares I Peter to the rest of the early Christian epistles, one notices on the one hand that there is no connection between it and the Johannine Epistles, while on the other hand there is express mention of it in II Peter. In addition to this, there are points of contact with the letters of James, Hebrews, and *I Clement*.

a. James agrees from place to place with I Peter in both vocabulary and structural arrangement:

I Peter	James
1:1	1:1
1:6f.	1:2f.
1:23–2:2	1:18-22
1:24	1:10f.
2:1	1:21
4:8	5:20
5:5f.	4:6, 10
5:9	4:7

The structure of these points of contact will have to await detailed explanation within the framework of the exegetical discussion;[86] that structure is to be explained on the basis of common parenetic tradition that for the most part comes from Palestinian origin and not on the basis of literary familiarity.[87]

b. In contrast to James, Hebrews does not have complete clauses with the same verbal structure as I Peter. But the two letters do share some characteristic expressions: the alien status of believers (I Pet. 1:1; 2:11; Heb. 11:13), the blood of sprinkling (1:2; Heb. 12:24), the living word (1:23; Heb. 4:12), the bearing up of sins (2:24; Heb. 10:10), Jesus the shepherd (2:25; 5:4; Heb. 13:20), Christ's suffering unto death ἐφ' ἅπαξ (3:18; Heb. 9:28), Christ as example (3:22; Heb. 12:17), the inherited blessing (3:9; Heb. 12:17), bearing the humiliation of Christ (4:14; Heb. 13:13; cf. 11:26), and generally Christ as model. What we have here primarily is a corresponding "spiritual atmosphere."[88] One can say in preliminary fashion: The two authors address similar situations with similar devices.[89]

c. *I Clement* gives expression for the first time to the Christianity associated with the church in Rome (ca. A.D. 96). Its correspondences

---

86. Cf. especially below, pp. 356ff.

87. In agreement with Selwyn, 462f., and Kelly, 11f., contra Zahn, *Introduction* I, 133f., n.3, and A. Meyer, *Das Rätsel des Jacobusbriefes* (BZNW 10; Gießen, 1930), 72-82, one should not assume I Peter's dependence on James, and still less dependence in the other direction.

88. So Selwyn, 464.

89. See below, pp. 68-70.

with I Peter consist mainly of a considerable number of words that are characteristic of both and that are only or almost only found in them within early Christian literature: ἀγαθοποιεῖν, ἀγαθοποιΐα, ἀδελφότης, ἄμωμος, ἄσπιλος, ἀπροσωπολήμπτως, ἀρκετός, παθήματα (Χριστοῦ), παροικία, τίμιος (regarding Christ's blood), and ὑπογραμμός. How are we to explain this kinship? There are no discernible indications that *I Clement* was familiar with I Peter any more than it was with I Corinthians. Similar or synonymous statements are rare: Of this type we have I Pet. 2:9 — *I Clem.* 59:2 (LCL AF I, 111): "called us from darkness to light," which is a piece of congregational liturgy, and I Pet. 4:8 — *I Clem.* 49:5 (LCL AF I, 92f.): "Love covers a multitude of sins," as well as discourse about the patriarchs as "fathers" (I Pet. 3:6 — *I Clem.* 4:8 [LCL AF I, 14f.]), which are both common formulas. The reference to the παροικία in the address of *I Clement* (LCL AF I, 8f.) is no more convincing as an argument for the appropriation of I Pet. 1:1 than is the commandment to subject oneself to the elders in 57:1 (LCL AF I, 106f.) as an appropriation of I Pet. 5:5. The portrayal of Christ according to Isaiah 53 in *I Clem.* 16:3-14 (LCL AF I, 34-37) does not point to contact with the portrayal in I Pet. 2:22ff. Hence, literary familiarity cannot be demonstrated.[90] But the surprising points of contact in terminology and concepts are not based on common formulaic tradition, as for example with James, but perhaps on the same locally conditioned linguistic and conceptual tradition.[91]

But while the linguistic and conceptual background in which I Peter thus may have taken shape, points, therefore, to the Western Church, especially to Rome, the first incontestable use of the letter was in the East.

d. The letter written by Polycarp from Smyrna around the year A.D. 112 to the church of Philippi makes direct use, as Eusebius already

---

90. So Usteri, 320-324; O. Knoch, *Eigenart und Bedeutung der Eschatologie im theologischen Aufriß des ersten Clemensbriefes* (Theophaneia 17, Bonn, 1964), 95f.; E. Massaux, *Influence de l'Évangile de S. Matthieu sur la litterature chrétienne avant S. Irénée* (Dissertation, Louvain; Paris, 1950), 42-44, 64; contra Knopf, *Lehre/Clemensbriefe,* 43 and passim; Hagner, *Use,* 239-246.

91. This traditional context is, of course, only one aspect of the complex prehistory of *I Clement,* which is pursued in K. Beyschlag, *Clemens Romanus und der Frühkatholizismus. Untersuchungen zu I Clemens 1–7* (BHTh 35; Tübingen, 1966), especially 201, 347.

made clear, of I Peter, though it does not quote it expressly.[92] These are the correspondences that can be seen:

Polycarp	I Peter
8:1f.	2:24, 22 (3:14); 4:16 (2:21)
10:2 (Latin)	2:12
1:3	1:8
2:1	1:13, 21
2:2	3:9
5:3	5:5; 2:11
7:2	4:7

Around A.D. 120 another representative of the Church in Asia, Papias of Hierapolis, "relied on testimonies" from I Peter (so *HE* III.16, with no indication of the passages involved).[93] Not much later II Peter, which also may have arisen in the East, refers to I Peter by calling itself Peter's "second letter" (3:1).[94]

All these varied points of contact with early Christian epistolary literature, which cannot yet be summed up in terms of structure, confirm that I Peter by no means arose out of the developing Pauline tradition, but made use of independent tradition, which has almost as many points of correspondence in James as it does in Paul. Its own roots become apparent when we compare it with the gospel tradition.

Relationship to the Gospel Tradition

The points of contact of I Peter with the gospel tradition involve Synoptic sayings of Jesus and Synoptic vocabulary and concepts. The Gospel of John is nowhere in evidence.[95]

---

92. Cf. P. N. Harrison, *Polycarp's Two Epistles to the Philippians* (Cambridge, 1936), 296ff.; W. Bauer, *Die Briefe des Ignatius von Antiochien und der Polykarpbrief* (HNT Supplement II; Tübingen, 1920), 284f.; Massaux, *Influence*, 183-187.

93. Cf. R. Heard, "Papias' Quotations from the NT," *NTS* 1 (1954/55), 130-134.

94. Further use of I Peter in second-century writings prior to Irenaeus is discussed by Massaux, *Influence*, 642f. *(Didache),* 131f. (Ignatius), 161f. *(II Clement),* 245f. *(Sibylline Oracles),* 321-323 (Hermas), 565-568 (Justin), 588, 590 (Athenagoras), and 602 (Theophilus of Antioch). It is noteworthy that Ignatius apparently did not encounter any traces of I Peter during his journey through Asia.

95. According to Gundry, "Verba Christi," I Peter contains numerous parallels to

I Peter reproduces Synoptic sayings of Jesus in the shape they took in parenesis and not directly in terms of the Synoptic tradition.[96] The restatement of the command to love enemies stands closer to the corresponding passages in Paul than to those of the Gospels. The pronouncement of blessing on the persecuted and the summons to the witness of action have close contact with the parenetic shaping of those sayings in the redaction of Matthew.[97] In most instances I Peter appropriates concepts and key words from Jesus as they had been shaped in ecclesiastical tradition: the image of the shepherd (2:25; 5:2, 4), invocation of God as Father (1:17), the interpretation of Jesus' death as a ransom (1:18f.), the designation of Jesus' suffering and death and that of his followers as πάσχειν (2:19f., 21, 23), and the portrayal of his suffering according to Isaiah 53 (2:22). Much the same can be said of the admonitions to be circumspect and to stay awake (5:8), not to be anxious (5:7), to be a good steward (4:10f.), and others.

The examples given here are sufficient to suggest the conclusion that the ecclesiastical tradition in which I Peter arose traveled the same road of development as did the Synoptic Jesus tradition. Like the latter

---

Johannine sayings of Jesus, mediated by Peter (similarly already Usteri, 305). In the passages referred to, however, one finds only similar thoughts or individual words: I Pet. 1:3, 23; 2:2 — Jn. 3:3, 7: rebirth; I Pet. 1:21 — Jn. 14:1: πιστεύειν with εἰς; I Pet. 1:22 (4:8) — Jn. 13:34; 15:12: mutual love; I Pet. 2:25; 5:4 — Jn. 10:11, 14; I Pet. 5:2 — Jn. 21:15-17: Jesus the Shepherd and his commission to shepherd. Best, "I Peter and the Gospel Tradition," correctly opposes Gundry's analysis, which is just as inadequate in regard to the Synoptics. Gundry's conclusion that I Peter makes extensive use of Jesus' sayings in their original form — sayings that stood in a special connection to the person of Peter — is entirely without foundation.

96. According to Best, "I Peter and the Gospel Tradition," 105f., I Peter used primarily two blocks of oral Jesus tradition, which approximate what is recorded in Lk. 6:22-33 (cf. I Pet. 2:19f.; 3:9, 16; 4:14) and 12:32-45 (cf. I Pet. 1:4, 13; 4:10f.; 5:2-4). Contact with Matthew, Best writes, is limited to two individual sayings: Mt. 5:10 (I Pet. 3:14) and 5:16 (I Pet. 2:12), perhaps Mk. 10:45/Mt. 20:28 as well (I Pet. 1:18f.), though a proximity to Mark in general is not discernible (pp. 111f.).

But this analysis cannot stand because it does not distinguish the types of contact, e.g., formula or only key words, and takes into account indirect mediation of the Jesus tradition through parenetic and other ecclesiastical traditions only in regard to I Pet. 3:9 (Best, 105). In order to clarify the relationship of I Peter to the Synoptic tradition, it is necessary to consider the parallel relationship and reciprocal influence of that which was passed on about Jesus in the gospel tradition and that which was passed on about him in christological, parenetic, and other ecclesiastical didactic traditions. Pursuing this aspect are D. L. Dungan, *The Sayings of Jesus in the Churches of Paul: The Use of the Synoptic Tradition in the Regulation of Early Church Life* (Oxford, 1971); J. Brown, "Synoptic Parallels." See also the comments below on 3:8-12.

97. Cf. Goppelt, *Typos,* 152-158; Selwyn, 24f.

it came out of the Palestinian Church and was embellished in the Hellenistic Church. Belonging to this ecclesiastical tradition were also an intensive appropriation of the OT and coloration by various religious influences from the world around.

The Background: Scripture and the Religious Environment

a. I Peter makes use throughout of the OT, both as linguistic influence and as support for points. It does so for the most part without express quotation. This sort of usage of the OT was already established within the traditions of I Peter and was prepared by *testimonia*.[98] With the aid of the OT I Peter understands the Christian message and the transformation of the human situation through it as eschatological fulfillment event (1:10f.). In typological references the community is characterized as the new holy, priestly people of God (2:9f.); it is reminded of the alien existence and the exodus (1:13; 2:11); baptism is interpreted as the counter-image of the deliverance of Noah (3:20f.); and Christians are obligated to maintain the posture of the fathers of Israel (3:5f.). The letter often refers to Psalm 34, but it did not arise as a homily on this passage.[99] In terms of self-understanding, in any case, the author of I Peter is first and foremost a theologian of Scripture.

Like Hebrews and *I Clement,* which are related to I Peter in linguistic style, I Peter made use of the OT in an intensive way, but formally and in terms of content in a way distinct from them. Hebrews and *I Clement* make use of the OT in exegetical argument, while I Peter uses it homiletically. In terms of content, the OT provides the writer of Hebrews with salvation-historical/typological correspondences, *I Clement* with authoritative moral analogies, and I Peter with wisdom sayings and images. Its hermeneutical approach places I Peter, like Hebrews, in the middle of the "apostolic" witness, since it announces that the eschaton is present in the dialectic of the now-but-not-yet. This cannot be said for *I Clement* or for the other documents of the Apostolic Fathers.

---

98. See the comments on 2:22; 4:8; 5:5.

99. Contra Bornemann, "Erster Petrusbrief," 146ff. (see n.43 above); Moule, "Nature and Purpose," 1ff. On other OT backgrounds in general see, among others, Deterding, "Exodus Motifs"; Osborne, "Utilisation"; Pryor, "First Peter and New Covenant"; Voorwinde, "OT Quotations."

b. The religio-historical background is felt in I Peter not directly but through the mediation of Christian traditions. What is mediated in this way confirms what has been said above in tradition-historical terms about the letter's origin. Behind the first part (1:3–2:10), in which the author expresses his understanding of the essence of being a Christian, stands a complex of tradition that proceeds from the self-understanding of the Qumran community. The Church is the holy, priestly people of the eschaton, who live in the present as foreigners. The second part (2:11–3:12) combines the household code tradition, which is connected to Stoicism, with this Palestinian description of Christian existence. In the interpretation of suffering (3:13–4:11), seen from the perspective of the history of religion, points of view from Jewish wisdom and apocalypticism, perhaps with some elements from the mystery religions, are mixed together. These points of view, however, here have been overlaid more thoroughly than in the two previously named parts with material from the Jesus tradition and from scriptural theology.

Thus, as in the letter of Polycarp to the Philippians, I Peter is furnished in many ways with early Christian streams of tradition and the religious backgrounds mediated to it by them. But in fundamental distinction to Polycarp, I Peter draws on a tradition going back directly to Palestinian origins that had been in conversation with the Hellenistic Christianity represented by Paul. I Peter then shaped this tradition independently into a fundamental, Church-wide form of address that nevertheless addressed a particular historical situation.

THE SITUATION OF THE ADDRESSEES' COMMUNITY

The historical situation of the communities addressed by the letter is characterized decisively by conflict with society.[100] To what degree are

---

100. See Dibelius, "Rom und die Christen"; E. A. Judge, *The Social Pattern of Christian Groups in the First Century* (London, 1960), especially 62-71; Selwyn, "Persecutions"; L. W. Barnard, "Clement of Rome and the Persecution of Domitian," *NTS* 10 (1963/64), 251-260; A. N. Sherwin-White, *Roman Society and Roman Law in the NT* (Oxford, 1963); Goppelt, *Apostolic,* 102-117; J. D. McCaughey, "Persecution Documents"; S. Sandmel, *The First Christian Century in Judaism and Christianity* (Oxford/New York, 1969); J. Molthagen, *Der römische Staat und die Christen im 2. und 3. Jahrhundert* (Hypomnemata 28; second ed., Göttingen, 1975); Brox, "Situation und Sprache"; Furnish, "Elect Sojourners"; Elliott, *1 Peter, Estrangement and Com-*

we able historically to identify this conflict and thereby the emergence of the letter? We are able to answer the question of historical situation only when we take into account the kerygmatic perspective in which this situation is portrayed in the letter.

The Kerygmatic Perspective

As has become clear, the three parts of the letter address the conflict in stages. The first part (1:3–2:10) mentions the conflict only in parenthesis: Those who are addressed stand in the eschatological salvation in spite of the trials of suffering that they experience on occasion through pressure from society. In the second part (2:11–4:11) the conflict becomes the reverse side of Christian behavior within institutions: One is to behave correctly even under sufferings. It is only in the concluding part (4:12–5:11) that conflict becomes a theme: Suffering under the pressures of society belongs to the very essence of Christian existence.

Therefore, the author's encouraging and exhorting address with respect to the conflict situation is developed progressively, while the terminology used remains the same. This terminology gives indication of the unity of the statements and their perspectives. The letter addresses "suffering" in a stereotypical way (2:19f.; 3:14, 17; 4:1, 15, 19; 5:10; less directly in 4:13; 5:9) that points to wrongs of various sorts arising from the aggressions of society. This affliction is not characterized by the LXX technical terms διωγμός ("persecution") and διώκειν ("to persecute"), which are used in various places of the NT, not even in 3:14, where the pronouncement of blessing upon the "persecuted" is appropriated.[101] Nor does I Peter appropriate the apocalyptic term for the eschatological affliction of the community of God, θλῖψις ("distress").[102] The concluding part of the letter, which directly addresses existing hardships, makes use only of παθήματα ("sufferings," 4:13; 5:9) and πάσχειν ("to suffer," 4:15, 19; 5:10) and refers to the activity of adversaries only with ὀνειδίζειν ("to revile," 4:13). The concluding

---

munity; Neugebauer, "Zur Deutung und Bedeutung"; Tarrech, "Milieu"; Aschcraft, "Theological Themes"; Winbery, "Ethical Issues"; Clark, "Persecution"; Senior, "First Letter of Peter" (comparing views of Balch, Elliott, and Goppelt); Neyrey, "First Peter and Converts"; J. H. Elliott, "1 Peter. Its Situation and Strategy."

101. A. Oepke, *TDNT* II, 229f.
102. H. Schlier, *TDNT* III, 141-148.

part's discourse on "suffering" ends with the reference to ἀγαθοποιΐα ("right behavior," 4:19), which is the key term for the second part, while the second part itself, in contrast, demonstrates the necessity for "suffering" as a consequence of "right behavior." In the concluding sentence, 5:10, just as in the introduction (1:6f.), suffering is mentioned only in parenthesis. The terminological structure of the whole letter is, therefore, consistent.

What are we to conclude from this unified use of terminology regarding the letter's kerygmatic perspective? The letter does not look on the situation of the Christians from the perspective of its environment as "persecution," but from the perspective of Christ as "discipleship." In 2:21-23 it portrays Jesus' experience in the same terms: "Christ also suffered . . . ; when he was reviled, he did not revile in return, when he suffered, he did not threaten." Because the historical situation has even terminologically been brought into the context of this christological perspective, the concrete circumstances are only observable in the context of this interpretation of them. It flattens out the historical particulars and allows the characteristic elements of the discipleship situation to emerge. In exactly this way, however, the character of the difficulties facing the Christians and the motivation for the pressures brought on them become more visible than they would through chronicled reporting.

The Nature of Their Suffering

I Peter refers to the addressees' experience with the technical term πάσχειν ("to suffer") in view of the course of Jesus' life. It refers thereby to wrongs done by society and its representatives up to and including execution.[103] Two things are said in essence with regard to the form in which Christians experience a limitation of life's possibilities, a limitation which can even lead to their eradication:

a. Christians were discriminated against by means of slanderous accusations: "if they speak against you as wrongdoers" (2:12); "when you are abused, those who revile your good behavior in Christ may be put to shame" (3:16); "they are surprised by . . . they abuse you" (4:4); "if you are reproached for the name of Christ" (4:14). This verbal

---

103. See below, pp. 335f.

hostility against the Christians comes from their fellow citizens, also and precisely from their relatives, colleagues, and acquaintances. It is more than personal insult: It takes from them the public respect on which existence in society depended, even more than in our time, and public officials have found action against them appropriate.

b. From the suspicion of Christians as "wrongdoers" followed accusations before the courts. This can be concluded from the pointed admonition in the concluding part of the letter: "Let none of you suffer as a murderer, thief, wrongdoer, or mischief-maker. But if one suffers as a Christian (ὡς Χριστιανός) . . ." (4:15f.). Murderers and thieves "suffer" because they have been handed over by the police to the courts and condemned there, normally to death. The admonition presupposes, therefore, that Christians were sometimes brought before the courts on the basis of slanderous accusations and could be condemned there for belonging to the Christian religion — even if the accusations proved to be without content.

According to the entire context these appearances in court were occasioned by police action initiated not by public officials, but by the verbal hostility of the general population, which is mentioned as affliction in the concluding portion of the letter (4:14) as well as earlier (2:12; 3:16; 4:4). Whenever Christians were "slandered" as "wrongdoers" the courts had to concern themselves with them, if these accusations were brought before the official agencies. Whenever official agencies and the courts were willing to take up these accusations, the instances of such accusations would increase and the situation would become more volatile. But the destiny of Christians apparently no longer depended only on such progressive circumstances conditioned by local and personal factors; for the public officials the Christian religion as such was already considered criminal, but the judgment was not yet followed out in a systematic plan.

What brought on this general social and official defamation of Christians? What was the point of the accusations?

The Motives for Hostility

One motive for the hostility of the addressees' neighbors is described in this declaration: "Let the time that is past suffice for doing what the Gentiles like to do. . . . They are surprised that you do not now join them in the wild profligacy, and they abuse you" (4:3f.). This motive is by no means contrived: It corresponds to the statements of Hellenistic critics and is, indeed, the decisive reason for the conflict. An essential principle of life in Hellenistic society was conforming tolerance, i.e., reciprocal acceptance, especially in religion and morals. Judaism sought to establish the absolute claim of its religion during the Maccabaean period and had opposed this principle in bitter confrontations with Hellenistic rulers. How Hellenistic people felt about Jews as a result can be seen in the pointed formulation of Philostratus, who referred to the Jews as

> a race that has made its own life apart and irreconcilable, that cannot share with the rest of humanity in the pleasures of the table nor join in their libations or prayers or sacrifices, are separated from ourselves by a greater gulf than divides us from Susa or Bactra or the more distant Indies.[104]

This posture of nonconformity was permitted generally for Jews, however reluctantly, on the basis of their ethnic peculiarity transmitted from the patriarchs. It did, however, create considerable outrage when it was experienced among one's own fellow citizens, acquaintances, and relatives: Hellenistic people expressed spiteful misunderstandings and misinterpretations of Christian statements and Christian life-style.[105]

Christian eschatological expectation of the collapse and judgment of the non-Christian "world" must have been entirely incomprehensible for a Hellenistic person. This together with a critical withdrawal from the customary forms of life must have called forth the impression that the Roman historians pass on as the reliable conclusion of the trials by the public officials: While Christians were not guilty of the criminal acts for which they were held in suspicion by the people and by Nero, who thus took advantage of public opinion, they *were* guilty of "hatred

---

104. *Vita Apollonii* 3.33 (LCL I, 541).

105. Typical is the polemic that the philosopher Celsus (ca. A.D. 160) directs against Christianity: Just as Judaism arose from a rebellion of inferior people against the commonwealth of Egypt, so also the Christian religion arose from an insurrection against the Jewish commonwealth (Origen, *Contra Celsum* III.5ff. [*ANF* IV, 467]). The Jews' laws and customs were, in all their peculiarities, the inherited practices of this people and were to be observed as such (III.5.25, 34 [*ANF* IV, 554]). Only the absurd claim to an absolute status is reprehensible (5.41 [561f.]). The Christian religion, however, teaches defection from all inherited religion. It is rebellion against the order of the world (5.33ff., 41; 8.14 [557, 644]).

against mankind,"[106] and the Christian religion was felt to be "a new and mischievous superstition."[107] The Roman governor Pliny summarized the conclusion of his own communications in the following judgment: a "depraved and excessive superstition" and an "inflexible obstinacy" in clinging to what is itself already punishable.[108]

These reports presuppose that the population actually held Christians in suspicion of criminal acts. The reasons for this were the withdrawal of Christians from the customary forms of society and their frequent gathering into closed assemblies, especially the sacred meal celebrations, in which one Christian greeted another with "the kiss of love" (5:14) and received the "body and blood" (I Cor. 10:16). In addition, there may have been within the Christian movement itself actual violations of law for various reasons; I Peter is certainly not thinking only of refined shortcomings when it warns that one should not misuse "the freedom" that the gospel brings as a "pretext for evil" (2:16), that no one should be brought before the court as "a wrongdoer or mischief-maker" (4:15), and that the Church offices are not to be misused for gain (5:2f.).

Adding to the feelings and expressions of aversion and suspicion were the resentments already present against westward-moving near eastern secretive religions and aroused by commercial losses that came about through repudiations of cult and magic (Acts 16:19-23; 19:23-40). Finally, there was the matter of Jewish polemic, which for internal and external reasons defended itself against this illegitimate child.[109] All these motives are, however, secondary in relation to the one named in I Peter: The decisive offense was that Christians were, in fact, fundamentally different.

Historical Location of the Conflict Situation

Where in the development of the conflict between Christianity and the Hellenistic-Roman world are we to locate the situation that I Peter presupposes?

---

106. See n.114 below.

107. Suetonius, *Nero* 16 (LCL II, 111).

108. Pliny, *Epistulae* 10.96.3 (LCL II, 401-405), accuses them of "pertinaciam certe et inflexibilem obstinationem" and "superstitionem pravam, immodicam." According to Knox, "Pliny," I Pet. 3:15 seeks to counter such accusations, but this is not to be assumed.

109. II Cor. 11:24f.; I Thess. 2:14ff.; Acts, passim; Rev. 2:9; 3:9; *Mart. Pol.* 12:2 (LCL AF II, 329, 335); 13:1; 17:2; Justin, *Dialogue* 131.2 (*ANF* I, 265).

a. As is evident in I Peter, the situation is fundamentally different from the time of Paul, above all, the time of his "missionary journeys" and the Epistles connected with the journeys. It is true that even during that Pauline period it was not only missionaries but also local churches (I Thess. 2:14) that encountered the hostilities of non-Christians. These hostilities developed out of slanders and led to the intervention of public officials (Acts 13:50; 14:19; 16:19f.; 17:5-9, 13; 18:12f.; 19:23f.). But that situation distinguishes itself fundamentally from what is presupposed in I Peter in two ways: First of all, the attacks in the Pauline period were particular, localized occurrences, so that, for example, no such difficulties in Corinth are mentioned in the extensive statements of the two Corinthian letters. According to I Peter, on the other hand, adversity has become the normal experience for Christians throughout the Empire (5:9). And the second difference corresponds to the first: In the Pauline period public officials proceeded on the basis of concrete incidents and accusations, while now in I Peter Christians are guilty on the basis simply of their membership in this religion group, apart from particular charges (4:16).

b. When did the situation thus change in relation to the Pauline period? To put it another way: When did Christians come to be socially discriminated against in the entire Empire and punishable as Christians in the view of public officials? In the year 112/113 Pliny the Younger, governor of the province of (Pontus-)Bithynia, which is named in the address of I Peter, inquired of Trajan whether membership in the Christian religion as such should be punishable or was so only when it was linked with certain deeds.[110] Trajan ruled for the former, adding, nevertheless, that Christians were not to be sought out, but were to be prosecuted only when properly indicted, and that they were to be set free when they repented. When Pliny published this correspondence, this policy of Trajan was generally known, and it remained the legal norm until Decius in 249/250.[111]

Does I Pet. 4:15f. presuppose this policy of Trajan? This is, for example, the assumption of Beare, who combines with it the hypothesis that the severe intervention of Pliny set in motion the situation that the letter of comfort addresses (not the "baptismal meditation" in 1:3–4:11).

---

110. Pliny, *Epistulae* 10.96.2 (LCL II, 401-403).
111. Goppelt, *Apostolic,* 113f.; cf. A. Wlosok, "Die Rechtsgrundlagen der Christenverfolgungen der ersten zwei Jahrhunderte," R. Klein, ed., *Das frühe Christentum im römischen Staat* (WdF 267; Darmstadt, 1971), 275-301; J. Moreau, *Christenverfolgungen,* 61ff.

For that reason, he thinks, the address in 1:1 included only the double province of Pontus-Bithynia.[112] But the letter clearly does not presuppose the criterion of action that Pliny applies, namely sacrifice for the emperor. Therefore, this hypothesis is generally rejected.[113]

The danger that already the name of "Christian" could by itself be the occasion for condemnation did not come about first following Trajan's decision. Pliny's inquiry itself presupposes that accusations against Christians were plentiful and that public officials could already regard membership in the religion alone as guilty of punishment. From what time was this possibility a reality?

Nero's police action against the Christians in Rome was the earliest known officially sanctioned action directed against Christians as Christians. It, too, was based on the bad reputation of Christians among the people.[114] This "persecution" was at first, to be sure, chronologically and locally limited and personally conditioned. But it shows that Christianity had now distinguished itself from Judaism in the eyes of the populace as an independent religion. Its members were now called "Christians," and their reputation was so unfavorable among the people that public officials could proceed against Christians merely on the basis of their being Christians. If an imperial measure affected Christians as Christians in this way in the capital city, the name certainly carried the same burden for all public officials of the Empire.

Therefore, the situation presupposed in I Peter was possible throughout the Empire from the time of Nero's action, but hardly before that.[115] Do we have any indications when it became acute? It is, of

---

112. Beare, 32-35.

113. So, with further counterarguments, Selwyn, 46; Spicq, 19f.; Kelly, 28f.

114. As Tacitus, *Annales* 15.44.2, 4 (LCL IV, 283), ca. A.D. 116-117, reports (largely accurately), Nero, seeking to divert the suspicion of the people from himself after the burning of Rome in A.D. 64, charged "a class of men, loathed for their vices, whom the crowd styled Christians" (see the comments below on 4:16) with starting the fire and had them seized in a police action, tried in court, and tortured to death in public games. At these court trials the Christians could not be convicted either of starting the fire or of the "shameful deeds" *(flagitia)* otherwise charged to them, but were convicted of "hatred against mankind" *(odium generis humani)*.

115. This must be emphasized even against the assumption that the letter might have been written just shortly before the Neronian "persecution," as is thought by Selwyn, "Persecutions," 48; Spicq, 19; Schelkle, 10. Such a dating cannot be based on an argument that the positive orientation toward the state in 2:14ff. was no longer to be expected after the experience with Nero, since this positive orientation was maintained even in *I Clement* (60:4–61:2) and thereafter (see above, pp. 21f.).

course, necessary that we separate ourselves from the understanding of history that developed in the second century, according to which after a first persecution under Nero there followed a second under Domitian.[116] This theory, which was strengthened by an orientation developing out of later persecutions, misconstrues the situation: Domitian did not suppress the Christian religion as such in a systematic fashion any more than Nero did. Both affected Christians, rather, through personally conditioned and very different measures of an individual sort. Under Domitian Christians were snared in the decisions that he made above all in the last years of his reign against all who did not take seriously his constantly increasing claim to divine honor. According to the sparse reports hardships for Christians occurred principally in two regions. It was in these parts of the Empire that the emperor's claim received especially emphatic support and that Christianity had expanded in an intensive way, i.e., mainly Rome and the western parts of Asia Minor.

According to Dio Cassius the emperor in Rome had his nephew, the consul Flavius Clemens, executed "because of atheism," had his wife Flavia Domitilla banished, and condemned many others to death or to confiscation of their goods because they had "drifted into Jewish ways."[117] Those who were involved were in reality Christians, as even Eusebius presupposes.[118]

The situation was intensified in western Asia Minor. Pliny knew about Christians who "twenty years ago," i.e., in the days of Domitian, had given up their faith, probably under official pressure.[119] In Ephesus a temple to Domitian has been discovered; it had a colossal statue of the emperor and was destroyed after his death.[120] The cult of the emperor probably provided the occasion for the writing of Revelation, as was thought even in the ancient Church.[121] The concern of Revelation is to warn its readers about worship of the eschatological ruler of the world (Rev. 13).

---

116. Melito developed this theory from the apologetic thesis that only the evil emperors persecuted the Christian religion: "The only emperors who were ever persuaded by malicious men to slander our teaching were Nero and Domitian" (*HE* 4.26.9 [LCL I, 391]). See below, n.122.

117. Dio Cassius 67.14.1f. (LCL VIII, 349).

118. *HE* 3.17-20 (LCL I, 238-241).

119. Pliny, *Epistulae* 10.96.6 (LCL II, 405).

120. Cf. B. Reicke, *The NT Era: The World of the Bible from 500 B.C. to 100 A.D.* (tr. D. Green; London/Philadelphia, 1978), 278f.

121. *HE* 3.20.9 (LCL I, 241).

So it was that under Domitian the dangers in which Christians from the end of the Pauline period on had been constantly living were intensified.[122] And yet, there is no reference in I Peter to the criterion that was decisive for determining if one were a Christian both for Revelation and for the public authorities, namely, one's position with respect to the cult of the emperor. Does I Peter belong to the time of Domitian? That question is frequently answered in the affirmative.[123] To be sure, Rome is for I Peter already "Babylon" (5:13), but it had become this according to Rev. 17:5f. through the Neronian persecution! But the particular focus of the Domitianic situation, especially in Asia Minor, i.e., the divine homage paid to the emperor, lies quite clearly outside the purview of I Peter.

Hence, the letter presupposes a situation, as is often said, between the years 65 and 90. All indications speak in favor of placing it in the first rather than the second half of this period of time. The situation introduced by the Neronian persecution is still alien for the readers and probably unexpected (4:12), while for the recipients of the Book of Hebrews it already has become customary (Heb. 10:32-39; 12:4). And in Luke-Acts the basis for affliction is developed in persecution sayings through one's connection to the "name"; this, too, represents a development subsequent to I Peter.[124] Thus, I Peter's emergence is to be dated, if one judges on the basis of the thematized struggle between Church and society, somewhere between 65 and 80.[125] Other indicators also speak in favor of this time frame.

---

122. Goppelt, *Apostolic,* 109-114; in the same sense, L. W. Barnard, "Clement of Rome and the Persecution of Domitian," correctly places the picture of a "persecution" by Domitian, which is buttressed above all by Eusebius's theory (*HE* 3.17f.; cf. 3.20 [LCL I, 235, 237-241]): "He was the second to promote persecution against us, though his father, Vespasian, had planned no evil against us." Additional traditions are in J. B. Lightfoot, *The Apostolic Fathers* I/1: *S. Clement of Rome* (third ed., London, 1890), 104-115.

123. Jülicher-Fascher, *Einleitung,* 196f.; Kümmel, *Introduction,* 424; see also below, n.125.

124. Cf. 5:13: ὀνειδίζεσθε ἐν ὀνόματι Χριστοῦ; 5:16: ὡς Χριστιανός, and Lk. 21:12: "[they will] persecute you, deliver you up to the synagogues and prisons, and you will be brought before kings and governors ἕνεκεν τοῦ ὀνόματός μου" (in Mk. 13:9 "persecute" is missing and the motivation is only of a substantive kind: ἕνεκεν ἐμοῦ; in 13:13 par., however: μισούμενοι . . . διὰ τὸ ὄνομά μου); cf. also Acts 5:41: "that they were counted worthy ὑπὲρ τοῦ ὀνόματος ἀτιμασθῆναι."

125. So also Wikenhauser-Schmid, *Einleitung,* 602 (cf., in contrast, Wikenhauser, *Introduction,* 504ff.); Kelly, 28-30; and Spicq, 18-21, who, however, for other reasons dates the letter to "the time of Nero toward the end of the apostle's life, perhaps in the year of his martyrdom" (p. 26). See also Glaze, "Introduction to 1 Peter." With similar considerations about the situation

THE ORIGIN OF THE LETTER

What we have learned so far about the situation addressed by the letter and about the traditional contexts in which it stands allows for certain deductions concerning its place in the early history of the Church. These deductions now need to be drawn together and compared with the letter's own claims about its origin, which were discussed at the beginning of this Introduction. In this way a picture of the emergence of the document, which from its beginning was conceived of as an entirety, i.e., as a letter, will become visible.

Time

a. When we concentrate on study of the conflict situation, mastery of which is the letter's immediate intention, we come upon discussion of the letter's time of emergence. This situation was, as we have seen, the intensive experience for Christians in Asia Minor and in Rome between the years 65 and 80.

b. The dissemination of Christianity throughout Asia Minor, which is presupposed in the opening of the letter, may have occurred as early as 65 and was certainly completed by 80. The letter does not go beyond this time of the basic mission; nowhere in it do the problems of the second generation come to the fore, or even, as in Hebrews, questions about enduring for a long period of time.

c. Furthermore, reliable references concerning the time of emergence can be derived from the two parenetic sections in I Pet. 4:10f. and 5:1-5, which concern themselves with Church offices. For the region in question we find rather closely clustered specific data about the development of Church organization.

I Peter is the only post-Pauline document still recognizing charismatic forms of service (4:10f.). In the churches addressed by the letter, such forms of service are mixed with an early form of organization under elders (5:1-5). This arrangement of Church offices existed before

---

of persecution, Knopf, 23, argues on the basis of the broad dissemination of Christianity presupposed by I Peter for a date of 81-90, and Windisch, 81, generally for the time of the Flavians. Dibelius, "Rom und die Christen," 189-192, assumes that the letter was written in the 90s in anticipation of the persecution through Domitian, which had not yet broken out. Also in support of the Domitianic persecution as the setting is Warden, "Imperial Persecution."

the stage of development reached in these regions in the days of Domitian (81-96). Already in 110 Ignatius found the monarchical episcopate to be operative in the western areas of Asia Minor. The Pastoral Epistles, which have the same region in mind, characterize the active elders as bishops, so that this group gains emphasis over against the larger body of elders (I Tim. 3:1; 5:17; Tit. 1:5-9); this preliminary stage of the monarchical episcopate was reached in Asia Minor probably as early as the years between 80 and 90. In Rome, where the development proceeded somewhat more slowly, *I Clement* presupposes similar relationships in around A.D. 96 as those seen in the Pastoral Epistles (*I Clem.* 54:2; 57:1 [LCL AF I, 100f., 106f.]).

I Peter comes close to the structure of offices represented by the Book of Acts, which does not correspond to the time portrayed in Acts but does lie chronologically before the circumstances out of which the Pastoral Epistles and *I Clement* emerged: I Pet. 4:10f. is most like Acts 6:2-4 and I Pet. 5:2a is most like Acts 20:28. Since the view of things in I Peter in relation to Acts is probably earlier rather than later, the latest chronological limit for I Peter is 80-85 and the earliest is the end of the Pauline period.

Thus, three independent criteria suggest to us a time of emergence for the letter between 65 and 80. This chronological location helps to clarify questions about the place of emergence and authorship, and these are confirmed by the following further reflections:

Place

Attempts to determine where the letter was written have led in various ways to the assumption that it was written in the East. It was from the East that we have our earliest references, namely by Papias and Polycarp, to I Peter.[126] And it was in the East that the name "Christian," which according to I Pet. 4:12 had become the ground for judicial condemnation, was first used to characterize the followers of Jesus (Acts 11:26). Thus, the letter could have been composed in Syrian Antioch[127] or in Asia Minor, where the greatest familiarity with the circumstances existed.[128]

---

126. Polycarp, *Phil.* 1:3; 8:1; 10:2 (LCL AF I, 283f., 293, 295); Papias in *HE* 3.39.17 (LCL I, 299).

127. M.-É. Boismard, *DBSuppl.* VII (Paris, 1966), 1415-1455, especially 1448-1453.

128. Beare, 50.

But against these assumptions is the fact that the problems that concern nearly all the Christian documents from Asia Minor and Syria play no role in I Peter. The Pastoral Epistles, the circular letters in Revelation, and the letters of Ignatius — but not I Peter — are concerned with the debate with Jews and Gnosticism. In this regard, I Peter is much like documents of that time coming out of the western Church.[129] The early attestation of the letter in Asia Minor merely substantiates the place to which it was addressed, the historical relevance of which no one contests.

Pointing to its place of emergence is the observation that its diction comes very close to that of three early Christian documents that are typical for the western Church, namely, *I Clement,* which represented the Roman ecclesiastical tradition, Hebrews, which was written in Italy (Heb. 13:24), and the Lukan documents, which in all probability came from that region of the Church, to which their basic frame of reference points. Indirect arguments, therefore, suggest that I Peter was written where it claims it was written, in "Babylon," i.e., Rome (5:13). The name "Babylon" is not intended merely to underscore the name of the author, on the assumption of familiarity with a residency of Peter in Rome. It illumines, rather, the concern of the letter, which is the situation of Christians in society, and probably also indicates the background out of which the letter emerged.[130]

Behind the letter stood the church in the capital of the world. This church came to be the first martyr community within the entire Church through the action of Nero. By the martyrdom of the two most important apostles it came to represent their will and testament. By all indications, I Peter was the first of a series of ecumenical writings addressed to the East from the Roman church.[131]

Author

Is it possible that the letter, as it claims (1:1; 5:12), was written by Peter through the mediation of Silvanus?

---

129. Goppelt, *Christentum und Judentum,* 224f.; *idem, Apostolic,* 123-134.
130. See the comments on 5:13.
131. A Roman origin is maintained by Kümmel, *Introduction,* 425 (as a possibility); Kelly, 33.

a. Over the years a series of doubts have been registered in connection with direct origin from Peter. Some are based on unreasonable expectations linked with his name, but on the whole they are persuasive.

1. Many have felt that a personal disciple of Jesus like Peter would make more of the image and words of his Master on the basis of personal recollection.[132] As it is, the letter describes Jesus' passion in the language of prophecy (2:22f.) and appropriates his words by way of Church tradition. Furthermore, this expectation *is* fulfilled by the undoubtedly pseudonymous II Peter. That document points in 1:16-18 emphatically to a personal experience with Jesus and even expressly mentions in 3:15, as one might expect of Peter, "our beloved brother Paul." But from the beginning the persons of the witnesses receded behind the Jesus tradition, which came about on the basis of their accounts; that tradition did not portray the course of Jesus' life in the biographical mode of "genuine reminiscence," but by probing for understanding in the light of Scripture. Even Acts does not have Peter reach back to his recollection of Jesus, and I John does not refer to the Jesus of the Fourth Gospel. In some ways, therefore, how I Peter treats the Jesus tradition says more for than against Peter as author.

It remains conspicuous, nevertheless, that the author applies his function as apostle in relation to the churches to a far lesser extent than Paul. This can be explained, as has become clear, on the basis of the letter's character: It seeks to apply tradition in a generalizing way — and is apparently not the word of an apostle in a direct sense.

2. Another argument that has been brought against Petrine authorship of the letter is that it betrays "throughout a strong dependent leaning upon Paul," makes use of his letters, and is "dependent on Pauline theology."[133] But tradition-historical analysis (above) has shown that the letter comes out of an independent tradition of Palestinian origin, which, while influenced by Paul, was nevertheless not determined by him. The roots of this tradition could speak for Peter as the source. But it is hardly thinkable that Peter was responsible for the further development of this tradition up to the stage represented in the letter, since it is shaped to a large extent by the reflective processes of the Hellenistic Church.

---

132. Jülicher-Fascher, *Einleitung,* 196, are able to ascribe I Peter only to one "who does not see in Jesus the powerful personality that ruled for a lifetime the person whom it once drew into its path"; so also Jülicher, *Einleitung* (fifth and sixth eds., 1906), 181; Knopf, 16.

133. Knopf, 17; so also Beare, 44f.; Kümmel, *Introduction,* 423f.

3. This last argument is especially valid if one takes into consideration the present linguistic shape of the letter. It is unthinkable that Peter
as a fisherman from Galilee had command of the Greek language to
the degree reflected in the letter, according to our stylistic analysis (see
above). Nor would one expect of Peter that the numerous allusions to
the OT should follow the LXX almost automatically.

4. Finally, the person of Peter does not fit into the situation of
the churches addressed in the letter. It is very difficult to imagine
Peter writing to missionary churches whose emergence did not
proceed from him but decisively from Paul, or that he would not be
mindful of this initiative. Finally, however, the expansion, the form
of government, and the affliction besetting these churches point to a
time following the Neronian persecution, in which Peter had in all
probability already died.

Thus, by all indications, the letter cannot come directly from Peter.

b. The letter also declares that it was written by Silvanus, though
as he was commissioned to do so by Peter (5:12). None of the doubts
expressed against Petrine authorship apply to Silvanus. To the contrary,
everything that is to be deciphered from the letter about the author would
correspond to Silvanus optimally.[134] He had traveled the path that the
tradition standing behind the letter had followed: He was a product of
the church of Peter in Palestine, and he had been temporarily a coworker
of Paul and thus had become a teacher in the Hellenistic Church. He
was from the beginning a Diaspora Jew, so he had all the linguistic
prerequisites. As Paul's coworker in the missionary work of Asia Minor
he also had personal contact with the core of the communities addressed
in the letter.

Therefore, it is often assumed with good reason that Silvanus
actually drafted the letter.[135] This is not a "secretarial hypothesis"
invented by a misguided apologetics. It is, rather, supported by in-

---

134. See the comments on 5:12.

135. Jerome explains, without mentioning Silvanus, the distinctiveness of I and
II Peter by saying that Peter made use of various *interpretes* (*Epistulae* 120.11 [*NPNF* second
series VI, 224]). More recently Zahn, *Introduction* II, 149-151 (cf. the exegetes mentioned
there on p. 158 and below in n.138); Radermacher, "Erster Petrusbrief und Silvanus," 293;
Selwyn, 9-17, 27-32; van Unnik, "Teaching," 92ff.; Spicq, 25 (listing other advocates of this
view). Kelly, 32, appropriates the hypothesis with reservations, as we do. The attempt of
Selwyn to prove the hand of Silvanus in both I Peter and I Thessalonians (cf. above, n.82)
does not succeed since I Thessalonians is stylized in a genuinely Pauline sense, as shown
by B. Rigaux, *Saint Paul: Les Épîtres aux Thessaloniciens* (Paris, 1956), 105-111.

dividual references and the manner in which the letter's content is shaped.[136]

c. And yet doubts can also be registered for the view that Silvanus is the letter's author. These doubts suggest that we should consider another possibility and keep the decision open.

1. These doubts focus first on the person of Silvanus. The letter was in all probability written later than Peter's death, possibly as much as ten to fifteen years later. So, one must assume that Silvanus carried out a commission of Peter only after Peter's death[137] or that he borrowed the authority of the apostle whom he knew so well for a written communique that appropriated the tradition shaped by Peter.[138] But could he not have written on the basis of his own responsibility? Could not the "faithful brother as I regard him" (5:12) be a self-recommendation? Is it thinkable that Paul's coworker should emphasize Peter exclusively in a letter to Asia Minor, not mentioning Paul at all? This would be very unlikely because of *I Clement*.[139]

2. Joining with these doubts regarding the person of Silvanus are those of a tradition-historical nature. The synthesis of traditions present in the letter has not been accomplished individually by one theologian, but by Church development as a whole. This does not exclude the possibility, however, that this development was represented by a teacher like Silvanus.

d. These reflections lead then to the following conclusions: The presence of the names of Peter and Silvanus are, measured in terms of the tradition-historical structure of the letter, unlikely to be a simple postulate of pseudonymous authorship, as if the actual author wanted just to prove a formal authority.[140] The letter utilizes, in any case,

---

136. This as well as the philological sense of the statement in I Pet. 5:12 is missed by the polemic that Beare, 47f., 209, 212-216, and Kümmel, *Introduction*, 423f., direct toward this possibility.

137. He would then assume a similar posture to that of Mark in the composition of his Gospel according to the legendary report of Papias.

138. E.g., Usteri, 345-347: soon after the death of Peter; Bornemann, "Erster Petrusbrief," 160: an address of Silvanus at a baptismal celebration between A.D. 80 and 90.

139. *I Clem.* 47:1ff. (LCL AF I, 89f.); Ignatius, *Eph.* 12:2 (*ibid.*, 187); *Rom.* 4:3 (*ibid.*, 231); Polycarp, *Phil.* 3:2; 9:1 (*ibid.*, 287, 295); II Pet. 3:15.

140. On the problem of pseudepigraphy see W. Speyer, *Die literarische Fälschung im heidnischen und christlichen Altertum* (Handbuch der Altertumswissenschaft I/2; Munich, 1971); M. Hengel, "Anonymität, Pseudepigraphie und 'Literarische Fälschung' in der jüdisch-hellenistischen Literatur," *Entretiens sur l'antiquité classique* XVIII (Geneva, 1972), 231-329; N. Brox, *Falsche Verfasserangaben. Zur Erklärung der frühchristlichen Pseudepi-*

tradition for which both names could stand as a seal. It is possible that it was known in Rome that this tradition was shaped in a decisive way by these two teachers and passed on under their names. Reference to them could be much like the concluding reference in Jn. 21:24. Be that as it may, the letter owes its existence to the tradition so characterized above and not to the musings of an unknown person of the second generation, even if it was written by a person of that time.[141]

The substantive relevance of an early Christian document, i.e., its "apostolic" or "canonical" character, depends not on the person of the author but on whether direct and genuine witness to Christ has been incorporated in accord with its intention.[142] This criterion applies to I Peter. Its witness is substantively "genuine" according to the criteria derived from the Jesus tradition as well as from the Pauline witness to Christ. It articulates the exclusive presence of eschatological salvation in Christ.[143] This salvation is present in the letter in its description of the already-and-not-yet in the dialectic of faith and sight and its mediation of it through address in the indicative and in the imperative.[144] The message of the letter is applied gospel, which accomplishes brotherly love in the Church and positive behavior in society as saving promise and summons. This gospel leads one, according to the letter, into affliction at the hands of the representatives of what has been formerly and enables one to overcome this affliction through the joy springing forth from the salvation that is, nevertheless, dawning.[145] The letter's proclamation of Christ is, therefore, to be designated as genuine and has not been appropriated from other early Christian documents available to us,

---

graphie (SBS 79; Stuttgart, 1975); *idem,* "Zur pseudepigraphischen Rahmung des ersten Petrusbriefes," *BZ* NF 19 (1975), 78-96; *idem,* ed., *Pseudepigraphie in der heidnischen und jüdisch-christlichen Antike* (WdF 484; Darmstadt, 1977); L. Donelson, *Pseudepigraphy and Ethical Argument in the Pastoral Epistles* (HUTh 22; Tübingen, 1986); D. G. Meade, *Pseudonymity and Canon: An Investigation into the Relationship of Authorship and Authority in Jewish and Earliest Christian Tradition* (Grand Rapids, 1986).

141. This should be said in any case in regard to the thesis that it was perhaps a "Roman Christian" around A.D. 100 (Jülicher-Fascher, *Einleitung,* 196f., 199f.) or "an unknown man of the second or third generation, who put this epistle together in hard times in the name of Peter" (Windisch, 81; similarly, Kümmel, *Introduction,* 424f.).

142. Goppelt, *Apostolic,* 162-167; *idem,* "The Plurality of NT Theologies and the Unity of the Gospel as an Ecumenical Problem," V. Vajta, ed., *The Gospel and Unity* (Göttingen, 1971), 106-130.

143. See the comments below on 1:10-12.

144. See the comments below on 1:8, 13.

145. See the comments below on 4:12f.

but has been shaped directly by the tradition emanating from the first witnesses.

Both criteria by which we are able to designate the letter as "canonical" and/or "apostolic" became effective, however, in various ways through the history of its canonization.

CANONIZATION (J. ROLOFF)[146]

I Peter established itself as canonical surprisingly early. As far as we can tell, its ecclesiastical validity was uncontested by the second century. In this regard, it represents something of an exception within the Catholic Epistles, in any event something comparable to I John.

The earliest witness to attest to the early valuation of the letter and to make known its reason for such is II Peter, which was written around A.D. 110. This pseudepigraphic letter not only testifies to the dissemination of I Peter, but also uses its authority to advantage (3:1).[147] In fact, with respect to its validity, it appears to place I Peter alongside the Pauline Epistles deliberately; these it presupposes, moreover, are generally known (3:15). This is all the more significant since II Peter is the oldest Christian document to refer to the Pauline Epistles with the technical term γραφαί, "Scriptures" (3:16), thus granting them the same rank as the OT Scriptures. According to II Pet. 3:1f. the function of the letters of the apostles, i.e., of the Epistles of Peter and Paul, is to recall "the predictions of the holy prophets and the commandment of the Lord and Savior through your apostles." Their authority does not depend on their content, but on the fact that they are, indeed, letters of the apostles, i.e., in the sense understood by II Peter, that they come from eyewitnesses of the great events of the first generation (1:16).

Irenaeus also considers I Peter to be composed by the apostle Peter and quotes it frequently. And yet, for him it clearly stands in the shadows

---

146. See B. F. Westcott, *A General Survey of the History of the Canon of the NT* (sixth ed., London/New York, 1889); T. Zahn, *Geschichte des Neutestamentlichen Kanons* II (Erlangen/Leipzig, 1892); A. von Harnack, *Das NT um das Jahr 200* (Freiburg, 1893); Massaux, *Influence,* 1950; Kümmel, *Introduction,* 475-510; K.-H. Ohlig, *Die theologische Begründung des neutestamentlichen Kanons in der alten Kirche* (Düsseldorf, 1972); B. M. Metzger, *The Canon of the NT* (Oxford, 1987).

147. Brox, *Falsche Verfasserangaben,* 18f.

of the Pauline corpus and has very little significance within the realm of scriptural truth against heretics.[148] Clement of Alexandria interprets the letter within the framework of his *Hypotyposes.*[149] Tertullian counts it in his Bible along with thirteen Epistles of Paul, the Book of Acts, the Book of Revelation, I John, and Jude among the *apostolicae litterae.*[150]

Origen lists the letter in his canon under the *homologoumena* and locates it directly after the Pauline Epistles and before I John, adding doubt concerning the apostolic origin of II Peter.[151] It is in Origen that I Peter appears for the first time under the heading "Catholic Epistles."[152]

Eusebius expresses a similar judgment. But his sequence is: I John, I Peter, and "if you will, the Book of Revelation."[153] He is quite decisive, moreover, about distinguishing I Peter as genuine, generally recognized, and uncontradicted by the other writings ascribed to the apostle Peter; the Acts of Peter, the Gospel of Peter, the Kerygma of Peter, and the Apocalypse of Peter he rejects entirely; he does acknowledge that II Peter appears to many to be "instructive," but rejects it as not genuine. Thus, of all the supposed Petrine writings "only one single letter is genuine and generally recognized by all teachers of the church."[154]

In view of this general recognition of apostolic authorship for I Peter, its absence from the Muratorian Canon is something of a riddle, since this index of documents recognized toward the end of the second century in Rome regards apostolicity as a decisive criterion.[155] If one does not argue on the basis of the fragmentary character of the Muratorian Canon or on the basis of the possibility of textual corruption, all

---

148. H. von Campenhausen, *The Formation of the Christian Bible* (tr. J. Baker; Philadelphia, 1977), 193f.

149. *HE* 6.14 (LCL II, 47-51); fragments in Latin translation in GCS III, 203-206.

150. H. Rönsch, *Das NT Tertullians* (Leipzig, 1871), 572; von Campenhausen, *Formation,* 275. Quotations in *Scorpiace* 12 (*ANF* III, 645f.: I Pet. 2:20f.; 4:12ff.); *De Oratio* 15 (*ibid.,* 685f.: I Pet. 3:3).

151. *HE* 6.25.7-10 (LCL II, 75-77).

152. Cf. *HE* 6.25.5 (LCL II, 75). The expression as such is older. It appears initially to have been added to I John. Cf. *HE* 7.25.7 (LCL II, 75) on Dionysius of Alexandria.

153. *HE* 3.25.2 (LCL I, 257).

154. *HE* 3.3.4; cf. 3.2 (LCL I, 193).

155. Kümmel, *Introduction,* 494, n.73; a different view in von Campenhausen, *Formation,* 253ff.

that is left is the assumption that I Peter was not yet known in Rome at the time of the Canon's emergence and that the letter was first able to establish itself in the course of the third century, coming from the East. This is not entirely impossible. The key voices of support are always in the East or among the Greek Fathers. In the Syrian Church, however, the Catholic Epistles gained entry at a late date. Its canon was limited until into the fourth century to the Gospels, Acts, and the Pauline Epistles. It was not until the creation of the Peshitta at the beginning of the fifth century that I Peter, James, and I John were included.

The Easter letter of Athanasius (367) conclusively established the canon of the Greek Church, refers to I Peter within a group of seven generally recognized Catholic Epistles, and determined the sequence followed by most ancient manuscripts: Gospels, Acts, Catholic Epistles (James, I and II Peter, I-III John, Jude). Behind this arrangement stood probably the intention to have the letters of the original apostles follow directly the history of the primitive Church.

In the canon of the Latin Church the Pauline corpus was placed before the Catholic Epistles; their individual sequences, however, remained unchanged. Later, Luther made a change in his translation of the Bible by putting Hebrews, James, and Jude together with Revelation at the end and I Peter directly after the Pauline Epistles.

THE TRANSMISSION OF THE TEXT (J. ROLOFF)[156]

The group of writings "Acts and Catholic Epistles" to which I Peter belongs is less widely attested in the ancient manuscripts, for obvious reasons, than the Gospels and the Pauline corpus. The complete text of the letter is, nevertheless, contained in nine uncial manuscripts and some five hundred minuscules.

The Egyptian text type is represented by the uncials ℵ, B, A, C,

---

156. See M. H. Lagrange, *Critique Textuelle* II: *La Critique Rationelle* (Paris, 1935), 529-578; H. Vogels, *Handbuch der neutestamentlichen Textkritik* (second ed., Münster, 1955); J. Duplacy, *Où en est la critique textuelle du Nouveau Testament?* (Paris, 1959); B. M. Metzger, *The Text of the NT* (second ed., New York, 1968); K. Aland, *Studien zur Überlieferung des NT und seines Textes* (Berlin, 1967); Kümmel, *Introduction*, 511-537; Wikenhauser-Schmid, *Einleitung*, 592f.; K. Aland and B. Aland, *The Text of the NT* (tr. E. Rhodes; second ed., Grand Rapids, 1989).

P, and Ψ and the minuscules 33 (ninth century), 81 (eleventh century), 326 (twelfth century), 1175 (tenth century), and 1739 (tenth century, the descendant of a fourth-century manuscript).

Witnesses of the Antiochene text are the uncials K, L, and S and the majority of the minuscules.

Witnesses of the Western text are almost entirely missing, since Codex D (Bezae) does not contain the Catholic Epistles (except for a fragment of III John), and the Old Latin tradition[157] is limited to fragments. Western influences could be present in the text of minuscule 383 (thirteenth century).

The papyrus codex of the Bodmer Library in Geneva (Bodmer Papyri VII and VIII), edited in 1959 by M. Testuz and bearing the siglum 𝔭[72], has drawn considerable attention.[158] It is a small format (15.5 × 14.2 cm.) codex of at least ninety leaves that apparently consists of several manuscripts bound together. Besides I and II Peter, Jude, and others, it contains the apocryphal correspondence between Paul and the Corinthians, eleven of the *Odes of Solomon,* the *Paschal Homily* of Melito of Sardis, an *Apology* written by the Egyptian martyr bishop Phileas (who died in 307), the *Protevangelium of James,* and Psalms 33 and 34 in the LXX text. The codex apparently was put together during the third or early fourth century in Egypt.[159] The significance of the codex is that it offers the only papyrus text of the Catholic Epistles to go beyond fragments; 𝔭[74] (= Bodmer Papyrus XVII) need not be considered here because of its late dating (seventh century). 𝔭[72] as text of I Peter belongs to the Egyptian type and often agrees with B, A, P, and 1739. With respect to reliability, one should not, on the whole, overestimate it.

We shall restrict ourselves in the following to a list of a few interesting variants from 𝔭[72].[160] *Unique readings:* 1:12: εὐαγγελι-σαμένων ὑμῖν instead of εὐαγγελισαμένων ὑμᾶς (apparently an accom-

---

157. Text editions: *Vetus Latina,* ed. by the Erzabtei Beuron, vol. 26/1, second installment: *Epistula I Petri* (Freiburg, 1958); W. Thiele, *Die lateinischen Texte des 1. Petrusbriefes* (Aus der Geschichte der lateinischen Bibel 5; Freiburg, 1965).

158. *Papyrus Bodmer VII-IX. Publié par M. Testuz* (Geneva, 1959).

159. F. W. Beare, "The Text of I Peter in Papyrus 72," *JBL* 80 (1961), 253-260; *idem,* "Some Remarks on the Text of I Peter in the Bodmer Papyrus (𝔭[72])," *Studia Evangelica* III/2 (1964), 263-265; J. D. Quinn, "Notes on the Text of 𝔭[72]," *CBQ* 27 (1965), 241-249; Aland, *Studien,* 134.

160. Extensive discussion in Beare, "Text of I Peter," 254ff.

modation to the preceding ὑμῖν); 1:17: καλεῖτε instead of ἐπικαλεῖσθε (this appears to be supported by the Old Latin witnesses that read "vocatis"); 2:3: εἰ ἐγεύσασθε ἐπιστεύσατε ὅτι χ͞ς (= χριστός) κύριος instead of εἰ ἐγεύσασθε ὅτι χρηστὸς ὁ κύριος (the quotation from Ps. 34:9 was not recognized by the copyist and was, therefore, interpreted as a christological formula; this made necessary interpretation of ἐγεύσασθε by the added ἐπιστεύσατε); 4:16: ὡς is missing before Χριστιανός, which breaks up the link between Χριστιανός and πασχέτω (v. 15) and alters the meaning (copyist's error?); 5:14 does not include the closing wish of peace.

Readings connected to already known variants: 1:22 (with ℵ, C, Ψ, and it): ἐκ καθαρᾶς καρδίας instead of ἐκ καρδίας (B, A, vg) (accommodation to I Tim. 1:5?); 2:20 (with ℵ, P, Ψ, and 1739): κολαζόμενοι instead of κολαφιζόμενοι (ℵ, B, A, and C) (simplification); 3:18 (with A, etc.): περὶ ἁμαρτιῶν ὑπὲρ ὑμῶν ἀπέθανεν instead of περὶ ἁμαρτιῶν ἔπαθεν (B and the majority of minuscules; but there are a number of other variants here,[161] this one apparently an accommodation to familiar christological formulas); 4:8 (with ℵ, B, L, P, 1739): καλύψει instead of καλύπτει (B, A, Ψ, and K); 4:14 (with A and Ψ): ἐπαναπαύεται instead of ἀναπαύεται (ℵ and B); 5:10 (with Old Latin, Sahidic, and Bohairic witnesses): στηρίξει θεμελιώσει instead of στηρίξαι σθενώσει θεμελιώσει (a simple error of omission?).

---

161. See below, p. 250, n.11.

Translation and Commentary

1:1f.: Epistolary Prescript:
To the Elect Foreigners in the Diaspora

1 *Peter, Apostle of Jesus Christ,*
to the elect foreigners in the Diaspora
of Pontus, Galatia, Cappadocia, Asia, and Bithynia,
2 *(who are elect)*
according to the foreknowledge of God the Father,
through the sanctification of the Spirit,
for obedience and for the sprinkling with the blood of Christ:

Grace and peace be apportioned to you richly![1]

Form and Style[2]

1. The prescript utilizes the two-stage oriental form of the ancient introduction to a letter also followed in the Pauline Epistles, II Peter, II John, Jude, Rev-

---

1. On the division of the translation into lines representing sense units see the Introduction, p. 25.

2. See P. Wendland, *Die urchristlichen Literaturformen* (HNT 1/3; Tübingen, 1912), 411-417; H. Lietzmann, *An die Römer* (HNT 8; fifth ed., Tübingen, 1971), 22; O. Roller, *Das Formular der paulinischen Briefe* (BWANT 4/6; Stuttgart, 1933), 55ff.; E. Lohmeyer, "Probleme paulinischer Theologie I: Briefliche Grußüberschriften" (1927), *idem, Probleme paulinischer Theologie* (Darmstadt, 1954), 7-29; correcting Lohmeyer: G. Friedrich, "Lohmeyers These über das paulinische Briefpräscript kritisch beleuchtet," *ThLZ* 81 (1956), cols. 343-346; J. Schneider, "Brief," *RAC* II, 1957, cols. 564-576; E. Peterson, "Das Praescriptum des 1. Clemensbriefes," *idem, Frühkirche, Judentum und Gnosis* (Freiburg, 1959), 129-136; C. Andresen, "Zum Formular frühchristlicher Gemeindebriefe," *ZNW* 56 (1965), 233-259; W. G. Doty, *Letters in Primitive Christianity* (Philadelphia, 1973); K. Berger, "Apostelbrief und apostolische Rede. Zum Formular frühchristlicher Briefe," *ZNW* 65 (1974), 190-231; F. Schnider and W. Stenger, *Studien zum Neutestamentlichen Briefformular* (Leiden, 1987).

elation (1:4), *I Clement,* Polycarp's letter to the Philippians, and the *Martyrdom of Polycarp.* Among letters in early Christian literature, only the letters in Acts 15:23 (the Apostolic Decree); 23:26 (the letter of a Roman officer) and Jas. 1:1 and the letters of Ignatius appropriate the Greek epistolary introduction. Another example of the customary form of the oriental prescript is Dan. 4:1 in the text of Theodotion (= 3:31 Aramaic): Ναβουχοδονόσοϱ ὁ βασιλεὺς πᾶσι τοῖς λαοῖς, φυλαῖς καὶ γλώσσαις τοῖς οἰκοῦσιν ἐν πάσῃ τῇ γῇ· εἰϱήνη ὑμῖν πληθυνθείη. The greeting is often expanded as, for example, in *II Bar.* 78:2 (*OT Pseudep.* I, 648): "Thus speaks Baruch, the son of Neriah, to the brothers who were carried away in captivity: Grace and peace be with you."

2. Paul expanded independently on the oriental formula. I Peter has only that part of this expansion that became generally typical for the early Christian Church letter and has nothing specifically Pauline:[3] (a) ἀπόστολος Ἰησοῦ Χϱιστοῦ is not made more specific as it is in Paul (and in the Pastorals). (b) The recipients of the letter are characterized by none of the typically Pauline expressions (ἀγαπητός, κλητός, ἅγιος, πιστός, ἐκκλησία). Instead, non-Pauline designations, which direct attention to the theme of the letter, are used;[4] but these terms appear elsewhere in epistolary addresses, namely in James (1:1: ἐν τῇ διασποϱᾷ) and in the Apostolic Fathers (*I Clement;* Polycarp, *Philippians; Martyrdom of Polycarp* inscription: τῇ ἐκκλησίᾳ τῇ παϱοικούσῃ), and thus show their affinity to a non-Pauline tradition. (c) The greeting formula of I Peter does not follow the one used consistently in the Pauline letters, I Thessalonians and the Pastoral Epistles excepted. In its use of the conspicuous πληθυνθείη, which appears already Dan. 4:1 (see above), 34, the formula is in contact with *I Clement,* Polycarp to the Philippians, the *Martyrdom of Polycarp,* and further with II Peter and Jude. χάϱις instead of the frequent ἔλεος was probably introduced into the greeting by Paul; it is found, however, in early Christian writings not influenced by Paul, for example, in Rev. 1:4. It may be considered in post-Pauline times as generally Christian.

3. Already the epistolary introduction to I Peter is stylized in sophisticated language. As is suggested by the translation, one can arrange it according to style and content into seven lines. Whether or not a poetic form is intended[5] may remain open. In the interest of the sophisticated style no definite articles are used.[6]

1   The address names as author "Peter, Apostle of Jesus Christ." Πέτϱος,

---

3. Schelkle, 18: "Here, too, the form created by Paul influenced I Peter (indirectly?)"; Beare, 73: " 'Grace and peace from God the Father' is almost the hallmark of the Pauline correspondence."

4. Paul does not use παϱεπίδημος; πάϱοικος is found only in Eph. 2:19 (not of Christians); ἐκλεκτός is very rare.

5. So, e.g., Windisch, 50.

6. BDF §261.6 (p. 137).

translation of Aramaic *kêpāʾ*,[7] originally a name of honor[8] then a cogno-
men, became in the Hellenistic Church the only name used.[9] The name is
supposed to insure a hearing among Christians in Asia Minor — independent of to what extent the apostle was a participant in the letter's composition. Even the Pauline Epistles give indication of the standing that Peter
had in their realm (Gal. 1:18; 2:9, 11, 14; I Cor. 1:12; 9:5). Peter was known
through the Easter kerygma (I Cor. 15:5), the gospel tradition, and the
animated exchange with the Palestinian Church as the first witness of Jesus
(Mk. 3:16 par.) and asthe representative of the primitive Church (Gal. 1:18;
2:9) — even though he was never himself actually involved in missionary
work in Asia Minor. Mt. 16:17ff. indicates how he was held in esteem
around A.D. 80 in Syria; the same is true of *I Clem.* 5f. and Ignatius, *Rom.*
4:3 in regard to A.D. 100 in Rome and Asia Minor.[10] But unlike II Peter,
I Peter does not lay claim on its own to the named author's formal authority
(cf. 1:8; 5:1); it argues only from the perspective of substance.[11]

The designation ἀπόστολος Ἰησοῦ Χριστοῦ is used almost formulaically and only here in the address. It does not, as in Paul, point to the
commission to the office and its legitimacy.[12] Only once does the author
refer to his office (5:1), placing himself among the Church's elders. Paul,
on the other hand, places himself among the charismatic leaders (I Cor.
12:28), which are recalled here only briefly (I Pet. 4:10f.).

---

7. Paul normally uses the Greek transliteration Κηφᾶς from Aramaic כֵּיפָא, "rock,"
"stone"; only in regard to the decision of the Apostolic Council (Gal. 2:7f.) does he use the
Greek translation Πέτρος. See O. Cullmann, "Πέτρος, Κηφᾶς," *TDNT* VI, 100f.

8. Cf. Mk. 3:16; Mt. 16:17ff.; Jn. 1:42.

9. Πέτρος appears in the NT as a surname with the original name Σίμων (Mk. 1:16)
only in the gospel tradition: Σίμων ὁ λεγόμενος Πέτρος, Mt. 4:18; 10:2; Σίμων Πέτρος, Mt.
16:16; Lk. 5:8; Jn. 6:8, 68; 13:6, 9, and passim. In the instructions to Cornelius in Acts 10:5,
18, 32; 11:13: Σίμων ὃς ἐπικαλεῖται Πέτρος and Σίμων ὁ ἐπικαλούμενος Πέτρος; in II Pet.
1:1, to secure the connection to the past: Συμεὼν Πέτρος. The author of Acts, when not
dependent on a source, uses only Πέτρος; so also the Apostolic Fathers: *I Clem.* 5:4 (LCL
AF I, 17); *II Clem.* 5:3 (*ibid.*, 135); Ignatius, *Rom.* 4:3 (*ibid.*, 231: Peter and Paul); *Smyrn.*
3:2 (*ibid.*, 255); Κηφᾶς only in *I Clem.* 47:3 (*ibid.*, 91), in a quotation from I Corinthians.

10. Strathmann, "Stellung des Petrus"; Cullmann, *Peter;* Gewalt, *Petrus,* 628f.

11. On the problem of pseudonymity see above. pp. 48-53.

12. That Peter was an "apostle" is certain for the entire NT. In what sense he was an
apostle is not said in I Peter, though it is surely to be understood here in accord with use of
the term at the close of the apostolic period, as seen in the gospel tradition: Apostles are the
twelve (Mt. 10:2; Mk. 6:30; cf. Eph. 2:20; Jude 17), though Paul is not excluded, as he is
in Luke's schematized arrangement. II Peter, which is based on I Peter, expressly includes
Paul (3:15). On ἀπόστολος see J. Roloff, *Apostolat-Verkündigung-Kirche* (Gütersloh, 1965);
F. Hahn, "Der Apostolat im Urchristentum," *KuD* 20 (1974), 54-77.

The letter addresses itself to the Christian movement in *Asia Minor* in the name of Peter from Rome[13] and is thus the first document that establishes and gives witness to the connection between these two regions of the Church. To be sure, the connection was prepared by the Pauline Prison Epistles[14] and even by Romans (15:19-24). It is out of this connection of the two regions that the early catholic Church was to grow in the second century. It is this ecumenical perspective that distinguishes the letter (cf. 5:9).

The Christians in Asia Minor are addressed as ἐκλεκτοὶ παρεπίδη-μοι διασπορᾶς, "elect foreigners who (live) as diaspora."[15] This address distinguishes itself from the Pauline address in a fundamental way: Paul characterizes his addressees in a vertical dimension as those who are "saints" "called" by God, who for their part "call upon the Lord's name" (e.g., I Cor. 1:2). I Peter characterizes them in the horizontal dimension in light of their relationship to the world around them: They have been set apart from the nations of the world by election and live scattered among them as foreigners who have no homeland here. The very address thus envisages the theme of the letter: Christians in society. It does not have particular churches in mind, but Christians in the everyday world living among their fellow human beings. The situation is brought into perspective by means of the visual model: They are living in society as "diaspora." In extrabiblical Greek ἡ διασπορά, the "scattering" and the "scattered ones," is found only in one context, in its use in Hellenistic Judaism as a technical term for that part of the Jewish people that lived outside the Palestinian motherland scattered among peoples from Persia to Spain.[16] As such it is applied here to the Church, as are the self-designations of Israel outlined in 2:9, without any noticeable polemic. To what degree has this use of the term appropriated its sociological and theological ingredients?

The *Jewish Diaspora*[17] came about through deportation and voluntary emigration and subsequently was encouraged by the granting of many privileges.

---

13. On the geographical references see above, pp. 3-7.
14. Cf. Goppelt, *Apostolic*, 102f.; *idem, Theology* II, 38.
15. διασπορᾶς is qualitative or epexegetical genitive, not partitive genitive.
16. Cf. K. L. Schmidt, "διασπορά," *TDNT* II, 98f.
17. *Sib. Or.* 3.271 (*OT Pseudep.* I, 368); Josephus, *Antiquitates Judaicae* 14.115 (LCL VII, 509), quoting Strabo: "This people has already made its way into every city, and it is not easy to find any place in the habitable world which has not received this nation." See J. Juster, *Les Juifs dans l'empire romain* I/II (Paris, 1914); A. Stuiber, "Διασπορά," *RAC* III, cols. 971-981; H. Hegermann, "Das hellenistische Judentum," J. Leipoldt and W. Grund-

Unlike the mystery associations of the oriental cults, the Diaspora did not merely serve the religious needs of individuals on a syncretistic basis; the Jews gathered, rather, into religiously exclusive communal organizations, the synagogue communities. Not only did they understand themselves as members of a people, but they were also connected organizationally with their center, the Temple in Jerusalem. But the Diaspora Jews participated in the commerce and life of their environment in accord with the picture given by the legends in Daniel and had considerable religious effect. It is the Jews' self-understanding in this situation that the technical term διασπορά expresses. In Hellenistic Judaism the term replaced what the Hebrew OT referred to as deportation, exile, and captivity, though in the LXX "the scattering" (διασπορά) is understood in the same way as in the Hebrew OT, as judgment that would be removed by the final gathering at the day of salvation.[18] What the Diaspora situation meant in a positive way is not linked in the LXX with the term; this positive note is emphasized in Jeremiah 29, in deutero-Isaiah, and in the stories of Daniel: Life in a society holding a different worldview motivates Jews to formulate an apologetic that represents conceptually the universal claim of "the Lord" on global society and that becomes an effective recruiting measure in the age of Hellenistic syncretism.

Out of this conceptual complex I Peter and other early Christian uses of "diaspora"[19] appropriate essentially only the sociological com-

---

mann, ed., *Umwelt des Urchristentums* I (second ed., Berlin, 1967), 292-345; M. Stern, "The Jewish Diaspora," S. Safrai and M. Stern, ed., *The Jewish People in the First Century* I (Compendia Rerum Iudaicarum ad Novum Testamentum; Assen/Philadelphia, 1974), 117-183; E. Schürer, *The History of the Jewish People in the Age of Jesus Christ* III/1 (ed. G. Vermes, et al.; Edinburgh, 1986), 1-176;

18. In all twelve LXX uses of διασπορά it is a technical term representing modification or enlargement of a Hebrew text threatening dispersion among the nations as a judgment (Dt. 28:25; 30:4; Jer. 13:14; 15:7; 34:17 = 41:17 LXX; Neh. 1:9; figurative in Dan. 12:7; cf. *Pss. Sol.* 9:2; 17:18 [*OT Pseudep.* II, 660, 666]) or promising gathering from among the nations (Isa. 49:6; Ps. 147[LXX 146]:2), particularly in response to repentance (Dt. 30:1-5; quoted in Neh. 1:8f.; Jdt. 5:19) or in a plea for repentance (II Macc. 1:27); cf. *Pss. Sol.* 8:28 (*OT Pseudep.* II, 660). More often the situation is addressed with the verb διασπείρω.

Philo and Josephus do not use διασπορά as a technical term. When the Diaspora Jews became homeless as a result of the destruction of Jerusalem in A.D. 70, Hebrew גּוֹלָה, which means "exile" and "exiled ones" in the OT, became the technical term for the Diaspora; cf. Str.-Bill. II, 490; A. Schlatter, *Der Evangelist Johannes* (Tübingen, 1930), 198f.

19. According to Jas. 1:1 ("to the twelve tribes in the dispersion") the technical term, in fact, signified a people in dispersion. According to the Agape prayer in *Did.* 9:4 (LCL AF I, 323): "As this broken bread was scattered . . . but was brought together and became one, so let thy Church be gathered . . . ," the Christian diaspora came about from the seed of the word and waits for a future, eschatological gathering. Self-understanding as diaspora has become a liturgical tradition and remained vital in Christianity until the fourth century, when both the self-understanding and the technical term disappeared. They reappeared for the first time in the nineteenth century, initially for confessional minorities, but in the world's new

ponents: Christians are diaspora as a people living in small communal organizations scattered among the peoples and waiting expectantly for its ingathering in the eschaton. The scattering, however, is not the product of judgment, but of an election that separates and estranges them from global society. And the ingathering is not described as a reuniting around Jerusalem or a return to the heavenly commonwealth (Phil. 3:20), but as a future gathering around the Lord, when faith becomes vision (I Pet. 1:8). The diaspora situation is an expression of the eschatological already-and-not-yet, an expression of being elected and being a foreigner. This characterization of Christian existence in the opening address of I Peter links up tradition-historically only remotely with OT and Jewish ideas about the Diaspora; its connections are much stronger with ideas about estrangement resulting from election.

The designation of the readers as παρεπίδημοι introduces the first part of the letter (1:3–2:10) programmatically and then is expanded in the second part (2:11–4:11) by πάροικοι (2:11). παρεπίδημος means "foreigner" (= ξένος), one who possesses neither rights of citizenship nor rights as a guest and who resides *temporarily* among another people;[20] πάροικος refers to the foreigner who lives *permanently* with an inferior status among the citizens of the land, i.e., the "resident alien."[21] The two terms are made graphic here by the reference to the model of the Diaspora[22] and

---

situation after World War II they characterize the situation of Christianity in world society. Even more, they declare that Christianity always remains a diaspora in nature, even in the Christian West, because it is such in accord with its essence. H.-J. Schoeps, *Barocke Juden, Christen, Judenchristen* (Bern/Munich, 1965), 117: Christians experience today what *galut* meant for the Jews throughout the centuries, "the bitterness of being 'only' guest-settlers in the whole wide earth." Cf. G. Niemeier, "Diaspora als Gestalt kirchlichen Seins," *EvTh* 7 (1947/48), 226-233; H. Kruska, "Zum neuen Verständnis der Diaspora," *TheolViat* 5 (1953/54), 299-321; K. Rahner, "A Theological Interpretation of the Position of Christians in the Modern World," *Mission and Grace: Essays in Pastoral Theology* (tr. C. Hastings; London, 1963), 3-55; R. Schnackenburg, "Gottes Volk in der Zerstreuung. Diaspora im Zeugnis der Bibel," *idem, Schriften zum NT* (Munich, 1971), 321-337.

20. So already in extrabiblical Greek; cf. W. Grundmann, "παρεπίδημος," *TDNT* II, 64f. As in I Pet. 2:11 it occurs with πάροικος in its two LXX occurrences: Gen. 23:4 (Abraham as πάροικος καὶ παρεπίδημος in the Promised Land); Ps. 38(39):13 (the Israelites in their land, since it belongs to the Lord; cf. Lev. 25:23; Ps. 119:19; I Chr. 29:15). In the NT otherwise only in Heb. 11:13 of the patriarchs: ξένοι καὶ παρεπίδημοι. The verbal form, frequently used in Greek literature, is absent from the LXX and the NT.

21. Cf. G. Stählin, "ξένος," *TDNT* V, 30f.; K. L. and M. A. Schmidt, "πάροικος," *TDNT* V, 841ff.

22. G. Stählin, *TDNT* V, 31, conjectures, without supporting references, that both

later by the allusion to Israel's situation in Egypt.[23] They were probably already familiar to the readers on the basis of Christian tradition as a designation for their situation.[24]

The idea that life in society is for Christians "the time of their παροικία" (1:17) is a basic motif throughout I Peter, above all in the first part. This designation is not so much occasioned by the conflict situation, i.e., by the "alienation" (ξενίζειν) of the environment regarding Christians (4:4), as developed in a substantive way out of the essence of Christian existence, in view, to be sure, of life in society: Christians are foreigners among their fellow human beings, even among relatives and acquaintances, because their existence has been established on a totally new basis. They are "elected" or — as is said subsequently in 1:3 — "born anew to a living hope through Jesus Christ's resurrection from the dead." Furthermore, they have been "ransomed from the futile ways inherited from your fathers as binding tradition" (1:18) and are called into community with the Holy One (1:15f.). They are, therefore, in the παροικία (1:17). They are "the elect, the holy people," who belong to God (2:9f.). To live in society on the basis of Jesus' resurrection means to have an eschatological existence in history.

In this way the image from OT and Jewish tradition of Christians as "foreigners" is expressed. There is no explicit reflection here concerning a home (Phil. 3:20); rather, according to I Pet. 1:4 one is to think of a future "inheritance" that is, nevertheless, already "preserved in heaven," that is, vouchsafed by God (cf. Hebrews 11). The sociological effect of being a foreigner is in view: Christians distance themselves as nonconformists from handed-down life-styles (1:17f.); therefore, those around them are "estranged" regarding them (4:3f.). In both Christians and those around them the effects of this foreignness can or

---

terms were also technical terms for the Jewish Diaspora. Possibly in favor of this could be such passages as Sirach prologue 34, where παροικία is used nearly synonymously with διασπορά (cf. *TDNT* V, 842f.). Philo uses παροικία exclusively, however, in a dualistic sense of the transcendent world above (*TDNT* V, 848f.).

23. See the comments on 2:11.

24. In the address portions of *I Clement*, Polycarp, *Philippians*, and the *Martyrdom of Polycarp*, παροικοῦσα has nearly become a stock term. Cf. further Dionysius of Corinth to the church at Gortyna (*HE* 4.23.5 [LCL I, 379-381]); the account of the martyrs of Lyons (*HE* 5.1.3 [LCL I, 405]); *Herm. Sim.* 1.1 (LCL AF II, 139); Origen, *Contra Celsum* III,29f. *(Origen: Contra Celsum,* tr. H. Chadwick [Cambridge, 1965], 146f.); *Diogn.* 5:5; 6:8 (LCL AF II, 359, 363). From the second century on παροικία, "parish, parochial," became a designation for the local church (cf. *TDNT* V, 852f.).

should be felt — the letter speaks of this in the parenesis — but the foreignness is established by election.

God's electing activity is in I Peter, especially in the first part of the letter, more of an orienting concept than it is anywhere else in the NT.[25] It is developed in 1:2 and 2:4-10 and then is appropriated once again at the end in 5:13. In 2:4-10 it links up in a central way with the calling of Israel in God's covenant, which in the OT, above all in Deuteronomy and deutero-Isaiah, was understood by the term "election" as an act of God's will.[26] That those "elected" in this sense become "foreigners" in society is traced out in a special form in connection with the OT and Jewish tradition of election.[27]

Elect Ones as Foreigners

1. The idea that elect ones become foreigners is to be found in the NT only in I Peter, Acts (7; 13:17), and Hebrews (11). And only in these same three documents does the NT use the terms used by I Peter for Christian existence as that of foreigners. Usage of these terms points to their OT usage: παρεπίδημος is used with ξένος in Heb. 11:13 for the patriarchs in the Promised Land, πάροικος in Acts 7:6 for Israel in Egypt and 7:29 for Moses in Midian, παροικεῖν in Heb. 11:9 for the patriarchs, παροικία in Acts 13:17 for Israel's time in Egypt.

Among these passages only Acts 13:17 links being a foreigner with election, but elsewhere, as in I Pet. 1:4, existence as foreigners is always shaped by the assurance of future inheritance, and this assurance is itself an expression of election. Precisely this assurance, as Acts 7 develops in a comprehensive way, leads Abraham (7:5), Israel (7:6f.), and Moses (7:29) into παροικία. According to Heb. 11:8-10, 13-16 as well the patriarchs become foreigners because they travel the path of faith, by following the nonverifiable promise of inheritance.

Hebrews inserts into this eschatological orientation of election and existence as foreigners two Hellenistic aspects with which I Peter is not familiar: In Heb. 11:10, 16 the promised inheritance is portrayed as the future city, which according to 12:22 (cf. 13:14) is at the same time the city that is already in existence in heaven. Here the concept of homeland and citizenship in the πόλις is combined with the OT apocalyptic expectation of inheritance and the city of God.[28] This motif is missing in I Peter. Also missing is any link with the ancient Hellenistic

---

25. Paul uses the term very rarely, perhaps because it was so overworked in Judaism and because its original meaning had become skewed. Cf. G. Schrenk, "ἐκλέγομαι, ἐκλεκτός," *TDNT* IV, 181ff.

26. Dt. 7:6-8; 14:1f.; Isa. 43:10; cf. G. Quell, "ἐκλέγομαι (OT)," *TDNT* IV, 146ff.

27. Cf. G. Schrenk, *TDNT* IV, 185f.; K. L. and M. A. Schmidt, *TDNT* V, 848f. (Philo).

28. So also Eph. 2:12, 19; Phil. 3:20; *Diogn.* 5:9 (LCL AF II, 361); *Herm. Sim.* 1.1 (*ibid.*, 139); cf. G. Stählin, *TDNT* V, 29.

dualism, according to which the soul dwells in the heavenly world and therefore is estranged from the material world of earth,[29] while Hebrews also has appropriated from this some aspects.[30]

While Acts and Hebrews leave the picture of existence as foreigners in its OT context and only indirectly bring it into relationship with Christians, I Peter applies this designation of the elect people directly to Christians.[31] It prepares the way for this by using πάροικος, which was a common self-designation in the second-century Church.[32]

2. When one inquires into the origin of this early Christian tradition one finds it — specifically in the form seen in I Peter — preformed in the self-understanding of the Essene community. A statement about that community's origin in CD 3:21–4:6 combines not only election (I Pet. 1:1; 2:9) and residence in a foreign place (I Pet. 1:1, 17; 2:11), but also adds other elements that constitute the first major part of I Peter: the exodus (I Pet. 1:13), the exile (standing for this the diaspora in 1:1), affliction (1:6), the true Israel (cf. 1:9f.), and total repentance (for this the second birth in 1:3, 23). This text reads (translation from G. Vermes, *The Dead Sea Scrolls in English* [third ed., London, 1987], 85):

> As God ordained for them by the hand of the Prophet Ezekiel, saying, The Priests, the Levites, and the sons of Zadok who kept the charge of my sanctuary when the children of Israel strayed from me, they shall offer me fat and blood (Ezek. xliv,15).
>
> The *Priests* are the converts of Israel who departed from the land of Judah, and (the *Levites* are) those who joined them. The sons of *Zadok* are the elect of Israel, the men called by name who shall stand at the end of days. Behold the exact list of their names according to their generations, and the time when they lived, and the number of their trials, and the years of their sojourn, and the exact list of their deeds. . . .

The same motifs return in CD 6:4f. (Vermes, *Scrolls,* 87):

> The *Well* is the Law, and those who dug it were the converts of Israel who went out of the land of Judah to sojourn [וַיָּגוּרוּ] in the land of Damascus.

"Damascus" here is not a geographical term, but the symbolic code name for residence in exile.[33] The community at Qumran understood itself, accordingly,

---

29. Stählin, *TDNT* V, 25ff., 32-35; Philo, *De Cherubim* 120f. (LCL II, 79f.), interprets Lev. 25:23, the most significant OT passage with regard to παροικία, with respect to the distance of the heavenly homeland.

30. Hebrews is regarded somewhat differently by K. L. and M. A. Schmidt, *TDNT* V, 852, n.64.

31. Cf. Bolkestein, "Kerk."

32. From the second century on, Christian Gnostics (Stählin, *TDNT* V, 32-35, refers, above all, to *Acts of Thomas* and the Mandeans) and — in a different sense — Catholic Christians confessed regarding themselves that they were foreigners in the world.

33. A. S. van der Woude, *Die messianischen Vorstellungen der Gemeinde von Qumran* (Studia Semitica Neerlandica 3; Assen/Neukirchen, 1957), 48-53.

as the holy people of God living in exile, in a foreign land, and in the desert and prepared itself for the imminent eschatological calling home: "when the exiled sons of light return from the Desert of the Peoples" (1QM 1:3 [Vermes, *Scrolls,* 105]; cf. 1QM 1:2).

    3. The Essene community's self-understanding shows itself here and elsewhere as a model that contains nearly all the motifs with which the structure of Christian existence is described in the first major part of I Peter. But even with respect to the points of contact already mentioned, the letter expresses these concepts not according to Hebrew terminology, but in the conceptual language of the LXX, of Hellenistic Judaism, finally in that of Hellenistic Christianity: It calls life in a foreign land διασπορά and not exile (גּוֹלָה) or residence in the desert. It speaks not of repentance, but of second birth. Even in this respect the content of its concepts is altered fundamentally, as we shall see. But in tradition-historical terms it is evident that the field of conceptual reference has not been appropriated directly from Essene tradition, but has been mediated through Christian tradition.

2a In three prepositional phrases the author clarifies how it is that election took place, how human beings came to be exiled among fellow human beings. These phrases are dependent on ἐκλεκτοῖς.[34] Election is based on the heavenly counsel of God the Father mediated through the Spirit and present as obedience and participation in Christ.

    The meaning of this sentence becomes clearer through form-critical analysis:
    1. According to its natural divisions the sentence belongs within the primitive Christian tradition of triadic formulas.[35] It is not related to the typically Pauline formulas in I Cor. 12:4-6; II Cor. 13:13; Eph. 4:4-6, nor to Jude 20f. It is, rather, more probably related to Mt. 28:19. It is most often linked to II Thess. 2:13f.: εἵλατο ὑμᾶς ὁ θεός . . . ἐν ἁγιασμῷ πνεύματος . . . εἰς περιποίησιν δόξης . . . Ἰησοῦ Χριστοῦ: If the same formulaic schema is utilized here as in I Pet. 1:2 then it has been filled out more vigorously in 2 Thessalonians. Most importantly, the surprising third element of I Pet. 1:2 has been adapted to general Christian concepts of the goal of election.
    2. When we ask how the peculiar substantive construction of the triadic

---

    34. Selwyn, 119, wants to connect them with ἀπόστολος; Beare, 75f., supplementarily with the wish for peace. But this is not justified on grammatical grounds.
    35. H. Windisch, *Der zweite Korintherbrief* (KEK 6; Göttingen, 1924), 429ff.; M. Dibelius, *An die Kolosser, Epheser, an Philemon* (HNT 12; third ed. rev. by H. Greeven, Tübingen, 1953), 14f.; E. Lohmeyer, *Das Evangelium des Matthäus* (KEK special vol.; fourth ed., Göttingen, 1967), 413f.; O. Cullmann, *Die ersten christlichen Glaubensbekenntnisse* (ThSt 15; second ed., Zurich, 1949), 30ff.; E. Stauffer, *NT Theology* (tr. J. Marsh; New York, 1955), 251-253 ("The Beginnings of a Trinitarian Creed"); Selwyn, 247-250; W. Nauck, *Die Tradition und der Charakter des ersten Johannesbriefes* (WUNT 3; Tübingen, 1957), 56-59; G. Kretschmar, *Studien zur frühchristlichen Trinitätslehre* (BHTh 21; Tübingen, 1956), 218, n.1.

formula, above all the third element, "for obedience and for strengthening with the blood of Christ," came about, then the Essene tradition, which is also operative in the context, offers a soteriological schema that is astonishingly similar in its construction and quite understandable as a possible source. In 1QS 3:6-8 the following arrangement is developed within the framework of determiners for the covenant renewal festival (1QS 1:16–3:12); according to the text salvation is to be obtained and, therefore, entry into the community is repeatedly made possible (Vermes, *Scrolls,* 64):

> For it is through the spirit of true counsel concerning the ways of man that all his sins shall be expiated. . . . He shall be cleansed from all his sins by the spirit of holiness uniting him to His truth. . . . And when his flesh is sprinkled with purifying water and sanctified by cleansing water, it shall be made clean by the humble submission of his soul to all the precepts of God.

This soteriological schema, which appears elsewhere, comes still closer to the substantive construction of I Pet. 1:2 if one keeps in mind that God's "knowledge" (עֵצָה) corresponds to his "counsel" (דַּעַת) according to 1QS 3:15[36] and that נזה, which is understood as sprinkling in the LXX, is represented above all by ῥαντίζω.[37] The similarity is, therefore, so conspicuous that it can hardly be coincidental.

3. This similarity suggests a similarity of situation, which might explain the conceptual similarity. In Qumran this soteriological schema was not only a teaching about salvation, but was also practiced as a ritual of entry. Therefore, we should inquire about the connection of the formula in I Pet. 1:2 with baptism. The formula's terminology clearly brings to mind the early Christian tradition of baptism: Sanctification through the Spirit begins according to general Christian understanding with baptism. The focal word of the formula, "sprinkling," refers in Heb. 10:22 to the inner aspect of the act of baptism;[38] I Peter, which is related in so many ways to Hebrews, speaks in 3:21 in the same way expressly about baptism.

Therefore, I Pet. 1:2 undoubtedly points to baptism, but in what sense? Does it reproduce a Christian ritual of baptism, which possibly was stimulated by Essene tradition?[39] A similar ritual can be traced in terms of the history of liturgy later in the old Syrian ritual of baptism. In it the communication of the Spirit and obligation

---

36. "From the God of knowledge (מֵאֵל הַדֵּעוֹת) comes all that is and will be. Before they existed he established their whole design, and when, as is ordained for them, they come into being, it is in accord with his glorious design that they accomplish their task without change" (1QS 3:15f.).

37. Lev. 6:20; IV Kgdms. 9:33; Ps. 50:9 LXX; cf. C. Hunzinger, "ῥαντίζω," *TDNT* VI, 977.

38. O. Michel, *Der Brief an die Hebräer* (KEK 13; thirteenth ed., Göttingen, 1975), 346f.; Hunzinger, *TDNT* VI, 982f.; Nauck, *Tradition und Charakter,* 59.

39. This is conjectured by Nauck, *Tradition und Charakter,* 59, and Hunzinger, *TDNT* VI, 982f.

toward obedience precede the water bath, the sprinkling (cf. *Did.* 7:1 [LCL AF I, 318-321]).[40]

4. I Pet. 1:2 does not describe, however, the individual acts of a baptism ritual. The first part, which is independent of the Essene schema, cannot refer to the first act of a ritual. Instead, it gives witness kerygmatically to the encounter of salvation, just like the entire formula; this encounter happens fundamentally in the act of baptism, but goes beyond baptism to encompass the rest of one's life. Such is also the result of the exegesis of the individual expressions.

In terms of tradition history, therefore, I Pet. 1:2 derives perhaps from a Palestinian-Syrian baptismal catechesis prompted by Essene precedents; such a catechesis continued to have influence within the circle of the Roman church (cf. Heb. 13:24). The statement here interprets baptism kerygmatically as calling into the condition of salvation. The translation of this tradition into the old Syrian rite of baptism is a second narrowing.

The three parts of the formula are accordingly held together not through the unity of a rite, but through the unity of God's activity and its goal: Election separates a person from the world and places him or her into the community of salvation, which lives yet as diaspora. This is encountered as the work of God the Father, the Spirit, and Jesus Christ and is, indeed, the demonstration of grace from the one God, ἡ εἰς ὑμᾶς χάρις (1:10). God is in I Peter, as for all of primitive Christianity, the One "from whom all things exist and for whom we exist," as the confessional formula in I Cor. 8:6 declares in connection with the Hellenistic Father-of-all formula and the OT and Jewish confession of God's uniqueness.[41] Election proceeds from God in a threefold shape. He is encountered as event, yet as event connected to word, which is the expression of One who is personally in relationship. Whether or not the Spirit is also thought of here, like the Father and the Word, already as a person, so that it is named between God and Christ, must remain open.[42]

θεὸς πατήρ is an expression of refined liturgical language which is used in the NT infrequently, appearing above all in the greeting formulas of letters.[43] It designates God as the Creator who now creates the new existence through the proof of his grace (1:3)[44] and, therefore, is addressed as Father in the name of Jesus (1:17). God's πρόγνωσις,

---

40. Nauck, *Tradition und Charakter,* 155-159. Acts 10:44-48 is, however, not a baptismal ritual, but a singular exception.

41. G. Schrenk, "πατήρ," *TDNT* V, 1012.

42. One cannot, however, say with Selwyn, 249, that the passage presupposes the doctrine of the "three persons of the Holy Trinity."

43. For the first time certainly in the wish for grace in most of the Pauline Epistles: "Grace and peace from God the Father" and further in II John 3; Jude 1; cf. Schrenk, *TDNT* V, 1006f. with n.368.

44. Cf. Schrenk, *TDNT* V, 1009f.

his "foreknowledge," is according to the OT not knowledge beforehand,[45] but predetermination, which is effective as election.[46] It makes its appearance in history, according to I Pet. 1:15; 5:10, as in Rom. 8:29f., as calling. Because calling — the leading of a person to faith — is encountered only as creative grace from the One who is in relation to us (cf. Rom. 9:11f., 16), i.e., coming not from one's own subjectivity, faith recognizes behind its so seemingly accidental emergence the eternal predetermination of the Father in keeping with the promise which gives it foundation; this predetermination bears it and carries it along to its goal (cf. Rom. 8:29f.; 11:2, 28f.).

The center of this calling is the ἁγιασμὸς πνεύματος, "the sanctification accomplished by the Spirit."[47] The Spirit is a power from beyond this world; through it God or the Exalted Christ takes hold of a person from the inside by addressing that one in a convincing way.[48]

---

45. As it is in Greek literature. Cf. R. Bultmann, "προγινώσκω, πρόγνωσις," *TDNT* I, 715f.

46. The noun πρόγνωσις is found in the LXX only in Jdt. 9:6 and represents there God's predetermining knowledge. Otherwise the verb γιγνώσκειν, "know, recognize," is used of God's electing predetermination: Amos 3:2: πλὴν ὑμᾶς ἔγνων ἐκ πασῶν θυλῶν; cf. Hos. 5:3; Num. 16:5; Jer. 1:5: "Before I formed you in the womb I knew (= chose) you (LXX ἐπίσταμαι), and before you were born I consecrated (ἡγίακα) you; I appointed you a prophet to the nations."

In postbiblical Judaism God's electing knowledge is emphasized, above all, in the Essene texts: The Creator is אֵל הַדֵּעוֹת, "the God of knowledge"; as such he has determined unchangeably the path of each person (1QS 3:15f. [cf. n.36 above]; 1QH 1:26-29; 12:10-12; cf. 1:19, 21: "In the wisdom of your knowledge you established their destinies before they existed. . . . I know this by the wisdom that comes from you, for you have opened my ears to marvelous mysteries"; CD 2:7: "From the beginning God did not choose them. He knew their deeds before they were created"). F. Nötscher, *Zur theologischen Terminologie der Qumrantexte* (BBB 10; Bonn, 1956), 175f., holds foreknowledge and predetermination (πρόθεσις, προορίζειν) apart too widely; the two cannot be separated sharply. In 1QH 9:26-36 God's (fore)knowledge and determining care as Father are linked impressively in the language of prayer:

> You have known me from my father's time, [and have chosen me] from the womb [Jer. 1:4]. . . . From the breast of the one who conceived me your mercies have been with me. . . . You have delighted me with your Holy Spirit. . . . Until I am old you will care for me, for my father knew me not and my mother abandoned me to you. You are a father to all [the sons] of your truth, and you rejoice over them as a mother over her children.

47. πνεύματος is, like both genitives parallel with it, subjective genitive or genitive of author. The expression is also found in II Thess. 2:13. ἁγιασμός, a *nomen actionis,* is without a clear equivalent in the LXX. Cf. O. Procksch, "ἁγιασμός," *TDNT* I, 113f.

48. On πνεῦμα in I Peter see E. Schweizer, "πνεῦμα," *TDNT* VI, 446f.

Whoever is taken hold of by the Spirit is thus taken from the realm of the profane and placed into the sphere of the holy, i.e., of God:[49] Such a one is "sanctified" (2:5, 9; 3:5). This "sanctification" corresponds in content to God's self-revelation. It expresses itself, therefore, in corresponding human conduct, determined by hope, faith, and love (1:15, 22). The Spirit's thus taking hold of a person is accomplished already during missionary proclamation (1:12), above all, however, fundamentally in the act of baptism[50] and furthermore in proclamation which proceeds from baptism, as the letter itself develops (see the comments on 1:13).

The central effect of the election that occurs in this way is characterized by the third part in two formulations: Election leads to "obedience" per se.[51] ὑπακοή is, as 1:22 declares, acknowledgment of the truth, i.e., faith that gives shape to conduct corresponding to reality. Election takes place, accordingly, as the summons to faith as obedience. This summons is experienced fundamentally through baptism.

When obedience proceeds from baptism in this sense its connection with "sprinkling" — a connection that is at first so surprising — becomes understandable. It arises not only from the tradition-historical origin of the formula and its OT background (covenant-making) but also from the content of the event of baptism. The expression ῥαντισμὸς αἵματος Ἰησοῦ Χριστοῦ, "sprinkling with the blood of Jesus Christ," calls to mind for the primitive Christian reader the making of the covenant at Sinai, which also comes into view at the end of the first part in 2:9. According to Ex. 24:7f. the people pledge obedience, are then sprinkled with "the blood of the covenant," and are taken up into the covenant. But this OT procedure is no longer directly in view here. I Peter does not develop the statement about sprinkling of blood typo-

---

49. In this way the letter itself in 1:15f. elaborates on this term, which is so central for it. ἅγιος is found in 1:12, 15f.; 2:9; 3:5; ἁγνίζειν in 1:22.

50. In I Cor. 1:30 as well ἁγιασμός represents baptism; cf. 6:11.

51. Windisch, 52, enlarges what follows in accord with Ἰησοῦ Χριστοῦ in II Cor. 10:5. But this is impossible, since there Ἰησοῦ Χριστοῦ is subjective genitive.

ὑπακοή is here, as in 1:14, absolute (cf. 3:20). Prior to Christian usage, the word cannot be documented in extrabiblical Greek, and in the LXX it is found only in II Sam. 22:36 (with no Hebrew term behind it). In the NT it occurs twelve times as a central theological term; it is used absolutely in Paul (Rom. 6:16; 15:18; 16:19; II Cor. 7:15; 10:6; Phlm. 21), and the other NT occurrences are in accord with Pauline usage (I Pet. 1:2, 14, 22; Heb. 5:8). I Peter gives new meaning to the concept, passed on to it through the formula tradition, that election expresses itself in obedience with the aid of development of this term in Hellenistic Christianity. Cf. Agnew, "I Peter 1:2."

logically from the perspective of the OT, as in Heb. 9:18-21.[52] It appropriates, rather, a Christian expression,[53] which was for the readers a well-known figure of speech. To "sprinkle with Christ's blood" means to take a person into the realm of influence of Christ's dying, to align him or her with the One who died.[54] This alignment accomplishes, as the figure expresses graphically, purification and thereby appropriation into a new connection to God. The figure announces, moreover, that the alignment has taken place fundamentally in baptism.[55]

The significance of Jesus' dying is developed further in I Pet. 1:18-20, where the scope of vv. 1f. is made clear, i.e., why election estranges one from the world. According to v. 18 Jesus' death redeems from the "conduct inherited from the fathers." Furthermore, the "obedience" to which election leads is, according to the rest of the letter (cf. 1:22; 2:21ff.; 3:14), also obedience in the sense of the Sermon on the Mount; whoever sets out on this path is estranged from "natural" humankind, as is Jesus himself (Mt. 8:20; Mk. 3:33ff.). This differentness also means conflict with society, but it is not based on presumption and willfulness, but on election: God has taken hold of those elected by him, and they can only thank him for that (1:3-12).

2b The greeting χάρις ὑμῖν καὶ εἰρήνη πληθυνθείη, which closes the prescript, appears to be quite brief after the extensive address. The greeting wishes the addressees the "demonstration of grace" and the

---

52. Contra Selwyn, 120; Beare, 77; Schelkle, 22f.

53. This expression forms the basis for the conceptual developments in Hebrews, applies the expression to various OT passages (cf. below, n.55), and is met again in *Barn.* 5:1 (LCL AF I, 354, cf. n.1): ἐν τῷ ῥαντίσματι αὐτοῦ τοῦ αἵματος.

54. αἷμα Χριστοῦ is a common primitive Christian figure for Jesus' death in its salvific significance. Heb. 9:16 has θάνατος in place of αἷμα in 9:18; so also Rom. 5:9f.

55. Sprinkling with Christ's blood is mentioned in the NT only in Hebrews and I Peter. Here the expression comes closest to Heb. 12:24: Whoever joins the Church approaches "Jesus, the mediator of a new covenant, and the sprinkled blood (αἵματος ῥαντισμοῦ) that speaks more graciously than Abel's blood." This sprinkling occurs, according to Heb. 10:22, at the same time as a washing of the body, i.e., baptism: "with our hearts sprinkled (with blood) clean from an evil conscience and our bodies washed with pure water." What this sprinkling mediates is made available through its typological background, namely, the sprinkling of blood on the great Day of Atonement (Leviticus 16), the water of reconciliation (Numbers 19), and the establishment of the covenant on Sinai (Ex. 24:3-8; so Heb. 9:13, 18-21). What is communicated in this typological picture is this: To align oneself with Jesus' death is to be cleansed from sins and set into covenant relationship with God. This goes far beyond God's gracious but insufficient provisions witnessed to in the OT. What is established through this sprinkling is nothing less than the promised new covenant, the eschatological relationship to God that truly means forgiveness and fellowship.

"salvation,"[56] whose content the triadic formula has described already in its particulars. The wish is intercession; yet more: powerful promise, blessing.

---

56. εἰρήνη in the greeting has the comprehensive meaning of the OT term שָׁלוֹם. Cf. G. von Rad and W. Foerster, "εἰρήνη," *TDNT* II, 403-406; see the comments below on 3:11; 5:14.

1:3–2:10: First Major Part: The Basis and Essence of Christian Existence in Society

1:3-12: Born Again to a Living Hope

3 *Praised be the God and Father of our Lord Jesus Christ,*
who has birthed us anew according to his great mercy,
to a living hope through the resurrection of Jesus Christ from
the dead,
4 *to an incorruptible, untainted, and imperishable inheritance,*
which is kept in heaven for us,
5 *who are preserved by God's power through faith*
for the salvation that is ready to be revealed at the last time.

6 *Then you will rejoice,*
you who are now, if it must be, experiencing pain through
many tests,
7 *in order that the genuineness of your faith,*
which is more precious than perishable gold, which is purified
(indeed) through fire,
may be found for praise, glory, and honor in the revelation of
Jesus Christ.

8 *Him you love, without having seen him,*
believing in him, without seeing him now,
you will rejoice in inexpressible and transfigured joy,
9 *if you receive the end of your faith, the salvation of souls.*

10 *After this salvation (the) prophets sought and searched.*
    They prophesied about the (particular) grace for you
11 *while they searched to which or what sort of time Christ's*
    Spirit (working) in them pointed,
    and his Spirit witnessed beforehand to the sufferings afflicting
    Christ and the glory following thereafter.
12 *To them it was revealed that they served not themselves but you*
    with that which has now been preached to you through those
    who brought the gospel to you in (the power of) the Holy Spirit
    sent from heaven
    — into which (even the) angels desire to have insight.

Form and Structure

1. The expressions of thankfulness and entreaty that normally follow the address and greeting in ancient letters[1] are formulated here as praise to God, as *eulogia*.[2] The eulogy is an OT and Jewish form of prayer.[3] I Peter appropriates this precedent by way of Christian tradition.

---

1. Cf. A. Deissmann, *Light from the Ancient East* (tr. L. Strachan; New York, 1927), 148-169; F. Schnider and W. Stenger, *Studien zum Neutestamentlichen Briefformular* (NT Tools and Studies 11; Leiden, 1987), 42-49.

2. The shaping of the thanksgiving and intercession in the opening of the letter as blessing is seen in the NT in II Cor. 1:3-11; Eph. 1:3-12 (13f.); and here (vv. 3-5). This appears to be a specifically primitive Christian epistolary phenomenon, since in pre-Christian literature it is only found in an ostensible letter of Suron (Hiram) to Solomon, which is quoted ca. 150 B.C.: Σούρων Σολομῶνι βασιλεῖ . . . χαίρειν. Εὐλογητὸς ὁ θεός, ὃς τὸν οὐρανὸν καὶ γῆν ἔκτισεν (Eusebius, *Praeparatio Evangelica* 9.34 [cf. *Preparation for the Gospel*, tr. E. Gifford [Oxford, 1903], 477]). Cf. Deichgräber, *Gotteshymnus*, 64.

3. OT eulogies frequently begin with εὐλογητός (the LXX translation of בָּרוּךְ) κύριος ὁ θεὸς Ἰσραήλ and refer to a saving act of God as the ground for praise in a concluding participial, relative, or purpose clause (III Kgdms. 1:48; 8:15, taken up in the Benedictus, Lk. 1:68; altered in Gen. 14:20; Ps. 65[66]:20; Dan. 3:28; II Macc. 15:34; in Gen. 9:26 the formula introduces the curse and blessing [cf. 1QM 13:2, 4]; in some psalms it is added as closing eulogy: Ps. 40:13 [= 41:14]; 71[72]:18; 88[89]:53; 105[106]:48).

While the blessing of God in the OT is usually in the third person, in Jewish literature the second person dominates. Thus each entreaty of the Eighteen Benedictions closes with a blessing that confesses God as the One who fulfills the entreaty (Str.-Bill. IV, 211-214). A similar form is utilized in part by the benedictions that bracket the *shema* liturgically (Str.-Bill. IV, 192-195). At table, food and drink are blessed as one confesses God as the Provider with a benediction: "Blessed are you, Yahweh our God, King of the world . . . who has . . ." (H. W. Beyer, "εὐλογέω," *TDNT* II, 760). Essene prayers give thanks in the same way for redemption: 1QM 14:8: "[Blessed is] your name . . ."; 1QH 5:20; 10:14; 11:27; occasionally also in the third person: 1QM 14:4: "Blessed be the God of Israel, who has maintained mercy toward his covenant and the appointed times of salvation with the people that he has delivered." Cf. Deichgräber, *Gotteshymnus*, 40-43.

The introductory formula of benediction in v. 3a (εὐλογητὸς . . . Ἰησοῦ Χριστοῦ) appears verbatim in II Cor. 1:3 and Eph. 1:3. Whether or not it is of Pauline origin, it represents Christian formulaic material.

The eulogy's foundation in v. 3b(-5) refers confessionally to the encounter with salvation: "who has birthed us anew. . . ." Even v. 4 makes the transition from the first person plural of the confession to the second person plural of kerygmatic-indicative address, which is maintained to the end of the section. The same stylistic forms can be found in Eph. 1:3-14. Thereafter the verbatim-parallel formula of benediction follows — also concluding with a participle[4] — a foundational confession of the salvation-enounter in the first person plural; though first appearing in 1:13f., it too makes the transition to kerygmatic address and in doing so manifests a departure from its otherwise sophisticated language.[5]

While both sections confess the salvation-encounter in the first person plural,[6] comparable sections in 1QH (e.g., 2:20-30; 3:19-36; 11:2-8) and in the *Odes of Solomon* (11; 15; 28f. = *OT Pseudep.* II, 744-746, 748, 759-761) picture the experience of redemption individually in the first-person singular. I Peter does not, as we shall see, describe an experience, but rather proclaims what encounters all who are called through baptism.

2. The entire section 1:3-12 is grammatically one complete sentence-thought, structured with stylistic care in a series of relative clauses. It speaks a sophisticated language.[7] According to Windisch what we have here is a hymn divided rhythmically into five strophes, each with seven or five lines.[8] Upon more exacting application of stylistic criteria this view can no longer stand. A clustering of the lines that corresponds to the sense content and the rhythm of the language (see the translation above) does bring clearly to light, however, the transparent arrangement.[9]

3. When one attempts to arrange the section by content, four groups of statements emerge distinctly. The first is vv. 3-5, the praising confession that God

---

4. Grounds for the blessing are identified in a participle also in II Cor. 1:4; in the LXX the participle is relatively uncommon (Pss. 71:18; 134:21; 143:1); in postbiblical Judaism it appears more often (I Macc. 4:30; II Macc. 15:34; *Pss. Sol.* 6:6b [*OT Pseudep.* II, 658]; 1QS 11:15; 1QM 14:4, 8; most of the entreaties of the Eighteen Benedictions).

5. On Ephesians 1 see Schille, *Hymnen,* 73-81; Deichgräber, *Gotteshymnus,* 64-76: a clear but not exclusive connection to baptism.

6. Similarities of vocabulary between Eph. 1:3-14 and I Pet. 1:3-5 may be explained on the basis of utilization of the same material in traditional expressions; so Deichgräber, *Gotteshymnus,* 78. See also C. L. Mitton, "Relationship"; Coutts, "Eph. I.3-14 and I Pet. I.3-12"; cf. further Cothenet, "Liturgie."

7. On the Greek style of I Peter see Radermacher, "Erster Petrusbrief und Silvanus," especially 288.

8. Windisch, 52. Following his lead is J. Schneider, 44. According to Preisker (Windisch-Preisker, 157) it is a psalm of prayer. Opposing this view, and rightly, is Deichgräber, *Gotteshymnus,* 77, n.1. Boismard, *Quatre hymnes,* 24ff., finds here, as in 2:22-25; 3:18-22; and 5:5-9, a baptismal hymn.

9. Chevallier, "I Pierre 1,1 à 2,10," makes every effort to demonstrate an artificial literary shaping that reaches beyond 1:3-12. Cf. more recently Kendall, "1 Peter 1:3-12."

has birthed us anew to a living hope. There follow then two identically structured sentences each with ἀγαλλιᾶσθε as the main verb and each containing a qualification: vv. 6f., hope, although it is challenged in the present by suffering (ἄρτι εἰ δέον λυπηθέντες), and vv. 8f., hope, although salvation cannot yet be seen in the present (ἄρτι μὴ ὁρῶντες). Nevertheless, what vv. 10-12 declare in closing has its validity: The grace that has already become the Church's portion is even now the eschatological salvation of prophecy.

Vv. 3-5: New Birth Based on God's Mercy

3 With the verbal adjective εὐλογητός, unknown in extrabiblical Greek, the LXX translated the Hebrew passive participle בָּרוּךְ, "blessed," "praised (be)." The NT appropriates the word in this sense and applies it exclusively in doxologies to God.[10] Whoever pronounces the eulogy actualizes the core of his or her faith: In a worshipful and praising manner he or she confesses God as God, namely as the One to whom one owes oneself.

The NT eulogy identifies God no longer as "the God of Israel," as the Benedictus still does (Lk. 1:68), but as "the God and Father of our Lord Jesus Christ" (II Cor. 1:3; Eph. 1:3).[11] This predicate for God, ὁ θεὸς καὶ πατὴρ τοῦ κυρίου ἡμῶν ᾽Ιησοῦ Χριστοῦ is from the liturgical language of prayer and expresses that God has now manifested himself as God no longer only through Israel's election,[12] but conclusively through the sending of his Son. "Through him," namely, through Jesus Christ, according to I Pet. 1:21, we have "come to faith in God." The perspective here is, therefore, not that of the theology represented by the quest for the historical Jesus, which emphasizes the discourse of the

---

10. εὐλογητός occurs in the NT in Lk. 1:68; Rom. 1:25; 9:5; II Cor. 1:3; 11:31; Eph. 1:3; I Pet. 1:3. It is intended as a wish; a supplementary εἴη or ἐστίν is to be expected here less than with other wish formulas (BDF §128.5 [p. 71]). It can be replaced in early Christian writings by εὐχαριστεῖν, αἰνεῖν, ὁμολογεῖν, or ἐξομολογεῖσθαι. Cf. H. Schlier, *Der Brief an die Epheser* (Düsseldorf, 1957), 42f.; H. W. Beyer, "εὐλογέω," *TDNT* II, 754; 758f.; 764.

11. The attributive genitive "of our Lord Jesus Christ" refers to θεός. This is suggested, if not proven, by the single article before θεὸς καὶ πατήρ and required for the formula in Rom. 15:6; II Cor. 11:31 by the context. Eph. 1:17 speaks expressly of "the God of our Lord Jesus Christ"; so Schlier, *An die Epheser,* 43, n.2; contra H. Windisch, *Der zweite Korintherbrief* (KEK 6; ninth ed., Göttingen, 1970), 36ff. That God was turning himself eschatologically toward humanity in Jesus' coming and in the establishment of the resurrected one as Lord does not exclude but includes that God remains God in relation to Jesus.

12. The attributive genitive "of Israel" in the OT refers to the elect one, who confesses Yahweh as his or her God and to whom God himself in return makes confession, e.g., the three men in the fiery furnace, Dan. 3:28.

earthly Jesus about God the Father. Instead, this passage has in mind the exalted One as the κύϱιος of the Church. In this Lord, the entire path of Christ, including the earthly One and what he has said, is present. The person who can believe in God and "invoke him as Father" (1:17) is not one who has received information about God, but one who has been bound to him through the Son.

Accordingly, the salvation-encounter on which the eulogy is founded is attested here in anthropological particularity: ὁ κατὰ τὸ πολὺ αὐτοῦ ἔλεος ἀναγεννήσας ἡμᾶς εἰς ἐλπίδα ζῶσαν δι' ἀναστάσεως Ἰησοῦ Χϱιστοῦ ἐκ νεκϱῶν. This clause attests to the foundational "whence" of Christian existence. It is appropriate that it uncovers the roots of that state of being in the style of doxological confession. Even in anthropological perspective, the basis for being a Christian is not a decision or the appropriation of a commandment, but a second birth established in God's mercy, the manifestation of a new being. How this second birth takes place becomes clear when we analyze the term ἀναγεννάω.

The Origin of the Statements about New Birth in 1:3, 23

1. The verb ἀναγεννάω, "birth again," "enable to be birthed again," occurs in the NT only in I Peter (1:3, 23), but the concept of new birth was known broadly in the Hellenistic Christianity of the post-Pauline period under terms like παλιγγενεσία (Tit. 3:5), ἀποκυέω (Jas. 1:18), and ἄνωθεν γεννᾶσθαι (Jn. 3:3, 5, 7) or ἐκ θεοῦ γεννᾶσθαι (Jn. 1:13; I Jn. 2:29, and passim in I John). While the verb ἀναγεννάω was not used in classical Greek or the LXX or by Philo, it was familiar in the Hellenistic environment in both colloquial and religious-technical senses.[13] The mystery religions probably thought of an ἀναγεννᾶσθαι.[14]

2. Not coincidentally the concept is absent from the earlier strata of NT documents and from Palestinian Judaism.[15] It arises from cyclical thought, which

---

13. In accord with Stoicism, Philo, *De Aeternitate Mundi* 8 (LCL IX, 190), refers by means of the noun ἀναγένεσις to the world's renewal, which elsewhere, including *De Aeternitate Mundi* 9, he refers to with παλιγγενεσία. Josephus uses ἀναγεννάω with the meaning "newly come about" for everyday matters.

14. See F. Büchsel, "γεννάω," *TDNT* I, 675-677; Windisch, 59; J. Dey, *ΠΑΛΙΓΓΕΝΕΣΙΑ;* M. Dibelius, "Die Isisweihe bei Apuleius," *idem, Botschaft und Geschichte* II (Tübingen, 1956), 30-79; R. Schnackenburg, *Die Johannesbriefe* (HThK 12/3; Freiburg, 1970), 178-182; Schelkle, 27ff.

15. E. Sjöberg, "Wiedergeburt und Neuschöpfung im palästinischen Judentum," *StTh* 4 (1951/52), 44-85; *idem,* "Neuschöpfung in den Toten-Meer-Rollen," *StTh* 9 (1956), 131-136; O. Michel and O. Betz, "Von Gott gezeugt," *Judentum, Urchristentum, Kirche* (FS J. Jeremias, BZNW 26; Berlin, 1960), 3-23; L. Goppelt, "Wiedergeburt II," *RGG* VI, cols. 1967-1969; cf. also G. Schneider, *Neuschöpfung oder Wiederkehr?* (Düsseldorf, 1961).

is foreign to OT tradition and according to which even human existence is absorbed in the circular flow of dying and becoming.[16] Yet because human existence — according to the OT — is indebted to the creation of God and is set on a teleological-historical course, an essentially new beginning as new creation is anticipated. In Palestinian rabbinic Judaism a "new creation" was announced for the eschaton in connection with the OT;[17] decisive changes in the circumstances of life before God, e.g., through conversion to Judaism, were characterized metaphorically as such a new creation already in the present.[18] The Essenes,[19] moreover, had in mind a transformation of one's personal life with eschatological relevance, when they characterized entry into their community not only as the

---

16. The statements about new birth in the mystery religions are considerably later than the NT, but may be taken as already applicable for NT times. According to Apuleius, *Metamorphoses* 11.21 (LCL 573, 575), the Isis initiation took place *ad instar voluntariae mortis et precariae salutis,* "like a voluntary death and a difficult recovery to health." Expected from the goddess was *sua providentia quodam modo renatos reponere rursus salutis curricula* ("by divine providence to make them as it were new-born and to reduce them to the path of heath"). According to the Mithras liturgy (ll. 719-721) the initiate was to say: κύριε πάλιν γενόμενος ἀπογίγνομαι αὐξόμενος καὶ αὐξηθεὶς τελευτῶ ἀπὸ γενέσεως ζωογόνου γενόμενος . . . (text in *The "Mithras Liturgy,"* ed. and tr. M. W. Meyer [Missoula, MN, 1976], 20f.; translation there and in H. D. Betz, ed., *The Greek Magical Papyri in Translation Including the Demotic Spells* I [Chicago, 1986], 52). According to an inscription of ca. A.D. 376 an initiate into the cult of Cybele became "taurobolio cribolioque in aeternum renatus." The only known non-Christian use of the verb ἀναγεννάω is in Sallust, *De Deis* 4 (fourth century A.D.; cf. *Concerning the Gods and the Universe,* tr. A. D. Nock [Cambridge, 1926], 8-9): At a point in the initiation after the fast the initiates were given milk to signify that they were reborn (ἀναγεννώμενοι).

Therefore, the Church Fathers are not projecting back a Christian concept when they say (often) that new birth took place in mystery initiations (Tertullian, *De Baptismo* 5.1 [*ANF* III, 671f.]: *in regenerationem;* Hippolytus, *Refutatio Omnium Haeresium* 5.8.10, 23 [*ANF* V, 59f.]: ἀναγεννᾶσθαι). The conversation about παλιγγενεσία in *Corpus Hermeticum* 13 (perhaps third century A.D.; cf. *Hermetica* I, tr. W. Scott [Oxford, 1924], 238-245) speaks of a γεννᾶσθαι or γένεσις from God (13.1, 3, 7); cf. R. Reitzenstein, *Hellenistic Mystery Religions, Their Basic Ideas and Significance* (tr. J. Steely; Pittsburgh, 1978), 46-52; A. D. Nock, *Corpus Hermeticum* II (Paris, 1945), ad loc.

17. Isa. 51:6; 65:17; 66:22; cf. *II Bar.* 32:6; 44:12 (*OT Pseudep.* I, 631, 634). There is no Hebrew-Aramaic word for new birth; cf. G. Dalman, *Die Worte Jesu* I (second ed., Leipzig, 1930), 145.

18. *Canticles Rabbah* 1 on 3:3 (*Midrash Rabbah, Song of Songs,* tr. M. Simon [London, 1939], 39): Abraham used to "bring them under the wings of the Shechina. You learn from this that if a man brings one creature under the wings of the Shechina, it is accounted to him as if he had created him and formed him and moulded him." *b. Yebamoth* 22b: "One who has become a proselyte is like a child newly born . . ." (cf. *The Talmud, Nashim* I, ed. I. Epstein [London, 1936], 131). Cf. Str.-Bill. II, 423; III, 763; Sjöberg, "Wiedergeburt." The idea of being begotten by God is encountered in the OT and Jewish literature only as a figure of speech; according to Prov. 8:25, wisdom was begotten by God, i.e., in accord with Sir. 24:8 (10), it was created by him. The king, according to Pss. 2:7; 109:3 LXX, was begotten by God, i.e., adopted.

19. Sjöberg, "Neuschöpfung."

realization of repentance and acceptance into the new covenant, but also as resurrection and new creation. The concept appears in 1QH 3:19-23 in the context of motifs that directly recall I Pet. 1:3-5 (translation from G. Vermes, *The Dead Sea Scrolls in English* [third ed., London, 1987], 172f.):

> I thank Thee, O Lord,
> for Thou hast redeemed my soul from the Pit,
> and from the hell of Abaddon
> Thou hast raised me up to everlasting height.
> I walk on limitless level ground,
> and I know there is hope for him
> whom Thou hast shaped from dust
> for the everlasting Council.
> Thou hast cleansed a perverse spirit of great sin
> that it may stand with the host of the Holy Ones, . . .
> that he may praise Thy name in a common rejoicing
> and recount Thy marvels before all Thy works.

This passage characterizes (also in the form of a eulogy) total repentance, i.e., entry into the sect, as resurrection and new creation toward hope, but not as new birth.

3. The statement about new birth in I Pet. 1:3 can be traced, therefore, to a context of motifs emerging from the self-understanding of the Qumran community. This context was undoubtedly transposed into the language of Hellenistic Christianity in a Christian tradition preceding I Peter. The technical term "new creation," which was alien to Hellenistic people, was replaced by the concept "new birth," which was more generally in vogue. This adaptation was enhanced by the inner-Christian tradition of the sonship relationship of baptized people to God the Father (cf. Gal. 4:6f., 28f.), although both concepts are from their inception independent of one another. This linguistic and tradition-historical background alone suggests that new birth is understood here neither as an empirical event, nor as the inspiration of a pneumatic supernatural dimension, nor as an experience of conversion. This is confirmed by the context.

As is initially developed in v. 3b, new birth occurs as transposition into a new life situation, namely as the dawn of an ἐλπὶς ζῶσα, of an unfailing and effective[20] "living hope." ἐλπίς here is not the act of hoping, but that which is hoped for, the promised saving future, since in vv. 4f. κληρονομία ("inheritance") and σωτηρία ("salvation") stand parallel to it. The newly born are all those to whom hope, i.e., the inheritance, the salvation, the promised saving future, has been given. Only an expectation such as this deserves the name of hope; according

---

20. ζῶσα in the sense found in Rom. 5:5, not "remaining," as in *Herm. Vis.* 3.12 (= LCL AF II, 56-59).

to primitive Christian perspective, without Christ humankind lives "without hope and without God in the world" (Eph. 2:12; cf. I Thess. 4:13).[21]

New birth as well as hope are established and accomplished "by the resurrection of Jesus Christ from the dead." Christian existence is established not by the miraculous revivification of a human being, but by the resurrection of Jesus, which integrates all of Christ's work (3:18-22); through it the captivity of humans and of human society to the fleshly existence that leads to death (1:24), to ignorance and passion (1:14), and thereby to futility (1:18) has been shattered, and the future, i.e., "the grace that is coming to you at the revelation of Jesus Christ" (1:13), has been made available.

But Jesus' resurrection accomplishes new birth only in connection with the two factors referred to elsewhere as causes: According to I Pet. 1:23 and Jas. 1:18, people are newly birthed by the word of God, the message of Jesus Christ, especially the message about his resurrection. According to Tit. 3:5 and Jn. 3:5 this new birth occurs by the baptism that links people to the resurrected One. When I Pet. 1:13 makes open confession: "he has caused us to be born anew," it does not have conversion in mind but baptism; it includes all baptized persons,[22] which can, however, only be expressed as confession.

The confession is characterized by the imperative following in 1:13 as a kerygmatic indicative pointing, not to empirical realities within this world, but, as in Rom. 6:3-10, to realities established by God, acknowledgment of which is the basis on which humankind lives (1:13ff., 22ff.). The meaning of this confession, which serves to introduce the letter, is delineated further by the promise at the conclusion of the letter; the two correspond to one another in content: In I Pet. 5:10 the concluding intercession begins: ". . . the God of all grace, who has called you to his eternal glory. . . ." A person is *newly birthed* when God *calls* him or her. Both occur fundamentally in baptism. New birth is the encounter with the persuasive promise of God. Accordingly, new birth makes its appearance as the new "I" that acknowledges this encounter and follows this calling, that hopes, believes, and loves (1:13, 21, 22f.).

---

21. Cf. R. Bultmann and K. H. Rengstorf, "ἐλπίς," *TDNT* II, 517-535; Cothenet, "Réalisme"; Kühschelm, "Lebendige Hoffnung."

22. The ἡμᾶς are all baptized persons. It is no mere coincidence that the other three instances in which the author includes himself with the readers in "we" (2:24; 3:18; 4:17; cf. Selwyn, 28) are also kerygmatic confessions.

In all, the new existence of humankind, the only existence that has a future, cannot be realized by humans on their own. It owes its debt of gratitude rather to "the great mercy of God" or, as it is stated in 5:10, to God's "grace."[23] It is no coincidence, therefore, that 1:3b begins with the expression ὁ κατὰ τὸ πολὺ αὐτοῦ ἔλεος, κτλ.

I Peter thus understands Christian existence primarily as oriented toward hope, not, as with Paul, toward faith. Paul singles out faith because it frees Christian existence from what preceded it. I Peter, like other documents of the post-Pauline period, emphasizes hope (much like Hebrews); after all, hope bears one along through the history that now, because of the delay of the parousia, confronts the Church in an oppressive way. The Church thus lives in the context of hope in a way similar to that of the OT-Jewish community of the exodus. Hebrews 11 refers explicitly to the patriarchs, but for the same substantive reason relevant Essene traditions are appropriated in the opening of I Peter. To be sure, the life oriented toward hope is established in an entirely different way than in the OT-Jewish community. This can be seen by the designation of its starting point as new birth through the resurrection of Jesus Christ, the language and content of which are foreign to the OT-Jewish community. And yet, it remains a life oriented toward hope. For this reason in vv. 4f. the reliability of hope is elaborated expansively.

4 That which is hoped for is described, as in Heb. 11:9ff., in accord with OT, Jewish, and primitive Christian tradition, as κληρονομία.[24] The

---

23. The expression corresponds to the OT רַב־חֶסֶד, LXX πολυέλεος, Ex. 34:6; Num. 14:18; Ps. 85(86):5. ἔλεος occurs only here in I Peter; otherwise I Peter uses the NT term χάρις.

24. κληρονομία, "inheritance," is used in the LXX of the land promised to the patriarchs (Dt. 12:9; 15:4; 19:10; cf. Dt. 5:9f.; Josh. 11:23, and passim) and for eschatological salvation, eternal life (Dan. 12:13 Theodotion; *Pss. Sol.* 14:10; 15:10f. [*OT Pseudep.* II, 664]; 1QS 11:7). In accord with this, the NT characterizes as "inheritance" or as that which is to be inherited: the earth (Mt. 5:5), the heavenly city (Rev. 21:2-7), the kingdom of God (Mt. 25:34; I Cor. 6:9f.; 15:50, and passim), the dominion of Christ (Eph. 5:5), glorification with Christ (Rom. 8:17), eternal life (Mk. 10:17 par Lk.; Lk. 10:25; Mt. 19:29; Tit. 3:7), immortality (I Cor. 15:50), and salvation (Heb. 1:14, etc.); cf. I Pet. 3:7: "joint heirs of the grace of life"; 3:9: "obtain a blessing [by inheritance]." "Inheritance" is, therefore, always a technical term for the eschatological salvation that God's faithfulness guarantees. The idea that the sons "inherit," i.e., the traditional designation of hope as inheritance, was not first prompted in 1:4 by the term ἀναγεννᾶσθαι, as Beare, 82f., and Schelkle, 31f., presuppose. It was, rather, occasioned foundationally through the Father-son relationship (v. 17; cf. Rom. 8:17; Gal. 4:7).

"inheritance" is guaranteed by a legally binding promise that reflects the Father-son relationship (1:10-12, 17).

This inheritance is — in contrast to anything that people acquire for themselves — ἀμίαντος, "not defiled by unrighteousness," ἀμάραντος, "unfading," and above all ἄφθαρτος, "imperishable," probably here "incorruptible," i.e., not subject to corruption (cf. Mt. 6:19f.).[25] What the eschaton brings can always only be defined in terms of the *via negationis* when viewed from the perspective of this world. According to I Pet. 3:7 the inheritance is "the grace of life"; according to 3:9 it is "the blessing," the gracious inclination of God that means life; and according to the nearby parallel in 1:5 it is σωτηρία, "salvation."

This illuminating, transcendent goal is not some distant utopia; rather, it is even now "kept in heaven." In τετηρημένη ἐν οὐρανοῖς the apocalyptic concept of the treasures of the time of salvation stored in heaven[26] has been appropriated as a figure. The future salvation is already now "for you" (εἰς ὑμᾶς) hidden with God; it is represented by the exalted Christ. With his "revelation" it will be manifest (1:7; cf. v. 5).

5 Just as God's faithfulness "keeps" salvation, so his power, according to v. 5a, also "guards" those who should receive it from missing it. God's guarding encompasses, as the wordplay τετηρημένη-φρουρούμενοι calls to mind, both salvation and its recipients.

That those who are called are also being guarded is assured by the indicative statements that precede the beginning of all parenesis. God's power holds them in protective custody: οἱ ἐν δυνάμει θεοῦ φρουρούμενοι. God's power is manifest as his activity that shapes his-

---

25. The same three adjectives are also used in Wisdom to distinguish God's giving from the world's giving: ἀμίαντος (appearing in the NT only in I Pet. 1:4), Wis. 4:2, of the reward of virtue; ἀμάραντος, Wis. 6:12, of wisdom; ἄφθαρτος (in I Peter also in 1:23; 3:4), Wis. 12:1, of the Holy Spirit, 18:4, of the Law. A sequence of adjectives with α-privatives is sophisticated Greek style; cf., e.g., Sophocles, *Antigone* 1071 (LCL I, 397): ἄμοιρον, ἀκτέριστον, ἀνόσιον νέκυν.

26. According to Jewish apocalyptic thinking the Son of man "has preserved the portion of the righteous" (*I En.* 48:7) and has "concealed" and "kept" it in heaven (48:6; 62:7 [*OT Pseudep.* I, 35, 43]); so also the Jerusalem above or paradise (*II Bar.* 4:2-6 [*ibid.*, 622]), so that it might come forth at the end (cf. II Esdr. 7:26; 10:27ff.). From this concept was developed the primitive Christian tradition according to which the "treasures of salvation" are hidden and preserved in heaven: so especially hope (Col. 1:5) and life (Col. 3:3); cf. H. Traub, "οὐρανός," *TDNT* V, 532f. In the process, the apocalyptic geography of heaven recedes so radically that "in heaven" really only means "with God." In II Cor. 5:1 ἐκ θεοῦ corresponds to ἐν τοῖς οὐρανοῖς.

tory; ultimately, however, it is manifest in the resurrection of Jesus and in the Spirit, who through the gospel prevails in human lives. This power leads those who are called not deterministically like the fates; rather, those who called are made participants as persons. They are guarded, therefore, διὰ πίστεως, i.e., by the preservation of their faith. This promise in the indicative becomes intercession at the end of the letter in 5:10: "May the God of all grace . . . himself restore, establish, and strengthen you." Between the opening in the indicative and the intercession at the conclusion, the letter gives to God's guarding the word of address in parenesis, since God desires the "thou" of faith that is "guarded . . . for . . . salvation."

The third phrase with εἰς (after two earlier ones in vv. 3b and 4a) characterizes the future that has been opened as σωτηρία,[27] as that coming to salvation which OT and Christian prophetic promises announce by means of this technical term and for which the Hellenistic world longed. σωτηρία is deliverance from all trials (1:6-9) and participation in the promised glory (1:10; 2:2).

Here in 1:5 as well as later in 1:9 and 2:2, what is described as "salvation" is not the deliverance that has already occurred and is especially present through baptism (3:21). Rather, εἰς σωτηρίαν ἑτοίμην[28] ἀποκαλυφθῆναι ἐν καιρῷ ἐσχάτῳ expresses, in view of the imminent expectation of the parousia, that "salvation" is close at hand (4:7). It will be "revealed" when it becomes manifest out of its hiddenness with Christ (1:7) and will then take on form visibly and concretely "at the last time," at that point in time determined by God for the end.[29]

---

27. Reference to salvation with σῴζειν and words from the same stem was well known to the Hellenistic Church. This terminology had its roots in the OT and Jewish tradition and was stimulated further by its usage in the Hellenistic environment. On the basis of the latter the nouns σωτηρία and σωτήρ came to the fore in the Hellenistic Church, while the Palestinian tradition generally used the verb. In I Peter the content of salvation, i.e., deliverance, is defined just as multidimensionally as elsewhere: In 1:5-9 it is, above all, deliverance from affliction; in 1:10 it is the realization of OT prophecy; in 2:2 it is the consummation. The verb is used in 3:21 of deliverance through baptism out of fleshly fallen existence and in 4:18 of deliverance from condemnation in the final judgment. Cf. W. Foerster, "σῴζω," *TDNT* VII, 995-997.

28. ἕτοιμος, "prepared," means here: "ready to be revealed" (BAGD s.v.).

29. The LXX translates the "day" or "hour" of judgment or of the end frequently with καιρός: Lam. 1:21: ἐκάλεσας καιρόν (for: "you have brought the day that you have announced"); Ezek. 22:3: "A city that sheds blood in the midst of her, that her time (καιρὸν αὐτῆς) may come"; cf. Gen. 6:13; Ezek. 7:12. Primitive Christianity appropriated this usage and frequently used καιρός of the point in time of the end: I Cor. 4:5 (cf. Gal. 6:9): "Do not

1:3-5 thus delineate that which establishes Christian existence: Christians are all those who are elected out of the stream of humanity, which is sunken under nihilism, those who have become strangers in society because they have been newly birthed to a living hope through the resurrection of Jesus. To them has been opened up that new life of which OT-Jewish and Hellenistic people spoke in various ways. But this new beginning is not empirically demonstrable; it remains only a new existence as summons and, as the following two groups of verses make clear, is constantly called into question.

The next two sections address the decisive inner struggles in such a way, however, that they are covered by the declaration of a promise. In both ἀγαλλιᾶσθε, "you shall rejoice," dominates as the main verb. What Christians are oppressed by is stated by two subordinate participles, ἄρτι ... λυπηθέντες (v. 6) and ἄρτι μὴ ὁρῶντες (v. 8). The letter was written in order to bring to completion the summons through that word, through which the summons, according to 1:23ff., was accomplished.

Vv. 6f.: Affliction and the Road to Praise of Those Made Complete

6 Here and in v. 8 ἀγαλλιᾶσθε does not, as the present tense suggests and as is often assumed, refer in either a consoling[30] or an imperatival[31] manner to a paradoxical contemporary joy: "you rejoice" or "rejoice. . . ." It promises, rather, as futuristic present tense,[32] a coming

---

pronounce judgment before the time," i.e., the point in time of the judgment; Rev. 1:3 (11:18); 22:10; Lk. 21:8: "the time," i.e., the end or the final judgment, "is at hand." In I Peter this usage is found in 5:6: "that in due time he may exalt you," i.e., at the point in time determined by him for the final judgment, and in 4:17: "the time has come for judgment to begin." Even the ἔσχατος καιρός in 1:5 is not, as in II Tim. 3:1; *Did.* 16:2 (LCL AF I, 333; cf. further I Jn. 2:18), the "end time," in the sense of the already present time extending to the parousia, but the point in time at which the end occurs. In contrast, Christ appeared, according to 1:20, ἐπ᾽ ἐσχάτου τῶν χρόνων (see the comments on 1:10ff.); the eschaton is thus said to be already present. Cf. G. Delling, "καιρός," *TDNT* III, 459-461.

30. So Schelkle, 34, nn. 3f.; Schneider, 45; Selwyn, 126f.; Knopf, 47f.; Wohlenberg, 13f.; Nauck, "Freude im Leiden," 71f.

31. So, referring to I Pet. 4:13; Jas. 1:2, occasionally since Augustine.

32. So Schlatter, *Petrus und Paulus*, 57; Windisch, 53; Moffatt, 96; T. Martin, "Present Indicative," 311f. Already Origen, GCS 1:36, and numerous Vulgate mss. translate with future tense ("exultabitis"). In v. 8, the future is already presupposed by Polycarp, *Phil.* 1 (LCL AF I, 283-285), certainly by Irenaeus, *Adversus Haereses* 4.9.2; 5.7.2 (ANF I, 472, 533). But the future is not the original reading here, as Selwyn, 259, would have it. Cf. "Additional Note C" in Selwyn, 258f.; BDF §323 (p. 168).

joy at the consummation. This is suggested, first of all, by the connection to what was said previously, since the ἐν ᾧ that introduces the sentence is to be linked to ἐν καιρῷ ἐσχάτῳ (as masculine gender) and not to the entire content of vv. 3-5 (as neuter).[33] Secondly, this explanation is required in terms of content by the parallel statement in 1:8 and decisively by 4:13. Rejoicing "with unutterable and exalted joy" (1:8) belongs to the consummation, not to the present. 4:13 differentiates carefully between present joy in spite of suffering — indeed, because of suffering — and joy at the revelation of Christ's glory.

ἀγαλλιᾶσθαι and ἀγγαλλίασις were technical terms already in the LXX for the eschatological rejoicing of the redeemed expressing itself as grateful worship.[34] According to the NT this rejoicing can manifest itself now as the work of the Spirit (Acts 2:46; 16:34; cf. Lk. 10:21); nevertheless, it is anticipated primarily at the consummation (Jude 24; Rev. 19:7 and throughout I Peter [1:6, 8; 4:13]).

The coming eschatological joy is announced with emphasis in order to increase consciousness of the significance of present affliction: That affliction is ὀλίγον "small," because compared to eternal glory it continues but a short time.[35] Furthermore, it stands under the εἰ δέον, "if it must be." In accord with 3:17, the intention here is: "if it is God's will." "Must be" signifies in primitive Christian tradition God's decision for eschatological salvation, not, as in Jewish apocalyptic literature, his unwavering plan for history, or, as in Hellenistic literature, fate.[36] If this

---

33. The latter is presupposed by the exegetes mentioned in n.30, who understand ἀγαλλιᾶσθε as present tense: "In this you rejoice, though now. . . ." Cf. also Best, 77.

34. In the liturgy of the enthronement Psalms the ἀγαλλιᾶσθε of the community and of all creatures is heard with the cultic-eschatological proclamation of God's royal dominion: Pss. 95(96):12; 96(97):1: ὁ κύριος ἐβασίλευσεν, ἀγαλλιάσθω ἡ γῆ (cf. I Pet. 1:8). Ps. 125(126):2, 5f. and Isa. 12:6 announce the eschatological jubilation in response to redemption; similar is Isa. 25:9; *Test. Lev.* 18:14; *Test. Jud.* 25:5; *Test. Benj.* 10:6 (*OT Pseudep.* I, 795, 802, 828). Cf. R. Bultmann, "ἀγαλλιάομαι," *TDNT* I, 19f.

35. ὀλίγον has here a chronological meaning with the temporal adverb ἄρτι, as in Prov. 24:33. In a different way Rom. 8:18 says generally about "the sufferings of this present time" that they "are not worth comparing with the glory that is to be revealed to us"; cf. II Cor. 4:17; Heb. 12:10.

36. δεῖ, δέον, can designate the hand of fate in extrabiblical Greek from the time of Herodotus 8.53 (LCL IV, 49f.) to *Corpus Hermeticum* 9.6a (Scott, tr., *Hermetica* I, 211). In the process of translation into Greek, Jewish apocalyptic literature appropriated this terminology without a Hebrew equivalent in order to express what determined God's revealed plan for history (Dan. 2:28f., 45). Primitive Christianity took over this terminology to express God's decision for eschatological salvation (Mk. 8:31 par.; 13:10;

"must be" stands above all affliction that might be expected, then those
who are called are no longer left to the caprice of fate or of humankind;
then they are themselves not to seek martyrdom but only the path of
obedience; then they are able to endure affliction as an expression of
God's decision for salvation (2:20; 5:6).

As is expressed first in a very general way, λυπηθῆναι encounters
Christians, i.e., they "are saddened," they suffer that which is painful
to them, above all in instances of social alienation.[37] As Christians
understand them, these painful experiences are ποικίλοι πειρασμοί,
"various trials."[38] πειρασμός and πειρασθῆναι are always used in the
NT of those who already have been called into fellowship with God.[39]
πειρασμός throws one's relationship with God into question; it is an
"inner struggle." As such, πειρασμός can be both "temptation" that can
cause one to stumble and "trial" that brings confirmation. Affliction
contains both possibilities; in I Pet. 5:8 the former is in view, while here
the latter is thought of.

7 Affliction in the sense of trial should bring forth τὸ δοκίμιον
τῆς πίστεως, "the genuineness of faith."[40] ἵνα . . . εὑρεθῇ: Affliction
should, like fire in which precious metal is purified, separate out
what is foreign waste and test what is pure. The image illustrates not
only the goal of the trial, but also its necessity: The genuineness of

---

I Cor. 15:25; Rev. 1:1, etc.). Luke also applied δεῖ to the everyday life of Christians,
which took place in the framework of this endtime counsel of salvation; thus Acts 9:16:
". . . how much he must suffer for the sake of my name"; 14:22: ". . . that through many
tribulations we must enter the kingdom of God." Our passage comes close to this usage.
Lit.: W. Grundmann, "δεῖ," *TDNT* II, pp. 21-25; E. Fascher, "Theologische Beobachtungen
zu δεῖ," *Neutestamentliche Studein für R. Bultmann* (BZNW 21; Berlin, 1954), 228-254;
H. Tödt, *The Son of Man in the Synoptic Tradition* (tr. D. Barton; Philadelphia, 1965),
161ff., 188ff.; Hahn, *Titles,* 54ff., 189ff.

37. The verb λυπεῖσθαι is found only here in I Peter; it is replaced in 2:19 by the
noun λύπη, which represents there suffering under social pressure, not, as usually in the NT,
emotional pain (Rom. 9:2; II Cor. 2:1-5; 7:8-11; Jn. 16:20ff.). The two words are otherwise
both found in one NT document only in II Corinthians. They are not technical terms, unlike
θλίψις, which is not found in I Peter. λυπεῖσθαι here specifies that the affliction of Christians
belongs to the "sufferings of this present time" (Rom. 8:18).

38. πειρασμός is found again in I Peter at 4:12; πειράζω does not appear in the letter.
The plural is found in the NT here and in a related passage, Jas. 1:2, and in Lk. 22:28; Acts
20:19; II Pet. 2:9 v.l.

39. Cf. H. Seesemann, "πεῖρα," *TDNT* VI, 28-36.

40. τὸ δοκίμιον is the neuter form of the adjective δοκίμιος used as an abstract noun:
"that which is genuine"; "genuineness" = τὸ γνήσιον in II Cor. 8:8. Cf. W. Grundmann,
"δόκιμος," *TDNT* II, 259.

faith[41] or (simply) faith[42] is "much more precious (πολυτιμότερον) than perishable gold"[43] and is therefore in need, all the more, of purification. Through the fire of affliction all secondary motives must be separated out of faith so that naive belief may become mature and solid faith (see the comments on 4:1f.). Already this first interpretation of affliction allows it to be recognized as the expression of a judging and above all forgiving will.

The Interpretation of Suffering in 1:6f.

This *interpretation of suffering* appropriates primarily an OT-Jewish and primitive Christian wisdom tradition that was already shaped within the same conceptual connections. Jas. 1:2f. has such close affinities to I Pet. 1:6f. — in a different way from Rom. 5:2-4, which is similar in content — that one must assume that a common primitive Christian tradition is behind them: πᾶσαν χαρὰν ἡγήσασθε . . . , ὅταν πειρασμοῖς περιπέσητε ποικίλοις, γινώσκοντες ὅτι τὸ δοκίμιον ὑμῶν τῆς πίστεως. . . .

A direct precursor of this primitive Christian tradition is Wis. 3:5f., though this Christian tradition does not appropriate the idea of education, which dominates in wisdom interpretation of suffering. Wis. 3:5f. says concerning the righteous who have placed their hope in God: καὶ ὀλίγα παιδευθέντες μεγάλα εὐεργετηθήσονται, ὅτι ὁ θεὸς ἐπείρασεν αὐτοὺς καὶ εὗρεν αὐτοὺς ἀξίους ἑαυτοῦ ὡς χρυσὸν ἐν χωνευτηρίῳ ἐδοκίμασεν αὐτούς. . . .[44] A more distant background to this interpretation is in Ps. 65(66):10 LXX: God's people are tested as silver, ὅτι ἐδοκίμασας ἡμᾶς, ὁ θεός, ἐπύρωσας ἡμᾶς, ὡς πυροῦται τὸ ἀργύριον.

Trial by affliction points toward eschatological assessment:[45] ἵνα . . . εὑρεθῇ εἰς ἔπαινον καὶ δόξαν καὶ τιμὴν ἐν ἀποκαλύψει Ἰησοῦ Χριστοῦ. "At the revelation of Jesus Christ,"[46] the genuineness of faith that comes forth through the trial of suffering "redounds to praise and glory and honor," when God allows it to emerge from hiddenness along with humankind's secrets (cf. Lk. 8:17; I Cor. 4:5). εὑρίσκειν expresses

---

41. Knopf, 49f.; Grundmann, *TDNT* II, 259.

42. Cf. Schelkle, 35f.

43. This conclusion *a minori ad maius* is also found in Plato, *Republic* 336E (LCL I, 41): δικαιοσύνην . . . πρᾶγμα πολλῶν χρυσίων τιμιώτερον.

44. This proverbial comparison is also found in Prov. 17:3; 27:21; Sir. 2:5; Rev. 3:18; Plato, *Republic* 413D/E, 503A (LCL I, 297; II, 79), and passim.

45. In the Psalms testing by God is also sought for the purpose of acquittal as "innocent" (Pss. 11:5; 17:3; 26:2; 139:23).

46. In this phrase, which is repeated in v. 13, "of Jesus Christ" is objective genitive; cf. 4:13; 1:5; 5:1.

here, as it often does, the outcome of a trial;[47] but it does not, as does Wis. 3:5f., refer directly to trial through suffering, but rather to its outcome in the final judgment.

The result becomes evident in its consequence: The genuineness of faith redounds to "praise, glory, and honor." The closest parallel to this unique expression is the reckoning of faith as righteousness.[48] Consequently the intention here is that "praise, glory, and honor" are accorded by God and Christ to faith that has endured.[49] God gives to those who are kept in faith what belongs to God himself: "praise" as recognition of their belonging to him,[50] "glory" as their participation in his being,[51] and "honor" as acceptance by him,[52] so that they "will not be put to shame" (2:6). When the trial through affliction leads to what is accorded to faith by God, the ἀγαλλιᾶσθαι, the song of praise, will leave far behind itself the painful experiences of the present. In the present, however, suffering and nagging doubts are the reverse side of reality, which indicates that salvation is present first in a hidden way.

Vv. 8f.: Through Faith to Sight

8 The Christian community does not depend for its life on Jesus' teaching but on fellowship with his person. For this reason the core of its affliction is that it "has not seen" him and "now does not see."[53]

---

47. Rev. 2:2: ". . . [you] have tested those who call themselves apostles but are not and have found them to be false" (εὗρες αὐτοὺς ψευδεῖς); II Pet. 3:14: "Therefore . . . be zealous to be found . . . without spot" (at the last judgment); cf. H. Preisker, "εὑρίσκω," *TDNT* II, 769f.

48. Rom. 4:9: ἐλογίσθη . . . ἡ πίστις εἰς δικαιοσύνην; cf. 4:3, 5, 22; Gal. 3:6. This Pauline phrase taken over from Gen. 15:6 was known, as seen in Jas. 2:23, in post-Pauline times as a formula. In contrast, Rom. 7:10 does not offer a verbal analogy to I Pet. 1:7, since εἰς there belongs with ἐντολή, not with εὑρέθη.

49. Rom. 2:7 (10) refers to the triad "glory, honor, and immortality (peace)" as the result of the final judgment; Phil. 1:11 says the same of "glory and praise," Rom. 2:29 and I Cor. 4:5 of "praise" of God.

50. H. Preisker, ἔπαινος," *TDNT* II, 587f.

51. I Pet. 5:4, 10; cf. G. Kittel, "δόξα," *TDNT* II, 247-250.

52. According to 2:7, "honor" results for those who believe through their belonging to the "honored" cornerstone, Christ (see below, p. 145).

53. Irenaeus, *Adversus Haereses* 5.7.2 (*ANF* I, 533), some Vulgate manuscripts, and the minuscule 441 insert πιστεύετε after ὁρῶντες. This reading was suggested by the paral-

Perhaps the aorist participle in the phrase ὃν οὐκ ἰδόντες also has in mind the distinction of most Christians from the witnesses (5:1) who did see Jesus during his earthly ministry and at Easter.[54] But that the Church has not seen Jesus in this way is addressed as a problem in the NT only in Jn. 20:29. What is decisive in I Pet. 1:8 is that Christ and thereby salvation (cf. vv. 5 and 7) neither were nor are directly visible for those who believe. This difficulty is addressed throughout the NT, since this not-seeing means that the renewal of the individual (II Cor. 4:18; 5:7)[55] and of creation (Rom. 8:24f.; Heb. 11:3, 27) have not yet taken shape concretely. According to I Jn. 3:2, one's own salvation becomes visible together with Christ's becoming visible.

Even this difficulty is addressed in the light of promise in the indicative mood: "Without having seen him you love him." Whether or not the (not) seeing is that of the earthly ministry and Easter, ἀγαπᾶν is not a feeling of attachment set in motion by personal acquaintance. It is, rather, the commitment that God elicits from one to whom he turns his attention. Therefore, "love" is parallel to "believe" in the next sentence. From the perspective of the tradition behind this statement in its entirety, love for Jesus Christ assumes the place where previously love for God stood.[56]

Here, too, the letter appropriates a sayings tradition, since both here and in the closest NT parallels enduring the inner struggle is mentioned first: Jas. 1:12: "Blessed is the one who endures trial (πειρασμός), for when he has stood the test (δόκιμος) he will receive the crown of life that God has promised to those who love him." In II Cor. 4:17f. the same sayings context is applied to those who "look not to things that are seen but to things that are unseen." The comprehensive OT-Jewish and primitive Christian background of this promise becomes clear in I Cor. 2:9, which, echoing Isa. 64:3, declares: "What no eye has seen and no ear heard . . . God has prepared for those who love him" (cf. Rom. 8:28).[57]

That this love, this total commitment that belongs to God (according to the basic OT commandment in Dt. 6:4f., quoted in Mk. 12:30 par.), is directed here

---

lelism with the preceding sentence and is an accommodating stylistic gloss. Cf. Harnack, *Beiträge zur Einleitung* VII, 87f.

54. I Cor. 9:1; 15:5; Lk. 1:2; Acts 1:21f.

55. Cf. G. Kittel, "εἶδος," *TDNT* II, 374f.

56. Otherwise still clear only in the formula of blessing in Eph. 6:24 (cf. Schlier, *An die Epheser,* 174ff.); in Phlm. 5 the antecedent is unclear; Eph. 3:19 is surely subjective genitive; II Tim. 4:8: "who have loved his appearing."

57. Polycarp, *Phil.* 1:3 (LCL AF I, 283f.) makes use of I Pet. 1:8 and is, therefore, not an additional supporting reference for this sayings tradition.

to *Christ* arises not from christological reflection, but from the Church's worship. The oldest of the few NT passages aside from the Johannine documents that speak of love for Christ is I Cor. 16:22, which cites the liturgy of the Lord's Supper and includes the prayer-address μαραναθά.

It was more usual to speak of "faith in him," i.e., in Christ, because his person — at his own initiative — became linked with faith in God. This was expressed, perhaps first in the theology of Christian mission, in an abbreviated way in this formula. The formula has in mind what I Pet. 1:21 says: "through him you have confidence in God" (see the comments below on v. 21). Faith is that utter confidence that God elicits by his promise, just as love is the total commitment that God summons forth through his demonstration of love.

Faith qualifies, for its part, the not-seeing: εἰς ὃν ἄρτι μὴ ὁρῶντες πιστεύοντες δὲ, κτλ. This does not refer to an invisibility on the part of God, which under favorable conditions could perhaps be penetrated by mystical or visionary experiences. It recognizes, rather, that all Christian experience is subject to more than one interpretation and that salvation is not an empirical given. Christ, and with him salvation, are, in the term coined by Luther, *absconditus*. Hence, the preceding aorist participle οὐκ ἰδόντες, "without having seen," also refers not merely to the now-absent historical objectification.

Whoever by faith holds fast to the hidden One because he or she has been laid hold of by that One (cf. I Cor. 8:3) will participate in the eschatological song of praise with "unutterable"[58] and "exalted"[59] joy (ἀγαλλιᾶσθε χαρᾷ ἀνεκλαλήτῳ καὶ δεδοξασμένη). That the consummation brings immeasurable joy is an OT and Jewish expectation, which was appropriated in a renewed way from the perspective of Jesus' appearance.[60]

9 Persons are led to the joy of praising God because they reach "the outcome[61] of faith, the salvation of souls": κομιζόμενοι τὸ τέλος

---

58. ἀνεκλάλητος, "that cannot be articulated," "beyond words"; similar is Rom. 8:26: ἀλάλητος. Cf. also I Cor. 2:9.

59. δεδοξασμένη; cf. G. Kittel, "δοξάζω," *TDNT* II, 253f. The transfigured joy corresponds to participation in glory in the consummation (4:13; 5:4, 10), although, according to 4:14, even now "the Spirit of glory" has taken hold of precisely those who are suffering for the sake of Christ.

60. Isa. 9:3; 61:3, 7; II Esdr. 7:98f.; *I En.* 51:5; 104:4 (*OT Pseudep.* I, 37, 85); Rom. 14:17, etc. Cf. R. Bultmann, *Theology of the NT* I (tr. K. Grobel; New York, 1951), 339f.

61. Here τέλος does not mean "end," as it generally does in the NT, but "goal," as in I Tim. 1:5, the completion of an event, in accord with the basic meaning of the word in Greek. Cf. G. Delling, "τέλος," *TDNT* VIII, 54. In Rom. 6:21f. τέλος is parallel to καρπός, "fruit," i.e., reward.

τῆς πίστεως, σωτηρίαν ψυχῶν. That faith directs itself toward salvation was opened up in a fundamental way when Jesus, as the healing stories report, declared deliverance to those who believe.[62] Now salvation is said to encounter the ψυχή, the "self," one's person.[63] Thus, faith for I Peter, as in Hebrews 11, is conduct directed toward the "outcome," the consummation, which therefore will be maintained amid inner struggles. Paul had developed πίστις as the decisively new thing that replaces what had gone before. I Peter speaks for the situation of the rising second generation. Its discourse about faith raises this question: Is salvation for Christians just as much a matter of the future, just as much given as promise, as for Israel? To this question the closing section of the eulogy addresses itself; this section appropriates anew the focal term σωτηρία, "salvation."

Vv. 10-12: The Presence of Salvation as Fulfillment

Style and Structure

1. The lofty style is now replaced by a more didactic tone. In unusually packed sentences the relationship of Jesus' appearance to OT prophecy, a relationship that has been proclaimed to the Church, is delineated[64] and thus the Church's situation is characterized as "fulfillment," i.e., it is described as eschatological in nature.

2. The structure of the complex statement becomes transparent if one takes note of the verbs. The statement sets in relationship to the prophesying of the prophets (προφητεύσαντες)[65] in vv. 10f. the proclamation of the gospel, the message of the fulfillment of prophecy in the Church (εὐαγγελισαμένων)[66] in v. 12. Both are proc-

---

62. Mk. 5:34; 10:52; Lk. 17:19: "your faith has saved you." It was from this assurance that the missionary formula in Acts 16:31; Rom. 10:9 arose; cf. Acts 15:11; Eph. 2:8; II Tim. 3:15. Cf. G. Fohrer, "σῴζω," *TDNT* VII, 976f.; L. Goppelt, "Begründung des Glaubens durch Jesus," *idem, Christologie und Ethik* (Göttingen, 1968), 44-65, especially 50ff.

63. ψυχή occurs relatively often in I Peter, namely six times. It signifies the self of a person, sometimes the self as person (1:9; 3:20; 4:19), sometimes as the guiding center of the person's conduct (1:22; 2:11, 25). I Peter uses this anthropological technical term, therefore, in a fundamentally different way from Paul. Cf. Dautzenberg, "Σωτηρία ψυχῶν."

64. The subsequent statements about the prophets cannot be traced back to the OT writing prophets. But they do not have Christian prophets in mind, as Selwyn, 134, assumes (followed by Warden, "Prophets"); correctly opposing this view are Kelly, 58f.; Best, 83f.; and Michaels, 41. Regarding the "salvation-historical" aspect of the statement, cf. Spicq, 53ff.

65. προφητεύειν has here as in Mk. 7:6 par.; 11:13; Jude 14 the special meaning "foretell." Cf. G. Friedrich, "προφήτης," *TDNT* VI, 828f.

66. εὐαγγελίζεσθαι occurs only here in I Peter (εὐαγγέλιον only in 4:17). In Paul's usage the verb refers to proclamation, in accord with the promise in Isa. 52:7 (= Rom. 10:15),

lamation generated by the Spirit (vv. 11, 12): Only thus is God's salvation encountered beforehand; there it is encountered as prophecy, here as gospel. The prophecy given to the prophets caused them to "search" and "inquire" about the time of fulfillment (vv. 10f.), but this was not to "serve" (v. 12) them, but the Church.

Vv. 10-12 introduce into the context the question regarding the sense in which salvation, which up to now (vv. 5, 7, 9) has been announced as future, is already present as fulfillment.

10 This verse supplies a suspenseful answer: περὶ ἧς σωτηρίας ἐξεζήτησαν καὶ ἐξηρεύνησαν προφῆται. Even the prophets[67] asked about the salvation that, according to v. 9 and v. 5, even for the Church is yet in the future, inquiring after the time of its appearance (v. 11a). That is to say, they prophesied περὶ τῆς εἰς ὑμᾶς χάριτος, "of the grace that was to be yours."[68] But this grace, this demonstration of God's love, has already been given fundamentally to the Church, even if according to v. 13 the Church still looks in hope for "the grace that is being brought to you at the revelation of Jesus Christ." Grace consists, after all, of the central content of the prophetic announcement, i.e., according to v. 11b, "the sufferings (experienced by) Christ and the subsequent glories," that is, in spite of the surprising plurals, the suffering unto death and the glorification of the promised One.[69]

This statement appropriates a basic line of the NT coming from Jesus himself. He characterized his work, especially his departure from this world, in

---

the news of the dawn of God's royal dominion — i.e., of Jesus' appearance as fulfillment — which comes through the proclamation (Rom. 1:2ff., 16f.; I Cor. 15:1-5).

67. The definite article is absent not only before προφῆται, but also in v. 12 before ἄγγελλοι.

68. The closest parallel is in I Cor. 15:10: ἡ χάρις αὐτοῦ ἡ εἰς ἐμέ, "the grace given to me"; cf. the comments on 1:2.

69. τὰ εἰς Χριστὸν παθήματα is a modification of the formula τὰ τοῦ Χριστοῦ παθήματα, which is seen in 4:13 and 5:1 and elsewhere in the NT only in Paul (II Cor. 1:5; Phil. 3:10). In Paul it refers to the sufferings that Christians share with their Lord, in I Pet. 5:1 to the sufferings of Christ himself, in which, according to 4:13, those who belong to him participate. The plural refers, therefore, to Jesus' suffering unto death, including the sufferings that he had to endure at various times before his death (2:23; see below on πάσχω), not also to the subsequent sufferings of Christians.

On the basis of plural παθήματα we have, then, plural δόξας — unique in the NT, though also found in the LXX (Ex. 33:5: στολὰς τῶν δόξων; 15:11: θαυμαστὸς ἐν δόξαις). This plural does not refer to different revelations of Christ's glory (I Pet. 3:22; so Selwyn, 137), different events of his glorification (Knopf, 56f.), or the co-glorification of the many. That glorification follows suffering is also expressed in Paul (Rom. 8:18), Hebrews (2:9), and Luke's Gospel (24:25f.); cf. I Pet. 4:13.

enigmatic terms as fulfillment of Scriptures referring to the time of salvation.[70] According to the Easter kerygma represented by Paul in I Cor. 15:3-5, which in all probability goes back to the primitive Palestinian Church,[71] Jesus' death and resurrection happened κατὰ τὰς γραφάς, "according to Scripture." From this emerged the concept that the prophecies of the prophets directed themselves in a central way to Jesus' dying and rising.[72]

It is decisive that I Peter defines eschatological salvation not, according to the thought structure of Jewish apocalyptic literature, as the end of history (II Esdr. 7:30f.), but "salvation-historically" as the fulfillment of prophecy. Eschatological salvation is to be found wherever "grace," the demonstration of God's love, encounters a person and makes the relationship to God whole in the manner that was prophesied. Then, however, eschatological salvation is already present with Christ according to the content of prophecy referred to here. Yet, it is still hidden "in heaven" (v. 4), "you do not now see him" (v. 8). It will first become visible in a concrete way with Christ; the future salvation (vv. 5, 9) corresponds to the revelation of Jesus Christ (vv. 7, 13), i.e., to the parousia. With this point of view I Peter agrees with the decisive soteriological mainstream of the NT, which flows from Jesus through Paul to John.[73] According to this mainstream, the eschatological salvation with Christ is already present for faith and is yet a future with Christ for sight. It is present, hidden in history, and calls forth, therefore, sociologically, the eschatological existence as exiles, as in I Pet. 2:11f.[74]

11f. The fulfillment character of Christian existence, which is fundamental for the entire NT, is described in particular in assertions made uniquely about prophecy: ἐρευνῶντες εἰς τίνα ἢ ποῖον καιρὸν

---

70. In Mt. 11:4-6 par. Jesus interprets his ministry as the hidden realization of prophecies such as Isa. 35:5f.; 61:1. In the saying about the cup in Mk. 14:24 par. Mt. he sees his departure from this world in the light of Isaiah 53: Behind ὑπὲρ πολλῶν stands Isa. 53:12. Cf. H. Patsch, *Abendmahl und historischer Jesus* (Stuttgart, 1972), 191; L. Goppelt, "τύπος," *TDNT* VIII, 255.

71. Cf. L. Goppelt, "The Easter Kerygma in the NT," *The Easter Message Today* (tr. S. Attanasio and D. Guder; New York, 1964), 36ff.; Hahn, *Titles*, 176ff.

72. This is especially prominent in Luke; cf. Lk. 24:25: ". . . all that the prophets have spoken. Was it not necessary that the Christ should suffer these things and enter into his glory?"; similar is Acts 3:18. Cf. G. Friedrich, "προφήτης," *TDNT* VI, 832ff.; Goppelt, *Typos,* 77f., 100-106, and 209-211 regarding the possibility of demonstrating this NT perspective historically.

73. Bultmann, *Theology* II, 161, 180f., also views it in this sense, though he defines the eschaton from an apocalyptic perspective. See on the discussion: Goppelt, *Typos,* 212ff.

74. See the comments on 2:11f., 13ff.

ἐδήλου τὸ ἐν αὐτοῖς πνεῦμα Χριστοῦ. Prophecy was given to the prophets, therefore, by "Christ's Spirit." Prophecy caused the prophets, therefore, "to search expressly and to inquire (exegetically)" (ἐκζητεῖν, ἐξερευνᾶν, v. 10a),[75] above all "when and under what circumstances" the prophecy given to them would occur (v. 11a).

That prophecy comes from the Holy Spirit, as does the proclamation of the gospel (v. 12a), is a well-known concept;[76] but that "the Spirit of Christ" speaks by the prophets is articulated only here in the NT. Similarly, it is frequently observed in the NT that the prophets longed to see the salvation prophesied by them,[77] not, however, that they searched out the time of fulfillment. It was made known to them at the same time that they should serve with their prophecy not themselves but the community of salvation: οἷς ἀπεκαλύφθη ὅτι οὐχ ἑαυτοῖς ὑμῖν δὲ διηκόνουν αὐτά. That prophecy was intended for the community of salvation is the common perspective of primitive Christianity,[78] but not that this also was revealed to the prophets. Where, then, do these special ideas come from?

The Special Ideas in 1:11f.

These ideas can be found to a certain extent in Daniel and in subsequent apocalypticism. The author of Daniel asks, as does later apocalypticism,[79] among the afflicted people of God about the end of the time of woe and the coming of the predicted salvation. The author attempts in relation to this, e.g., to interpret

---

75. ἐρευνάω (v. 11) and ἐξερευνάω (v. 10) were already, in classical Greek, terms for scientific investigation. In the LXX (Ps. 118:2, 69), in Philo (*Quod deterius potiori insidiari soleat* 13 [LCL II, 211]), and in Jn. 7:52 they are used of inquiry into scriptural revelation. Cf. G. Delling, "ἐρευνάω," *TDNT* II, 655ff. Cf. also on v. 11, Kilpatrick, "1 Peter 1:11."

76. Again, especially important for Luke: The "Spirit sent from heaven" (as here in v. 12) effects, according to Acts 2:4, the proclamation of the gospel (Acts 1:8; 4:8; 6:10; 13:4, 9; also Eph. 3:5f.). This Spirit also "announced beforehand" through the prophets (Acts 1:16; 28:25; cf. 7:51). That the prophets were inspired by the Spirit is a common Jewish concept (Sir. 48:12f., 24; *I En.* 91:1 [*OT Pseudep.* I, 72]; II Esdr. 14:39ff.; *Test. Lev.* 2:3 [*OT Pseudep.* I, 788]; cf. Str.-Bill. II, 129; F. Baumgärtel, "πνεῦμα," *TDNT* VI, 382ff.). This idea was already stated in the OT, though hardly among the writing prophets (*TDNT* VI, 362), and was taken over in primitive Christianity (Heb. 3:7; 9:8; 10:15; II Pet. 1:21, and passim).

77. Mt. 13:16f. par. Lk.: ". . . many prophets . . . longed to see what you see and did not see it"; cf. Jn. 8:56.

78. E.g., Rom. 4:23f.; I Cor. 10:11; Acts 3:24; 13:26: "to us has been sent the message of this salvation." On the grammatical issues see Shimada, "Critical Note."

79. II Esdr. 4:33-36: "How long and when?"; 4:51; in II Esdr. 13:13-24 the seer asks whether he will experience that day.

the prophecy of the seventy-year duration of the exile (Jer. 25:11; 29:10) in light of the delay (Dan. 9:2, 22-27; cf. 12:6-13). He takes as his point of departure thereby, as do apocalyptic writings following him, the idea that prophecy is to be weighed in terms of the community of the eschaton.[80]

This focus on the time of fulfillment and on the eschatological community is encountered with still greater emphasis in the Qumran community's self-understanding; there the expressions seen in I Pet. 1:10a are used formulaically[81] according to the scriptural sense of "search" and "inquire." One inquired, as 1QpHab 7:1-8 expresses programmatically, "when time would come to an end," referring to the time of the eschatological turn of events, the time "not made known" by God to the prophet. That time and thereby the intended sense of prophecy was first made known by the Teacher of Righteousness, "in whose heart God set understanding, so that he might interpret all the words of God's servants the prophets, through whom God foretold everything that would happen to his people . . ." (1QpHab 2:6-10).[82] Here the focus is not on the "spirit of prophecy," as in rabbinic Judaism, but on a revelation that brings prophecy to fulfillment.[83]

From this perspective the work of the Spirit in prophecy could have been seen in primitive Christianity as a preliminary expression of the work of the Spirit — of the Spirit of Christ[84] — that has already been experienced, i.e., beginning from the moment that preexistence christology saw everything up to the consummation of the world from the standpoint of God's activity through the Son.[85]

---

80. *I En.* 1:2 (cf. *OT Pseudep.* I, 13): ". . . I understood as I saw, but not for this generation, but for a remote generation to come."

81. 1QS 5:11: "inquired" (בקש) and "sought" (דרש) in the Torah. The two verbs stand together in an entirely different sense in I Macc. 9:26: καὶ ἐξεζήτουν καὶ ἠρεύνων. Schutter, *Hermeneutic,* 100-109 and passim sees in vv. 10-12 the hermeneutical key for I Peter and especially for the "homiletic midrash" of 1:13–2:10 in its connections to OT interpretation at Qumran.

82. The point of contact between this statement and I Pet. 1:10ff. is also observed by G. Jeremias, *Der Lehrer der Gerechtigkeit* (StUNT 2; Göttingen, 1963), 142; on the whole issue see O. Betz, *Offenbarung und Schriftforschung in der Qumransekte* (WUNT 6; Tübingen, 1960), 75-82.

83. The scriptural prophets received God's revelation "by his Holy Spirit" (1QS 8:16); the teacher of righteousness, who interpreted them, received his understanding from God himself (1QpHab 2:2f.; 7:4f.). Philo speaks of the Spirit of the prophets (πνεῦμα προφητικόν) and in his exegesis sees himself in the grasp of the same Spirit as Moses (*De somniis* 2.252 [LCL V, 555f.]; cf. W. Bieder, "πνεῦμα," *TDNT* VI, 374).

84. "The Spirit of Christ" appears elsewhere in the NT only in Rom. 8:9, where it refers to the Spirit in whom the exalted Christ and God through him now work in a person (cf. v. 10; II Cor. 3:17). Here I Peter has in mind a corresponding working of the preexistent one. A Spirit christology is not presupposed thereby (contra Kelly, 60).

85. Thus Paul is able in I Cor. 10:4 to interpret the "spiritual rock" as the preexistent Christ. In the second century that the preexistent one was at work in the prophets became a view shared by the Church Fathers: The prophets were fulfilled, according to *Barn.* 5:6 (LCL AF I, 355f.); Ignatius, *Magn.* 9:2 (*ibid.*, 205f.) by "his grace." According to Justin, the Logos speaks forth out of them (*Apologia* 1.33.6; 36.1 [*ANF* I, 174f.]; so also Irenaeus, *Adversus*

In accord with these reflections on the origin of these ideas, it remains an open question in v. 12 how the revelation that provides the prophets their destiny is to be perceived.[86] Here, what is ascribed to the prophets, as in the representation of the content of prophecy in v. 11b, is that which first became evident from the perspective of fulfillment.

These unique (in the NT) statements about the prophets are intended, perhaps, to discourage the Church from a similar apocalyptic searching after the "end."[87] But most of all they are intended to illustrate indelibly the "already" of salvation's presence, of fulfillment, so that the Church, even within the delay of the parousia, might hold fast the tension between this "already" and its own existence in the world. After all, to overcome this tension is the decisive problem of Christian existence in history, which became acute in the latter part of the apostolic period.

The actual role given to the prophets is to "serve" the Church, to which the fulfillment of their prophecy was announced in the new day through the apostles. The "Spirit of Christ" given to them has announced ahead of time Christ's suffering and glorification: προμαρτυρόμενων τὰ εἰς Χριστὸν παθήματα καὶ τὰς μετὰ ταῦτα δόξας. Therefore, it was revealed to them that they were not to serve themselves but "you" (plural). διακονεῖν is used, as in 4:10, as an ecclesiological technical term meaning: help one to believe.[88] Prophecy enables the Church to understand the Christ-event preached to it as fulfillment, as eschatological salvation, and, therefore, to appropriate proclamation as gospel.[89]

But the proclamation of the gospel itself is decisive: ἃ νῦν ἀπηγγέλη ὑμῖν διὰ τῶν εὐαγγελισαμένων ὑμᾶς ἐν πνεύματι ἁγίῳ ἀποσταλέντι ἀπ' οὐρανοῦ. This proclamation emerges "now," νῦν being qualified eschatologically for the sake of the message of salvation. Those who are referred to are the messengers of joy promised in Isa. 52:7; Nah. 2:1, those who broadcast this message (Rom. 10:15). They

---

Haereses 4.20.4 [*ANF* I, 488]). It is "our Christ" who speaks forth out of the burning bush (*Apologia* 1.62.3f. [*ibid.*, 184]; cf. *Dialogue* 61f. [*ibid.*, 227f.]). But never do the Fathers say, as here, that it is the "Spirit of Christ."

86. The OT passages adduced by Schelkle, 42, Gen. 49:10; Num. 24:17; Dt. 18:15; Hab. 2:1-3, express various matters and do not cover the concept.

87. Cf. Acts 1:6; Rev. 6:9-11.

88. Mk. 10:44f.; I Cor. 12:4-6; Cf. E. Schweizer, *Church Order in the NT* (tr. F. Clarke; London, 1961), 171-173; Goppelt, *Apostolic*, 177f.

89. προμαρτύρεσθαι appears only here in the NT and is not found in in classical Greek or the LXX.

do so because the Holy Spirit is "sent from heaven" for this purpose and gives them strength and authority.

The final clause in v. 12 adds yet more: Not only the prophets, but even "angels long," bending over, as it were, "to look"[90] into that which has been given to the Church (εἰς ἃ ἐπιθυμοῦσιν ἄγγελοι παρακῦψαι).[91] The angels, the representatives of the heavenly world already honoring God (Heb. 12:22; Rev. 4), wait for the redemption of the entire creation (Rom. 8:19); they rejoice, therefore, over the sinner's repentance (Lk. 15:10) and join in the hymn of praise at the consummation of redemption (Rev. 5:11-14; 19:1ff.).

Therefore, what the prophets prophesied, without being able to touch the fulfillment, and what angels long for — namely the realization of salvation from God — has become reality for Christians, who live in society as aliens afflicted on many sides. They have been born anew within the time remaining to an effective hope. The whole description in vv. 3-12 of Christian existence is of nothing that is demonstrable. It is, rather, of proclaimed promises, kerygmatic indicatives, which are developed imperatively in the material that follows.

1:13–2:10: The Basic Conduct That Corresponds to New Birth

Arrangement, Form, and Meaning of the Imperatives in 1:13–2:10

1. Up to this point in 1:3-12 the essence of Christian existence was expressed in the style of confession and promise in the indicative mood. From 1:13 through 2:8 all the main verbs, except in Scripture quotations and remarks on them (1:25b;

---

90. The formulation is similar to the Greek of *I En.* 9:1 according to the *Chronographia* of Georgius Syncellus (cf. *OT Pseudep.* I, 16): The four archangels παρέκυψαν ἐπὶ τὴν γῆν ἐκ τῶν ἁγίων τοῦ οὐρανοῦ. But I Peter does not have curious watching in mind, but rather a longing for the revelation of salvation. Perhaps the statement, for which there are no closer parallels in content, transfers to angels what the saying in Mt. 13:16f. par. Lk., which already stands behind I Pet. 1:10, says about the prophets: "(They) longed (ἐπεθύμησαν) to see what you see." That the transferal came about through philological confusion, מלאכים = ἄγγελοι for מלכים = βασιλεῖς, as conjectured by Manson, "Review of Selwyn," 220, is not to be assumed. A different idea — that knowledge of salvation history is denied to angelic powers — is seen in apocalyptic writings (*I En.* 16:3; *II En.* 24:3 [*OT Pseudep.* I, 22, 142f.]; Mk. 13:32; I Cor. 2:6; Ignatius, *Eph.* 19 [LCL AF I, 193]); therefore, according to Eph. 3:10, the wisdom of God is announced to angels through the Church. And yet, there appears at the same time the *angelus interpres* in the apocalyptic visions!

91. εἰς ἃ = ἃ νῦν ἀνηγγέλη = the content of the prophecy, the promised salvation.

2:7a, 8b), are imperative (1:13: ἐλπίσατε, 1:15: ἅγιοι . . . γενήθητε, 1:17: ἐν φόβῳ . . . ἀναστράφητε, 1:22: ἀλλήλους ἀγαπήσατε, 2:2: ἐπιποθήσατε, 2:5: οἰκοδομεῖσθε). In 2:9f. an indicative promise concludes this series.

All but the last of these imperative verbs are in the aorist tense; therefore, they summon the readers not into a condition but to active initiative in various situations.[1] "Hope" (1:13) does not mean "have hope," but "show that hope has been given to you." "Love one another" (1:22) does not mean "cherish love as an attitude," but "show one another brotherly love in every situation." These two imperatives, together with the present tense imperative in 2:5, which summons the readers to abiding incorporation into the community, announce the themes for the three parts of this section.

2. The form-critical and theological character of the imperatives is based on their connection to the preceding indicatives, as the introductory διό, "therefore" (1:13) shows. The instruction "hope fully" in 1:13 introduces the new section and shapes the theme up to v. 21. It appropriates imperatively what the leading sentence of the previous section, 1:3, had confessed in the indicative mood as encounter: "He has birthed us anew to a living hope" (διό thus picks up on all of the preceding section). The imperative summons the readers to realize precisely what is, according to the indicative, already given. The indicative section (1:3-12) and the imperative section (1:13-21) thus correspond to each other and describe the essence of Christian existence from the two perspectives. The extent to which the remaining imperatives in 1:22–2:10 belong in this context will be examined when the character of this form of address is given closer attention.

3. This speaking of Christian experience in the dialectic of indicative and imperative[2] as promise and summons is encountered in the NT otherwise only in Paul, but what is meant by it is an essential element of the entire NT proclamation.[3] In Paul it is often seen in baptismal parenesis, i.e., in what is addressed to the baptized with respect to their baptism. Thus, Rom. 6:3-5 (10), like I Pet. 1:3-5, confesses in the first person indicative what is encountered in baptism, and Rom. 6:11-14, like I Pet. 1:13-25, gives as a conclusion a second-person imperative summons to view oneself and conduct oneself according to this encounter. Similar

---

1. BDF § 337 (pp. 173f.).

2. See O. Merk, *Handeln aus Glauben. Die Motivierungen der paulinischen Ethik* (MbThSt 5; Marburg, 1968), 34-41; K. Kertelge, *"Rechtfertigung" bei Paulus* (NTA NF 3; Münster, 1967), 251-263; F. Neugebauer, *In Christus* (Göttingen, 1961), 53ff., 61; H. M. Schenke, *Das Verhältnis von Indikativ und Imperativ bei Paulus* (dissertation, Berlin, 1956), 8-40 (overview of literature); W. G. Kümmel, *Römer 7 und die Bekehrung des Paulus* (1929), 98ff., reprinted in *idem, Römer 7 und das Bild des Menschen im NT* (ThB 53; Munich, 1974); R. Bultmann, "Das Problem der Ethik bei Paulus" (1924), *idem, Exegetica* (Tübingen, 1967), 36-54; *idem, Theology of the NT* I (tr. K. Grobel; New York, 1951), 330-333; H. Windisch, *Taufe und Sünde im ältesten Christentum bis auf Origines* (Tübingen, 1908); P. Wernle, *Der Christ und die Sünde bei Paulus* (Freiburg/Leipzig, 1897).

3. Even Jesus' summons to discipleship is in the first instance always an indicative, the offer of fellowship. But fellowship is infectious only to the extent that it comes on a person through the imperative.

baptismal paranesis is also found in Rom. 6:17f., 19b; 8:9f., 12f.; Gal. 5:25a, b; Col. 3:3, 5. This form of statement is not, however, restricted to baptismal parenesis. According to II Cor. 5:18f., 20 God has given, with the offering up of his Son, the commission to announce that he has reconciled humanity with himself through the cross and, therefore, to persuade all people to allow themselves to be reconciled with him. That this form of statement is thus applied, beyond baptism, also to the cross, i.e., to God's activity encountered there, is especially important for interpretation of this form of statement. The content of the indicative in II Corinthians 5 is not empirically demonstrable, neither cosmologically nor anthropologically. It is, rather, a new relationship of God to humanity, a relationship that he has originated. The imperative summons the reader to acknowledge this reality — not merely to accept a commandment.[4]

4. This applies in I Peter 1 as well: New birth toward hope is given as a call toward glory, the call that was encountered empirically solely through the human word of preaching and through the symbolic action of baptism. The imperative obligates one to appropriate this calling ever anew through conduct generated by hope. This form of statement is used because God's eschatological turning toward humankind came about, not as a phenomenon that changed relationships by a show of power, but within history through the "foolishness and weakness" of Jesus' appearance and proclamation of that appearance.[5] The indicative gives witness to God's hidden eschatological activity for salvation through the cross or through baptism, and the imperative summons one to appropriate it through faith[6] and to let it become an active reality. I Peter 1 characterizes the content of the indicative expressly as that which one "does not see" (v. 8) and the imperative as the summons to faith (v. 21). To characterize Christian existence in the interrelatedness of indicative and imperative is the most direct expression of the *theologia crucis*.

5. Why is the imperatival summons important as summons to faith beyond the

---

4. The approach of "purely historical" exegesis tried to explain the indicative as a condition and the imperative as moral appeal. For this approach, the indicative gives expression to the abstract idea, communicated to the apostle Paul through the experience of conversion, that the baptized person is transported in terms of the psyche or naturally into a condition in which sin should actually be impossible. But Paul was, as this line of interpretation goes, compelled to use the imperative by the "harsh reality" that baptized persons continued to sin; it was, therefore, a repetition of the parenesis of mission. This explanation, which misunderstands the content and character of Paul's statements, was put forward in numerous variations in the leading stream of research from F. C. Baur to the history-of-religions school, especially by P. Wernle and H. Windisch. Opposing this approach in detailed debate was the foundational article of R. Bultmann (cf. the literature mentioned in n.2 above). On the designation "purely historical exegesis," see Goppelt, *Theology* I, 257.

5. I Cor. 1:21-25. This phenomenon should not be called the coming of the new aeon, since the new aeon is an empirically new world. For this reason, Paul does not appropriate this term.

6. The exemplary imperative in Rom. 6:11, "consider yourselves . . . ," signifies faith. Cf. Goppelt, *Theology* II, 102f.

indicative promise? The imperative allows two things to come to the fore: God does not wish — as the indicative witnesses — to act only for humankind and in relationship to humankind, but also together with humankind. A person should not acknowledge a new situation in his or her natural state; he or she should, rather, become a covenant partner and thereby a new "I," one who allows himself or herself to be taken into service for his or her Creator. At the same time, by means of the imperative the hidden eschatological situation witnessed to by the indicative should, without losing its nondemonstrability, become historically active in order to overcome the old person and the way of life of the present aeon. Neither is in the past for the baptized; the baptized person is always free from them only to the extent that he or she allows the kerygma to become active with respect to his or her person.[7] Through this content the character of the statement's form becomes clear: The indicative does not only give information and the imperative is not merely an appeal to the human will; both are, rather, address from God. They are — "in, with, and under" the human word, as I Pet. 1:23ff. develops — the active word of God. The indicative is God's enduring promise and the imperative is God's effective invitation.[8]

6. Along with the theological meaning of the imperatives in I Pet. 1:13-21 their form-critical character also becomes clear. Through them the section, in accord with its form, does not become ethical parenesis, as in Romans 12–13, i.e., a list of traditional ethical directives in a Christian framework. It is, rather, like Rom. 6:11-14, baptismal parenesis: In this section, therefore, the starting point of Christian existence is set forth parenetically.

7. Do the imperatives following in 1:22–2:10 also cohere with this formal schema of baptismal parenesis? According to form and content they are based on the summons to hope in 1:13-21, within the theme of the social dimension of Christian existence (cf. 1:1). It is critical that instruction about the decisive social relationship, which is membership in the Christian Church, be integrated into this broader social dimension. In a corresponding way, the imperative in Rom. 6:11 is developed in 6:12-14, and especially in Col. 2:20–3:17 the imperative receives broad attention.[9]

---

7. The σῶμα τῆς ἁμαρτίας in Rom. 6:12 is not — as appears to be the case according to Merk, *Handeln,* 36f. — transformed by baptism in terms of everyday experience into a merely temptable σῶμα τοῦ θανάτου in the old aeon.

8. Since righteousness, new birth, and the Spirit are always encountered only as the personal, gracious turning of God (so also Merk, *Handeln,* 39f.) in the form of effective consolation, and not as infused potentialities, we should not identify what is expressed in the indicative — as does Merk, appropriating Käsemann's categories — objectively as a gift that shows itself as power and corresponds to that change in dominion to which the imperative summons (38). To be sure, the imperative is also not, on the other hand, only a summons to decision that obligates one to acknowledge the paradox expressed in the indicative, namely, that God's word is encountered in the word of humans.

9. Perhaps it is not coincidental, but, rather, conditioned by early Christian parenetic tradition, that in I Pet. 2:11ff., as in Colossians 3, a household code parenesis comes in the next major part. Munro, *Authority; idem,* "Interpolation," posits textual interpolations and a pastoral stratum in 1:13, 20f. Dijkman, "Pastoral Stratum?" opposes this view.

8. In the process of developing the baptismal parenesis in I Peter 1–2, various parenetic traditions play supportive roles in content. Only to a minor extent does the traditional triad "faith, hope, love," whose key words appear in 1:13, 21f., make a contribution.[10]

9. The most important tradition-historical factor is seen in a motif that permeates and shapes the entire section, namely, the motif of the exodus: The elect set out from the world toward their destiny. "Gird up your minds" (1:13) appropriates its motif from Ex. 12:11: Israel eats the Passover with "loins girded"; turning away from the worldly form of life (vv. 14ff.) recalls in content Ex. 16:3; redemption from slavery (v. 18) recalls Ex. 13:3; and the blood of the Lamb (v. 19) recalls the Passover (Ex. 12:5). Furthermore, the scriptural quotation in 1:24f. is from Isaiah 40, the chapter on the second exodus, which the Essenes claimed as the scriptural basis for their own exodus.[11] And the closing proclamation in 2:9, which supports the third part of the section ("You are the elect generation, the royal priesthood . . .") transfers the covenant promise given to Israel at Sinai (Ex. 19:5f.) to Christians.

These points of contact with the exodus are not derived from a conscious typological evaluation of OT statements.[12] Nor did they grow merely, like I Cor. 5:7f., out of a tradition of the Christian Passover homily in which the concept of exodus was active.[13] The references came about, rather, unintentionally from the context that has again and again been seen as the tradition-historical background for the entire first major part of the letter (1:3–2:10), namely, the self-understanding of the Qumran community, understanding itself as the community of exodus. But the character of the imperatives indicates that I Pet. 1:13ff. has in mind, not a once-for-all historical emigration, but the eschatological exodus to be realized ever anew, which is experienced in a fundamental way through "hoping fully."

1:13-21: Unlimited Hope

13 *Therefore, gird the loins of your understanding, be sober,*
   place your hope fully on[14] the grace
   that is being brought to you at the revelation of Jesus Christ.[15]

---

10. The triad of faith, hope, and love is found in I Thess. 1:3; 5:8; I Cor. 13:13; Col. 1:4f.; Eph. 1:15-18; I Tim. 6:11; II Tim. 3:10; Heb. 10:22-24; *Barn.* 1:6 (LCL AF I, 343); cf. H. Conzelmann, *I Corinthians* (tr. J. Leitch; Hermeneia; Philadelphia, 1975), 229ff.

11. 1QS 8:13f.; 9:19.

12. Contra J. Daniélou, *From Shadows to Reality: Studies in the Biblical Typology of the Fathers* (tr. W. Hibberd; Westminster, MD, 1960), 162f.

13. W. Huber, *Passa und Ostern* (BZNW 35; Berlin, 1969), 31ff.

14. ἐπί + the accusative with ἐλπίζω: toward a goal, not only with respect to a foundation; e.g., *Barn.* 6:9 (LCL AF I, 361).

15. φερομένην does not mean, as in BAGD s.v. φέρω 4aβ (p. 855): "hope for the grace that is *proclaimed* for you at the revelation of Jesus Christ."

14 *As children of obedience*
shape[16] yourselves (that is, your conduct) not in accord with
the lusts that earlier in the (time of) ignorance (dominated) you,
15 *but as the One who called you is holy,*
so also yourselves become holy in your entire conduct.
16 *For it is written: "You should be holy since I am holy." (Lev.*
11:44)

17 *And if you call upon as "Father" that One*
who without regard for person judges with respect to the work
of each,
so conduct yourselves in fear during the time of your existence
as foreigners.

18 *For you realize that you were redeemed not with a perishable*
thing, with silver or gold,
from your vain way of living passed on from your fathers,
19 *but through the costly blood of Christ as a lamb without*
shortcoming or blemish,
20 *who was destined before the foundation of the world,*
but for your sake has appeared at the end of time,
21 *you who have come through him to faith in God,*
who raised him from the dead and gave glory to him,
so that your faith and hope may be directed toward God.

The *theme and arrangement* of the section are apparent. It begins and ends (vv. 13 and 21) with the summons to hope. This summons is motivated in vv. 13-17 from the perspective of the goal of Christian existence and in vv. 18-21 from the perspective of the origin of Christian existence. Hope is seen here as the fundamental posture of Christian conduct. What is expected is the grace to be encountered in the parousia (v. 13) and the judgment according to works that will come with the parousia (v. 17); the imperative "hope fully" goes with the first expectation, "walk in fear" with the second. The obligation of sanctification is inserted between the two (in vv. 14-16). After these two expectations are spoken of, vv. 17-21 gives the christological foundation.

---

16. Perhaps this participle — and in the same way ἀναζωσάμενοι and νήφοντες in v. 13 — stands in place of the imperative. Cf. in this regard D. Daube, "Participle and Imperative in I Peter," in Selwyn, 467-488.

V. 13: Hope Directed toward Grace

13 V. 13b, τελείως ἐλπίσατε κτλ., is decisive. According to Greek thought it is appropriate for a person to have ἐλπίδες, expectations, both good and bad, regarding the future.[17] But here the imperative ἐλπίσατε, "have hope," is not oriented toward utopias postulated for the sake of humankind; rather, in accord with OT, Jewish, and primitive Christian tradition,[18] it is oriented toward God's promise of salvation, which is addressed to humankind.

This goal, which shapes the content and structure of hope, is "the grace that is being brought to you at the revelation of Jesus Christ." The ἀποκάλυψις ᾿Ιησοῦ Χριστοῦ, his "becoming visible," is, as in 1:7 and 4:13, his manifestation in the parousia. This manifestation is itself fundamentally "the grace," the demonstration of God's love, that "meets" (ἡ φερομένη ὑμῖν χάρις) those who are called. "Grace" brings with it, according to 1:10, σωτηρία, the universal salvation event, the new creation itself (vv. 5, 9), the "inheritance" promised through the resurrection of Jesus Christ to those who are called (vv. 3f.). I Peter also has in mind — with these "physical"-sounding OT terms — God's love, which embraces in an ultimate sense those who are called (1:21), and "being with the Lord" (I Thess. 1:8; cf. I Pet. 1:8).

The goal that defines hope is thus understood in the sense of universal eschatology, as in 4:7, as the expectation of an imminent parousia, but its content, which is shaped personally and soteriologically, makes it independent of chronological and spatial concepts. It is thus without the goal being spiritualized, since God shows himself as, in fact, God when he "gives life to the dead and calls into existence things that do not exist" (Rom. 4:17). The content and certainty of this hope are identified in the indicative mood, which gives them foundation, through the promise that accomplishes new birth, the promise that came through the resurrection of Jesus.[19]

This content shapes the structure of the action of hoping, which can only be done τελείως,[20] "entirely," "undividedly," like the orientation

---

17. R. Bultmann, "ἐλπίς," *TDNT* II, 517ff.

18. *Ibid.*, 521-530.

19. On the issue of content see J. Moltmann, *Theology of Hope* (tr. J. Leitch; New York, 1967), 202f.

20. τελείως, "whole," "complete," "total," "lacking nothing" (G. Delling, "τέλος," *TDNT* VIII, 74f.) belongs with ἐλπίσατε (Kelly, 66; Schelkle, 44f.; Selwyn, 140, et al.), not with νήφοντες (Windisch, 55; Beare, 96).

toward the coming reign of God required by Jesus. Hope here is not flight to life's fulfillment held in reserve in the beyond; in fact, it is precisely the act of refusing every form of reserve, since the goal is not fortune in the next world, but the creature going home to his or her Creator. Hence for I Peter, as often after Paul,[21] hope, as an expression of being a Christian (3:15), stands virtually in place of faith.[22] In structure it is similar to hope in the OT: moving in trust toward the future promised by God, holding fast to one's calling toward that promised future. It is determinative for one's entire conduct and is expressed in particular ways, as Hebrews 11 illustrates, through OT examples: It takes the risk of exodus into the existence of foreigners and holds fast to the afflicted people of God without fearing the powerful, even if this costs one standing in society (Heb. 11:8ff., 23-26). For I Peter it is important, moreover, that such unreserved commitment to God's future not lose sight, out of spiritual enthusiasm, of the duties of historical existence; rather, hope places one squarely before such duties, as 2:11–3:7 develops. It does so, however, regarding them as "penultimate" (Bonhoeffer), that toward which Christians should not accommodate themselves in conformity. Such hope does not avoid fear of the powers and injustice, but it overcomes them; it does so, however, without, to be sure, thereby becoming fixed on the alteration of the structures toward God's future.

In this way, hope determines the orientation expressed in both prominent participles in v. 13a: διὸ ἀναζωσάμενοι τὰς ὀσφύας τῆς διανοίας ὑμῶν, νήφοντες. We have here two conventional images in primitive Christian parenesis. One who "girds the loins"[23] is one who hems up the long garment which hinders one's stride; thus, διάνοια, one's thinking and willing, should be "rolled up" in preparation for departure. One who is intoxicated loses his or her dream world, while one who "is sober"[24] sees what is real and accommodates himself or herself to

---

21. Bultmann, *TDNT* II, 532f.; H. Conzelmann, "Hoffnung II: im NT," *RGG* III, cols. 417f.

22. See the comments on 1:21.

23. In early Christian literature ἀναζώννυμι occurs only here and in the quotation of this passage in Polycarp, *Phil.* 2:1 (LCL AF I, 285). Prov. 31:17 LXX: ἀναζωσαμένη . . . τὴν ὀσφύν. The verb means "buckle up, tuck up"; in content it is largely synonymous with ζώννυμι in Jn. 21:18; Acts 12:8 and περιζώννυμι in Lk. 12:35; 17:8; Eph. 6:13; cf. already Ex. 12:11; Jer. 1:17 (LXX). The closest parallel in content to I Pet. 1:13 is Lk. 12:35: "Let your loins be girded and your lamps burning" in expectation of the Lord. So too Eph. 6:14, though without a direct eschatological focus.

24. νήφω "be sober," in contrast to drunkenness, otherwise figurative in I Pet. 4:7;

the assured future; i.e., such a person has hope. The direct consequence of hope, as is expressed frequently in parenesis, is sanctification, which vv. 14-16 take up.

Vv. 14-16: Sanctification of Daily Life instead of Conformity

The *antithetical pair of sentences in vv. 14f.* summons one toward a fundamental decision that puts into practice "total hoping"; in the conduct of daily life hope leads one not to live "profanely," but "in a holy manner." The antithesis comes from parenetic tradition. The closest early Christian parallel is the ethical key principle in Rom. 12:2: Do not conform to the ways of life in this aeon, but on the basis of faith examine rationally from case to case what is God's will. Since μὴ συσχηματίζεσθε appears in the NT only in these two places, there is perhaps a common parenetic tradition which has been developed independently by the two writers.[25]

The form of the antithesis presented here reminds one centrally of the self-understanding of the Qumran community, which was constituted on the basis of the fundamental decision for total holiness. "Those of perfect holiness" (1QS 8:20f.; CD 20:2, 7) separate themselves from the realm of wickedness and delusion (1QS 3:9-11). The Scripture quotation added in v. 16, Lev. 19:2, points to the OT background: Preceding this directive about the law of holiness is the prohibition of following the ways of life of the peoples among which Israel lives (Lev. 18:1-5, 30).

14 This verse prohibits συσχηματίζεσθαι, one's "conforming oneself," not in general terms, as in Rom. 12:2, in relation to the ways of life "of this aeon," but more specifically in relation to the habits of one's own old self: μὴ συσχηματιζόμενει ταῖς πρότερον ἐν τῇ ἀγνοίᾳ ὑμῶν ἐπιθυμίαις. This special focus is characteristic of I Peter (cf. 2:11; 4:2f.). It does not reject the forms of historical existence as such, but only their shaping through ἄγνοια, "ignorance,"[26] and ἐπιθυμία, "craving." Both of these are characteristics of paganism according to OT, Jewish, and primitive Christian tradition.[27] "Pagans" succumb to "craving" because

---

5:8, and the rest of the NT occurrences (I Thess. 5:6, 8; II Tim. 4:5). Cf. O. Bauernfeind, "νήφω," *TDNT* IV, 937f.

25. In *I Clem.* 29:1–30:1 (LCL AF I, 57-59) the summons to sanctify oneself in contrast to the peoples of the world is developed not as a fundamental decision, but as individual parenesis.

26. ἄγνοια in the NT otherwise in Acts 3:17; 17:30; Eph. 4:18, always of failure to know God.

27. Jer. 10:25; Ps. 79:6; Wis. 14:22; Acts 17:30; Eph. 4:18; I Thess. 4:5: "not in the passion of lust like heathen who do not know God." The Jews boast of their knowledge of God and his law (Rom. 2:17-20) and yet do not know him (10:3).

they do not know God. God is recognized only where he is acknowledged as the Creator who gives life (Rom. 1:21; I Cor. 8:3) and
not when — as frequently in the Hellenistic world — a divine world-
principle is accepted.

In I Peter ἐπιθυμίαι are not merely the vices listed in 4:3, but
according to 4:2 the manifold strivings of humans to procure life for
themselves. Conduct according to lusts characterized the "former" (πρότερον) life, namely, before baptism. What is the purpose, then, of this
participial imperative? This striving that denies God is not, for baptized
people, behind them in a simple chronological sense. Neither does it
encounter them merely as temptation from the world around them;[28]
after all, it is only at death that one is released from fleshly existence,
i.e., from the human existence that is oriented toward death and characterized by striving in one's own strength (4:1, 6). Hence, this summons to nonconformity is not aimed at strengthening recent converts,[29]
but at stimulating continued confirmation of baptism that has already
taken place.

The summons makes its appeal in language that alludes to baptism:
ὡς τέκνα ὑπακοῆς, "as children of obedience. . . ."[30] According to 1:10
baptism delivers one into "obedience," into the life of faith, and through
it — as the corresponding foundational introduction of v. 15 expresses
— the summons comes.

15 The summons binds the readers to the summoning One. For
this reason, those who are summoned should become holy in their
"entire walk," in their entire conduct,[31] as God is holy:[32] κατὰ τὸν

---

28. So Schelkle, 45.

29. Contra Windisch, 56: "The readers are apparently addressed as recently converted
Gentiles."

30. The expression is surely patterned after Hebrew use of "child" and "son," so that
the genitive refers to the rooted connectedness that has a determinative effect: Hos. 10:9:
ἐπὶ τὰ τέκνα ἀδικίας; *I En.* 91:3 (*OT Pseudep.* I, 72): "children of righteousness"; Eph. 2:2:
ἐν τοῖς υἱοῖς τῆς ἀπειθείας. ὡς is causal as in I Pet. 1:19; 2:2, 11f., 13f., 16; 3:7; 4:10f., 16.

31. ἀναστροφή occurs six times in I Peter, twice in II Peter, and only five times in all
the rest of the NT. The noun has, like the verb ἀναστρέφειν (I Pet. 1:17) and about seven
other occurrences in the NT), already in classical Greek the figurative meaning "conduct,
behavior" (cf. BAGD s.v.). But this meaning is represented in the NT more often by
περιπατεῖν (about 48 occurrences; in this meaning not found in I Peter). Both terms correspond to Hebrew הלך. For bibliography see Brandt, "Wandel als Zeugnis."

32. The formal comparison between the Holy One and the holy ones in vv. 15f. does
not, therefore, point to imitation of the deity as taught, for example, in Plato (cf. Selwyn,
141f.), but to appropriation of the sanctification that has been encountered.

καλέσαντα ὑμᾶς ἅγιον καὶ αὐτοὶ ἅγιοι ἐν πάσῃ ἀναστροφῇ γενήθητε. According to 1:12, they were laid hold of by his Holy Spirit. The ἅγιος is the one who belongs to God (2:9); only God is by nature holy. Holiness is not an "attribute" of God, but an expression of his being: God is untouchably pure and loyal and rejects — this in light of the context — the impurity that denies him. 3:5 illustrates conduct made holy by pointing to the "holy" wives of the patriarchs: These women lived "in this world" as wives, but their way of life, including their attire and adornment, was shaped by the fact that they unreservedly "hoped in God" and feared only God, not man. Holiness manifests itself, therefore, not within a realm of religiosity bracketed from the world, but in daily life. It also shows itself, not, as in Qumran, as the life of a specialized community, but as historical existence lived toward its Creator-Redeemer.

16 In this sense the basic OT principle of Lev. 19:2, with which the parenesis is emphasized here, is understood and reinterpreted in a NT manner: ἅγιοι ἔσεσθε, ὅτι ἐγὼ ἅγιος. The call to sanctification of everyday life stands in this section appropriately between the call to hope directed toward grace (v. 13) and the call to fear before the judge (v. 17), since holiness encompasses both.

V. 17: Fear before the Judge

17 Fear in light of judgment according to works is now added to hope directed toward grace (v. 13) as a primary theme of conduct. Paul and the rest of the NT also mention the final judgment in parenetic frameworks.[33] Therefore, concepts that appear to be in conflict, namely, total hope toward grace and fear with respect to judgment according to works, are linked together for the sake of establishing ethical goals.[34] But it is important to see how and why they came to be linked.

According to the eschatological expectations of rabbinic Judaism,

---

33. II Cor. 5:10f.; cf. Rom. 14:10f.; I Cor. 3:12-15; 4:4.

34. Thus in the sense of the liberal theology of A. Ritschl, e.g., H. J. Holtzmann, *Lehrbuch der Neutestamentlichen Theologie* II (second ed., Tübingen, 1911), 222ff.: "A judgment based on a standard of demonstrated works is the unavoidable postulate of the religion of law and belongs in any case already to the pre-Christian stratum of [Paul's] conceptual development, while justification by faith can first be understood from the dimension of Christian experience." See H. Lietzmann and W. G. Kümmel, *An die Korinther I/II* (HNT 9; fifth ed., Tübingen, 1969), at II Cor. 5:10; H. Braun, *Gerichtsgedanke und Rechtfertigungslehre bei Paulus* (UNT 19; Leipzig, 1930).

one who is circumcised should make every effort to be acquitted in the final judgment on the basis of both fulfillment of the law and the repentance that eradicates his trespasses; finally, however, he should have hope for the grace that will save him for the sake of election and the fathers.[35] In 1:13, I Peter challenges the reader to hope for grace "fully," i.e., for grace "alone." But grace can only be grasped through judgment according to works and not by bypassing it. I Peter suggests this through its theology of suffering, according to which even those who believe must pass through the judgment of persecution (4:6, 17-19).

According to Paul, however, judgment according to works and salvation by grace are related to one another as the law is related to Christ: The law is abrogated by Christ only eschatologically, i.e., for the one who lives by faith (Rom. 10:4); it continues to apply conclusively in the final judgment (2:5-11). Those who are justified through Christ, however, have hope that they will be delivered ultimately through Christ — through him alone — "from the wrath" of the final judgment according to works (5:9f.). Similarly the visionary image of Rev. 20:12-15 declares that all will be judged according to the books of works; those who are delivered will be only those who are found in the book of life, the book of the "Lamb that was slain" (Rev. 13:8).

Therefore, I Pet. 1:17 in fact links things that belong together: Hope for grace (v. 13) belongs together with fear (ἐν φόβῳ . . . ἀναστράφητε). After all, the One whom the summoned address as Father is also the Judge: εἰ πατέρα ἐπικαλεῖσθε τὸν ἀπροσωπολήμπτως κρίνοντα κατὰ τὸ ἑκάστου ἔργον . . . , "if [i.e., "since"] you call upon as 'Father' that One who without regard to persons judges with respect to the work of each. . . ." (This clause recalls the common formula "call on the name of the Lord," which at an early date became a Christian self-designation [I Cor. 1:2, etc.]; the expression originally connected to God [cf. Joel 3:5] was thereby applied to Jesus Christ as κύριος.) The clause πατέρα ἐπικαλεῖσθαι is found in early Christian literature only here;[36] it was, therefore, not a standing

---

35. *Pss. Sol.* 9:5f. (*OT Pseudep.* II, 660f.): "The one who does what is right saves up life for himself with the Lord, and the one who does what is wrong causes his own life to be destroyed. . . . To whom will you be good, O God, except to those who call upon the Lord?"; *Midrash Canticles* to 1:5 (87b): "The Community of Israel said . . . I am black through my own deeds, but comely through the works of my ancestors" (*Midrash Rabbah* IX, tr. M. Simon [London, 1939], 51; cited in Str.-Bill. I, 118). Cf. E. Sjöberg, *Gott und die Sünder im palästinischen Judentum* (Stuttgart, 1939).

36. In the LXX only Ps. 88:27: ἐπικαλέσεταί με Πατήρ μου εἶ σύ, θεός μου. Jer. 3:19 (God to Israel): "And I thought you would call me 'My Father.' "

formula. Nonetheless, the address "Father" in prayer is the most direct expression of certainty about God that was transmitted from Jesus to the disciples according to the gospel tradition, especially Matthew.[37] According to Paul (Rom. 8:15; Gal. 4:6) it was understood in the Hellenistic Church as the most important witness of the Spirit for one's relationship to God, the witness that summons one to freedom from fear (cf. I Jn. 4:17c, 18). And yet, Paul "knows" at the same time "the fear of the Lord" (II Cor. 5:11) precisely because he also expected judgment according to works for Christians (II Cor. 5:10).

God's judgment inquires "without respect of persons" (ἀπϱο-σωπολήμπτως),[38] also without consideration of Church membership. It focuses exclusively on conduct, ἔϱγον, "work," the singular noun representing one's entire conduct, the course of one's life.[39] Even one who tries to live by faith can only think about this question with trepidation. This trepidation in light of accountability before God is the fear[40] that according to this parenesis belongs to a Christian's awareness of reality. This φόβος is not, however, the resignation to fearfulness to which the author of II Esdras succumbs because the judgment according to works appears to him to be final (7:69). This fear is also not an expression of a post-Pauline "vulgar piety,"[41] but the necessary dialectical antithesis to Christian hope; without it what emerges out of *certitudo* is a *securitas* that is alien to reality. Fear corresponds to life in the "time of existence as foreigners" (ὁ τῆς παϱοικίας ὑμῶν χϱόνος),[42] since it is the time of inner conflict and confirmation.

---

37. J. Jeremias, *NT Theology* I (tr. J. Bowden; London, 1971), 61-68.

38. ἀπϱοσωπολήμπτως appears only here in the Bible. It is used of God's judgment also in *Barn.* 4:12 (differently in *I Clem.* 1:3 [LCL AF I, 353, 11]). The same idea is otherwise expressed by the nouns πϱοσωπολημψία (Rom. 2:11; cf. Eph. 6:9; Col. 3:25) and πϱο-σωπολήμπτης (Acts 10:34; cf. already Dt. 10:17).

39. In addition to the usual plural κατὰ τὰ ἔϱγα from Ps. 61(62):13 in Rom. 2:6; Rev. 20:12f., we also find the singular in I Cor. 3:13ff.; Gal. 6:4; Rev. 22:12: ἀποδοῦναι ἑκάστῳ ὡς τὸ ἔϱγον ἐστὶν αὐτοῦ. So also already Isa. 40:10; 62:11; cf. Mt. 16:27: ἀποδώσει ἑκάστῳ κατὰ τὴν πϱάξιν αὐτοῦ. The plural is used in I Pet. 2:12: ἐκ καλῶν ἔϱγων.

40. To speak of conduct "in fear" (namely, before God) is in the NT peculiar to I Peter: 1:17; 2:18; 3:2, 16. The closest parallel is Acts 9:31: ποϱευομένη τῷ φόβῳ τοῦ κυϱίου; cf. II Cor. 7:1; Eph. 5:21. This figure of speech comes, like the Pauline expression "with fear and trembling" (Phil. 2:12, and passim), from the OT: Ps. 2:11 LXX: δουλεύσατε τῷ κυϱίῳ ἐν φόβῳ. The φόβος κυϱίου is a major motif in proverbial wisdom: Ps. 110(111):10; Prov. 1:7; 9:10; Sir. 1:11f., 18, and passim. Cf. H. Balz and G. Wanke, "φοβέω," *TDNT* IX, 189-219.

41. So Knopf, 68f.; similarly Windisch, 56f.

42. See above, p. 67.

Vv. 18-21: Christ's Act of Redemption as the Origin of Hope[43]

Thought Development and Form

1. Vv. 18-21 consists of a series of relative clauses linked together under the participle εἰδότες in v. 18. Its content, redemption through Christ, does not give foundation, nevertheless, to the challenge to conduct one's life in fear (v. 17);[44] rather, out of it faith and hope are derived in v. 21. Accordingly in vv. 18-21 the fundamental form of conduct, which in vv. 13-17 was developed out of the goal of Christian existence, is now derived from its origin: God has redeemed us through Christ from past human existence. Thereby faith and hope directed toward him have been made possible.[45]

2. In two other places, in 2:21-25 and 3:18-22, I Peter will motivate its parenesis with corresponding formulaic christological statements. Often it has been assumed that it uses in these three sections not just christological formulaic traditions but "Christ hymns."[46] In support of this hypothesis two primary arguments are given: (a) The sections are formulated in lofty, "poetic" language. This is true, nevertheless, also for other parts of I Peter. Decisive, is, therefore, (b) the impression that these christological expressions say much more than is necessary as a basis for parenesis. This impression must be examined exegetically. Only then will a form-critical and tradition-historical judgment be possible.

18f. εἰδότες, "since you know," was a common expression. Paul uses it to remind his readers of an understanding of faith, well known within it, but does not introduce formulas with it.[47] Here as well, the writer uses it to direct attention to the original encounter, i.e., to redemption through Jesus' death: ἐλυτρώθητε, "you were ransomed" or "redeemed" (by God),[48] an expression that was already familiar to the readers from the gospel tradition.

The meaning of the verb oscillates here between "ransomed" and "redeemed." V. 18 names a purchase price and thereby suggests the

---

43. See van Unnik, *Verlossing 1 Petrus 1:18-19; idem,* "Critique of Paganism"; Miller, "Deliverance and Destiny"; Davies, "Primitive Christology"; see also Andrianopoli, *Mistero di Gesù.*

44. So Schelkle, 47: The exhortation (to childlike fear, v. 17) "is strengthened through the added thought about redemption through Christ (1:18-21)."

45. See Delling, "Bezug der christlichen Existenz"; Krafft, "Christologie und Anthropologie."

46. See below, pp. 207-210.

47. Rom. 5:3; 6:9; I Cor. 15:58; II Cor. 4:14; 5:6; Eph. 6:8f.

48. One should understand "God" as the subject, since Isa. 52:3, used in the formulation of v. 18, speaks of God redeeming. God is also the subject of the connecting προεγνωσμένου in v. 20.

basic Greek meaning "ransom." But the religious meaning, "redeem," which was associated with the word in the LXX and in early Christianity[49] fits better with the OT background of the passage, Isa. 52:3, and above all with the concept of vicarious sacrifice in v. 19. Nevertheless, the meaning of the word remains ambivalent. This is conditioned by the statement concerning Jesus' death in early Christian tradition. The saying about ransom (λύτρον) in Mk. 10:45 par. Mt. interprets his death as representative atonement: The Son of man gives his life as atonement for the peoples of the world. In content, this interpretation appropriates in free meditative association with the Hebrew text — not as quotation — the (unique in the OT) statement in Isa. 53:10-12 about the suffering to death of the Servant of God, which accomplishes atonement universally.[50] Isaiah 53 is used elsewhere in the NT only in the saying over the cup in Mk. 14:24 par. Mt., which cannot be derived from early Christian Scripture interpretation; it may very well go back to Jesus himself.[51] In I Tim. 2:6 the saying is inserted in Hellenistic form into a confessional formula.

Here a tradition coming from the Mk. 10:45 saying has been developed further, with both sides of the statement expanded: On the one hand, it is underscored that the legal release through ransom has been accomplished "not with perishable things such as silver or gold (οὐ φθαρτοῖς, ἀργυρίῳ ἢ χρυσίῳ)"[52] but as redemption through Jesus' atoning death (ἀλλὰ τιμίῳ αἵματι ὡς ἀμνοῦ ἀμώμου καὶ ἀσπίλου Χριστοῦ),[53] as is emphasized, on the other hand, through comparison

---

49. λυτροῦσθαι (middle voice), "purchase the freedom (of a slave or a prisoner of war) in exchange for a ransom," and (passive) "be ransomed," was common in Hellenistic language (F. Büchsel, "λύω," *TDNT* IV, 340, 349f.). In the LXX the verb is especially important in deutero-Isaiah, as in the passage appropriated here, for גאל, speaking of Israel's liberation from the Babylonian exile, and in Deuteronomy (7:8, and passim) for פדה, of the liberation from Egypt (cf. Ex. 6:6; 15:13; on this cf. O. Procksch, "λύω," *TDNT* IV, 331-334). The verb goes thereby beyond "ransom" to the sacral sense "redeem," in which there is often no longer thought of a ransom.

50. J. Jeremias, "Das Lösegeld für viele (Mk 10,45)," *idem, Abba* (Göttingen, 1966), 216-229; E. Lohse, *Märtyrer und Gottesknecht* (FRLANT NF 46; second ed., Göttingen, 1963), 117ff.

51. Support on particulars is in H. Patsch, *Abendmahl und historischer Jesus* (Stuttgart, 1971), 175-180.

52. This statement was surely developed in reliance on Isa. 52:3. Therefore, as in the LXX, the price is indicated by the dative, not, as in Tit. 2:14 and elsewhere, the genitive.

53. This further development of the λύτρον saying of Mk. 10:45 has no parallel in the Pauline passages, which treat the image of conveyance through ransom: I Cor. 6:20 (ἠγοράσθητε τιμῆς); 7:23. On the other hand, it does have a contextual parallel in some

with a lamb of offering. The simile of the lamb does not refer here, however, to Isa. 53:7 — although this text is appropriated in the next christological section (I Pet. 2:22) — but incorporates the tradition that characterizes Jesus as the Passover lamb.[54] The death of the Passover lambs was regarded in rabbinic Judaism as an atonement offering making possible the redemption from Egypt.[55] Here in I Peter the release from prison is not a release from guilt for sin, as in Isaiah 53. Jesus' death, the "blood of Christ,"[56] was τίμιος, "precious," "of high value,"[57] because he was, as was required of OT offerings, ἄμωμος, "without spot,"[58] ἄσπιλος, "without blemish,"[59] namely, without sin and holy.[60]

The comparison with the Passover lamb contributes to the understanding of Jesus' death, which God himself made possible as atonement and thus legally: Jesus' death makes possible the liberating exodus, in accord with God's gracious institution in the Old Covenant. The deeper sense of this atonement first becomes clear from the perspective of the prophecy in Isaiah 53, which stands behind the origin of this Christian tradition, namely Mk. 10:45. The atoning death of the Servant of God is not, like the suffering to death of martyrs according to IV Macc. 6:28f.; 17:20ff., a substitutionary achievement for the God who calculates one achievement for another. It is also not, like OT offerings, an objective rite that according to God's gracious institution obliterates guilt. It is, rather, the demonstration of God's faithfulness, which sets

---

respects in Tit. 2:14, the only other NT passage in which the word (the verb λυτροῦσθαι in Titus) interprets Jesus' death. A parallel in content is found in Rev. 5:9, where the images of ransom and "slaughtered lamb" are again joined: ἐσφάγης καὶ ἠγόρασας. Cf. Heb. 9:12: Through sacrificial atonement Christ secured αἰωνίαν λύτρωσιν, "an eternal redemption." ἀπολύτρωσις, "redemption," is frequently encountered, but does not express the meaning of Jesus' death but its present and future soteriological effect; it appears in I Cor. 1:30 with "sanctification" and in Eph. 1:7; Heb. 9:15 with "forgiveness."

54. I Cor. 5:7; cf. Jn. 19:36 = Ex. 12:46.

55. Str.-Bill. IV, 40; cf. J. Jeremias, *The Eucharistic Words of Jesus* (tr. N. Perrin; New York, 1966), 225f.

56. See the comments on 1:2.

57. So also *I Clem.* 7:4 (LCL AF I, 21): τίμιον τῷ πατρί.

58. According to Lev. 22:17-25 sacrificial offerings must be ἄμωμος, "unblemished"; so also Ex. 29:1; Ezek. 43:22f. So also of Christ's self-offering in Heb. 9:14.

59. ἄσπιλος, "unspotted," does not appear in the LXX. It is used figuratively in Jas. 1:27 of Christians: "keep oneself unstained from the world"; cf. I Tim. 6:14; *II Clem.* 8:6 (LCL AF I, 141).

60. I Pet. 2:22: "he committed no sin . . . ," an idea shared in early Christianity: II Cor. 5:21; Heb. 4:15; 7:26; I Jn. 3:5.

aside the first promise in a second and brings about the desired result without rendering void the first. Jesus brings "as a servant" forgiveness and salvation as fellowship with God mediated through his person; what he brings can for this reason be transmitted further after his departure from this world only through him as the resurrected One.[61]

Through Jesus' death God makes possible the exodus from fallenness to "the vain way of living passed on from your fathers" (v. 18b): ἐλυτρώθητε ἐκ τῆς ματαίας ὑμῶν ἀναστροφῆς πατροπαραδότου. This expression elaborates on the image sketched in v. 14 of the pre-Christian situation: μάταιος, "futile," elaborates on ἄγνοια, "ignorance" (of God), and on ἐπιθυμία, "craving": "Futile" is already in classical Greek what a world of mere appearance erects against reality, what therefore is deceptive, pointless, and senseless. Greek tragedy, like the LXX and the NT, speaks of a form of human conduct that strides senselessly into the void; only the standards of measure differ. According to the LXX everything is futile by which a person denies his or her creatureliness, e.g., human-made idols.[62] According to the NT all are futile who in point of fact deny God, Christians included (I Cor. 15:17; Tit. 3:9; Jas. 1:26). Those who do not draw their life from God lose themselves in their world to unrelatedness, since they understand neither themselves nor those with whom they come in contact in terms of their origin and destiny. Choosing ἐπιθυμία over the claim upon them coming from reality, they try to erect a world for themselves.

Humankind is unable to free itself from the conduct thus characterized by these three key words, which is "inherited from your fathers" (πατροπαράδοτος), i.e., a binding tradition.[63] The term describes "sociologically" what the Adam-Christ typology in Rom. 5:12-21 says theologically. The expression has Gentile Christians in mind, but does not reflect particularly on paganism but on human existence as such. Because people are bound together in this way, I Peter does not direct

---

61. L. Goppelt, "Geschichtlich wirksames Sterben," *Leben angesichts des Todes* (FS H. Thielicke; Tübingen, 1968), 61-68; Patsch, *Abendmahl und historischer Jesus,* 183ff.

62. Lev. 17:7; Jer. 8:19; 10:15; cf. Eph. 4:17 (O. Bauernfeind, "μάταιος," *TDNT* IV, 519-522). Wis. 13:1 reminds one directly of the key words in our passage: "For by nature all were foolish (μάταιοι) and had no perception of God (οἷς παρῆν θεοῦ ἀγνωσία)."

63. Therefore πατροπαράδοτος, "inherited from one's father," "handed down" (in the NT only here; LXX), must be understood negatively on the basis of its contextual link to "ransom." Here it refers not only, as in Diodorus Siculus 4.8.5 (LCL II, 367), to obligatory tradition, which one can abandon: μηδὲ τὴν πατροπαράδοτον διαφυλάττειν. II Tim. 1:5; 3:15 does not describe simply the opposite of that which I Pet. 1:19 intends.

moral and religious appeals toward them; rather, redemption through Jesus' death is preached to them.

20 Jesus' death is the universal redemption only because it has come forth from God's plan for the world: προεγνωσμένου μὲν πρὸ καταβολῆς κόσμου, φανερωθέντος δὲ ἐπ' ἐσχάτου τῶν χρόνων δι' ὑμᾶς. This confessional statement formulated in antithetical parallelism appropriates apocalyptic schemata and places Jesus' death in the context of God's plan for the world: Jesus was "known beforehand," i.e., in accord with 1:2, he was destined beforehand (to be the agent of salvation),[64] "before the foundation of the world," before its creation or its beginning;[65] he has "appeared," become active in history, at the end of time,[66] i.e., at the beginning of the endtime.[67]

This antithesis speaks not of preexistence and incarnation, but of "predetermination" and "appearance." The two verbs do not correspond to one another exactly. According to 1:2 God's eternal predetermination is realized among Christians through the historical summons. Here, however, φανεροῦσθαι, "appear," speaking of Christ, is placed in relation to predetermination. What does this mean in the context before us?

---

64. προγινώσκειν (see the comments on 1:2), "foreknowledge," "precognition." God's precognition is also always predetermination or election since it attends not to what others do, but to that which happens through God; so Rom. 8:29; 11:2 of Christians (Eph. 1:4: ἐξελέξατο), here only of Christ (cf. R. Bultmann, "γινώσκω," *TDNT* I, 715f.).

65. καταβολή appears in the NT in post-Pauline writings and always, except in Heb. 11:11, in the phrase ἀπὸ/πρὸ καταβολῆς κόσμου. The phrase is closely connected to extrabiblical Greek: καταβολή, "laying down," e.g., the laying down of the foundation for a building (F. Hauck, "καταβολή," *TDNT* III, 620f.). ἀπὸ καταβολῆς can mean "from the beginning" (H. Sasse, "κοσμέω," *TDNT* III, 885, n.62), e.g., Diodorus Siculus 12.32.2 (LCL IV, 441). Hellenistic Judaism appropriated the word κόσμος and spoke of the beginning of the world with other expressions (Sasse, 878, 881f.). In contrast, *Test. Mos.* 1:12-14 (*OT Pseudep.* I, 927) corresponds even in context to I Pet. 1:20: "[God] created the world on behalf of His people, but he did not make this purpose of creation openly known from the beginning of the world. . . . But he did design and devise me, who (was) prepared from the beginning of the world, to be the mediator of his covenant."

66. ἐπ' ἐσχάτου (with no article for neuter ἔσχατον) τῶν χρόνων, "at the end of time(s)," in the NT only here; the synonymous expression in Heb. 9:26 is ἐπισυντέλεια τῶν αἰώνων, otherwise often the LXX expression ἐπ' ἐσχάτου τῶν ἡμερῶν (Heb. 1:2, and passim; cf. G. Kittel, "ἔσχατος," *TDNT* II, 697f.); further, Jude 18: ἐπ' ἐσχάτου τοῦ χρόνου; I Pet. 1:5: ἐν καιρῷ ἐσχάτῳ.

67. With Jesus' death and rising the eschatological event begins (see the comments on 1:10-12). I Peter clearly recognizes the chronological tension between the φανεροῦσθαι that has already occurred (1:20) and the future φανεροῦσθαι (5:4; cf. 1:5, 7) of the eschaton, referring, thereby, to a chronological span for the eschaton. But the writer does not calculate time periods.

In a christological formula found in several places among the Apostolic Fathers the emergence of the preexistent One is characterized as follows: "Who was from eternity with the Father and was made manifest at the end of time."[68] This formula is fashioned in the sense of preexistence christology and appropriates at the same time the Jewish apocalyptic idea that the Son of man and other figures of salvation, who have been hidden in heaven since the primeval beginning, would come forth at the end of time.[69] Here the formula differs from this objectification and speaks theocentrically of God's predetermination. The formula here is also not identical with an expression in the inauthentic ending to Romans (16:25f.): The mystery of salvation, "which was kept secret for long ages but is now disclosed (φανερωθέντος)."[70]

According to the context the Greek word in I Pet. 1:20 does not mean only that something present has been unveiled or has made its appearance, or only that a promise has been fulfilled; rather, it means that what was predetermined has been made manifest and thereby realized historically. The passage that comes closest is Heb. 9:26: νυνὶ δὲ ἅπαξ ἐπὶ συντελείᾳ τῶν αἰώνων . . . πεφανέρωται, which reflects not directly on the incarnation of the preexistent One, but, like I Tim. 3:16, on the active involvement of the preexistent One in the historical context (Heb. 1:2). I Pet. 1:20 speaks even less of an emergence of that which is already present. Rather, it emphasizes that in Jesus' ministry, especially in his suffering to death, God's eternal plan of salvation was accomplished[71] — because Christ became actively involved historically by design as the predetermined One. For this reason Jesus' less than spectacular ministry and suffering in history is the eschatological redemption; and thus through him the world is not only subsequently reinstated, but is also brought to the goal determined for it from eternity.

This soteriological intention of the statement is articulated directly

---

68. Ignatius, *Magn.* 6:1 (although with ἐφάνη [LCL AF I, 203]); but *Herm. Sim.* 9.12.2f. (φανερὸς ἐγένετο [*ibid.* II, 249]); *II Clem.* 14:2 (ἐφανερώθη [*ibid.* I, 151]); cf. *Odes Sol.* 4:14 (*OT Pseudep.* II, 737).

69. *I En.* 62:7 (*OT Pseudep.* I, 43).

70. Cf. Goppelt, *Typos*, 127; E. Käsemann, *Commentary on Romans* (tr. G. Bromiley; Grand Rapids, 1980), 421-428; R. Bultmann and D. Lührmann, "φανερόω," *TDNT* IX, 4f.

71. This concept grew out of the theology of history in OT and Jewish apocalyptic literature, which had its precursor in the theology of deutero-Isaiah (Isa. 45:21; 46:8ff., and passim): Isa. 37:26; *I En.* 48:6 (*OT Pseudep.* I, 35); II Esdr. 6:1-6: "Before the world's portals were standing . . . , even then had I these things in mind, and through me alone and none other they were created. So also the end will come through me alone and none other."

in the closing δι' ὑμᾶς, "for your sake." In apocalyptic and Essene traditions as well[72] redemption occurs for the sake of the elect. This exclusive consciousness of election is linked to the Church in I Pet. 2:9f. even more than it is here. It is a matter, however, not of a pre-destination theory that serves self-justification. It is rather the pledge of salvation's final revelation, the pledge that brings one under the obligation of universal mission because Jesus' commission — as I Peter holds in dialectical tension[73] — applies to everyone.

21 Christ's eschatological work of salvation spanning all of cre-ation places an obligation on all who have become believers through him: τοὺς δι' αὐτοῦ πιστοὺς[74] εἰς θεόν. Believing is established "through him,"[75] through his work of salvation, because his work makes access to God possible: "Christ also suffered . . . in order to lead you to God" (3:18). Jesus' death has this significance because it was death directed toward the resurrection; according to 1:3, new birth toward hope and thereby also the experience of believing became reality through the resurrection.

Therefore, the basis of faith is identified here as its content: εἰς θεὸν τὸν ἐγείραντα αὐτὸν ἐκ νεκρῶν. Already according to the formulaic tradition[76] in Rom. 4:24, to "believe" means to hold fast to the One who raised Jesus from the dead and has thereby shown himself ulti-mately as God, as the Creator "who gives life to the dead and calls to existence things that do not exist" (Rom. 4:17) — and thus to become certain of his promise, which gives access to salvation (Rom. 4:18-21). Jesus' resurrection was indeed, as the expression added here, καὶ δόξαν αὐτῷ δόντα,[77] implies, not a revivification but an eschatological becom-ing-new and thereby a reception into "glory": Jesus was — in a unique way — taken up into God's essence, "exalted to God's right hand."[78]

---

72. *I En.* 62:8; 45:3f. (*OT Pseudep.* I, 43, 34); CD 4:3f.; cf. G. Schrenk, "λέγω," *TDNT* IV, 170f.

73. See the comments on 2:12; 3:1, 19. See also Spörri, *Gemeindegedanke*.

74. Here πιστός is not passive "trustworthy," but, as already in classical Greek and often in the NT, active "believing." The equally well-supported variant πιστεύοντας and especially the modestly supported πιστεύσαντας are appropriate mitigations. According to Selwyn, 146f., the expression here is, as often in the NT, a conventional designation: "believers"; opposing this assumption, however, are other matters of detail.

75. Faith "through Christ" otherwise in Acts 3:16; Jn. 1:7.

76. Rom. 8:11: "him who raised Christ Jesus from the dead"; II Cor. 4:14; Gal. 1:1; Eph. 1:20; Col. 2:12; I Thess. 1:10; cf. Rom. 10:9.

77. Raise and glorify together also in Acts 3:13, 15.

78. See the comments on 3:21f.

The concluding statement in v. 21b directs attention back to the beginning of the section: ὥστε τὴν πίστιν ὑμῶν καὶ ἐλπίδα εἶναι εἰς θεόν. Like faith, so also hope[79] is directed, not to a better world, but to God, who will glorify those who belong to him with Christ (4:13).

When one looks back at the christological foundation for believing and hoping in vv. 18-21, one has the impression that everything that is said was necessary to give faith and hope their foundation from the perspective of the origin of Christian existence, from Jesus' death and resurrection.[80] At the same time it serves to strengthen and to intensify the imperatives of vv. 13, 14-16 as well as the reference to fear of God in v. 17.

1:22–2:3: Brotherly Love

22 *You who have cleansed your souls through obedience to the truth*
for unhypocritical brotherly love,
love one another from the heart with total commitment.

23 *For you have been born anew —*
not from perishable but from imperishable seed,
(that is) through the living and abiding word of God;
24 *For "all flesh is like grass*
and all its glory as the flower of grass.
The grass is withered
and the flower has faded,
25 *but the Word of the Lord remains forever." (Isa. 40:6-8)*
This is the word that was preached to you as good news.

2:1 *So now put away all malice*
and all guile, insincerity, and envy
and all slander.

---

79. R. Bultmann, "πιστεύω," *TDNT* VI, 207f., 210f.; Knopf, 78f., and many earlier exegetes take ἐλπίδα as predicative: "so that your faith is, at the same time, hope in God." It is true that in I Peter believing and hoping are two aspects of the same conduct (cf. 3:5). But here the progression of thought goes from faith in the God who glorified Jesus to the God who will glorify with him those who are his own. Further counterarguments are in Kelly, 77f.

80. Contra Schelkle, 51: "The context of the section 1:17-21 would require merely a statement about the saving death, for which 1:19 would be enough." But then there would be no explanation of how Jesus' death is able to become faith's foundation.

2 *As newborn children long for spiritual, genuine milk,*
  so that you may grow to salvation through it,
3 *for you have, indeed, tasted how good the Lord is.*

Theme, Structure, and Tradition

1. Bound inextricably to one's turning to God in hope and faith as exodus from this world's ways of life (1:13-21) is the mutual demonstration of love among the members of the exodus community. The imperative "Love one another" (1:22), which sets the theme for the section 1:22–2:3, adds this dimension to the picture of fundamental Christian conduct described thus far.

Love within the community is also part of the self-understanding of the exodus community at Qumran. 1QS 1:9-11 proclaims as a rule for the community: "Love all the children of light, each according to his place in God's design, and hate all the children of darkness, each according to his guilt in God's vengeance." Acceptance into the community is described then in 1QS 3:4-9; 4:20f., which, like I Pet. 1:22a (see the comments below), give the basis for brotherly love.

But the Qumran community's inward-facing bond of solidarity has a different character from what is seen in I Peter. This becomes clear from the very different views of conduct toward outsiders.[1] Apparently a complex of expression from Essene tradition was appropriated here on the basis of materials transmitted within the Church and was given new content. Jesus himself had, in fact, already emphasized the place of one's neighbor in one's relationship to God, mediated by him, because God himself draws people into his fellowship, demonstrating love without restriction.[2]

This principle also directed members of the Church from the very beginning in their relationships with one another, so that they understood themselves to be obligated to the mutual demonstration of love.[3] The realization of this obligation was, however, never taken for granted. For this reason, the thematic imperative, "Love one another," in 1:22b is given extensive foundation.

2. From the foundation supplied here emerges the arrangement of the brief

---

1. See n.12 and the comments on 2:11.

2. Mt. 6:12 par. Lk.; Mk. 11:25f.; Mt. 6:14f., and passim. Particularly important is Mk. 10:43ff.

3. Cf. Acts 4:32–5:11; Jn. 13:35: "By this will all know that you are my disciples: if you have love for one another," and the sharp warnings in I John about failure to show brotherly love. This difference from the Qumran ideal is also shown by the recognition even by outsiders that the Christian community was based on love — and was held in suspicion by outsiders. Tertullian, *Apologeticus* 39 (*ANF* III, 46): Even because they willingly supported afflicted fellow believers, Christians were held in suspicion by outsiders: " 'See,' they say, 'how they love one another,' for they themselves are animated by mutual hatred; 'how they are ready even to die for one another,' for they themselves will sooner put to death." In Minucius Felix, *Octavius* 9.2 (*ibid.* IV, 177) the accusation of outsiders is recorded: The Christians "know one another by secret marks and insignia, and they love one another almost before they know one another. . . . They call one another promiscuously brothers and sisters." See below, n.13.

section: The imperative ἀγαπήσατε in v. 22b is motivated by preceding and following participial sentences clauses: v. 22a: ἡγνικότες; v. 23: ἀναγεγεννημένοι. The second of these clauses is reinforced in vv. 24f. by an OT quotation. Then in 2:1-3 the readers are admonished to turn away from what has gone before, from failure in living in relationship to their neighbors, and toward the word that calls forth what is new.[4]

3. The key words of this parenesis — "cleanse," "brotherly love," "love one another," "born anew through the word," "lay aside," and "grow," are all clear elements of Christian parenetic tradition. But there is here no direct appropriation of prior formulas. In vocabulary and style the section follows in every detail the ideas developed initially in 1:1. The Scripture quotation, which reinforces the impression of a more didactic style, introduces once again a loftier style.[5]

Vv. 22-25: Mutual Love as Sign of the New Birth

22 ἀλλήλους ἀγαπᾶν, demonstration of love mutually, is the signpost of φιλαδελφία, "brotherly love." The two expressions appear here, as usual,[6] alongside each other to explain each other. Mutuality differentiates brotherly love from love for neighbor. Only those who have been addressed by the prescript of the letter, namely the members of the Church, are able to be called to mutual love. They are "brothers" with one another. Just as Israel according to OT and Jewish concepts,[7] so also the community of Jesus' disciples understood themselves as family.[8] For this reason, its members characterized themselves and addressed one another as brothers and sisters.[9] Therefore, they saw themselves called upon to show especially to each other that love to which they were obliged to have for every neighbor.[10] φιλαδελφία is

---

4. Spicq, 59, 77, divides the first main part, 1:13–2:10, into two sections: 1:13-25 and 2:1-10.

5. The demarcation and thesis of Danker, "I Peter 1,24–2,17," are problematic.

6. I Jn. 3:11: "love one another"; 3:14: "love the brethren"; so also 4:11f., 20f.; cf. Rom. 12:10: τῇ φιλαδελφίᾳ εἰς ἀλλήλους φιλόστοργοι.

7. "Brother" as fixed designation: Lev. 19:17; Dt. 18:15 (= Acts 3:22; 7:37); Ps. 22:23 (= Heb. 2:12; cf. 7:5); Zech. 7:9f.; Jer. 31:34; as address: Jer. 22:18, and passim; so also in rabbinic writings (Str.-Bill. II, 766) and the Qumran literature: 1QS 6:22; 1QM 13:1; 15:4, 7; CD 6:20; 7:1f.

8. Probably Jesus already applied the image of the family of God, which was used in the OT of Israel (Hos. 2:1-3, 4-6; cf. Str.-Bill. III, 682), to his disciples: Mk. 3:31-35 par.; cf. Mt. 23:8; Lk. 22:32.

9. As a designation: I Pet. 5:12; Rom. 8:29; 14:10, 13, 15, 21, and passim; as address: Rom. 1:13; 7:1, 4; 8:12; 10:1, and passim throughout all NT church documents.

10. Cf. Gal. 6:10.

never used figuratively in non-Christian writings,[11] but in the NT is applied with emphasis — in relation to the spiritual brotherhood.[12]

This terminology is more prominent in I Peter than in the rest of the NT, even though the theme is not emphasized as much as in I John. Only I Peter characterizes the Church as ἀδελφότης, "brotherhood" (2:17; 5:9), and only I Peter appeals to the Church with the adjective φιλάδελφος, "brotherly" (3:8). This emphasis of the brotherhood arises out of the Jewish and early Christian tradition that influences I Peter's discourse about community as well as out of the situation of the community in relation to its environment, which made inner solidarity a necessity.

But I Peter does not by any means seek with the emphasis on brotherly love to suppress, as did the Essenes, the demonstration of love beyond its own circle toward the particular neighbor. Instead, I Pet. 3:8f. combines brotherly love with love for neighbor in the form in which Jesus expressed it according to the Sermon on the Mount (Mt. 5:45 par. Lk.): Even with respect to the persecutor evil is to be repaid with good.[13]

Because love within the Church is applied without limits as the standard, the hypocrisy that accompanies all regulation is a constant possibility.[14] Quite deliberately, therefore, brotherly love is qualified here by the predicate adjective ἀνυπόκριτος, "unhypocritical," which elsewhere in the NT is also connected primarily with love within the Church.[15] The demonstration of love is "unhypocritical," not merely gestures of benevolence without a personal turning toward the other person, when it comes ἐκ καρδίας, "from the heart,"[16] from the core of

---

11. H. von Soden, "ἀδελφός," *TDNT* I, 146.

12. I Thess. 4:9; Rom. 12:10; Heb. 13:1; II Pet. 1:7. For bibliography see K.-H. Schelkle, "Bruder," *RAC* II, cols. 631-640; C. Spicq, *Agape in the NT* II (tr. M. McNamara and M. Richter; St. Louis, 1965), 346-353; H. Kosmala, *Hebräer —Essener —Christen* (Leiden, 1959), 44-50; C. Brady, *Brotherly Love: A Study of the Word φιλαδελφία and its Contribution to the Biblical Theology of Brotherly Love* (dissertation, Fribourg, 1961).

13. So also Rom. 12:10, 14, 17-21. This directive reminds one of the similarly worded but, in terms of starting point, differently intended confession in 1QS 10:17-21: "I will pay no one the reward of evil. I will pursue him with goodness. For judgment of all the living belongs to God, and he it is who will render to each his reward."

14. The fundamental model for feigned demonstration of love under the pressure of regulation is the conduct of Ananias according to Acts 5:1-6 (see above, n.3).

15. Rom. 12:9; II Cor. 6:6; otherwise, I Tim. 1:5 and II Tim. 1:5 of faith and Jas. 3:17 of wisdom.

16. J. Behm, "καρδία," *TDNT* III, 611f.

reflection and will, and ἐκτενῶς, "honestly," which here means not so much "intensely" as "undividedly," "with total commitment."[17]

The demonstration of love in this pointed sense among members of the Church is by no means to be taken for granted. It is precisely one who is called by the gospel to devote himself or herself to God in complete solitude, i.e., through faith, that is always in danger of religiously embellishing his or her "fleshly" way of thinking, the egocentric need to assert oneself, as can already be seen in the turbulent debates within the Pauline communities.[18] For this reason, the imperative to demonstrate love to one another is given intensive motivation by means of two participles that underscore the indicative of the salvation encounter.

In the first participle (v. 22a), the readers are told that their ψυχαί, the core of their lives as persons,[19] are "purified"[20] permanently (so the perfect tense): τὰς ψυχὰς ὑμῶν ἡγνικότες. It is purified ἐν τῇ ὑπακοῇ τῆς ἀληθείας, "through obedience to the truth," i.e., as Acts 15:9 explains, through faith. "The truth" that one obeys is not, as in Greek thought, some verifiable content, but in accord with OT and Jewish thought it is reliable reality that places one under obligation,[21] namely God's self-revelation, seen conclusively in Jesus' death and resurrection and represented by the gospel. "To obey the truth" is, therefore, the same as to obey the gospel,[22] i.e., to devote oneself to God through faith (1:21). This turning to God purifies from the tendency of wanting and

---

17. Some translate "fervently," e.g., BAGD s.v.; Schweizer, 42. Others translate "earnestly," e.g., Schelkle, 52, or "unremittingly," e.g., Michaels, *1 Peter*, 75f. Evang, "1 Petr 1,22f.," 117f. and passim opts for a temporal translation in the context of some broader syntactical and structural arguments.

18. I Cor. 1:11f.; 11:18-21.

19. The object of ἁγνίζειν here is ψυχαί, "souls," in Jas. 4:8 it is καρδίαι, "hearts," and in I Jn. 3:3 it is ἑαυτός "himself/herself"; in substance they mean the same.

20. ἁγνίζειν in the LXX is the technical term for ritual purification that enables one to participate in the cult (Ex. 19:10; Josh. 3:5, appropriated in Jn. 11:55; Acts 21:24, 26; 24:18). In the NT, in accord with Jesus' fundamental directive in Mk. 7:15, it is the technical term for spiritual purification of one's life from all that is opposed to God (Jas. 4:8; I Jn. 3:3; cf. F. Hauck, "ἁγνός," *TDNT* I, 122f.). The verb corresponds in this context somewhat to the "holy One" in I Pet. 1:14ff. A close parallel to the expression in 1:22, perhaps pointing to a traditional context, is 1QS 3:4-9 (cf. 4:20f.): "He shall be cleansed from all his sins by the Spirit of holiness uniting him to its truth. . . . When his flesh has been sprinkled with purifying water and sanctified by cleansing water, it will be made clean by the humble submission of his soul to God's precepts."

21. G. Quell and R. Bultmann, "ἀλήθεια," *TDNT* I, 232f., 238f.

22. In Paul similar statements stand together: Gal. 5:7: not to obey the truth; Rom. 10:16 and II Thess. 1:8: not to obey the gospel, i.e., not to believe. See the comments above on 1:2, 14.

needing to get one's own way and leads, therefore, to "unhypocritical brotherly love," since in turning to God one gives oneself to the Lord of all that happens, the Lord who now seeks human beings in a love without preconditions and limitations.

When and how does this purification "through obedience to the truth" become a reality? The perfect tense of the participle points to an event that has ongoing validity. Formulaic pointers to experienced purification can be found already in Paul, and there they call to mind baptism.[23] But neither here nor there is baptism expressly mentioned. The implicit pointer to the event of baptism does not establish an empirical change. Rather, that which is already a reality from God through baptism, namely, the connection to God's act of love through the summons to faith, which frees from all previous connections, is promised anew.

23 The second perfect participle indicates that the new birth through the word corresponds to this purification through obedience to the truth:[24] ἀναγεγεννημένοι . . . διὰ λόγου ζῶντος θεοῦ καὶ μένοντος. They are two sides of the same event. As purification this event frees one from all that has gone before, and as new birth it opens a person to that which is new. "Through obedience" characterizes the event as human conduct, while "new birth" characterizes it as the gift of the Creator. Even new birth is not linked simply with baptism as a rite, but with the activity of God encountered through baptism; in 1:3 new birth is linked with the resurrection of Jesus, here with the "word of God,"[25] which in 1:25, in general accord with early Christian usage, is identified with the gospel proclamation of Jesus' resurrection. The event of baptism is, as was made clear in 1:3, summons and deliverance over to the active word.

God's word does its work in a way comparable to that of a natural seed, which, however, like the birth that it brings forth, belongs to what is passing away. Therefore, it is said: οὐκ ἐκ σπορᾶς φθαρτῆς, ἀλλὰ ἀφθάρτον. The word is "incorruptible seed,"[26] because it is "living"

---

23. I Cor. 6:11; cf. further Eph. 5:26; Tit. 3:3-7; Heb. 10:22.

24. So also Jas. 1:18: ἀπεκύησεν ἡμᾶς λόγῳ ἀληθείας. Cf. I Jn. 3:9: πᾶς ὁ γεγεννημένος ἐκ τοῦ θεοῦ ἁμαρτίαν οὐ ποιεῖ, ὅτι σπέρμα αὐτοῦ ἐν αὐτῷ μένει. Cf. also Jn. 1:12f.

25. ὁ λόγος τοῦ θεοῦ, only here in I Peter. In 2:8; 3:1, as otherwise in earliest Christianity, we find the absolute form ὁ λόγος.

26. The image of "seed" and "new birth" (cf. I Jn. 3:9), which is interpreted here in terms of the creating word in an OT sense, has its analogies in the Hellenistic world: *Corpus*

(ζῶν),[27] i.e., creatively active,[28] and "abiding" (μένων).[29] Because the word abides, the "I" that lives from it also has durability. This new "I" is capable of demonstrating love, since it no longer lives in a selfish direction but for the One who has called it forth.

24f. This speech-phenomenon of God, articulated through human beings and giving shape to historical existence, was for the ancient world characteristic only of the biblical concept of God, but by the same token was quite fundamental to it. Thus, this statement about "the word of God" — expressed through human beings and yet, unlike all human speech, transcending imminence, and being "incorruptible" and "abiding" — is interpreted and supported by a Scripture quotation, Isa. 40:6-8.[30] The "word of the Lord" (ῥῆμα κυρίου, v. 25a) as "that which remains" is placed in relation to history as that which passes away. "All flesh" (πᾶσα σάρξ), human beings in their totality,[31] make their appearance as active and passive figures of history. History, which threatened to overwhelm the people of God in the situation of Isaiah 40, and now for I Peter the Church, is compared to grass and to all the splendor of the flower of grass: It will pass away. Only "the word of the Lord," which goes forth in history, "abides," not as a general truth suspended above history, but as the promise that is carried out and is effective in history to accomplish the exodus into a new existence for the afflicted Church, just as it did in the past for Israel in its exile.

The "word" in this sense is, as v. 25b explains, what was and is being proclaimed to the Church as gospel: τοῦτο δέ ἐστιν τὸ ῥῆμα τὸ

Hermeticum 13.1: ἀγνοῶ, ὦ Τρισμέγιστε, ἐξ οἵας μήτρας . . . ἀναγεννήθης, σπορᾶς δὲ ποίας; 13.2: ἡ σπορὰ τὸ ἀληθινὸν ἀγαθόν (*Hermetica* I, tr. W. Scott [Oxford, 1924], 238f.).

27. God is characterized as "living and abiding" in Dan. 6:20. But here, in accord with v. 25, these adjectives are used of the λόγος, not θεοῦ, which is inserted peculiarly into the expression. Cf. la Verdière, "Grammatical Ambiguity."

28. Cf. Ps. 33:9; Isa. 55:10f.; Heb. 4:12.

29. Cf. Mt. 24:35: "Heaven and earth will pass away, but my words will not pass away."

30. Isa. 40:6-8 is quoted with insignificant modifications according to the LXX text. Twice the quotation deviates from both the Hebrew and the LXX texts: In the first line ὡς is inserted and in the last line — perhaps to facilitate the application — κυρίου is used instead of τοῦ θεοῦ ἡμῶν (LXX). In the second line αὐτῆς corresponds more closely to the Hebrew text than it does to ἀνθρώπου in the LXX.

31. πᾶσα σάρξ, Hebrew כָּל־בָּשָׂר, "all flesh," represents all people, humankind (cf. F. Baumgärtel, "σάρξ," *TDNT* VII, 106f.); σάρξ is humankind as God's creation, which is subject to death (E. Schweizer, "σάρξ," *TDNT* VII, 123f.). Concerning the further use of the term in I Peter see the comments on 3:18, 21; 4:1f., 6.

εὐαγγελισθὲν εἰς ὑμᾶς (cf. 1:12). It is what promises a new existence; it relieves one of the need to constitute one's own life; it makes one, thereby, free to come to the assistance of one's "brothers." 2:1-3, which is added here, draws the conclusion from this meaning of the word and makes the transition to the next section, 2:4-10.

2:1-3: Putting Away All Malice, Longing for Genuine Nourishment

2:1 At this point it is appropriate, not in a legalistic way but in consistency with what is being said, to conclude by means of a standard formula of primitive Christian parenesis: "Lay aside"[32] (like an old garment) everything that destroys the relationship to one's neighbor: ἀποθέμενοι οὖν, κτλ. The catalogue of vices that follows[33] is just as traditional as the threefold "all"[34] added as prefix. The catalogue refers to κακία, the "evil deed," which contemplates harm for others,[35] and δόλος, "guile," which uses all the resources of deception in order to get one's way. From both of these follows conduct expressed in the plural, i.e., expressions of "hypocrisy," "envy," and "slander." These are all present in the Church, not according to some sociological statistic, but certainly potentially ever present.

2 This verse counters not with a catalogue of virtues but with reference to the word that gives as gift what human wilfulness unsuccessfully seeks to force, which is life. The image of the continual and intense longing of a newborn for its mother's milk refers to the preached word: ὡς ἀρτιγέννητα βρέφη τὸ λογικὸν ἄδολον γάλα ἐπιποθήσατε. The image is not freely drawn up as comparison, parable, or allegory, but like the images of "growing" (v. 2b) and "taste" (v. 3) is a traditional metaphor.

---

32. The participle is to be translated as an imperative (cf. p. 106, n.16). The expression takes as its point of departure the metaphor of discarding old garments (Rom. 13:12; Col. 3:8f.; Eph. 4:22f.), but becomes here, as in Jas. 1:21 (cf. Eph. 4:25), a fixed formula distinct from the image; cf. Selwyn, 19, 98f., 393-400.

33. The Hebrew equivalents of the key words are found already, except for φθόνος, in the vice catalogue in 1QS 10:21-23 and, except for ὑπόκρισις, in Rom. 1:29-31, and partly in other NT catalogues. *Barn.* 20:1 (LCL AF I, 407) has ὑπόκρισις, δόλος, and κακία with other terms. Cf. S. Wibbing, *Die Tugend- und Lasterkataloge im NT* (BZNW 25; Berlin, 1959), 87f., 93f.

34. Cf. A. Vögtle, *Die Tugend- und Lasterkataloge im NT* (NTA 16, 4-5; Münster, 1936), 45, 218ff.

35. So also I Pet. 2:16; cf. W. Grundmann, "κακός," *TDNT* III, 483f.

The Image of Mother's Milk

In early Christianity as in its environment "mother's milk" was a standard image for a spiritual "nourishment" that mediates life:

1. In primitive Christianity it symbolizes in I Cor. 3:1f. and Heb. 5:13 initial instruction in contrast to the solid food for those who are mature. But in I Pet. 2:2 it represents the message of salvation and its content as such.[36] The closest parallels are in the *Odes of Solomon* and in the Essene texts and move in the direction of this nuance to the image.

2. Two texts in the *Odes of Solomon* recall I Pet. 2:2 and are at points even verbatim:[37]

And before they had existed,
I recognized them;
and imprinted a seal on their faces.
I fashioned their members,
and my own breasts I prepared for them,
that they might drink my holy milk and live by it.
. . . .
For my work are they,
and the power of my thoughts. (8:13-16)

A cup of milk was offered to me,
and I drank it in the sweetness of the Lord's kindness.
The Son is the cup,
and the Father is he who was milked;
and the Holy Spirit is she who milked him. (19:1f.)

Here the symbolic drinking of milk, through which participation in the divine is expressed or mediated in the mysteries and in magic, has become an image for a particular nourishment that stands in dualistic antithesis to literal nourishment. But in I Pet. 2:2 this dualistic aspect is missing, as is the mystic undertone. Therein I Peter is like the Essene texts.

3. Also in the Essene texts care for the infant becomes an image not only for spiritual nourishment but for a new existence:[38]

. . . my father knew me not
and my mother abandoned me to Thee.
For Thou art a father
to all [the sons] of Thy truth,

---

36. Its conveyance is portrayed in I Thess. 2:7 by the metaphor of a wet nurse.

37. Translations from *OT Pseudep.* II, 742, 752. The points of contact with I Pet. 2:3 (ὅτι χρηστὸς ὁ κύριος) are surely the result not of direct incorporation of I Peter (Schelkle, 56, n.2) but of a common tradition.

38. Translations from G. Vermes, *The Dead Sea Scrolls in English* (third ed., London, 1987), 192, 185. So also *Odes Sol.* 35:5 (*OT Pseudep.* II, 765); differently in 4:10 (*ibid.*, 736): "bountiful springs which abundantly supply us with milk and honey."

and as a woman who tenderly loves her babe,
so dost Thou rejoice in them;
and as a foster-father bearing a child in his lap
so carest Thou for all Thy creatures. (1QH 9:35f.)

Thou hast made me a father to the sons of grace,
and as a foster-father to men of marvel;
they have opened their mouths like little babes . . .
like a child playing in the lap of its nurse. (1QH 7:20-22)

4. In I Pet. 2:2 the image draws closer to the depicted existence of those who believe, not only through the style of the metaphor but also through the labeling of milk as "spiritual" and "pure"; thereby — intended or unintended — a point of contact with the forms of speech of the Hellenistic environment has been established, but in no way has the terminology of Gnosticism or of the mystery religions been appropriated.[39] Even the supplementation of the image with references to growing and tasting is more compatible with an enlarging of this Essene tradition[40] than with an involution of the language of the mystery religions.[41]

The very structure of the image discourages the understanding of the introductory expression "as newborn children" as a pointer to the immediately preceding occurrence of new birth in the act of baptism,[42] so that it would reproduce the text of a baptismal address.[43] ἀρτιγέννη-

---

39. In the mythical account the Egyptian god-king is nourished with the milk of Isis unto immortality (cf. H. Schlier, "γάλα," *TDNT* I, 646f.). The initiates of the cult of Cybele declare: ". . . we . . . abstain from bread and all other rich and coarse food . . . after this we are fed on milk as though being reborn" (Sallust, *De Deis* 4 = *Concerning the Gods,* tr. A. Nock [Cambridge, 1926], 9). And in a magical papyrus it says: "And take the milk with the honey and drink it before the rising of the sun, and there will be something divine in your heart" (K. Preisendanz, ed., *Papyri Graecae Magicae* (second ed., Stuttgart, 1973), papyrus I, l. 20. [p. 5]; translation here from H.-D. Betz, ed., *The Greek Magical Papyri in Translation* I [Chicago, 1986], 3); further material in Schlier, *TDNT* I, 646.

40. O. Michel and O. Betz, "Von Gott gezeugt," *Judentum, Urchristentum, Kirche* (FS J. Jeremias; Berlin, 1960), 14, suppose that the sect developed this image out of Num. 11:12. On the critical dialogue concerning Qumran backgrounds see, among others, Snodgrass, "Formation."

41. With Kelly, 85f., contra Schlier, *TDNT* I, 647.

42. That I Pet. 2:2 presupposes the custom coming into practice toward the end of the second century of giving milk and honey to the newly baptized in the baptismal eucharist is not to be assumed. According to Hippolytus, *Apostolic Tradition* 23.2 (= *Hippolytus,* tr. G. Cuming [Grove Liturgical Study 8; Bramcote, England, 1976], 21), this was done to remind those baptized of their new birth and the eternal future; cf. Tertullian, *Adversus Marcionem* 1.14; *De Corona* 3.3 (*ANF* III, 281, 94).

43. With Selwyn, 41, and Kelly, 87, contra the representatives of the liturgical interpretation (see above, pp. 16-18). Far off the mark is the view of Windisch, 58, that here a reinstatement of the innocence of children is at work, by which he imposes his theory of sinlessness.

τος, "new born,"[44] reinforces first of all the image: the βρέφη are "sucklings,"[45] who "crave" intensely their mother's milk.[46] Above all, however, it makes clear in view of the substantive issue that this longing for life-giving nourishment comes from a new birth (1:3, 23) and is now indispensable in order for life to continue. Because new birth is not itself the new nature there must be added to it not only the imperative to live in accord with it (1:13, 22f.), but also the demand to attend further to the word that creates new birth and thereby to come to a condition of growth. "The spiritual and pure milk" is, according to 1:25, "the word" that is preached in the Church and, according to 2:3a, its content, "the Lord." This nourishment, which communicates life, is λογικός, i.e., of the kind coming from God's word and Spirit,[47] and is also, therefore, in contrast to everything that comes from human beings, ἄδολος, "without deception," reliable and true.[48]

"Growth" comes about by this continual appropriation of the word: ἵνα ἐν αὐτῷ αὐξηθῆτε εἰς σωτηρίαν. Whereas the previous indicative and

---

44. ἀρτιγέννητος, one of many compounds with ἄρτι in post-classical Greek: "recently, just now, newly born."

45. A βρέφος is a nursing child. βρέφος is linked with ἀρτιγέννητον also in Lucian, *Dialogues of the Sea-Gods* 12.1 (LCL VII, 221).

46. On ἐπιποθεῖν, cf. Pss. 41:2; 118(119):174 LXX.

47. λογικός apppears in the NT only here and in Rom. 12:1. In Stoic philosophy it means "belonging to the logos, to reason," "rational," "reasonable" (G. Kittel, "λέγω, λογικός," *TDNT* IV, 142f.). In the mystery religions and Gnosticism it signifies that which is spiritual-internal, what corresponds to the mystical type of religion. For example, the Gnostic says in *Corpus Hermeticum* 13.18 (cf. *Hermetica*, tr. Scott, I, 253): ὁ σὸς Λόγος δι' ἐμοῦ ὑμνεῖ σέ. δι' ἐμοῦ δέξαι τὸ πᾶν λόγῳ, λογικὴν θυσίαν (cf. *TDNT* IV, 142).

Accordingly, λογικός in I Pet. 2:2 indicates not just formally that "milk" is a metaphor for what is "spiritual" (so Epictetus, *Dissertationes* 1.16.20; 3.1.26 [LCL I, 113; II, 15]; Philo, *De Migratione Abrahami* 185 [LCL IV, 241]), but also that what is offered is spiritual nourishment corresponding to the logos of the Christians, i.e., to the gospel (1:25): This nourishment has precisely that quality which was at that time sought in philosophy and mysticism. In substance λογικός has the same meaning as πνευματικός in 2:5; it is used here because what one drinks is the Word (cf. Kittel, *TDNT* IV, 142f.).

48. ἄδολος occurs only here in the NT. In Greek literature it meant "without guile/deceit," e.g., of words, Euripides, *Supplices* 1029 (LCL III, 583), passive "genuine," in later inscriptions of food (W. Dittenberger, ed., *Sylloge Inscriptionum Graecarum* [third ed., Hildesheim, 1915-24], 736, l. 101; Oxyrhynchus papyrus 729, l. 19 = *The Oxyrhynchus Papyri* IVB, ed. B. P. Grenfell and A. S. Hunt [London, 1904], p. 217). It characterizes proclamation as "undeceiving," also as "genuine," in contrast to the deceit that holds sway throughout the human sphere (2:1, 22; cf. Eph. 4:14), not, like ἀληθινός in Jn. 6:32, as genuine in dualistic antithesis to unreal earthly nourishment. Cf. BAGD s.v.; F. J. Dölger, *Antike und Christentum* I (Münster, 1929), 170, n.39.

imperative sentences allow Christian existence to appear as a decision always to be repeated anew, so by means of this image it is characterized as a process. The gospel as spiritual nourishment allows the new "I," which expresses itself through hope, faith, and love, to "grow," i.e., to endure and mature (cf. 5:10),[49] toward the goal of σωτηρία, the future salvation (1:5, 7, 9). That those who are born from the word continue to seek the word as a child seeks its mother's milk is not only a life-sustaining obligation; it also corresponds to their actual need.

3 They have in fact[50] tasted that the Lord who is to be encountered in this word is kind: εἰ ἐγεύσασθε ὅτι χρηστὸς ὁ κύριος. The expression deliberately echoes Ps. 34:9 (LXX Ps. 33:9: γεύσασθε καὶ ἴδετε ὅτι χρηστὸς ὁ κύριος). But no individual biblical saying is taken up, but rather an entire Psalm present in the recollection of the author comes to expression, a Psalm that finds echoes elsewhere in the letter.[51] To a considerable extent, the author finds in the OT hymn of thanksgiving the assurance that he wishes to communicate: God delivers from affliction one who perseveres with God to the end. Perhaps the motivation to interpret the Church's situation on the basis of this Psalm was mediated through Essene tradition.[52] It is possible that the Essenes themselves spoke of tasting God's grace[53] and derived this from the

---

49. αὐξάνομαι was already a fixed expression for a child's growth in the LXX (Gen. 21:8, 20, and passim; Lk. 1:80). It is also used of coming into being, i.e., of the emergence and development of Christian existence out of the word, for the first time in the parable of the sower (Mk. 4:8; cf. 4:20), and of the "growth" of the baptized "in faith" (II Cor. 10:15; cf. II Thess. 1:3), "in every good work" (Col. 1:10), "in every way into him" (Eph. 4:15), and comprehensively "in the grace and knowledge of our Lord" (II Pet. 3:17f.). In I Pet. 2:2 growth is connected to the time of inner struggle preceding the consummation; it consists, therefore, above all of "restoring, establishing, and strengthening" (5:10), of standing the test — not of increasing. I Pet. 2:2 is linked in terms of motifs above all with Eph. 4:11-16, but with no traditional context observable.

50. εἰ is not conditional, but causal: "since," as in 1:17; Mt. 6:30; Rom. 6:8, and passim.

51. The expression appended here in 2:4, πρὸς ὃν (sc. τὸν κύριον) προσερχόμενοι is found also in Ps. 33:6 LXX: προσέλθατε πρὸς αὐτόν. I Pet. 3:10-12 quotes Ps. 33:13-17 LXX (so also *I Clem.* 22:1-8 [LCL AF I, 49] = Ps. 33:12-18 + 31:10 LXX; *Did.* 4:9 [*ibid.*, 317] alludes to Ps. 33:12 LXX); see below, p. 139, n.22.

52. Apparently the Psalm, though not quoted directly, provided key words and concepts to the self-understanding of the Essene community, as described in Kosmala, *Hebräer—Essener—Christen*, 128f. Of those terms and concepts these are also characteristic of I Peter: the poor and the humble (Ps. 34:3, 7), those who fear God (vv. 8, 10, 12), the holy ones (v. 10); those who trust/hope in God (vv. 9, 23), joy in God (v. 3), the sufferings of the righteous (v. 20), and, more distantly, many statements regarding rescue and redemption.

53. Josephus, *De Bello Judaico* 2.158 (LCL II, 383) reports that for a long time they

Psalm, which alone in the OT sketches this image. For I Peter this image is already a Christian tradition.[54] That it also played a role in the mystery religions[55] constitutes once again only a remote background.

Here the image is used to say: You have "tasted," i.e., recognized through experience,[56] "that the κύριος (no longer as in Psalm 34[33] God, but the exalted Christ) is good."[57] The addressees experienced this when through the word a new existence from grace and for grace was given to them (1:3, 13, 18f.; 2:23ff.). This experience was mediated to the NT community over and over again through baptism and the eucharist. The graphic term "taste" and the subsequent cultic image of "approaching" (v. 4) could be echoes of the eucharist, though this is hardly intentional.[58] Substantively, the constant appropriation of the word to which this sentence obligates one, as well as the fitting of oneself into the Church, to which the subsequent section directs one, are realized primarily — though not exclusively — in the eucharistic worship celebrated in house-churches.

To this point it has been made clear that Christian existence comes about in the context of solitary hardship out of faith that cannot be secondhand. In what follows the point is made that Christian existence can only be lived in the Church. The readers are summoned, therefore, to incorporate themselves into the Christian fellowship.

---

kept in line with their teaching those who once had tasted their wisdom (τοῖς ἅπαξ γευσαμένοις τῆς σοφίας αὐτῶν). The expression does not, however, occur in the Essene writings (cf. Kosmala, *Hebräer —Essener —Christen*, 118).

54. It is found otherwise in the NT in Heb. 6:5: καλὸν γευσαμένους θεοῦ ῥῆμα, cf. v. 4: γευσαμένους τε τῆς δωρεᾶς τῆς ἐπουρανίου. Here it recalls rabbinic references to the "foretaste of the future world" (Str.-Bill. III, 690).

55. R. Perdelwitz, *Mysterienreligion*, 65ff.; J. Behm, "γεύομαι," *TDNT* I, 675f.

56. γεύομαι, "taste," "savor," was already used figuratively in classical Greek (BAGD s.v.; Behm, *TDNT* I, 675f.).

57. χρηστός, "useful," "good," is used of God also in extrabiblical Greek (Herodotus 8.111 [LCL IV, 113f.]), thus meaning "gracious." So elsewhere in the NT only in Lk. 6:35 and Rom. 2:4 (substantively) of the Creator's goodness through which the creature is upheld undeservedly; of Jesus in Mt. 11:30 in a figure of speech: "My yoke is easy." It is wrong to translate it here according to the figure as "tasting good" because of the quotation character of the passage (contra Kelly, 86). Cf. χρηστότης in Rom. 11:22; II Cor. 6:6; Eph. 2:7; Tit. 3:4, of God the redeemer. Cf. Stevick, "Matter of Taste."

58. Later, Psalm 34 was sung during the eucharist (*Apostolic Constitutions* 8.13.16 [*ANF* VII, 491]; Cyril of Jerusalem, *Catechesis Mystagogica* 5.20 [*NPNF* second series, VII, 156]; Jerome, *Epistulae* 71.6 [*NPNF* second series, VI, 154]). Kelly, 87, concludes from the context of I Pet. 2:3 that it already presupposed an eucharistic interpretation of the Psalm.

2:4-10: Life in the Eschatological Community[1]

4 *Come to him, the living stone*
   who, rejected by human beings,
   is, however, elect and precious before God
5 *and allows you to be built into a spiritual house,*
   as living stones into a holy priesthood,
   in order to offer spiritual sacrifices,
   which are pleasing to God through Jesus Christ.

6 *For it stands in Scripture:*
   "Behold I lay in Zion an elect stone, a precious cornerstone,
   and whoever believes in him will not be put to shame." (Isa.
   28:16)
7 *Now to you who believe the honor is granted.*
   But for those who do not believe,
   "the stone that the builders rejected has become the
   cornerstone" (Ps. 118:22)
8 *and "a stone of stumbling and a rock of offense."* (Isa. 8:14f.)
   They stumble over it because they do not obey the word,
   to which they also are destined.

9 *But you are (the) elect generation, (the) royal priesthood,*
   (the) holy people, (God's) own people,
   so that you proclaim the mighty deeds
   of the One who has called you from darkness into his
   wonderful light.
10 *You were once no people, now, however, are God's people,*
   who once had not experienced mercy, but now have
   experienced mercy.

Form and Tradition

1. The section can be divided into three parts: In vv. 4f. the individuals who are called to Christ are urged to let themselves be built on him, the foundation stone, into a spiritual temple and to serve God in priestly fellowship. Vv. 6-8 give foundation to this admonition through a commented quotation of three OT passages about Christ, the stone: He is established for all as the foundation of salvation or

---

1. Elliott provides a thorough analysis of 2:4-10 in *Elect and Holy*. See also Coppens, "Sacerdoce royal"; Best, "I Pet. II,4-10"; Minear, "House"; Kohler, "Communauté."

of stumbling. In vv. 9f. those who are called to faith are characterized in complementary fashion as the elect people of God who are to be his witness.

2. How is the relationship of these three parts to be understood? The content suggests that the imperatival first part is supported by the indicatives in the second and third parts, especially through the direct pointers to Scripture in the second. But the second and the third parts are not the same: The second points directly to Scripture, while the third, like the first, does so only indirectly. The third is, again like the first, stylized in lofty language, while the second begins didactically with a reference to Scripture. Thus, the impression could arise, which Preisker developed into an hypothesis, that vv. 4f. and 9f. are two strophes of a hymn from a baptismal worship service, while vv. 6-8 are a later addition, perhaps from a collection of *testimonia* with explanatory glosses.[2] But seen more precisely, as Selwyn points out, even vv. 6ff. are in a lofty style.[3]

Furthermore, Preisker's hypothesis is entirely refuted by the observation that vv. 4f. anticipates key words in vv. 6ff. (λίθον, ἀποδεδοκιμασμένον, ἐκλεκτόν, and ἔντιμον) and vv. 9f. (ἐκλεκτόν, ἱεράτευμα, and ἅγιον). On the basis of this observation Elliott concludes correctly: The author of I Peter has not added the quotation complexes around the motifs of elect stone (vv. 6ff.) and elect people (vv. 9f.) as after-the-fact "proofs from Scripture." He has, rather, taken them over from Jewish and Christian tradition and used them in relation to the letter's situation in the thematic sentences in vv. 4f. as well as in the midrashic footnotes in vv. 6-10.[4] In this way they also lay a foundation in content for the imperative in vv. 4f.

3. But from the standpoint of tradition history the author has not, as he apparently did in what preceded, taken up only the two quotation complexes. They were available to him already with the thematic focus developed here in the stream of tradition that becomes visible again and again behind the first major part of the letter. The motifs in vv. 4-10, like other elements therein, are seen together in the self-understanding of the Qumran community. Therefore, a traditional context — to be sure, already developed in a Christian direction — is to be presupposed.

The Qumran community also characterized itself as the true temple and relied thereby on Isa. 28:16. The conduct of the Qumran community was described as priestly service through which true offerings are offered.[5] The references to temple and priesthood are not randomly selected images. They were constitutive for the Essene movement, which arose, as it is, out of rejection of the temple (cf. CD 3:19–4:4). The same is true of the motifs in I Pet. 2:9f.: The sect understood itself as the true Israel, as "the enlightened ones," who take their stand with the teacher "rejected" by Israel and give witness to God's "great" and "wonderful" deeds.[6] In a way differing from v. 9,

---

2. In the appendix to Windisch's commentary, p. 158.
3. Selwyn, 277, 281.
4. Elliott, *Elect and Holy,* 16-49.
5. Above all, 1QS 8:4-11; 9:3-6 (true sacrifices and true temple); see below, nn. 30, 45.
6. See above, pp. 69f.

however, they transferred to themselves the characterization "people of God" only in the situation of the imminent eschatological battle.[7] In accord with this Exodus 19, the passage basic for v. 9, plays a small role in Qumran, as does Ps. 118:22, which is so important for vv. 4, 7.[8]

These indicators alone make clear that I Pet. 2:4-10 is not linked directly to Essene traditions or, for that matter, Essene text sources.[9] It presupposes not only some elements missing there but also a new interpretation of the concepts that are present. Both are undoubtedly of Christian origin. The inner consistency of the entire complex of thought already in Essene statments suggests, however, that the author of I Peter not only linked individual traditional Christian concepts, but also appropriated a Jewish Christian complex of tradition.

4. Along the path of this stream of tradition in early Christianity it can be determined that individual traditions in I Pet. 2:4-10 made their appearance in Paul as well: In Rom. 9:32f. (as here in vv. 6, 8) Isa. 8:14 and 28:16 are connected, and in Rom. 9:25f. (as here in v. 10) Hosea 1–2 is appropriated. But I Pet. 2:4-10 is not aligned with the shaping of these passages in Paul. Moreover, the tradition from which I Peter takes its departure contains motifs that are foreign to Paul and belong to the tradition of the Palestinian Church: Ex. 19:6 (here in vv. 5, 9) is missing from Paul, certainly not coincidentally; it derives nevertheless from the covenant at Sinai (Gal. 4:24f.; cf. Heb. 12:18-24). It is appropriated otherwise in the NT only in Rev. 1:6; 5:10, primarily with the central expression βασίλειον ἱεράτευμα. Also Ps. 118:22f. (here in vv. 4, 7) represents Palestinian traditional material that is not given an interpretive function in Paul.[10]

Thus, on the whole, I Pet. 2:4-10 utilizes a complex of tradition from the Hellenistic Church that comes from Palestine and makes its appearance in Paul only in asides. It applies this complex of tradition to its situation in a unique way, in comparison with other early Christian usage.

Vv. 4f.: Incorporation into the Spiritual Temple and True Priesthood

Christ, on whom — according to that which was just said in vv. 2f. — the person who believes depends for life, like the child on milk, is at the same time λίθος, "stone." What is referred to here is the foundation stone of a building.[11] Therefore, one can be connected to him only by

---

7. 1QM 3:13; 10:9f.; 13:7; see below, p. 148 with n.61.

8. Elliott, *Elect and Holy,* 210 and n.14.

9. Elliott, *Elect and Holy,* 210f., is right in opposition to D. Flusser, "The Dead Sea Sect and Pre-Pauline Christianity," *Scripta Hierosolymitana* 3 (1958), 215-266 (p. 235).

10. See below, n.45.

11. Beare, 121, gives an analogy for the linking of the two images of nourishing with milk and the supporting stone: Artemis of Ephesus was portrayed as the mother goddess and was, at the same time, represented through a meteorite. But Beare himself rejects any

allowing oneself to be part of the edifice founded by him, the congregational community. Vv. 4f. adds to the picture of Christian life developed thus far this fundamental element of Christian existence with the aid of traditional concepts of Christ as the stone and the church as the edifice.

4 The new theme is introduced with an imperatival participle:[12] πρὸς ὃν προσερχόμενοι, λίθον ζῶντα. The attributive "living," the opposite of natural stones, indicates that "stone" here is a metaphor and that it explains the content: Christ is the resurrected One who lives in order to communicate life.[13]

This is, to be sure, not historically visible. It is said of the stone: ὑπὸ ἀνθρώπων μὲν ἀποδεδοκιμασμένον παρὰ δὲ θεῷ ἐκλεκτὸν ἔντιμον. For the public he is and remains — ἀποδεδοκιμασμένος is a perfect participle — the stone rejected by humankind, not only by Israel. He is deemed by human critical examination to be unfit for the future edifice of humankind.[14] "With God however," and that means not only before him but through him, he is — expressed graphically — "chosen and precious": God has chosen him and established him in "honor" — ἔντιμον belongs together with τιμή — to be the foundation stone of the edifice of a new humanity. Thus the early Christian reader would understand this anthitesis, since its first half calls to mind Ps. 118:22, the second Isa. 28:16 — even if the passages were not quoted in vv. 6f. Ps. 118:22 was well known as a saying of Jesus about his rejection, and the christological interpretation of Isa. 28:16 was already known by Paul as tradition.[15] Both announce that Jesus was destined according to God's plan of salvation to become the "cornerstone," i.e., at least in this context, the foundation stone[16] of an edifice.

---

connection. The same applies even more to the analogies mentioned by Perdelwitz, *Mysterienreligion,* 69f.

12. See below, n.28.

13. ζῶν has in connection with λίθος in vv. 4f. the same double meaning as πνευματικός with οἶκος and θυσία in v. 5. In the same way Paul speaks of θυσία ζῶσα in Rom. 12:1 and of πνευματικὴ πέτρα in I Cor. 10:4. The "dualistic" background of the Johannine ζῶν in Jn. 4:10f.; 6:51; 7:38 is not seen here. On the discussion see Elliott, *Elect and Holy,* 34.

14. So ἀποδοκιμάζειν, according to W. Grundmann, "δόκιμος," *TDNT* II, 256, 260f.

15. See below, n.45.

16. According to v. 5, baptized persons are to "allow themselves to be built" on him into a house. But Isa. 28:16 LXX clearly does not refer to a foundation stone (ἐμβαλῶ εἰς τὰ θεμέλια Σιὼν λίθον). In I Pet. 2:4, Ps. 118:22 can also only be connected to a foundation stone. This is admitted by J. Jeremias, who otherwise understands the cornerstone as the

The Christological Interpretation of the Stone Motif[17]

1. Ps. 118:22 was connected to Jesus' rejection already in the Aramaic-speaking Church, since the key word "reject" is passed on in Jesus' saying in Mk. 12:10 par. in accord with the LXX by ἀποδοκιμάζειν, and in the kerygma Acts 4:11 by ἐξουθενεῖν, i.e., on the basis of free translation. Whether or not the pointer to the Scripture passage goes back beyond the Aramaic Church to Jesus himself is questionable. Mk. 12:10 in its present form cannot come from him, since it is a formal quotation, not a free usage corresponding to oral speech. The saying was probably formulated when Jesus became the "cornerstone" of the new community. But since Jesus found his path in the Psalms prefigured by the humiliation and exaltation of the righteous one, it must remain open whether or not the key word "reject" in the announcements of coming suffering (Mk. 8:31: ἀποδοκιμάζειν; Mk. 9:12: ἐξουθενεῖν) was educed from a reference to Ps. 118:22 or preceded it as the starting point.

2. In Lk. 20:17f., the parallel to Mk. 12:10, further words about stones are added to Ps. 118:22, namely, Isa. 8:14, the "stone of stumbling," and Dan. 2:44f., the "stone of judgment." Perhaps the very early Christian interpretation of "the stone" in Psalm 118 occasioned also the interpretation of Isa. 8:14; 28:16.

3. This interpretation of Scripture passages about the "stone" began in Judaism: (a) By echoing Isa. 28:16 the Qumran community characterized itself as "the precious cornerstone" (1QS 8:7; less clear is 1QS 5:5; 4QpIsa[d] 1; 1QH 6:26; 7:8f.). The image there, as in Eph. 2:20, is connected with the image of the community as edifice.[18] An echo from Ps. 118:22 is present perhaps in 2Q23:6.[19] (b) In rabbinic literature the OT passages are rarely cited. The cornerstone in Ps. 118:22 and Isa. 28:16 is in "a king" in the targums and is thereby linked to David or the Messiah.[20] Isa. 8:16 is interpreted in a rabbinic discussion of about A.D. 200 with reference to "the Son of David," the Messiah.[21] A messianic interpretation in second-century Judaism is presupposed also by Justin, *Dialogue* 34, 36 (*ANF* I, pp. 211-213).

4. Thus undoubtedly the Qumran statements connecting the stone of Isa. 28:16

"keystone" ("λίθος," *TDNT* IV, 274ff.). R. J. McKelvey, "Christ the Cornerstone," *NTS* 8 (1961/62), 352-359, opposes Jeremias and makes a strong case that even in Eph. 2:20 a "foundation stone" is meant. See more recently H. Merklein, *Das kirchliche Amt nach dem Epheserbrief* (StANT 33; Munich, 1973), 144-152.

17. See J. Jeremias, "λίθος," *TDNT* IV, 270-280; Moule, "Reflections"; Betz, "Felsenmann und Felsengemeinde"; J. Maier, *Die Texte vom Toten Meer* (Basel, 1960) II, 93f.; McKelvey, "Christ Cornerstone"; H. Braun, *Qumran und das NT* I (Tübingen, 1966), 190, 283ff.; Elliott, *Elect and Holy*, 23-33; Hillyer, "Rock-Stone"; Oss, "'Stone' Passages."

18. See Maier, *Texte vom Toten Meer* I, 189; II, 93f.

19. See M. Baillet, "Les 'Petit Grottes' de Qumrân" (Discoveries in the Judaean Desert 3; Oxford, 1962), 83.

20. See Str.-Bill. I, 876; III, 276; Elliott, *Elect and Holy,* 27.

21. See Str.-Bill. II, 139f.

with the image of the edifice and linking both to the eschatological community come the closest to I Pet. 2:4f. The only other NT passage in which the "cornerstone" in Isa. 28:16 is connected with the edifice of the community is Eph. 2:20.

If Christ is the foundation stone of an edifice then one is able "to come" to him only by being incorporated into the edifice erected by him. From "come to" follows necessarily: "let yourselves be built" (v. 5). The expression πρὸς ὃν προσερχόμενοι is perhaps derived from Psalm 34[33] (v. 6: προσέλθατε πρὸς αὐτόν),[22] which was quoted earlier in v. 3, where it refers to the coming to God that communicates illumination and deliverance. According to Hebrews this coming to God happens now through Jesus; in the Synoptics, especially Matthew, to come to God is to join oneself to Jesus.[23] "Coming to" is, therefore, the turning of the entire person to Christ, not only in moral-religious orientation; it is for the baptized person the constant realization of baptism through hope and faith and through discipleship (1:13, 21; 2:21).

5   Coming to God communicates participation in Christ: through the "living stone" Christians become "living stones":[24] καὶ αὐτοὶ ὡς λίθοι ζῶντες οἰκοδομεῖσθε. They are "living" as he is living, but they are living not from within themselves, but always in a "transferred" sense. ὡς, "as," which is prefixed here, but not with Christ, also indicates this.[25]

The "coming to" must then become a οἰκοδομεῖσθε. "Allow yourself to be built" is not connected here individualistically to a particular person as edifice — as in ecclesiastical language and already in Paul — but collectively to the edifice of the community.[26] "Allow yourselves

---

22. See above, p. 132, n.51. Ps. 33:6 LXX, departing from the Masoretic Text: προσέλθατε πρὸς αὐτὸν καὶ φωτίσθητε. The last word reminds one of I Pet. 2:9b (see the comments there).

23. προσέρχομαι (see J. Schneider, "ἔρχομαι," *TDNT* II, 683f.) does not occur elsewhere in the NT with πρός, which is good classical Greek, but with the dative of the person. In the Synoptic Gospels, above all in Matthew, it is often used of the approach of the disciples or others to Jesus (Mt. 5:1; 18:1, 21; 24:3, and passim). In Hebrews it is used of "those who draw near to God through him" (7:25; cf. 4:16; 10:1, 22; 11:6; 12:18, 22). πρός is used similarly in the Synoptic Gospels only in the synonymous expression in Mt. 11:28: δεῦτε πρός με πάντες (cf. Mk. 1:17 par. Mt.: δεῦτε ὀπίσω μου) and in John in the expression ὁ ἐρχόμενος πρός ἐμε (Jn. 6:35, 37, 44f., 65; 7:37; cf. Schneider, *TDNT* II, 672f.).

24. The image of members of the community as stones is found already in 1QH 6:26: "You will set the foundation on rock and the structure by the measuring cord of righteousness. You will lay tried stones by the plumb line of truth to build a mighty wall." It occurs in the NT only in Mt. 16:18, though it is also found in Ignatius, *Eph.* 9:1 (LCL AF I, 183): "stones of the temple of the Father" and *Hermas*, passim.

25. ὡς indicates a transferred sense also in 1:19; 2:2, 11.

26. οἰκοδομεῖσθε is derived here from the image, as is συνοικοδομεῖσθε in Eph.

to be built" is an admonition to baptized persons to maintain membership in the body of Christ in the way illustrated in 4:7-11 and more
extensively in I Cor. 12:12-27. The membership in the Church established by baptism (I Pet. 3:20f.) is actualized centrally through the
eucharist (I Cor. 10:17). But the idea in I Peter is more likely that of
making common cause with the Church through nonconforming conduct in society (4:4), by following the One who "was rejected by human
beings, but exalted by God" (2:20f.; 3:8f.; 5:9f.). The middle voice of
the verb "let yourselves be built" indicates perhaps that the Church —
as throughout the NT — is constantly being built by God or Christ.[27]
This does not exclude the imperative, but includes it.[28]

The house that is built in this way is οἶκος πνευματικός, a "spiritual
house,"[29] i.e., a "house" in a transferred sense, an organism of living
people (as "house" was already in everyday language used of the
family), above all, however, a house created, shaped, and sustained by
the Holy Spirit (4:10f.; I Cor. 12:13). It is the dwelling place of God's
presence among human beings, the eschatological and new temple,
which is spoken of here neither polemically over against Judaism, nor
apologetically in relation to Gentile temples, nor "salvation-historically"
in relation to the temple of the Old Covenant. The point of view here
is, as in the entire context, sociological: Christians should understand
and maintain themselves as members of the fellowship established on
the great "living stone" that has been rejected by human beings.

2:20. This word usage is related only loosely to the technical sense, which is found in an
especially pronounced form in the Pauline writings and in Acts; it was already in use in the
LXX and in 4QpPs37 3:16 (cf. O. Michel, "οἶκος, οἰκοδομέω," *TDNT* V, 139-143).

27. Mk. 14:58; Mt. 16:18; Acts 20:32; I Cor. 3:16f.; I Tim. 3:5; according to Jn.
6:44f., coming to Christ is always possible only through the "drawing of the Father," through
the eschatological dimension of being taught by God.

28. οἰκοδομεῖσθε is understood by some as indicative (Selwyn, 159; Beare, 119; Kelly,
89) and by others as imperative (Windisch, 58; Schelkle, 57; Prigent, "2,4-10," 56). The
context, the sequence of imperatives beginning in 1:13, the indicative-based foundation in
vv. 6ff., and the content (see above) all suggest the latter.

29. πνευματικός expresses, with οἶκος and θυσία, in accord with the context, not a
spiritual opposition to an earthly, physical worship setting made by human beings, but simply
the distinction with respect to the established worship setting, i.e., the transferred character
provided by the Spirit. In this respect, Elliott, *Elect and Holy,* 154ff., and E. Schweizer,
"πνεῦμα, πνευματικός," *TDNT* VI, 437, n.706 are correct. The latter refers to I Cor. 10:3f.;
Did. 10:3 (LCL AF I, 325: spiritual food and spiritual drink); *Barn.* 16:10 (*ibid.,* 397: spiritual
temple) as analogies; see above, n.13, and cf. Schröger, "Haus."

Character and Origin of the Image of the "Spiritual House"[30]

1. According to Elliott, οἶκος here means "house" as edifice or as family, but not as temple.[31] The image of stone excludes, however, the sense common in the LXX as in the NT of house as family. That the author is thinking, with no emphasis to be sure, of the temple is suggested by the earlier history of the image: The only other οἶκος-passage in I Peter (4:17) appropriates the common LXX designation οἶκος θεοῦ for the temple (cf. Judg. 17:5; Isa. 56:7, and passim). In the immediate context the key word "priesthood" points to the temple, as does Isa. 28:16, echoed in v. 4.

2. Early Christian tradition often likens the Church to an edifice. It thereby points, not ultimately on the basis of Jesus' saying about the temple in Mk. 14:58 par., above all to the new temple (so expressly I Cor. 3:16f.; II Cor. 6:16; Eph. 2:20ff.; I Tim. 3:15 [house of God]; Heb. 3:6 [his house]; 10:21f. [the great high priest over God's house]; II Clem. 9:3; Barn. 16:10; Ignatius, Magn. 7:2 [LCL AF I, 142f., 398f., 202f.]).

3. The way was prepared for this early Christian image for the Church above all by the self-understanding of the Qumran community, which likened itself to an edifice erected by God. This edifice is according to 1QH 6:25-29 a city, in CD 7:11ff.; 20:10, 13 a house, and in 1QS 5:6 the temple. The community is according to 1QS 8:5: "a house of holiness for Israel, an assembly of supreme holiness for Aaron." To the concept of the heavenly edifice in Gnosticism[32] there exists no affinity in I Peter.

The Church is then characterized[33] as ἱεράτευμα ἅγιον, "holy priesthood,"[34] which points in the same direction. ἱεράτευμα does not,

---

30. See P. Vielhauer, *Oikodome, Das Bild vom Bau in der christlichen Literatur vom NT bis Clemens Alexandrinus* (Karlsruhe-Durlach, 1940); P. Bonnard, *Jésus Christ édifiant son Église. Le concept d'édification dans le Nouveau Testament* (third ed., Paris, 1948); Selwyn, 285-291; T. Schneider, "Bauen," *RAC* I, cols. 1265-1278; O. Michel, "οἶκος," *TDNT* V, 119-159; Maier, *Texte vom Toten Meer* II, 93f.; J. Pfammatter, *Die Kirche als Bau. Eine exegetisch-theologische Studie zur Ekklesiologie der Paulusbriefe* (Analecta Gregoriana 110; Rome, 1960); Y. M. J. Congar, *The Mystery of the Temple* (tr. R. Trevett; London, 1962); B. Gärtner, *The Temple and the Community in Qumran and the NT* (SNTS Mon. Ser. 1; Cambridge, 1965); Elliott, *Elect and Holy,* 157ff.; *idem,* "Salutation and Exhortation"; *idem, Home* (see reviews by B. Olsson, *SvExÅ* 49 [1984], 89-108; and A. C. Wire, *RelStRev* 10 [1984], 209-216); W. Dalton, "Church"; Klinzing, *Umdeutung des Kultes,* 50-93, 167-213; W. D. Kilpatrick, "Theology."

31. Elliott, *Elect and Holy,* 159; different is Michel, *TDNT* V, 129f.

32. See M. Dibelius, *An die Kolosser, Epheser, an Philemon* (HNT 12; third ed. rev. by H. Greeven, Tübingen, 1953), 71ff.; H. Schlier, *Der Brief an die Epheser* (Düsseldorf, 1957), 143ff.; Michel, *TDNT* V, 127, n.31.

33. εἰς should be taken with οἰκοδομεῖσθε, not, in analogy to v. 9c (εἰς περιποίησιν), with οἶκος (pace Elliott, *Elect and Holy,* 160, n.2): The "spiritual house" is not set aside for a "holy priesthood," but is identical with it. Hence, some manuscripts leave out εἰς in order to let the two terms appear in apposition.

34. ἱεράτευμα, derived from Ex. 19:6, the passage quoted in I Pet. 2:9, is an LXX

in relation to other concepts of priesthood, convey to every baptized person priestly rights and functions, the "priesthood of all believers," which was imposed on this passage by the Reformation. It impresses on the readers, rather, that belonging to the house of God never means quietistic participation, but always active service.[35] All are empowered and obligated to do what is otherwise reserved for priests, namely to serve God. This service, as the OT regulations concerning priests emphasize,[36] was possible only for the "holy one," one who was pure and who belonged to God. Those summoned to faith through baptism are, however, "made holy" for the service of God (1:2, 15f.).[37]

It is their service ἀνενέγκαι πνευματικὰς θυσίας, "to offer spiritual sacrifices."[38] These are offerings in a transferred sense, not material accomplishments but dedication of the entire person to God prompted by the Spirit. The content of such "offerings," as they are also referred to already in the OT and in Qumran,[39] is specified in the NT in various ways. So, e.g., Rom. 12:1, where it is said that "bodies" — whole persons, including all of conduct — are to be given to God. On this basis praise of God, sharing with one's neighbor, the winning of persons through mission, and the ministry and martyrdom of the apostle are called offerings.[40]

---

construction not found in other Greek documents; it occurs only here in the NT. It designates the priesthood as a body, not as a function (cf. G. Schrenk, "ἱερός, ἱεράτευμα," *TDNT* III, 249f.). See Cerfaux, "Regale Sacerdotium"; Blinzler, "IEPATEYMA"; H. von Campenhausen, "Die Anfänge des Priesterbegriffs in der alten Kirche," *idem, Tradition und Leben* (Tübingen, 1960), 272-289; Elliott, *Elect and Holy,* 159-198.

35. Cf. Pesch, "Priestertum der Getauften," esp. 306ff. See also Ketter, "Allgemeine Priestertum."

36. Ex. 29:44ff.; Leviticus 8.

37. See the comments on 1:2, 15f.; 2:9: ἔθνος ἅγιον.

38. On "spiritual sacrifice" see Wenschkewitz, "Spiritualisierung"; J. Behm, "θύω," *TDNT* III, 183-189; P. Seidensticker, *Lebendiges Opfer* (NTA 20/1-3; Münster, 1954); H. Kosmala, *Hebräer—Essener—Christen* (Leiden, 1959), 150, 363-378; Elliott, *Elect and Holy,* 174-179; Best, "Spiritual Sacrifice"; Feuillet, "Sacrifices spirituelles"; Colecchia, "Rilievi su 1 Piet. 2,4-10"; Hill, "To Offer."

39. Pss. 40:9ff.; 50:14; 51:16-19; 69:31f.; 107:22; 141:2 (Hos. 6:6; Amos 5:24f.; Mic. 6:6ff.). According to 1QS 9:3-5 prayer and a just manner of life are fitting sacrifices; see also 1QS 10:6; 4QFlor 1:6f. Further material in Str.-Bill. I, 413f.; K. G. Kuhn, "ἅγιος," *TDNT* I, 97f.

40. Heb. 13:15f. (cf. Rev. 8:3f.; Phil. 4:18; Eph. 5:2); Rom. 15:16; II Tim. 4:6. According to Selwyn, 160f., 294-298, and Kelly, 91f., what is intended by the sacrifices is especially the eucharist (contra Best, 104), since already in the time of I Peter the concept is to be assumed (which can be demonstrated from the turn of the second century) that the eucharistic prayers were regarded as sacrifices (*I Clem.* 44:4; Ignatius, *Eph.* 5:2; *Phld.* 4

These are according to I Peter "offerings that are pleasing to God through Jesus Christ" (θυσίας εὐπροσδέκτους θεῷ).[41] An offering is nothing if it is not accepted by God.[42] Whether an offering is welcomed is an issue throughout the OT and into the NT.[43] The offerings of Christians, their priestly service, are welcomed "through Jesus Christ" (διὰ Ἰησοῦ Χριστοῦ), not as human achievements or as achievements made possible through the power of Christ or of the Spirit, but because they are mediated through Jesus Christ, which they are when they represent service based on the freedom of faith. They are welcomed as a result of the grace of "redemption" and in expectation of the grace that receives even that which is inadequate (1:13, 18). This priestly service directed to God is at the same time the Church's witness for God, which v. 9 designates as the Church's mission.

The imperative in vv. 4f. thus rounds off the portrayal of the essence of Christian existence. Christian existence is lived out as the realization of community through κοινωνία and διακονία in the midst of society as one follows in discipleship the exalted Christ, who was rejected by society and now has become the foundation of a new humanity. This imperative will then be reinforced and explained in indicative constructions in the two groups of verses that follow, in which it is said that God provides two things: the foundation stone in relation to which the future is decided and the people to whom, as the new humanity, the future belongs.

[LCL AF I, 85, 179, 243]). Probably *Did.* 14:1ff. (*ibid.*, 331), where the concept of sacrifice is underscored through use of Mal. 1:11, 14, also has in mind the eucharistic prayers, which, of course, are not to be separated from the presentation of the elements. Justin characterized the elements themselves as θυσία (*Dialogue* 41; 117 [*ANF* I, 228, 257f.]), emphasizing, however, at the same time that the prayers are the sacrifices of Christians (*Dialogue* 117 [*ibid.*, 257f.]). Hence, one can say that the eucharistic prayers also belong to the "spiritual sacrifices," but I Peter does not focus on them (cf. Behm, *TDNT* III, 189f.).

41. The word order suggests that θεῷ διὰ Ἰησοῦ Χριστοῦ is to be taken with εὐπροσδέκτους (Selwyn, 162f.), not (in analogy to Heb. 13:15f.) with ἀνενέγκαι (Beare, 123; Elliott, *Elect and Holy*, 161).

42. εὐπρόσδεκτους occurs four times in Paul, including Rom. 15:16: "quite acceptable," "welcome." Paul uses δεκτός for the same idea in Rom. 12:1; Phil. 4:18. Heb. 13:16 has εὐάρεστος, "pleasant," "well-pleasing."

43. Gen. 4:4f.; 15:17; Lev. 9:24. The ὀσμὴ εὐωδίας, the "sweet-smelling sacrificial fragrance," is mentioned not only in Gen. 8:21; Lev. 2:2, but also in II Cor. 2:15f.; Phil. 4:18; cf. Eph. 5:2.

Vv. 6-8: Christ as Cornerstone and Stone of Stumbling

Now both Scripture passages that the author had in mind in the formulation of vv. 4-5a and appropriated in key words there are quoted expressly[44] and supplemented by Isa. 8:14. In v. 4 Ps. 118:22 comes before Isa. 28:16, but now they are reversed.

It is clear that this linking of quotations already existed in early Christian tradition. Isa. 28:16 and 8:14 are also connected in Rom. 9:33, where they are reproduced, as here, in a text form varying from that of the LXX; but Paul and the author of I Peter do not present the same portion of the text or the same sequence.[45] The quotation from Ps. 118:22 inserted here was a christological *testimonium* from the earliest time.[46] Therefore, the three Scriptures concerning Christ the stone were certainly transmitted orally as a small collection of *testimonia.*[47] Different parts of them were reproduced in different sequences according to the intention of different contexts.

Here the intention is to be derived from the quotations, the words introducing them, and from the three midrashic glosses that are inserted as commentary. The introductory words are linked to v. 5 by causal διότι. Scripture is to give the foundation, then, to the admonition to let oneself be built upon Christ the living stone, i.e., to give one's confession to Christ and his community while coming to terms with society. Although the connection to Scripture is essential for the author — as περιέχει ἐν γραφῇ shows — the quotations are not cited merely as proof texts for what has already been said. Through commented restatement in a new sequence a declaration is developed that advances the matter in a unique way: Christ is laid across the path of humanity on its course into the future. In the encounter with him each person is changed: one for salvation, another for destruction. The positive possibility is developed first in vv. 6-7a by use of Isa. 28:16;[48] the

---

44. περιέχει is ordinarily transitive in Greek and Semiticized Greek: "contain." But here it is intransitive, "it is contained," "it stands" (BAGD s.v.). Though it is anarthrous here, γραφή is Scripture as a whole (BAGD s.v.), not a Scripture passage (BDF §258.2 [pp. 134f.]) or a collection of quotations (Selwyn, 163).

45. The texts are compared in Selwyn, 270f.; exegetical comparison of the seven NT stone passages is in Elliott, *Elect and Holy,* 28-32; Prigent, "2,4-10."

46. See above, p. 138.

47. So also Kelly, 95; Elliott, *Elect and Holy,* 32; Selwyn, 268-277; 4QTest is a characteristic example of a collection of scriptural messianic testimonies.

48. The passage originally announced that Yahweh will lay the foundation stone for

negative possibility is then articulated in vv. 7b-8 by use of Ps. 118:22 and Isa. 8:14f.

6 Christ was established ἐν Σιών, i.e., in Jerusalem, as λίθος ἀκρογωνιαῖος, as the foundation stone lying at the corner, he who is to support the new edifice of humanity redeemed by God. He is, as was emphasized already in v. 4, ἐκλεκτός and ἔντιμος: He is "elect" as the eschatological Deliverer and established "in honor" (1:20). For this reason it can be said: καὶ ὁ πιστεύων ἐπ' αὐτῷ οὐ μὴ καταισχυνθῇ: "Whoever believes in him,"[49] i.e., whoever bases one's existence on the promise given in him, "will not be ashamed," will not be disappointed, but will receive acceptance and honor with God.[50]

7a The first gloss applies the statement understood in this sense to the reader and thereby prepares the way for the promise in vv. 9f.: ὑμῖν οὖν ἡ τιμὴ τοῖς πιστεύουσιν. "Honor" is given to those who are addressed because they believe. This honor is the same as not being ashamed before God. Those who believe and belong to the eschatological community of salvation are acknowledged before God because they have received their share in Christ's honor. According to v. 5 they are even now joined to him, and according to v. 9 they are members of the "elect people" and will, therefore, also endure in the judgment (1:7, 11, 13; 4:13f.; cf. Rom. 10:11).

7b Here a further gloss introduces the negative possibility: ἀπιστοῦσιν δὲ, "But for those who do not believe. . . ."[51] Such persons are, as the third gloss in v. 8b explains, those who reject the gospel, not those who do not know it. For those who reject the gospel Christ becomes the stone that proves to be their undoing, as is concluded from the linking together of the two other stone passages from Scripture. What has happened is what was promised in Ps. 118:22:[52] λίθος, ὃν ἀπεδοκίμασαν οἱ

a new temple in Jerusalem. Corresponding to this new founding is the watchword "Whoever believes will not be confounded."

49. ἐπ' αὐτῷ is missing in the Masoretic Text and LXX B; it is surely a Christian interpretation that has worked its way into LXX A ℵ (contra J. Jeremias, "λίθος," *TDNT* IV, 272).

50. Cf. R. Bultmann, "αἰσχύνω," *TDNT* I, 189ff.

51. ἀπιστέω, in classical literature "be incredulous," in Hellenistic literature also in a religious sense; in the early Christian sense still in Mk. 16:16; Ignatius, *Eph.* 18:1 (LCL AF I, 191; cf. Rom. 3:3; II Tim. 2:13: "be unfaithful"; cf. BAGD s.v.).

52. Ps. 118:22, perhaps a proverbial expression, originally referred to miraculous deliverance by Yahweh (v. 23): A stone that was scorned has been put in an important place in the construction. Application of the verse to Jesus is in accord with the Psalm's intention.

οἰκοδομοῦντες. "The builders," according to v. 4 those who want to construct their own world for themselves, have rejected Jesus as an inadequate stone for their edifice. But God has made him into the "cornerstone" (οὗτος ἐγενήθη εἰς κεφαλὴν γωνίας),[53] i.e., the stone that is the starting point from which the edifice of a new humanity is erected. Jesus has not been swept from the path by the judgment on humanity that is shown in the cross. God has exalted the crucified One to become the "Lord" through whom all are to be called home into his eschatological saving reign (Phil. 2:9ff.). I Peter still thinks in this universal breadth,[54] even if it has in mind above all the special community of salvation. Christ is not the "cornerstone" here in the sense that a few choose him as their foundational basis; he is laid in the path for all.

8 Because he is the foundation of the universal edifice he is at the same time, according to Isa. 8:14, λίθος προσκόμματος καὶ πέτρα σκανδάλου, "stone of stumbling and rock of offense."[55] One cannot simply step over Jesus to go on about the daily routine and pass him by to build a future. Whoever encounters him is inescapably changed through the encounter: Either one sees and becomes "a living stone," or one stumbles as a blind person over Christ and comes to ruin,[56] falling short, i.e., of one's Creator and Redeemer and thereby of one's destiny. This taking offense is expressed not only in the alienation felt toward those who are disciples of Jesus (4:4 and elsewhere), but also in the resistance that comes from indifference (cf. 3:1).

---

53. κεφαλὴ γωνίας, the "cornerstone" (what constitutes the point of the angle). According to J. Jeremias, "γωνία," *TDNT* I, 793, I Pet. 2:7 refers to "a sharp stone at the corner of the building against which men stumble and fall"; thereby, the image is fixed in an objective sense.

54. This is seen by Beare, 125. He interprets, however, too much in an exclusively "political" direction, too little in an eschatological direction, when he explains that Christ is "the keystone of the divine order of human society" or the barrier to building this order, according to one's own devising.

55. Isa. 8:14 originally announced that Yahweh himself becomes the stone of falling for Israel, which failed to keep faith. This announcement is applied in the NT in Rom. 9:33 and I Pet. 2:8 in keeping with the original meaning, while the LXX inserts a negative (οὐχ ὡς λίθου προσκόμματι συναντήσεσθε) and thus makes an announcement of salvation out of the saying about judgment.

56. σκάνδαλον, in Greek literature "snare," is used in the LXX with πρόσκομμα for מוֹקֵשׁ, "trap," but also (as here) for מִכְשׁוֹל, a "block" over which one falls. Both Hebrew words are used figuratively of occasions for sin and destruction (cf. G. Stählin, "σκάνδαλον," *TDNT* VII, 339-344). The NT aligns itself exclusively with this LXX word usage and understands by σκάνδαλον that which hinders one from coming to faith or causes one to stray from it.

The gloss in v. 8b explains the theological structure of this offense: οἳ προσκόπτουσιν τῷ λόγῳ ἀπειθοῦντες εἰς ὃ καὶ ἐτέθησαν. It is refusal to believe, both disobedience to the call of the word (of God)[57] and hardening by God.[58] The two cannot be combined rationally, but both obedience and election are necessary for faith, since faith must make its confession, on the one hand, as a new "I" created by God (1:2; Rom. 8:28ff.), and is as such, on the other hand, a responsible "I" in relation to God (1:17; II Cor. 5:10). Rejection of the gospel message is, therefore, a responsible act of the will, disobedience, and blindness from God.

Vv. 7b-8 thus repeat in relation to the rejection of the gospel among the peoples of the world what Romans 9–11 develops about rejection of the gospel by Israel. In Romans also Isa. 28:16 and 8:14 are linked to unbelief — on the part of Israel (Rom. 9:33) — and there also unbelief is described as disobedience (10:14, 16) and hardening (9:14-18, 27-29; 11:7-10). The application of this to the peoples of the world conditions another direction of development in I Peter. Romans 9–11 leads to the prophetic horizon of 11:25ff.: In a short time "the fullness of the Gentile peoples" will come to faith and then "all Israel will be saved." But for I Peter and the other post-Pauline documents of the NT this expectation for Israel is pushed into the background by society's rejection of the Church and its message.[59] I Peter seeks to sustain the small special community drawn from Israel and from the peoples of the world; this community is afflicted because it is different from its neighbors; it is not preserved for its own sake but for its mission to all. This election and mission are pledged to Christians in conclusion in vv. 9f.

Vv. 9f: Election to God's People and Mission into the World

Here expressions that are focused in the OT on Israel's election and mission are transferred to the Church.[60] They are selected without direct

---

57. τῷ λόγῳ belongs with ἀπειθοῦντες, not προσκόπτουσιν; the connection in 3:1; 4:17 is a fixed expression.

58. τιθέναι refers here and in 2:6, as often in the LXX and the NT, to placement by God; εἰς ὃ has in mind stumbling, refusal of faith, not its consequences (contra J. Jeremias, "λίθος," *TDNT* IV, 277, n.71); cf. I Thess. 5:9: οὐκ ἔθετο ἡμᾶς ὁ θεὸς εἰς ὀργήν (on this see C. Maurer, "τίθημι," *TDNT* VIII, 154, 156ff.).

59. See Goppelt, *Apostolic,* 109-117.

60. The texts are compared in Selwyn, 277-281.

quotation, composed anew, and woven together with explanatory remarks. This promise to Christians begins with the covenant promise to
the Israelites who departed from Egypt (Ex. 19:6), which according to
the LXX says: ὑμεῖς δὲ ἔσεσθέ μοι βασίλειον ἱεράτευμα καὶ ἔθνος ἅγιον.
Together with this promise are interlaced expressions from Isa. 43:20f.,
the promise of the second exodus: ὅτι ἔδωκα ἐν τῇ ἐρήμῳ ὕδωρ . . .
ποτίσαι τὸ γένος μου τὸ ἐκλεκτόν, λαόν μου, ὃν περιεποιησάμην τὰς
ἀρετάς μου διηγεῖσθαι.

In all probability the author also takes this *interpretation of Ex. 19:6* from
Christian tradition, since it stands as a hymnic tradition behind Revelation that is
quite remote from I Peter (Rev. 1:6; 5:10). Also, the usage of Hosea 1–2 in v. 10
is, like what precedes it, demonstrably traditional.

The statements in these two verses can be found in part, like what has gone
before them, in the Essene tradition, and yet here also there remains a noteworthy
distance: The Qumran sect understood itself as the true Israel, to which belongs the
covenant of the fathers (CD 8:17f.; 19:29ff., 33ff.). They separated themselves from
the way of life of the majority and were witnesses for God (CD 8:17; 19:20, 29f.).
They were "enlightened" and took their stand with the one who was "rejected" by
the majority (1QH 4:5, 8, 23). They gave witness to the "great" and "wonderful"
deeds of God (1QM 14:12f.; 18:7, 10), who elected their fathers alone out of love
(CD 8:15). In spite of this claim the characterizations "people of God" and "Israel"
are first transferred to "the sons of light" when they step forward for the eschatological
battle against "the sons of darkness" (1QM 3:13; 10:9f.; 13:7; see above, p. 136, n.7).
Thus it is understandable that Ex. 19:6 played no role in these texts.[61]

9 This verse begins in antithesis to v. 8b: ὑμεῖς δέ, "But you. . . ."
In relation to a society for which rejection of the gospel becomes more
and more characteristic, the Christians living in that society should
understand themselves as God's people.

The terms γένος, ἔθνος, and λαός are used side by side. In accord
with Greek usage γένος characterizes a people as having a common
origin (cf. Phil. 3:5), ἔθνος describes a group of people with the same
customs, and λαός represents a body of people pursuing a common goal.
In the LXX λαός is used only of Israel, the people summoned by God;
τὰ ἔθνη are the Gentile peoples or the Gentiles as a whole. λαός is also
given special emphasis here by being repeated in v. 10. ἔθνος, which
can also be used in biblical Greek interchangeably with λαός (cf. Acts

---

61. The few instances in Jewish literature in which Ex. 19:6 has been appropriated
from the LXX are analyzed by Elliott, *Elect and Holy,* 50-107.

4:25, 27), is taken over here from Ex. 19:6, where it is used in terms of its literal translation as in the LXX. Since Christians are thus no longer characterized, as in Paul, as a "people" in "salvation-historical" antithesis to Israel (Gal. 6:16) but in view of a society that rejects them, the term assigns to them a social-political position in history. They are not — as it might seem — a secret society cultivating personal religiosity, but rather a body of people oriented toward historical conduct. But the goal is not a "Christian" world.

As the attributives state, Christians are a people only through election and sanctification in the eschatological sense that has already been set forth.[62] They are γένος ἐκλεκτόν, an "elect people,"[63] elect like the "stone," who was established through exaltation (2:6). They are ἔθνος ἅγιον, "a holy people," "holy" because they "belong"[64] to the One who has redeemed them through the death of Jesus (1:18). Therefore, they are also λαὸς εἰς περιποίησιν (cf. Acts 20:28: ἣν περιεποιήσατο . . .). For this reason the Church does not stand as a political entity alongside others in history, but as βασίλειον ἱεράτευμα, the "royal priesthood." Its activity in history is first and last vertically oriented. Christians are "royal"[65] because they have been taken into the βασιλεία of God, into his eschatological saving reign, and are thereby empowered to serve (cf. Rev. 5:10). But their service is only that of witness to all, because the βασιλεία is intended to include all.

The Church's mission is to proclaim God's "great deeds" (Acts

---

62. See the comments on 1:2, 15f.

63. γένος ἐκλεκτόν is from Isa. 43:20, and is found only here in the NT; 1QM 12:1 is close: "the elect of your holy people. . . ."

64. Isa. 43:21 (ὃν περιεποιησάμην) is altered in accord with Mal. 3:17 to εἰς περιποίησιν. Ex. 19:5: λαὸς περιούσιος ἀπὸ πάντων τῶν ἐθνῶν: Therefore they are a "holy" people (Dt. 7:6), and this came about only through Yahweh's electing love (Dt. 7:8), as CD 8:15 also emphasizes. See H. Strathmann, "λαός," *TDNT*, 35f.

65. βασίλειον can be a noun, "royal house," "palace," or an adjective, "royal." The former option is chosen by Selwyn, 165f., and with additional arguments also by Elliott, *Elect and Holy*, 149-154, and Kelly, 96f., who understand it in context as an interpretive parallel to οἶκος πνευματικός in v. 5. In favor of this view it can be said that βασίλειον is often used in extrabiblical Greek, as in the LXX, much more often as a noun than as an adjective and that in Hellenistic Jewish writings (II Macc. 2:17; Philo, *De Sobrietate* 66; *De Abrahamo* 56 [LCL III, 479; VI, 33]) its occurrence in Ex. 19:6 is understood as a noun (so also in Rev. 1:6; 5:10). Furthermore, the adjectives in v. 9 all follow the corresponding nouns.

On the other hand, it must also be noted that this arrangement is dictated by the OT passages. The context in I Peter, which both before and after uses two-part personal designations, speaks in favor of taking βασίλειον as an adjective. Therefore, even in the Old Latin this view was already represented. But no major substantive difference results (cf. n.34).

2:11),[66] Jesus' death and resurrection as the liberating alteration of the human creature and the world (1:18ff.): ὅπως τὰς ἀρετὰς ἐξαγγείλητε — the exodus spoken of in Isaiah 43 in eschatological form. The Church's members proclaim this alteration because they have encountered it themselves. Those who are addressed are also to proclaim the miraculous deeds of the One "who has called you out of darkness into his wonderful light": τοῦ ἐκ σκότους ὑμᾶς καλέσαντος εἰς τὸ θαυμαστὸν αὐτοῦ φῶς. In an extension of OT and Jewish traditions[67] early Christians understood the summons to faith as transferal from darkness into light.[68] "Darkness" was blindness of perception, the erring will, decay linked with evil and death. "His light" is the illumination of all existence shining forth from God. This light is "wonderful" (θαυμαστός)[69] because it is the miracle of deliverance from this decay. The Church is to "proclaim" (ἐξαγγέλλειν)[70] that through Jesus this great deed of God

---

66. ἀρετή, actually "excellence," when used of God, assumes in extrabiblical Greek the meaning "miraculous act of power" or, as throughout the LXX, "renown"; thus it is used in Isa. 43:21 for תְּהִלָּה. Despite the echo here of Isaiah 43, one is to assume, in accord with "proclaiming," the more Greek meaning "demonstration of power." The expression has (apart from II Pet. 1:3) no analogy in the NT, though surely in Qumran: 1QM 14:13; 18:7.

67. The Jewish terminology of mission referred to conversion as illumination: Joseph and Asenath 15:12 (*OT Pseudep.* II, 227): εὐλογητὸς κύριος ὁ θεός σου, ὁ ἐξαποστείλας σε τοῦ ῥύσασθαί με ἐκ τοῦ σκότους καὶ ἀναγαγεῖν με ἀπὸ τῶν θεμελίων αὐτῆς τῆς ἀβύσσου εἰς τὸ φῶς; 8:9 (*ibid.,* 213): "the Most High, the Powerful One of Jacob, who gave life to all (things) and called (them) from the darkness to the light, and from the error to the truth and from the death to the life"; so also Rom. 2:19: "a light to those who are in darkness." In I Pet. 2:9, however, the tradition-historical starting point is probably the corresponding characterization of conversion in the Qumran writings, which stands in a similar context (1QH 4:5f., 23; see above, p. 148). Already in the OT light is a common image for salvation; one encounters here especially the expression: "your (God's) light," Pss. 36:10; 43:3; cf. Isa. 2:5, etc., the "light of the Lord." On the other hand, only a remote background for I Pet. 2:9 is seen in Hermetic Gnosticism (*Corpus Hermeticum* 7.2A = *Hermetica,* tr. W. Scott [Oxford, 1924] I, 173) and in the mystery religions (Perdelwitz, *Mysterienreligion,* 77ff.) where communication of knowledge and initiation are portrayed as illumination. See H. Conzelmann, "σκότος," *TDNT* VII, 426-438; S. Aalen, *Die Begriffe Licht und Finsternis im Alten Testament, im Spätjudentum und im Rabbinismus* (Oslo, 1951).

68. The closest parallel is Acts 26:18, speaking of Paul's mission: "to open their eyes, that they may turn from darkness to light and from the power of Satan to God"; cf. I Thess. 5:4f.; Eph. 5:8; *I Clem.* 59:2; *II Clem.* 1:4ff.; *Barn.* 14:5f. (LCL AF I, 111, 129, 391f.). Accordingly, the emergence of the perception of faith (II Cor. 4:6) and later baptism (Justin, *Apologia* 1.61.12f.; 65.1 [*ANF* I, 183, 185]; *Dialogue* 122.1 [*ibid.,* 260]) were characterized as illumination (possibly both: Heb. 6:4; 10:32; cf. Ps. 33:6 LXX; see above, n.22).

69. θαυμαστός, "wonderful," as in Mk. 12:11 par. Mt., in accord with Ps. 117:23 LXX, of the exaltation of the hidden stone; Rev. 15:3.

70. LXX διηγεῖσθαι is replaced by ἐξαγγέλλειν, which Greek readers could more easily understand as "proclaim."

has taken place and is encountered. This proclamation takes place through the preaching by which the Church is supported and all the more through its very existence and conduct.[71]

10   The change that the Church's members have undergone is, like the new birth spoken of in 1:3, not a physical-natural transformation, but a new and strictly personal connection to God, a new covenant, which works itself out, however, in terms of total existence and conduct. For this reason it can be said: οἵ ποτε οὐ λαός, νῦν δὲ λαὸς θεοῦ, οἱ οὐκ ἠλεημένοι, νῦν δὲ ἐλεηθέντες. The key words are from Hos. 1:6, 9f.; 2:1, 27. There God's relationship to Israel is portrayed in personal terms as the rejection and acceptance of a wife and her children. Here this image of the renewed acceptance of Israel is connected, as in Rom. 9:25f.,[72] to acceptance of Gentiles. But while Paul expresses thereby the paradoxical fulfillment of the promise given to Israel, I Peter speaks of the eschatological "becoming a people" of Christians in history. While those living in the Church's environment became a public entity or individuals through the Hellenistic-Roman imperial structure, Christians are called to be a new shared community oriented toward the future; they are this because God out of his free mercy has bound them to himself and thereby to one another.

That Christians are the "people of God" because they are people of the new covenant is emphasized by Paul in order to distinguish them as the eschatological fulfillment of Israel. Hebrews does the same thing in order to make the readers certain of that which is eschatological/ultimate and is given to them to counter the inner doubt caused by not seeing. But I Peter emphasizes identity as "God's people" in order to characterize the addressees' place in society and their historical mission. From the basis for Christian existence thus described in the first major part of the letter are now drawn in the second major part the consequences for the behavior of Christians in the structures of society.

---

71. Cf. Mt. 5:14-16; see the comments below on 2:11f., 13ff.

72. Though Rom. 9:25f. cannot have been the literary source for I Pet. 2:10, since I Peter presents a different passage from Hosea, partly in a different translation (with LXX, οἱ οὐκ ἠλεημένοι; Rom. 9:25: οὐκ ἠγαπημένην).

2:11–4:11: Second Major Part:
The Realization of Christian Existence
in the Structures of Society

Structure, Theme, and Tradition

1. The direct address in 2:11, like that in 4:12, indicates a new beginning, and the catchword "I beseech you" introduces parenesis, as it often does in the NT.[1] Here the parenesis extends all the way to 4:11. It is developed in two subparts, the transition between which is not clearly indicated: Christians are to be engaged responsibly in the institutions of society (2:11–3:12) and are to overcome the conflicts that come about from their engagement through their willingness to suffer (3:13–4:11). Both subparts close with parenesis on life together in the Church (3:8-12; 4:7-11).

2. The author already had in mind the theme of this part when he addressed the readers in 1:1 as "foreigners in the Diaspora." This address is taken up again in 2:11. Its meaning and basis were made clear in the first main part of the letter: To be a foreigner is the *signum* of Christians in society, since it is the sociological expression of the eschatological character of their existence.

Now the letter can answer the question toward which it has been pointing: How are the addressees, as "foreigners," to conduct themselves in relation to the society in which they live as "diaspora" and which for its part is increasingly more "alienated" in relation to them (4:4)? The answer that is given grows out of the first part. There Christians were consistently, in accord with the self-understanding of the Qumran community, the community of exodus. But, unlike the people of Qumran, they did not experience the exodus literally as emigration out of society. That which is new cannot be described, as it is in the Qumran literature, as an existing condition that can be demonstrated empirically; it can only be described in the dialectic of indicative and imperative.[2] This differentiates Christian existence

---

1. Rom. 12:1; I Cor. 1:10; I Thess. 4:1, and elsewhere.
2. See the comments on 1:13.

in a far-reaching way from that of the Essenes, although formally it can be portrayed to a great extent with the same expressions. The new existence has an entirely different origin and therefore a different character for the two contexts: In Qumran the origin is the law, radically interpreted, the ascertainable fulfillment of which is made possible through the power of grace. For I Peter, on the other hand, it is the gospel of the redemption that has taken place in hiddenness and will come forth visibly in the near future (1:18f., 13; 4:7). In Qumran the point of beginning is the experience of conversion which was reinforced every year;[3] in I Peter it is the summons to faith, the hidden new birth through the resurrection of the crucified One (1:3; 2:9). For this reason in Qumran the exodus was experienced as emigration in view of the anticipated realization of the new being.

But in the community of I Peter the exodus was experienced as confession with respect to the world of the resurrection that has already dawned (indicative!); indeed, it was an exodus experienced in the manner of life that is based on faith that leaves behind one's ties to evil in society in order to make others free as well (cf. I Cor. 5:6ff.). But this manner of life is never a possession at one's disposal but is always action (imperative!) to be experienced always anew, since the baptized ones still live "in the flesh" (4:2). Conduct in society is described programmatically in 2:11f. as exodus in this sense and is also so characterized in the first subpart in detail.

3. This departure from the understanding of the Qumran community, which manifests itself in social-ethical consequences, is also seen in terms of religious history. From this point on contact with the Qumran texts ceases. From the first verse of this part on a close association with Hellenistic social ethics is felt. Like the Qumran tradition, this tradition has also come to the author through the medium of material transmitted in the Church.

I Peter as a whole thus produces something new by combining the Hellenistic tradition, which was oriented toward society and politics and open to the world, with the tradition from Qumran, which was turned away from the world and "monastic." Christian existence in society is for I Peter thus oriented both eschatologically and historically. But in the course of Church history this new orientation split again and again into its pre-Christian antecedents: In the fourth century, e.g., the significance of Christianity was fulfilled for some in the state Church and for others in anchoritism; in the nineteenth century it was fulfilled for some in culture-Protestantism and for others in pietistic groups.

---

3. 1QS 1:16–3:12: the ritual of annual covenant renewal (J. Maier, *Die Texte vom Toten Meer* (Basel, 1960) I, 22ff.; II, 13.

2:11–3:12: RESPONSIBLE PARTICIPATION IN THE INSTITUTIONS OF SOCIETY

2:11f.: Engagement for the World in Inner Freedom from the World as the Basic Principle of Christian Activity

11 *Beloved, I beseech (you),*
that you as foreigners and sojourners
keep yourselves from fleshly lusts,
which militate against the soul.
12 *Conduct your manner of life well among the Gentiles,*
so that they — on account of which they slander you as
evildoers —
(nevertheless) observe (your posture) from your good works
and praise God on the day of visitation.

In mutually complementary fashion, these two verses provide fundamental direction — first negatively and then positively — for the behavior of Christians in society.

11 The parenesis is announced by παρακαλῶ, "I beseech you," addresses the readers as ἀγαπητοί, "beloved," and describes them as πάροικοι καὶ παρεπίδημοι," "foreigners and sojourners." The address ἀγαπητοί is specifically Christian; it is found hardly anywhere else in the Jewish and Hellenistic environment. It is used in most early Christian letters in the body of their thought development, and not at the beginning, in order to make what is said all the more emphatic.[4] Christians are for our author "beloved" because they are loved, as in 1:22, by him, by the brothers, and above all by God (cf. Rom. 1:7).

The appeal that begins here applies to them because they are "foreigners and sojourners."[5] The expression, which is perhaps formulaic in char-

---

4. So Paul in Rom. 12:19; I Cor. 10:14; II Cor. 7:1; I Thess. 2:8, and elsewhere, as well as later in Heb. 6:9; Jas. 1:16, 19; 2:5 (here always with ἀδελφοί); II Pet. 3:1; Jude 3; I Jn. 2:7, and elsewhere. See C. Spicq, *Agape in the NT* II (tr. M. McNamara and M. Richter; St. Louis, 1965), 429-439.

5. ὡς παροίκους καὶ παρεπιδήμους can be connected with παρακαλῶ (so Schweizer, 54; Kelly, 102f.), though a preceding ὑμᾶς would then be expected. Therefore, it surely belongs to ἀπέχεσθαι (so Knopf, 101; Schelkle, 69, n.2). But the expression not only gives the basis for the ἀπέχεσθαι, but also, reaching back to the first part, establishes the heading for the second. Thus παρακαλῶ not only introduces the second sentence, but also announces the entire parenesis that follows.

acter,[6] appropriates catchwords from the first part of the letter (παρεπίδημοι from 1:1 and παροικία from 1:17) and thereby recalls its content. Christians are "foreigners" because they are called into eschatological existence and "sojourners" because they are to live this existence in history.[7]

Because they are "foreigners" in this sense, this surprising and possibly sobering instruction is directed to them: ἀπέχεσθαι τῶν σαρκικῶν ἐπιθυμιῶν," "keep yourselves from fleshly lusts." To be a foreigner to the world, to experience the exodus, means first of all, therefore, that Christians are to become estranged to the world in themselves. "Keep yourselves from lusts" is a rule of classical Greek–Hellenistic ethics from the time of Plato that is appropriated by Hellenistic Christianity, perhaps through the mediation of Hellenistic Judaism.[8] Abstinence was for Greeks an expression of σωφροσύνη, "circumspection," but for Christians the experience of sanctification (I Thess. 4:3), which corresponds to existence as a foreigner (I Pet. 1:14ff.).

"Fleshly lusts" are the "human lusts" (4:2) that shaped pre-Christian existence (1:14; 4:2). They are, however, also a possibility for Christians since they do not simply lie in the past: Those summoned to faith still live ἐν σαρκί, "in the flesh" (4:2). The σάρξ is not evil as such; it is human existence yoked to death.[9] What is σαρκικός, "fleshly,"[10] is the craving

---

6. In the LXX Gen. 23:4 and Ps. 38:13, similarly Heb. 11:13: ξένοι καὶ παρεπίδημοι.

7. See above, pp. 68-70 ("Elect Ones as Foreigners").

8. Middle voice ἀπέχομαι is "keep oneself at a distance from," "abstain from" (Plato, *Phaedo* 82C: ἀπέχονται ν τῶν κατὰ τὸ σῶμα ἐπιθυμιῶν ἁπάσων, similarly 83B; *Leges* 8.835E [LCL I, 287, 289; X, 149]; Aristotle, *Ethica Nicomachea* 2.2.9 [LCL XIX, 79]: ἐκ . . . τοῦ ἀπέχεσθαι τῶν ἡδονῶν γινόμεθα σώφρονες, καὶ γενόμενοι μάλιστα δυνάμεθα ἀπέχεσθαι αὐτῶν). There is no corresponding formulaic use in the LXX (Job 28:28: ἀπέχεσθαι κακῶν; cf. 1:1, 8; 2:3; Wis. 2:16), but the Greek formula does appear to have had an influence in the NT (I Thess. 4:3: "This is God's will, your sanctification: that you abstain from unchastity . . ."; 5:22: "abstain from every form of evil"). The prohibitions in Acts 15:20, 29, in the apostolic decree, take on this sense ("abstain from") in its allegorical reinterpretation; in the first instance it pertained, like I Tim. 4:3, to matters of ritual. Selwyn, 369-375, conjectures that the verb was the catchword of a traditional baptismal catechesis and that its appearance in NT passages connected with Silvanus is not coincidental. But it is likely only that use of the verb, like use of ἀποτιθέναι (2:1), was customary in baptismal parenesis and did not have an OT-Jewish origin, but a Greek-Hellenistic origin.

9. So not only in 1:24, but also in 3:18 and 4:1f.

10. σαρκικός, otherwise in the NT six times in Paul; it is not found earlier (E. Schweizer, "σάρξ," *TDNT* VII, 101, n.25). But I Peter does not appropriate the adjective directly from Paul, but from early Christian tradition. The counterpoint to ψυχή, which it subsequently develops, has no point of correspondence in Pauline anthropology. I Peter does not follow Pauline anthropology in particular, but rather the basic line of thought of biblical anthropology, which is distinguished fundamentally from Greek-Hellenistic anthropology: Plato defines the lust from which one should abstain as κατὰ τὸ σῶμα (cf. n.8), while Epictetus,

determined by this human life, which desires to constitute its own life instead of expecting it from the Creator's hand; it expresses itself, therefore, especially in excess and idolatry (4:2f.).

These ἐπιθυμίαι, "lusts," promise and desire life, but accomplish the opposite: αἵτινες στρατεύονται κατὰ τῆς ψυχῆς," "they go to war against the soul." The ψυχή is the heart of one's life as a person, the "I" that should be delivered into eternal life.[11] This "I" is suppressed and destroyed by passions; the "going to war" is thought of as a struggle to the death (στρατεύεσθαι),[12] not simply as a a struggle between competing claims.[13] Partial analogies to this statement are in Mk. 8:36: ". . . and forfeit one's soul [i.e., one's life]," and Rom. 7:9ff.: if sin lives the "I" dies. If the "I" that is delivered through Christ is not to be lost, then the exodus must be accomplished continually as "keeping oneself."

The meaning of this for one's behavior in relation to society is that the exodus cannot be accomplished by emigration out of society. Alien existence cannot be lived as flight from the world, since one who flees from the world denies thereby that he or she is still part of the world. Christians, like all people, are still dependent on those institutions of society that in spite of "fleshly craving" make earthly life possible. Therefore, they are obligated to participate in them for their own sakes. They are also obligated to participate in them, and even more, for the sake of their positive commission in relation to society, toward which the next verse points.

12 Christians should see to it that their "manner of life among the Gentiles" is "well ordered": τὴν ἀναστροφὴν ὑμῶν ἐν τοῖς ἔθνεσιν ἔχοντες καλήν. They live as foreigners in the Diaspora, as did Israel among the "Gentiles," i.e., among people who do not know God, who

---

Dissertationes 3.7.3 (LCL II, 51), Plutarch, *Moralia* 101B (LCL II, 99), and Diogenes Laertius 10.145 (LCL II, 669f.) speak of "joys of the flesh," referring thereby to material bodily existence expressing itself in excess and uncontrolled passion, which must, therefore, be made subject to the spiritual intellect.

11. See the comments on 1:9, 22; 2:25; 3:20; 4:19.

12. Thus, O. Bauernfeind, "στρατεύομαι," *TDNT* VII, 711; the verb is used otherwise in the NT figuratively in I Tim. 1:18 and, as here regarding passions, in Jas. 4:1.

13. It is not the opposition of σάρξ and ψυχή, as in the struggle between "flesh" and "thought" (νοῦς) in Rom. 7:14ff., between "flesh" and "the (Holy) Spirit" (πνεῦμα) in Gal. 5:17, or even between the bodily and the intellectual side of humankind in Greek-Hellenistic philosophy (e.g., Plutarch, *Moralia* 101B [LCL II, 99]). This differentiation between the bodily and the intellectual sides of a person was taken over in Hellenistic Judaism (IV Macc. 1:20ff.; 3:1ff.; 7:16ff.; cf. Philo, *Legum Allegoriae* 2.106 [LCL I, 291]). It is noteworthy that the Qumran documents speak only of a battle of the various spirits in the flesh, never of a battle between flesh and spirit (R. Meyer, "σάρξ," *TDNT* VII, 114).

indeed reject him together with his people.[14] Christians are to address themselves positively to this situation and conduct themselves "well" in secular society. This instruction can be followed throughout the subsequent parenesis like a scarlet thread: 3:1f., 16 also require that one be ἀγαθή or ἀγνὴ ἀναστροφή, 2:12: καλὰ ἔργα, 2:15f., 20; 3:6: ἀγαθο-ποιεῖν (cf. ἀγαθοποιός in 2:14), 3:13: τοῦ ἀγαθοῦ ζηλωταί.

The sense in which Christians' conduct should be καλός or ἀγαθός, i.e., "good,"[15] is to be deciphered from the context. The decisive crite-rion was already named in 1:15: One's manner of life, one's entire behavior, should correspond to the summons from "the holy One" to be "holy." As now becomes clear with the aid of different terminology, this behavior is distinguished fundamentally from that of the Gentiles, which is stamped by "lusts," by striving to stake out one's own existence by one's own power without God (1:14; 2:11; 4:3).

But this different orientation of Christians does not make sense to outsiders: Quite deliberately now the letter describes social-ethical con-duct no longer as "holy" but as καλός and ἀγαθός, terms common to the classical Greek-Hellenistic tradition. But it is said at the same time that society judges Christians not as "good" but, quite to the contrary, as v. 12b develops, as "evildoers" (κακοποιοί). Such judgment is to be refuted by "good conduct." The goal is, therefore, not self-justification but the liberation of all for acknowledgment of their Creator. But how is this possible for others in view of the limited evidence for the quality of Christian conduct? What is decisive becomes clear in terms of the reflection that follows.

Why are Christians slandered as "evildoers"?[16] There is alienation toward Christians not because they are bad but because they are differ-ent, because they no longer conform to the way of life shaped by craving (4:4). Their critically distanced posture is seen as "hatred for the human race," and this uneasiness is articulated in accusations of every possible wrongdoing that must avoid the light: καταλαλεῖν ὑμῶν ὡς κακοποιῶν. Christians were looked on not only as morally suspect, but even as

---

14. See above, p. 64.
15. The two words are, as already in the LXX, synonymous: "good" (W. Grundmann, "καλός," *TDNT* III, 544).
16. κακοποιός appears in the NT only in I Pet. 2:12, 14; 4:15. According to I Pet. 2:14 it is the responsibility of government leadership to punish the κακοποιοί; cf. 4:15; Jn. 18:30 (Koine reading); Rom. 13:4: ἐὰν τὸ κακὸν ποιῇς. In I Pet. 3:9-12 κακόν, "evil," acquires a more comprehensive moral-religious sense (see the comments there).

criminals who transgress against the order of society; therefore, they could be brought before the courts as "dangerous to the public" (4:15). This situation can be deciphered from the statements of Roman historians about the reasons for the Neronian persecution.[17]

The concern of I Peter is that those who are alienated toward Christians and their orientation and who, therefore, make slanderous remarks should observe the opposite on the basis of this very orientation (ἐν ᾧ) as "good works" and praise God: ἵνα ἐν ᾧ καταλαλοῦσιν ὑμῶν ὡς κακοποιῶν ἐκ τῶν καλῶν ἔργων ἐποπτεύοντες δοξάσωσιν τὸν θεόν.[18] 3:1f. refers to a practical example for this ἐποπτεύειν, "observation," "seeing" (the verb is encountered only in these two passages in the NT): The husband who rejects the faith of his wife "observes" her maritally honorable behavior and should thereby be won over for faith. Thus, according to our verse, the true character of Christians' conduct should be grasped over a longer period of time[19] through thoughtful observation[20] prompted "by the good works" of Christians. This can only happen in such a way that one who observes comes to faith in response to this on his or her own; only then the offensive distinctiveness of Christians becomes understandable. ἐποπτεύειν is, therefore, not to establish something through what appears on the surface but — without this being a matter of conscious reflection here — truly seeing, as the Gospel of John describes it, in terms of the blind person's recovery of sight through faith,[21] or, in terms of Greek

---

17. Tacitus, *Annales* 15.44 (LCL IV, 285, ca. A.D. 110): Nero was able to deflect suspicion of starting the fire from himself to the Christians because they were "loathed for their vices *(per flagitia invisos)*." But the police investigation did not convict them of starting the fire, but only of "hatred of the human race" *(quam odio generis humani)*. Suetonius, *Nero* 16 (LCL II, 111): "a new and mischievous superstition."

18. The difficult sentence construction in v. 12b surely resulted from the appropriation of the tradition in Mt. 5:16 (see below, n.28) and application of it by ἐν ᾧ . . . κακοποιῶν to the current circumstances of the addressees. Hence, "see[ing] your good works" (Mt. 5:16) becomes "seeing [perceiving] based on good works" that counters any slander. Both ἐν ᾧ and ἐκ καλῶν ἔργων are, therefore, connected with ἐποπτεύοντες (Windisch, 62), not with δοξάσωσιν (Schweizer, 54). ἐν ᾧ is, therefore, not temporal "while" (Schelkle, 68) or "whenever" (Selwyn, 170), but, as in 3:16, ἐν τούτῳ, ἐν ᾧ = "wherein."

19. Present participle.

20. ἐποπτεύω, "observe"; ἔργα ἐποπτεύειν, "inspect": Hesiod, *Opera et Dies* 767 (LCL, 59). The LXX has only ἐπόπτης, always of God as an expression of his omniscience: II Macc. 7:35: τοῦ παντοκράτωρος ἐπόπτου θεοῦ. See below, n.22.

21. Jn. 9:39; W. Michaelis, "ὁράω," *TDNT* V, 361f. See also F. Hahn, "Sehen und Glauben im Johannesevangelium," *NT und Geschichte* (FS O. Cullmann; Zurich/Tübingen, 1972), 125-141.

philosophy, as grasping that which truly exists through rational seeing.[22]

Because faith breaks forth in this "observing," the observing leads people to their destiny: ἵνα . . . δοξάσωσιν τὸν θεὸν ἐν ἡμέρᾳ ἐπισκοπῆς. They turn to their Creator, who now becomes their Redeemer, and confess with songs of praise that they owe him their very selves.

This is to happen on "the day of visitation," on the day in which the Creator lays hold of his creatures. This can be the day of judgment, on which God announces himself to the world in punishment as God, or the day on which God graciously visits the individual.[23] According to 4:11, 16 the serving as well as the suffering of Christians should flow even now into "songs of praise." Even the closest parallel to our passage, the saying in Mt. 5:16, has in mind songs of praise in the present. Therefore, the day of the gracious visitation of the individual could be intended here.[24] In contrast the expression "day of visitation" as such allows one to think of the future day of judgment.[25] According to 4:7, 17f., the day of judgment stands directly in the author's field of vision, and presumably he wishes to take it up here in the context of the tradition behind Mt. 5:16 together with reference to the Church's present persecution by the Gentiles. The statement is, therefore, ambiguous. In any case the "song of praise" is the expression of those who have discovered from the Christians' "good works" the truth about them and have thereby found that truth also for themselves.[26]

The question of what "good works" this eschatological turning

------

22. Michaelis, *TDNT* V, 321f. The verb ἐποπτεύω was already in the Eleusinian mysteries used in a technical sense of visions during initiation (Plato, *Phaedrus* 250C [LCL I, 485]: μυούμενοί τε καὶ ἐποπτεύοντες; cf. Michaelis, *TDNT* V, 373f.). In I Pet. 2:12 the verb is not used in a technical sense but does indicate not only attention given to something by means of personal observation, but also observation that evokes reflection.

23. The noun ἐπισκοπή, which is rare in extrabiblical sources, stands in the LXX for Hebrew פְּקֻדָּה, "visitation." On the ἡμέρα τῆς ἐπισκοπῆς God will show himself as God to the unjust in a punishing way (Isa. 10:3); in the same sense, Jer. 6:15; 10:15; Sir. 18:20 speak of the καιρός or ὥρα ἐπισκοπῆς. But in Wis. 3:7 it can also be said that the deceased just ones shine brightly ἐν καιρῷ ἐπισκοπῆς αὐτῶν, "at the time of their visitation"; visitation becomes for them, as Wis. 4:15 expressly declares, χάρις and ἔλεος, "a demonstration of grace." In this sense, Jesus' coming to Jerusalem is in Lk. 19:44 "the time of your [gracious eschatological] visitation." The verb is used in the same sense in Gen. 50:24f.; Lk. 1:68. Cf. W. H. Beyer, "ἐπισκέπτομαι," *TDNT* II, 606ff. Nothing is to be derived from other uses of the term in I Peter, since in 5:6 ἐπισκοπή is a secondary textual reading, and ἐπίσκοπος in 2:25 belongs to another branch of the term's history.

24. See Knopf, 103f.; Schweizer, 57; Selwyn, 171; Spicq, 99.

25. So van Unnik, "Teaching," especially 103ff.; F. Hahn, *Mission in the NT* (SBT 47, tr. F. Clark; London, 1965), 141, n.6. See also Schelkle, 72.

26. A forced singing of praise would be absurd.

point sets in motion leads into the substantive and traditional context of the entire statement. "Good works" are in rabbinic Judaism unusual acts of benevolence and intercession which go beyond what is required by the law.[27] But here the expression is taken over from the tradition behind Mt. 5:16: ". . . that they see your good works and praise your Father in heaven."[28] In this tradition coming from Jesus "good works" represent conduct required by Jesus and described in terms of example, in which eschatological repentance shows itself.

But in I Peter 2 the expression refers specifically to conduct that arises from faith and is appropriate to the situation in the institutions of society: not unusual humanitarian accomplishments but the most elementary "service of worship in the everyday life of the world" (E. Käsemann). Later I Peter replaces καλὰ ἔργα, "good works," with ἀγαθοποιεῖν, "to conduct (oneself) properly,"[29] and thus comes close to Hellenistic thought, according to which the spiritual-ethical as well as the political-social ideal type is the καλὸς κάγαθός.[30]

This terminology, which emerges still more emphatically in the Pastoral Epistles,[31] is characteristic of the attempt to gain for Christians a place in Hellenistic society. It shapes the theology of I Peter in a decisive way: The author develops this place in society in terms of the missionary-eschatological sending of Christians. That Christians should strive to have a good reputation among non-Christians is emphasized regularly in early Christian tradition.[32] But that their conduct should become a witness in society is expressed programmatically only in Mt.

---

27. See below, p. 178.

28. The two statements agree in important expressions:

| Mt. 5:16: | ὅπως | ἴδωσιν ὑμῶν τὰ καλὰ ἔργα καὶ | δοξάσωσιν |
| I Pet. 2:12: | ἵνα | ἐκ τῶν καλῶν ἔργων ἐποπτεύοντες | δοξάσωσιν |

The points at which they differ correspond respectively to the kerygma of Matthew and I Peter (see above, n.18). This observation suggests that Matthew and I Peter have shaped in redactionally different ways a common tradition.

In its other echoes of the Gospels, I Peter comes close to Matthew only once (3:14 = Mt. 5:10), while in others it approaches Luke (see the comments on 2:19f.; 3:16). Therefore, its author did not use our Gospel of Matthew directly. So also Best, "I Peter and the Gospel Tradition," especially 103-111. Best is in critical conversation with Gundry, "Verba Christi"; see also Gundry's reply, "Further Verba"; Maier, "Jesustradition."

29. In 2:15 ἐκ καλῶν ἔργων is replaced by ἀγαθοποιεῖν.

30. W. Grundmann, "καλός," *TDNT* III, 538ff.

31. Grundmann, *TDNT* III, 549f.

32. I Cor. 10:32; Col. 4:5; I Thess. 4:12; I Tim. 3:7; 5:14; 6:1; Tit. 2:5-10; also I Pet. 2:15; 3:16; 4:15.

5:16 and here.[33] The OT and Jewish tradition that Israel is to sanctify and glorify God's name among the peoples is thereby appropriated.[34] This takes place in Judaism through obedience to the law. The community at Qumran can, therefore, understand it in such a way that it arms itself in the context of emigration for the holy war against the unrighteous. But by righteous living in relation to the institutions of Hellenistic society Christians give witness to the God who now wants to redeem all. How righteous living should be manifested is developed in the next section on the basis of the household code tradition.

2:13–3:7: Conduct in the Institutions of Society

Excursus: The Station Code Tradition[1]

Station Codes in Early Christian Parenesis

Listings of directives to people in various stations like that in I Pet. 2:13–3:7 can be found repeatedly in early Christian parenesis. If one compares the texts three different groups according to form and content emerge:

---

33. Applied to social-ethical practice in I Pet. 3:1f. (see the comments there); perhaps already also in I Cor. 7:13f., 16f.; later in Ignatius, *Eph.* 10:1 (LCL AF I, 185; cf. *Trall.* 3:2 [*ibid.*, 215]); *Herm. Mand.* 3.1 (*ibid.*, II, 75).

34. Isa. 49:3; Str.-Bill. I, 411ff.; especially *Test. Naph.* 8:4 (*OT Pseudep.* I, 813): "If you achieve the good, my children, men and angels will bless you; and God will be glorified through you among the gentiles. The devil will flee from you." The last statement appears in Jas. 4:7 and was, therefore, known in early Christianity. Rom. 2:19f., 23f. presuppose similar concepts from the Jewish theology of mission. See D. Daube, "Jewish Missionary Maxims in Paul," *StTh* 1 (1947), 158-169; R. Schnackenburg, " 'Ihr seid das Salz der Erde, das Licht der Welt.' Zu Mt 5,13-16" (1964), *idem, Schriften zum NT* (Munich, 1971), 177-200; J. Blauw, *The Missionary Nature of the Church* (London, 1962); van Unnik, "Rücksicht."

1. See M. Dibelius, *An die Kolosser, Epheser, an Philemon* (HNT 12; third ed. rev. by H. Greeven, Tübingen, 1953), 48ff., 91f. (excursus on Col. 4:1 and Eph. 5:14); Weidinger, *Haustafeln;* Wendland, "Sozialethischen Bedeutung"; Schroeder, *Haustafeln;* O. Merk, *Handeln aus Glauben. Die Motivierungen der paulinischen Ethik* (MbThSt 5; Marburg, 1969), 214-224; E. Lohse, *Colossians and Philemon* (Hermeneia, tr. W. Pöhlmann and R. Karris; Philadelphia, 1971), 154ff. (excursus on Col. 3:18); P. Stuhlmacher, "Christliche Verantwortung bei Paulus und seinen Schülern," *EvTh* 28 (1968), 165-186; Philipps, *Kirche in der Gesellschaft;* Crouch, *Origin and Intention of the Colossian Haustafel;* Goppelt, "Prinzipien neutestamentlicher Sozialethik"; *idem,* "Jesus und die Haustafel"; Schrage, "Ethik"; Munro, *Authority* (cf. the response by Dijkman, "1 Peter: A Later Pastoral Stratum?"); Balch, *Let Wives Be Submissive* (history-of-religions bibliography; cf. the review by A. C. Wire, *RelStRev* 10 [1984], 209-216); *idem,* "Early Christian Criticism"; *idem,* "Hellenization/Acculturation"; Senior, "Conduct"; Motyer, "Codes."

1. The series in I Peter is to be linked closely with the ones in Col. 3:18–4:1 and Eph. 5:22–6:9. The same genre is present here, as it is usually called, that of the "household code."[2] The same oral tradition must be the basis of all three texts.[3] Frequently included in this genre and tradition are two other groups of texts[4] which can, however, be fundamentally differentiated from it by careful examination.[5]

2. First, the series of directives for stations in the Church found in the Pastoral Epistles and the Apostolic Fathers (I Tim. 2:[1]8-15; 6:1f.; Tit. 2:1-10; *I Clem.* 1:3; 21:6-9; Ignatius, *Pol.* 4:1–6:1; Polycarp, *Phil.* 4:2–6:3 [LCL AF I, 10f., 46-49, 270-275, 286-291]) clearly constitute a separate group and speak to a different social situation from that of the "household codes." Here Christians are addressed not in their "worldly station" but as members of stations and groups within the congregation. Thus, alongside married couples, widows, young people, and slaves are always mentioned leaders, elders, and deacons of the Church as well. Therefore, the household code parenesis, as represented in I Pet. 2:13–3:7, has been combined with the congregational parenesis developed in I Pet. 5:1-5 and has thereby been altered in its structure. Furthermore, the polar pairing of stations characteristic of the household codes has disappeared to a large extent, and the typical arrangement of particular directives is gone entirely. Therefore, this group of texts no longer belongs to the genre of the household codes; it has only appropriated a few elements of the household code tradition. This is even more the case for a further group:

3. In *Did.* 4:9-11 (LCL AF I, 316f.), paralleled in many respects in *Barn.* 19:5-7 (*ibid.,* 402-405) we find directives to people in their stations — worldly stations, fathers and children, slaves and masters, to be sure, but according to form and content they belong to the classification of proverbial wisdom. Only *Did.* 4:11 (*ibid.,* 317) takes over a "household code tradition": "You who are slaves be subject to your masters. . . ."

This differentiation, which has received too little attention, is explained and confirmed by analysis of the structure of the household code schema as distinguished in this fashion.

---

2. Luther labeled as "Haustafel" ("household code") a number of biblical passages relating to various stations in life (the second appendix to the Shorter Catechism = *The Book of Concord* [tr. and ed. T. G. Tappert; Philadelphia, 1959], 354-356: "Table of Duties"; cf. P. Schaff, ed., *The Creeds of Christendom* [sixth ed., New York, 1931] I, 249). In Luther Bibles from the end of the sixteenth century "Haustafel" has been the heading over the corresponding sections of Colossians and Ephesians. This word became, primarily because of M. Dibelius, the designation for a genre of early Christian parenesis (Weidinger, *Haustafeln,* 1f.). As such it has been adopted in English-language exegetical literature.

3. So fundamentally Dibelius, *Kolosser, Epheser,* 48ff.; Weidinger, *Haustafeln,* 5f.; cf. Goppelt, *Apostolic,* 153f. The point of contact is not, as is often assumed, based on literary dependence or use of a primitive Christian catechism; the first hypothesis is analyzed and refuted by E. Percy, *Die Probleme der Kolosser- und Epheserbriefe* (Lund, 1946), 433-440 and Schroeder, *Haustafeln* II, 16ff. (n.67), the second by Schroeder, I, 7-16.

4. So from Weidinger, *Haustafeln,* 2, to Lohse, *Colossians,* 154.

5. So also Schroeder, *Haustafeln* I, 81. The similarities and differences between the NT passages under question can be seen in the synoptic tables in Selwyn, 419-439.

The "Household Code" Schema

Common Identifying Marks

The household code tradition is found in its most brief and ancient form in Colossians. There it is distinguished stylistically so completely from the rest of the letter, even from the rest of the parenesis, that it is recognizable as appropriated material. In Ephesians and I Peter the tradition is reworked in varying ways. In view of this distinctive expansion the common marks of identification can be distinguished quite clearly.

1. The theme is always the Christian in his or her relationships with others established through the basic forms of historical existence, i.e., through marriage, parenthood, the workplace, and the relationship to civil government.

2. As regards form, the directives in Colossians and Ephesians are arranged in pairs, each pair starting with the subordinate person. Thus they address the two partners of some basic social relationship: wives and husbands in marriage, children and parents, slaves and masters. This polarity is not developed in I Peter except in relationship to marriage, but is probably presupposed. Thus the directives are focused on relationships, not on stations considered in isolation.

3. In the three codes, particular directives are all arranged in the same way: An apodictic imperative follows the address directed to the members of the station, and the imperative is usually supported by some rationale (e.g., Col. 3:18: Αἱ γυναῖκες, ὑποτάσσεσθε τοῖς ἀνδράσιν, ὡς ἀνῆκεν ἐν κυρίῳ).[6] A considerable number of similarly worded characteristic expressions, e.g., the stereotypical imperative "subject yourselves," correspond to this agreement in thematic focus and form.[7]

The common structure comes into still sharper relief when we analyze the expansion of this schema in I Peter.

The Expansion of the Schema in I Peter

In comparison to Colossians and Ephesians, I Peter has altered the household code tradition in order to clarify kerygmatically the social situation of Christians, which is acute for this letter. What the other letters have principally in view — but certainly not exclusively[8] — is the Christian household, "the extended family." I Peter has in mind individual Christians in the institutions of a non-Christian society that discriminates against them. This different viewpoint is seen by the following alterations of the schema:

1. The sequence of directives in Colossians and Ephesians proceeds from the middle of the household — marriage — outward to slaves. But in I Peter the sequence is reversed, moving from the civil order surrounding all society to the smallest unit, marriage.

---

6. This form of instruction was given precise analysis for the first time by Schroeder, *Haustafeln* I, 91-108. See more recently Schroeder on 2:11–3:12 in "Once You Were No People."

7. See below, pp. 174-176.

8. Contra Rengstorf, "Neutestamentlichen Mahnungen," 136f.

2. In Colossians and Ephesians all stations of the household are addressed in pairs while in I Peter, husbands excepted, only the subordinate partners are addressed, since for them the tie to non-Christians is especially problematic. The relationship of children to parents is left out since Christian children of non-Christian parents would be hardly thinkable in the situation at hand.

In contrast, the relationship with political authority is added. Instruction in this regard was not only necessary, but formally belonged in this series: Instruction on the relationship to government includes, as early as Rom. 13:1, the same elements of form as the individual directives of the household code schema, except for direct address.[9]

3. The individual directives in I Peter are developed in terms of content with a view to the conflict situation, which surprisingly arises neither in the household codes of Colossians or Ephesians nor in the instructions in Rom 13:1-7. By including this aspect I Peter is more thoroughgoing in dealing with reality, since injustice and, therefore, conflict and the matter of witness in the stations of society are always acute issues.

The Term "Household Code"

When all is said and done the designation "household code" is inadequate for this genre and tradition. I Pet. 2:13–3:7 is in any case not a "household code," but a "station code." The designation "station code" also does more justice to the sequence in Colossians and Ephesians, since they are not restricted fundamentally to the Christian household and conform, moreover, to the instruction in Rom. 13:1. This designation recommends itself even if it may be subject to misunderstanding today, since it uses the term "station" not in the modern sense but in that of the Reformation. One's "station" is here the place in society's institutions to which one is assigned by God's sovereignty in history, the "role" with which one is charged.[10]

This social-ethical schema came to be of cental importance at the end of the Pauline period in the correspondence between Rome and Asia Minor. But it disappeared as early as the Pastoral Epistles and the Apostolic Fathers. Its structure and meaning become clear on the basis of inquiry into its origin.

---

9. The similarity of structure prohibits the assumption of substantive differences between Paul and Colossians (contra Stuhlmacher, "Verantwortung," 180f.).

10. What the Reformation called "stations," more recent Lutheran social ethics has called "order of creation" or "order of preservation," and sociology has called "institution." These specialized terms refer in essence to the same established data, but see them according to different aspects and criteria.

11. A. Alt, "Die Ursprünge des israelitischen Rechts," *Kleine Schriften zur Geschichte des Volkes Israel* I (Munich, 1953), 278-332; E. Gerstenberger, *Wesen und Herkunft des "apodiktischen Rechts"* (WMANT 20; Neukirchen, 1965); H. Gese, "Der Dekalog als Ganzheit betrachtet," *ZThK* 64 (1967), 121-138 (= *idem, Vom Sinai zum Zion* [Munich, 1974], 63-80).

The Origin of the Station Codes

Other Structures of Popular Station Ethics

1. In the OT and in Palestinian Judaism we do not find any parallels to the station codes. The institutions addressed in the codes — marriage, relationships in the workplace, the civil order — are ordered in the OT through the sacred justice of God, through apodictic commandments and casuistic principles of justice,[11] which were applied to the present casuistically in Judaism in the Halakah.

Along with these, proverbial wisdom influenced broad strata of the Jewish population through the centuries on how one should behave constructively in terms of one's own life and that of one's community; such pertains to the forms of life within community as they exist in the context of history and are guaranteed legally. On the basis of life experience it describes how one is to live out one's role in society, the world into which one "is born" and which is "to a great extent conditioned and determined by community considerations."[12] Wisdom describes that which is generally valid, that "which survives no matter what the social circumstances."[13] Thereby it is asserted: " 'Good' is that which does good; 'evil' is that which causes harm."[14] Proverbial wisdom emerged in Israel, from Proverbs to Sirach, to a large extent from the trickling in of Near Eastern wisdom, which was also consciously appropriated. In modified form it lives on in Judaism in the minor tractates of the Talmud.[15]

2. These two forms of social-ethical directive are also found in Hellenistic Judaism. Non-Israelite justice is again developed in proverbial wisdom that depends on classical Greek-Hellenistic traditions, above all in the Wisdom of Solomon and in the proverbial collection of pseudo-Phocylides, which is more important for the question of the origin of the NT station codes.[16] The latter borrows its title from the collection of proverbs by Phocylides, which came into being as early as the sixth century B.C. among the Greeks; this collection was used for teaching throughout the centuries alongside that of Theognis. This classical Greek-Hellenistic proverbial tradition was appropriated in the second century A.D. in the Christian *Sentences of Sextus.*[17] Alongside this there arose in Hellenistic Judaism,

---

12. G. von Rad, *Wisdom in Israel* (tr. J. Martin; London, 1972), 75.

13. *Ibid.,* 76.

14. *Ibid.,* 77.

15. I.e., *m. Aboth, Aboth de Rabbi Nathan, Derek Erets Rabbah, Derek Erets Zuta.* See H. L. Strack, *Introduction to the Talmud and Midrash* (Philadelphia, 1931), 53f., 73f.; H. L. Strack and G. Stemberger, *Introduction to the Talmud and Midrash* (tr. M. Bockmuehl; Edinburgh, 1991), 129, 245-247, 250f.

16. Text in D. Young, ed., *Anthologia Lyrica Graeca II (Theognis, Ps.-Pythagoras, Ps.-Phocylides, Chares, Anonymi Aulodia, Fragmentum Teliambicum)* (second ed., Leipzig, 1961), 95-112; English translation in *OT Pseudep.* II, 574-582.

17. Ed. H. Chadwick (Cambridge, 1959); ed. and tr. R. Edwards and R. Wild (Chico, CA, 1981); see G. Delling, "Zur Hellenisierung des Christentums in den 'Sprüchen des Sextus,' " *Studien zum NT und zur Patristik* (FS E. Klostermann, TU 77; Berlin, 1961), 208-241.

above all in Philo, in dependence on the great classical Greek-Hellenistic exemplars, the beginnings of a Jewish philosophical ethics. This form of ethics played, however, a considerably smaller role than justice, custom, and proverbial wisdom, except for popular philosophical moments of illumination for the ethos of everyday life.[18] In early Christianity an ethics comparable to this philosophical ethics emerged for the first time among the Christian Alexandrians.

3. Of these forms of ethical directive, the literature of proverbial wisdom offers itself as the closest analogy to the station codes, but we also find in it no true parallels. Proverbs does already address social life, above all marriage and the family,[19] but the statements there are different in both form and content. At least in terms of the longer series of directives for various stations, one finds parallels in Hellenistic Judaism. Pseudo-Phocylides begins directives for conduct in work and marriage and in relation to children, friends, relatives, parents, servants, and slaves with: "Work hard so that you can live from your own means" (153); "Do not remain unmarried, lest you die nameless" (175); "Do not be harsh with your children, but be gentle" (207); and "Love your friends till death, for faithfulness is a good thing" (218 [*OT Pseudep.* II, 579-582]). The sequence of directives in Tob. 4:3-21 is of the same kind. Also similar are the directives that Josephus gives in the context of an apologetic explanation of the law for married couples, children and parents, young and old, friends and strangers (*Contra Apionem* 2:198-210 [LCL I, 372-379]). He calls them stipulations of the Law that are, however, to a large extent proverbial wisdom. Of a different structure is the sequence that Philo, *De Decalogo* 165-167 (LCL VII, 192-195), derives from the fourth commandment.[20]

4. When one compares these Hellenistic Jewish series dealing with stations with early Christian series, the third group of the latter, that represented by *Did.* 4:9-11 and *Barn.* 19:5-7 (LCL AF I, 316f., 402-405), offers a direct correspondence. Both groups belong by form and content to proverbial literature, and both are distinguished structurally from the station code schema.

5. Proverbial wisdom and station codes have in mind different social situations. Wisdom advises how one should conduct oneself in the social contexts to which one belongs by birth or placement; according to form, each bit of advice stands by itself as a proverbial pronouncement and is self-contained. The station codes, however, give instruction for entry into social relationships and leave the how up to the individual; they are directives which are open, pointed toward polarity. Such instruction is necessary where the one addressed is not fundamentally at home in the ways of life of society. It is, indeed, for "foreigners and sojourners"

---

18. This differentiation corresponds to a degree to the confrontation, first pointed out by Plato, of common inherited ethics and philosophical ethics; see A. Dihle, *Die goldene Regel. Eine Einführung in die Geschichte der antiken und frühchristlichen Vulgärethik* (Göttingen, 1962), 5-7.

19. E.g., Prov. 6:23-35; 12:4; 18:22.

20. See below, pp. 170-172.

(I Pet. 2:11). It is by no means a coincidence that we find, therefore, a close correspondence to the station codes in the duty codes of Stoicism.

The Stoic Duty Codes

1. The social ethics of Stoicism operates on the basis of a sociological presupposition similar to that of the early Christians. Stoic philosophy frees its students fundamentally from inherited ways of life, e.g., from civil laws[21] or from the station of a slave,[22] and makes them autonomous in relation to society by connecting them to the logos, the spirit that shapes the cosmos and at the same time resides in humankind.[23] But the student who has become wise and has found the correct fundamental orientation or understanding is instructed (this is portrayed above all in Epictetus) to fulfill τὰ καθήκοντα, the obligations of σχέσεις, the relationships with others which by accident or choice have fallen to the student's lot.

The result of correct philosophical activity is

> that each person passes his life to himself, free from pain, fear, and perturbation, at the same time maintaining with his associates both the natural and the acquired relationships, those namely of son, father, brother, citizen, husband, wife, neighbour, fellow-traveller, ruler and subject.
> I ought not to be unfeeling like a statue, but should maintain my relations, both natural and acquired, as a religious man, as a son, a brother, a father, a citizen. See . . . whether they observe what becomes them as men, as sons, as parents, and then, in order, through all the other terms for the social relations. (Epictetus, *Dissertationes* 2.14.8; 3.2.4; 4.6.26 [LCL I, 309; II, 23, 355])

Epictetus does consider the duties that emerge in particular out of these relationships, or, as is also said, from one's role, one's πρόσωπον, but does not narrow them down,[24] since one is to acknowledge only what corresponds to the nature of the one who is acting and of the particular relationship. One who is wise — and only this one — can discover his or her own particular duties.[25] Epictetus points therefore to duties by means of questions that invite the reader to contemplation:

---

21. Seneca, *De Otio* 8.3; *Epistulae Morales* 28.4 (LCL II, 201; IV, 201).

22. Epictetus, *Dissertationes* 1.19.7; 29.60; 4.7.17 (LCL I, 131, 203; II, 367); Seneca, *De Beneficiis* 3.20; *De Ira* 3.15.3 (LCL III, 165; I, 293-295).

23. Epictetus, *Dissertationes* 2.10.3; 3.23.4 (LCL I, 275; II, 171); M. Pohlenz, *Die Stoa* I (Göttingen, 1970), 338. See J. Stelzenberger, *Die Beziehungen der frühchristlichen Sittenlehre zur Ethik der Stoa* (Munich, 1933).

24. Epictetus, *Dissertationes* 2.10 (LCL I, 275-283); also Seneca, *Epistulae Morales* 94.1 (LCL VI, 11): Philosophy "supplies precepts appropriate to the individual case, instead of framing them for mankind at large," and "for instance advises *(suadet)* how a husband should conduct himself towards his wife, or how a father should bring up his children, or how a master should rule his slaves. . . ." It is Hierocles who makes the most detailed effort to consider relationships according to priority and to give advice regarding fulfillment of the duties of each relationship; see Weidinger, *Haustafeln*, 29-33; K. Praechter, *Hierokles der Stoiker* (Leipzig, 1901).

25. Schroeder, *Haustafeln* I, 44-46; II, 40, n.82 (references).

Consider who you are. To begin with, a Man; that is, one who. . . . In addition to this you are a citizen of the world, and a part of it. . . . What, then, is the profession of a citizen? . . . Next bear in mind that you are a Son. What is the profession of this character (πρόσωπον)? . . . For each of these designations (ὀνομάτων), when duly considered, always suggests the acts that are appropriate to it. (Epictetus, *Dissertationes* 2.10.1, 3f., 7, 11 [LCL I, 275, 283, 285]).

2. Undeniably this Stoic duty ethic overlaps to a considerable extent with the early Christian station ethic in content and form: Both are addressed to people who are fundamentally free in regard to social obligations. They instruct such people as free persons to fulfill the obligations of the social ties that bind them through origin or choice. How they are to fulfill these obligations is not spelled out in rules; the one who is free is, rather, to decide from the nature of the relationship what the obligation is. Thus, it is in both the Stoic lists and the Christian lists characteristic for the form of the directive that the name of the station is addressed with emphasis and that a series of stations is developed in order to represent the variety of relationships that bring a person into obligation.

3. These formal points of contact caused Martin Dibelius and his student Karl Weidinger to suppose that the household code schema in Col. 3:18–4:1 was taken over directly or through the mediation of Hellenistic Judaism from the popularized schema of the Stoic duty codes. It was initially Christianized only superficially by incorporation of motivating references to the Kyrios; in Ephesians and I Peter it was Christianized further. The occasion for taking over this parenesis was the delay of the parousia. The communities originally shaped by the imminent expectation and pneumatic enthusiasm (here I Corinthians 7 is unjustifiably generalized) had to adjust themselves again to the routine of the world and took over, therefore, the moral principles of those around them. The household codes "show . . . that Christian parenesis preserved for the average ethics of western culture the moral principles of the family espoused by popular Greek philosophy and the Jewish Halakah."[26]

---

26. Dibelius, *Epheser, Kolosser*, 49 (quoted); Weidinger, *Haustafeln*, 6-12. Merk stands very close to this view: The primary occasion for adopting the Hellenistic duty schema is not maintenance of the civil order, but the eschatological aspect: "Ἐν κυρίῳ are included both civil relationships and duties within the Church, but a new order under Christian considerations is no longer needed. . . . These admonitions 'seek not to transform the world but to change people toward the kingdom of God . . .'" (*Handeln aus Glauben*, 223, quoting M. Dibelius, "Das soziale Motiv im NT," *idem, Botschaft und Geschichte* [1956] I, 200). Differing is H. D. Wendland, "Vom Menschenbild des NT," *Dienst unter dem Wort* (FS H. Schreiner; Gütersloh, 1953), 306-327: "The Haustafeln proclaim rather: Here the Lord Jesus Christ begins . . . to change the world, as when, for example, forgiving love begins to operate . . . in the realm . . . of justice" (319).

But, despite individual points of contact noted with thoroughness, this basic view overlooks the different structures present in Hellenistic ethics. In I Peter, the stations in this world are not merely where the future kingdom of God is verified; they function, rather, as the witness for which the world is looking.

Heinz Dietrich Wendland also maintained that the station code was taken over from Hellenistic culture, but evaluated the Christian motivation for doing so differently. According to him, Christian adoption of the code schema altered the character of the conduct in the inherited life contexts. This conduct was fused into Christ's dominion and was, therefore, no longer "mere legality" and "joyless subordination to human domination and power." The directives are now "an application of the commandment to love one's neighbor and brother in the *oikos* and among the membership of the household."[27]

Undoubtedly this new motivation also changed conduct, but Wendland's explanation promotes a christocratic misunderstanding of social ethics, namely, a flattening out of the differences between the way of life in the Church and that in the worldly stations. This difference is, however, for Paul (cf. Rom. 12:19 and 13:4) as well as for I Peter (cf. 1:22f.; 4:8-11 and 2:13–3:7) clearly presupposed. Wendland does not recognize the peculiarity of NT social ethics because he uncritically appropriates Dibelius's tradition-historical hypothesis and thus overlooks the unique Christian shaping of the station code schema.[28]

4. These points of contact between the early Christian station ethic and the Stoic duty ethic, which greatly exceed those that were noted in regard to the OT and Jewish writings, can be made use of in looking at the emergence of the station code schema, if one also pays attention to the differences:[29]

a. The Stoic duty ethic speaks in the formal style of diatribe, while the NT station codes speak in the style of God's apodictic justice. The imperative "obey your parents" in Eph. 6:1 is, e.g., just as apodictic as the imperative of the fourth (fifth) commandment, which is added as confirmation. It is no coincidence that

---

27. Wendland, "Sozialethischen Bedeutung," 104-114, quotations from 107, 110.

28. Similarly, Lohse, *Colossians,* 156f., also sees what is new only in the motivation for conduct, but he interprets this more in the sense of the individual, personal ethos of decision:

> It is true that the content of the directives was taken from the cultural environment. The phrase "in the Lord," however, which introduces the new motivation, is not a mere formal element whose only function is to Christianize the traditional material. Rather, the entire life, thought and conduct of believers is subordinated to the lordship of the Kyrios. At the same time the words "in the Lord" set forth a critical principle which makes it possible to determine which ethical admonitions were considered binding for the community. Man's relationships with his fellow men are the field upon which the Christian proves his obedience to the Lord insofar as he conducts his life in "love" (ἀγάπη).

29. These differences were first observed clearly by David Schroeder and became the starting point of his fundamentally new structural analysis of the household code tradition. It is not his intention, as Merk (*Handeln,* 216f., especially n.115) and Lohse (*Colossians,* 154, n.4) misunderstand him, to replace the derivation from the Stoic duty codes with one from Jesus or from the OT justice of God, but to expand the tradition-historical connection to the Stoic duty codes with additional factors and, thereby, to correct the overly simplified concept of "transferal." See below, pp. 172-174 with n.43 on p. 175.

this formal style is also found in corresponding statements in Hellenistic Jewish writings on the stations: Pseudo-Phocylides (153-227 [*OT Pseudep.* II, 579-582]) gives words of advice from proverbial wisdom in the form of apodictic commandments. A reshaping of the Stoic ethics of relationships corresponding to the NT is apparently seen in the instructional sequence on the stations in Philo, *De Decalogo* 165-167.[30] To be sure, Philo does not formulate apodictic imperatives, but he does characterize the ethics of relationships, which he develops on the basis of Stoic tradition, as commandments that enlarge on the fourth commandment. Perhaps this pairing of directives outside the NT, which surfaces especially here and is characteristic of the NT station codes, is determined by the subordination of social partners to God's commandment, which is a factor in both the NT and Philo. Thus, the formulation of the station codes as apodictic imperatives is to be attributed without doubt to an OT and Jewish element of style.[31] This is also supported by the fact that in I Peter the Semiticizing imperatival participle is often used.[32]

b. Even the distinctive formal style, not simply the express reference to the Kyrios, articulates a fundamental substantive difference in structure from the Stoic duty codes. Stoicism urges one who is wise to achieve realization by accepting social relationships in accord with one's own logos. In the station codes, on the other hand, apodictic commandments instructs those who, in regard to social ties

---

30. LCL VII, 89:

In the fifth commandment on honouring parents we have a suggestion of many necessary laws drawn up to deal with the relations of old to young, rulers to subjects, benefactors to benefited, slaves to masters. For parents belong to the superior class of the above-mentioned pairs, that which comprises seniors, rulers, benefactors and masters, while children occupy the lower position with juniors, subjects, receivers of benefits and slaves. And there are many other instructions given, to the young on courtesy to the old, to the old on taking care of the young, to subjects on obeying their rulers, to rulers on promoting the welfare of their subjects, to recipients of benefits on requiting them with gratitude, to those who have given of their own intitiative on not seeking to get repayment as though it were a debt, to servants on rendering an affectionate loyalty to their masters, to masters on showing the gentleness and kindness by which inequality is equalized.

31. Also pointing to this commandment character as well as this background to the household code is Stuhlmacher, "Verantwortung," 179, n.21; he concludes that Colossians takes "at least the schema and the individual directives of its station code from Hellenistic Judaism. More precisely: it takes them from the Decalogue interpretation of the Diaspora synagogue, above all from the world-oriented interpretation of the fourth commandment current in that context" (177f.). This hypothesis is not supported by the material from Hellenistic Judaism and from early Christianity. It fails to take into account that the references to the Decalogue in both instances, including Eph. 6:1f., are secondary in terms of the history of tradition. It gives the NT station ethics a too narrow, Halakic character. It is quite probable, nevertheless, that the Decalogue, which is often quoted as a summary of the OT Law in early Christian parenesis, helped to provide the form in the shaping of the station codes.

32. See below, pp. 218f.

are, according to Paul, "free" (I Cor. 7:22) or, according to I Peter, "foreigners" (1:1; 2:11) in their stations and their corresponding obligations.

c. An immediate consequence of this difference of structure is that the NT station codes address considerably fewer stations than the Stoic duty codes or even the corresponding proverbial series in the wisdom tradition. This is, as in Rom. 13:1-7, an aspect of the "Christianizing" of the appropriated material.[33] Only the fundamental and indispensable forms of historical existence in society — marriage, parenthood, the workplace, and the civil order — are included. In these relationships one can be directed apodictically — if it is true that Christians are obligated to historical existence. For this question, however, it is decisive that the instructions in the station codes apply, according to the principle of relationship ethics, only to the social situation given historically, to one's station; they do not address an arrangement or order in the abstract, e.g., the existence of slavery as such. But within this limitation it can be said that the decision concerning the substantive presupposition of Christian ethics had been made long before the relationship ethics of the Stoic duty codes was appropriated (by way of popular Stoic philosophy and Hellenistic Judaism) and augmented in this independent way — certainly not without the participation of Paul[34] — by the Hellenistic Church.

The Contribution of the Jesus Tradition and the Earliest Christian Parenesis

1. Early Christianity did not begin just in its second generation to concern itself with the institutions of society as it adapted to a longer journey in history on account of the delay of the parousia. Already Jesus himself took a very clear and fundamentally new position toward marriage and the political order. His directives were expressed within the eschatological call to repentance: His saying against divorce (Mk. 10:11f. par. Mt.; Mt. 5:32 par. Lk.) intends primarily to eliminate "hardness of heart," which is predicted for the day of salvation (Mk. 10:1-9 par. Mt.). And the saying about paying taxes to the emperor is directed toward the total commitment of oneself to God (Mk. 12:13-17 par.). This eschatological perspective gives a new shape to social-ethical directives: It dislodges social-ethical questions from law and its casuistic application and from the pragmatic lessons of experience and orients them directly to the will of the Creator, i.e., the Lord of history. With regard to marriage, it regards the relationship between a man and a woman as established by the Creator; with regard to taxes, it points to the relationship of the people of Palestine to the Roman emperor as established in terms of history, just as the coin indicates: The coin declares that the emperor,

---

33. Cf. Merk, *Handeln,* 221: "Primary for the act of 'Christianizing' — however one may wish to judge it — was that . . . a selection was made and what was appropriated was only that which was useful and which demonstrated itself as necessary for the ordered life of the community while living within the organized relationships of this world."

34. The station code tradition is an application and extension of I Cor. 7:10, 20; Rom. 13:1-7.

as the possessor of civil power in this realm, makes commerce and travel possible; therefore, all are obligated to do justice to this relationship by paying taxes.[35] Jesus' eschatological summons to repentance thus removes the matter of obligation within the institutions of society from law and custom and transfers it in the manner of an ethics of relationship.

2. In Paul the directives of Jesus' eschatological summons to repentance have already become the parenetic tradition of the eschatological community. In I Cor. 7:10 he places Jesus' saying against divorce in the midst of a parenesis that prohibits — as a misunderstanding of that which is new — defection from marriage for the sake of the new existence and of Christian freedom. Paul emphasizes three times the principle that he — as he assures — presents in all the churches: "Let each remain in (the station of) one's calling in which he has been called (to faith)" — even the slave (7:20-24).[36]

This principle is applied positively in Rom. 13:1-7: Christians, like "everyone," are to subject themselves to the political authorities. In all probability Jesus' saying about paying taxes to the emperor contributed to the shaping of this parenesis; it stands certainly behind v. 7. It is essential, however, not that it echoes the wording of the saying, but that the parenesis emerges in harmony with Jesus' intent through a selection and reworking of Hellenistic principles about the civil order, principles that describe what has come about historically.[37]

The station code tradition that comes to the fore in Colossians is, therefore, in structure a direct application of these Pauline beginnings developed from the Jesus tradition.

3. The station code schema is, therefore, to be regarded as a genuinely Christian composition of a social ethic precisely because in it we have, not the application of an OT and Jewish tradition, but the reworking of a Hellenistic ethos on the basis of principles developed by Jesus and Paul. To put the matter pointedly: The station codes are not the result of a disappearance of eschatological self-understanding, but, to the contrary, the direct expression of such a self-understanding. Not coincidentally the genuine station code tradition recedes together with this self-understanding at the end of the first century. It is reduced, on the one hand, to congregational regulations and suppressed, on the other, in favor of traditional Jewish and Hellenistic proverbial wisdom.[38]

4. I Peter gives the station code tradition its own special focus. In this letter the code is intended to point the reader to a critical and responsible manner of life

---

35. According to the same principle, i.e., by reference to the relationships established in history, the parable of the Good Samaritan explains who one's neighbor is and the commandment to love one's neighbor is understood in a comprehensive sense (Lk. 10:30-37). See Goppelt, "Freiheit zur Kaisersteuer."

36. On I Cor. 7:20-24 and the issues of interpretation connected with it see P. Stuhlmacher, *Der Brief an Philemon* (EKK 18; Zurich/Neukirchen, 1975), 43ff.

37. See below, p. 181.

38. Cf. Weidinger, *Haustafeln,* 77ff.

in the institutions of society, which becomes a missionary witness. Responsible entry into the various structures of society for the Lord's sake, not an interim adaptation to that which remains for the present, was from the very beginning the intent of this parenetic tradition. This social-ethical principle is profoundly flexible. Social-ethical obligation is derived here neither from a legitimation principle nor from a social theory, but is located in practical realization within the structures existing from place to place. That the scope of the station code tradition intends this responsible entry into the structures of society that exist historically is made clear by the key clause of the instruction, which is not used comparably elsewhere, the stereotypical "subject yourselves."

The Obligation to Subject Oneself

1. Where the narrower ὑπακούετε, "be obedient," is not used, the polar directives of the station codes begin typically with the imperative ὑποτάσσεσθε,[39] "subject yourselves." Subjection is always required in relation to the emperor and his officials (Rom. 13:1, 5; I Pet. 2:13; cf. Tit. 3:1) and of wives in relation to their husbands (Col 3:18; Eph. 5:22, 24; I Pet. 3:1, 5; cf. Tit. 2:5). I Peter (2:18; cf. Tit. 2:9) also requires it of slaves, while Colossians (3:22) and Ephesians (6:5) require obedience (ὑπακούετε) of slaves and children (Col. 3:20; Eph. 6:1).[40] The two terms are not interchangeable; subjection can be demonstrated in obedience, e.g., among wives (I Pet. 3:6), but it speaks of a broader and more flexible relationship.

ὑποτάσσεσθαι, which is not found in classical Greek, is often used in Hellenistic Greek of subjection to rulers[41] and on occasion of subjection of wives to their husbands. Its use is, therefore, unlike that in I Peter, of situations involving constraint, not choice. Nowhere outside the NT station ethic does it refer to moral obligations in sequence; the Stoic duty codes never use it to instruct the reader in relationship obligations.[42] Therefore, use of the word was not transferred over

---

39. The grammatical form changes; see below, p. 175. See G. Delling, "τάσσω, ὑποτάσσω," *TDNT* VIII, 27–48; E. Kamlah, "'Υποτάσσεσθαι."

40. Subjection of children is also mentioned outside the station codes: Lk. 2:51 (of Jesus); I Tim. 3:4.

41. In the LXX only I Chr. 29:23f. is relevant: After Solomon was anointed king, ἐπήκουσαν αὐτοῦ πᾶς Ἰσραὴλ . . . ὑπετάγησαν αὐτῷ (they "pledged their allegiance/subjected themselves to him"). οἱ ὑποτεταγμένοι are often "vassals": *Ep. Arist.* 205, 207, and passim (*OT Pseudep.* II, 12ff.); Epictetus, *Dissertationes* 4.2.10 (LCL II, 309); further passages of this sort are listed in G. Delling, *TDNT* VIII, 39f.; cf. W. Dittenberger, ed., *Sylloge Inscriptionum Graecarum* supplement II (Leipzig, 1905), 718; see also below, p. 181.

42. It was first used of the wife by Plutarch, *Praecepta Coniugalia* 33 (LCL II, 323): ὑποτάττουσαι μὲν γὰρ ἑαυτὰς τοῖς ἀνδράσιν ἐπαινοῦνται, κρατεῖν (to have control) δὲ βουλόμεναι μᾶλλον τῶν κρατουμένων ἀσχημονοῦσιν; Pseudo-Callisthenes I.22.4 (*The Life of Alexander of Macedon*, tr. E. Haight [New York, 1955], 28), Alexander speaking to his mother: πρέπον γάρ ἐστι τὴν γυναῖκα τῷ ἀνδρὶ ὑποτάσσεσθαι, "to be subject [willingly] to her husband."

from the ethos of the environment; it articulates specifically Christian intentions.[43] But what are these intentions?

2. In the two oldest passages in which ὑποτάσσεσθαι is used in the manner of the station codes, it is linked with emphasis to other words from the root τάξις, "order." In Rom. 13:1f. four words of this root are clustered together.[44] It is, therefore, undoubtedly to be translated here and elsewhere in the station code tradition as "subject yourself."

Does this point to a binding order?[45] In relation to this question it is useful to consider a point made in another passage: In I Cor. 16:16, as in I Pet. 5:5 (see the comments there), one is directed to subject oneself within the congregation: εἰς διακονίαν τοῖς ἁγίοις ἔταξαν ἑαυτούς· ἵνα καὶ ὑμεῖς ὑποτάσσησθε τοῖς τοιούτοις. In I Corinthians this directive has an instructive background: Already in 14:40 the principle was put forward that in the congregation "everything should happen decently and in order (εὐσχημόνως καὶ κατὰ τάξιν)." This is the only passage in which the word τάξις itself, which is encountered in the NT only occasionally, is used of social relationships. The context in I Corinthians 14 brings τάξις together with εἰρήνη: "The spirit of the prophets should subject itself (ὑποτάσσεται) to the prophets; for God is not a God of disorder but of peace" (14:32). God wills "peace," שָׁלוֹם, a relationship of wholeness for all toward one another (cf. I Cor. 7:15)[46] and, in this sense, "order."

3. Already *I Clement* 20 (LCL AF I, 42-45) appropriates the Hellenistic concept of order, according to which order is the discernible principle of organization in the cosmos.[47] In the NT directive "to subject oneself," as in the OT[48] and Judaism,[49] order is a fundamentally historical entity. According to the NT this historical order is established by God in different ways. In Rom. 13:1 ὑποτάσσεσθαι is to place "oneself into an order established by God."[50] But more precisely, the political authorities, who are to maintain law and order and not just the state in

---

43. Schroeder, *Haustafeln* I, 117-121. See, among others, Refoulé, "Bible et éthique sociale"; Cothenet, "Réalisme."

44. According to the four occurrences of words of the root ταξ- in Rom. 13:1f., "Christians are to be 'subordinated,' for the powers are 'ordained' of God; whoever 'resisteth' (is subordinate) resists the 'ordinance' of God" (E. Brunner, *Justice and the Social Order* [tr. M. Hottinger; New York, 1945]; see further O. Cullmann, *Christ and Time* (tr. F. Filson; Philadelphia, 1964), 198ff.; O. Michel, *Der Brief an die Römer* (KEK 4; fifth ed., Göttingen, 1978), 393ff.

45. τάσσω is frequently used of appointment of representatives of the state, etc.; see Delling, *TDNT* VIII, 28.

46. See W. Foerster, "εἰρήνη," *TDNT* II, 412f.; Delling, *TDNT* VIII, 30, n.22.

47. H.-U. Minke, *Die Schöpfung in der frühchristlichen Verkündigung nach dem 1. Clemensbrief und der Areopagrede* (Dissertation, Hamburg, 1966), 27-36.

48. H. H. Schmid, *Gerechtigkeit als Weltordnung* (Tübingen, 1968), 169. Behind the OT terms צדק, שלם, and אמת stands the ancient oriental concept of world order.

49. Philo, *De Decalogo* 166 (LCL VII, 89), distinguishes between parents and children, rulers and ruled, masters and slaves as greater and lesser τάξεις, "classes."

50. Delling, *TDNT* VIII, 43f.

itself, are established by God, i.e., by his sovereignty in history. Among the other stations, lifelong monogamy is described as established by the Creator (Mk. 10:7f., par. Mt.; cf. I Cor. 6:16). But slavery is nowhere expressly derived from God: It is accepted as a historical reality that like all history is brought about by God under various conditions. Thus, subjecting oneself is necessary in the contingent situations established by God in history, by which it is made possible for people to live together on earth. Why these particular established relationships call for subjection is not reflected on. The question of the basis of subjection is combined with that of its shaping. It is not clarified, in any case, by a concept of order.

4. What is intended by the instruction "subject yourselves" can be understood from the situation of proclamation. The instruction is not directed against the zealot's rebellion against authority, but, according to the only direct data from the early period, I Corinthians 7, against ascetic-pneumatic emigration out of life's stations. The disorder in worship referred to in I Corinthians 14 is evidence of a misunderstood pneumatic-eschatological existence, as is the question that I Cor. 7:12ff., 20f. answers, namely, can a wife who is sanctified through faith (cf. 7:14) continue to live with a non-Christian husband in marriage? Can a slave who has become free through faith remain obligated to a non-Christian master? The Pauline principle states, as has become clear: "Each is to remain in the station in which he or she was called" (7:17, 20, 24).

This basic principle is applied positively in Rom. 13:1f. and in the station codes: "Subject yourselves" means primarily: Arrange your lives in terms of these stations. That this also means simply "subjection" is in accord with the customs of the period, as, e.g., Col. 3:18 declares in regard to marriage: "Subject yourselves . . . *as is seemly.*" It is for the first time in I Tim. 2:13-15 that the argument is against pneumatic-Gnostic emancipation, and there, on the basis of a speculative view of the history of creation, a misunderstanding of the wife's ὑποταγή is set forth.[51]

5. Subjection of oneself means primarily that the person who has become a "foreigner" in relation to society through the summons to faith nevertheless enters into the ways of life of the society in which he or she stands. The question then arises: How is this involvement to be shaped so that it does not become conformity? Conformity is, in fact, rejected in principle by NT ethics (Rom. 12:2; I Pet. 1:18; 4:3f.). I Peter introduces a word into the household code tradition that takes this into account: Christians are to "conduct themselves properly" (ἀγαθοποιεῖν) in the stations.

---

51. In Eph. 5:22f. such a misinterpretation is avoided by understanding the established order of creation in terms of its structure along the lines of the eschatological relationship of the Kyrios to his community: "The husband is the head of the wife as Christ is the head of the Church." In contrast, I Timothy 2 comes close to a tradition that appears in Josephus, *Contra Apionem* 2.201 (an interpolation? LCL I, 373): "The woman, says the Law, is in all things inferior to the man. Let her accordingly be submissive, not for her humiliation, but that she may be directed; for the authority has been given by God to the man."

"Proper Conduct" in Life's Stations

1. In the introduction to the station code in I Pet. 2:12, Christians are admonished first of all quite generally with respect to καλὴ ἀναστροφή, "good conduct," in society; such behavior should counter the accusation that they are κακοποιοί, "evil doers," "criminals," because it declares itself, as is initially said in a traditional expression, in καλὰ ἔργα, "good works." This directive is motivated in terms of apologetic-missionary appeal as well as pastoral care (cf. 4:15) and is summarized and specified by ἀγαθοποιεῖν, "proper conduct." This word is used of the conduct of the emperor's subjects (2:15), of slaves (2:20), of wives (3:6), and finally of all in their social relationships (3:17). It is encountered only rarely in the rest of the NT[52] and almost takes on the character of a technical term here in I Peter. Used along with it are also the cognate nouns ἀγαθοποιός (2:14) and ἀγαθοποιΐα (4:19), which do not appear elsewhere in the NT.

2. The verb is not used of conduct within the Church, which is described with the technical terms "brotherly love" (1:22f.; 3:8) and "serve" (4:10f.). ἀγαθοποιεῖν characterizes, instead, the conduct of Christians within society's structures. This conduct should be "good" or (better) "proper" in the sense that it supports and acknowledges in every way those representatives of the state who do justice to their vocation, since they are sent εἰς ἐκδίκησιν κακοποιῶν, ἔπαινον δὲ ἀγαθοποιῶν (2:14). It is also the behavior of a Christian in his or her worldly station on the basis of a "conscience bound to God," even as a slave (2:19f.). It is "the pure manner of life" (3:2) by which a Christian wife acts in accord with her marriage, without allowing herself to be influenced by human fear (3:6). "Proper conduct" is, therefore, the Christian way to do justice to the requirements of the worldly stations. It is linked with the demonstration of neighborly love in relation to all who are in need of such — even the enemy (3:9), but it is not identical to this love. For the author of I Peter, as for Paul, Christian involvement has a different shape in relation to the stations than it does in relation to the Church or one's neighbor (cf. Rom. 12:4-8, 10, 14; 13:4-6); yet, here too I Peter does not depend on Paul, as the differing terminology shows.[53]

3. Comparison of word usage elsewhere shows that the distinctiveness of ἀγαθοποιεῖν gives to I Peter a significant place in the history of Jewish and Christian ethics. I Peter developed this technical term, to be sure, from the unspecialized use of the word in Hellenistic Judaism[54] by modifying the Jewish and

---

52. Mk. 3:4 v.l. par. Lk. 6:9; Lk. 6:33, 35; III Jn. 11; Acts 14:17.

53. Paul does not use ἀγαθοποιεῖν (ποιεῖν ἀγαθόν, as in I Pet. 3:11, only in Eph. 6:8). He does use analogous constructions, such as ποιεῖν τὸ καλόν (Rom. 7:21; II Cor. 13:7; Gal. 6:9) and expressions with (κατ-)ἐργάζομαι and ἔργον; the Pastoral Epistles have καλὰ ἔργα and ἀγαθὸν ἔργον; occasionally one encounters ἀγαθοεργέω (I Tim. 6:18; Acts 14:17); ἀγαθοεργός as v.l. in Rom. 13:3; κακοποιέω in II Thess. 3:13.

54. In the LXX throughout for היטיב, usually of God's acts (Num. 10:32; Judg. 17:13; Zeph. 1:12; II Macc. 1:2; so also *Ep. Arist.* 242 [*OT Pseudep.* II, 28]), further of political acts of favor (I Macc. 11:33 A), of the good works of Judaism (Tob. 12:13 B), and of the

primitive Christian tradition of "good works" (2:12); it wished thereby to address also Hellenistic peoples who were oriented toward καλοκἀγαθία.[55]

After the NT ἀγαθοποιεῖν was used in *I Clement* and *Hermas* of Christian social conduct, but in fundamentally different ways. In *I Clem.* 2:2, 7 and similarly in 33:1; 34:2f. ἀγαθοποιΐα is used of life in the Church, which is given special recognition in 1:2f. (LCL AF I, 10-13, 48-51, 8-11). In *Hermas,* on the other hand, ἀγαθοποίησις is conduct which has validity in an especially Christian way, namely, intercession for those in need of help.[56] This understanding of ἀγαθοποιεῖν is also found in later Fathers[57] and corresponds to a great extent to the concept of "good works" in Judaism.

In rabbinic literature "good works" are referred to both in a wider sense as the fulfillment of the law and, more narrowly, as "alms," i.e., acts of benevolence and above all the "works of love," e.g., visiting the sick, giving hospitality to strangers, and helping at weddings and funerals.[58] The differentiation between "works of the law" and "works of love" was according to *m. Aboth* already current at the time of the NT, and already in Tob. 12:13 B the latter is called ἀγαθοποιεῖν. The differentiation is explained more precisely in *b. Berakoth* 32b baraita (translation from *The Babylonian Talmud. Seder Zera᾽im,* tr. I. Epstein [London, 1948], 200): "Our Rabbis taught: Four things require to be done with energy, namely, [study of] the Torah, good deeds, praying, and one's worldly occupation."

When one takes note of these shifting concepts about what good social conduct is,[59] then it becomes clear to what degree ἀγαθοποιεῖν represents in

---

demonstration of good that wins over one's opponent (*Test. Benj.* 5:2; *Test. Jos.* 18:2: ἀγαθοποιΐα [*OT Pseudep.* I, 826, 823]; cf. I Pet. 3:13). ἀγαθοποιός in Sir. 42:14 is not made more specific.

55. In early Christian writings only in Jas. 5:10 v.l.; Ignatius, *Eph.* 14:1 (LCL AF I, 189).

56. *Herm. Mand.* 8.10 (LCL AF II, 105f.):

To minister to widows, to look after orphans and the destitute, to redeem from distress the servants of God, to be hospitable, for in hospitality may be found the practice of good [ἀγαθοποίησις], to resist none, to be gentle, to be poorer than all men, to reverence the aged, to practise justice, to preserve brotherhood, to submit to insult, to be brave, to bear no malice, to comfort those who are oppressed in spirit, . . . those who are offended in the faith, give them courage, to reprove sinners, not to oppress poor debtors, and whatever is like to these things.

ἀγαθοποίησις has the same meaning in *Herm. Sim.* 5.3.4 (LCL AF II, 158f.; cf. 5.5-9 [*ibid.,* 158-161]) and ἀγαθοποιεῖν in *Vis.* 3.5.4; 3.9.5; *Sim.* 9.18.1f. (*ibid.,* 39, 51, 267f.), as well as probably in *II Clem.* 10:2 (*ibid.* I, 142f.).

57. Cyprian, *De Opere et Eleemosynis* (MPL IV, 602ff. [*ANF* V, 476-484]); Chrysostom, *Homiliae de Pentecoste* 1.6 (MPG L, 462f.): "After baptism are necessary . . . confession, alms, prayers, and other good works"; Cyril of Jerusalem, *Catecheses Illuminandorum* 15.26 (*NPNF* VII, 112f.).

58. *t. Pe᾽a* 4:19 (24) (*The Tosefta,* ed. J. Neusner [Hoboken, 1986], I, 73); cf. Str.-Bill. IV, 536f.

59. Seeing the same differences is van Uunik, "Teaching," 108f.: "Good works" are

the station code of I Peter a specifically NT statement of a Christian social ethic.[60]

4. How the proper conduct of Christians in the stations of society achieves shape in its realization is to be derived from the decisive key words of the station code: Involvement in the stations and in their particular rules for getting along (cf. ὑποτάσσεσθαι) is to be practiced according to criteria for which the decisive motivation is made clear in the words πάσῃ ἀνθρωπίνῃ κτίσει and διὰ τὸν κύριον (2:13). These criteria are applied in the practice of involvement through συνείδησις θεοῦ (2:19), the conscience directed toward God, and are thus made possible in life's stations by critical and responsible conduct.

2:13-17: The Civil Order[1]

13 Subject yourselves for the Lord's sake to every human creature,
  whether it be the emperor as the magistrate
14 or the governors as those sent by him
  in order to punish evildoers,
  but to commend those who conduct themselves properly;
15 for it is thus the will of God
  that you should bring to silence through proper conduct the
  foolishness of people who do not understand.

---

not in I Peter, as in Judaism, special works in relation to the poor, the deceased, etc.; rather, they apply to all. They are also not, as in the Church Fathers, specifically Christian, but secular. They correspond to the Greek understanding of that which is socially good, not to the ancient oriental understanding. Nor are they, as is sometimes claimed, signs of a de-eschatologizing. They are also not (this objection must be raised regarding the further developments in van Uunik's thinking) as generally intended as in Phil. 4:8, but are connected to the stations. ἀγαθοποιεῖν also does not stand simply as the Greek word for OT "love of neighbor," even if Lk. 6:33, 35 brings it into close proximity with love of neighbor.

60. Contra D. Georgi, "Predigt über 1 Petr 3,18f.22," *EvTh* 31 (1971), 187-192, specifically 188: "We wish to make our decision in favor of the aggressiveness of the statements about Christ in the early Christian Christ-hymn and against the fainthearted ethics of I Peter."

1. See Dibelius, "Rom und die Christen"; A. Strobel, "Zum Verständnis von Rm 13," *ZNW* 47 (1956), 67-93; E. Käsemann, "Röm 13,1-7 in unserer Generation," *ZThK* 56 (1959), 316-376; *idem*, "Principles of the Interpretation of Romans 13," *idem, NT Questions of Today* (tr. W. J. Montague; Philadelphia, 1969), 196-216; O. Cullmann, *The State in the NT* (tr. F. V. Filson; New York, 1956); G. Delling, *Römer 13,1-7 innerhalb der Briefe des NT* (Berlin, 1962); L. Goppelt, "Die Herrschaft Christi und die Welt," *idem, Christologie und Ethik* (Göttingen, 1968), 102-136; *idem*, "Der Staat"; *idem*, "Freiheit zur Kaisersteuer"; Souçek, "Gegenüber von Gemeinde und Welt"; Sleeper, "Political Responsibility"; Schrage, *Die Christen und der Staat*; Goldstein, "Politischen Paränesen"; Załęski, "Posłceszeństwo"; Botha, "Christian and Society"; Légasse, "Soumission aux Autorités"; Winter, "Seek the Welfare of the City."

16 *(Do this) as those who are free,*
    and not as those who use freedom as a pretext for evil,
    rather as servants of God.

17 *Honor all,*
    love the brotherhood,
    "fear God,
    honor the emperor."

Tradition and Form

The parenesis in I Pet. 2:13-17 overlaps with, among other passages in the NT, frequently with Rom. 13:1-7; I Tim. 2:1-3; and Tit. 3:1-3. There is apparently a common tradition behind these passages, which had its beginning in Jesus' saying on paying taxes to the emperor (Mk. 12:14-17 par.) and is continued in *I Clement* 61 (LCL AF I, 114-117) and in other Church Fathers.[2]

1. These NT passages not only agree in content by calling on Christians to acknowledge the state; they also formulate this directive to a large extent in similarly worded expressions.[3] What is required is always ὑποτάσσεσθαι (I Pet. 2:13; Rom. 13:1, 5; Tit. 3:1). Rulers are referred to variously as "supreme, governing over" (I Pet. 2:13: ὑπερέχων; Rom. 13:1: ὑπερεχούσαι; I Tim. 2:2: ἐν ὑπεροχῇ) and are designated in part by their titles (I Pet. 2:13: βασιλεύς; I Tim. 2:2: βασιλεῖς) and in part by their ranks (Rom 13:1: ἐξουσίαι; Tit. 3:1: ἀρχαὶ ἐξουσίαι).[4] Further, tending to justice is singled out as the task of the rulers (I Pet. 2:14: εἰς ἐκδίκησιν κακοποιῶν, ἔπαινον δὲ ἀγαθοποιῶν; Rom. 13:3f.: τὸ ἀγαθὸν ποίει . . . ἔπαινον . . . , ἔκδικος . . . τῷ τὸ κακὸν πράσσοντι; cf. I Tim. 2:2: ἵνα ἤρεμον καὶ ἡσύχιον βίον διάγωμεν). To be sure, these expressions represent, for the most part, customary Hellenistic terminology.[5] But this close contact among early Christian remarks in this area is the result not merely of customary forms of speech but of common ecclesiastical tradition. As it is, I Peter 2 has much closer contact in content and formulation with Romans 13 than with either passage from the Pastoral Epistles.

2. In formal style as well I Peter 2 and Romans 13 come very close. I Peter 2 follows the form of the station codes while Romans 13 prepares the way for this form structurally. The passages in the Pastoral Epistles, on the other hand, represent instructions to a pastor regarding either parenesis (Tit. 3:1-8) or intercession (I Tim. 2:1-3).

---

2. R. Knopf, *Die Lehre der zwölf Apostel. Die zwei Clemensbriefe* (HNT supplement 1; Tübingen, 1920), 146f. (excursus on *I Clem.* 61:1).

3. See the synoptic tables in Selwyn, 423-433.

4. In Lk. 12:11 τὰς ἀρχὰς καὶ ἐξουσίας replaces the Markan phrase (Mk. 13:9 par. Mt.) ἐπὶ ἡγεμόνων καὶ βασιλέων, in Lk. 21:12 the Markan phrase is retained, and in Lk. 20:20 the two are joined: παραδοῦναι αὐτὸν τῇ ἀρχῇ καὶ τῇ ἐξουσίᾳ τοῦ ἡγεμόνος.

5. See below, p. 187, n.41, and pp. 181f., nn. 9-11.

3. It is all the more noteworthy that I Peter and Romans 13 are very different in their placement of the theological-kerygmatic accent. I Peter does not refer to God's establishment and commissioning of rulers, as does Rom. 13:1f., 4. Paul makes his point — presumably in view of a lingering Jewish reservation about paying taxes and a Christian fanaticism that would relativize the importance of civil government[6] — that Christians are obligated to the civil officials as commissioned by God "for the sake of conscience" (Rom. 13:5). I Peter describes the emperor and his officials in view of the situation of conflict as "creatures" (2:13) to whom honor is due, as to all people (v. 17). It understands the subjection that is required as a demonstration of Christian freedom, intended also to counter suspicions (vv. 15f.). It is hardly coincidental that along with this 5:13, with the key word "Babylon," brings an entirely different parenetic tradition to bear on the political realm. In I Peter 2 and Romans 13, therefore, a single early Christian tradition is shaped differently in view of different situations of proclamation.

4. Regarding the origin of this parenetic tradition two sources can be named: (a) This sort of position toward the state was given to Christians in Jesus' saying about paying taxes to the emperor in Mk. 12:13-17 — in opposition to both nomistic reservations and a euphoric view of the state that extends even into Hellenistic Jewish literature. It is no coincidence that this saying of Jesus appears to be echoed in Rom. 13:7.[7] (b) In this way the Hellenistic, especially Hellenistic Jewish, tradition of political ethics was adopted and aided the development of the content of these early Christian parenetic traditions. In the political ethos of the Hellenistic world one spoke of ὑποτασσόμενοι, the *subjecti*,[8] in relation to the ὑπερέχοντες, those who rule,[9] and of ἔπαινος, "praise," for good citizens.[10] That enforcing justice by prosecuting evildoers and commending those who do good is the main task of rulers is emphasized in the broadly developed portrayal of the magistrate in the *Letter of Aristeas* (187-300), which comes out of Hellenistic Judaism.[11]

---

6. The Scillitan martyrs declared: *Ego imperium huius seculi non cognosco,* "I do not recognize the empire of this world"; Latin in: R. Knopf and G. Krüger, ed., *Ausgewählte Märtyrerakten* (third ed., Tübingen, 1929), 28f.; English translation in H. Musurillo, *The Acts of the Christian Martyrs* (Oxford, 1972), 86-89.

7. Delling, *TDNT* VIII, 44: "R. 13 itself would also appear to be an interpretation of Jesus' answer to the question as to His attitude to Roman rule, Mk. 12:17 and par."

8. See below, n.17.

9. Cf. BAGD s.v.; e.g., Diogenes Laertius 6.78 (LCL II, 81).

10. Antoninus Pius says in a letter: ἔτι καὶ διὰ τοῦτο προθυμοτέρους ἡγεῖσθε τοὺς πολείτας ὑμῶν ἔσεσθαι τῶν καλῶν τοῦ ἐπαίνου χάριν (L. Lafoscade, *De epistulis (aliisque titulis) imperatorum magistratuumque Romanorum* (Insulis, 1902), no. 38, 19; additional material in Strobel, "Rm 13," 84f. Philo apparently combines this thought with the next when he remarks in *Legatio ad Gaium* 7 (LCL X, 7) that the law fulfills its role as it brings "honours for things good and punishment for things evil."

11. *Ep. Arist.* 291f. (*OT Pseudep.* II, 32):

What is the most important feature in a kingdom? To this he replied, "To establish the subjects continually at peace, and guarantee that they obtain justice quickly in

These points of correspondence also cover essentially the scope of the NT statements, though, compared to the Hellenistic ethos of the state, they represent but
a meager assortment. Even *Aristeas* has more to say; e.g., that those who rule
should maintain and promote life among the people.[12] The NT tradition identifies
as the reason for subjection only the most basic function of civil order.

5. Alongside the NT tradition nourished by these sources and utilized in
I Pet. 2:13-7, there emerges in 5:13 a tradition developed from OT and Jewish
apocalypticism in early Christian apocalypticism and finding expression in the NT
above all in Revelation 13 and 17.[13] I Peter shows that the two traditions do not
exclude one another at a substantive level — when one is able to understand the
letter itself as a unity.[14]

Vv. 13-15: Subjection for the Sake of the Lord

13   The imperative ὑποτάγητε, "subject yourselves," which as the guiding directive continues through the following parenesis (2:18; 3:1), its
motivation, "for the Lord's sake," which also continues to be presupposed, and the very general object, "every human creature," which is
made specific in the following clause, allow this verse to be the programmatic introduction of the entire station code. This is the case even
though the verse introduces directly only the first part, i.e., the directive
for conduct in relation to representatives of the state.

The subjection to which one is obligated in the station code tradition is πάσῃ ἀνθρωπίνῃ κτίσει, "to every human creature." κτίσις is for
Hellenistic people above all the "foundation," e.g., the foundation of a
city, in which the architectural, economic, and social intentions of the
founder take shape.[15] In biblical Greek it is always seen from the
perspective of God as "creation" or the "created thing."[16] But this

---

verdicts. The sovereign brings about these aims when he hates evil and loves good
and holds in high esteem the saving of a human life. In the same way that you consider
injustice the greatest evil. . . .

One should appoint as governors, "Men who hate wickedness, and . . . do justice. . . ."
(280; *ibid.*, 31).

12. *Ep. Arist.* 240 (*OT Pseudep.* II, 28): "By realizing that God has given to legislators the
purpose of saving men's lives, you would follow them"; 279 (*ibid.*, 31): "Whose guidance must
kings follow? . . . The laws, so that by practicing justice they may improve the lives of men."

13. See the comments on 5:13.

14. In this regard see above, pp. 19f.

15. W. Foerster, "κτίζω," *TDNT* III, 1025, 1027f.

16. *Ibid.*, 1027f.

interpretation appears to provide no meaning here.[17] But the word in this context becomes immediately understandable once it is recognized that it expresses, as "foundation," not only a genetic fact of life but primarily an intention. "Created thing" means not only that human existence comes from God and is not self-generated, but also that humanity is destined to a course of life in history. Thus, the subjection is "to every human creature," i.e., to every human being in the destiny that the Creator, as Lord of history, has given to that one. Thus, it applies first of all "to the emperor as sovereign."

Subjection is commanded διὰ τὸν κύριον, "for the Lord's sake." This motivation, which is part of the station code tradition from the very beginning, sounds rather paradoxical here after what has appeared in the letter to this point — and linked to the emperor, who was also called κύριος.[18] Has not the exalted Christ (Christ, not God, is meant here by ὁ κύριος)[19] freed those who belonged to him from the ties of "the ways of conduct inherited from the fathers," which shape the physical existence of creatures in their historical destiny (1:18; cf. 4:3f.) and transferred them into the eschatological existence "of foreigners" (2:11)? But it is just for this reason that Christians should, in fact, subject themselves, not to any person in his or her physical existence, but to that person in the destiny given to him or her as a created one.

This is commanded, however, really for the sake of the exalted Redeemer, as became clear above all in the debate over the "chris-

---

17. For this reason, the following meanings have been deduced from Greek usage: "every human order" (Windisch, 63), "every human institution [of civil authorities]" (BAGD s.v. κτίσις 2), "every fundamental social institution" (Selwyn, 172). These translations, which are not otherwise to be found, run counter, however, to the context, which speaks of subjection to persons, not institutions. Already the Syrian and, in part, the Latin versions follow biblical usage with "every human *creature*" (Vulgate: "subiecti igitur estote omni humanae creaturae"). This translation is held emphatically by Schlatter, *Erläuterungen zum NT* III (Stuttgart, 1928), 37; J. Jeremias, "ἄνθρωπος," *TDNT* I, 366f.; Foerster, *TDNT* III, 1034f.; Kelly, 108 ("human creature").

18. A. Deissmann, *Light from the Ancient East* (tr. L. Strachan; second ed., London, 1927), 353-361; cf. Acts 25:26.

19. So also Schlatter, *Erläuterungen* II, 37f.; Preisker in Windisch-Preisker, 15, 154. The counterarguments that 2:15a points to "God's will" (Schelkle, 73 with n.2) and that subjection beneath the creature is given foundation through the Creator (Kelly, 109) are not convincing, since the will of the Creator is now carried out for the sake of the exalted Lord. The constant motivation of the household code tradition, appropriated here, refers, therefore, to the "Kyrios" (Col. 3:20, 22, 23, 24; 4:1; Eph. 6:7, 8, 9; "Christ" in Eph. 5:25, 29, 32; 6:5). This traditional context points to a corresponding meaning in I Pet. 2:13, even though absolute ὁ κύριος is not otherwise used in I Peter of the exalted Christ.

tocratic" interpretation.[20] After all, this One is one with the Creator; through him everything has been created, as the early Hellenistic Church confessed.[21] Therefore, those who belong to him are also subject to the will of the Creator, who sustains historical life in patience for the realization of the redemption already accomplished in the counsel of God. The biblical person knows this will of God from Genesis 9.

Though it is not stated explicitly in I Peter or elsewhere in the NT, the idea that historical life is held together by working within life's stations is known to Judaism.[22] I Peter is quick to develop a soteriological foundation here which includes this concept indirectly: Christians should prepare the way for the "visitation" of all by proper behavior within society's structures (2:12, 15f.).[23] They serve the achievement of redemption also by obeying the will of the Creator[24] — "for the sake of the Lord." Thus, this motivation, though adopted through formulaic channels, points to a comprehensive and substantive context. Obviously this motivation implies decisive criteria for the nature of subjection.

Accordingly, emphasis continues to be given just as clearly to the side of being duty bound as to that of critical distance in consideration of the "human creations" first named here — the emperor and his officials.[25] The motivation "for the Lord's sake" removes from the βασιλεύς,

---

20. This interpretation was represented in NT research primarily by O. Cullmann, "The Kingship of Christ and the Church in the NT," *idem, The Early Church* (London, 1956), 103-37; *idem, Christ and Time* (tr. F. Filson; Philadelphia, 1950), 191-194. In systematic theology it is represented by E. Wolf, "Was heißt 'Königsherrschaft Christi' heute?" *Unter der Herrschaft Christi* (BEvTh 32, ed. E. Wolf; Munich, 1961), 67-91. Opposing it have been certain representatives of "kerygmatic theology": G. Bornkamm, "Christ and the World in the Early Christian Message," *idem, Early Christian Experience* (tr. P. L. Hammer; London/New York, 1969), 14-28; in a modified way, E. Käsemann, "On the Subject of Primitive Christian Apocalyptic," *NT Questions of Today* (tr. W. Montague; Philadelphia, 1969), 108-137, particularly 132-137. A third point of view is represented by L. Goppelt, "The Lordship of Christ and the World according to the NT," *Lutheran World* 14 (1967) 15-39, especially 30-33. Reports on the status of research are found in W. Schrage, *Die konkreten Einzelgebote in der paulinischen Paränese* (Gütersloh, 1961), 13-48; H. J. Gabathuler, *Jesus Christus, Haupt der Kirche — Haupt der Welt. Der Christushymnus Colosser 1,15-20 in der theologischen Forschung der letzten 130 Jahre* (AThANT 45; Zurich/Stuttgart, 1965).

21. I Cor. 8:6; Col. 1:16.

22. On Jewish tradition see pp. 166f.

23. Elsewhere in the NT, Rom. 3:26 speaks of the time "of God's patience" (cf. 2:4), Acts 14:15-17 and 17:24-28 of God's preserving providence, and I Tim. 2:1-5 of the preservation of the life of Christians for the deliverance of all.

24. A soteriological aspect of Christian conduct in relation to government is also encountered in I Tim. 2:2f.

25. I Tim. 2:1f. also moves from the obligation for "all" to the obligation for "kings."

the "king," the sacral and ideological splendor with which both the continuation of the ancient oriental cult of the ruler and political philosophy and poetry had surrounded him.[26]

The βασιλεύς is here,[27] as earlier in oriental usage,[28] the "great king," the Roman emperor, who is called Καῖσαρ in Mk. 12:14, 16 par. and elsewhere in the NT; the designation βασιλεύς has here a different ring than in usage of the same word for local princes.[29] But I Peter uses the designation, as does the parallel tradition in I Tim. 2:2 and *I Clem.* 37:3, merely as a civil-legal term precisely because the author, as the following indirect disclaimer shows, is well aware of the term's sacral and ideological association. The emperor is the ὑπερέχων, i.e., in a common civil-legal technical term, the "one placed over," the "sovereign."[30]

14 The ἡγεμόνες, the provincial "governors,"[31] are "sent," i.e., commissioned by the emperor: δι' αὐτοῦ πεμπόμενοι. Their commission is described here, like the position of the emperor, only in civil-legal terms and is not, as in Rom. 13:1f., 4f., traced directly back to God. The commission "to prosecute evildoers and to commend those who conduct themselves properly" (εἰς ἐκδίκησιν κακοποιῶν, ἔπαινον δὲ ἀγαθοποιῶν) corresponds to the Hellenistic, especially Jewish Hellenistic, ethos of the state,[32] as does the early Christian tradition in Rom. 13:3f., which makes use of the same ethos. I Peter refers to the emperor's commission of governors, not in order to analyze empirical circumstances, but in order to describe the historical destiny of the civil executive according to the will of God. "Commending the upright" referred actually to freely con-

---

26. "The early Greek idea of the divinity of a politically creative personality linked up in Hellenism with the views of divine kingship current among different civilised peoples of the Orient" (H. Kleinknecht, "βασιλεύς," *TDNT* I, 565).

27. As in 2:17; I Tim. 2:2; Rev. 17:9ff.; *I Clem.* 37:3 (LCL AF I, 73).

28. Deissmann, *Light,* 367f.; cf. Rev. 17:9f.

29. So, e.g., Mt. 2:1, 3; 14:9, and passim. See K. L. Schmidt, "βασιλεύς," *TDNT* I, 576f.

30. See n.4 above.

31. They could be referred to — each according to his position — as "proconsul," i.e., civil governor of a senatorial province, as "legatus," i.e., military commander in an imperial province, or as "procurator," i.e., administrator of taxation revenues and judge in important cases. See BAGD s.v.; G. Wesenberg, "Pro consule," PW XXIII/1, cols. 1232-1234; H.-G. Pflaum, "Procurator," PW XIII/1, cols. 1240-1279; B. Reicke, "Statthalter," *BHH* III, cols. 1857f.; G. R. Watson, "Legati," *OCD* 591; E. Badian, "Pro Consule," *OCD* 880f.; F. G. B. Millar, "Procurator," *OCD* 881f.; A. N. Sherwin-White, *Roman Society and Roman Law in the NT* (Oxford, 1963), 1-23.

32. See n.10 above.

ferred commendations,[33] which were bestowed on worthy citizens in public documents and inscriptions and which conveyed political esteem. But here it is used formulaically of merely civic recognition and thereby the legal protection that all who conduct themselves properly can expect.[34] The references to this commission and to the emperor's position in history provide additional foundation, as the twofold ὡς in vv. 13-14 indicates, to subjection "for the sake of the Lord."[35]

15 This verse supplies an additional motivation in a causal ὅτι clause, which applies the principle of 2:12 to the political situation and describes it as θέλημα τοῦ θεοῦ. It is, as in 4:2, "God's will" that claims Christians for the good, for that which brings salvation to all,[36] even as it also causes them to experience suffering (3:17; 4:19). Christians are to[37] "bring to silence" (φιμοῦν) through ἀγαθοποιεῖν the discrimination mentioned in 2:12.

Such discrimination arises from "the ignorance of foolish people." One who is ἄφρων, "foolish," is, according to a typical statement in Jewish wisdom,[38] one who does not see God or, therefore, truth and justice. Such a person is found in ἀγνωσία, "ignorance,"[39] and does not know what he or she is doing. Therefore, such a person's steps are not without guilt, but are certainly forgiveable before God and humans.[40] For this very reason, Christians have no cause "to return evil for evil" in relation to society;

---

33. Since importance was enjoyed only by the person who was recognized in the political community, ἔπαινος, "praise," "recognition," was a life goal in the polis culture, as, e.g., "righteousness" was the highest of life values for the OT community; in Sir. 39:10; 44:8, 15 "praise" stands for righteousness. Cf. H. Preisker, "ἔπαινος," *TDNT* II, 586f.

34. Strobel, "Rm 13" (see n.1 above), 80-83, rejects with regard to Rom. 13:3 the explanation of "recognition" (so Kühl, K. Barth, and Althaus on that verse) and sees there merely a reference to commendations, for which he offers numerous documentary supports. In parenesis addressed to Christians, however, the statement only makes sense in the extended meaning developed above.

35. On usage of ὡς see below, p. 188, n.46.

36. To do God's will and to be receptive to God's encounters is, according to the entire NT, the destiny of being a Christian. In this regard, cf. G. Schrenk, "θέλω, θέλημα," *TDNT* III, 57ff.

37. The οὕτως does not reach back to what has gone before (contra Selwyn, 173; Kelly, 110), but introduces, like τοῦτο in I Thess. 4:3; Jn. 6:40 and the similar expression in Mt. 18:14, that which follows.

38. ἄφρων occurs seventy-five times in the LXX of Proverbs, which thus has more than half of all LXX occurrences. In the NT the word is used elsewhere with similar meanings in Lk. 11:40; 12:20; Rom. 2:20. Cf. G. Bertram, "φρήν," *TDNT* IX, 225.

39. ἀγνωσία occurs elsewhere in the NT only in I Cor. 15:34. ἄγνοια has the same sense in I Pet. 1:14; Acts 3:17; 17:30; Eph. 4:18, as does the verb ἀγνοεῖν in Acts 13:27; 17:23 (Rom. 10:3); I Tim. 1:13; Heb. 5:2; II Pet. 2:12.

40. Cf. Lk. 23:34 v.l.; Acts 3:17; 17:30; I Tim. 1:13; Heb. 5:2; 10:26.

rather, they should "overcome" evil "with good" (3:9; cf. Rom. 12:21). Here this is done by countering suspicions with proper conduct.

ἀγαθοποιεῖν is, as in the preceding verse, not the demonstration of love for one's enemy, e.g., "blessing" (3:9), which outdistances categories of law, but the proper conduct according to which the civil authorities judge citizens when they do justice to their commission. This proper conduct includes observation of civic laws — v. 14 and 4:15 have these primarily in mind — but first and foremost "subjecting oneself," i.e., loyalty as such.

Are suspicions thereby "silenced"? The apologetics of the pre-Constantinian Church teaches otherwise. Suspicions are not dispelled when in court Christians are found guilty of nothing illegal (4:15), since their overall conduct remains open to various interpretations by others. The "foolish" are really first brought to silence when they become wise — "on the day of visitation" (2:12). When the expectation of success[41] reaches this deeper level, then "proper conduct" actually receives its foundation, i.e., in the sense conveyed in 2:12.

Vv. 16f.: The Freedom of Christians as the Basis for Social-Political Conduct

16 Proper conduct is not only grounded in the goal of Christian existence but also in its root: Christians are ἐλεύθεροι, "free," but they are so only as δοῦλοι θεοῦ, "servants of God." It is not coincidental that the letter addresses the problem of freedom at the beginning of its message concerning the institutions of society and especially in view of the tense political situation; it does not otherwise mention the problem of freedom.

The Background of the Statement about Freedom in 2:16f.[42]

1. That only the δοῦλος of God is an ἐλεύθερος and that for this reason freedom cannot be a pretext for living in excess calls to mind, in both terminology and content, Paul's words: "You have been freed from sin and have become God's slaves" (Rom. 6:22); "You were called to freedom, but do not use your freedom as an opportunity for the flesh, but through love be servants (δουλεύετε) of one

---

41. Indeed going beyond *Ep. Arist.* 257 (*OT Pseudep.* II, 30): "The human race deals kindly with those in subjection."

42. See M. Dibelius, *James* (Hermeneia, tr. M. Williams, ed. H. Koester; Philadelphia, 1975/76), 116f. (excursus on Jas. 1:25); H. Schlier, "ἐλεύθερος," *TDNT* II, 487-502; K. Niederwimmer, *Der Begriff der Freiheit im NT* (Berlin, 1966); D. Nestle, *Eleutheria* I (Tübingen, 1967); E. Käsemann, *Jesus Means Freedom* (tr. F. Clarke; London, 1969).

another" (Gal. 5:13; cf. I Cor. 9:19; II Pet. 2:18f.). But even in this statement I Peter is not directly dependent on Paul, in neither terminology nor perspective.

2. Freedom, associated as it is here with the political realm, was in Palestinian Judaism at the center of discussion. According to Josephus's apologetic report the Zealots had a "passion" for liberty and were "convinced that God alone [was] their leader and master."[43] Pharisaic Judaism practiced a quietistic freedom in relation to the Roman authorities because it followed the rule that "no one is a free man but he who is occupied with study of Torah."[44] The term "freedom," which was foreign to the OT, was appropriated even in Palestinian Judaism from the Greek world.

3. Philo varied this connection between freedom and obligation to the law in his work *Quod Omnis Probus Liber Sit,* which is contemporaneous with I Peter, along the lines of Stoic philosophy: Just as those living not under tyranny but according to the law are free from government, so those who live according to the law are free in distinction to those over whom wrath and passion dominate (*Quod Omnis* 45 [LCL IX, 36f.]). According to Stoicism the wise person becomes inwardly free when he applies himself to the law of world reason.[45]

The freedom that I Peter calls on as the ground and means of "subjection"[46] comes not from voluntary subordination to a law, but according to the explanation in 1:18, using OT and Jewish terminology, from "redemption": Those who believe are free from inherited ways of behavior because they were ransomed by God to be his possession, i.e., they became his servants.[47] Therefore, even in the political realm they are no longer dependent on securing their existence by being time-servers. But through their relationship with God, their Creator and Redeemer, they bear, nevertheless, an obligation to civil authorities, as well as to justice.

---

43. Josephus, *Antiquitates Judaicae* 18.23 (LCL IX, 21); cf. *De Bello Judaico* 2.118 (LCL II, 366-369).

44. *m. Aboth* 6:2 (cf. Str.-Bill. II, 522).

45. Seneca, *De Vita Beata* 15.7 (LCL II, 141): "deo parere libertas est"; Epictetus, *Dissertationes* 4.1.158 (LCL II, 299), of Diogenes: . . . ὅτι οὐδενὸς δέομαι, ὅτι ὁ νόμος μοι πάντα ἐστὶ καὶ ἄλλο οὐδέν. ταῦτα ἦν τὰ ἐλεύθερον ἐκεῖνον ἐάσαντα.

46. The threefold ὡς in v. 16, like the twofold ὡς in v. 14, has a causal meaning; the subject and predicate are found with ὑποτάγητε in v. 13.

47. θεοῦ δοῦλοι is an OT expression for those whom God takes into service and thereby blesses. As such it is not found in Paul's letters, as in Lk. 2:29; Acts 16:17; Tit. 1:1; and Rev. 1:1. Regarding the content of the statement, cf. I Cor. 7:22f.: "He who was free when called is a slave of Christ. You were bought with a price: Do not become slaves of humans." According to Rom. 6:18, speech about "being a slave" as a designation for freedom is actually inappropriate; this is especially the case when it is understood in Greek terms: "How can a man be happy if he is a slave to anybody at all?" (Plato, *Gorgias* 491E [LCL V, 411]). Cf. Mt. 17:26: "Then the sons are free"; similarly Jn. 8:36.

Freedom would be ἐπικάλυμμα τῆς κακίας, "a pretext for evil,"[48] were it understood libertinistically or ascetically as exemption from this obligation to civil authorities. This misunderstanding of Christian freedom came into the Church from Gnostic streams of thought.[49] It arose, however (even without theoretical development), out of human failure; the author may be thinking here primarily about this (in light of 4:15).

17 Social-political obligation is finally summarized in a four-part sentence, which has its focus in the last part.[50] The four clauses belong together in pairs.

The first pair is quite consciously stated, like v. 13a, in general terms: πάντας τιμήσατε, τὴν ἀδελφότητα ἀγαπᾶτε. Christians demonstrate honor[51] to all people, not only to the powerful and the rich but also to slaves, who are without honor and without rights; all are taken seriously as creatures of God and are thus recognized as human beings.[52] But love, a mutual, deliberate posture of assistance, binds the members of the Church to one another as "brotherly love" (ἀδελφότης).[53] This distinction — honoring all, loving the brothers — is not a renunciation of love for neighbor:[54] The differentiation became necessary from the term for love, since ἀγαπᾶν means "demonstrate love," referring not merely to an orientation like the philanthropy of Stoicism.[55] The demonstration of love is necessarily restricted to the immediate and regular shared life in the community of faith and to the actual and immediate encounter with the neighbor.

---

48. ἐπικάλυμμα in the NT only here (four occurrences of κάλυμμα in II Cor. 3:13-16), otherwise a known phrase: Menander, fragment 90 ("The Boetian Girl" = LCL, 322f.): πλοῦτος δὲ πολλῶν ἐπικάλυμμ' ἐστὶν κακῶν; Philo, *De Decalogo* 172 (LCL VII, 91): τὸ μὴ ποιεῖσθαι προκάλυμμα πίστιν ἀπιστίας.

49. I Cor. 7:17-24; I Tim. 4:1-5: "who forbid marriage . . . ; everything created by God is good . . ."; cf. II Pet. 2:18f.

50. See E. Bammel, "Commands."

51. This general giving of honor is not mentioned elsewhere in the NT and comes close to statments in proverbial wisdom about honor; see G. von Rad, *Wisdom in Israel* (tr. J. Martin; London, 1972), 81f.

52. See the comments on 2:7; 3:7.

53. ἀδελφότης appears in the NT only here and in 5:9, also in *I Clem.* 2:4 (LCL AF I, 11, 13); already in the LXX it is used both literally (IV Macc. 9:23; 10:3, 15, and elsewhere) and figuratively (I Macc. 12:10, 17, of a brotherhood established by a covenant). Just as the members of the OT and Jewish community called themselves ἀδελφοί, so also according to the NT did the members of the Christian community; see the comments on 1:22; 3:8; 4:8. See H. von Soden, "ἀδελφός," *TDNT* I, 145f.

54. See the comments on 1:22; 3:9.

55. M. Pohlenz, *Die Stoa* I (fourth ed., Göttingen, 1970), 316: For Seneca *humanitas* is "philanthropy, the disposition that is stirred deep inside by everything that affects the other person."

The second double line, τὸν θεὸν φοβεῖσθε, τὸν βασιλέα τιμᾶτε, is directed, perhaps in dependence on Prov. 24:21,[56] to the expression that concludes the whole sequence: "Honor the emperor." This was appropriate according to the Hellenistic ethos.[57] That obligation is now placed, however, in proper perspective: "Honor" is due to the emperor as fundamentally to all people, but "fear" is due, however, only to God. This is so because God alone determines existence and non-existence. Fear before God also stands out in I Peter, with an emphasis found in no other NT document, as a motivation for parenesis — above all, for social ethics; this becomes evident again immediately afterward in v. 18. Therefore, the letter is silent about the fear that, according to Hellenistic tradition, is due to human authorities.[58] It thereby distances itself clearly from both preceding and (especially) later early Christian statements, particularly from Rom. 13:(3f.)7, which appropriates this Hellenistic ethos and thereby lends support to the view that earthly masters are representatives of the heavenly master.[59]

2:18-20: The Position of Slaves[1]

18 *You slaves,*
     subject yourselves in all fear to (your) masters,
     not only to the good and kind ones, but also to those who are
     unpleasant.
19 *For this is grace,*
     if one on account of one's conscience (bound) to God endures
     suffering
     while suffering unjustly.
20 *For what sort of glory is it*
     if you commit an offense and, being punished (for it), endure?
     But if you conduct yourself properly and suffering (for that)
     endure,
     this is grace with God.

---

56. φοβοῦ τὸν θεόν, υἱέ, καὶ βασιλέα. If this was the model then it is all the more significant that I Peter differentiates between God and the emperor.

57. Strobel, "Rm 13," 83f.

58. H. Balz, "φοβέω," *TDNT* IX, 193.

59. Eph. 5:33: A woman should fear her husband; vv. 21f.: She should subject herself to him "out of fear of [RSV 'reverence for'] Christ" "as to the Lord." Still stronger is *Did.* 4:11 (LCL AF I, 317; cf. *Barn.* 19:7 [*ibid.*, 493, 495]): "But you who are slaves be subject to your master, as to God's representative, in reverence and fear."

Tradition and Social Situation

1. Instruction for slaves becomes in I Peter the focal point of the station code. The conflict situation of Christians in society, which the letter addresses, comes into sharp relief especially among slaves. The detailed instruction to them has exemplary meaning, therefore, for all Christians in all earthly stations.

2:18 follows the station code tradition for slaves as it was given substantive foundation in I Cor. 7:21, took prominent shape in Col. 3:22 and Eph. 6:5, and was repeated in *Did.* 4:11 and *Barn.* 19:7 (LCL AF I, 316f., 402-405). In all these passages the parenesis is presented as address followed by imperative and motivation. The motivation always refers to fear (before God) or to the heavenly Lord. According to Colossians and Ephesians slaves should conduct themselves in relation to their earthly masters ὡς τῷ κυρίῳ or Χριστῷ, according to the *Didache* and *Barnabas* ὡς τύπῳ (likeness) θεοῦ. But in I Pet. 2:19 slaves are instructed to be prepared διὰ συνείδησιν θεοῦ to suffer injustice.[2] In I Tim. 6:1, Tit. 2:9f., and Ignatius, *Pol.* 4:3, the tradition has been altered significantly.

2. The common tradition in Col. 3:22-25 and Eph. 6:6-8 is developed kerygmatically in a different direction in I Pet. 2:19-21. In Colossians and Ephesians "eye service" is proscribed. In I Peter the slave is encouraged to nonconformity even in relation to difficult masters. In Colossians and Ephesians total obedience in one's respective station is connected to the exalted Lord in order to give foundation to deliberate and honest conduct in relation to the earthly master. I Peter, on the other hand, refers to the "conscience-bond to God" in order to urge slaves toward "proper conduct" — even in situations of injustice and even if this brings "suffering" with it. The different directions of development condition in particular the different formulations, e.g., in Ephesians and Colossians "obey" over against "subject yourselves" in I Peter.

---

1. See H. Gülzow, *Christentum und Sklaverei in den ersten drei Jahrhunderten* (Bonn, 1969; further bibliography); Str.-Bill. IV, 698-744 (excursus on "Das altjüdische Sklavenwesen"); H. Greeven, *Das Hauptproblem der Sozialethik in der neueren Stoa und im Urchristentum* (Gütersloh, 1935), 28-41; T. Wiedemann, *Greek and Roman Slavery* (Baltimore, 1981); W. L. Westermann, "Sklaverei," PW Suppl. VI, 894-1068; *idem, The Slave Systems of Greek and Roman Antiquity* (Philadelphia, 1955); J. Vogt, *Sklaverei und Humanität im klassischen Griechentum* (AAWLM.G; Wiesbaden, 1953); E. Häusler, *Sklaven und Personen minderen Rechts im Alten Testament* (Dissertation, Cologne, 1956); G. Kehnscherper, *Die Stellung der Bibel und der alten christlichen Kirche zur Sklaverei* (Halle, 1957); C. Haufe, "Die antike Beurteilung der Sklaven," *Zeitschrift der Karl-Marx-Universität* 9 (1959/60), 603-616; F. Bömer, *Untersuchungen über die Religion der Sklaven in Griechenland und Rom* (AAWLM.G; four volumes, Wiesbaden, 1957-63); M. I. Finley, *Slavery in Classical Antiquity* (Cambridge, 1960; texts); D. B. Davis, *The Problem of Slavery in Western Culture* (Ithaca, NY, 1966); R. H. Barrow, *Slavery in the Roman Empire* (New York, 1968); S. Schulz, *Gott is kein Sklavenhalter* (Zurich/Hamburg, 1972); E. Schweizer, "Zum Sklavenproblem im NT," *EvTh* 32 (1972), 502-506; M.-L. Lamau, "Exhortation aux esclaves"; Thompson, "Masters."

2. Comparison of the particulars is made possible by the synopsis in Selwyn, 430.

The distinctive shaping of the tradition corresponds to an altered social situation. In the Pauline Epistles the situation in relation to a non-Christian master, the situation of marriage to a non-Christian spouse (I Cor. 7:13-16), is never addressed as a problem. From I Peter 2 onward servitude to Christian and non-Christian masters came to be considered again and again.[3] The unique shaping of the instruction in I Peter is determined not by the particular composition of the communities addressed,[4] but by the general social situation of the Christian slave. Probably the churches of the early period included mainly slaves who had been baptized together with the "whole house."[5] Individual Christian slaves were tolerated in non-Christian households (e.g., Acts 16:16ff.), undoubtedly as members of a religion regarded as a Jewish sect, even if they did not adapt in every way to custom like Jewish slaves.[6] Even for members of larger slave groups, e.g., the emperor's slaves (Phil. 4:22), there remained latitude for individuals. But in the second generation, especially in Asia Minor and Rome, the more intensive dissemination of Christian faith was accompanied by discrimination against Christians. I Peter applies the early Christian slave parenesis to this new situation and deepens it to form an instruction that was unique even in the NT and that has no parallel in Jewish or Hellenistic literature.

3. The OT and rabbinic Judaism, like the Hellenistic and Roman legal system, described the position of the slave in legal terms. The station of slave was not merely a vocational or an economic institution; it was a legal state, sanctioned by civil law, that made people who were born into slavery or caught by circumstances or who sold themselves into a marketable product, though not without special legal protections.

In broad terms neither Jewish or Hellenistic wisdom nor the Stoic duty codes address the issue of slavery directly.[7] There are various reasons for this. Even in the context of wisdom slaves are not considered as persons with responsibility; pseudo-Phocylides itself offers only regulations for the conduct of masters (224ff.). In Stoicism the station of slave is treated with indifference on the theory that according to nature no one is a slave and all are alike.[8] The only one truly enslaved is one who forgoes freedom, i.e., who does not live as a wise person: "One is a slave to lust, another to

---

3. I Tim. 6:1f.; Ignatius, *Pol.* 4:3 (LCL AF I, 273). According to the *Canons of Hippolytus* 4:46f., a slave disciplined by his master because of his faith should be recognized as a confessor.

4. Contra Selwyn, 431.

5. Acts 11:14; 16:15, 16, 31, 32ff.; 18:8; Jn. 4:53. See P. Weigandt, "Zur sogenannten 'Oikosformel,'" *NovTest* 6 (1963), 49-74. The idea that Christianity was originally disseminated by those in bondage is an unhistorical construction, contra K. Kautsky, *The Foundations of Christianity* (tr. J. Hartmann; New York, 1986), and others (cf. Gülzow, *Christentum und Sklaverei*, 26, n.3).

6. Philo, *Legatio ad Gaium* 155 (LCL X, 79); cf. Bömer, *Untersuchungen* IV, 918, n.1.

7. Schroeder, *Haustafeln* I, 50-53, 72f.

8. Seneca, *De Beneficiis* 3.28.1-4 (LCL III, 177f.); Epictetus, *Dissertationes* 1.13.4 (LCL I, 99).

greed, another to ambition, and all men are slaves [to hope,] to fear" (Seneca, *Epistulae* 47.17 [LCL IV, 310f.]). Philo makes use of the Stoic principle that by the nature of things no one is a slave (*De Specialibus Legibus* 2.69 [LCL VII, 350f.]), but condones at the same time holding foreigners as slaves, in accordance with the Mosaic law (2.123 [*ibid.,* 378-381]) and recommends humane treatment of slaves (3.137-140 [*ibid.,* 388-391]). It is worthy of note that in Judaism only the monastic community at Qumran fundamentally rejected slavery.[9]

4. The Christian message of freedom, even for the slave (I Cor. 7:22f.), does not try to treat the historical situation with indifference; it also does not aim at an ascetic emigration out of that situation. The station code parenesis applies the message in such a way that slaves are obligated to do justice to the historical situation in view of the eschatological Lord of history. But it is precisely through this direct address that the parenesis turns the slave into a human being standing in society as responsibly as the one who is legally free. This point of view, which is unique over against the Hellenistic and Jewish environment, applies to the realm of social ethics in a substantially consistent way the following principle: For faith in the Church the distinction between free and slave has been removed just as much as that between male and female (Gal. 3:28; Col. 3:11). The parenesis is shaped according to the structure of society, not that of the form of life belonging to the Church, but it does honor the slave as a human being, i.e., as a responsible creation (2:13) before God, destined for eternal fellowship with him (3:7).

5. On the basis of the NT station codes for slaves it would have to be concluded — in only apparent contrast to the actual wording of the codes — that Christians were obligated to work for the abolition of slavery wherever they were able to influence the structures of society. And yet even among the Apostolic Fathers the slavery question was bracketed off from the realm of social-ethical responsibility and placed among the issues involved in "works of love": The NT line of thought was not pursued further.[10] Within the Church's realm of influence

---

9. Josephus, *Antiquitates Judaicae* 18.1.5 (LCL IX, 19): "They neither bring wives into the community nor do they own slaves, since they believe that the latter practice contributes to injustice and that the former opens the way to a source of dissension."

10. In *Did.* 4:11 and *Barn.* 19:7 (LCL AF I, 317, 403, 405) the NT directives are merely repeated without kerygmatic development and are accentuated in such a way that they support subservience. In *I Clem.* 55:2 (*ibid.,* 103), moreover, selling oneself into slavery is apparently called a work of love: "Many have delivered themselves to slavery, and provided food with the price they received for themselves." Hermas, who refers to himself as a former slave in *Vis.* 1.1.1 (*ibid.* II, 7), advises in *Sim.* 1.8 (*ibid.,* 141): "Therefore instead of lands, purchase afflicted souls," and in *Mand.* 8.10 (*ibid.,* 105): "Redeem from distress the servants of God." In *Apostolic Constitutions* 4.9.2 (= *Didascalia* 18 [*ANF* VII, 435]), manumission of Christian captives and slaves, wherever possible and necessary, is a duty; but in 2.57.62 (*ibid.,* 421f.) Christians are expressly permitted to purchase slaves; according to 4.12 (*ibid.,* 436) a slave of a non-Christian house is to be baptized only when proper conduct vouches for him that such is in order.

slavery (not serfdom) was first abolished, particularly under the influence of monasticism, in the twelfth and thirteenth centuries in northwestern Europe. Else-where slavery was first abolished generally around the turn of the nineteenth century under the influence of Christianity, primarily from the Quakers and Puritans in England and North America, together with the Enlightenment understanding of human rights.[11]

V. 18: Service in Fear of the Lord

18 Slaves and masters are not designated in the conventional way as δοῦλοι and κύριοι but as οἰκέται and δεσπόται, probably in order to avoid the religious terms δοῦλος (2:16) and κύριος (2:13).[12] Perhaps the situation of the house church, where association among classes would be especially difficult amid conflicts, is thought of.[13] Even the custom-ary imperatives of the station code tradition[14] are focused on conflict by the attributives attached at the end of the sentence: ὑποτασσόμενοι ἐν παντὶ φόβῳ τοῖς δεσπόταις, οὐ μόνον τοῖς ἀγαθοῖς καὶ ἐπιεικέσιν ἀλλὰ καὶ τοῖς σκολιοῖς. The slave should subject himself or herself, therefore, not only to a "good" (ἀγαθός) and "kind" (ἐπιεικής) master, but also to a "twisted," "perverted" one, i.e., an "unpleasant" (σκολιός) one, one that is unjust (cf. v. 19: ἀδίκως) and not merely ill-tempered.[15]

It is in view of such masters that the qualification "in all fear" (ἐν παντὶ φόβῳ) takes on special importance: With such masters it is par-ticularly important that in every respect[16] one should fear God[17] and

---

11. E. von Dobschütz, "Sklaverei und Christentum," *RE* XVIII, 431ff.; R. Budden-sieg, "Wilberforce," *RE* XXI, 275-283; H. D. Wendland, "Sklaverei und Christentum," *RGG* VI, cols. 101-104 (bibliography).

12. It is on account of this differentiation that masters are already called οἱ κατὰ σάρκα κύριοι in Col. 3:22 and Eph. 6:5, and ἴδιοι δεσπόται in I Tim. 6:1 and Tit. 2:9.

13. οἰκέτης, actually "member of the household," was already in Greek culture also a "household slave"; the counterpart in Greek authors in general and Philo was the δεσπότης, the "master," or "owner." Cf. BAGD s.v.; F. Gschnitzer, *Studien zur griechischen Termino-logie der Sklaverei* (AAWLM.G; Wiesbaden, 1964), 17.

14. οἱ οἰκέται is vocative, as often in the NT with the definite article (J. H. Moulton, *A Grammar of NT Greek* I: *Prolegomena* [Edinburgh, 1906], 70). The participle ὑποτασ-σόμενοι is a Semiticizing imperative formulation (see the comments on 2:12). See D. Daube in Selwyn, 467-488; E. Lohse, "Parenesis and Kerygma," 44ff.

15. Actually "crooked" (Lk. 3:5), figuratively: "twisted," "perverse," perfidious." In Dio Chrysostom 58(75).1 (LCL V, 241) the word is used with πονηρός; Phil. 2:15 (cf. Acts 2:40, in accord with Dt. 32:5): γενεὰ σκολιὰ καὶ διεστραμμένη.

16. Thus understanding ἐν παντί in accord with κατὰ πάντα in Col. 3:22.

17. The objects of fear are not — as Schlatter, *Petrus und Paulus,* 115, and Selwyn, 175, suppose — the earthly masters.

not humans — but precisely because of this one should obey human masters. This characteristic line of argumentation became apparent already at 2:17; it is appropriated again in 3:5f., 14f., and provided the reason that I Peter bases subjection in the various relationships of the station code (2:17, 18; 3:2) on fear of God — going beyond Col. 3:22 and Eph. 5:21 in this way. The same is true at 3:16 of the general responsibility of Christians in relation to adversaries. In 1:17 the letter introduces this fear before God as a fundamental motif of Christian conduct. This emphasis of fear before God is especially conspicuous in that Paul never, in any passage stemming directly from him, uses it as a motivation for parenesis,[18] while among the Apostolic Fathers it frequently comes to the fore.[19] In comparison with the latter, the reference in I Peter is less interested in providing the basis for social-ethical conduct than it is in defining such conduct more closely. This "fear" has a special place in social ethics, since it places ethics into the realm of the Creator's sovereign rule over history, the τέλος of which is judgment (4:17f.); this judgment announces itself in advance in painful encounters (4:17-19; cf. Rom. 13:4; Lk. 13:1-5).

Vv. 19f.: Statement and Development of the Command

19   The Christian slave with a "twisted" master must suffer "unjustly" (ἀδίκως).[20] Such a slave is insulted, disciplined, tormented, and otherwise tortured without cause (cf. v. 23). That a slave in such a situation suffers because he or she has been called to freedom and righteousness is not what is thought of here.[21] To bear such pains, λύπαι, is χάρις,

---

18. The exceptions are the occurrence, which does not directly derive from him, in II Cor. 7:1 (cf. H. Balz, "φοβέω," *TDNT* IX, 216, n.149) and the station code tradition in Col. 3:22; Eph. 5:21. On this score, for Paul, in view of God's act of judgment, felt in anticipation in what befalls a person in history, fear belongs to faith (Rom. 3:20; 11:20; II Cor. 5:10f.; 7:11), though being afraid does not (Rom. 8:15; cf. I Jn. 4:18). Therefore, Paul's own historical conduct — his risky undertakings — is accompanied again and again by "fear and trembling" (I Cor. 2:3; differently Eph. 6:5).

19. Balz, *TDNT* IX, 216, n.149.

20. The word is common in Greek but appears in the NT only here (cf. BAGD s.v.). In substance it should be noted that even for Aristotle there was no such thing as injustice toward a slave, since a slave was a possession (*Ethica Nicomachea* 5.10.8 = 1134b.8ff. [LCL XIX, 292f.]). This orientation was altered considerably by NT times, mainly through the influence of Stoicism.

21. Ignatius, *Pol.* 4:3 (LCL AF I, 273): "Do not let them [slaves] be puffed up" — by reproaching the church with their harsh fate, for which they as Christians are too good.

grace, the demonstration of God's love, not because he rewards the suffering as if it were an achievement, but because the suffering is an expression of the call to salvation, as is stated in v. 20b and given foundation in vv. 21-25.[22]

The bearing of sufferings takes place διὰ συνείδησιν[23] θεοῦ. This expression, which is without parallel in the NT and its environment,[24]

---

22. According to this continuation, χάρις cannot be defined here as "recognition" (as in Lk. 6:32ff.) — which Kelly, 116, following Selwyn, 176, assumes — in a way different than in Paul (see the comments below on v. 20b).

23. See C. Maurer, "σύνοιδα," *TDNT* VII, 898-919; C. A. Pierce, *Conscience in the NT* (SBT 15; London, 1958); R. Bultmann, *Theology of the NT* I (tr. K. Grobel; New York, 1951), 211-220; O. Kuss, *Der Römerbrief* (Regensburg, 1957), 76-82; J. Stelzenberger, *Syneidesis im NT* (Abhandlungen zur Moraltheologie 1; Paderborn, 1961), especially the report on research, 11-27.

24. συνείδησις (with the cognate verb σύνοιδα) refers in Greek literature to "consciousness" of something, "awareness," and further to "awareness of oneself," i.e., self-understanding in an intellectual and then also in a moral sense. When it is used of a person's decision-making knowledge about his or her own conduct in a moral context, we translate it as "conscience," but without thereby identifying it with understandings of conscience in Western philosophy. In this sense συνείδησις was connected in the Hellenistic environment of the NT only with negative judgments ("bad conscience"), while the verb σύνοιδα was connected also with positive judgments (Maurer, *TDNT* VII, 898-907; Stelzenberger, *Syneidesis*, 27-36).

σύνοιδα occurs in the NT only twice: in Acts 5:2, "have knowledge of," in I Cor. 4:4, "I am not aware of anything [as regards questionable behavior] against myself."

συνείδησις, on the other hand, appears thirty times in the NT (Jn. 8:9 is a secondary reading). In Paul it is both that by which Christians and non-Christians judge regarding their previous conduct, as in Hellenistic Judaism (Rom. 2:15; 9:1; II Cor. 1:12; 4:2; 5:11), and the Christian's religious and moral decision-making capacity with respect to what is yet to be done (eight occurrences in I Cor. 8:7-13; 10:25-30 and one in Rom. 13:5). In the sixteen occurrences in post-Pauline documents συνείδησις is, except in I Pet. 2:19, that by which a Christian judges concerning his or her total relationship to God and neighbor; the goal is always that the Christian have through grace in faith a conscience that is "good" (Acts 23:1; I Tim. 1:5, 19; Heb. 13:18; I Pet. 3:16, 21) or "pure" (I Tim. 3:9; II Tim. 1:3; cf. Heb. 9:14). "Something absent altogether from the surrounding Greek world and exceptional in Hellenistic Judaism is now proclaimed as the norm of life. This is the good and clear conscience as the healing of the inwardly divided man . . ." (Maurer, *TDNT* VII, 919). Two of the three occurrences in I Peter fit into this pattern in post-Pauline NT documents, expecting of Christians a "good conscience" (3:16, 21).

I Pet. 2:19 is the only passage in this group of writings to set itself apart from this usage. Indeed, some copyists tried to assimilate it by putting ἀγαθήν in place of θεοῦ (C, 614, al, sy) or after θεοῦ (A*, Ψ, 33). Since in all other NT occurrences, i.e., in all earlier Christian usage available to us, the word refers to a person's religious and moral decision-making capacity with respect to his or her conduct and thereby has the technical sense of "conscience," it is reasonable to assume this meaning here as well. But how are the unique connection to genitive θεοῦ and the relationship of συνείδησις to its context here to be understood? Can συνείδησις, since it is used differently than in other post-Pauline documents,

is interpreted and linked to the context in many different ways in exegetical studies.[25] The discussion becomes all the more confused by the problem of translation: Some translate "consciousness of God" or "God's consciousness" and mean by this a consciousness that makes moral judgments on the basis of its relationship to God, i.e., "conscience."[26] Others translate it with "conscience," but mean by this merely knowledge of God.[27] When we disregard the merely verbal differences and inquire about the intended substance, we find in most commentaries the interpretation that Kelly put forward with particular consistency: θεοῦ can only be objective genitive; therefore, συνείδησις must have here its fundamental Greek meaning of "cognizance": Cognizance (or knowledge) of God — of God's relationship to those who belong to him and of his goal for them — makes it possible for slaves to take upon themselves grievous treatment.[28]

But elsewhere in the NT συνείδησις is used of critically discerning awareness, i.e., "conscience," and the causal διά used here suggests that the expression should be connected to the context in the sense of cause and not only of enabling. These philological concerns can be appropriated if συνείδησις is given here the meaning that Paul developed in a new direction after modest beginnings in Hellenistic Judaism:[29] The conscience not only judges critically (as was already thought in Hellenistic Judaism) as ἔλεγχος regarding prior conduct, but also decides whether a Christian may eat meat sacrificed to idols (I Cor. 8:10 and passim) or should be subject to rulers (Rom. 13:5). A statement parallel to I Cor. 8:10 in Rom. 14:1 ascribes the same capacity for critical discernment to faith: Just as I Cor. 8:12 speaks of the "weak conscience," so also Rom. 14:1 speaks of one "who is weak with respect

---

have one of the two meanings that appear in Paul, or must one have recourse finally to general Greek usage here?

25. An overview of the discussion is found in Stelzenberger, *Syneidesis,* 45f.

26. So Wohlenberg, 74f.; Windisch, 64.

27. So Selwyn, 176ff.; Schelkle, 79ff.

28. Kelly, 117: " 'because of the knowledge of God' . . . in the strength of which the Christian slave cheerfully bears affliction." The expression is also understood in this sense by Schweizer, 61; Selwyn, 176ff.; and Schelkle, 80, though they use the then incomprehensible translation "conscience." Schweizer: "Whether it is done in relation to God or not, it turns the same act or experience into grace or . . . the activity of self-accomplishment"; Schelkle says: "The Christian slave endures, whatever is laid upon him . . . in the conscience . . . and, therefore, in patience."

29. Maurer, *TDNT* VII, 912.

to faith." Conscience in this sense is, therefore, the rationally discerning "I" of faith, which analyzes and decides what God's will is in the particular situation for the one who believes (cf. Rom. 12:1f.).[30] This conscience is directed toward God, as is faith; it is — as the genitive συνείδησις θεοῦ,[31] which at first seems so puzzling, expresses — a conscience directed toward God or bound to him.[32]

Because of this conscience directed toward God the Christian slave can "bear" (ὑποφέρειν) sufferings.[33] This conscience obligates one to be in subjection (cf. Rom. 13:5), but in a subjection that takes place for the Lord's sake and that sees in the earthly master only God's "creation" (2:13). It thus differs in its posture and not infrequently also in its practical realization from what the earthly master expects. Because the Christian slave as a free person follows his or her conscience and thus "behaves properly," a situation of conflict arises. The obligation to subjection and to a higher order of obedience in relation to God can only be maintained by preparedness "to suffer unjustly" (πάσχων ἀδίκως) according to the will of God.[34] The conscience directed toward God obligates one also to the very same thing. This interpretation is supported by v. 20: Arising out of the conscience bound to God is primarily "proper conduct" and then also "suffering" within the stations of life. Suffering comes forth not only from the fits of caprice and the malice of one's master.

20 The social-ethical parenesis reaches here its focal point for slaves and thereby in exemplary fashion for all. The hearers are addressed now directly in the style of diatribe. There is no reason to magnify the situation and to expect glory[35] when one is able to absorb with defiance or with a kind of stoic superiority the blows[36] brought on

---

30. Cf. also Maurer, *TDNT* VII, 914-916.

31. It is objective genitive; in the same way πίστις is used in Rom. 3:22 with the genitive and in Acts 20:21 with εἰς.

32. Similarly, Windisch, 64: "the inner constraint toward God that requires one to renounce obedience to evil and endure injustice patiently." Maurer, *TDNT* VII, 916: "the first commentary" on Rom. 13:5.

33. ὑποφέρω, literally "remove," "bear," figuratively "endure," has then more the sense "take upon oneself."

34. The biblical example for this situation is Joseph's conduct in relation to his master's wife (Gen. 39:7-20).

35. τὸ κλέος, "fame," in the NT only here.

36. κολαφίζω, "strike with the fist," "slap in the face," "abuse"; the use of the word in the Passion narrative (Mk. 14:65 par.) is not part of the purview here (contra Selwyn, 178).

by offenses: ποῖον γὰρ κλέος εἰ ἁμαρτάνοντες καὶ κολαφιζόμενοι ὑπομενεῖτε.

This statement of fact clothed in a rhetorical question serves only as an antithetical foil for the social-ethical chief point on which the entire parenesis is now focused: ἀλλ' εἰ ἀγαθοποιοῦντες καὶ πάσχοντες ὑπομενεῖτε, τοῦτο χάρις παρὰ θεῷ.[37] Among Christian slaves a situation of suffering under their masters should arise only in spite of — indeed, on account of — the slaves' proper conduct. V. 20b is parallel to v. 20a: Just as offense and discipline are not merely coordinated but bound to one another, so also proper conduct and suffering are linked together not only concessively but also causally.

To bear suffering without wavering is χάρις παρὰ θεῷ, "grace before God."[38] Why? According to some interpreters[39] it is such because it is made possible by and accomplished by the strength of grace; according to others[40] because it achieves recognition from God. In support of the latter it can be said that "grace before God" at the end of the verse represents to a degree the antithesis to "glory," prestige among one's fellow human beings, in the earlier part of the verse. But the precise and intensive use of the term in I Peter and the substantive interpretation of Christian suffering suggest a different meaning.[41] Whoever bears unjust affliction from people in the way that Christ did, according to vv. 21ff., participates in his path (4:13), in the path leading to salvation (3:17-22). That is to say, such a person is surrounded and borne along by "grace," by God's bestowal of himself, which accepts that person in love (5:12). Grace summoned this person to such conduct (v. 21; cf. Phil. 1:7, 29), and grace brings him or her to its goal (5:10). Even while that person is afflicted by fellow human beings, God is not against but for him or her (3:14; cf. Rom. 8:37-39). The reference to grace in vv. 19f. draws attention thereby to the other central statements of the letter about χάρις; these as well as the present context further illumine the importance of the term.

---

37. Cf. van Unnik, "Classical Parallel."

38. παρὰ θεῷ, literally "with God," here as in 2:4 and Rom. 2:13 "before God," i.e., from the perspective of relationship to God or from God.

39. E.g., Schelkle, 80.

40. E.g., Beare, 147; Kelly, 116, on 2:19: " 'this is grace,' i.e. an act which is intrinsically attractive and thus wins God's approval. . . . For this sense of 'grace' . . . cf. Lk. vi.32-34."

41. Similarly Windisch, 64: Innocent suffering . . . "testifies to the grace that holds sway over the righteous one, Heb. 12:6."

Grace in I Peter[42]

1. The Greek word χάρις designates in its root meaning that which gladdens, e.g., "sweetness" or "kindness"; in the Greek world it becomes above all the usual expression for the ruler's "demonstration of favor."[43] This word is for Paul a theological technical term for God's bestowal of himself through Jesus' work of redemption (Rom. 3:24), the bestowal that bears and shapes the destiny of the person who gives himself or herself over to it, i.e., who believes (Rom. 6:14) — just as the "righteousness" of God (Rom. 6:18f.) or his Spirit (II Cor. 13:13) are also Pauline technical terms. Hence, Paul calls the abilities that the Spirit communicates by taking the natural gifts of a person into service for God's work of salvation χαρίσματα, "gifts of grace" that issue forth from the one (singular) grace (Rom. 12:6; I Cor. 12:4-6). In the early Christian term χάρις essential components are brought in from the content of the OT term חֶסֶד; even חֶסֶד is not a state of mind but an event, the moment when one person turns to another to offer the other person help on the basis of spontaneous kindness and in keeping with a prior relationship.[44] חֶסֶד is translated in the LXX, however, with ἔλεος[45] so that the Pauline term χάρις is linguistically — and to a considerable extent also in terms of content — a new formation.

2. No other NT document appropriates this technical term as densely and in a similarly broad variety of usage as does I Peter. Outside the Pauline corpus in the NT it alone speaks of the χαρίσματα that grow out of χάρις (4:10). χάρις in this letter is, moreover, the formal essence of the saving, eschatological turning of God to humankind that bestows life (3:7). This turning took place in Christ's suffering unto death, is now proclaimed in the gospel (1:10), and will encounter finally us at his parousia (1:13). In 5:12 the point of the entire letter is summarized with the term χάρις: The author wants to assure the readers that the existence into which they have been placed through Christ is truly grace. Even proper conduct in one's station in this world and especially the suffering connected with it are, indeed, grace (2:19f.). "The God of all grace," the One who summoned them, will bring them through everything to the finish (5:10). He gives — as it is said by reaching back to the OT — "grace to the humble" (5:5). Therefore, the introductory wish for grace (1:2) is not only a formula; the wish for grace at the end, however, is anticipated by 5:10, so that there remains in 5:14 only a brief wish for peace.

---

42. See H. Conzelmann and W. Zimmerli, "χάρις," *TDNT* IX, 372-406 (bibliography); G. Stählin, "Gnade," *RGG* II, cols. 1634ff.; K. Rahner, "Gnade," *LThK* IV, 977ff.; Bultmann, *Theology* I, 288-314; L. Goppelt, "Grace" (tr. J. E. Alsup), *Baker's Dictionary of Christian Ethics* (ed. C. F. H. Henry; Grand Rapids, 1973), 273-275. An opposing view is held by Elliott, "Backward," 189f.

43. Conzelmann, *TDNT* IX, 372-376.

44. Zimmerli, *TDNT* IX, 376-387, especially 386f.

45. χάρις is used in the LXX sometimes for חֵן, so that it does not become a theological term (*TDNT* IX, 389).

Just as the parenetic references to grace in 2:19f. are clarified by the letter's whole understanding of grace, so now they are clarified finally by the christological foundation that follows.

2:21-25: The Christological Foundation

21 *For you were called to this;*
Christ suffered, indeed, for you
and has (thereby) left you a guiding image,
that you should follow his footprints:
22 *"He did no sin,*
and in his mouth was found no deceit." (Isa. 53:9)
23 *When he was abused, he did not abuse in return,*
when he suffered, he did not threaten;
rather, he relied on the One who judges rightly.
24 *He "bore our sins himself" in his body on the wood* (Isa. 53:4)
in order that we who have died to sins might live to
righteousness.

"By his wound you have been healed." (Isa. 53:5)
25 *For you were "like sheep going astray,"* (Isa. 53:6)
but now you have been turned toward the Shepherd and
Herdsman (overseer) of your souls.

V. 21: Christ as Guiding Image

21 εἰς τοῦτο γὰϱ ἐκλήθητε connects the preceding parenesis to the christological foundation that follows: "Since for this," i.e., to maintain just conduct under suffering,[1] "you have been called." καλεῖν, actually "to summon," is here, as in 2:9; 3:9; 5:10, an early Christian technical term[2] for the electing and determining summons of God (1:15) to eschatological salvation, the call to faith in Christ (1:5, 8; cf. I Cor. 7:20) and to hope in him (1:13). This link to Christ (cf. 2:4), which is established in baptism (which is why aorist ἐκλήθητε is used), directs

---

1. εἰς τοῦτο appropriates τοῦτο from v. 20b, where it refers to the previous conditional clause.

2. This NT usage is based on LXX occurrences of the word, e.g., Isa. 41:9: ἐκάλεσά σε καὶ εἶπά σοι Παῖς μου εἶ, ἐξελεξάμην σε; cf. 42:6; 43:1; 46:11; 50:2; 51:2. See K. L. Schmidt, "καλέω," *TDNT* III, 487-491.

one toward Christ's path also within the institutions of society, namely in the suffering of injustice (cf. 4:13).

"For Christ also suffered for you and left for you a guiding image. . . ." This causal ὅτι clause establishes two connections between the suffering Christ and the suffering of believers, one by ὑπὲρ ὑμῶν, the other by the terms "model" and "following in discipleship." How do these two connections relate to one another in content?

The first clause, Χριστὸς ἔπαθεν ὑπὲρ ὑμῶν, reflects the common confessional formula "Christ died for us," which interprets Jesus' death as vicarious atonement.[3] Under the influence of this formula even reliable manuscripts read ἀπέθανεν here; the original text is, however, without doubt ἔπαθεν.[4]

As early as the Pauline period the verb πάσχειν had become a Christian technical term for Jesus' suffering, especially his suffering unto death,[5] though it was also used of afflictions that Christians experienced on account of being believers.[6] In I Peter πάσχω comes to the fore — announcing the thematic focus of the letter — more prominently than in any other NT document: It occurs twelve times in the letter — always in a specifically Christian expression — and only thirty times in the rest of the NT.[7] τὰ παθήματα is also used of both Christ's suffering

---

3. I Cor. 15:3; Rom. 5:6; 8:34; 14:9, 15; I Pet. 3:18. See W. Kramer, *Christ, Lord, Son of God* (tr. B. Hardy; Naperville, IL, 1966), 26f.

4. So ℵ, al, sy, and Ambrose. The correct reading is in 𝔭⁷² B, and Koine. ℵ* and others have ἀποθανεῖν for παθεῖν also in 3:18 and 4:1 (see the comments there). For the same reason, the first person is substituted in various manuscripts for ὑμῶν and ὑμῖν.

5. It is used of Jesus' suffering unto death in Luke (Lk. 24:15; 24:26, 46; Acts 1:3; 3:18; 17:3) and Hebrews (9:26; 13:12), for his suffering prior to death in Heb. 2:18 (temptation) and 5:8 (Gethsemane). In Jesus' announcements of his coming suffering in the Synoptics the formula πολλὰ παθεῖν (Mk. 8:31 par.; 9:12; Lk. 17:25) refers in its present context to his suffering before death, but originally it referred to the entire suffering unto death, so that the expression is older than Mark; it is to be found before this in the *Testament of Moses*, which goes back to a Semitic original (3:11 [*OT Pseudep.* I, 928]; cf. Ps. 33:20 LXX; Josephus, *Antiquitates Judaicae* 13.268 [LCL VII, 361f.]). See W. Michaelis, "πάσχω," *TDNT* V, 913ff.; H. Patsch, *Abendmahl und historischer Jesus* (Stuttgart, 1972), §46, especially nn. 296-299 (see n.29 below). Absolute πάσχειν is Hellenistic; see *TDNT* V, 907f.; J. Jeremias, *The Eucharistic Words of Jesus* (tr. N. Perrin; New York, 1966), 162.

6. The verb has this sense in Paul, except perhaps in I Cor. 12:26 (cf. II Cor. 1:6; Gal. 3:4; Phil. 1:29; I Thess. 2:14; II Thess. 1:5), just as also in Acts 9:16 (cf. II Tim. 1:12) and Rev. 2:10. Only in a few instances does it refer to ordinary suffering (Mt. 27:19; 17:15 v.l.; Mk. 5:26; Lk. 13:2; Acts 28:5). See Michaelis, *TDNT* V, 919-924.

7. Of the "persecution sufferings" of Christians in I Pet. 2:19; 3:14, 17; 4:1, 15, 19; 5:10; the possibility of suffering unto death is included at least in 4:1, 15, 19 (Michaelis, *TDNT* V, 921ff.). These passages are linked to subsequent statements about Jesus' suffering

unto death (1:11; 5:1) and the sufferings of Christians (5:9) as participation in his suffering (4:13).[8] The martyrological use of both noun and verb frequently recalls Paul (see the comments on 4:13). But Paul does not use the verb christologically: He never speaks of a πάσχειν of Christ, though he does speak of Christ's παθήματα. The verb is used prominently of Christ in the Synoptic announcements of his approaching suffering, in Luke, and in Hebrews. These uses and thereby the entire terminological tradition probably go back to the Palestinian Church, possibly to Jesus himself.[9] This use of πάσχειν suggests that the christological formulas grew up in the same stream of tradition. It was with the aid of these formulas that the author of I Peter formulated 2:21-25. The term that was available to the author from the tradition was at the same time, however, his own. For this reason alone the ὑπέρ phrase is not just a formula appropriated automatically. This statement about the turning of Christ to his own has, rather, substantive meaning for its parenetic context.

The two images in verse 21b, which draw the line of connection between Christians and Christ from two directions, are obviously directed to this context: ὑμῖν ὑπολιμπάνων ὑπογραμμόν, ἵνα ἐπακολουθήσητε τοῖς ἴχνεσιν αὐτοῦ. These two clauses have often been understood as calling for an "imitation" of Jesus' suffering,[10] so that here the ethic of *imitatio Christi* was thought to be established. This view has had many notable representatives in the history of the Church.

The Hellenistic world was permeated with the moral-religious principle of imitation of deity.[11] The *imitatio* or μίμησις was motivated

---

unto death (2:21; 3:18; 4:1) or the mistreatment of him before his death (2:23; cf. *TDNT* V, 918f.).

8. Michaelis, *TDNT* V, 934f.; see the comments below on 4:13.

9. See n.5 above.

10. Windisch, 65: "Slaves [are] the born imitators of Christ"; A. Schulz, *Nachfolgen und Nachahmen. Studien über das Verhältnis der neutestamentlichen Jüngerschaft zur urchristlichen Vorbildethik* (StANT 6; Munich, 1962), 176-179; H. D. Betz, *Nachfolge und Nachahmung Jesu Christi im NT* (BHTh 37; Tübingen, 1967), 181f.

11. The corresponding Stoic principle, e.g., states: ἀκολουθεῖν φύσει/θεῷ (Epictetus, *Dissertationes* 1.30.4 [LCL I, 205]; μιμεῖσθαι is used by Epictetus only in a pre-philosophical sense: "imitate") or ἕπεσθαι θεοῖς (*Dissertationes* 1.12.5, 8; 20.15 [LCL I, 91, 139f.]). It is developed in this way: "Ipsa . . . cogitatio de vi et natura deorum studium incendit illius aeternitatem imitandi" (Cicero, *Tusculan Disputations* 5.70 [LCL XVIII, 497]). Hence, it follows for Seneca, *Epistulae Morales* 95.50 (LCL VI, 91): "Vis deos propitiare? Bonus esto. Satis illos coluit, quisquis imitatus est." See Schulz, *Nachfolgen,* 178f., 206-213; Betz, *Nachfolge,* 107-136; Michaelis, *TDNT* IV, 661-664.

by the mythical-cosmological connection between the human micro-cosm and the macrocosm and by paideia, the necessity for education. In Philo, that humankind is in God's likeness, as understood by Philo, is the basis for this obligation of imitation.[12]

In the NT "model" (usually τύπος) and "imitation" (μιμεῖσθαι) are Pauline terms for the isomorphic fashioning of one's life mediated by the shaping influence of the word of God and by the obedience of faith.[13] Here in I Peter as well the Greek concept of *mimesis* has been appro-priated in at most a formal sense.[14] This is to be deduced already on the basis of the meaning of both images in 2:12b. Jesus' suffering is a ὑπογραμμός that he has "left behind" for his own.[15] ὑπογραμμός is literally a student's traced or copied reproduction of the alphabet, and figuratively the "paragon" or "guiding image" that, once it is given, places one under obligation. It is not an "example" or "model" toward which one strives on the basis of free choice.[16] Here the obligation comes from the summons.

A similar point is made by the second image: Whoever follows the "footprint" (τὰ ἴχνη)[17] of another does not emulate a partner, but sets out in the direction indicated, indeed journeyed, by the one fol-lowed.[18] Like the first image this one is from a Hellenistic context: The moral-religious direction that one takes was often portrayed as a journey down a path. The image of following a footprint is more common in

---

12. On Philo see Michaelis, *TDNT* IV, 664-666; Schulz, *Nachfolgen*, 215ff.

13. Cf. I Thess. 1:6; I Cor. 4:16; 11:1. See Michaelis, *TDNT* IV, 666-673; L. Goppelt, "τύπος," *TDNT* VIII, 248f. The model is effective to the extent that the word speaks forth from it, through which it took shape.

14. The root of μιμεῖσθαι is not used by I Peter; in 3:13 v.l. it is a secondary reading.

15. ὑπολιμπάνω, used only here in the NT, is a cognate of ὑπολείπω, "bequeath," "leave behind" (cf. BAGD s.v.).

16. The noun ὑπογραμμός appears first in II Macc. 2:28, the verb ὑπογράφειν from Plato, *Protagoras* 326D (LCL II, 145) on for alphabet characters traced by students (cf. Clement of Alexandria, *Stromateis* 5.49.1 [*ANF* II, 456]: ὑπογραμμὸς παιδικός), figuratively in *Leges* 4.711B (LCL X, 276): πάντα ὑπογράφοντα τῷ πράττειν. The noun appears in the NT only in I Pet. 2:21. It is used of Christ in *I Clem.* 16:17; 33:8; Polycarp, *Phil.* 8:2 (LCL AF I, 37, 65, 293), of Paul in *I Clem.* 5:7 (*ibid.*, 17). Cf. G. Schrenk, "ὑπογραμμός," *TDNT* I, 772f. Later the Church Fathers correctly use it almost synonymously with τύπος (see Schrenk, *TDNT* I, 773), which Paul uses in connection with the root of μιμεῖσθαι in the sense of "shaping model" (Phil. 3:17; I Thess. 1:6f.; II Thess. 3:9; cf. I Tim. 4:12; Tit. 2:7; so also I Pet. 5:3 [see the comments there]).

17. τὸ ἴχνος, the "imprint" (of a foot), plural "footprints"; frequently of footprints that one follows. See A. Stumpff, "ἴχνος," *TDNT* III, 402f.

18. See also E. Schweizer, *Lordship and Discipleship* (London, 1960), 11.

the Greek and Hellenistic context than in the OT and Jewish realm;[19] the expression is found verbatim only in Philo.[20]

Use of this Hellenistic image in reference to Jesus connects it to the early Christian concept of discipleship: "Following" (ἐπακολου-θεῖν) comes close here to the technical meaning "following in discipleship," i.e., going behind someone, becoming that person's student, and thereby participating in his destiny. The verb had taken on this meaning already in the Jesus tradition on the basis of its OT and Jewish prehistory.[21] I Pet. 2:21 and Rev. 14:4 are the only two passages in the NT or the Apostolic Fathers in which (ἐπ-)ἀκολουθεῖν, a technical term for following in discipleship during the earthly days of Jesus in the Synoptic Gospels and in John, is directly applied to the post-Easter Church;[22] in the Gospels this takes place only in a coded manner through redaction. After Easter this "going along behind" is indeed possible only in a figurative sense. For this reason Paul describes what "following in discipleship" now means with other terms.[23] Once again, however, I Peter (so also Rev. 14:4) appropriates Palestinian tradition in Hellenized form. The redaction of the gospel tradition paved the way for such appropriation, especially for seeing the affliction of

---

19. In the LXX ἴχνος is used figuratively only rarely, e.g., Sir. 50:29: ἐὰν γὰρ αὐτὰ ποιήσῃ, πρὸς πάντα ἰσχύσει. ὅτι φῶς κυρίου τὸ ἴχνος αὐτοῦ; cf. 14:22: ἔξελθε ὀπίσω (behind wisdom) ὡς ἰχνευτής; 51:15. In contrast, pursuit of intellectual or moral direction was from Plato on often spoken of as adopting a track: *Republic* 553A (LCL II, 270f.), of a son: ζηλοῖ τε τὸν πατέρα καὶ τὰ ἐκείνου ἴχνη διώκῃ (cf. also *Theaetetus* 187E [LCL VII, 171]). Philo, *De Virtutibus* 64 (LCL VIII, 201f.): ἐπακολουθῆσαι τοῖς ἴχνεσιν (cf. *De Fuga et Inventione* 130 [LCL V, 78-81]). In the OT, this verb is linked with the image of a path only in Isa. 55:3: καὶ ἐπακολουθήσατε ταῖς ὁδοῖς μου.

In the NT the image of a track is also appropriated in Rom. 4:12 and II Cor. 12:18. In the Apostolic Fathers, Ignatius, in *Eph.* 12:2 (LCL AF I, 187), wants to be found following Paul's path (as a martyr); but here the image serves, as already in various ways in Greek and Hellenistic literature, the idea of mimesis (e.g., Aelius Aristides 46.160): "He imitated his father and followed his works like footprints." See Stumpff, *TDNT* III, 402-405.

20. Cf. Philo, *De Virtutibus* 64 (LCL VIII, 201).

21. G. Kittel, "ἀκολουθέω," *TDNT* I, 213f.; M. Hengel, *The Charismatic Leader and His Followers* (tr. J. Greig; Edinburgh/New York, 1981); Schweizer, *Lordship;* F. J. Helfmeyer, *Die Nachfolge Gottes im Alten Testament* (BBB 29; Bonn, 1968); H. Kosmala, "Nachfolge und Nachahmung Gottes II: im jüdischen Denken," *ASTI* 3 (1964), 65-110.

22. G. Kittel, *TDNT* I, 214f.; H. Kraft, *Clavis Patrum Apostolicorum* (Darmstadt, 1963), s.v.

23. See n.13 above and Schweizer, *Lordship,* 91f.; E. Larsson, *Christus als Vorbild* (ASNU 23; Uppsala, 1962); A. Schulz, "Leidenstheologie und Vorbildethik in den paulinischen Hauptbriefen," *Neutestamentliche Aufsätze* (FS J. Schmid; Regensburg, 1963), 265-269.

Christians by society from the perspective of the discipleship sayings.[24]

The nature and especially the motivation of discipleship in the particular situation can be derived from the context of I Pet. 2:21. The concrete "how" is developed in vv. 22f. on the basis of the situation previously addressed parenetically in vv. 19ff. The motivation is developed, on the one hand, in accord with "for you" (v. 24) and, on the other hand, in accord with "you were called" (v. 21a; cf. v. 25). Even in the Jesus tradition following in discipleship is always initiated by Jesus' turning to people, not by the choice of the one encountered by him.[25] In the same way, for Paul the σὺν Χριστῷ follows from the ὑπὲρ ἡμῶν.[26] So also here, according to vv. 24f., Christ leads into proper conduct through his suffering unto death "for us" and thereby leads us into suffering. But to those whom he has bound to himself in this way he shows, through the nature of his suffering (vv. 22f.), that — and how — they should take on themselves the affliction that they encounter. It is in this sense that he is for them a "guiding image" and that they are to "follow in his footsteps." The affliction of Jesus' disciples at the hands of society was thus already in the Synoptic tradition and in Paul understood from the perspective of Jesus' suffering unto death as encounter and obligation.[27] Not until post-NT Christianity was ἀκολουθεῖν equated with μιμεῖσθαι and both often understood in the sense of an *imitatio*.[28]

---

24. The saying about bearing one's cross in Mk. 8:34 par. Mt. 16:24 (different in Lk. 9:23) becomes an admonition to discipleship under the cross by being connected with the announcement of coming suffering (Mk. 8:31ff.); in Mt. 10:37 (different in Lk. 14:26) it is placed in the context of the disciples' situation of persecution. The same connection is found independently of the Synoptic tradition in Jn. 12:24-26; see Schweizer, *Lordship,* 80-92; Elliott, "Backward," 195-198.

25. The rabbi's disciple seeks out his teacher. But discipleship to Jesus begins by the unique word of command "follow me" (Hengel, *Charismatic Leader,* 50-73); cf. Jn. 15:16.

26. II Cor. 5:14f.; Rom. 5:6ff.; 6:3f.

27. Mk. 8:34ff. (see n.24 above); 10:45 par. Paul interpreted both his afflictions (e.g., II Cor. 1:5-7; 4:10; Phil. 3:10; Col. 1:24) and those of the Church (II Cor. 1:5-7; I Thess. 1:6, and elsewhere) as participation in Jesus' fate. Closer to I Peter, however, is the parenesis that comes out of a similar social situation in Heb. 12:2; 13:13. In the Apostolic Fathers the parenesis in Ignatius, *Eph.* 10:3; Polycarp, *Phil.* 8:1f. (LCL AF I, 185, 293) and elsewhere approaches the mimesis concept (see n.11 above) and that in *I Clem.* 16:17 (*ibid.,* 37) the ethics of model. In Polycarp, *Phil.* 8:1f., I Pet. 2:22, 24 is quoted verbatim and an admonition is added: "Let us then be imitators of his endurance. . . ." See also the comments on 4:13.

28. Augustine, *De Sancta Virginitate* 27 (*MPL* XL, 411 [*NPNF* first series III, 426]): "Quid est enim sequi nisi imitari?" See further Kittel, *TDNT* I, 214, n.29; Stumpff, *TDNT* III, 404f. The *imitatio* concept emerges clearly for the first time when Polycarp's death is

The exegesis of v. 21 produces accordingly already far-reaching conclusions about the structure of the christological section now to follow in 2:22-25.

Structure and Origin of the Christ Hymn in 2:22-25[29]

I Peter 2:22-25 is the second christological section of the letter, after 1:18-21 and before 3:18-22. Like the other two such sections, it calls for reflection on its structure and its tradition-historical origin.

Structure

It was H. Windisch[30] who designated vv. 21-25 as a "Christ hymn." R. Bultmann[31] developed the widely accepted hypothesis that these verses are an edited Church "hymn." He based this on among other things the view that the content of these verses was not entirely connected to the parenetic context: "For you" in v. 21a and the vicarious significance of Jesus' death (vv. 24f.) have no significance "for the context."[32] But our exegesis has reached the opposite conclusion. Without diminishing from this the following observations suggest that tradition has, indeed, been appropriated here.[33]

1. V. 24a-b departs from the parenetic context by shifting from the second person plural to the first person plural. Vv. 24c-25 returns to second person plural, but speaks thereby not only to the slaves addressed in v. 21 but to the entire community. This corresponds in fact to the implied exemplary character of this parenesis, but not to its explicit developments. In all probability, therefore, the references to the community in vv. 21a and vv. 24c (25) were also originally in the first person plural.

---

portrayed as like Jesus' Passion: "[For one might almost say] that all that had gone before happened in order that the Lord might show to us from above a martyrdom in accordance with the Gospel" (*Mart. Pol.* 1 [LCL AF II, 313]). Thereafter it is certain that Christ alone is worshipped, since he alone suffered for all, but martyrs are honored as his μαθηταὶ καὶ μιμηταί. See H. D. Betz, *Nachfolge*, 181f.; H. von Campenhausen, *Die Idee des Martyriums in der alten Kirche* (second ed., Göttingen, 1964), 87.

29. See Bultmann, "Bekenntnis- und Liedfragmente"; Deichgraber, *Gotteshymnus*, 140-143; E. Fascher, *Jesaja 53 in christlicher und jüdischer Sicht* (Aufsätze und Vorträge zur Theologie und Religionswissenschaft 4; Berlin, 1958); Hahn, *Titles*, 54-67; J. Jeremias, "παῖς θεοῦ," *TDNT* V, 677-717; E. Lohse, *Märtyer und Gottesknecht* (FRLANT NF 46; second ed., Göttingen, 1963); *idem*, "Parenesis and Kerygma"; H. Patsch, *Abendmahl und historischer Jesus; idem*, "Zum alttestamentlichen Hintergrund," 278f.; K. H. Schelkle, *Die Passion Jesu in der Verkundigung des NT* (Heidelberg, 1949), 81-104; Schille, *Hymnen*, 45f.; Shimada, *Formulary Material;* Wengst, *Christologische Formeln und Lieder;* H. W. Wolff, *Jes 53 im Urchristentum* (second ed., Berlin, 1950); Osborne, "Guide Lines"; Richard, "Functional Christology"; Tuni, "Jesus of Nazareth."

30. Windisch, 65.

31. Bultmann, "Bekenntnis- und Liedfragmente," 294f.

32. *Ibid.*, 295.

33. See also Wengst, *Christologische Formeln und Lieder,* 83ff.

2. Therefore, the address in v. 21b (ὑμῖν ὑπολιμπάνων, κτλ.), which was parenetic from the beginning, and naturally the transition εἰς τοῦτο γὰρ ἐκλήθητε in v. 21a (cf. 3:18) are to be differentiated from these broader references to the whole community. V. 23, on the other hand, may not have been introduced for the sake of parenesis,[34] but might itself have occasioned the appropriation here of the traditional piece.[35] The ἵνα clause in v. 24b clearly has a general parenetic point, but it could hardly have been introduced by the author on the basis of the tradition.[36] But v. 25, which is similarly worded, could be the author's addition,[37] so that the hymn concluded with v. 24c. But even in v. 25 it is not possible to exclude a source without question; the rhythm is not precise and there are no style-critical differences to be observed. The author has incorporated into the context a tradition that has already become his own.

3. On the basis of form Bultmann characterized the source "as a consequence of the graphic description" as "a hymn, not a confession."[38] Deichgräber makes a case for the same conclusion, "Christ hymn" or "Christ song," because the christological statements are in sophisticated diction and style.[39] The clauses are, in fact, composed in sophisticated language formulated rhythmically. The four parts — one should probably not speak here about strophes — are relative clauses, three with ὅς and one with οὗ. A clear division of lines can be made. This division is underlined in v. 22 and v. 23a by *parallelismus membrorum,* and in v. 23a rhetorical antithesis comes to the fore.

4. In conclusion, one may describe the structure of the source, in regard to both form and content, in this way: The confessional statement in v. 21a, the old ὑπέρ formula, has been developed didactically with the aid of Isaiah 53 (LXX) within a hymn: "Christ has suffered" (vv. 22f.) "for us" (v. 24).

Origin

1. This structure explains why the reference to the Passion in the formula never comes into contact with Jesus' announcements of his coming suffering, the summaries of the Passion, or the Passion narratives of the Gospels: The reference to the Passion does not report the Passion but develops the kerygma of the Passion's significance. Even in v. 23 the author probably does not think about individual aspects of the Passion story but only about the general tenor of the Passion.

---

34. This is considered possible by Bultmann, "Bekenntnis und Liedfragmente," 295, and assumed by Schille, *Hymnen,* 46.

35. So Lohse, "Parenesis and Kerygma," 58, n.108; Deichgräber, *Gotteshymnus,* 141.

36. So Bultmann, "Bekenntnis- und Liedfragmente," 296f.; Schille, *Hymnen,* 46; contra Deichgräber, *Gotteshymnus,* 141.

37. So Bultmann, "Bekenntnis- und Liedfragmente," 296f.; Deichgräber, *Gotteshymnus,* 142; Kelly, 125, in regard to v. 25b.

38. Bultmann, "Bekenntnis- und Liedfragmente," 297.

39. Deichgräber, *Gotteshymnus,* 140ff., cf. 106.

40. The translation above agrees with Bultmann, Schille, and Deichgräber.

2. In the Gospels the Passion is portrayed above all in dependence on the Psalms (22, 69, and others) as the path of the suffering just One.[41] But here the ὑπέρ formula is explicated, more exclusively and intensively than anywhere else in the NT, by expressions from the hymn of the Suffering Servant of God in Isaiah 53. Two aspects are taken from this OT text:

(a) Jesus' suffering unto death corresponds in its type to that of the Suffering Servant: V. 22 appropriates verbatim Isa. 53:9 (LXX), and in content v. 23 is perhaps inspired by Isa. 53:7 ("He opened not his mouth") and the key word παρεδόθη of Isa. 53:12 (LXX).

(b) Because Jesus was without guilt as he gave himself in suffering to God, his suffering unto death was vicarious atonement: V. 24a, b is based on Isa. 53:4, 12 (LXX); vv. 24c-25 is based on Isa. 53:5f. (LXX). What is said corresponds exactly, therefore, to what is in the first Christ hymn in I Peter: According to 1:19 Jesus' suffering unto death was an offering to God "without blemish or spot" (cf. vv. 22f.), and according to 1:18 it was the atoning sacrifice that "redeems" from the obligation of debt and service in relation to sin (cf. 2:21a, 24f.). In the third christological section as well vicarious atonement is the point of departure (3:18).

3. What then is the source of this interpretation of the ὑπέρ formula with the aid of Isaiah 53? The oldest christological formula tradition on the meaning of atonement with regard to the death of Jesus, in, e.g., I Cor. 15:3 and Rom. 4:25, does not reach back, surprisingly, to Isaiah 53.[42] Since by all indications this earliest tradition came from the Palestinian Church,[43] its emergence has been explained by many as follows: The concept of an atoning significance of martyrdom was widely accepted in Palestinian Judaism[44] and was transferred to Jesus by the Church.[45] But it has been shown that the concept of a martyr's death having an atoning effect for others came to the fore in NT times only in Hellenistic Judaism; on the basis of this observation it has been concluded that the ὑπέρ formula emerged in the Hellenistic Church.[46] But this conclusion is in conflict with the tradition-historical criteria that lead back to Palestine. This difficulty is resolved by the understanding that Jesus himself, in the cup saying in Mk. 14:24 par. and probably also in the ransom saying in Mk. 10:45 par., interpreted his approaching Passion in intuitive dependence on Isaiah 53 and with an immediacy that was foreign to later reflection. It was on the basis of Jesus' interpretation, then, that

---

41. Goppelt, *Typos*, 100-104; Schelkle, *Passion Jesu*, 81-104.

42. So correctly Hahn, *Titles*, 55f.

43. *Ibid.*

44. Lohse, *Märtyrer und Gottesknecht*, 64-104; he attempts to reconcile the absence of direct Jewish textual support from the time of Jesus by inferences (76f.) and postulates that the explanation of the cross as atonement in the Palestinian Church grew out of Isaiah 53 (145).

45. Cf. Hahn, *Titles*, 55f.

46. Wengst, *Christologische Formeln und Lieder*, 56f.

the early Christian ὑπέϱ formula came into being. It was then transmitted through the tradition of the Lord's Supper.[47]

4. At a later stage the formula was developed theologically with the aid of OT declarations. This occurred in a particular way in each part of the NT, above all in Paul, Hebrews, and I Peter. Only in I Pet. 2:21-25 has Isaiah 53 been applied extensively in this way. A corresponding evaluation of Isaiah 53 can be found elsewhere in the NT only in Matthew (8:17) and Luke (Luke 22:37; Acts 8:32f.), which are in content quite distinct.[48] The hymn in I Peter 2 may therefore have arisen within a stream of tradition in which the Synoptic tradition was elaborated. It grew, to be sure, in its verbal formulation out of the Hellenistic Church; the quotation following the LXX, the absolute use of πάσχειν[49] in vv. 21a, 23, and the echo of Pauline theology in v. 24 all point in that direction.

Vv. 22-24b: Christ's Innocent Suffering for the Atonement of Our Sins

22 Except for the first two words, this sentence appropriates Isa. 53:9 (LXX), which begins with ὅτι ἀνομίαν, while here we have ὅς ἁμαρτίαν. This difference probably reflects not merely a textual variant;[50] rather, ἀνομία, which was difficult to understand from the perspective of early Christian usage,[51] was replaced by ἁμαρτία, which fit better with the christological statement. V. 24 is thus linked directly with what precedes: He bore not his sins, but ours.

The OT statement is applied to Christ to indicate that in his total conduct, especially in his words, he followed God's will.[52] Within the christological statement this explains the efficacy of his death (1:18f.; 2:24), but within the context of the parenesis for slaves it calls for corresponding "right conduct" on the basis of a "conscience bound to God" (v. 19). ἁμαρτία, used here for the first time in I Peter, refers in

---

47. So, on the basis of extensive history-of-religion and tradition-historical analyses, Patsch, *Abendmahl und historischer Jesus,* §§41f.; on the earlier discussion see Schelkle, 84, n.1.

48. See also *I Clem.* 16:3-14 on Christ as model of the humble, 16:1f., 17; *Barn.* 5:2 for the atoning death, often in Justin (*Apologia* 1.50.2-11; 51.1-5, and passim) and in Melito (LCL AF I, 34-37, 355; *ANF* I, 179f.; VIII, 751-762).

49. See n.5 above.

50. According to Schelkle, 84, n.2, the variant is supposed to have been introduced under the influence of Zeph. 3:13 LXX: καὶ οὐ ποιήσουσιν ἀδικίαν. There is little likelihood of this.

51. Heb. 10:17 also comments on OT ἀνομία (cf. 8:12) with ἁμαρτία. Cf. I Jn. 3:4.

52. It is because the NT witnesses are certain of this unity, not because of empirical analysis, that they confess Jesus' "sinlessness" (II Cor. 5:21; Heb. 7:26; Jn. 8:46; I Jn. 3:5); it is not a dogma about Jesus' essence, but a soteriological statement.

the letter to transgression against God;[53] δόλος is speech that deceives others,[54] that which destroys community among people and for that reason with God.

23 According to v. 22 Christ suffered innocently, i.e., in the sense of Mt. 5:39, "not resisting the one who is evil." He did not return evil for evil. He himself practiced what is urged for Christians in I Pet. 3:9, in accord with his command to love one's enemy (Lk. 6:27f.). It was this parenetic tradition, perhaps in combination with Isa. 53:7 (LXX: διὰ τὸ κεκακῶσθαι οὐκ ἀνοίγει τὸ στόμα), that brought about the formulation of this verse.[55]

The three parts of the verse reflect fundamental aspects of the Passion narrative without representing particular parts of the narrative. (a) "Abuse" (ὃς λοιδορούμενος οὐκ ἀντελοιδόρει)[56] summarizes the impression that the accounts themselves give, such as the slander after the condemnation in the Sanhedrin (Mk. 14:65 par.), the ridicule by the guards (Mk. 15:17-20a par.), and the derision by the crucified thief (Mk. 15:29-32 par.). (b) Acceptance of all injustice without retort[57] impressed even outsiders such as Celsus[58] with the Passion story. When Jesus "did not threaten as he suffered" (πάσχων οὐκ ἠπείλει), he conducted himself in a way unlike that of the Jewish martyrs,[59] who laid claim to the *ius*

---

53. See the comments on 4:1.

54. "Deceit," "cunning," as in 2:1 (see the comments there); 3:10 — the opposite of veracity, not of "faultlessness."

55. V. 23 by no means directly gives, as Selwyn, 95 assumes, the impression of an eyewitness. Even if the author were "a witness of Christ's sufferings" (see the comments on 5:1) in a historical sense, he would, as a member of the Church, reproduce his impression only through the medium of the tradition.

56. λοιδορέω means here, as otherwise in Greek, "reproach," "abuse," also "slander," not as in the LXX. E.g., Acts 23:3f.; Jn. 9:28; Josephus, *War* 6.307 (LCL III, 465), referring to a prophet of doom: "He neither cursed any of those who beat him. . . ." Cf. H. Hanse, "λοιδορέω," *TDNT* IV, 293ff.

57. Jesus did not answer the charges: Mk. 14:61 par.; 15:5 par.; Lk. 23:9; otherwise in Jn. 18:19-22; Josephus gives a similar report about Joseph in *Ant.* 2.60 (LCL IV, 195): "[He] silently underwent his bonds and confinement, confident [in] God. . . ."

58. Origen, *Contra Celsum* 2.33 (*Contra Celsum*, tr. H. Chadwick [Cambridge, 1965], 94): If Jesus had been divine, he would thus at least have had to punish his tormentors with a gaze.

59. The Maccabaean youths die with the announcement or plea that God would punish their tormentors (II Macc. 7:17, 19, 31, 35ff.; IV Macc. 10:11); cf., however, *Test. Benj.* 5:4: "For if anyone wantonly attacks a pious man, he repents, since the pious man shows mercy to the one who abused him, and maintains silence"; *Test. Gad* 6:7 (an interpolation?): "But even if he is devoid of shame and persists in his wickedness, forgive him from the heart and leave vengeance to God" (*OT Pseudep.* I, 826, 816).

talionis, which was also valid in the Greek world.[60] He was silent, however, not "like an immovable rigid stone"[61] in the sense of Hellenistic self-control ("ataraxia"); he was silent because he did not wish to accuse his enemies, but to show them love. (c) "He trusted" the judgment[62] "to the One who judges justly" (παρεδίδου δὲ τῷ κρίνοντι δικαίως).[63] He leaves the judgment to God in a different sense than the Jewish martyrs: They expected compensatory revenge for what befell them. But Jesus set in opposition to evil not recompense but unlimited forgiveness;[64] he could do this because he left the preservation of justice to God. It was the goal of his own conduct to overcome evil through good and to remove the adversary thereby from judgment (cf. 2:12). Even this statement probably comes from the parenetic tradition behind 3:9,[65] which Rom. 12:19 develops into a corresponding directive: "Never avenge yourselves, but leave it to God's wrath," which, like I Pet. 2:23c, is to be understood not in terms of the OT and Jewish background that is clearly echoed but in terms of the parenetic context developed here (cf. Rom. 12:14, 21; I Pet. 3:9).

24a, b According to vv. 22f. Jesus suffered innocently as the righteous One like the Servant of God. For this reason his suffering unto death was, like that of the Servant, vicarious atonement. Now in vv. 24f. this idea is developed further in two clauses that are parallel in content. Both statements begin with relative pronouns referring to Jesus: v. 24a: ὃς τὰς ἁμαρτίας ἡμῶν αὐτὸς ἀνήνεγκεν, κτλ.; v. 24c: οὗ τῷ μώλωπι ἰάθητε. The first comes closer to Pauline terminology while the second

---

60. Aeschylus, *Choephori* 301 (LCL II, 189): " 'For word of hate let word of hate be said' crieth Justice aloud as she exalteth the debt, 'and for murderous stroke let murderous stroke be paid' "; cf. Marcus Aurelius 6.30 (LCL, 145-147).

61. *Odes Sol.* 31:10f. (*OT Pseudep.* II, 763): "But I endured and held my peace and was silent, that I might not be disturbed by them. But I stood undisturbed like a solid rock, which is continuously pounded by columns of waves and endures."

62. Not as Kelly, 121; Selwyn, 179: "himself," "his cause."

63. The v.l. τῷ κρίνοντι ἀδίκως in six lectionaries may well have come about quite early through an inadvertent approximation to the end of v. 19. It was taken up by Cyprian, *Ad Quirinum* 3.39; *De Bono Patientiae* 9 (*ANF* V, 545, 486), and Clement of Alexandria, *Adumbrationes* (*ANF* II, 572), and was adopted by the Vulgate ("tradebat autem iudicanti se iniuste"). It would express a submission of Jesus to Pilate's authority, which I Peter (see the comments on 2:17) precisely does not wish. It is in any case not, as Harnack assumed (*Beiträge zur Einleitung* VII, 89f.), original.

64. Different is Polycarp, *Phil.* 2:1 (LCL AF I, 285): "whose blood God will require from them who disobey him." See n.59 above.

65. Is it inspired by Isa. 53:8f. LXX, as v. 23 is by Isa. 53:7? That παραδιδόναι in Isa. 53:6, 12 prompted it is very improbable.

is closer to Synoptic terminology. Both begin by quoting Isaiah 53 (LXX), and according to both atonement relieves one not finally from the guilt of sin, but from bondage to sin. These two clauses are, therefore, fundamentally cast in a parenetic direction.

The statement in v. 24a explains with a verbatim quotation of Isa. 53:4 (12, LXX)[66] that Christ "bore," like the Servant of God, not his own sins but "our sins." He bore them, as is explained in an addition to the quotation, "in his body on the tree" (ἐν τῷ σώματι αὐτοῦ ἐπὶ τὸ ξύλον).[67] ἀναφέρειν, which in Isa. 53:12 (LXX) means only "bear," is interpreted as "bear upon." ξύλον, which can refer to an instrument of punishment already in the Greek language,[68] is a technical term here, as otherwise in early Christianity, for Jesus' cross.[69] This "taking upon" is, therefore, Jesus' suffering unto death. The connection to Isaiah 53 (LXX) uncovers the meaning of Jesus' suffering and explains what the formula ἔπαθεν ὑπὲρ ὑμῶν in v. 21a intends: Jesus bore our sins by suffering the judgment for them; he took the judgment ἐν τῷ σώματι,[70] i.e., in his bodily and human existence, upon himself. The formulation of this clause recalls not only Isaiah 53 (LXX) but also other OT concepts of offering and atonement, but they are not in view here.[71]

The effect for the baptized of this vicariously atoning suffering unto death is, according to v. 24b, death to sin leading to life for righteousness: ἵνα ταῖς ἁμαρτίαις ἀπογενόμενοι τῇ δικαιοσύνῃ ζήσωμεν. The parenetic outcome of this recalls Romans 6 and similar Pauline

---

66. The formulation combines LXX Isa. 53:4 (οὗτος τὰς ἁμαρτίας ἡμῶν φέρει . . .) and 12 (. . . αὐτὸς ἁμαρτίας πολλῶν ἀνήνεγκεν . . .).

67. I Peter refers to the whole Passion, not, like Paul, only to Christ's death; therefore, there is no reason to understand ἐπί with the accusative, as is possible in Hellenistic Greek, to be like επί with the genitive: "He bore our sins . . . on the wood." So Beare, 149f.; Kelly, 122f.

68. J. Schneider, "ξύλον," *TDNT* V, 37.

69. Thus on the basis of a reinterpretation of Dt. 21:22 in Gal. 3:13; Acts 5:30; 10:39 (κρεμάσαντες ἐπὶ ξύλον); cf. also Acts 13:29; Schneider, *TDNT* V, 39f.

70. So also Col. 1:22; Rom. 6:12; cf. Num. 14:33.

71. Two points of contact can be considered here: (1) In I Pet. 2:5 the author uses the LXX formula ἀναφέρειν θυσίας ἐπὶ τὸ θυσιαστήριον (Gen. 8:20; Lev. 3:5ff.; 11:16; 14:20, and passim), which is used in Heb. 9:28 in connection with Isa. 53:12: ἅπαξ προσενεχθεὶς εἰς τὸ πολλῶν ἀνενεγκεῖν ἁμαρτίας. But the point in I Pet. 2:24 is not, as in Hebrews, a high-priestly self-sacrifice, nor does I Peter regard the cross as an altar on which Jesus offers himself as sacrifice; the object of ἀναφέρειν is sins, not the body (with Selwyn, 180; Kelly, 122; contra Wohlenberg, 81ff.; Schelkle, 85). (2) The author is also not thinking of the scapegoat, on which, according to Lev. 16:21, the guilt of the people is laid by Aaron (with Kelly, 122f.; Beare, 149f.; contra Windisch, 65f.).

statements.[72] According to Romans 6 the baptized have died through baptism with Christ to the dominion of sin (vv. 2, 11) in order to live under righteousness (v. 18). But the similarly structured expressions here in I Pet. 2:24 are used in an entirely different way and in a different sense than in Romans: "Sin" and "righteousness" here are not powers, but conduct that is sinful[73] or righteous,[74] to which a person is bound or devoted. ἀπογενόμενοι means, in contrast to ζήσωμεν, "having died from"; but this "death from" does not occur by a "crucifixion with" (Rom. 6:6), but as the word intends,[75] by redemption from the realm of sin. It does not occur by a punctiliar verdict of judgment by God that is appropriated by faith (Rom. 6:11), but by one separating oneself from sinning. How this is done is explained in I Pet. 4:1f.,[76] mainly by the calling into discipleship until one's own suffering unto death (v. 21), which is acknowledged and practiced. The same experience is described in the following parallel statement with ἐπεστράφητε.

Vv. 24c-25: Turning to the Shepherd and Herdsman of Our Souls

24c The second clause begins like the first (v. 24a) with a quotation from Isaiah 53 (LXX): "By his wound you have been healed."[77] The "wound" (μώλωψ)[78] is parallel to "bore upon," which represents Christ's suffering unto death.[79] Whether these two terms allude here, as is often assumed,[80] to the wounds of slaves is very questionable. That Christ's

---

72. Rom. 7:4; II Cor. 5:14f.; Gal. 2:19; Col. 2:20; 3:3, 5.

73. In I Pet. 2:22, 24a, b; 3:18; 4:1 (see the comments there), 8.

74. Otherwise in I Peter in 3:14; δίκαιος with it with the same meaning in 3:12 (= Ps. 34:16), 18; 4:18.

75. ἀπογίνομαι only here in the LXX and NT: "be distant/absent" (Thucydides 1.39 [LCL I, 71]: τῶν ἁμαρτημάτων ἀπογενόμενοι, "not participating in . . .") or "distance oneself," "die" (Thucydides 2.98 [*ibid.*, 449]; Herodotus 2.136; 5.4 [LCL I, 439-441; III, 4f.]; Mithras liturgy l. 719 [text in *The "Mithras Liturgy,"* ed. and tr. M. W. Meyer (Missoula, MN, 1976), 20f.; translation there and in H. D. Betz, ed., *The Greek Magical Papyri in Translation Including the Demotic Spells* I (Chicago, 1986), 52; cf. p. 82 above, n.16]: πάλιν γενόμενος ἀπογίγνομαι). Cf. BAGD s.v.; F. Büchsel, *TDNT* I, 686.

76. See the comments there.

77. Isa. 53:5f. LXX: τῷ μώλωπι αὐτοῦ ἡμεῖς ἰάθημεν πάντες ὡς πρόβατα ἐπλανήθημεν.

78. μώλωψ occurs only here in the NT and refers to a "welt" raised by blows; cf. BAGD s.v.

79. *Barn.* 7:2 (LCL AF I, 365): ἔπαθεν, ἵνα ἡ πληγὴ αὐτοῦ ζωοποιήσῃ ἡμᾶς.

80. Selwyn, 181; Beare, 149f.; Kelly, 122.

wound effects healing (ἰάθητε) represents an unclear image for the healing of the illness of sinning through his vicarious suffering.[81]

25 Healing from sinning is interpreted as an ἐπιστραφῆναι, a turning, of those who like sheep have been wandering about, to the shepherd Christ. The connection provided by Isa. 53:5f. to both images is developed with the aid of early Christian traditions: ἐπεστράφητε νῦν ἐπὶ τὸν ποιμένα καὶ ἐπίσκοπον τῶν ψυχῶν ὑμῶν. The connection of the two verbs in v. 24c and v. 25 corresponds to a commonly used early Christian tradition.[82] The image of the herd and of the shepherd has a broad OT background.[83] But I Peter appropriates not this, but the early Christian tradition that developed from it. Jesus himself had explained his work of salvation through a parable of the discovery of a lost sheep.[84] His ministry was very early likened indirectly to the shepherd's (ποιμήν) work of finding the lost sheep,[85] but only in relatively late strata of the NT is Christ called "shepherd."[86] Just how common the tradition of the image seen here in I Peter was can be seen in its application to Church leadership in 5:2, 4: ποιμάνατε τὸ ἐν ὑμῖν ποίμνιον τοῦ θεοῦ (ἐπισκοποῦντες) . . . καὶ φανερωθέντες τοῦ ἀρχιποίμενος. . . . From this it may be concluded that in 2:25 ἐπίσκοπος is intended to interpret the image of the shepherd; this is also the case of the corresponding early Christian tradition in Acts 20:28 and its OT background.[87] The term designated in the Greek language the "overseer," often the divine Overlord who looked out for his people in a merciful and beneficent way;[88] such overlordship was expected especially of the salvation deities called upon as κύριοι (cf. I Cor. 8:5f.). ψυχή represents here, as in I Pet. 1:9, the whole person.

Therefore the overlordship of the glorified Christ, which protects

---

81. That Christ is thought of here, in extension of Mk. 2:16f. par., as a physician, is inserted by the Church Fathers, e.g., Theodoret (cf. *NPNF* second series III, 114): ὁ ἰατρὸς ἐδέξατο τὴν τιμὴν καὶ ὁ ἄρρωστος ἔτυχε τῆς ἰάσεως (cf. Windisch, 66).

82. Isa. 6:10 LXX, which is appropriated in Mk. 4:12; Mt. 13:15; Jn. 12:40; Acts 28:27: μήποτε . . . ἐπιστρέψωσιν, καὶ ἰάσομαι. . . .

83. J. Jeremias, "ποιμήν," *TDNT* VI, 487-500.

84. Lk. 15:2, 3-7 (par. Mt. 18:12-14); cf. Mt. 10:6; 15:24; Lk. 19:10; cf. Ps. 119:176.

85. Mk. 6:34 par.; for further passages see Jeremias, *TDNT* VI, 493f.

86. Heb. 13:20; Rev. 7:17; Jn. 10:11f. (cf. 21:15-17).

87. Ezek. 34:11, of God: ἐκζητήσω τὰ πρόβατά μου καὶ ἐπισκέψομαι αὐτά.

88. H. W. Beyer, "ἐπίσκοπος," *TDNT* II, 608-614. God is characterized as ἐπίσκοπος already in the LXX (Job 20:29; Wis. 1:6), as well as in Philo (*De Mutatione Nominum* 39.216; *De Somniis* 1.91 [LCL V, 255, 345]). God is also spoken of in the Hellenistic world as shepherd (Philo, *De Agricultura* 50-52 [LCL III, 135]).

from evil and is beneficent, now surrounds those who once wandered about like sheep (ἦτε γὰρ ὡς πρόβατα πλανώμενοι), those who had fallen prey to "their own manner of life" (cf. 1:12). Now, however, their path has been redirected toward that one center. The aorist passive ἐπεστράφητε corresponds to the expressions with which the letter otherwise designates the transition to the saving νῦν (1:12; 2:10; 3:21): "You were ransomed" (1:18), "newly birthed" (1:23, 3), "called" (2:9; 5:10). For this reason it is probable that the passive voice, not the middle, is intended:[89] they were led by God to Christ in order to follow him in discipleship (v. 21) as the Shepherd and Overlord so that their life now has this direction determined by him.

3:1-6: Responsibilities of Married Women[1]

1 *Similarly, you wives,*
subject yourselves to your husbands,
so that even those who do not obey the word
may be won through their wives' manner of life without a word,

---

89. ἐπιστρέφω in the LXX usually represents שׁוב and thus becomes a technical term meaning "turn around," "convert"; cf. G. Bertram, "ἐπιστρέφω," *TDNT* VII, 723-726. It was taken up in this sense in early Christianity in formulas of the Gentile mission (I Thess. 1:9) and is used often in Acts (3:19; 14:15; 15:19; 26:18, and elsewhere), though usually μετανοέω stands in its place. ἐπιστρέφω appears in Jas. 5:20 as the opposite of being lost: ἐκ πλάνης. The aorist passive can be used as middle "convert" (so in I Pet. 2:25 according to BAGD s.v., referring to Epictetus, *Dissertationes* 2.20.22 [LCL I, 376]) or as passive "be turned or led to" (so Bertram, *TDNT* VII, 728). In favor of the latter is the immediately preceding ἰάθητε.

1. See, in general: H. Baltensweiler, *Die Ehe im NT* (AThANT 52; Zurich, 1967); H. Greeven, "Ehe nach dem NT," *NTS* 15 (1969), 365-388; E. Kähler, *Die Frau in den paulinischen Briefen* (Zurich, 1960); K. H. Rengstorf, "Die neutestamentliche Mahnung an die Frau, sich dem Mann unterzuordnen," *Verbum Dei manet in aeternum* (FS O. Schmitz; Witten, 1953), 131-145; Rengstorf, *Mann und Frau im Urchristentum* (Cologne, 1954); J. Leipoldt, *Die Frau in der antiken Welt und im Christentum* (Leipzig, 1955); S. Terrien, *Till the Heart Sings* (Philadelphia, 1985; cf. Bibliography 233-250); R. F. Collins, "Marriage (NT)," *ABD* 4 (1992), 569-572.

On 3:1b-2 see: R. Allen, *The Spontaneous Expansion of the Church and the Causes Which Hinder It* (Grand Rapids, 1962); Bieder, *Grund und Kraft der Mission;* J. Blauw, *The Missionary Nature of the Church* (tr. W. Holladay, et al.; New York, 1962); W. Brandt, "Wandel als Zeugnis"; E. Güttgemanns, *Der leidende Apostel und sein Herr* (FRLANT 90; Göttingen, 1966); F. Hahn, *Mission in the NT* (tr. F. Clarke; London, 1965); J. Jeremias, "Die missionarische Aufgabe in der Mischehe (1 Cor. 7,16)" (1954), *idem, Abba. Studien zur neutestamentlichen Theologie und Zeitgeschichte* (Göttingen, 1966), 292-298; Lippert, "Leben als Zeugnis"; van Unnik, "Rücksicht"; E. Peterson, "Theologie des Kleides," *Marginalien zur Theologie* (Munich, 1956), 41-56; Niederwimmer, *Askese und Mysterium;* Balch, *Let Wives Be Submissive;* Achtemeier, "Newborn Babes," 218-222; Patterson, "Roles in Marriage."

2 *when they see your holy manner of life (conducted before God)*
in fear.

3 *Let your adornment not be the outer (adornment)*
of braiding of hair, putting on of gold (jewelry), and wearing of
garments,
4 *but of the hidden person of the heart*
in the incorruptible (essence) of a gentle and quiet spirit:
This is precious before God.

5 *For so the holy women who hoped in God adorned themselves*
then
and subjected themselves to their husbands,
6 *just as Sarah obeyed Abraham by calling him "lord";*
you have become her children if you conduct yourselves
properly
and fear no intimidation.

Tradition and Structure

This prosaically styled and extensive parenesis for wives appropriates to a large extent elements of transmitted material that also make an appearance in station codes in Col. 3:18; Eph. 5:22f., and in the congregation regulations in I Tim. 2:9-15; Tit. 2:4f.; *I Clem.* 1:3; 21:7; Polycarp, *Phil.* 4:2 (LCL AF I, 10f., 46f., 286-289). Its missionary aspect (vv. 1b-2) is at the same time its overall point of view. In terms of particulars the following structural elements stand out:

1. The instruction in v. 1a follows in its structure the station code tradition and thereby corresponds largely in wording to Col. 3:18 and Eph. 5:(21)22. The expression repeated in v. 5, ὑποτασσόμεναι τοῖς ἰδίοις ἀνδράσιν, can also be found in the differently structured congregation regulation of Tit. 2:4f., and it is echoed in the key word ὑποταγή in I Tim. 2:11 and *I Clem.* 1:3 (LCL AF I, 10f.).

2. Grammatically the imperative is not causal, as is normally the case in the station code schema, the ground for the imperative being stated (as in 3:7) in a final clause. In this way it is able to call attention to the conflict situation, i.e., the religiously mixed marriage. In such a situation the proper conduct is for the wife to become a missionary witness in her actions. This instruction is like I Cor. 7:16 in content, but it has no direct contact with I Corinthians. The key phrase for the station code in I Peter, "proper conduct," summarizes in v. 6b what has been said; for the Christian wife what "proper conduct" is in marriage is developed in vv. 3-6a with the aid of parenetic traditions.

3. What is said about the wife's conduct, especially in regard to adornment in vv. 3f., makes verbatim use of the same tradition as the congregation rule in

I Tim. 2:9-15.[2] This Church tradition lays hold for its part of a topos of proverbial ethics that was common in the Hellenistic world.[3] Even the references to OT examples in vv. 5-6a, which illustrate and underscore what has been said about conduct, are traditional; they are to be found in a similar context in I Tim. 2:13f.

Vv. 1f.: The Married Woman as Witness

1 ὁμοίως, "similarly," as previously in 2:13, 18 and later in v. 7 (there again ὁμοίως) wives are addressed[4] along with their male counterparts (v. 7), unlike slaves (2:18-20), and are also to position themselves in terms of their station. The imperatival participle[5] ὑποτασσόμεναι (τοῖς ἰδίοις ἀνδράσιν) here means, as in 2:18, that that "positioning of oneself" amounts to "subjecting oneself."

According to the station code tradition, subjection is appropriate because of neither a fundamental quality of marriage[6] nor a fundamental quality of womanhood[7] as marriage and womanhood emerged from God's creation, but quite clearly because of custom.[8] Subjection corresponds to the structure of society of that time; Christians were to place themselves into their historical situation even in this respect. The directive stands thereby in tension with Jesus' sayings, which make husband

---

2. Cf. I Pet. 3:3-5 and I Tim. 2:9-15:

v. 3:	ἐμπλοκὴ τριχῶν	ἐν πλέγμασιν (v. 9)
	χρυσίων	χρυσίῳ (v. 9)
	ἱματίων κόσμος	ἱματισμῷ (v. 9)
v. 4:	ἡσυχίῳ	ἡσυχίᾳ (vv. 11f.)
v. 5:	ἐκόσμουν	κόσμῳ κοσμεῖν (v. 9)

3. Plutarch, *Moralia* 141e (LCL II, 316-318); Epictetus, *Enchiridion* 40 (LCL III, 476-479); Seneca, *De Beneficiis* 7.9 (LCL III, 476-479; cf. Ausonius, *Ludus Septem Sapientum* 1.4 [LCL I, 311]); Quintilian, *Institutio Oratia* 8, proem 20 (LCL III, 189); Diodorus Siculus 12.21 (LCL IV, 416-419); pseudo-Lucian, *Amores* 40ff. (LCL VIII, 212-217); cf. *Ep. Arist.* 229f. (*OT Pseudep.* II, 28); Philo, *De Virtutibus* 39f.; *De Migratione Abrahami* 97; *De Vita Mosis* 2.243 (LCL VIII, 187-189; IV, 187; VI, 571).

4. One should include the article here (to indicate address), as in 2:18 and 3:7: αἱ γυναῖκες. ἰδίοις is used in 3:1, 5 in place of the personal pronoun to underscore that this concerns the situation of marriage.

5. See above, p. 128, n. 32.

6. It is not an "order of creation" (contra Schelkle, 88; Kelly, 127); the gospel tradition calls indissoluble monogamy an institution of the Creator (Mt. 19:4-6 par.), but not subjection.

7. The pointed argument in I Cor. 11:3 should not be generalized for the station code tradition; the "proof from Scripture" in I Tim. 2:13-15 represents a decline into anti-heretical polemics.

8. Col. 3:18: ὡς ἀνῆκεν, "as is fitting."

and wife equal in accord with what creation originally established (Mt. 19:4-6 par. Mk.) and with creation's eschatological goal (Mk 12:24f. par.). This equality was appropriated in the post-Easter proclamation for Church membership (Gal. 3:28f.; I Cor. 12:13; Col. 3:11), but was also adapted to custom (I Cor. 11:2-16).

I Peter maintains this fundamental equality of the wife more than the rest of the parenetic tradition, since wives are not only addressed here in terms of personal responsibility, as are husbands, but are also summoned to give the witness in deed, with which all are charged here, to serve as example in the conflict situation. The station-code tradition, which is articulated in general terms in 2:12 (let there be a Christian witness through personal presence in society) is modeled in the case of wives for the conflict situation.

Many[9] Christian women are married to men who "are disobedient to the word" (εἴ τινες ἀπειθοῦσιν τῷ λόγῳ),[10] i.e., who deprive themselves of the gospel. This situation, which Paul already reflected on in I Cor. 7:12-16, created considerable difficulties. While a woman should, in the opinion of ancient ethicists, follow the religion of her husband,[11] these Christian women separate themselves exclusively from the husband's religion and its corresponding custom and place themselves into the close life shared by the Church. Tertullian, writing to his wife, portrays the permanent conflict that came out of such a situation in terms of later Church custom.[12] I Peter has a deeper understanding of the conflict, in accord with all that has been said up to this point (cf. 2:19). Apart from the reference to intimidation in 3:6b, I Peter speaks not of the negative aspects of the situation (as with slaves) but of the positive possibilities: A husband who deprives himself of "the word" should "without a word"[13] be won over by his wife's manner of life, won over, i.e., for faith: ἵνα . . . διὰ τῆς τῶν γυναικῶν ἀναστροφῆς ἄνευ λόγου κερδηθήσονται.[14] Such a husband would be familiar with the content of the gospel — as much as one is able to recognize that content

---

9. εἴ τινες has the same meaning here as in Phil. 4:8, where it alternates with ὅσα.

10. ἀπειθεῖν, as in 2:8 (see the comments there); 3:20; 4:17.

11. Plutarch, *Praecepta Conjugalia* 19 (LCL II, 311).

12. Tertullian, *Ad Uxorem* 2.4f. (*ANF* IV, 46f.); cf. Justin, *Apologia* 2.2 (*ANF* I, 188f.).

13. Not, of course, "without the word" (contra Knopf, 122).

14. κερδαίνω became a "missionary term" (H. Schlier, "κέρδος, κερδαίνω," *TDNT* III, 673): I Cor. 9:19-22; cf. Mt. 18:15. D. Daube, "Κερδαίνω." On ἵνα with the future as in Dan. 3:10, 11; 6:6 LXX, cf. BDF §369 (pp. 186ff.).

from the outside. He would perhaps have heard that content together with his wife, from his wife, and from other Christians (cf. 3:15), but then rejected it. Now the reality of this content should encounter him as lived word and win him over, not for an empirical understanding of her behavior but for faith.

2   Such men are won over for faith because they constantly have before their eyes[15] that which is shaped by the "word," and out of which, therefore, the "word" speaks. Their being won over is based, therefore, not on their capacity for moral decision,[16] but on the gospel's power to convince:[17] ἐποπτεύσαντες τὴν ἐν φόβῳ ἁγνὴν ἀναστροφὴν ὑμῶν, "when they see your pure manner of life (conducted before God)[18] in fear." The conduct they observe is "pure"[19] in that it arises from fear of God, which shuns evil but does not fear humankind (3:6), and especially by grace (1:17f.).

The content of this witness in deed is by no means the eschatological ethos of the Sermon on the Mount, but conduct that does justice to marriage. As is clarified in what follows, this conduct in marriage is first of all according to vv. 3f. the way in which the wife tries to achieve a natural partnership and to relate lovingly to the other person. It is, in general terms, according to vv. 5f., to place oneself or subject oneself within marriage; it is "proper conduct" in this station of life. On this basis, the next two verses explain how the Christian wife is to adorn herself in order to win over her husband for herself and for the gospel.

Vv. 3f.: Convincing Adornment

3   The Church Fathers quoted v. 3 as a prohibition of feminine jewelry;[20] more recently it has been explained as an expression of a

---

15. ἐποπτεύω, as in 2:12.

16. Contra Windisch, 66f.; Selwyn, 183.

17. Further: Ignatius, *Eph.* 10:1 (LCL AF I, 185): "Suffer them therefore to become your disciples, at least through your deeds"; cf. *Trall.* 3:2 (*ibid.*, 215). The most impressive example is the conversion of Augustine's father through the conduct of his mother: *Confessions* 1.11.17 (*NPNF* first series I, 50). Cf. Philo, *De Josepho* 86 (= 2.54 [LCL VI, 182f.]).

18. See the comments on 2:18.

19. On this word see F. Hauck, "ἁγνός," *TDNT* I, 122.

20. Clement of Alexandria, *Paedagogus* 3.66.3 (II.127.2 [*ANF* II, 287, 269]: I Tim. 2:9 quoted as I Peter); Tertullian, *De Oratione* 20; *De Cultu Feminarum* 1.6; 2.2, 7-13 (*ANF* III, 687; IV, 16f., 19); Cyprian, *De Habitu Virginum* 8 (*ANF* V, 432).

"puritanical" mentality.[21] The statement develops, however, merely a vivid picture of contrast that Christian parenesis took over from Hellenistic ethics[22] in order to impress on the reader the positive statement, which appears here in v. 3: ὧν ἔστω οὐχ ὁ ἔξωθεν . . . κόσμος. It is not to be assumed from this sentence, therefore, that many wealthy women who could afford expensive coiffures, gold jewelry, and conspicuous apparel belonged to the churches addressed by I Peter.[23] The genitive nouns of action[24] depict the expenditure of work and time that this way of making oneself attractive requires: ἐμπλοκῆς τριχῶν καὶ περιθέσεως χρυσίων ἢ ἐνδύσεως ἱματίων.

4 The positive antithesis is not intended to heighten the impression that spiritual inwardness is more valuable than physical appearance.[25] It contrasts, rather, what a person can make of herself with what she becomes through Christ: ὁ κρυπτὸς τῆς καρδίας ἄνθρωπος, κτλ. "The hidden person of the heart" is one whose being is determined by faith. The key words of this unique expression are encountered elsewhere in the NT only in Rom. 2:29 and in Matthew. In Matthew what impression a person makes on his or her environment is contrasted with that which is "hidden" (Mt. 6:3f.), that which comes "out of the heart" (6:21; 15:8, 18f.), and that which alone has lasting importance before God (6:4, 6, 18). Therefore, here genitive καρδίας explains the adjective κρυπτός and vice versa: "The hidden person" is not the inner side of the person,[26] but the whole human being as it is determined from within, "from the heart," i.e., from believing thoughts and desires.[27] This heart is "hidden" because its essence cannot be confirmed; it is not empirically demonstrable because it comes forth from faith and from the Spirit.[28]

---

21. Knopf, 123, quotes Gunkel, 555: "The early Christian Church was puritanically disposed, not at all differing in this respect from the pious Judaism of that time."

22. See above, nn. 2f.

23. Contra Beare, 155; Kelly, 129f.

24. The construction is: ὧν (sc. ὁ κόσμος) ἔστω οὐχ ὁ ἔξωθεν ἐμπλοκῆς κτλ. τὸ χρυσίον, "gold," is here "gold jewelry"; so also I Tim. 2:9; Rev. 17:4; 18:16.

25. Contra Windisch, 67: "an attempt to sever the spiritual essence of a person from his or her external appearance."

26. Contra Knopf, 124 (possessive genitive), and Selwyn, 184 ("genitive of definition").

27. So Kelly, 129, and Knopf, 124, as a second possibility: appositional genitive (see BDF §167 [pp. 92f.]).

28. The expression, which is in accord most often with the terminology of the Matthean special source (M), has a certain correspondence in the Pauline differentiation between the "outer" and the "inner" person (II Cor. 4:16; cf. Rom. 7:20-22).

This person is encountered ἐν τῷ ἀφθάρτῳ τοῦ πραέος καὶ ἡσυχίου πνεύματος, "by the incorruptible means[29] of a gentle and peaceful spirit." The outward expressions of the "hidden person" derive from the spirit; this does not refer to the inner human realm, a person's disposition,[30] or to the Spirit of God as such,[31] but to the human spirit as it is shaped by God's Spirit.[32]

This spirit is to be "gentle and quiet." πραΰς is in OT thought the humble person who does not insist on his or her way, but awaits from God the result of his or her conduct.[33] In classical Greek and Hellenistic thought it is used of gentle friendliness, which has worth as a social virtue, above all on the part of women.[34] Here, as in 3:16 (μετὰ πραΰτητος), I Peter refers to the latter, the friendly conduct of a person in relation to the neighbor. It understands this, however, from the perspective of Christian presuppositions, as the application of these principles to all Christians in 3:14-16 indicates: "Gentle friendliness" is now an expression of love even of one's enemy (cf. I Cor. 13:4-7), not of pliant indulgence.[35] With friendliness of this kind in the face of offenses and aggression[36] early Christian parenesis combines here and elsewhere the "calm and quiet state of being"[37] that does not become agitated and

---

29. ἐν τῷ ἀφθάρτῳ is a substantivized neuter: that which is "immortal," the "imperishable quality" (see BAGD s.v.).

30. BAGD s.v.: "disposition"; cf. *Pss. Sol.* 12:5 (*OT Pseudep.* II, 662): ψυχὴ ἡσυχίας. Kelly, 130: "frame of mind," as probably in I Cor. 4:21 and Gal. 6:1 as well.

31. Knopf, 125: In 1:2, 11f.; 3:18; 4:6, 14 "it is the Holy Spirit of God or the Spirit of Christ." In 3:19, however, we are faced, in any case, with a different meaning for πνεῦμα (see the comments there).

32. The closest parallel is in the Pauline expression πνεῦμα πραΰτητος (I Cor. 4:21). Gal. 6:1: "If anyone is overtaken in a trespass, you who are spiritual are to restore him in a spirit of gentleness." This expression, like ἡσύχιον πνεῦμα in I Pet. 3:4, is to be understood along the lines of OT and Jewish tradition, according to which the human spirit receives its particular shape from external activity, finally from God's Spirit. See E. Sjöberg and E. Schweizer, "πνεῦμα," *TDNT* VI, 381, 447f.

33. This tradition is appropriated in the Matthean special source, Mt. 11:29; 21:5, of Jesus, 5:5, of those pronounced blessed; see R. Bultmann, "πείθω," *TDNT* VI, 6.

34. F. Hauck and S. Schulz, "πραΰς, πραΰτης," *TDNT* VI, 646; cf. Plutarch, *Praecepta Conjugalia* 45 (II.144e [LCL II, 333]); *Consolatio ad Uxorem* 2 (2.608d [LCL VII, 583]).

35. ταπεινός is used of humility before God in 5:5f.

36. I Cor. 4:21; II Cor. 10:1; Gal. 6:1.

37. ἡσύχιος, "quiet," is used elsewhere in the NT only in I Tim. 2:2; there as here, and as in *I Clem.* 13:4; *Barn.* 19:4 par. *Did.* 3:7f. (LCL AF I, 31, 403, 315), it appears alongside πραΰς. Both NT occurrences utilize Isa. 66:2 LXX: "on whom shall I look except one who is humble and contrite and who trembles at my words." *Herm. Mand.* 5.2.3; 6.2.3; 11.8; cf. 5.2.6 (LCL AF II, 91, 97, 121, 93): ἡσυχία with πραΰτης.

does not answer "invective with invective" (cf. 2:22f.; 3:9). It is an expression of the "nonresistance" that overcomes evil with good (Mt. 5:39). Outward expressions of a "gentle and quiet spirit" have a lasting quality before God and human beings; they are "imperishable" (ἄφθαρτος) like "treasure in heaven" (Mt. 6:19f.). They[38] are an adornment that is "precious before God": ὅ ἐστιν ἐνώπιον τοῦ θεοῦ πολυτελές. For God "looks on that which is hidden" (Mt. 6:4, 6, 18; cf. I Sam. 16:7), on the authentic substance by which a person shows himself or herself to be God's creation, one who "hopes in him" (v. 5).

Vv. 5f.: Old Testament Examples

5 οὕτως γάρ ποτε καὶ αἱ ἅγιαι γυναῖκες . . . ἐκόσμουν ἑαυτάς, "for so the holy women adorned themselves." These women are "holy" like the "holy people" (2:9)[39] "once upon a time" in antiquity,[40] "holy" like the "saints" of now because they were elect and belonged thereby to the Holy One (1:15f.; 2:9). This relationship shows itself in their "hope in God": αἱ ἐλπίζουσαι εἰς θεόν. They await their continued existence from God's promise (1:3, 13; 3:15; cf. Heb. 11:13). This orientation, i.e., this hope and faith (1:21), is seen in the way in which these women adorn themselves and conduct themselves in marriage. Here the reason for the reference to these OT models becomes clear: The conduct of the "holy women" of the OT is not a model worthy of imitation just for general human reasons,[41] as in *I Clement,* which lists series of examples from the OT together with examples from secular history (*I Clem.* 55:1 [LCL AF I, 120f.]). I Peter seeks, like Hebrews 11, to direct attention to a "cloud of witnesses" who have travelled the same path of hoping faith (Heb. 12:1).

---

38. In content, ὅ can only be connected to the entire preceding sentence (so Beare, 155), not to ἐν τῷ ἀφθάρτῳ alone (Bengel, ad loc.; Knopf, 125) or to πνεύματος (Kelly, 129f.).

39. ἅγιοι is commonly used to characterize Christians. It appears only rarely as an attribute of particular groups or individuals. It is used of OT persons only here, in II Pet. 3:2 (cf. Ignatius, *Phld.* 9:2 [LCL AF I, 248f.]) of "the holy prophets," and in Mt. 27:52 of many "saints." It is used of NT persons in Acts 4:27, 30: "your holy servant Jesus"; Eph. 3:5: "holy apostles and prophets" (Ignatius, *Magn.* 3:1 [*ibid.,* 199]: "the holy elders").

40. ποτέ thus also in 3:20; in 2:10 of the time before Christ, thus often in Paul (Gal. 1:13, 23; 2:6; Col. 1:21; 3:7, and passim).

41. Contra Knopf, 126: "It was also one of the great merits of the OT that it furnished the young Church the great book of ethical patterns." See more recently G. Ghiberti, "Sante donne."

6 I Peter links Christian women, moreover, with a particular person who is named expressly, Abraham's wife, and understands them as her descendants (ἧς ἐγενήθητε τέκνα). They do not become Sarah's "children" when they behave like her.[42] They are, rather, already her children because they are heirs of the same promise (1:10-12). But the author does not reflect critically on this relationship in the way that Paul does (in Romans 4 and Galatians 3), but applies it as accepted on the basis of Christian tradition, as in 2:9. The OT figures are not thought of as types[43] pointing to the time of fulfillment (I Cor. 10:11), but as spiritual progenitors. What is decisive here is that the women of the elect people conduct themselves in accord with their marital ties (ὑποτασσόμεναι τοῖς ἰδίοις ἀνδράσιν) just as the women of that people with whom election and promise began.

In Sarah's case subjection was seen in her obedience[44]: ὡς Σάρρα ὑπήκουσεν τῷ 'Αβραάμ. This is demonstrated by an OT passage that does not exactly fit, but which was also adduced by the rabbis in the same sense: According to Gen. 18:12 Sarah called Abraham (her) "lord"[45] (κύριον αὐτὸν καλοῦσα). It was customary in the ancient Orient for women to refer to or address their husbands with this title.[46]

"You become her children when you conduct yourselves properly and fear no intimidation." The participles ἀγαθοποιοῦσαι καὶ μὴ φοβούμεναι express not the *ground*,[47] but a *demonstration* of this relationship to Sarah. Christian women became "her children"[48] through

---

42. Philo, *De Virtutibus* 195 (LCL VIII, 283-285): ". . . kinship is not measured only by blood, but by similarity of conduct. . . ."

43. Sarah is not seen "typologically," as Kelly explains it, 130ff.

44. In the station code tradition ὑπακούειν stands in place of ὑποτάσσεσθαι. It is used elsewhere in respect to children (Col. 3:20; Eph. 6:1) and slaves (Col. 3:22; Eph. 6:5). See above, p. 174.

45. Gen. 18:12 LXX: ὁ δὲ κύριός μου πρεσβύτερος. Cf. *Midrash Tanḥuma* (Vienna, 1863) חיי שרה 29a: "Abraham's wife honored him and called him 'lord,' as it says in Gen. 18:12: . . ." (Str.-Bill. III, 764). Sly, "Philo and Josephus," interprets v. 6b in the context of Hellenistic Jewish narrowing of the role of wives and of the biblical record of Sarah. See also below, n.50.

46. Cf. Hahn, *Titles,* 78ff.

47. Contra Windisch, 67: "The thought is formulated in an un-Pauline way, since not faith but good works and fearlessness (Prov. 3:25) are named as conditions. . . ." Even μή does not indicate a conditional meaning, since it is normally used in koine Greek with the participle.

48. The unique formulation is modeled on "children of Abraham," which is encountered in the NT above all in the gospel tradition (Mt. 3:9 par. Lk.; Jn. 8:39; cf. Gal. 3:7: υἱοί). Much more common is the corresponding designation of Abraham as father (Rom. 4:11f.; Jas. 2:21; Mt. 3:9 par.; Jn. 8:39, 53; *I Clem.* 31:2 [LCL AF I, 61]; *Barn.* 13:7 [*ibid.*, 389]). The corresponding reference to Sarah as mother occurs already in Isa. 51:2: "Look

baptism (that this was so apart from whether they were Gentiles or Jews is not mentioned by I Peter) and thereby through the summons to hope: The aorist verb ἐγενήθητε clearly looks back to a single past event. That they became her children in this way demonstrates itself in "proper conduct," as the roughly connected present participle ἀγαθοποιοῦσαι[49] indicates. ἀγαθοποιοῦν stands here in place of ὑποτάσσεσθαι from v. 5. This confirms what has been stated for other uses of the verb in I Peter: "Proper conduct" is doing justice to the demands of society's institutions in accord with a Christian conscience. Here this proper conduct is subjection in accord with conscience. It is possible only if fear of humankind is overcome. A Christian woman married to a non-Christian man is in danger of threats of being forced, openly or otherwise, to give in to wishes of her husband that conflict with her faith. The women are urged, therefore, as are all Christians, in accord with a fundamental line of thought of I Peter, in fear of God (3:2), to fear "no intimidation"[50] from the human side[51]: μὴ φοβούμεναι μηδεμίαν πτόησιν.

3:7: *Responsibilities of Married Men*[1]

7 *Similarly, you husbands,*
 live together in understanding with the female sex as with the weaker one.
 Render honor (to your wives) as fellow heirs of the (gift of) grace of life,
 so that nothing will stand in the way of your (common) prayers.

---

to Abraham your father and to Sarah who bore you." In the NT she is mentioned elsewhere only in Rom. 4:19; 9:9; Heb. 11:11.

49. This rough connection is, however, no reason for taking the aorist in a present sense (so Beare, 156), which would be linguistically possible, or reading ὡς Σάρρα . . . τέκνα as a parenthesis (so Bengel, ad loc.; Beare, 156f.; Knopf, 129f.).

50. ἡ πτόησις occurs in the NT only here. Here it could be either active "frightening action," "intimidation," or passive "fear," "fright," as cognate accusative. The former is more probable; examples of such usage are in Tertullian, *Ad Uxorem* 2.5 (*ANF* IV, 46f.): A non-Christian man threatens his wife with denunciation; Justin, *Apologia* 2.1 (*ANF* I, 188). See further Schlosser, "1 Pierre 3,5b-6"; Kiley, "Like Sara."

51. This second expression is not illustrated by the Sarah story; it draws on Prov. 3:25 LXX: καὶ οὐ φοβηθήσῃ πτόησιν ἐπελθοῦσαν. Proverbs 3 was used repeatedly in early Christianity for parenetic purposes (cf. Selwyn, 408ff.). Prov. 3:34 is quoted in I Pet. 5:5.

1. Reicke, "Gnosis der Männer."

Form and Tradition

1. The brief word addressed to husbands follows in form the schema of the station code as it is shaped in 3:1f.: address, imperative, and purpose clause giving the ground of the imperative.

2. The directive has apparently, as was the case in 3:3f., been filled out by a wisdom tradition that also stands behind I Thess. 4:4f.: "that each of you know how to take a wife for himself in holiness and honor, not in the passion of lust like Gentiles who do not know God." In both places an appeal is made to reason (κατὰ γνῶσιν, εἰδέναι, μὴ εἰδότα τὸν θεόν), the wife is referred to as σκεῦος, and the husband is told to give τιμή to her. The connection between the two passages is to be explained on the basis of the use of related parenetic Church tradition. Selwyn's suggestion that Silvanus's participation in the writing of both letters produced the connection is improbable. Comparable in terms of the wisdom background is *Ep. Arist.* 250 (*OT Pseudep.* II, 29): "How can one reach agreement with a woman? 'By recognizing,' he replied, 'that the female sex is . . . of naturally weak constitution. It is necessary to have dealings with them in a sound way. . . .'"

3. The first imperative[2] of the complicated sentence in 3:7 is backed up by the appeal to understand the natural and historical difference between men and women. The second is backed up by knowledge of the soteriological-eschatological status of equality. The two imperatives flow into the purpose clause that supplies the rationale for the whole: "so that nothing will stand in the way of your (common) prayers."

7 Like all Christians living within the earthly stations (ὁμοίως), husbands are directed (v. 7a) to the responsibilities that fall to them by virtue of their station. This is the case even though they are the only ones in the station code in this letter who do not belong to the ὑποτασσόμενοι, the subordinate side of a relationship. The married life they share with their wives[3] is supposed to be lived out "in accord with understanding," συνοικοῦντες κατὰ γνῶσιν. γνῶσις here does not signify the verification of some factual content — empirical analysis[4] — or, in a Gnostic sense, a superior concept of reality (I Cor. 8:1). It is, rather, the sensitive understanding that develops in love for God and one's fellow human beings when one knows oneself to be loved

---

2. συνοικοῦντες and ἀπονέμοντες are participial imperatives.

3. συνοικέω, "live together," i.e., in marriage, so already in Herodotus I.93; IV.168 (LCL I, 120-123; II, 372-375); Sir. 25:8. Acts 10:27 replaces it with συνομιλοῦντες, which was used of purely spiritual community. The same ascetic tendency also is seen in NT textual alterations, including Lk. 2:36: seven "days" instead of "years"; I Cor. 7:3: τὴν ὀφειλομένην εὔνοιαν instead of τὴν ὀφειλήν; I Cor. 9:5: "a wife as sister" instead of "a sister as wife."

4. R. Bultmann, "γινώσκω," *TDNT* I, 691f.

by God.[5] For this reason it expresses itself especially in consideration for others.

As in all the traditional formulas of that paternal society, the wife is called "the weaker vessel": ὡς ἀσθενεστέρῳ σκεύει τῷ γυναικείῳ.[6] The author of I Peter does not intend with this formulas all that Greek and Jewish authors had said about the supposed physical[7] and psychological[8] weakness of women. The author intends, rather, to make the point that the wife belongs to those who, even according to the Jesus-tradition,[9] are to receive the special attention and care of *agape*. And this was the case especially in light of their social and legal standing in marriage in the ancient world and in an economic structure that was heavily dependent on physical labor. What is expected morally and religiously of a woman, according to 3:1f., is not cancelled.

Accordingly, v. 7b sets the understanding of marriage that comes from a Christian understanding of the natural and historical givens alongside the understanding of marriage that arises from the eschatological viewpoint: A man should give his wife "honor" as an equal in her status as a person[10] (cf. 2:17), since she is "fellow heir[11] of the gift

---

5. Thus I Cor. 8:1-13 describes the Christian γνῶσις that determines one's conduct in precise terms. The noun γνῶσις occurs in I Peter only in 3:7, which does not presuppose such reflection (Reicke makes reference too directly to I Corinthians 8), but implies its foundation as Christian tradition. The recognition coming forth from faith and love, which guide one's conduct, belongs parenetically to the structure of Christian existence; cf. Phil. 1:9f.: ". . . that your love may abound more and more with knowledge . . . so that you may approve what is excellent"; Phlm. 6: ". . . that the sharing of your faith may promote knowledge of all the good"; Col. 1:9f.; 3:10: ". . . put on the new nature, which is being renewed in knowledge"; II Pet. 1:3, 5f.; 3:18; *Barn.* 2:3; 21:5 (LCL AF I, 343, 409); cf. Bultmann, *TDNT* I, 707f.

6. τὸ σκεῦος, "instrument," "vessel," is used figuratively for (1) a human being as a tool (Acts 9:15), (2) the body as the vessel of the Spirit (*Herm. Mand.* 5.1.1-7; *Barn.* 7:3 [LCL AF II, 86-91; I, 365]), (3) in the OT and Judaism from the parable of the potter in Jer. 18:1-11, often of mankind as creation, (4) in rabbinic Judaism, כְּלִי, "vessel," for a man's wife (Str.-Bill. III, 632f.; C. Maurer, "σκεῦος," *TDNT* VII, 360f.). In I Thess. 4:4 the fourth meaning is seen; I Pet. 3:7 stands between this and the third meaning. Therefore, one best translates it as "vessel" (so also Maurer, *TDNT* VII, 367; BAGD s.v.).

7. Plato, *Republic* 5.455D, E; 457A (LCL I, 447-449, 451); *Leges* 781A (LCL IX, 487): τὸ θῆλυ διὰ τὸ ἀσθενές; Philo, *De Ebrietate* 55 (LCL III, 344-345); Oxyrhynchus Papyrus 261, ll. 11-13 (B. Grenfell and A. Hunt, *The Oxyrhynchus Papyri* II [London, 1899], 231).

8. Plato, *Leges* 6.781B (LCL IX, 489): "[but insofar as] females are inferior in goodness to males . . ."; *Ep. Arist.* 250f. (*OT Pseudep.* II, 29).

9. Mt. 11:28; 18:10; also in I Cor. 8:9; Rom. 14:1, 13, 20. Rom. 15:1 has the summons to consideration for the weak, but in contrast to I Pet. 3:7 it is the spiritually weak who are referred to.

10. ἀπονέμειν τιμήν, "assign honor," occurring frequently in classical Greek; in early Christian literature also in *I Clem.* 1:3; *Mart. Pol.* 10:2 (LCL AF I, 11; II, 327).

11. A group of manuscripts has nominative instead of dative because the dative of

(of the grace) of life": ἀπονέμοντες τιμὴν ὡς καὶ συγκληρονόμοις χάριτος ζωῆς. Like her husband, to whom she is united in faith, she receives in the new world the "gift of grace," namely "life,"[12] as an inheritance that is already now accorded her (1:4f.).

This new eschatological viewpoint is valid not only in regard to marriage, but also in regard to all the stations of this world. In each of them the partner must finally be recognized as the one who is intended to be "fellow heir of the grace of life." This is the final criterion of Christian social ethics. In marriage as elsewhere, it does not cancel the historical forms of life. But it does give them a boundary and a goal.

The double imperative should be noted, especially in regard to the purpose clause in v. 7c: εἰς τὸ μὴ ἐγκόπτεσθαι τὰς προσευχὰς ὑμῶν, "so that nothing will stand in the way of your (common) prayers." "Your prayers" are certainly not those of husbands alone, but the common prayers of husband and wife. Jesus himself taught that prayer is impeded when a relationship with a fellow human being is troubled.[13] Whenever the most intimate human relationship — marriage — is not lived out satisfactorily the prayers of those involved are "hindered"; they do not achieve the proper stature and do not reach oneness with God's will and provision.[14]

Thus, the directives of I Peter regarding the living out of marriage in view of both the present conflict and the new existence develop principles of NT social ethics that to this day give guidance. More than the previous parenetic statements these instructions have illustrative significance for the other stations.

---

object in v. 7a is singular. But the nominative, which connects the statement with the man, distorts its meaning.

12. χάριτος is objective genitive, and ζωῆς is epexegetical genitive.

13. Mt. 5:23; 6:12, 14f.; cf. I Cor. 11:33f.; Jas. 4:3. The directive has, therefore, a different meaning than the regulation in I Cor. 7:5, which is not a "commentary" on I Pet. 3:7 (contra Kelly, 134), but corresponds to the rule in *Test. Naph.* 8:8 (*OT Pseudep.* I, 814): "There is a time for having intercourse with one's wife, and a time to abstain for the purpose of prayer." Gross, "Wives," extends to v. 7 the conflict situation for wives and slaves addressed in the code and suggests that the wives addressed are non-Christians married to Christian men; Michaels, *1 Peter,* 172, considers both suggestions possible.

14. ἐγκόπτω, "hem in," "hinder." The meaning is narrowed one-sidedly in W. Bauer's translation: "in order that your prayers not be robbed of success" ("damit nicht eure Gebete des Erfolges beraubt werden," *Griechisch-deutsches Wörterbuch zu den Schriften des NT . . .* [fourth ed., Berlin, 1952], s.v.; this translation is not in later German editions and is not reflected in either English version [BAGD and its 1957 predecessor]), and in G. Stählin's explanation in "ἐγκοπή," *TDNT* III, 856 (cf. 857): The ascent of prayers to God is hindered. See also on this passage Fridrichsen, "I Peter 3:7."

3:8-12: Social Conduct of All[1]

8 *Finally, be of one mind (among yourselves),*
compassionate, brotherly, forgiving, and obliging.
9 *Do not return evil for evil or invective for invective;*
but rather bless, because you have been called so that you
should receive blessing.

10 *For "whoever wishes to love life and to see good days*
should henceforth keep the tongue from evil
and the lips so that they do not speak deceit.
11 *But let that one cease from evil and do good,*
seek peace and pursue it." (Ps. 34:13-15)
12 *For "the eyes of the Lord (attend) to the righteous*
and his ears to their prayer,
but the face of the Lord (is turned) against those who do evil."
(Ps. 34:16f.)

Structure and Tradition

1. By means of the introductory adverbial clause τὸ δὲ τέλος, "finally," "conclusively," the author announces that he wishes to conclude the parenetic sequence. With πάντες, "all," he indicates that he is now addressing all members of the Church together. He refers to the fundamental social distinction always accepted by all: In relation to both brothers (v. 8) and adversaries (v. 9) one has to overcome all that separates and seek life together by means of demonstrations of love. Perhaps a parenetic schema is reflected when the station code is concluded with this general reference: In Romans 13 as well one finds the writer calling all to love that surpasses what has been practiced before (13:8-10), after addressing each person in his or her particular station (13:1-7).

2. To a great extent, the arrangement of this section resembles formally the arrangement of the preceding parenetic expressions: After the address (πάντες) comes a series of imperatival adjectives or participles that conclude in v. 9b with a unique basis for the imperatives. As a general basis (vv. 10-12) a Scripture quotation (Ps. 34:13-17a) has been added to the particular basis.

3. This section is clearly appropriating the parenetic tradition that we meet also in I Thess. 5:13b-15 and especially in Rom. 12:10, 14, 16f. In Col. 3:12-15 and Eph. 4:1-3, 31f. there are substantive points of correspondence that do not, however, indicate a common tradition.

---

1. See Best, "I Peter and the Gospel Tradition"; D. L. Dungan, *The Sayings of Jesus in the Churches of Paul: The Use of the Synoptic Tradition in the Regulation of Early Church Life* (Oxford, 1971); C. H. Talbert, "Tradition and Redaction in Romans XII.9-21," *NTS* 16 (1969/70), 83-94; J. P. Brown, "Synoptic Parallels"; Piper, "Hope."

a. Here as in Romans 12 love for one's enemies is mentioned after love for one's brothers. In both places the parenesis has been redactionally enlarged by OT directives; in Romans 12 they are woven into the fabric, while here they are added at the end.

b. In the individual parenesis the same key words are used quite extensively, though in differing sequences:

I Peter 3	Romans 12
v. 8 ὁμόφρονες	v. 16 τὸ αὐτὸ . . . φρονοῦντες
συμπαθεῖς (εὔσπλαγχνοι)	v. 15 χαίρειν μετὰ χαιρόντων κλαίειν μετὰ κλαιόντων
φιλάδελφοι	v. 10 τῇ φιλαδελφίᾳ . . . φιλόστοργοι
ταπεινόφρονες	v. 16 μὴ τὰ ὑψηλὰ φρονοῦντες, ἀλλὰ τοῖς ταπεινοῖς . . .
v. 9 μὴ ἀποδιδόντες κακὸν ἀντὶ κακοῦ	v. 17a μηδενὶ κακὸν ἀντὶ κακοῦ ἀποδιδόντες (cf. I Thess. 5:15)
τοὐναντίον . . . εὐλογοῦντες	v. 14 εὐλογεῖτε τοὺς διώκοντας (cf. I Cor. 4:12)

c. In regard to the differences between these two passages, the five adjectives in v. 8 consistently reproduce in Hellenistic formulation what is stated in Romans 12 in a more OT-Jewish manner. The first two adjectives, ὁμόφρονες and συμπαθεῖς, are found only here in the LXX, NT, and Apostolic Fathers; they are from later Greek ethics, but in content they represent Jewish and Christian expressions.[2] The remaining three adjectives, φιλάδελφοι, εὔσπλαγχνοι, and ταπεινόφρονες, also represent words current in Hellenistic colloquial language. They are used here, however, in the sense that they or their linguistic roots had acquired in Jewish and Christian parenesis. Only the second of these three makes even one other appearance in the NT, in Eph. 4:32; the second and the third are sometimes used in the Apostolic Fathers in parenesis.[3] The linguistic-historical process shows that in

---

2. ὁμόφρων, "like-minded," "harmonious" (from Homer on; Plutarch, *Moralia* 432c [LCL V, 469-471]; Strabo, *Geographia* 6.3.3 [LCL III, 111-113]: ὁμόφρονας ὡς ἂν ἀλλήλων ἀδελφούς; W. Dittenberger, *Orientis Graeci Inscriptiones Selectae* [Leipzig, 1903-05], 515, l. 5), is used in place of τὸ αὐτὸ φρονοῦντες (Rom. 12:16; 15:5; Phil. 2:2; cf. I Cor. 1:10).

συμπαθής, "showing sympathy" (from Aristotle on; Plutarch, *Moralia* 536a [LCL VII, 84-86]; Dittenberger, *op. cit.*, 456, l. 66; in the LXX of uncertain textual originality) represents what the expression in Rom. 12:15 states: "rejoice with those who rejoice, weep with those who weep," which comes from Jewish tradition (Sir. 7:34; *Derek Erets* [Str.-Bill. III, 298; *Minor Tractates*, ed. A. Cohen (London, 1965), II, 529-566]; *Test. Iss.* 7 [*OT Pseudep.* I, 804]); similarly worded Hellenistic expressions speak of what politeness requires: συγχαίρω σοι (= *gratulor tibi*, CorpGlossLat III, 227, l. 23; cf. O. Michel, *Der Brief an die Römer* (KEK 4; fifth ed., Göttingen, 1978), 387, n.27.

3. φιλάδελφος, "loving one's brother/sister," used in Greek literature positively and only of literal siblings; figuratively in pseudo-Socrates, *Epistle* 28.12: "in openness toward

content this parenesis was connected to concepts of human community that developed out of the OT revelation of God. But it presents the early Christian tradition that was developed on this basis in more deliberately Hellenized language in comparison with Paul.

d. The decisive point of departure for this parenetic tradition becomes clear in v. 9: This directive corresponds in content to Jesus' saying in the Sermon on the Mount about love for one's enemy. But verbally it has far less in common with the form of this saying that has been handed on in the Gospels than it has with the form found in the parenesis in Romans 12: I Pet. 3:9a corresponds almost word for word to Rom. 12:17a (see above) and to a large extent to I Thess. 5:15a; the second part of the verse resembles I Cor. 4:12, but especially Rom. 12:14. In contrast, v. 9a is not at all verbally similar to Jesus' command to love one's enemy in the gospel tradition (Lk. 6:27a par. Mt. 5:44: ἀγαπᾶτε τοὺς ἐχθροὺς ὑμῶν; 6:27b: καλῶς ποιεῖτε τοῖς μισοῦσιν ὑμᾶς; Mt. 5:39: μὴ ἀντιστῆναι τῷ πονηρῷ). In I Pet. 3:9b there is contact in at least a few key words (Lk. 6:28a: εὐλογεῖτε τοὺς καταρωμένους ὑμᾶς; 6:28b par. Mt. 5:44b: προσεύχεσθε περὶ τῶν ἐπηρεαζόντων/ὑπὲρ τῶν διωκόντων; cf. I Pet. 3:16: ὑμᾶς).

The comparison indicates that two traditions developed out of the saying of Jesus, namely, what is represented in the gospel tradition and what is in the Church parenesis.[4] The Church parenesis in I Pet. 3:9 probably grew out of a form of the saying that stood closer to Lk. 6:27f. than to the Matthean parallel. What factors were at work in the reshaping of the dominical saying into Church parenesis can only be touched on here: The total change of direction required by Jesus (Lk. 6:27): "Love your enemies, do good to those who hate you," was fused for parenetic use with the example that follows in Lk. 6:28 and was formulated for memory with the aid of familiar phrases from the wisdom tradition[5] for use in everyday encounters with opponents of the faith. In this way, the "cursing" (καταρᾶσθαι), which was originally mentioned in the example and which was critical in the

---

humankind"; II Macc. 15:19: loving the members of God's people (BAGD s.v.; H. von Soden, "ἀδελφός," *TDNT* I, 144-146; see the comments above on 1:22).

εὔσπλαγχνος has in Greek literature only a medical meaning. Here it means "gracious," "generous," so also Eph. 4:32 (cf. Col. 3:12: σπλάγχνα οἰκτιρμοῦ); *I Clem.* 54:1 (LCL AF I, 101: of God); Polycarp, *Phil.* 5:2; 6:1 (*ibid.,* 289, 291); so also already *Test. Zeb.* 9:7; *Test. Sim.* 4:4 (*OT Pseudep.* I, 807, 786). The use of the stem σπλάγχνα takes on here the meaning of Hebrew רַחֲמִים, in accord with NT linguistic custom; cf. H. Koester, "σπλάγχνον," *TDNT* VII, 551f.

ταπεινόφρων in Greek literature often means "faint-hearted"; here it is "humble," as already in Prov. 29:23; so also *Barn.* 19:3; *Herm. Mand.* 11.8; Ignatius, *Eph.* 10:2 (LCL AF I, 403; II, 121; I, 185). Elsewhere in the NT only the noun ταπεινοφροσύνη appears: Col. 3:12; Eph. 4:2; so also *I Clem.* 19:1; 38:2 (LCL AF I, 43, 73), which represents OT עֱנָו, which in 1QS 4:3 stands together with רַחֲמִים (see above): "a spirit of humility (וְרוּחַ עֲנָוָה), patience, abundant charity (וְרוֹב רַחֲמִים), unending goodness" (cf. S. Wibbing, *Die Tugend- und Lasterkataloge im NT* [BZNW 25; Berlin, 1959], 104f.).

4. *Did.* 1:3 (LCL AF I, 308f.) attempts to advance the former further, Polycarp, *Phil.* 2:2 (LCL AF I, 284f.) the latter.

5. Prov. 17:13: "if a man returns evil for good . . ."; 24:29: "Do not say, 'I will do to him as he has done to me, I will pay the man back for what he has done' "; cf. 20:22;

Jewish realm, was still appropriated at the end in Rom. 12:14, but in I Pet. 3:9 it was replaced exclusively by "invective" (λοιδορία). Hence, the proverbial wisdom of which Paul availed himself for redactional purposes in Rom. 12:16f., 19f. as he expanded Church parenesis was itself already active as it took shape growing out of the saying of Jesus. The central saying of Jesus appropriated in this way was the criterion under which this parenetic tradition was shaped in conversation with OT and Jewish traditions; this is true, in any case, for its coinage by Paul and in I Peter.

4. The parenesis taken up in I Pet. 3:8f. was subsequently developed and supported still further in vv. 10-12 by quotation of a wisdom Psalm passage. This lay within the preceding lines of development. The parenesis was by no means prompted by the Psalm.[6] The OT expressions were understood from the viewpoint of the Christian parenesis, which was already in existence. Furthermore, it is not within the NT perspective to call this parenesis an interpretive commentary on Ps. 34:13-17;[7] the author's point of view proceeds fundamentally not from the OT text but from the Christian tradition; he seeks, as the addition of causal γάρ in v. 10 indicates, in Scripture a basis for that tradition. The meaning of this OT foundation is derived no longer from the wisdom experience of life, but from the experience of Christ that finds articulation in the christological foundation described in I Pet. 2:21-25.

5. Tradition-historical analysis thus enables us to recognize the foundation and goal of the entire section. Both are fundamentally misunderstood when one sees the section as instruction on virtue by which ideals of the autonomous personality of Church-political shrewdness are sacrificed: "The leaders of this community try not to let any hateful sectarian spirit arise. . . . In a situation like this gentleness and modesty are more effective than clever veracity and noble pride."[8] This explanation fails to recognize that the parenesis has its roots in the revelation of God that came about through Jesus and that finds its locus of meaning therein. As has become clear from the history of the terms used, it is from the vantage point of this revelation of God that the author understood the Hellenistic and OT and Jewish expressions that aided in the formulation of this concluding directive on social engagement.

Vv. 8f.: Instruction in Keeping with Jesus' Sermon on the Mount

8 In this series of five imperatival adjectives the author thinks first of all, as is indicated by the centrally located φιλάδελφος ("loving one's brother"), of the relationship of Church members to one another.

II En. 50:4 (*OT Pseudep.* I, 176f.). In contrast, Lev. 19:18, which is close in substance, has no after-effect in the formulation.

6. Contra Selwyn, 413f. (see the comments above on 2:3). According to Bornemann, "Erster Petrusbrief," Psalm 34 was the text of the baptismal address (cf. 146ff.).

7. Contra Schweizer, 72.

8. Knopf, 133f., following Gunkel, 557.

Brotherly love is, according to consistent use of the term in the NT, the mutual demonstration of love among Church members, not a more abstract brotherly orientation toward all people.[9] The five adjectives express, therefore, the practice of κοινωνία that is essential for the Church (cf. Acts 2:42; Gal. 2:9; I Jn. 1:3a, 7).

It is consistent with this that all be ὁμόφρονες ("of one mind"). As τὸ αὐτὸ φρονοῦντες, which stands in the place of ὁμόφρονες in Rom. 12:15 and elsewhere, indicates, the Church members' thinking and striving are to have the same content and be directed toward the same goal,[10] not by coordination according to one program, but by dialogical orientation toward the commission of the one Lord. Through this orientation φρονεῖν, thinking and striving, according to Phil. 2:2-6, are not directed toward self-realization (Rom. 12:16), but toward service with differing gifts. What results from this is not uniformity but unanimity. Because of this, the competing parties customary in philosophy and in Jewish religious life, the σχίσματα and αἱρέσεις, are reprehensible in the Church (I Cor. 1:10), because they serve one's individuality and not the Lord. Dialogical engagement with one's brother where a common goal cannot be seen is focused on in the subsequent expressions.

συμπαθής ("compassionate") is connected to that which causes someone else distress or joy; it "rejoices with those who rejoice and weeps with those who weep," as the corresponding OT-Jewish expression puts it in Rom. 12:15.[11] In a community of brothers it is not only necessary that each be involved in relation with the other, but also that each be constantly and charitably open to the other in such a way that the other's failings are covered.

For this reason, all members of the Church are to be εὔσπλαγχνοι, "charitable." τὰ σπλάγχνα, originally the internal organs, became a term in the NT, as already in the *Testaments of the Twelve Patriarchs,* for that inner turning of one's attention toward one's neighbor in which one not only gives something, but also gives one's self.[12]

---

9. See the comments on 1:22.

10. See above, n.2; cf. Phil. 4:2: "I entreat Euodia and Syntyche to agree in the Lord" (τὸ αὐτὸ φρονεῖν ἐν κυρίῳ); cf. Rom. 15:5; II Cor. 13:11; Gal. 5:10.

11. With respect to the more difficult side, this conduct is motivated in Heb. 4:15 explicitly in christological terms: "We do not have a high priest who is unable to sympathize (συμπαθῆσαι) with our weaknesses, but one who in every respect has been tempted . . ."; accordingly, Heb. 10:34: "You had compassion (συνεπαθήσατε) on the prisoners." Cf. W. Michaelis, "πάσχω," *TDNT* V, 935; see above, p. 230, n.2.

12. So II Cor. 7:15; Phil. 1:8; 2:1; Col. 3:12; Phlm. 12 (cf. Koester, *TDNT* VII, 555f.).

Such turning of one's attention is only possible in the conduct of the ταπεινόφρων, of the one who is "meek," i.e., of the *anaw,*[13] the one who considers the other more important than himself or herself, who does not look after his or her own concerns but after those of the other (Phil. 2:3), because he or she lives from the love of God. In this posture Jesus as the *anaw* calls to himself those who are burdened (Mt. 11:29).[14]

9 The love that shapes positively the relationship of the Church's members to one another, while it makes itself concrete in this manner, also overcomes the evil that comes to it from without: μὴ ἀποδιδόντες κακὸν ἀντὶ κακοῦ. The command to counter slanders with blessing — ἢ λοιδορίαν ἀντὶ λοιδορίας, τοὐναντίον δὲ εὐλογοῦντες — is then directly connected. As becomes clear in the example of Jesus in such a situation (2:23) and in the additional thought developments in 3:13-17, this command has in mind opponents who attack Christians because of their Christian conduct. The saying of Jesus that was the point of departure for this parenetic tradition was already focused on religious adversaries. I Peter applied the saying directly to the situation of those addressed, i.e., to expressions of alienation encountered from society. Christians should, as was said in the introduction to the parenesis in 2:11f., not avoid such expressions in a resigned and bitter way, but overcome them through "right conduct" within life's stations. This conduct is an application of the fundamental commandment that encompasses the whole range of contacts with one's neighbor: Evil, especially insults and accusations, should not be returned in kind or even echoed in attitude or conduct, but should be countered with blessing.

"Blessing" and "to bless," which are found only here in I Peter, are defined by the subsequent supporting rationale: ὅτι εἰς τοῦτο ἐκλήθητε ἵνα εὐλογίαν κληρονομήσητε, "for you have been called for this:[15] that you should inherit blessing."[16] What the blessing consists of is to

---

σπλαγχνίζεσθαι has the same meaning in the Synoptic parables of the unmerciful servant (Mt. 18:27), the prodigal son (Lk. 15:20), and the Good Samaritan (Lk. 10:33), so that again the christological foundation and shaping of the intended manner of conduct become clear.

13. See above, the third paragraph of n.3.

14. The substantive context is overlooked in many manuscripts (P, Koine, others) that replace ταπεινόφρων with φιλόφρων, "loving," "amiable," because the latter apparently fits only in the relationship with God, not into this sequence on relationship to the brother.

15. τοῦτο connects itself not, as in 2:21, to what has gone before, so that one could translate: "since for this [namely, to bless] you have been called, in order that you also receive blessing" (so Knopf, 134). The sense is, rather, as in 4:6: "you should bless because you have been called to inherit blessing" (so Kelly, 137).

16. "Inherit blessing" also in Heb. 12:17, there in regard to patriarchal history (Gen. 27:30-40; cf. 48:15; 49:25f.; Sir. 3:9).

be derived from what the letter says about "inheriting." Inheritance, according to 1:4, is the hope made accessible through the resurrection of Jesus, the encounter with salvation, the conclusive turning of God toward humankind (1:5, 13); this turning of God was already according to the OT the actual content of blessing. The eschatological salvation is encountered as blessing because it is mediated through the active consolation of God (cf. Mt. 25:34; *I Clem.* 35:3 [LCL AF I, 66f.]). Because they have been called[17] to receive the consolation of salvation, the addressees are also able to respond to their opponents only with blessing, i.e., with the active consolation of salvation that rests on intercession oriented toward salvation.[18] Such consolation takes place in the speech and deed that witnesses to each person about the salvation that is also effective for him or her (I Pet. 3:15; cf. Acts 7:56, 60; 26:29; Ignatius, *Eph.* 10:2f. [LCL AF I, 184f.]). Whoever meets an opponent as one who is destined to be "a fellow heir of the grace of life" (3:7) is acting as one who blesses.

The Scripture quotation that is added underscores this directive in vv. 8f., which is utterly decisive for the entire conduct of Christians in a society that discriminates against them.

Vv. 10-12: Expansion in a Scripture Quotation

The quotation of Ps. 34:13-17a now strengthens the antithesis in 3:9. Whoever wishes to receive (v. 9c) life (v. 10a) or God's consolation (v. 12) abstains from any word (v. 10b) and more generally any action

---

17. See the comments on 2:9.

18. εὐλογεῖν in Greek literature "speak well, praise," in the NT only in the LXX sense of "bless," which is foreign to Greek thought. Cf. H. W. Beyer, "εὐλογέω," *TDNT* II, 754f. NT use of the verb is also linked in substance with the OT development of its own view of blessing out of the ancient Near Eastern idea of the autonomous causal word: The Bearer and Dispenser of all blessing is Yahweh (Gen. 49:25). Blessed, therefore, is one whom the Lord is "with." So, e.g., Gen. 17:7f.; 26:3: "I will be with you." This authoritative and effective consolation is "blessing."

In the NT, Hebrews refers directly to the OT blessing of people through people (Heb. 7:6f.; 11:20f.). Jesus himself obligated his disciples — differently than in the OT — only to bless, not to curse. This directive (Lk. 6:28 par.) finds its way into parenesis (Rom. 12:14; I Cor. 4:12; I Pet. 3:9). Giving blessing, moreover, is now no longer, as in the later layers of the OT and in Judaism, the special right of the priests (Sir. 50:22; based especially on Num. 6:22-26), but is assigned to all as a charge (cf. I Pet. 2:5). See Beyer, *TDNT* II, 754-763; L. Brun, *Segen und Fluch im Urchristentum* (Oslo, 1932); F. Horst, "Segen und Fluch im AT," *RGG* V, cols. 1649ff.; W. Schenk, *Der Segen im NT* (ThArb 25; Berlin, 1967); C. Westermann, *Der Segen in der Bibel und im Handeln der Kirche* (Munich, 1968).

(v. 11a) that would do harm to another person (v. 9a). Such a person demonstrates good (v. 11a) to others and seeks peace (v. 11b = v. 9b). With this directive the basic point of reference for the whole parenesis that precedes, namely, the antithesis of κακοποιεῖν (2:16; 3:9) and ἀγα-θοποιεῖν (2:14f., 20; 3:6; cf. v. 11a: ποιησάτω ἀγαθόν), is underscored. The quotation thus also prepares the way for the next section, which begins with the application of this antithesis to the pressure exerted by the world (3:13). The quotation has, therefore, been selected strategically for this context.

The quotation probably came to the author through the parenetic tradition.[19] The OT text of the LXX (Psalm 33) is not quoted word for word but, as in 1:24, is woven into the parenesis. But it is, nonetheless, presupposed that the hearer will recognize the words as a scriptural quotation. To fit into the parenesis in v. 10a the question in Ps. 33:13 LXX becomes a conditional participle. In vv. 10b-11 the imperatival address corresponding to the question becomes a third person imperative.[20] V. 12, on the other hand, follows the LXX exactly. Even from this weaving itself of the OT text into the Christian parenesis it follows that the expressions of the quotation were understood according to the usage of the Christian context and not of the OT context.[21]

10a   In Ps. 34:13 the psalmist uses the style of proverbial wisdom to address the deeply rooted and generally accepted longing of humankind for a safe and pleasant existence.[22] For the Christian reader ζωή, "life," is the abiding and whole existence of the creature with its Creator, the existence that, as was just stated in 3:7,[23] was given as an inheritance. For Christians the only "good days" are those that signify "blessing," the consolation of God. In the following verses "good" is used repeatedly for that which grows out of fellowship with God (3:13, 16, 21). But it is not simply that from a Christian perspective "life" and "good days" are not "supraterrestrial" and "future," while the psalmist thinks in merely "terrestrial" and "present" terms. "Life" and "good days" are, rather, already present as the result of new birth (1:3ff., 22ff.),

---

19. Cf. Selwyn, 413f.

20. Selwyn, 190, supposes that even this approximation was already present in Christian parenetic tradition.

21. Because Ps. 33:17b LXX ("to cut off the remembrance of them from the earth") could not be inserted, the quotation concluded with v. 17a.

22. H. J. Kraus, *Psalms 1–59: A Commentary* (tr. H. Oswald; Minneapolis, 1988), 385f.; G. von Rad, *Wisdom in Israel* (tr. J. Martin; London, 1972), 81.

23. The word occurs in I Peter only in these two passages.

i.e., as hidden fellowship with Christ (1:8f.; 4:13), the revelation of whom I Peter, nevertheless, waits more expressly for than does Paul (cf. Col. 3:3f.).

10b Whoever seeks this life[24] keeps his or her tongue and lips from speaking evil and deceit. This warning from Ps. 34:14 is developed in Jas. 1:26; 3:1-12 as it was intended in the Psalm. But here the reader is to understand the warning as general confirmation of the directive in v. 9 that one is not to respond in like manner to acts of discriminatory aggression.

11 In v. 11a the tenor of the preceding parenesis is strengthened along the same lines: One should not κακοποιεῖν, but should ἀγαθο-ποιεῖν in various situations. In v. 11b the author thus addresses the core of his parenesis: ζητησάτω εἰρήνην καὶ διωξάτω αὐτήν. In the midst of manifold conflicts the proper course is to seek peace. This is an aspect of fundamental early Christian instruction: "If at all possible, whenever you can do anything about it, be at peace with all people" (Rom. 12:18); such instruction is anchored in Jesus' preaching (Mt. 5:9).

12 If all that is said in vv. 10b-11 about "doing evil" or "doing good" is thus to be understood in the context of Christian parenesis, then the "righteous ones" (δίκαιοι) here are those who on the basis of new birth "conduct themselves rightly" and act in accordance with the command to love the enemy (v. 9). They are those who according to 2:24 "live to righteousness" and according to 3:14 "suffer for righteous-ness' sake." Those who "do evil" are, on the other hand, those who do the opposite of all this, in spite of redemption.

When God's gracious turning and thereby life becomes the portion of the righteous ones (v. 10a) this does not correspond to a primitive theory of recompense,[25] since they respond to the grace through which they were originally sought and empowered for ἀγαθοποιεῖν. In the same way, God's opposition is judgment of those who spurn grace by their conduct. The God of the Bible does not leave us to our autonomous selves, but encounters each of us as a person: "Eye," "ear," and "face" express in visual imagery God's active and personal involvement. The

---

24. ἀγαπᾶν, v. 10a: "love," "desire," as in Sir. 4:12; Rev. 12:11. Bengel, ad loc., indicates the reverse of the frustrated weariness with the world in Eccl. 2:17: "I hated life, since what is done under the sun is grievous to me: All is vanity and striving after wind."

25. So, e.g., Tob. 4:6f.: "If you do the truth, success will attend your work. . . . Do not turn your face away from a poor man and God's face will not be turned away from you." The author of Psalm 34 announced his experience of salvation with such statements.

reward of righteousness abides in God's gracious turning; judgment of evil is the withdrawal of grace so that God is no longer "for us" but against us (5:5; cf. Rom. 5:10; 8:31).[26]

3:13–4:11: PREPARED FOR SUFFERING IN SOCIETY FOR THE SAKE OF GOOD

Theme and Structure

1. In the course of the generalizing statements of the parenesis about conduct in society, which began in 3:8, what was said in 2:18-25 to Christian slaves in regard to the conflict situation is now developed for all members of the Church. The opening question, "And who will do evil to you?" introduces the new theme of suffering as a result of social discrimination. To this point this theme has been in the background all along, but has received attention only at individual points (1:6f.; 2:12, 15, 19ff.; 3:9). Now it comes to the fore as the main theme. But it is still related in polarity to the previous main theme of just conduct in society. In view of this polarity, one should not designate the developments of thought that follow as the "main part" of the letter.[1]

2. The new thematic focus is treated first here in three sections: In 3:13-17 the watchword is issued: Be ready also to suffer for just conduct in society. This watchword is given a christological basis in 3:18-22 and a soteriological basis in 4:1-6. In 4:7-11 the thought developments are concluded for the moment with the summons for the Church to maintain its existence to the end that is drawing near. After this conclusion, the letter begins in 4:12, as it did earlier in 2:11, with a new address and takes up in 4:12-19 the theme of suffering once again, but from a different perspective. For this reason it does not really conform to the arrangement of the letter to include, as do Selwyn, Spicq, and Best,[2] 4:12-17 in this major part of the letter.

3:13-17: Prepared To Suffer for Just Conduct in Society

13 *And who then is going to do evil to you if you are zealous for good?*

---

26. Knopf, 136, misunderstands this NT concept, which had its beginning in Jesus' words about reward, when he explains: "God sees, therefore, all, good and evil, and gives to each according to what is deserved." Cf. G. Bornkamm, "Der Lohngedanke im NT," *idem, Studien zu Antike und Urchristentum* (third ed., Munich, 1970), 69-92; W. Pesch, *Der Lohngedanke in der Lehre Jesu* (MüThSt 1/7; Munich, 1955).

1. Contra Kelly, 139.

2. Selwyn, 191; Spicq, 129; Best, 131. For Kelly, 139, 3:13–5:11 belongs together as well. In general see Omanson, "Suffering."

14 *But if you must suffer for the sake of righteousness — blessed*
   are you!
   "Do not be afraid of them and do not become troubled";
15 *"sanctify" rather "the Lord," Christ, in your hearts.* (Isa.
   8:12f.)
   (Be) ready at all times to give account to anyone
   who asks you to answer for the hope that is in you.
16 *(Do this) however, with gentleness and fear,*
   as those who have a good conscience,
   so that for what you are slandered they will be shamed,
   those who discredit your good manner of life in Christ.
17 *For it is better that you — if God so wills it —*
   suffer as those who conduct themselves rightly,
   and not as those who do evil.

Structure and Tradition

1. This section was arranged with great care. In vv. 13 and 14a the watchword
is advanced to the fore thematically, and in v. 17 it is underscored conclusively.
In vv. 14b-16 the consequences for a truly "apologetic" form of conduct are drawn
from it.

2. This line of thought is developed in parenetic prose. The author thus
brings to expression matters that for him were quite specific, even though he
consistently formulates them in traditional terms. In vv. 13 and 17 he uses maxims
of the sort found in proverbial wisdom. In v. 14a he draws on a beatitude passed
on as tradition from Jesus, and in vv. 14b and 15a he applies to the situation an
OT saying that was probably already at home in Christian parenesis. In vv. 15b
and 16 he takes up again in altered form the thesis that in 2:12 he derived
programmatically from a saying of Jesus.[3]

Vv. 13-14a: Zealous for Good

13 This verse introduces the new theme, but is also linked to what
precedes it by a concessive καί[4]: "And who will then (under the given
circumstances) harm you?" (καὶ τίς ὁ κακώσων ὑμᾶς;). The circumstance
that has just been underscored by an OT quotation (vv. 11f.) is summarized again in a conditional clause: "If you are zealous for the good"
(ἐὰν τοῦ ἀγαθοῦ ζηλωταὶ γένησθε). The expression "zealous for the

---

3. See above, p. 161.
4. As in Mk. 10:26; Jn. 5:36; cf. BDF §448.2 (p. 233).

good," which was familiar in Hellenistic as well as in Jewish and Christian usage,[5] indicates that persistent and total, even passionate, giving of oneself for good, as the letter commanded thematically in the preceding section. This demand works its way through this new section in altered forms: V. 14 requires "righteousness," v. 16 "a good manner of life in Christ," and v. 17 "just behavior." The last of these expressions was the key phrase of the preceding section (2:12) and indicates that the essence of the just social conduct thought of here becomes especially clear in reference to the Christian slave (2:20) and the Christian wife (3:6). It is conduct that does justice to the institutions within which one lives and generally to the *justitia civilis* (cf. 4:15). It does not conform to the commonly accepted middle-class morality but, according to v. 16, is practiced with a "good conscience" before God or "in Christ," i.e., in fellowship with Christ.

When Christians are asked with a view toward such conduct: "and who then will harm you?" the question sounds naive in light of the experiences that the letter consistently presupposes, i.e., if the question is taken as a wisdom saying, as the form suggests, i.e., as an expression of one's experience of life. Hence, many exegetes[6] insist that κακόω ("harm") cannot mean the same here as πάσχω ("suffer") in vv. 14 and 17; it must, rather, have in mind, they contend, an inner harm that believers, as those who are inwardly free, are spared (Pss. 41:4; 118:6; Mt. 10:28; Rom. 8:28, 31). But this explanation does justice neither to word usage nor to the context: κακόω here extends what was said about those who do κακά, "evil" (vv. 9 and 12), and is used in Acts[7] consistently to mean "persecute," and therefore as a counterpart of πάσχειν. According to what precedes here (v. 12), *sub specie Dei* good follows good and evil follows evil. Furthermore, the author voices in 2:12 and 3:1f. the certainty coming from the Jesus tradition of Mt. 5:16 that it is also possible among people to overcome evil through good. Thus, he is able here, although he is quite familiar with suffering for the sake of righteousness (2:19f.), to encourage the readers to trust the protective and conquering power of good because in it the gospel is at work

---

5. Epictetus, *Dissertationes* 2.11.25 (LCL I, 288f.; cf. 2.12.25 [296f.]); Philo, *De Virtutibus* 175 (LCL VIII, 271), and passim: ζηλωτὴς τῆς ἀρετῆς; Tit. 2:14: ζηλωτὴς καλῶν ἔργων.

6. Kelly, 139f.; Schelkle, 100; Beare, 163; Knopf, 136f.; additional material in Knopf.

7. Acts 7:6, 19; 12:1; 14:2; 18:10; among the Apostolic Fathers only *I Clem.* 16:7 (LCL AF I, 35; = Isa. 53:7): διὰ τὸ κεκακῶσθαι οὐκ ἀνοίγει τὸ στόμα.

(3:9).[8] His formulation reminds one of Isa. 50:9 (LXX): τίς κακώσει με, where, however, the writer was thinking of the future, as in Lk. 12:7; 21:18, of God's outward support.

14a When it comes, nevertheless, to "suffering for the sake of righteousness," then what was said in the beatitude passed along from Jesus in Mt. 5:10 applies:[9] "Blessed are those who suffer." Thus the author continues: ἀλλ' εἰ καὶ πάσχοιτε διὰ δικαιοσύνην, μακάριοι. In the case of Christian slaves, as an example, it has already been made clear how not only in spite of but also "on account of" righteousness, on account of just conduct,[10] it is possible to come into social conflict, with all its consequences.[11] The author sees a similar situation of conflict and its manifold results — discrimination, ostracism, occupational disadvantages, accusations, and legal proceedings before the courts (not official governmental persecution)[12] — as a possibility at any time for all members of the Church. But he leaves open the possibility, as in v. 17, that such "suffering" might happen by formulating his statement in the rare and, therefore, especially noteworthy optative mood:[13] εἰ καὶ πάσχοιτε. He emphasizes the openness of the situation in order to protect the Church from fatalistic resignation and to encourage it toward a positive form of conduct in the sense of the principle advanced in 2:12. If one keeps in mind this kerygmatic goal then one need not reconstruct from this use of the optative a different situation than the one seen in the "must" in 1:6 (cf. 2:21; 4:12).[14]

Whoever has been afflicted and wronged for the sake of righteousness by his or her social environment is blessed. μακάριος, "happy," "blessed,"[15] indicates here as in 4:14 and in the remaining NT beati-

---

8. So Schlatter, *Petrus und Paulus,* 132f.; so also philologically, but in the sense of proverbial wisdom, Windisch, 69.

9. Mt. 5:10: μακάριοι οἱ δεδιωγμένοι ἕνεκεν δικαιοσύνης. I Pet. 3:14: εἰ καὶ πάσχοιτε διὰ δικαιοσύνην, μακάριοι. This and 2:12 are the only passages in I Peter in which clear points of contact with Matthew exist (cf. Best, 111; see above, p. 229, n.1); Mt. 5:10 is quoted verbatim, moreover, in a context similar to I Pet. 3:14, in Polycarp, *Phil.* 2:3 (LCL AF I, 285).

10. δικαιοσύνη, as in 2:24, "just conduct."

11. See the comments on 2:19f.

12. Contra Knopf, 137f.

13. BDF § 385 (p. 194f.).

14. So Kelly, 140f.; Selwyn, 191; contra Beare, 163, and those named by him on p. 162.

15. Here I Peter does not place μακάριος in the predicate position, as it does in 4:14 in accord with most of the rest of the NT, but uses it as the final clause of a conditional sentence, without a copula as is often the case (BDF § 127.4 [p. 70]); so also *Herm. Mand.* 8.9 (LCL AF II, 105; cf. BAGD s.v.).

tudes, in accord with the concept of good fortune mediated by the gospel, that person who participates in God's salvation, who is safe within God's blessing (4:14; cf. 3:9).[16] Just why this applies in the case of such suffering is spelled out in 3:18–4:6. But from this watchword — "While being prepared to suffer, accomplish good in society" — which concerns the conflict in a thoroughly positive way, the author draws the consequence for the struggle.

Vv. 14b-17: Positive "Apologetics" instead of Fear of Humankind

14b-15a   With a view toward the confrontation the author first states the principle: Do not fear not any person, only God/Christ. He thus echoes what he said earlier[17] within the broad realm of the conduct of "God-fearers" in relation to the powers of world society. He formulates the principle with the aid of Isa. 8:12f., thereby not only formally underscoring it by scriptural quotation, but even doing so in terms of specific content. The context of the passage is quite familiar to the author.

He cites the OT passage according to the LXX and applies it to the current situation by minor alterations of the text: τὸν δὲ φόβον αὐτῶν μὴ φοβηθῆτε μηδὲ ταραχθῆτε.[18] In v. 14b he links it to the opponents of the Christians by means of αὐτῶν, "of them" (rather than αὐτοῦ).[19] In v. 15a, τὸν Χριστόν is inserted after κύριον, and thus "Lord," which stands in the LXX for Yahweh, the name of God, is interpretively applied to the exalted Christ,[20] in whom God is manifest as the Church's eschatological Ruler.

The two sides of the directive, which the author has received through

---

16. Of the literature on μακάριος we mention here just E. Lipinski, "Macarismes et psaumes de congratulation," *RevBibl* 75 (1968), 321-367; J. Dupont, *Les Béatitudes* (three volumes, Études Bibliques; Paris, 1969-1973).

17. I Pet. 1:17; 2:17; 3:2.

18. The letter makes use here of Isa. 8:14 as it did earlier in 2:7f. and as Rom. 9:33 does. The words that come immediately before in Isa. 8:12f. are surely familiar to the author, not only in terms of this one occasion. The passage reads according to the LXX (with the alterations in I Peter noted in parentheses): τὸν δὲ φόβον αὐτοῦ (αὐτῶν) οὐ (—) μὴ φοβηθῆτε οὐδὲ μὴ (μηδὲ) ταραχθῆτε, κύριον αὐτὸν (δὲ τὸν Χριστὸν) ἁγιάσατε [καὶ αὐτὸς ἔσται σου φόβος].

19. αὐτῶν is objective genitive, not subjective genitive, which is, however, philologically possible (cf. BAGD s.v. "αὐτός" 3b) and which Schelkle, 100, n.1, assumes: "Do not fear their terrors." The LXX already changed the original warning to share the fear of the people into an admonition not to be afraid of the Assyrians.

20. τὸν Χριστόν is appositional and explains the designation "Lord." It is not a predicate ("sanctify Christ as Lord"), which word order might suggest.

the mediation of long OT, Jewish, and Christian tradition,[21] condition one another: Fear of society's pressure toward conformity, which comes with a high degree of emotion, is overcome when the true and ultimate Lord of history, the exalted Christ, comes to be "sanctified": κύριον δὲ τὸν Χριστὸν ἁγιάσατε. Like God in the first petition of the Lord's Prayer (Mt. 6:9), Christ is "hallowed" when he is acknowledged as "the Lord," i.e., as the One in whom God's deity makes its appearance in the form of his eschatological universal message of salvation; this is the salvation that destroys all evil, for holiness is God's essence.[22]

This acknowledgment takes place ἐν ταῖς καρδίαις ὑμῶν, "in your hearts," a phrase added to the OT quotation. That is, it occurs through the conduct that results from faith. Faith enables fear of humans to disappear from the "heart,"[23] from the center of a person's life. Faith does not close doors to relationship with other people out of either fear or hate. It turns, rather, in openness to others just as it turns to God. Out of the principle developed here follows in vv. 15b-16 the treatment of preparedness for apologetic-missionary responsibility.

15b This sentence recalls one of the sayings about persecution in Lk. 12:2-12 (par. Mt.), in which the admonition to fear not humankind but God (Lk. 12:4f.) stands alongside the promise that the Spirit will give the appropriate word during the trial before the legal authorities (12:11f.). Nonetheless, it addresses a different situation with different words. It speaks with Hellenistic terminology primarily of instances of private conflict, not merely of trials before legal authorities.

The clause αἰτεῖν τινα λόγον περί τινος, "require from someone an accounting about something," is familiar to Plato,[24] as is the word ἀπολογία, "defense," "justification." This terminology demonstrates an openness to the Hellenistic world, even if Plato's *Apology* did not enter into the horizons of Christian apologists until the second century.[25] The

---

21. IV Macc. 13:14f.: "Let us not fear the one who thinks he kills, for a great struggle and destruction of the soul await in eternal torment." Cf. Wis. 16:13-15; Lk. 12:4f. par. Mt. Selwyn, 193, while considering v. 15a, refers to the quite similarly worded passage in Seneca, fragment 123 in Lactantius, *Divinae Institutiones* 6.25 (*ANF* VII, 192): "[God] is to be consecrated by each man in his own breast."

22. See the comments on 1:16.

23. See the comments on 1:22.

24. Plato, *Politicus* 285E (LCL III, 107).

25. See A. Harnack, "Socrates und die alte Kirche," *idem, Reden und Aufsätze* I (Giessen, 1904). 27-48.

two expressions can have juridical meanings,[26] but the more detailed description of the situation here points to a running debate in everyday life with people who have a different way of thinking. Such debates can lead to legal trials, as is reported in Acts with regard to the earliest period[27] and is presupposed as well in I Pet. 4:15. But this is not the situation that is primarily in view here. Here every Christian is summoned to be prepared at all times in relation to every person to give an account about the meaning of being a Christian:[28] ἕτοιμοι ἀεὶ πρὸς ἀπολογίαν παντὶ τῷ αἰτοῦντι ὑμᾶς λόγον. The *"always"* and "in relation to *everyone"* lead one out of the narrow perspectives of the persecution sayings into the breadth of a universal missionary apologetic.

All who seek information about the meaning and essence of Christian existence ask, from the Christian perspective, about the "hope" that lives "in you," i.e., in the Christian community or more probably in the individual Christian: περὶ τῆς ἐν ὑμῖν ἐλπίδος. Hope, not faith, is, as has been seen in 1:3 and 1:21, for I Peter *the* distinguishing mark of Christian existence.[29] That Christians take their orientation from a future expectation was familiar even to outsiders, but the author clearly does not reflect much on this fact.

16 Everyone who inquires aggressively, out of curiosity, or with interest about the content of the Christian life is to be given information from a posture that is described from three perspectives. First it is said: μετὰ πραΰτητος καὶ φόβου. In relation to others Christians are to be "gentle."[30] That is, they do not condemn others but seek to win them over to the grace in which they themselves have become participants. They encounter the other person in this way by conducting themselves in "fear"[31] before God, i.e., in responsibility before God and in view of God's judgment.

---

26. αἰτεῖν τινα λόγον is used only here in the NT. λόγον δοῦναι, "to give account," corresponds to it elsewhere and is used juridically in I Peter as in Rom. 14:12 and passim; it is used in Plato, *Politicus* 285E (LCL III, 107), however, of a private defense. So also ἀπολογία, "defense," "justification," refers in Acts 25:16; 26:2; II Tim. 4:16 to defense before the court, but in I Cor. 9:3; II Cor. 7:11, and elsewhere to other dispute situations.

27. Acts 16:19-40; 17:6-10; 19:24-40; Lk. 12:11f. par. Mt. 10:19.

28. Cf. *m. Aboth* 2:18: "Rabbi Eliezer [ca. A.D. 90] said: Be alert to learn Torah and know what answer you will give to an Epicurean."

29. See the comments on 1:3, 21; cf. I Thess. 4:13; Eph. 2:13; I Cor. 15:16f.; Acts 23:6; 26:6.

30. See the comments on 3:4.

31. As in I Pet. 1:17; 2:18; 3:2.

Second, the Christians' conduct must be consistent with their apologetics: They must have in relation to their own selves a "good conscience,"[32] συνείδησιν ἔχοντες ἀγαθήν. This is possible if, like Paul in I Cor. 4:1-4, they have the certainty of living by faith, without being perfect therein (Phil. 3:12-16; Rom. 12:3). In this context a "good conscience" would include, above all, *justitia civilis* and would thereby exclude suspicions.

Third, and corresponding to the good conscience, is a "good manner of life," one that contradicts the slanders mentioned in 2:12.[33] One's manner of life, one's conduct, is "good" when it is carried out ἐν Χριστῷ, "in Christ"; for this reason the author speaks of the ἀγαθὴ ἐν Χριστῷ ἀναστροφή. I Peter is the only non-Pauline NT document to appropriate the formula ἐν Χριστῷ, which by all indications was coined by Paul. The formula is found about 164 times in Paul's letters.[34] But this letter, as has become increasingly clear, does not belong to the Pauline tradition. In Paul's writings the formula has a considerably broad spectrum of meanings: The ἐν can have an instrumental and a modal sense, but it is never used in a local-mystical sense. In principle, the formula means for Paul instrumentally that one's course is determined by the death and resurrection of Christ.[35] All three occurrences in I Peter describe modally the shaping fellowship with Christ that is a central theological tenet of the letter.[36] Relationship to him now distinguishes "one's manner of life in Christ" (3:16) or in the future "the glory in Christ" (5:10); "those who are in Christ" (5:14) are those who are connected to him, his

---

32. συνείδησις has the same meaning here as in 3:21: "conscience" (unlike 2:19; see the comments there), which was also known in Greek and Jewish writings. The expression "good conscience" is found otherwise also in Rom. 2:15; 9:1; II Cor. 1:12; 5:11; Acts 23:1 (cf. 24:16); I Tim. 1:5, 19; 3:9; II Tim. 1:3; Heb. 13:18.

33. ἐν ᾧ (as in 2:12) καταλαλεῖσθε provided occasion for textual alterations because the verb is usually linked elsewhere with an objective genitive and is used in the passive voice neither in the NT nor in the LXX and only occasionally in other Greek literature (Polybius 27.12.2 [LCL III, 67]). Hence, G, Koine, and many others read καταλαλῶσιν- (οὖσιν) ὑμῶν ὡς κακοποιῶν, which is a secondary approximation to 2:12. Selwyn, 194, supposes that the original reading was, as in the Vulgate, ἐν ᾧ καταλαλοῦσιν ὑμῶν; this is not probable.

34. It is nowhere to be found before Paul. See A. Deissmann, *Die neutestamentliche Formel in Christo Jesu* (Marburg, 1892); F. Neugebauer, *In Christus. Eine Untersuchung zum paulinischen Glaubensverständnis* (Göttingen, 1961); A. Oepke, "ἐν," *TDNT* II, 541f.

35. This point of departure is found quite clearly in I Cor. 15:22: "As in Adam all die, so also in Christ will all be made alive."

36. See the comments on 4:1, 13.

community. In none of these three uses does the expression stand — as becomes especially clear in the future-oriented statement of 5:10 — as a pale, formalized expression for "Christian,"[37] but it represents precisely that relationship to Christ which precedes every expression of the life lived out of faith.

Slanders are to be refuted and opponents are to be "shamed"[38] by conduct shaped by fellowship with Christ: ἵνα ἐν καταλαλεῖσθε καταισχυνθῶσιν οἱ ἐπηρεάζοντες ὑμῶν τὴν . . . ἀναστροφήν. That such opponents might also be brought to repentance in the same manner is expected in 2:12.

17 The admonition to encounter discrimination with positive apologetics is supported, as γάρ indicates, by the repetition in a different form of the watchword that was developed at the outset in vv. 13-14a. Here the statement is a maxim in wisdom style, a phrase that was transmitted in similar form already as a saying of Socrates:[39] κρεῖττον γὰρ ἀγαθοποιοῦντας . . . πάσχειν ἢ κακοποιοῦντας. It applies more generally what was said in 2:20 to slaves: If it should come, nevertheless, to "suffering" (3:14), thus going beyond the requirement of just conduct in society (the ἀγαθοποιεῖν of 2:15, here emphasized once again), then that is still "better" than if one were to experience suffering as the deserved punishment for wrong behavior (2:12).[40] This is "better," i.e., more helpful, more useful for the Christians, though not to be ranked morally higher,[41] since in such suffering they may, as 2:20 pointed out, be confident that God is for them, that the μακάριοι of 3:14 applies to them. As the next section develops, they are travelling thereby the path of blessing opened to them by Christ.

But such suffering encounters them only when God, the Lord of history, wills it:[42] εἰ θέλοι τὸ θέλημα τοῦ θεοῦ. Once again the optative

---

37. So *I Clem.* 1:2; 21:8; 38:1; 46:6; 48:4; 49:1 (LCL AF I, 9, 47, 73, 89, 93).

38. καταισχύνειν, passive, "to be shamed"; so also Lk. 13:17; II Cor. 7:14; 9:4.

39. Plato, *Gorgias* 508C (LCL V, 471): τὸ ἀδικεῖν τοῦ ἀδικεῖσθαι . . . κάκιον.

40. See the comments on 2:12, 15; 3:14. A different interpretation of the passage is found in Michaels, "Eschatology."

41. κρεῖττον here as in I Cor. 7:9, 38; II Pet. 2:21; cf. Phil. 1:23.

42. εἰ θέλοι τὸ θέλημα τοῦ θεοῦ corresponds to εἰ δέον in 1:6. "If God wills" is a standard Greek formula. It is understood here, as is the δεῖ, from the perspective of the Father of Jesus (Lk. 12:6f. par. Mt.); cf. Plato, *Alcibiades* 135D (LCL VIII, 221), and passim: ἐὰν θεὸς ἐθέλῃ, so that Minucius Felix, *Octavius* 18.11 (*ANF* IV, 183), can call the expression "si deus dederit" a "vulgi naturalis sermo." Cf. Windisch-Preisker, 29 (on Jas. 4:15).

mood of the verb deliberately leaves open the possibility here, as in v. 14, that it will come to suffering.

3:18-22: Christ's Path of Salvation[1]

18 *For Christ also has suffered once and for all for sin,*
the Just for the unjust,
in order to lead you to God,
put to death in the flesh, but made alive in the Spirit.

19 *So he also went and preached to the spirits in prison,*
20 *who once had been disobedient as God's patience waited in the*
days of Noah as the ark was being built,
in which a few — namely eight souls — were delivered through
the water;
21 *as an antitype to this baptism now also delivers you —*
not as a putting away of dirt from the flesh,
but as the entreaty to God for a good conscience —
through the resurrection of Jesus Christ,
22 *who is at the right hand of God*
after having gone into heaven,
while the angels, authorities, and powers were made subject to
him.

Structure and Tradition

1. 3:18-22 is the third christological section of I Peter. Like the earlier christological sections, 1:18-21 and 2:22-25, it takes as its starting point Christ's atoning suffering unto death. But in contrast to the earlier sections, this one does not enlarge on the nature of this suffering and of the redemption,[2] but on the range of the suffering's saving effectiveness.

It is no accident that so many elements of the course of Christ's life are addressed here, more than in any other NT christological section. Nowhere else are so many aspects of the second article of the Apostles' Creed found in a preliminary stage of development. In v. 18 a faint echo of "suffered" can be heard, in v. 19 "descended into the underworld," and in vv. 21f. "raised," "ascended into heaven, sitting at the right hand of God." But this section does not depict a

---

1. See above, p. 207, n.29 for bibliography; see further: Boismard, *Quatre hymnes,* 60-67; Sanders, *NT Christological Hymns,* 95f.; Shimada, "Christological Creedal Formula"; Galot, "Vittoria di Cristo."
2. See the comments on 1:18 and 2:21.

redeemer's journey, the individual steps of which, as such, alter the cosmic situation; it shows, rather, the universal saving effectiveness of the suffering unto death "of the Just for the unjust," which is present in Christ as "the One who was killed and made alive" (v. 18).

2. The results of Christ's suffering unto death are introduced three times by καί, "also": "For Christ also" (v. 18), "So he also went" (v. 19), and "baptism now also" (v. 21). The saving effectiveness of the righteous One's suffering unto death is thus seen from these perspectives: V. 18 speaks of his constant leading of people to God, vv. 19-20a of his proclamation of salvation to "the spirits in prison," vv. 20b-21 of the deliverance he accomplished from the judgment now underway through baptism, and v. 22 of his saving dominion over the cosmic powers. This is, to be sure, no systematic arrangement. It is more likely that the author compiled, in accord with certain associations, a series of traditional concepts and formulas that sought to make visible the universal saving effectiveness resulting from the suffering unto death of the righteous One.

Therefore, this section gives less attention than the two earlier christological sections to constructing in the parenetic context an example to be imitated: The suffering of the righteous One is characterized expressly as a one-time occurrence (v. 18). Here the author seeks, rather, to include in the participation in Christ's sufferings (κοινωνεῖν, 4:13) the aspects of sharing and participating in this path of blessing and, thus, to lay the foundation for the pronouncement of blessing on those afflicted for the sake of righteousness (3:13-17).

3. This understanding of the structure of the section anticipates suggestively what the exegesis of the section will confirm, namely, that the section in its entirety has been shaped with a parenetic intention and has been incorporated here for that reason. Of course, the difficult conceptual arrangement and the stylization and formulaic character of the statements lead us to suppose that preexisting materials were utilized here.

a. Bultmann, who was first to carry out a thorough analysis,[3] came to the conclusion that a single connected traditional piece, consisting of vv. 18 (without δίκαιος ὑπὲρ ἀδίκων), 19, and 22, was utilized. He thought that it should probably be characterized according to genre as credal, not, like 2:22-25, as hymnic. The text, which Bultmann thought should perhaps be enlarged at its beginning by 1:20, was presumably worded as follows:

ὃς ἔπαθεν ἅπαξ περὶ ἁμαρτιῶν,
   ἵνα ἡμᾶς προσαγάθῃ τῷ θεῷ,
θανατωθεὶς μὲν σαρκί,
   ζῳοποιηθεὶς δὲ πνεύματι,
ἐν ᾧ καὶ τοῖς ἐν φυλακῇ πνεύμασιν ἐκήρυξεν,
   πορευθεὶς (δὲ) εἰς οὐρανὸν ἐκάθισεν ἐν δεξιᾷ θεοῦ,
      ὑποταγέντων αὐτῷ ἀγγέλων καὶ ἐξουσιῶν καὶ δυνάμεων.

---

3. Bultmann, "Bekenntnis- und Liedfragmente."

This reconstruction of the text has been obtained by means of a substantial number of conjectures but is still not unified stylistically.[4] Schille agreed largely with Bultmann, but excluded v. 19 to smooth things out.[5] Boismard inserted for v. 19 — on a purely hypothetical basis — 4:6.[6]

b. Wengst takes Bultmann's analysis as his point of departure, though he thinks that the preexisting material has been altered more strongly by editorial glosses:[7] The formula about Christ's death in v. 18 and the subsequent ἵνα clause did not belong, says Wengst, to the original traditional piece, but the parallelism of θανατωθεὶς μὲν σαρκί, ζῳοποιηθεὶς δὲ πνεύματι does appear to be formulaic; Wengst thinks that vv. 19f. are the author's editorial glosses and that mention of the great flood led him in v. 21 to a baptismal typology. While Bultmann included all of v. 22 in the preexisting material, Wengst includes only v. 22a and c. Wengst, like Bultmann, considers 1:20 (without δι' ὑμᾶς) to be the beginning of the traditional piece. Therefore, the text available to the author read:

ὁ προεγνωσμένος μὲν πρὸ καταβολῆς κόσμου,

  φανερωθεὶς δὲ ἐπ' ἐσχάτου τῶν χρόνων,

θανατωθεὶς μὲν σαρκί,

  ζῳοποιηθεὶς δὲ πνεύματι,

πορευθεὶς εἰς οὐρανόν,

  ὑποταγέντων αὐτῷ ἀγγέλων καὶ ἐξουσιῶν καὶ δυνάμεων.

This hymn consisted only of participial predicates to which ὁ must then be prefixed. This traditional piece could be compared with I Tim. 3:16 in form, while in content it described (as a "journey hymn") a journey in terms of its individual stations.

c. These unsatisfactory attempts at reconstruction[8] caused Deichgräber to conclude that the author did not utilize a block of preexisting tradition, but only individual hymnic, credal, and catechetical pieces. He identifies only v. 18b and perhaps portions of v. 22 as constitutive parts of a Christ hymn.[9]

4. The assumption that we see here individual elements of tradition may come the closest to the actual tradition-historical circumstances. In the exegesis of the letter it can be seen repeatedly that the author applied various traditions and bound them securely within the context of his parenesis toward a meaningful overall statement.

V. 18a, like 2:21, appropriated the primitive kerygma. The phrase paralleling

---

4. This was already asserted in opposition by J. Jeremias, "Zwischen Karfreitag und Ostern," 323f.

5. Schille, *Hymnen,* 38f.

6. Boismard, *Quatre hymnes,* 57ff., especially 66.

7. Wengst, *Christologische Formeln und Lieder,* 161ff.

8. See also Hunzinger, "Struktur," 142-145, who accepts Bultmann's reconstruction, but also ascribes δίκαιος ὑπὲρ ἀδίκων (v. 18) to the source in order to achieve a hymn with three strophes, each having three lines (v. 18a-c, vv. 18d-19, v. 22b, a, c).

9. Deichgräber, *Gotteshymnus,* 173.

it in v. 18b: "the Just for the unjust," appears to be an accommodation to the parenetic context and, yet, sounds like a formula. Similarly, the result clause in v. 18c belongs to the letter's parenesis of discipleship, but could already have indicated the goal of v. 18a. V. 18d, which in many ways reminds one of 1:20, is a formula cast in antithetical *parallelismus membrorum;* it is related to the christological formula tradition in Rom. 1:3f. and I Tim. 3:16.

The statements in vv. 19, 20a, b, and 21, which shift over into prose, certainly appropriate catechetical tradition; they utilize a complex of tradition that was grouped around the typology of the great flood (Lk. 17:26ff. par.). This traditional complex contained preexisting material that is seen in the apocalypticism of *I Enoch* and that is also used in Heb. 11:5-7 and II Pet. 2:4f.[10]

The three expressions in v. 22 are shown to be fixed statements by their formulaic style, i.e., relative clause or participial formulation. The first has a verbatim parallel in Rom. 8:34. πορευθείς in v. 22b corresponds to the same participle in v. 19 and shows, like καί at the beginning of vv. 18, 19, and 21, how the author did his editorial work of combining traditions.

V. 18: The Death of the Righteous One as the Opening of the Path to God

18a The christological foundation for the preceding parenesis is introduced, as in 2:21, with the expression ὅτι καὶ Χριστὸς . . . ἔπαθεν, "for Christ also . . . suffered." In both places the most likely reading is ἔπαθεν, "he suffered," not ἀπέθανεν, "he died,"[11] but πάσχειν here also includes the suffering of death.

This suffering unto death happened ἅπαξ, "once for all time." With this word the author emphasizes, like Paul in Rom. 6:10, that the sins that separate from God have been overcome ultimately and that the path to God, on which Christ takes us (v. 18c), has been opened up for all time.[12]

This release from sins was made possible through Christ's death περὶ ἁμαρτιῶν. This expression, which derives from the primitive ke-

---

10. See below, nn. 41f., 68.

11. So Selwyn, 196; Beare, 167; Schelkle, 102f.; contra Windisch, 70; Kelly, 147f. The manuscript support for both readings is good and either could be explained as an accommodation: ἔπαθεν (B, Koine, others) could be an adaptation to the context in 3:17 and 4:1. ἀπέθανεν (𝔭72, ℵ, A, others, Vulgate) could be an adaptation to the traditional formula (Rom. 6:10). In all probability, however, the latter came about from later usage, as a result of which ἔπαθεν was no longer understood as referring to suffering unto death.

12. Here ἅπαξ does not, as in Heb. 9:26-28; 10:10 (ἐφάπαξ), define what is spoken of over against other repeated acts of atonement.

rygma reflected in I Cor. 15:3, is found elsewhere in the NT only in Gal. 1:4 and Heb. 10:12. The two prepositions περί (in Galatians) and ὑπέρ (in Hebrews and I Corinthians) were used interchangeably without change of meaning as early as the LXX of sacrifice for sin.[13] I Peter appropriates, not this OT expression for sacrifice περὶ/ὑπὲρ ἁμαρτίας, but the NT formula of "death for." But the preposition "for" indicates in both contexts that sins[14] were blotted out through death as vicarious atonement[15] so that they no longer separate from God; therefore, the way is cleared for access to God. Here the "religious" consequence of atonement is stressed, while in 2:24 the ethical and ecclesiological consequences were emphasized. In each case, however, not only is guilt blotted out, but also wrong conduct is removed.

18b δίκαιος ὑπὲρ ἀδίκων establishes in a parallel statement to the preceding statement about Christ's suffering unto death a still closer connection to the preceding admonition to suffer "for the sake of righteousness" (v. 14; cf. δικαίους in v. 12). Jesus suffered as "the Just for the unjust." In this formulation I Peter follows once again Greek linguistic sensibilities,[16] though it understands the familiar Greek distinction between just and unjust along the lines of the OT distinction between "righteous ones" and "sinners" or "godless ones." This distinction is appropriated by the author in 4:18, quoting Prov. 11:31, and radicalized here in reference to Christ. In Greek-Hellenistic thought, an ἄδικος is one who trespasses against legal and moral standards. But in OT thought an "unrighteous" person is one who breaks out of the realm of divine justice and, thereby, breaks away from God.[17] Here Christ is "the just One" and all others are the "unjust ones"; as in the previous

---

13. Reference can be made here especially to Ezek. 43:21 LXX (περὶ ἁμαρτίας), 22, 25 (ὑπὲρ ἁμαρτίας); cf. also Lev. 5:7; 6:23; Ps. 39:7, and passim. The author of I Peter probably intends to alternate between this περί before ἁμαρτιῶν and the concluding ὑπέρ before ἀδίκων (as in 2:21 before ὑμῶν).

14. No article is used with ἁμαρτιῶν, as with δίκαιος and ἀδίκων, but the expressions are used undoubtedly in an encompassing way. Some manuscripts enlarge with (clearly secondary) ἡμῶν or ὑπὲρ ἡμῶν.

15. Similarly in Isa. 53:5 LXX: διὰ τὰς ἁμαρτίας ἡμῶν, and 53:10: περὶ ἁμαρτίας (as guilt offering "for sin").

16. The Synoptic tradition distinguishes, in accord with Palestinian linguistic usage, between "the righteous" and "sinners"; only in later formulations do we see "the righteous and the unrighteous" (Mt. 5:45; Acts 24:15). This distinction was familiar in Greek from the earliest times, e.g., Xenophon, *Memorabilia* 4.4.13 (LCL IV, 315): ὁ μὲν ἄρα νόμιμος δίκαιός ἐστιν, ὁ δὲ ἄνομος ἄδικος.

17. G. Schrenk, "ἄδικος," *TDNT* I, 149f.

material, the definite article is to be added. According to early Christian tradition[18] Jesus suffered as the just One, like the Servant of God in Isa. 53:11. As the idea is developed in I Pet. 2:22, Christ did justice without qualification to his relationship with God and humankind and remained in no wise a debtor to either.[19] The preposition "for" in 3:18a speaks primarily, in view of sins, of the atonement, but here, as in 2:21, the preposition focuses on a representation (along the lines of the prophecy, known to the author, in Isa. 53:4f., 11) that happened for the benefit of the unjust ones and that consisted in atonement.

18c The effect of the vicarious atonement is expressed here, as in 2:24 and 4:6, in the final clause ἵνα ὑμᾶς προσαγάγῃ τῷ θεῷ. I Peter takes up in this clause the early Christian image of the opening of access to God through Christ and extracts from it a new perspective. According to Paul, προσαγωγή, "access" (not "conveyance"), became operative through atonement because peace was achieved (Rom. 5:1; cf. Eph. 2:18; 3:12). According to Heb. 10:19-22 the path into the holy of holies to God has been opened up so that we may make our approach (προσερχώμεθα, 10:22; cf. 4:16; 10:25; 12:22). But according to I Peter Christ is the One who leads the redeemed to God. He is not, as in Hebrews, a forerunner and a preparer of the way,[20] but the One who leads. This special shaping of the image corresponds to the concepts of discipleship (2:21) and of participation in Christ's path (4:13) that are characteristic for I Peter.[21] The "lead-

---

18. Elsewhere in the NT only in Acts 3:14; 7:52; 22:14 (cf. 2:23), and in a different sense in Mt. 27:19 (v. 24 v.l.) and I Jn. 2:1, 29; 3:7. The formulation in I Pet. 3:18 was perhaps inspired by Isa. 53:11f., which is adapted also in I Pet. 2:24; there δίκαιος represents the ἄνομοι. In 4:18, I Peter uses the same two designations: δίκαιος stands there and in 3:12 for Christians; ἄδικος is no longer found. Peters, "Gospel," 26, calls 3:18 "the Gospel in a single sentence and its significance in a single statement."

19. That Jesus' death was valid for "sinners" is emphasized otherwise in the NT chiefly in Rom. 5:6-8; nevertheless, the accent there is on the demonstration of God's love, while here it is on the suffering of the righteous one.

20. The closest parallel is Heb. 2:10: "It was fitting that he for whom and by whom all things exist, in bringing (ἀγαγόντα) many sons to glory, should make the pioneer (ἀρχηγόν) of their salvation perfect through suffering." Cf. 5:7-10; 12:1ff.

21. It is occasionally thought that the concept of leading is to be enriched by the technical uses of this verb: προσάγειν is used in the LXX of cultic leading of animals to sacrifice (Ex. 29:10; Lev. 1:2, and passim; *I Clem.* 31:3 [LCL AF I, 61]) and of people to dedication (Ex. 29:4; Lev. 8:14; Num. 8:9) and of bringing a person before the courts (Ex. 21:6; Num. 25:6; Acts 16:20) or to an audience before the king (Xenophon, *Cyropaedia* 1.3.8 [LCL I, 33]). But all these ideas lie beyond the purview of I Pet. 3:18 (so Selwyn, 196; Kelly, 149; contra K. L. Schmidt, "ἀγωγή, κτλ.," *TDNT* I, 131-133; Schelkle, 103). προσάγειν occurs elsewhere in the NT only in Luke-Acts (Lk. 9:41; Acts 16:20; 27:27) and has here as there the ordinary meaning "lead to" (and intransitive "go to").

ing" of Christ encounters the one who is called into the Church (2:9) —
which lifts its voice to God as Father (1:17) — especially the one who is
linked with Christ through suffering for the sake of righteousness (4:13)
and who understands this suffering as an expression of his or her calling
(2:21).[22]

18d The fellowship that brings salvation is fellowship with the
"just One" who suffered "for the unjust." It is possible because he
encounters people as the One who "was put to death in the flesh but
made alive in the Spirit": θανατωθεὶς μὲν σαρκί, ζωοποιηθεὶς δὲ
πνεύματι. The antithesis of flesh and Spirit aided the anthropological
interpretation of Jesus' death and resurrection already in the Palestinian
formula in Rom. 1:3f., which has undergone further Hellenistic expansion in I Tim. 3:16.[23] "Flesh" and "Spirit" are used here in the sense
given them in early Christian anthropology;[24] they do not refer, as in
Greek tradition, to the constituent parts of a human being[25] or to realms
of existence, but primarily to modes of existence:[26] Jesus was killed
insofar as he belonged to "the flesh," to mortal human existence,[27] and

---

22. The ancient Near Eastern idea of the redeemer-deity who enables the redeemed
to travel through the spheres of the world to the realm of light (Perdelwitz, *Mysterienreligion,*
86; H. Gressmann, *Altorientalische Bilder zum Alten Testament* [second ed., Berlin/Leipzig,
1927], illustrations 92, 95), represents only a distant background to the NT image of access
to God; I Peter appropriates the image, in any case, as already Christian tradition (contra
Perdelwitz, 86).

23. Hellenized further in Ignatius, *Eph.* 7:2; *II Clem.* 9:5; *Herm. Sim.* 5.6.5-7 (LCL
AF I, 181, 143; II, 167-169); cf. E. Schweizer, *Lordship and Discipleship* (StBiblTh 28;
London, 1960), 67; W. Kramer, *Christ, Lord, Son of God* (tr. B. Hardy; Naperville, IL, 1966),
108-111.

24. See the comments on 1:24.

25. This tradition usually distinguishes between σῶμα and ψυχή, but can also refer,
instead, to σάρξ and πνεῦμα; so Euripides, fragment 971 (*Tragicorum Graecorum Fragmenta,*
ed. A. Nauck [second ed., Leipzig, 1889], 674): "Swollen in the flesh (σάρξ) he died, the
spirit (πνεῦμα) being released into the other" (cf. E. Schweizer, "σάρξ," *TDNT* VII, 102f.).
The Church Fathers interpret I Pet. 3:18 according to this anthropology: The "flesh" is
Christ's body, which dies; the "spirit" is his soul (Origen, *Contra Celsum* 2.43 [*MPG* 11,
864f.; *Contra Celsum,* tr. H. Chadwick (Cambridge, 1965), 99f.; Cyril of Alexandria, *Fragmenta in I Petrum* [*MPG* 74, 1012ff.]) or his divinity in connection with his human soul
(Epiphanius, *Panarion* 69.52 [*MPG* 42, 281f.; Augustine, *Epistola* 164.17-21 [*MPL* 33,
716ff.; *NPNF* first series I, 520f.]), which is immortal and, therefore, survives or is revived.
Schelkle, 103f., comes close to this explanation.

26. So Kelly, 150f.; contra Beare, 169 ("spheres of existence"); Schweizer, *TDNT* VI,
417 ("in the carnal sphere, in the spiritual sphere").

27. σαρκί is dative of relationship, expressing the same thought as κατὰ σάρκα in
Rom. 1:3f. and ἐν σαρκί in I Tim. 3:16, i.e., Christ's belonging to a particular mode of
existence.

"made alive," raised, insofar as he belonged to the Spirit, i.e., as in Rom. 1:3f., to the Spirit of God; according to I Pet. 1:11, his Spirit had even already spoken through the prophets. The Spirit was not something like an immortal soul in him, but his connectedness to God: He was raised, then, even more because he was Spirit.[28]

It is in this sense that flesh and Spirit are used of Christ within the anthropological thesis of 4:6 in order to interpret the course of mortals through death and resurrection.[29] Here what is seen with the aid of this anthropology is a picture of Christ in which his execution and resurrection are separate acts and, yet, in which they are integrated into the unity and continuity of his being as person.

The gospel calls a person, not to acknowledge individual facts of salvation, but to align oneself with the person of Jesus; in this person the event of salvation is effectively present. As such Christ leads people into fellowship with God, and the people he leads in this way are those who are called into his fellowship and who continue to be connected to him through suffering for the sake of righteousness. θανατωθείς and ζωοποιηθείς are verbs which elsewhere in the NT and in the Apostolic Fathers are used hardly ever of Christ, but rather always of believers, especially "the persecuted";[30] these verbs thus give what is stated here a focus on the commonality between the One who leads to God and those who follow in discipleship.

This saving effectiveness of the resurrected One that comes from Jesus' suffering unto death applies now, however, not only to those who are reached during the time that the gospel is preached, but, as the

---

28. Dative πνεύματι takes on an instrumental meaning, going beyond the modal sense, since it is nearly a fixed expression: The πνεῦμα accomplishes the ζωοποιεῖν (Rom. 8:11; I Cor. 15:45; II Cor. 3:6; Jn. 6:63).

29. See the comments on 4:6.

30. ζωοποιεῖν is here, as consistently in the NT (Rom. 4:17; 8:11; I Cor. 15:22, 36; Jn. 5:21), synonymous with ἐγείρειν, but is used with regard to Jesus only here. It stands in antithesis to θανατοῦν, "kill," which is used in the Passion narrative in regard to the intention of Jesus' opponents (Mk. 14:55 par. Mt.; Mt. 27:1) and in Jesus' sayings about persecution of his disciples (Mk. 13:12 par.); in Paul it occurs in statements about bodily (Rom. 8:36; II Cor. 6:9) and spiritual (Rom. 7:4; 8:13) participation in the cross. According to Windisch, 71, the original meaning of ζωοποιεῖν has been altered here: "By inserting the death-journey and by first referring expressly to the resurrection in v. 22, the author is apparently differentiating being made alive in the Spirit from the resurrection: As a spirit made alive again Christ went into the underworld to the spirits who were likewise bodiless; thereafter, he rose, i.e., with his body." This explanation fails to recognize the structure of the section, especially ἐν ᾧ in v. 19.

kerygma proclaimed from the very beginning, to all people. Accordingly, as 4:6 puts it, "the gospel was also preached to the dead." This universal scope of the saving effectiveness of Jesus' suffering unto death is brought to awareness now by means of an extreme example.

Vv. 19-20a: The Preaching to the "Spirits in Prison"[31]

The statement in vv. 19-20a has been interpreted in so many ways, even in contemporary discussion, that one is reminded of Luther's comment:[32] "This is a strange text and certainly a more obscure passage than any other passage in the NT. I still do not know for sure what the apostle means." Understanding the passage depends above all on clarification of two exegetical questions: To what does v. 19 refer with ἐν ᾧ? And who are the πνεύματα ἐν φυλακῇ?

19 ἐν ᾧ is connected by a number of exegetes with the preceding πνεῦμα, something that is quite possible philologically. They translate then "in which" or "as which." That is to say, Jesus went as a bodiless spirit, before his bodily resurrection, to likewise bodiless spirits.[33] But "spirit" in v. 18 does not refer to a part of the person existing unto itself, but to one's manner of existence, i.e., one's relationship with God.

Therefore, ἐν ᾧ must, if it is connected to πνεῦμα, be understood as instrumental; so Schlatter: "In the power of the spirit" Christ went there. Then, however, dative πνεύματι in v. 18d must also have primarily an instrumental meaning. But this is made impossible by the parallel σαρκί.[34]

One must, therefore, with a number of other exegetes understand ἐν ᾧ, as in 1:6 and 4:4, as a conjunction[35] and translate the construction

---

31. See Gschwind, *Niederfahrt;* Selwyn, 314-362; Reicke, *Disobedient Spirits;* Bieder, *Höllenfahrt;* Jeremias, "Zwischen Karfreitag und Ostern"; S. E. Johnson, "Preaching to the Dead"; Dalton, *Christ's Proclamation* (contra Rubinkiewicz, "Duchy zamknięte"); *idem,* "I Peter 3:19 and 4:6"; *idem,* "3:19 Reconsidered"; Strynkowski, *Descent of Christ;* Grillmeier, "Gottessohn im Totenreich"; Vogels, *Christi Abstieg;* Scharlemann, "'He Descended into Hell'"; Michaels, 205-213. Cf. BAGD s.v. "πνεῦμα" 2.

32. The 1523 commentary, as translated in M. H. Bertram, "Sermons on the First Epistle of St. Peter," *Luther's Works* XXX: *The Catholic Epistles* (ed. J. Pelikan and W. A. Hansen; St. Louis, 1967), 113 = XII, 367 in the Weimar edition.

33. So, e.g., Knopf, 147f.; Windisch, 70; Beare, 171; Schelkle, 104; Kelly, 152. See also Hanson, "Salvation Proclaimed."

34. Schlatter, *Petrus und Paulus,* 137f.

35. The relative pronoun with a preposition in Greek often assumes the sense of a conjunction (BAGD s.v. "ἐν" IV.6); in 3:21 as well, before the next καί (= "also"), the relative pronoun is again used in this way (see below, n.78).

as "wherein," "thereby," or "thus."[36] This expression thus appropriates what precedes in its entirety: "Thus," i.e., as one who died and rose, Christ went "also" to the spirits in prison. Like the "leading" of the "unrighteous" to God (v. 18c), this going is "also" an accomplishment of his suffering unto death. But nothing is said in the words ἐν ᾧ καί about the time and manner in which Christ went to the spirits in prison.

The understanding of τὰ ἐν φυλακῇ πνεύματα followed in the Western Church up to the beginning of the twentieth century was formulated by Augustine in opposition to an older interpretation.[37] According to Augustine the spirits in prison are the unbelieving contemporaries of Noah, who were held in the prison of sin and ignorance. To them the Spirit of the preexistent Christ (1:11) preached through Noah. But this allegorization is contrary to the scope of the context, which does not point, like 1:11, to prophecy, but to the saving effectiveness of Christ's suffering unto death.

Today two interpretations remain as serious possibilities:

1. In terms of philology and the history of religions much speaks for the explanation put forth in 1890 by Friedrich Spitta,[38] which since then has been appropriated by many:[39] Since Christ preaches to them, the πνεύματα are to be thought of as personal entities. But plural πνεύματα usually represents in the NT suprahuman spirit entities, i.e., angels or demons.[40] Within this sense of the word v. 19 is understood on the basis of a Jewish apocalyptic myth[41] that was known in early Christianity.[42] The brief remarks about the fall of angels in Gen. 6:1-4

---

36. So Bieder, *Höllenfahrt*, 106; Schweizer, *TDNT* VI, 447; similarly Selwyn, 197.

37. Augustine, *Epistola* 164.14-17 (MPL 33, 715f.; *NPNF* first series I, 519f.); more recently represented by Wohlenberg, 113 (on the history of research see Reicke, *Disobedient Spirits*, 37-42). See also Feinberg, "1 Peter 3:18-20"; Grudem, "Christ Preaching Through Noah."

38. Spitta, *Predigt an die Geister;* H. Gunkel, *Zum religionsgeschichtlichen Verständnis des NT* (FRLANT 1; Göttingen, 1910), 72f.

39. Knopf, 149ff.; Windisch, 71; J. Jeremias, *Abba. Studien zur neutestamentlichen Theologie und Zeitgeschichte* (Göttingen, 1966), 325f.; Reicke, *Disobedient Spirits*, 90f.; Selwyn, 326 (with reservations); Kelly, 153f.

40. Of spirit beings designated good or not expressly as evil in Acts 23:8f.; Heb. 1:14; 12:9; cf. Rev. 1:4; 3:1, and passim; of evil spirit beings in Mk. 1:23, 26; Acts 19:15f.; 16:16, and passim (see BAGD s.v. "πνεῦμα" 4b, c). On evil spirits see Kvanvig, "Bruken av Noahtradisjonene."

41. *I En.* (6) 10-16; 21; *II Bar.* 56:12f.; *Jub.* 5:6 (*OT Pseudep.* I, 15-22, 24, 641; II, 64); CD 2:18-21; 1QapGen 2:1, 16.

42. Jude 6 and II Pet. 2:4 refer to it explicitly.

was developed further in apocalyptic writings into a cosmic myth: The angels "transgressed the commandments of the Lord" (*I En.* 21:6; cf. 106:13f. [*OT Pseudep.* I, 24, 87]) and were thus "disobedient" (I Pet. 3:20). They then led humankind astray to such great wickedness that God had to destroy the first humanity in the flood. Therefore, the angels were bound and delivered over into the underworld[43] "in a prison" (*I En.* 18:14; 21:10 [*ibid.*, 23f.]) until the day of judgment. God sent Enoch to tell them not to expect mercy and that they are, rather, condemned eternally: "You will have no peace" (*I En.* 16:4 [*ibid.*, 22]). What the apocalyptic writers said about Enoch, their mediator of revelation, has been transferred, it is claimed, to Christ by Christians, and the resulting concept was, it would have to be assumed, so widely diseminated in early Christianity that the author of I Peter could point to it in formulaic brevity: "He preached to the spirits in prison."

What did he "preach" to them? The majority of those who take this position[44] say that, like Enoch, he announced to the spirits their rejection and dethronement through his exaltation. I Peter reminds the afflicted Church of this event because their opponents are only repeating the rebellion of the "spirits." But throughout the NT κηρύσσειν, "preach," is used of the proclamation of salvation in Christ and the Christian message.[45] For this reason, many representatives of the angelological interpretation of the passage assume that though Enoch preached judgment, Christ preached salvation. In the NT, however, it is never suggested that Christ redeemed fallen angels. Indeed, Heb. 2:16 comments expressly: "Surely it is not with angels that he is concerned but with the descendants of Abraham."[46]

The angelological interpretation of πνεύματα falls thereby into difficulties. It stands in conflict with what these πνεύματα are supposed to encounter, which is the saving proclamation of Christ.[47] Furthermore,

---

43. So *Jub.* 5:6 (*OT Pseudep.* II, 64); others locate the place of punishment at the end of heaven (*I En.* 18:12-14 [*ibid.* I, 23]) or in the second of the seven heavens (*II En.* 7:1-3; cf. *Test. Lev.* 3:2 [*ibid.* I, 112-115, 789]).

44. So Reicke, *Disobedient Spirits,* 90f.; Selwyn, 326; Kelly, 156f. See also Lindars, "Enoch and Christology."

45. So G. Friedrich, "κηρύσσω," *TDNT* III, 708. That the word can have a neutral sense in some passages with another subject (Lk. 12:3; Rom. 2:21; Rev. 5:2) proves nothing to the contrary (contra Kelly, 156).

46. At any rate Col. 1:20 (Rom. 8:21) does not refer to a reconciliation through the preaching of salvation.

47. Cf. Jeremias, *Abba,* 326.

the angels of Gen. 6:1-4 were "disobedient" not "in the days of Noah" (so I Pet. 3:20), but long before that.[48] Therefore, the interpretation does not deal with either of the statements about "the spirits in prison." Moreover, it is unlikely that I Pet. 3:18-22, which closes with the confession that the angels have been subjected to Christ, would present at an earlier point a statement about a similar event.[49]

2. These and other exegetical difficulties are resolved if the interpretation already developed by exegetes of the early Christian centuries is judged to be acceptable philologically and in terms of the history of religion. In this view the "spirits in prison" are the souls of Noah's unrepentant contemporaries.[50] Can πνεύματα have this meaning? The souls of the departed are, of course, usually called ψυχή in the NT. But I Peter, like Hebrews and Luke, tries always to present biblical concepts in Greek terms, and πνεῦμα is an ancient Greek synonym for ψυχή.[51] It is not coincidental that this usage is found perhaps in Luke (24:37, 39), certainly in Hebrews,[52] and very probably here in I Pet. 3:19. That with this term the author of I Peter refers to the continued existence of humans as individuals is also suggested by

---

48. That this chronology became unclear for the uncritical perspective of apocalyptic thinkers (Kelly, 154f.) is not to be concluded on the basis of *I En.* 106:13-18 (*OT Pseudep.* I, 87) since *I En.* 106:17 is surely a gloss; *Test. Naph.* 3:5 (*ibid.* I, 812) notes, as does *Jub.* 5:1-6 (*ibid.* II, 64) the connection between the fall of the angels and the depravity of the generation of the Flood.

49. This is also not suggested by the fact that in the related confession in I Tim. 3:16 ὤφθη ἀγγέλοις follows ἐδικαιώθη ἐν πνεύματι (contra Reicke, *Disobedient Spirits*, 234f.).

50. Clement of Alexandria, *Stromateis* 6.6.44-46 (*MPG* 9, 268a; *ANF* II, 490f.) refers to I Pet. 3:19 (6.45.4) in support of the idea that Christ offers salvation to all, even Gentiles (6.46.3); cf. *idem, Adumbrationes* (*MPG* 9, 731b; *ANF* II, 571-573); these are the oldest express references to I Pet. 3:19. According to Hippolytus, Christ preached to the righteous in Hades, even those "who were once disobedient," but had already repented apparently before his coming (fragment of an Easter sermon in Reicke, *Disobedient Spirits*, 23-27). In contrast, Origen refers to the passage repeatedly in the same universal sense as Clement: *Principia* 2.5.3 (*MPG* 11, 206c; *ANF* IV, 279f.); *Contra Celsum* 2.43 (*MPG* 11, 864f.; *Contra Celsum*, tr. Chadwick, 99f.); *Fragmenta in Commentariis in Mattheum* 132. This interpretation, which was of wider effect in the Eastern Church, appears to reduce the importance of the decision in time. Augustine developed his allegorical interpretation in opposition to it.

51. ἄνω τὸ πνεῦμα διαμενεῖ κατ' οὐρανόν (Epicharmus, fragment 22, H. Diels and W. Kranz, *Die Fragmente der Vorsokratiker* [fourteenth ed., Berlin, 1969], 202, l. 5); cf. H. Kleinknecht, "πνεῦμα," *TDNT* VI, 336.

52. Heb. 12:23: πνεύματα δικαίων τετελειωμένων, "spirits of the righteous made perfect" (in heaven), as in Dan 3:86a LXX: εὐλογεῖτε, πνεύματα καὶ ψυχαὶ δικαίων, τὸν κύριον. Cf. also *I En.* 22:3-13 (*OT Pseudep.* I, 24f.): πνεύματα τῶν ψυχῶν τῶν νεκρῶν (22:3; cf. BAGD s.v. "πνεῦμα" 2).

4:6, which says expressly that the gospel was proclaimed "to the dead."[53]

Is it possible then to support the idea that the souls of the flood generation continued to exist in the world of the dead in a prison? Several passages from Roman Church tradition, which until now have not been taken into account and with which I Peter has affinity, point this way. *II Clem.* 6:8 explains: If we are disobedient to Christ's commandments, nothing can save us from eternal punishment; "And the Scripture also says in Ezekiel that, 'if Noah and Job and Daniel arise, they shall not rescue their children in the captivity (ἐν τῇ αἰχμαλωσίᾳ)' " (LCL AF I, 136f.). αἰχμαλωσία is used literally of the "captivity" of prisoners of war, but here is thought of as a place of punishment in the hereafter. *Herm. Vis.* 1.1.8 threatens: "But they who have evil designs in their hearts bring upon themselves death and captivity (αἰχμαλωτισμός)" (*ibid.* II, 8f.). Here, as in *Sim.* 9.28.7 — ". . . lest you deny him and be delivered into prison (δεσμωτήριον)" (*ibid.*, 286f.) — what is referred to is a place of punishment in the hereafter.

"The spirits in prison" are, therefore, the souls of the flood generation preserved in a place of punishment after death. I Pet. 3:19f. contains, therefore, an important kerygmatic statement. In rabbinic tradition the generation of the flood were regarded as thoroughly and ultimately lost: "The generation of the Flood have no share in the world to come" (*m. Sanhedrin* 10:3a, *The Mishnah,* tr. H. Danby [Oxford, 1958], 397). But I Peter declares: Even to this most lost part of humanity Christ, the One who died and rose, offers salvation.[54] The saving effectiveness of his suffering unto death extends even to those mortals who in earthly life do not come to a conscious encounter with him, even to the most lost among them. I Pet. 4:6 expresses this directly: "The gospel was preached even to the dead." This kerygmatic statement represents the fundamental line of I Peter: It sets in contrast to the "excommunication" of Christians by society the missionary witness that determines their entire conduct in society and appropriates thereby the saying "You are the light of the world" (cf. 2:12), in the midst of a "disobedient" generation — to which, nonetheless, God's salvation applies! Apparently, this "nonetheless" is to be derived from

---

53. So also Friedrich, *TDNT* III, 707.

54. The Enoch myth may also have had a secondary influence in the shaping of this statement as an antithetical conceptual model.

the example of the flood generation in v. 20a, even though it is intended to give foundation primarily to the added typological summons to the exodus into the "ark."

But even though the statement has thereby a noteworthy kerygmatic sense, the idea that Christ preached to the dead is, nevertheless, very time-bound and mythical. Its character becomes clear when we place it in the context of its prehistory and subsequent history.

Excursus: Christ's Hades Proclamation in the Context of the History of Religion

Wilhelm Bousset integrated the Hades proclamation of Christ into his religio-historical reconstruction of NT christology with the following hypothesis: "The acceptance of the three-day interval between death and resurrection" also produced "the fantasy of the descent of Jesus into Hades." It comes to the fore on the one hand in the popular concept of a "battle of the prince of life with the prince (and the powers) of the underworld and of death," which is found for the first time literarily in *Odes Sol.* 42. On the other hand, it is found in the "theologoumenon 'sicklied o'er with the pale cast of thought' " (*Hamlet* III,1) about Jesus' preaching in Hades, which represses this mythology. This proclamation takes its point of departure above all, it is claimed, from an OT saying quoted by Justin (*Dialogue* 72 [*ANF* I, 235]) and no less than six times by Irenaeus (*Adversus Haereses* 3.20.4 [*ibid.* I, 450f.], and passim) and is presupposed in *Gospel of Peter* 41 (= 10; *NT Apoc.* I, 225).[55] This hypothetical construction marks off the horizon against which I Pet. 3:19 and 4:6 were understood within the presuppositions of and the information available to the "history-of-religions school." What can we say today about this?

1. The idea that the dead lived on in particular regions of the cosmos, above all in the underworld, was known to the entire ancient world. According to OT and Jewish tradition[56] the שְׁאוֹל, the ᾅδης, is an underworld realm of the dead, where the dead are not differentiated. They remain there as substanceless shadows until they, as was expected from the time of the apocalyptic writings, are raised to a new life.[57] Subsequent layers of the tradition refer to a preliminary separation already in Sheol between the just and sinners on the basis of a schema of recompense (e.g., *I En.* 22 [*OT Pseudep.* I, 24f.]; Lk. 16:24ff.). As a place of punishment Sheol became the permanent abode of the condemned (*II Bar.* 36:10f. [*ibid.*, 632]).

Hellenistic Judaism generally believed in the immortality of the soul. This

---

55. W. Bousset, *Kyrios Christos* (tr. J. Steely; Nashville, 1970), 60-68; on the discussion at that time see *ibid.,* 60, n.82. The quotations and references are from 60ff.

56. Cf. Str.-Bill. IV, 1016-1165.

57. E.g., *I En.* 51:1f. (*OT Pseudep.* I, 36); cf. Str.-Bill. IV, 1016f.

gave rise to the idea that the souls of the just, already at death, enter a heavenly blessedness that is occasionally called "paradise," which is the name of the place of final blessedness (Lk. 23:43), while the godless enter Hades as the place of punishment.[58] In the rabbinic literature Sheol is replaced by Gehinnom/Gehenna as the intermediate and final place of punishment.[59] In *II Esdras* and *II Baruch,* as in the NT, Hades is generally the location of the intermediate state, and Gehinnom/Gehenna is, as already in *I En.* 90:26f. (*OT Pseudep.* I, 71), the place of final perdition. Gehinnom/Gehenna is located differently in the cosmos in different traditions: According to *III Bar.* 4 and *II En.* 10 (*ibid.,* 666-669, 118-121) it is in the third heaven; *II En.* 40:12 (*ibid.,* 166) places it in the underworld, as is usually the case in other writings.[60]

The statements of I Peter about Christ's proclamation to the dead do not indulge in such graphic geography about the beyond. They only refer to persons with whom Christ has concerned himself and not to cosmic settings. The author does not describe his concepts, but witnesses to the meaning of the kerygma for deceased generations.

2. Corresponding to ideas about a place of residence for the dead in the cosmos, which were found among Gentiles as well as in Judaism, were myths of deities or heroes who went into the world of the dead in order to set them free. Such myths find themselves in nearly all religions of the environment of early Christianity:[61] The sending of Enoch to the angelic beings in the place of punishment of the underworld is only one example.

3. Christian post-NT writings speak of a ministry of Jesus in the world of the dead in two forms:

a. From the beginning of the second century a Hades proclamation of Christ was spoken of throughout the whole Church. "Have you preached to them that sleep?" is asked of Christ at the resurrection in *Gospel of Peter* 41f. (= 10), and he answers "Yes" (*NT Apoc.* I, 225). According to both eastern and western tradition Christ thus preached salvation to the righteous of the Old Covenant who had waited for him. This is presupposed by Ignatius, *Magn.* 9:2 (LCL AF I, 207): "And for

---

58. Wis. 1:1, 3, 5; 4:7; IV Macc. 5:37; 9:8; so also Philo, passim, and parts of *I* and *II Enoch* (cf. Str.-Bill. IV, 1020f.).

59. Str.-Bill. IV, 1022.

60. Str.-Bill. IV, 1085ff.; G. Friedrich, *TDNT* III, 707.

61. Kroll, *Gott und Hölle,* is a comprehensive but unfortunately undifferentiated collection of comparative material; further literature in Reicke, *Disobedient Spirits,* 231f. A neo-Babylonian text that comes into contact somewhat with I Pet. 3:19 says, e.g., about a deity, perhaps Marduk (Bousset, "Hadesfahrt Christi," 57f.):

He descends into the prison,
he arises (?) and reaches the prison,
he opens the gates of the prison, he comforts them;
then he looked on them, on all of them; he rejoiced.
Then the captive gods gazed on him,
friendly all of them — they observed him.

this reason he whom they waited for in righteousness, when he came raised them from the dead" (cf. *Phld.* 9:1 [*ibid.*, 248f.]). In *Herm. Sim.* 9.16.5 (*ibid.* II, 262f.) the apostles preach to the righteous of the Old Covenant and baptize them. Already in the first half of the second century a Jeremiah apocryphon of Christian origin is quoted by Justin (*Dialogue* 72 [*ANF* I, 235]): "The Lord God remembered His dead people of Israel who lay in the graves; and He descended to preach to them His own salvation."[62] Marcion twisted this Church tradition ironically into its opposite and taught that Christ saved all the sinners mentioned in the OT, including Cain and the people of Sodom and Egypt, but not the righteous ones of the OT.[63]

b. While the Hades proclamation of Christ is found primarily in theological reflection, the battle of Hades is encountered in homily and hymn. The oldest clear statement of this is in the Gnostic *Odes of Solomon* (42:11-20):[64]

Sheol saw me and was shattered,
and Death ejected me and many with me.
I have been vinegar and bitterness to it,
and I went down with it as far as its depth.
Then the feet and the head it released,
because it was not able to endure my face.
And I made a congregation of living among his dead. . . .

And those who had died ran toward me;
and they cried out and said, "Son of God, have pity on us.
"And deal with us according to your kindness,
and bring us out from the chains of darkness.
"And open for us the door
by which we may go forth to you. . . ."
Then I heard their voice. . . .
And I placed my name upon their head,
because they are free and they are mine.

Alongside this kind of hymnic statement (see also *Odes Sol.* 17:8ff.; 22; 29:4 [*OT Pseudep.* II, 750f., 754f., 761]), in which the Gnostic redeemer myth takes form, stands the homiletical portrayal of the Easter event in the paschal homily of Melito of Sardis: "I am the one that destroyed death and triumphed over the enemy and trod down Hades and bound the strong one and carried off man to the heights of heaven" (102f.).[65]

---

62. Cf. Grillmeier, "Gottessohn im Totenreich," 77f.

63. Irenaeus, *Adversus Haereses* 1.27.3 (*ANF* I, 352); Epiphanius, *Panarion* 1.3.42.4 (*The Panarion of Epiphanius of Salamis*, tr. F. Williams [Leiden, 1987], 274ff.). See A. von Harnack, *Marcion: The Gospel of the Alien God* (tr. J. E. Steely and L. D. Bierma; Durham, NC, 1990), 85ff.

64. *OT Pseudep.* II, 771.

65. *Melito of Sardis: On Pascha and Fragments,* ed. and tr. G. Hall (Oxford, 1979), 59; *The Homily on the Passion,* ed. C. Bonner (Studies and Documents 12; London/Philadelphia, 1940), 163; *Die Passa-Homilie des Bischofs Meliton von Sardes,* ed. B. Lohse (Textus

c. The structures of these various statements primarily represent soteriological developments clothed in the mythical concepts of the surrounding world. Only in the *Odes of Solomon* is a redeemer myth shaped by the soteriology of the Gnostic movement of much influence. Detailed analysis of these differences would take us too far afield.

4. How do early Christian traditions relate to these statements of the second century. What is said in the NT about a journey of Christ into Hades?

a. The NT documents consistently presuppose that death, even for Jesus, means a journey into the world of the dead (Mt. 12:40; Acts 2:27; Heb. 13:20).

b. But nothing is said about a ministry of Christ in the world of the dead, except in I Peter, neither in Rom. 10:7 nor in Eph. 4:8-10, and certainly not in Rev. 1:18 or Mt. 16:18.[66]

c. Therefore, I Pet. 3:19 and 4:6 are the only NT passages that speak of a ministry of the dead and resurrected Christ among the dead. But I Peter would not be able to make such brief reference to this idea if it were not already known in the churches as tradition. What I Peter says in regard to this tradition is, in comparison with the traditions of the second century, quite "apostolic." There is nothing in I Peter about a battle and triumph in the world of the dead; indeed, simply on the basis of his vicarious death the resurrected One is able to bring all to God (3:18). All that is proclaimed to the dead is the gospel, i.e., the message of Jesus' death and resurrection (4:6). But I Peter does not restrict the audience of this proclamation, in contrast to early catholic tradition, to the righteous of the OT; Christ preaches, rather, more generally "to the dead" (4:6), even to the most lost among them (3:19). According to the "apostolic" primitive confession, all are saved only through the grace that emerges in Jesus' death for all.

d. I Peter gives witness, therefore, with the aid of modestly applied but time-bound language to the universal saving effect of Christ's suffering unto death, in the sense of the "apostolic" gospel. If one understands the *descendit ad inferna,* which has stood in the Apostles' Creed since the fourth century,[67] as a reference to the statements in I Pet. 3:19 and 4:6, then it has a useful function.

Minores 24; Leiden, 1958). Cf. fragment 13 in J. C. Otto, *Corpus Apologetarum Christianorum Saeculi Secundi* IX (Jena, 1872), 419, 497.

66. That which E. Stauffer, *NT Theology* (tr. J. Marsh; New York, 1956), 133f., concludes about Christ's descent into Hades in the NT rests on a massive mythologizing of the NT statements.

67. For the first time in the "semi-Arian" "dated creed" of Sirmium from the year 359 (Socrates Sozomenus, *Historia Ecclesiastica* 2.37; Athanasius, *De Synodis* 8 [*NPNF* second series II, 61f.; IV, 454]), though the christological formula in the eucharist preface of Hippolytus already says: "Who when he was being betrayed to his voluntary suffering, that he might destroy death, break the chains of the devil, tread Hell underfoot, bring forth the righteous [therefrom] and set a bound [to it], and that he might manifest his Resurrection . . ." (R. H. Connolly, *The So-Called Egyptian Church Order and Derived Documents* [Texts and Studies 8/4; Cambridge, 1916], 164; translated in H. Bettenson, *Documents of the Christian Church* [second edition, Oxford, 1963], 107). For bibliography see Bieder, *Höllenfahrt;* A. Adam, "Apostolikum," *RGG* I, cols. 512f.; H. Thielicke, *The Evangelical Faith* II (tr. G. W. Bromiley; Grand Rapids, 1977), 415f.

20a   The generation of the great flood, like the society living around the Christian community, lived in a time of God's expectant patience before imminent judgment.[68] It was "disobedient" (ἀπειθήσας; cf. 2:8; 3:1; 4:17) and withdrew from the summons of its Creator, which had already gone out to it through the very conduct of Noah. This typological image of the present was familiar to the Church as part of its Jewish and Christian traditional heritage, especially through the gospel tradition: "They ate and drank . . . until the day on which Noah went into the ark, and there came a great flood and they were all destroyed."[69] By means of this image one is able to measure, on the one hand, the breadth of grace of the "just One who died for the unjust" to which vv. 18f. referred. On the other hand, the image provides the foundation for the admonition following in vv. 20b-21 to join the exodus, which baptism introduces into human existence.[70]

V. 21 adds in a relative pronoun with καί, as in v. 19, a further consequence of Christ's suffering unto death: It rescues "also you through baptism." As the key word ἀντίτυπον in v. 21 expressly indi-

---

68. Gen. 6:3 is understood by Targum Onkelos (*Targum Onqelos to Genesis* [The Aramaic Bible VI, tr. B. Grossfeld, Wilmington, DE, 1988], 52) and in *m. Aboth* 5:2 as a period of grace. The early Christian mission understood its own present in the same way (Rom. 2:4f.; II Pet. 3:9).

69. Lk. 17:26f. par. Mt. 24:37-39. As in Jewish apocalyptic literature (*I En.* 10:2; 54:7ff.; 66; 89:5; 106; *II En.* 34:3; cf. *Jub.* 5:11f. [*OT Pseudep.* I, 17, 38, 45f., 64, 86f., 158f.; II, 65]), the great flood is a type of the final judgment in early Christianity as well (II Pet. 3:6). In the same way, Noah is a type of the righteous person living in a decadent society (Heb. 11:7: "He built an ark to save his household; by this faith he condemned the world"; II Pet. 2:5: "herald of righteousness"; *I Clem.* 9:4 [LCL AF I, 23; as in Hebrews 11 Noah is placed after Enoch!]: "Noah was found faithful in his service, in foretelling a new beginning to the world, and through him the Master saved the living creatures which entered in concord into the ark"). These early Christian statements reflect the Jewish legend of Noah; cf. Josephus, *Antiquitates Judaicae* 2.74 (LCL IV, 35):

> For many angels of God now consorted with women and begat sons who were overbearing and disdainful of every virtue, such confidence they had in their strength; in fact the deeds that tradition ascribes to them resemble the audacious exploits told by the Greeks of the giants. But Noah, indignant at their conduct and viewing their counsels with displeasure, urged them to come to a better frame of mind and amend their ways; but seeing that, far from yielding, they were completely enslaved to the pleasure of sin, he feared that they would murder him and, with his wives and sons, quitted the country.

So also Philo, *Legum Allegoriae* 3.77; *De Migratione Abrahami* 125; *Quis Rerum Divinarum Heres Sit* 260; *De Abrahamo* 27, 46 (LCL I, 351-353; IV, 203-205, 417; VI, 147-149, 157-159); cf. *Sib. Or.* 1.125-198 (a Christian interpolation).

70. See the comments on 1:13; 4:3.

cates, this statement is developed in the form of a typology. The image of the generation of the great flood not only interprets what preceded, but also stamps what follows typologically; hence, the further development in v. 20b.

Vv. 20b-21: The Deliverance of Noah as a Type of Baptism[71]

20b The reference to baptism as deliverance is introduced in the relative clause that concludes v. 20: εἰς ἣν ὀλίγοι, τοῦτ' ἔστιν ὀκτὼ ψυχαί. "Only a few,[72] namely eight souls,"[73] went into the ark and thus "were delivered." The phrase δι' ὕδατος, "through the water," i.e., out of the water, is not instrumental but locative. To interpret the water as *means* of deliverance, "because it caused the ark to float, and [by it] those who had entered into the ark were separated out from those who died in the flood,"[74] is artificial and contradicts biblical tradition. In that tradition the water of the great flood was a means of judgment and not of deliverance. One only does justice to the tradition and to διεσώθησαν, "they were delivered out of,"[75] by viewing "through the water" as locative.[76] This understanding is confirmed by Jewish visual represen-

---

71. See Goppelt, *Typos*, 155-157; H. Greeven, "ἐπερώτημα," *TDNT* II, 687f.; Lundberg, *Typologie baptismale*, 98-116; Reicke, *Disobedient Spirits*, 174-187; Daniélou, *Sacramentum Futuri*, 69-94; Beasley-Murray, *Baptism in the NT*, 258-262; G. Kretschmar, "Die Geschichte des Taufgottesdienstes in der alten Kirche," *Leiturgia* V (Kassel, 1966), 1-348, especially 42-45 (bibliography); M.-É. Boismard, "La typologie baptismale dans la première épître de Saint Pierre," *VS* 94 (1956), 339-352; Cook, "I Peter iii.20." For orientation see J. E. Alsup, "Typology," *ABD* VI, 682-685.

72. Cf. Bishop, "Oligoi."

73. Unlike in 1:9, 22; 2:11 ψυχή here is the "living being," the "person," as in Acts 2:41 and classical Greek (BAGD s.v.). The "eight" are, according to Gen. 7:13, Noah, his wife, their three sons, and their sons' wives. There is no play here on the eighth day, the day of resurrection, on which one entered Church membership through baptism, as conjectured by Kelly, 159. This number symbolism is presupposed·by Justin, *Dialogue* 138.1 (*ANF* I, 268), and by the octagonal construction of early Christian baptistries. The same kind of allegorical approach interpreted the ark as representing the cross (*Dialogue* 138.2). But even interpreting the ark as representing the Church (Tertullian, *De Baptismo* 8.4 [*ANF* III, 672f.]; Cyprian, *De Ecclesiae Unitate* 6 [*ANF* V, 423]) goes beyond the typological correspondence.

74. So Schlatter, *Petrus und Paulus*, 141. Kelly, 158f., adds that εἰς ἣν can also mean "in it" and διασώζειν "bring safely through" in Hellenistic Greek.

75. "Deliver all the way through" or "redeem" (cf. BAGD s.v.), here as in v. 21, the former.

76. So also Knopf, 155; the same idea in *Herm. Vis.* 3.3.5 (LCL AF II, 35): ζωὴ ὑμῶν δι' ὕδατος ἐσώθη, καὶ σωθήσεται (through water).

tations of the flood. According to midrashic tradition,[77] Noah and his family went into the ark only after the water had already approached his knees. So, he was delivered "out of the water" in the ark. The baptismal typology in I Cor. 10:1f. develops the same idea, again with help from midrashic tradition: "Our Fathers also went through the sea," which brought ruin on the Egyptians; thus, they were "baptized into Moses."

21   If the OT image is understood in this way, then the ὅ which introduces its application cannot refer to ὕδωρ; it must, rather, refer to the preceding statement as a whole[78] (like the relative pronouns in 1:6 and 3:19): ὅ καὶ ὑμᾶς ἀντίτυπον νῦν σῴζει βάπτισμα, "as an antitype to this, baptism now also delivers you." ἀντίτυπον,[79] with the conjunctional ὅ, is a predicate noun, not an adjective. In v. 21b as well, deliverance is ascribed not to the baptismal water but to the baptismal act (ἀπόθεσις, ἐπερώτημα).

The manner in which baptism is the antitype of the OT event is expressed by ἀντίτυπος. This word is probably being used already as a technical term, since through Paul τύπος became in early Christianity an hermeneutical technical expression for OT pre-representations of the eschatological event beginning with Christ (I Cor. 10:6, 11; Rom. 5:14).[80] The OT event is viewed here, as in I Cor. 10:1f., not as merely an illustration of or analogy for the event of baptism, but as God's pre-representation of it witnessed to by Scripture.

The antitype indicates, therefore, that the God of the OT, the One who delivered Noah, is the One who is now at work in baptism. This is the point of the passive voice in διεσώθησαν. Baptism is finally not a symbol; in baptism, God becomes historically active, i.e., through human activity, just as in the days of Noah. And yet God does not leave people to their own devices through magical means, as I Cor. 10:1-13 makes clear by contrasting the concepts of the Hellenistic Church, drawn from the mystery religions, through typology.

---

77. Genesis Rabbah 32 on Gen. 7:7 (*Midrash Rabba, Genesis I,* tr. H. Freedman and M. Simon [London, 1939], 252f.).

78. So Knopf, 155; Hauck, 67f.; contra Windisch, 71; Kelly, 159. א* removes ὅ, and some minuscules replace it with ᾧ (accepted by Beare, 174), thus reflecting the difficulty of the sentence construction.

79. ἀντίτυπος was in use from Anaximander on as an adjective: "antitypical"; ἀντίτυπον, "antitype," "likeness," Heb. 9:24; *II Clem.* 14:3 (LCL AF I, 151f.).

80. L. Goppelt, "τύπος," *TDNT* VIII, 251-253.

To what extent should the accompanying circumstances of the saving event in the time of Noah also be related to baptism? In both cases God delivers by leading people through and out of water. What results, and this is quite important to I Peter (4:3), is separation from the rest of humanity, which, like the generation of the great flood in the time of God's patience that gave opportunity for repentance, is "disobedient" and, therefore, subject to judgment (4:17f.). To begin with, only "a few" (ὀλίγοι), a small minority,[81] is set apart for a new existence that has a future.

The saving activity of God in the time of Noah took place within the framework of historical time and space. Now God's salvation is eschatological. Here as well the antitype supersedes the OT type:[82] As is stated at the end of v. 21, the deliverance in baptism occurs δι' ἀναστάσεως Ἰησοῦ Χριστοῦ.[83] The deliverance "through the resurrection of Jesus Christ" is, according to 1:3, nothing less than new birth. According to the context here in ch. 3, deliverance occurs through Christ's resurrection because Christ brings us to God as the One who "was made alive" (v. 18), because he has achieved dominion over all powers (v. 22), and most of all because, according to 1:3, through the resurrection the new is made accessible.

Baptism is all this from God's perspective.[84] V. 21b adds in a parenthesis what occurs in baptism from the perspective of the baptized person:[85] "not a putting away of dirt from the flesh, but an appeal to God for a good conscience" (οὐ σαρκὸς ἀπόθεσις ῥύπου ἀλλὰ συνειδήσεως ἀγαθῆς ἐπερώτημα εἰς θεόν). The distinction between "flesh" and "conscience" corresponds, to a degree, to the distinction between the outer person and the "inner person of the heart" in 3:3. It

---

81. This idea that only a "few" are delivered, which was still foreign to Paul, is also found in Mt. 7:14; 22:14. That only few would be delivered out of the "corrupt" world troubled also (during the same period) the author of II Esdras (7:47; 9:14f., 20-22).

82. Goppelt, *TDNT* VIII, 251, 254.

83. δι' ἀναστάσεως is to be connected to σῴζει.

84. On I Peter's understanding of baptism see Reicke, *Disobedient Spirits,* 173-201; Kuss, "Paulinische und nachpaulinische Tauflehre," 144-147; Delling, *Taufe im NT,* 82-89; Nixon, " 'Baptism' in I Peter 3:21"; Dunn, *Baptism in the Holy Spirit,* 215-223; Dinkler, "Taufaussagen," 118-121; Brooks, "I Peter 3:21."

85. To explain that "baptism has its saving power; yet, it is — according to I Peter — only an appeal for God's action; it only has its power out of Christ's work of salvation" (Schelkle, 109; similarly Beasley-Murray, *Baptism in the NT,* 262), would contradict the preceding typological interpretation of baptism as divine intervention.

does not set body and spirit, as in ancient Greek thought, over against one another, but contrasts what is determinative for a person in outward and inward terms, in the same way as Jesus' saying about pure and impure (Mk. 7:15 par. Mt.). In baptism, a person is concerned not with the former but with the latter; he or she does not wash away dirt clinging to the "flesh," to the body.[86] Perhaps the point is that he or she is not striving for the ritual purity that was important to the entire ancient world.[87] But the disclaimer is intended less in an apologetic sense than as a contrast to give emphasis to the subsequent positive statement.

In baptism one seeks a συνείδησις ἀγαθή. One's conscience, one's discerning self-knowledge, is "good" when one's relationship to God, to fellow human beings, and to oneself is covered and shaped by God's gracious turning through Christ.[88] One seeks this peace through baptism: a person's ἐπερώτημα has its sights on peace. συνειδήσεως ἀγαθῆς can only be objective genitive, not subjective genitive,[89] since the "good conscience" that is an expression of being a Christian is mediated not

---

86. σάρξ has here, as in Heb. 10:22, the meaning of σῶμα, "body." ἀπόθεσις, "laying aside," occurs in the NT only here and in II Pet. 1:14. The author uses it instead of "washing away" (cf. Heb. 10:22) surely because ἀποτίθημι is a key word in early Christian parenesis for the "laying aside" of the old person (see the comments above on 2:1). One cannot get rid of the "old person" like dirt on the body by washing: This association stands perhaps alongside in the background. In Jas. 1:21 the image is used differently: ἀποθέμενοι πᾶσαν ῥυπαρίαν καὶ περισσείαν κακίας.

87. Kelly, 161f., appropriating an impulse from Dalton, *Christ's Proclamation,* 215-224, conjectures that the passage was taken from a baptismal catechism and is intended as a polemic against circumcision, which was thought of in the OT and Jewish context as a removal of impurity (Jer. 4:4; 9:25; I Sam. 17:26, 36; Str.-Bill. IV, 31-37; Philo, *De Specialibus Legibus* 1.2-7 [LCL VII, 101-105]). This conjecture is supported in no way by the meaning of the terms or by the intention of I Peter.

88. The first NT documents to speak of "good conscience" are post-Pauline (Acts 23:1; I Tim. 1:5, 19; I Pet. 3:16, 21). Used with συνείδησις are: καθαρά (I Tim. 3:9; II Tim. 1:3), καλή (Heb. 13:18), and ἀπρόσκοπος (Acts 24:16) as opposites of πονηρά (Heb. 10:22). In I Tim. 1:5f., the "good conscience" is explained by a mutually clarifying sequence: "love that issues from a pure heart, a good conscience, and sincere faith." "Conscience" combines, in extension of the Pauline understanding, the Greek concept of human reflective self-knowledge with the OT and early Christian concept of human determination by the "heart," the reflective desire either directed toward God or diverted from God (cf. C. Maurer, "σύνοιδα, συνείδησις," *TDNT* VII, 917-919). The "good conscience" expresses, therefore, the new being of the justified person. With the retreat of the theme of justification the formulas take on a moralistic sense among the Apostolic Fathers (*TDNT* VII, 919). See above, p. 196, nn. 23f.

89. Contra Selwyn, 205, and Beasley-Murray, *Baptism in the NT,* 261 (cf. n.3), who translate in agreement with G. C. Richards, "the pledge to God proceeding from a good conscience" ("1 Pet iii.21," *JThSt* 32 [1931], 77). Cf. Kelly, 162f.

through conversion, but through baptism; on this all NT documents are agreed.[90] The ἐπερώτημα does not, therefore, proceed from a good conscience, but seeks it.

ἐπερώτημα is much debated and difficult to explain in philological terms. In traditional usage it usually refers to an "inquiry" that takes place under the assumption that an answer will be given and that this answer will be binding for the questioner. In relation to the God of the Bible this inquiry becomes "entreaty," but it becomes entreaty that obligates those making entreaty; it still does not become an agreement or vow. If we understand the word here as an entreaty by which the one making it binds himself or herself to the answer on the grounds of the preceding offer, then we come closest to doing justice to the context of the passage and to the baptismal tradition behind it.

Ἐπερώτημα appears only here in the NT. It is derived from the verb ἐρωτάω, "ask, entreat." The following meanings offer themselves:

1. "Inquiry," "question" (e.g., Thucydides 3.53 [LCL II, 93-95]; *Herm. Mand.* 11.2 [LCL AF II, 118f.]). The verb ἐπερωτάω is often used of inquiry made of the gods through an oracle (Herodotus 1.53.1 [LCL I, 59-61] and passim); in the LXX it is used of asking about God's will. But ἐπερώτημα refers not to the inquiry itself (this is documented only for the synonym ἐπερώτησις in Herodotus 6.67; 9.44 [LCL III, 215-217; IV, 213]: μετὰ τὴν ἐπερώτησιν τῶν χρησμῶν), but to its result, the divine decision, as in both LXX occurrences (Sir. 33:3: "the law is as faithful as an ἐρώτημα [the result of an inquiry, the decision] of the Urim"; Dan. 4:17 [Theodotion]). This is the case also for W. Dittenberger, ed., *Sylloge Inscriptionum Graecarum* (third ed., Leipzig, 1915-24), no. 856 (second century): κατὰ τὸ ἐπερώτημα τῶν . . . Ἀρεοπαγείτων.[91]

2. The meaning "entreat" was established for ἐπερωτάω just as for ἐρωτάω. Only two biblical passages, however, come close to this meaning, Ps. 136:3 LXX v.l. and Mt. 16:1. On this philologically narrow basis numerous exegetes also see in I Pet. 3:21 the meaning "entreaty" for the noun.[92]

3. Other exegetes prefer a specialized juridical meaning, though this can only be documented from the second century A.D. on. ἐπερώτημα stands in this

---

90. Quite close tradition-historically is Heb. 10:22, according to which cleansing from an "evil conscience" takes place precisely through baptism. But even in Acts 2:38 repentance is realized in baptism, not prior to it, since repentance is always possible only to the extent that the one returning home is received, that he or she is forgiven; baptism, however, takes place "for forgiveness." See below, n.94.

91. Additional supporting material in Reicke, *Disobedient Spirits*, 183.

92. So BAGD s.v.; Knopf, 158; Windisch, 73; Schelkle, 109.

case for Latin *stipulatio,* "contractual agreement," specifically the binding question addressed to another, whose affirmative response completes the contract, e.g., ἐπερωτηθεὶς ὡμολόγησα, Oxyrhynchus papyrus 905 (*The Oxyrhynchus Papyri,* ed. B. P. Grenfell and A. S. Hunt), and passim; cf. a papyrus from Cairo: ἐὰν γὰρ μηδὲν ἐπερώτημα ἢ ἐγγεγρα[μμέ]νον] (F. Preisigke, *Griechische Urkunden des Ägyptischen Museums zu Kairo* [Schriften der Wissenschaftlichen Gesellschaft zu Strassburg 1911/18; Strassburg, 1911], 1).[93]

The designation of baptism as an obligating entreaty has no counterpart in the rest of the NT.[94] Such a designation refers to something other than the baptismal confession, which presupposes quite ancient NT formulas (Rom. 10:9; I Tim. 6:12; Heb. 4:14; cf. Acts 8:37). It calls to mind the *abrenuntiatio,* the renunciation of the devil, i.e., of the gods and the life that goes along with them, which, according to witnesses from the end of the second century, preceded the threefold immersion linked to the confession in the baptismal service of the catholic Church.[95] Earlier traces of the renunciation point to a tradition that comes out of Palestinian Jewish Christianity, traces of which are found in the baptismal practices of the Elkesaites and in the traditional matrix of the pseudo-Clementine letters;[96] they recall, moreover, the oath-like vow in the rite of admission among

---

93. From this the translation "pledge to God" is derived by LSJ, 618 (s.v. ἐπερωτάω); Selwyn, 205; Beare, 175; Kelly, 162. Beasley-Murray, *Baptism in the NT,* 261, translates: "the pledge to God . . ."; Reicke, *Disobedient Spirits,* 185: "an undertaking to a loyal attitude of mind" or "a good will" (183ff. has further Hellenistic supportive references). Schlatter, *Petrus und Paulus,* 147, in contrast, "the request of a good conscience toward God." See also Arvedson, "Syneideseos"; Aalen, "Oversettelsen"; Tripp, "Eperōtēma."

94. In both concept and terminology the closest NT parallel is Heb. 10:22f., where, as here (v. 18), the image of the open path is also used: "Let us draw near [to God] with a true heart in full assurance of faith, with our hearts sprinkled clean from an evil conscience [cf. 9:14] and our bodies washed with pure water. Let us hold fast the confession of our hope." Missing, however, is precisely the element that characterizes the passage in I Peter: In Hebrews baptism is interpreted as a cleansing that happens to the baptized one, while in I Peter 3 it is an ἐπερώτημα εἰς θεόν issuing forth from the baptized one.

95. It is referred to for the first time by Tertullian (*De Corona* 3; *De Pudicitia* 9 [*ANF* III, 94, 82-84]) and in the church order of Hippolytus (B. S. Easton, *The Apostolic Tradition of Hippolytus* [Cambridge, 1934], 45f.; texts also in Kretschmar, *Geschichte des Taufgottesdienst,* 89-91). Besides this interpretation through the two theologians (Kretschmar, 96-101) the remark of Tertullian, *De Resurrectione Carnis* 48.11 (*ANF* III, 582), reminds one of I Pet. 3:21: "Anima enim non lavatione, sed responsione sancitur."

96. Hippolytus, *Refutatio* 9.15.6; *Pseudo-Clementine Recognitions* 1.2 (*ANF* V, 134; VIII, 77). Whether or not Pliny's report of a morning worship service of the Christians (*Epistulae* 96.7 [LCL II, 401-405]) presupposes a baptismal celebration with a renunciation vow is uncertain (see Kretschmar, *Geschichte des Taufgottesdienst,* 42-45).

the Essenes.[97] In the realm of the catholic Church the key word characteristic for this understanding appears in the *Shepherd of Hermas*, i.e., in Roman tradition, reminiscent in many ways of the Essenes: "you see . . . that it is good to follow (ἀκολουθεῖν) the angel of righteousness, but to keep away from (ἀποτάξασθαι) the angel of unrighteousness" (*Mand.* 6.2.9 [LCL AF II, 99]).

What I Pet. 3:21 emphasizes about baptism belongs within this baptismal tradition. Yet, the ἐπερώτημα is not a vow, as it was in Qumran or in the early catholic Church, but an obligating entreaty by means of which the baptized person engages in the baptismal promise, i.e., in the pledge of God "to save" (σῴζειν; v. 21a), which for I Peter always means not only a new relationship to God, but also a new way of conducting oneself (2:24f.); the *signum* of this salvation is the "good conscience."[98] In baptism the one baptized thus turns to God, and the act of baptism "delivers," transports such a person into the existence for which he or she has made entreaty, "through the resurrection of Jesus Christ" — because through baptism Jesus' exaltation to become eschatological Lord of the universe is introduced.

V. 22: The Exaltation of Christ and the Dethroning of the Powers

The author focuses attention here on the goal of Christ's life. Without developing further soteriological aspects, he writes here in traditional formulas, which in terms of articulated content were familiar to the Church from their worship. These formulas reproduce in three lines[99] the confession of Christ's exaltation.

22a ὅς ἐστιν ἐν δεξιᾷ θεοῦ is found verbatim in Rom. 8:34 as well. It was a fixed formula[100] of considerable antiquity, developed at

---

97. They swear "to return with all [their] heart and soul to every commandment of the Law of Moses" (1QS 5:8-10; cf. CD 15:8; 16:7; 1QH 14:17).

98. The explanations of ἐπερώτημα in the ancient Church contribute nothing essential to that which has been ascertained here: Cyril of Alexandria, *Homiliae Paschales* 30.3; pseudo-Oecumenius (*MPG* 119, 514), who in the tenth century adhered to ancient traditions, spoke of ἐπερώτημα as οἷα ἀρραβῶν καὶ ἐνέχυρον [security] τῆς πρὸς θεὸν ἀγαθῆς συνειδήσεως.

99. After ἐν δεξιᾷ θεοῦ the Vulgate inserts: "deglutiens mortem ut vitae aeternae heredes efficeremur," "by swallowing up death [I Cor. 15:54] so that we might become heirs of eternal life" (Tit. 3:7). Harnack, *Beiträge zur Einleitung* VII, 83-86, reconstructs the Greek text behind this addition and regards it as original. But this is, on the basis of both textual tradition and stylistic form, out of the question.

100. (Acts 2:34; 5:31) Eph. 1:20 (Col. 3:1); Heb. 1:3; 8:1; 10:11; 12:2.

an early date in connection with Ps. 110:1a.[101] The image of "sitting at God's right hand"[102] brings to expression the functions of the exalted One in relation to God (cf., e.g., Rom. 8:34ff.), above all, that God's eschatological dominion in relation to the cosmos has now been given over to Christ (cf. Isa. 45:21-24 and Phil. 2:9-11).

22c Corresponding to the eschatological dominion of the exalted One is the subjection of "the angels, authorities, and powers" to him: ὑποταγέντων αὐτῷ ἀγγέλων καὶ ἐξουσιῶν καὶ δυνάμεων. This statement is prefigured in Ps. 110:1b: ἕως ἂν θῶ τοὺς ἐχθρούς σου ὑποπόδιον τῶν ποδῶν σου. It was then often formulated together with the words of Ps. 8:7, which are even more suitable: πάντα ὑπέταξας ὑποκάτω τῶν ποδῶν αὐτοῦ. In I Cor. 15:25, 27 the two Psalm passages are quoted together, as in Eph. 1:20, 22; in Heb. 2:8 only Psalm 8 appears. As in I Pet. 3:22a, here in v. 22c only the Christian formula has been appropriated.

The subjugation of the powers is announced as the yet-to-be-accomplished goal of Christ's dominion in I Cor. 15:25-27 and Heb. 2:5-9; but here in I Peter, as in Col. 2:10-15 and Eph. 1:20-22, the subjugation is confessed as having already taken place with the exaltation of Christ. This "already" is not an expression of a fanatical perfectionism like that countered by Paul in I Cor. 4:8. It is, rather, an expression of the kerygmatic indicative: What is confessed is what God has established in hiddenness through the exaltation of Jesus to his own right hand. This confession is particularly important for the churches addressed by I Peter, since the struggle with the effects of the "powers" in history was still underway (4:3f.; 5:8f.).[103]

---

101. The fact of the exaltation is presupposed by the address μαραναθά (I Cor. 16:22) and the confession in Rom. 1:3f., which also comes from the primitive Palestinian Church. Here, too, Ps. 110:1 was probably used of Jesus' new position of honor, which was accomplished through the exaltation (cf. Acts 7:55; Mk. 14:61f.). See Hahn, *Titles*, 100-103; L. Goppelt, "The Lordship of Christ and the World according to the NT," *Lutheran World* 14/1 (1967), 20-22.

102. The image is derived from ancient oriental coronation ceremonies; see H. J. Kraus, *Psalms 60-150: A Commentary* (tr. H. C. Oswald; Minneapolis, 1989), 90f.; for the Church it became a symbol, without detriment to its function as a means of representing supernatural visions (cf. Acts 7:56). In Hellenistic Judaism, according to Aristobulus, it was interpreted: "with a mighty hand . . . it is necessary that the hands be explained as the power of God" (fragment 2 [Eusebius, *Praeparatio Evangelica* 8.10.7f.]); "He is entirely Heavenly, and he brings everything to completion on earth" (fragment 4 [13.3.5]); "we have familiar intercourse with God everywhere" (fragment 4 [13.3.6]; *OT Pseudep.* II, 838, 841 [n.f]).

103. On the question of the "already" and "not-yet," see O. Cullmann, *The Christology of the NT* (tr. S. C. Guthrie and C. A. M. Hall; revised ed., Philadelphia, 1963), 223-226;

I Peter is the only non-Pauline NT document to use a specifically Pauline form of expression in "angels, authorities, and powers." While the rest of the NT sees only good or evil angels at work behind what happens in nature and history, Paul refers to powers, which he designates with terms like "authority," "power," and "dominion." ἐξουσία and δυνάμεις are used side by side here, as in I Cor. 15:24,[104] and only here and in Rom. 8:38 are ἄγγελοι mentioned prior to the "authorities" (ἐξουσία).

Already on occasion in Jewish apocalyptic writings angels have the character of cosmic powers, under the influence of astrological religion.[105] Paul developed these ideas conceptually as he preached the lordship of Christ to Hellenistic hearers who saw themselves in relation to a cosmos of powers (I Cor. 8:5f.). For Paul the powers were not merely the fantasy-borne constructions of unbelief, but realities; they were something like what we think of in terms of regulatory legal standards and powers beyond the individual in nature and history, as soon as we see them in terms of God's relationship to the world.[106]

Unlike Paul, I Peter does not draw a line from these powers, which it mentions only here, to the Church's situation. In contrast to Col. 2:20, it sees only "the will of the Gentiles" (4:3) behind the pressure to conform. And behind the "persecutions," in contrast to Rom. 8:38, it sees the devil as the only superhuman authority (5:8). Therefore the reference to the powers in v. 22c, which is a formula adopted from a liturgical context, has only an indirect role in the parenesis.

22b Between Christ's resurrection and his sitting at God's right hand, the latter of which signifies the subjugation of the powers, this verse inserts: πορευθεὶς εἰς οὐρανόν, "after he entered heaven." It

---

E. Käsemann, "A Critical Analysis of Philippians 2:5-11," *JThC* 5 (1968), 78-82 (45-88); *idem*, "The Problem of the Historical Jesus," *Essays on NT Themes* (SBT 41; London, 1964), 45ff.; Goppelt, "Lordship," 21-22, 25-31; H. J. Gabathuler, *Jesus Christus, Haupt der Kirche —Haupt der Welt. Der Christushymnus Col 1,15-20 in der theologischen Forschung der letzten 130 Jahre* (AThANT 45; Zurich, 1965).

104. Otherwise in Col. 1:16; 2:10, 15; Eph. 1:21; 3:10; 6:12.

105. The formulation in I Pet. 3:22c is found verbatim only in *Ascension of Isaiah* 1:3 (*OT Pseudep.* II, 156), where it is, however, probably interpolated. Cf. *I En.* 61:10; *II En.* 20:1; *Test. Lev.* 3:8 (*OT Pseudep.* I, 42, 134f., 789); further, Str.-Bill. III, 583.

106. H. Schlier, *Der Brief an die Epheser. Ein Kommentar* (Düsseldorf, 1957), 87; G. H. C. MacGregor, "Principalities and Powers: The Cosmic Background of Paul's Thought," *NTS* 1 (1954/55), 17-28; H. Berkhof, *Christ and the Powers* (tr. J. H. Yoder; second ed., Scottdale, PA, 1977), 18-26.

thereby prefigures the corresponding statement of the Apostles' Creed. What was intended by this "entry"? Similar early Christian statements provide three possibilities:

1. Hebrews maintains that Christ as High Priest with his self-offering "passed through the heavens" (4:14) or "entered" "heaven itself" (εἰσῆλθεν, 9:24). This high-priestly ascension is intended to clarify in a typological image the soteriological meaning of Christ's exaltation to God's right hand (8:1; 10:12).[107] For Hebrews, the exaltation belongs together with the resurrection, which it does not mention except in 13:20.[108] From this perspective, the "entry" in I Pet. 3:22b is clearly an act subsequent to the resurrection (v. 21) and prior to Christ's sitting at God's right hand (v. 22a).

2. This recalls the account of the ascension in Acts 1:9-11, which is the only other passage in the NT or the Apostolic Fathers in which πορεύεσθαι εἰς (τὸν) οὐρανόν is found.[109] The clause is parallel in Acts 1:10f. with ἀνελήμφθη, "he was taken up" (vv. 2, 11, 22).[110] But in the Acts account the "ascension" is the end of an Easter appearance and marks for the disciples the conclusion to such appearances: They will not see Christ again until his coming "on the clouds of heaven" (1:11). With respect to the exaltation, the author of Acts never again refers to the disciples' having seen the "ascension" (not in 2:33-36 or anywhere else). But the exaltation (τῇ δεξιᾷ τοῦ θεοῦ ὑψωθείς, Acts 2:33) is spoken of in Acts 2:34 in the phrase ἀνέβη εἰς τοὺς οὐρανούς, "he ascended into heaven." In this way an OT technical term[111] has been appropriated and the ascension has been represented pictorially in accord with the ancient conception of the universe.

3. The identification of the exaltation and the "ascension," suggested in Acts, is seen for the first time in the Easter report of the inauthentic ending of Mark, Mk. 16:19 (ἀνελήμφθη) and then in *Barn.* 15:9 (ἀνέβη [LCL AF I, 396]), *Gospel of Peter* 56 (= 13; *NT Apoc.* I, 225f.), the *Epistula Apostolorum* 51 (= 62; *NT Apoc.* I, 278), and in a christological formula that became established during the second century and is seen in the original form of the Apostles' Creed.[112] This formula was a statement

---

107. On this use of πορεύομαι see F. Hauck and S. Schulz, *TDNT* VI, 576.
108. Cf. Phil. 2:9-11, but also Rom. 1:3f.; 10:9.
109. Cf. also *I Clem.* 5:4, 7 (LCL AF I, 17).
110. Lk. 24:51 v.l.: καὶ ἀνεφέρετο εἰς τοὺς οὐρανούς.
111. עָלָה הַשָּׁמַיִם, Dt. 30:12; Am. 9:2; II Ki. 2:11, and passim; Jn. 20:12; cf. Jn. 3:12f.; J. Schneider, "ἀναβαίνω," *TDNT* I, 520f.
112. According to H. Lietzmann, "Symbolstudien," *ZNW* 21 (1922), 23 (= *idem,*

of matters surrounding the Easter celebration and is not preformed anywhere in the NT more extensively than in I Pet. 3:22. But, like Acts 2:34f., I Peter 3 does not refer to a visible event of Christ going into heaven any more than it does in regard to the descent into the world of the dead in v. 19. It does not ascribe any saving effect to either event as such; nor does it consider either event what the ascension became in the Gnostic redeemer myth, i.e., a triumphant breaking through the cosmos.[113] The "entry" is in I Peter a time-bound expression for the exaltation, which is the inception of Christ's sitting at God's right hand.

When one looks back over this section, which is so packed in terms of content, it becomes clear that the path of suffering for righteousness has become through Christ a path of blessing and triumph. In this path those who believe are to have a share as those who follow in discipleship, even for their own sakes. This last aspect is developed in the next section, which adds to the christological foundation of the parenesis an anthropological foundation.

4:1-6: The Fruit of Discipleship: The Suffering of Believers

1 *Since, therefore, Christ has suffered in the flesh,*
   so arm yourselves also with the same understanding
   —for whoever has suffered according to the flesh has ceased
   from sin —
2 *so that you live no longer for human lusts,*
   but for God's will during the remaining time in the flesh.

3 *For it is sufficient that in former times you carried out the will*
   of the Gentiles,
   by living in indecency, lusts, drinking parties, feasts,
   drunkenness, and wanton idolatry.

Kleine Schriften III [Berlin, 1962], 211f.), the original form of the Apostles' Creed in the Western Church had at this point: ἀναβάντα εἰς τοὺς οὐρανούς, καθήμενον ἐν δεξιᾷ τοῦ πατρός; in the Eastern Church: ἀνελθόντα εἰς τὸν οὐρανὸν καὶ πάλιν ἐρχόμενον. See Goppelt, *Apostolic,* 18; P. Benoit, "The Ascension," *idem, Jesus and the Gospel* I (tr. B. Weatherhead; London, 1973), 209-253; B. M. Metzger, "The Ascension of Jesus Christ," *idem, Historical and Literary Studies, Pagan, Jewish and Christian* (NT Tools and Studies 8; Leiden, 1968), 77-87; G. Kretschmar, "Himmelfahrt und Pfingsten," *ZKG* 66 (1954/55), 209-253.

    113. Nothing suggests that the subjection of the angelic powers took place during this passing through the world spheres (contra Kelly, 164).

4 *They are estranged*
   because you no longer join in this flood of godlessness, and
   they blaspheme.

5 *They will have to give account to the One*
   who is ready to judge the living and the dead.
6 *For it was for this reason that the gospel was preached even to*
   the dead,
   that they might be judged humanly according to the flesh,
   but with regard to God might live according to the Spirit.

Structure and Tradition

1. This section is constructed transparently: In 4:1 the anthropological basis of the parenesis to follow is derived from the christological guiding principle of the preceding kerygmatic section (3:18), and at the end of 4:6b the anthropological basis is repeated: "Since Christ has suffered in the flesh, so arm yourselves also with the same understanding." From this foundation the consequences are drawn in 4:(2)3-5 for the conduct of Christians in society: They are to distance themselves from society's way of life even if society responds with discrimination and the result is "suffering for the sake of righteousness" (3:13, 17). Preparedness for such suffering is the thematic heading over the section, from which it begins and toward which it leads. As this theme was developed christologically in the previous section, so it is developed here anthropologically.

2. 3:18-22 and 4:1-6 are distinguished from the rest of I Peter in that only in these two sections does the letter speak anthropologically (except for a quite different sort of word usage in 1:24, conditioned by an OT quotation) of σάρξ (3:18, 21; 4:1a, b, 6) and, with the addition of 3:4, πνεῦμα (3:18, 19; 4:6). The thought developments begin and end with antithetical statements about σάρξ and πνεῦμα (3:18b; 4:6b). Furthermore, only in these two sections does the author refer to the proclamation in Hades (3:19f.; 4:6). Finally, these two sections emphasize the same side of the relationship to society: In the first, baptism separates a person from society and obligates one to behave in accord with a "good conscience" (3:16); in the second, the readers are admonished to separate themselves from the way of life of those around them, even if the response is discrimination. Separation, like suffering (hereby the first group of ideas is utilized), should be understood as the sacrifice of one's own fleshly existence. Christians should see the "situation of persecution," moreover, as a necessary purification for the sake of one's personal situation. This anthropological aspect is peculiar to this section, even though certain matters are also repeated in 4:12-19.

3. What traditions stand behind these thought developments?

a. The christological guiding principle in 3:18d, "put to death in the flesh but made alive in the Spirit," which is appropriated anthropologically in 4:1, 6, takes the christological formula of the Palestinian Church as its point of departure, which is known to us from Rom. 1:3f. and which was in general circulation in the Church of the second generation (see the comments above on 3:18). Already in the tradition this principle was more or less firmly connected to the rest of the christological formulaic material concerning the course of Jesus' life. In 3:18f., 22 it constitutes the soteriological center of that life.

b. Was the anthropological application of this christological formula in 4:1, 6b and its parenetic utilization also traced out in tradition? Behind these thought developments appears to stand a terminology of "repentance" that makes use of expressions of the Essenes and of the mystery religions: Quite possibly the designation of baptism as ἐπερώτημα (3:21), which is unique in the NT, belongs to this terminology; there are parallels to it not only among the Essenes, but also among the mystery religions.[1] The thesis that a person becomes free from sin only through suffering or through the death of the flesh (4:1) presupposes both the Jewish idea that death is judgment and that it separates from sin and the initiations into the mystery religions, which led the initiate through darkness and death in order to bring him or her to light and life.[2] As in 4:2, so the life of misdeed before repentance and the "rest of one's life" thereafter are also confronted in the mystery religions[3] and in another form among the Essenes.[4] That the flesh must be fought after this repentance (4:1) was familiar to the Essenes,[5] as well as to the piety of the mystery religions; the latter also used in this context the imagery of use of arms.[6] Release from the world of the dead, which is mentioned in 4:6 (cf. 3:19) in the context of this repentance terminology, belongs to the conceptual realm of the mystery religions, though there, of course, it does not occur for the physically dead by a journey into Hades,[7] but is anticipated for the living through symbolic imitation.[8] To conceive of this "act of repentance" as corresponding to the redeemer's

---

1. Apuleius, *Metamorphoses* 11.2, 6, 15 (LCL II, 541f., 549f., 563f.); see G. Wagner, *Pauline Baptism and the Pagan Mysteries: the Problem of the Pauline Doctrine of Baptism in Romans vi.1-11* (tr. J. Smith; London, 1967), 104-114. See also the comments on 3:21.

2. So, referring to the Dionysiac mysteries, Johannes Stobaeus, *Florilegium* 4.107M (cf. *Eine Mithrasliturgie*, tr. and ed. A. Dieterich [third ed. by O. Weinreich; Darmstadt, 1923], 163f.): διὰ σκότους τινὲς ὕποπτοι πορεῖαι καὶ ἀτέλεστοι . . . ἐκ δὲ τούτου φῶς τι θαυμάσιον ἀπήντησε . . . (cf. I Pet. 2:9); see below, n.8; Perdelwitz, *Mysterienreligion*, 83-85.

3. Apuleius, *Metamorphoses* 11.5, 15 (LCL II, 547, 563f.).

4. But only of the brief remaining period until the end (1QpHab 6:7f.).

5. 1QS 11:9-12b; 1QpHab 7:6-15.

6. Apuleius, *Metamorphoses* 11.15.5 (LCL II, 565): "quo tamen tutior sis atque munitior, da nomen sanctae huic militiae, cuius non olim sacramento etiam rogabaris . . ." (". . . and to the end that thou mayest live more safe and sure, make thyself one of this holy order, to which thou wast but a short time since pledged by oath").

7. There was in the Orphic mysteries a poem with the title Ὀρφέως εἰς Ἅιδου κατάβασις (Dieterich, *Nekyia*, 128ff.), but there is no further knowledge of it. See also Perdelwitz, *Mysterienreligion*, 90.

8. Apuleius, *Metamorphoses* 11.23.8 (LCL II, 581): "Accessi confinium mortis et calcato Proserpinae limine . . . remeavi, . . . nocte media vidi solem candido coruscantem lumine . . . ("Thou shalt understand that I approached near unto hell, even to the gates of

experience, as is the main idea of 4:1, was a fundamental notion of the mystery religions. But the focus on the redeemer's experience came to I Peter and its tradition by way of the concept of discipleship (2:21). I Peter does not draw its repentance parenesis, in any case, directly from the mystery religions[9] or from Qumran, but from Christian baptismal parenesis. The parenesis appears in that setting — in altered forms, to be sure — in Rom. 6:1-13; Gal. 5:24; 6:14 (cf. I Pet. 4:1).

c. The parenesis in 4:1-6 is related in content in several ways to the parenesis in 3:20f. Behind 3:20f. stands, to be sure, a catechetical utilization of the typology of the flood and Noah, the beginnings of which go back to Jesus and beyond him to Judaism. This catechetical tradition is connected to repentance parenesis not only by the link to baptism, but also through the ideas of separation and of ultimate deliverance. This catechesis included, because of the influence of Jewish tradition, the idea of the proclamation to the spirits in prison (3:19),[10] which was the starting point for the statement about the Hades proclamation in 4:6. It is possible that this catechetical tradition in 3:20f., therefore, was already connected with the repentance parenesis that emerges alongside it before they were incorporated into I Peter.

d. But peculiar to the author of I Peter, in addition to the shaping of these traditions, is their application to the social situation of the Christians in 4:3-5. Into this is woven a transmitted catalogue of vices (4:3) and a traditional phrase about the judgment (4:5b).

Vv. 1f.: Overcoming the Old Person

The watchword handed on in these verses reverses, as it were, one given before (most recently in 3:13f.). Doing right does on occasion lead to suffering, it was said. Now it is said that suffering leads to doing right. It does so because it destroys and judges the flesh. Suffering is, therefore, not only an attack by evil from the surrounding world, but also a battle with the wickedness in one's own flesh, just as the struggle with the world, according to 2:11, is always a struggle with one's own craving. This dialectical correspondence to the previous watchword is developed in vv. 1f. and is brought back in circular fashion to it in v. 4.

1 In the midst of the difficult sentence in vv. 1f. is in v. 1b the imperative τὴν αὐτὴν ἔννοιαν ὁπλίσασθε, "arm yourselves with the same understanding." ἔννοια does not mean here "disposition," but, as in the

Proserpine [and after that I was ravished throughout all the elements, I returned to my proper place]: about midnight I saw the sun brightly shine . . .").

9. Perdelwitz assumes incorrectly here as well as with respect to similar "statements of repentance" (especially at 1:3; 2:2, 3:3) a direct influence of the mystery cults.

10. Supporting texts in Str.-Bill. I, 961-966; III, 766.

wisdom speeches in Proverbs, "understanding" that produces conduct in accord with that understanding (here the conduct is described in v. 2).[11] The baptized are to "arm" themselves with this understanding, as if for battle.[12] According to v. 2, such understanding is necessary for the addressees as armament in the battle against "lusts" in their own human existence, not only in the struggle against the pressure from those around them to conform (vv. 3f.). Already the Pauline corpus appropriated for baptismal parenesis the well-known image of moral armament from OT and Jewish tradition and used it as a variation on the image of taking off the old garment and putting on the new.[13]

What is the content of the understanding that serves as armor against craving? That it is "the same"[14] points to what precedes in v. 1a: Χριστοῦ οὖν παθόντος σαρκί, "Since Christ, therefore, has suffered in the flesh."[15] This statement appropriates the decisive catch-phrase from 3:18: "Christ has suffered, . . . put to death in the flesh." The significance of this pointer to the earlier reference is that it includes with it what is said about the meaning and effect of Christ's suffering unto death in 3:19-22.[16] What comes from Christ's whole path of blessing is the understanding that the flesh must be handed over to suffering unto death so that it may come to a life "according to the Spirit" (3:18; 4:6).

V. 1c explains why this handing over of the flesh is necessary from the human perspective in order for, according to v. 2, lusts to be overcome

---

11. So Windisch, 73; contra Schelkle, 114. ἔννοια, "reflection," "thought," "knowledge," "disposition"; in Greek philosophy "concept," "term"; in the LXX almost exclusively in Proverbs for "knowledge" that obligates morally (1:4; 3:21; 23:4, and passim); in the NT only here and (used differently) in Heb. 4:12; cf. J. Behm, "νοέω, ἔννοια," *TDNT* IV, 968ff. Phil. 3:10 is parallel in content to I Pet. 4:1f.: "that I may know him and the power of his resurrection and may share his sufferings, becoming like him in his death," less so Phil. 2:5: τοῦτο φρονεῖτε ἐν ὑμῖν, ὃ καὶ ἐν Χριστῷ Ἰησοῦ, "reflect among yourselves about that which also in Christ Jesus (is suitable for reflection)." So J. Gnilka, *Der Philipperbrief* (HThK; Freiburg, 1968), 108; but the meaning of ἐν Χριστῷ Ἰησοῦ is uncertain.

12. ὁπλίζεσθαι, in the NT only here, "arm yourselves," also figurative with accusative of relationship in Sophocles, *Electra* 995f. (LCL II, 203): ὁπλίζεσθαι θράσος ("boldly").

13. I Thess. 5:8; Rom. 6:13; 13:12-14; II Cor. 6:7; 10:4; Eph. 6:11-17; cf. Isa. 59:17; Wis. 5:17ff.; cf. Selwyn, 396-400, 456-458; K. G. Kuhn and A. Oepke, "ὅπλον, πανοπλία," *TDNT* V, 298-302.

14. Cf. next to τὴν αὐτήν (ἔννοιαν) also the emphasized καὶ ὑμεῖς.

15. After παθόντος important manuscripts insert ὑπὲρ ἡμῶν (ℵ[1], A, P, Koine, many others, syr[h]) or ὑπὲρ ὑμῶν (ℵ*, 69, others, Peshitta). But neither addition is (with Kelly, 165; contra Selwyn, 208) to be taken as original, since Christ's suffering "for" cannot be imitated by Christians. The readings arose through accommodation to the familiar formula.

16. That is, it does not "skip over it."

and life to be lived in keeping with the Creator's will: ὅτι ὁ παθὼν σαρκὶ πέπαυται ἁμαρτίας, "for whoever has suffered in the flesh has ceased from sin." ὅτι cannot be translated with "that," as would otherwise be suggested philologically,[17] and the sentence cannot thus be understood as parallel to the previous statement as a paraphrase of the content of ἔννοια.[18] This is so because those who have "ceased from sin" cannot include Christ. In contrast, the statement fits meaningfully in the context if it is understood as giving parenthetically a general basis.

But how is this statement to be understood under such a view? In what sense does middle perfect "has ceased from sin" apply with respect to aorist "whoever has suffered in the flesh"?[19] What does it mean for a person to "cease from . . . ?" This expression has been paraphrased as "renounce," "desist from," and "be separated from."

The sentence as a whole has been interpreted in these ways:

1. Understood cognitively-psychologically it means that innocent suffering documents the break with sin.[20] Alternatively, with the decision to suffer a person has renounced fundamentally the path of sin.[21] But παθών does not mean "submitting to suffering":[22] It refers to what happens to a person, not to what a person does.

2. If the perfect tense of πέπαυται is taken gnomically, the statement could express a general truth: Through suffering, the flesh — the autocratic mortal — is brought into subjection and thereby sin is eliminated.[23] But experience alone shows that suffering can also, to the contrary, provoke sin. Most importantly, however, all Christian tradition agrees[24] that a person does not become free from sin through "one's own agony," but through Christ.[25]

---

17. So also Philo in *De Praemiis et Poenis* 42 (LCL VIII, 337): . . . εἰς ἔννοιαν ἦλθον . . . , ὅτι ἄρα τοσαῦτα κάλλη καὶ οὕτως ὑπερβάλλουσα τάξις οὐκ ἀπαυτοματισθέντα γέγονεν, ἀλλ᾽ . . . καὶ ὅτι πρόνοιαν ἀναγκαῖον εἶναι.

18. Contra Windisch, 72; Kelly, 166, and others.

19. It should be translated thus in agreement with BAGD; πέπαυται is surely not, as Kelly, 168, thinks, passive: "this one has been liberated" from sin.

20. Windisch, 73; so also W. Grundmann, "ἁμαρτάνω," *TDNT* I, 315.

21. E. Schweizer, "σάρξ," *TDNT* VII, 143, n.339.

22. So Windisch, 73.

23. Schelkle, 114, as one possibility.

24. See the comments on 1:18f.

25. Therefore, what Schelkle, 114, proposes as a second possibility also cannot be upheld: By means of innocent suffering a person makes atonement, thus becoming free from sin. Even in I Cor. 5:5 dying is not thought of as atonement, but, as in I Pet. 4:6, as judgment.

3. Therefore, others find here once again the Pauline statement: We "have died to sin" through baptism with Christ (Rom. 6:2; cf. Col. 2:11: "laying aside the body of flesh").[26] I Pet. 4:1c stands, to be sure, in the context of baptismal parenesis, and παθών does refer to suffering unto death, as it does in v. 1a. But in I Peter suffering unto death is never purely spiritual, but is always also bodily suffering.[27] And ceasing from sin[28] is never simply freedom from sin but always also desisting from offenses, as in v. 2a, according to which one should live no longer "for human lusts." Also in 2:24f. dying "to sin" is applied to offenses. "Sin," which except in 2:22 (tradition) is plural in I Peter (2:24; 3:18; 4:8), is singular here,[29] but it does not refer, as in Paul, to an authority that rules humanity, but as elsewhere to offense, though typically, generally.

4. The sentence does not correspond as a whole to the baptismal kerygma in Rom. 6:3f., but more closely to the general anthropological statement in Rom. 6:7: "For whoever has died has been justified from sin," which does not proclaim what happened in baptism from the standpoint of Christ, but gives the reason for what has happened. I Pet. 4:1c also names the reason, i.e., why one is called by Christ (v. 1a-b): The flesh must be handed over to suffering unto death in discipleship to Christ because only one who has suffered death has ceased from sin. The flesh and committing sin belong together and therefore only come to an end together (cf. Rom. 7:18, 24). This thesis, like the one in Rom. 6:7, is indebted to OT and Jewish concepts,[30] but Christian anthropology

---

26. Wohlenberg, 121-124; W. Michaelis, "πάσχω," *TDNT* V, 922f.

27. See below, nn. 30f.

28. The linking of παύομαι with the genitive is not found otherwise (Selwyn, 209); the closest verbal parallel in the NT is I Pet. 3:10: παυσάτω . . . ἀπὸ κακοῦ. Otherwise the word is used in the NT only of external cessation, especially in Luke. See A. Strobel, "Macht Leiden von Sünde frei?"; on p. 421 he refers to the formulation of Gen. 5:29 among the Ebionites, who understood it to say of Noah, the type of Christ: . . . οὗτος ἀναπαύσει ἡμᾶς ἐκ τῶν ἁμαρτιῶν ἡμῶν ἤτοι σκληρῶν ἔργων ἡμῶν (Epiphanius, *Panarion* 30.32.6ff. = 1.2.159 [*The Panarion of Epiphanius of Salamis*, tr. F. Williams (Nag Hammadi Studies 35; Leiden, 1987), 149]).

29. B, a few other Greek manuscripts, some Old Latin manuscripts, the Vulgate, and the Peshitta have the plural.

30. According to rabbinic understanding, by dying a person becomes free from the guilt of sin because death atones (K. G. Kuhn, "Rm 6,7," *ZNW* 30 [1931], 305-310) and free from fulfillment of the commandments because a dead person now "rests" (Str.-Bill. III, 232). The formulations in the Qumran scrolls come closer than these perspectives to I Pet. 4:1, describing, e.g., the demise of the generation of the flood in Gen. 7:22f. thus: "All flesh on dry land perished. It was as if they had never existed, since they did their own will and did not keep their Maker's commandment, so that His wrath was kindled against them" (CD 2:20). 1QM 12:11f. says of the eschatological battle with the sons of

was first established from the dimension of Jesus' death.[31] According to 2:24, Christ died for us "in order that we who have died to sins might live to righteousness." In the same way that the parenetic kerygma is based there on Jesus' death, so it is based here on this anthropological "teaching." The teaching is emphasized in order to give an anthropological basis (ὅτι) for preparedness for suffering that corresponds to Christ's suffering. And it also turns this preparedness into "understanding," i.e., into a confession of faith that places one under obligation.

Thus, the true sense of v. 1b also comes to the fore: One who "arms" himself or herself with the "understanding" belonging to Christ is one who places himself or herself under faith's judgment that one's "flesh," one's mortal human existence, must be subjected to suffering because it ceases from sin only when it is judged through suffering unto death.

The meaning of this statement becomes clearer through its prior history. The parenetic admonition of v. 1a-b says something with the term "suffer" that corresponds to and yet differs from what Paul says in Gal. 5:24 with the term "crucify" ("those who belong to Christ have crucified the flesh together with its passions and desires"; 6:14 is similar). This crucifixion is faith's act of decision: Faith places the flesh under the death sentence from God that was carried out in the cross of Christ. It is a second action, then, when Paul on the basis of this decision of faith willingly also takes on himself outward sufferings, which affect his earthly human existence, his flesh (II Cor. 4:10). Here in I Peter the relationship between the decision of faith and the experience of suffering is actually the opposite: In both places the "understanding" to be derived from Jesus' suffering is faith's judgment, but this does not imply that in God's eyes the flesh has already died — though this happens to a degree in 2:24 — but that, in accord with God's will, it should die through suffering in discipleship. One who willingly bears the "suffering of persecution" with this understanding anticipates this conclusion for himself or herself.

The summons to this understanding is developed in 4:1 directly from Christ's suffering (v. 1a) and not from the event of baptism, although the wider context is that of baptismal parenesis. Paul also derived this judgment directly from Jesus' death on one occasion (II Cor. 5:14) and on another occasion from its mediation through baptism (Rom. 6:2).

---

darkness: ". . . devour the flesh of the sinner with your sword." Cf. R. Meyer, "σάρξ," *TDNT* VII, 111-114.

31. The statement is formulated on the basis of Jesus' death, but it does not — contra Strobel, "Macht Leiden von Sünde frei?" 420 — speak directly of Christ's suffering, indicating that "his suffering means a break with sin that produces an after-effect right into the present."

2   This exegesis of the complex v. 1 is confirmed by the final clause in v. 2, toward which v. 1 is aimed: One who gives over the flesh in terms of this developed understanding is free of its jurisdiction for "the remaining time in the flesh." ὁ ἐπίλοιπος ἐν σαρκὶ χρόνος[32] is one's earthly span of life after baptism. This expression indicates that there is a short remainder of earthly life prior to the imminent end (4:7) and that there is still something left "in the flesh." But what now applies is this: εἰς τὸ μηκέτι ἀνθρώπων ἐπιθυμίαις ἀλλὰ θελήματι θεοῦ . . . βιῶσαι. "Human lusts" are identical with the "will of the Gentiles" (4:3) and with "fleshly lusts" (2:11). ἄνθρωπος represents here, therefore, the pre-Christian, "Gentile" (i.e., non-Christian) person. For the baptized living in this world's time-frame, ἄνθρωπος is never past chronologically, since the baptized still live "in the flesh." σάρξ represents here, also on the basis of this correspondence, as in 3:18 and 4:1, earthly human existence, that which is subject to death.

This human existence is not as such sinful; Christ belonged to it without committing sin (3:18; 2:22f.). But when this existence is determinative for a person it leads to craving. Craving that expresses itself in "lusts" (ἐπιθυμίαι) is nothing other than the hopeless, self-consuming preoccupation with the existence that is heading toward death (cf. 1:14; 2:11). It is the attempt to seize life defiantly without God and against God. It is thereby an expression of the "will of the Gentiles," of those "who do not know God";[33] it is the opposite of "the will of God."

To this θέλημα θεοῦ the baptized are obligated, even though they still live "in the flesh." How the content of God's will is to be recognized in the Church's concrete situation was developed extensively in the preceding parenesis. The vital question here is how the baptized can follow at all, against the will of God, the still-active claim of their own "flesh." The time after baptism is not a definitively existing new being of the repentant or redeemed one. It is not the time of the completed but only of the initiated πειρασμός, the situation of inner struggle (1:6f.; 4:12f.). The struggle with fleshly oppression is only won when the one called through baptism into a new existence (1:3, 9) "arms" himself or herself in connection with Christ's suffering unto death as just instructed in v. 1.

---

32. ἐπίλοιπος, "remaining," in the NT only here, substantival in Lk. 24:43 v.l. The whole expression was already classical: Herodotus 2.13 (LCL I, 289); Plato, *Leges* 1.628A (LCL X, 13f.). On its use in parenesis of repentance see above, p. 277.

33. I Thess. 4:5; cf. I Cor. 12:2; Gal. 2:15; Eph. 2:11; 4:17. See the comments above on 2:12.

This fundamental indicator of direction for living out Christian existence in the midst of affliction from society and with the inner struggle brought about by one's own old human life is now applied to the situation in society.

Vv. 3f.: Renunciation of Non-Christian Forms of Life

3 To overcome the old self-consuming human existence also means concretely to distance oneself from society's manner of life, even while one places oneself in its structures and institutions. "The will of the Gentiles" (τὸ βούλημα τῶν ἐθνῶν) manifests itself especially in those forms of social and religious custom that become requirements through the power of habit and the pressure for conformity.

It is precisely these areas of behavior that are named by the catalogue of vices in this verse as examples of the "will of the Gentiles" that Christians will have to face: The catalogue characterizes the vices from a Christian perspective, even while it appropriates a catalogue tradition.[34] Thus it does not point merely to the excesses that Hellenistic popular philosophy also condemned.[35] It would probably also include to a considerable extent, e.g., the wisdom for everyday life reflecting the spirit of Ovid that is recorded in the houses of Pompeii.[36]

---

34. Already πορεύεσθαι ἐν, which introduces the vice catalogue in v. 3b, was a fixed expression for ethical conduct, as in Ps. 1:1 LXX and Jude 11, 16, 18. Here the perfect tense stands in place of the customary περιπατεῖν. The catalogue has been taken, undoubtedly, from parenetic tradition. This is indicated already by a terminological discrepancy: The catalogue speaks of human ἐπιθυμίαι (v. 2), but also lists ἐπιθυμίαι — using the word in a narrower sense — as one among other transgressions. The tradition from which it was taken can be shown directly: Of the six transgressions listed here, the catalogues in Gal. 5:20 and Rom. 13:13f. mention the first and fourth (ἀσέλγεια and κῶμοι) verbatim, and the fifth (πότοι) with the synonym μέθαι and sixth (εἰδωλολατρίαι) are represented at least in Galatians 5. Already the Qumran vice catalogues, which are similar to those in Paul, have the first and sixth from the list in I Pet. 4:3 (cf. Wibbing [see below], 93f.); other Jewish catalogues have the third, fourth, and fifth (*ibid.*, 97f.). In contrast, the second transgression in the list (ἐπιθυμίαι) is found only in Hellenistic catalogues (cf. Epictetus, *Dissertationes* 2.16.45; 2.18.8 [LCL I, 334, 350]; IV Macc. 1:22f.). On the specific points of contact see the statistical overview in Wibbing, 87f., 92-94. See also A. Vögtle, *Die Tugend- und Lasterkataloge im NT* (NTA 16/4-5; Münster, 1936); S. Wibbing, *Die Tugend- und Lasterkataloge im NT* (BZNW 25; Berlin, 1959) (bibliography); E. Kamlah, *Die Form der katalogischen Paränese im NT* (WUNT 7; Tübingen, 1964).

35. Wibbing, *Tugend- und Lasterkataloge,* 20-23; Kamlah, *Paränese,* 145-148.

36. See L. Friedländer, *Darstellungen aus der Sittengeschichte Roms* (four volumes; Leipzig, 1922), §§IV (vol. I), VIII (vol. II), and XIII (vol. III).

"The will of the Gentiles," craving (v. 2), manifests itself first elementarily in giving free rein to desires for sex and for food and drink. The former is addressed by the phrase "in indecency and lusts" (ἐν ἀσελγείαις, ἐπιθυμίαις), the latter by "drinking parties, feasts, and drunkenness" (ἐν . . . οἰνοφλυγίαις, κώμοις, πότοις). The degree to which these types of conduct are seen from a Christian perspective then becomes clear at the end of the catalogue when all nonbiblical religious expression is disqualified as ἀθέμιτοι εἰδωλολατρίαι, "wanton idolatry." This designation, first coined by Christians,[37] characterizes all non-Christian religious expression except Judaism as worship of idols, of εἴδωλα in the OT and Jewish sense, i.e., of numinous constructs created by humans in God's place in order to exchange, as Paul explains in Rom. 1:23, in concealed fashion God's self-witness in the events of the world for the opposite.[38] Although the designation εἰδωλολατρία itself expresses the reprehensibleness of such conduct, I Peter underscores this with the attribute ἀθέμιτος, "wanton,"[39] in order to obviate the masking effect of linguistic habit. The last phrase of the verse makes it clear that the manner of life addressed by the whole catalogue is not one of "vices" on the edge of society, but of the social and religious life-style of society as a whole. By renouncing this way of life, Christians remove themselves from the life in society that they have shared before.

Therefore they are told beforehand ironically, as it were, "for comfort": ἀρκετὸς γὰρ ὁ παρεληλυθὼς χρόνος τὸ βούλημα τῶν ἐθνῶν κατειργάσθαι,[40] "it is sufficient that in former times you carried out the will of the Gentiles." That is: You will not miss it much, as the hunger for life imprisoned by mortality would deceive you into thinking, if you do not participate any longer in this way of extracting life's meaning

---

37. The word is found only in the NT and in subsequent Christian literature. It draws on OT and Jewish tradition and corresponds to the rabbinic term עֲבֹדַת אֱלִילִים (F. Büchsel, "εἴδωλον," *TDNT* II, 379f.).

38. Cf. I Thess. 1:9; Gal. 4:8; additional material in Büchsel, *TDNT* II, 377f.

39. ἀθέμιτος, "unlawful" (Acts 10:28), "wicked" (*I Clem.* 63:2 [LCL AF I, 119]; cf. *Did.* 16:4 [*ibid.*, 333]). The word does not refer to especially disgraceful practices linked with certain cults (contra Beare, 180). Even the previously named vices are not thought of in terms of excesses at cultic celebrations.

40. ἀρκετός, "enough," "sufficient," (cf. BAGD s.v.); regarding the construction of the sentence, cf. BDF §405.2 (p. 209); regarding the substantive issue see above on v. 2. The same viewpoint is motivated differently in *II Bar.* 83:5f. (*OT Pseudep.* I, 649f.): "And we should not look upon the delights of the present nations, but let us think about that which has been promised to us regarding the end."

from that which is immanent, even if "the flesh" claims the opposite and "craves" (cf. v. 2).

4 To distance oneself from the usual life-style of society not only makes one an opponent of one's own old human existence. It also unleashes conflict with those around. Nonconformity is responsible, finally, for the conflict between Christians and society, which is a central theme in I Peter: "They are estranged because you no longer join in." ἐν ᾧ is adverbial,[41] "over which," i.e., over the renunciation of their life-style, just demanded in v. 3, they are surprised and astonished (ξενίζονται).[42] It was on the basis of this "estrangement," not from any accidental socio-political situation, that the social discrimination against Christians arose. For this reason, the Christians were accused of *odium generis humani*.[43]

But from the perspective of Christian parenesis this isolation is seen very differently. This is expressed by the participle in v. 4b: μὴ συντρεχόντων ὑμῶν εἰς τὴν αὐτὴν τῆς ἀσωτίας ἀνάχυσιν, ". . . that you no longer join in this flood of godlessness." συντρέχω, "join in," does not indicate here a crowding together into one place, e.g., at a public ceremony, as in Acts 3:11.[44] It indicates, rather, going along in company with someone, being a "fellow traveler."[45] "Traveling" is, therefore, as is often the case, an image for conduct.[46] To be a fellow traveler here is to be in conformity with others. Doing so leads one into "the flood of godlessness," that "broad stream of a godless life."[47] ἀσωτία (from σῴζειν), "dissipation,"[48] is excess in compensation for meaninglessness, a way of life that is, as the root of the word indicates, godless.

---

41. See the comments on 2:12 and 3:19; 1:6 is different.

42. ξενίζω used in a second meaning, passive "be estranged," "be amazed," "become resentful (over)," here with ἐν (BDF §196 [p. 105]), in 4:12 with the dative (as in Polybius 1.23.5 [LCL I, 63]), v.l. ἐπί (as in Polybius 2.27.4 [LCL I, 309]); this meaning occurs in the NT only in these two passages.

43. See above, p. 159, n.17.

44. Contra Selwyn, 212f.; Perdelwitz, *Mysterienreligion*, 92, who refers to the organized cultic procession as an example.

45. So BAGD s.v.; Beare, 180f. Thus even as in Ps. 49:18 LXX: εἰ ἐθεώρεις κλέπτην, συνέτρεχες αὐτῷ . . .; *Barn.* 4:2 (LCL AF I, 349): μετὰ ἁμαρτωλῶν . . . συντρέχειν.

46. I Cor. 9:24; Gal. 2:2; 5:7; Heb. 12:1.

47. ἀσωτίας is not objective genitive "expulsion from . . ." (Beare, 180f.).

48. In the NT also in Eph. 5:18 (the consequence of excessive wine-drinking) and Tit. 1:6 (children to whom it does not apply, as it did, according to Lk. 15:13, to the prodigal son: ζῶν ἀσώτως); cf. Prov. 28:7; II Macc. 6:4; *Test. Jud.* 16:1; *Test. Ash.* 5:1 (*OT Pseudep.* I, 799, 818) and the definition of ἄσωτοι in Aristotle, *Ethica Nicomachea* 4.1.3f. (LCL XIX, 188f.): τοὺς γὰρ ἀκρατεῖς καὶ εἰς ἀκολασίαν δαπανηροὺς ἀσώτους καλοῦμεν.

Estrangement over the nonconformity of Christians manifests it-self in expressions that the author finally designates as βλασφημεῖν,[49] i.e., "slanderous discrediting," like that mentioned in 2:12 and 3:16.[50] The specifically NT meaning of "blaspheme," i.e., offense against the deity of God, may play a part here as well,[51] since what is said against behavior that seeks to correspond to "God's will" (v. 2) affects God himself (Mt. 5:11; Acts 9:4). The fundamental opposition against Chris-tian behavior affects the claim of God that establishes itself here within world events. That the author also has this in mind is suggested by the continuation of the parenesis, which calls to mind the words of Jesus about blasphemy (Lk. 12:10; Mt. 12:31f.; Mk. 3:28) and about the "careless word" concerning which one must give account on the day of judgment (Mt. 12:36).

Vv. 5f.: God's Judgment of the Dead and the Living

5 Because this reaction of society to the conduct of Christians ulti-mately affects God, God will also require an account for it. But Chris-tians are not able and should not take on this divine role. It is true that society requires Christians to account for themselves (3:15), but it is unable to understand their behavior. Like the suffering Christ (2:23c), Christians are to leave the judgment in all cases to God. In order that this perspective might be conveyed to the Church, the Church's conflict with society is placed here at the end of the parenesis in the light of the final judgment: οἳ ἀποδώσουσιν λόγον τῷ ἑτοίμως ἔχοντι κρῖναι ζῶντας καὶ νεκρούς. The judgment is near (4:7), the judge is even now "ready."[52]

Judgment is to be universal. It will encompass, as is expressed here in a familiar confessional formula,[53] those who are alive at the end as well as those who have died, since before the judgment all will be called to life again (I Cor. 15:51f.).

---

49. Some manuscripts smooth out the style by replacing the participle βλασφημοῦντες with βλασφημοῦσιν.

50. The word is used absolutely, as here, in Lk. 22:65.

51. So also Kelly, 170f.; in contrast, only for the latter are Selwyn, 213; Schelkle, 115f.; Beare, 181.

52. ἑτοίμως ἔχοντι, as in Acts 21:13; II Cor. 12:14 and already in Dan. (LXX) 3:15.

53. "Judge the living and the dead" is used of Christ in II Tim. 4:1; *Barn.* 7:2 (LCL AF I, 365); and in the Apostles' Creed; substantively in Acts 10:42; *II Clement* 11 (*ibid.*, 129); Polycarp, *Phil.* 2:1 (*ibid.*, 285); cf. Rom. 14:9 ("that he might be Lord of both the dead and the living").

Who is thought of here as the Judge? "Judge the living and the dead" is often a christological formula in early Christianity and is present as such in the Apostles' Creed. But since I Peter uses the formula in parenesis that summons to preparedness for suffering from the perspective of the suffering Christ (4:1), it also has undoubtedly in mind, as elsewhere (1:17; 2:23), God as judge.[54] For NT proclamation based on Lk. 12:8 par. it was understood that Jesus "was appointed judge by God" (Acts 10:42); for this reason, it is possible for the Father or the Son to be named as judge, depending on the context.

6 The concluding verse of this section[55] gives the basis (γὰρ καί, "then also") to what precedes and points with the introductory εἰς τοῦτο, "to this," as in 3:9, to the concluding sentence of the section. That sentence appropriates in altered fashion the guiding principle of the entire section from 4:1. The point of both references depends on the debated content of the main statement: νεκροῖς εὐηγγελίσθη, "to the dead the gospel was preached."[56] Which dead are intended here?

Many Church Fathers spiritualized "the dead," thinking it referred to those who are spiritually dead.[57] But "dead" can hardly have a completely different sense here from what it has directly before this in v. 5. Moreover, aorist εὐηγγελίσθη points to a past event.

Therefore, others assume that "the dead" are deceased Christians. The statement seeks, in this interpretation, to comfort the Church with regard to Christians that have died, just as the previous sentence seeks to do with regard to the opponents of the Christians. If the dead should "in the eyes of human beings," especially by suffering persecution or martyrdom, "be condemned," nonetheless "in God's eyes they live in the Spirit." This statement might have a parallel in Wis. 3:1-9; 5:15.[58]

---

54. With Windisch, 75; Schelkle, 116; in contrast to Selwyn, 213f.; Beare, 181f.; and Kelly, 171f.: Christ. God as Judge also in Rom. 2:6; 3:6; 14:10, as in the similar statement in *m. Aboth* 4:29: "It was not of your will that you were formed . . . , and not of your will will you give a just account and reckoning before the King of kings, the Holy One. . . ."

55. For bibliography see the excursus on 3:19, pp. 260-263 above.

56. The addressee of passive εὐηγγελίσθη (see the comments on 1:12) is dative here, in 1:25 accusative with εἰς, otherwise in the NT a personal subject in the nominative: Mt. 11:5; Lk. 7:22; Heb. 4:2, 6; *I Clem.* 42:1 (LCL AF I, 79). Here the passive is impersonal, as otherwise in the NT only in Rom. 10:10.

57. As in Lk. 9:59f.; Jn. 5:25; Eph. 2:1, 5. So Clement of Alexandria, *Adumbrationes,* on this passage (*ANF* II, 571f.); Augustine, *Epistola* 164.21 (*NPNF* first series I, 515-521); most recently, Gschwind, *Niederfahrt,* 26ff.

58. So Kelly, 175, following thereby Selwyn, 214f., 337-339; so also Wohlenberg and others.

But the death of Christians before the parousia is for the generation of
I Peter no longer a pressing question, as it was for the Thessalonian
church (I Thess. 4:13-18).

That the suffering of Christians is also judgment is explained in
4:(1f.)17f., but not here. The wording of the text suggests that the
proclamation of the gospel is encountered by the dead when they are
dead and that their death here, as in v. 5, is literal.[59]

Thus v. 6a says, in the context of 3:19, that the Hades proclamation
of Christ applies not only, as 3:19 made clear, to the most lost but to
all the dead. But should not then the present tense be used? This Hades
proclamation is for I Peter not an ongoing evangelization among the
ones not reached in history but an eschatological event that together
with Christ's suffering unto death and exaltation introduced the final
event, whose imminent conclusion is expected by the letter (1:10-12;
4:7). All this means that the sentence is a kerygmatic statement, not a
brief summary of objective facts about the Hades proclamation and the
path to salvation of the dead.[60]

Understood in this sense, v. 6a gives the basis with γὰρ καί first
of all to the universalism of judgment to which v. 5 pointed, by pointing
now to the universalism of the gospel: In the judgment all people, as
4:17f. declares, will finally be judged according to their relation to the
gospel. The "godless" of the OT judgment sayings (4:18) are now those
who "are disobedient to the gospel" (4:17). For this reason, the deliverance making possible the proclamation of the gospel is encountered by
all. In this encounter it is especially seen — and this is the decisive
matter given foundation in this reference — that salvation also encounters the dead according to the guiding principle established in 4:1b (on
the basis of 3:18): ὁ παθὼν σαρκὶ πέπαυται ἁμαρτίας.

This guiding principle in v. 6b is developed further with regard to
the dead in antithetical parallelism: Among the dead as well judgment
according to the flesh precedes the new and enduring life: ἵνα κριθῶσι
μὲν κατὰ ἀνθρώπους σαρκί. The dead were "with respect to the flesh,"[61]
i.e., in view of their mortal humanity, to which craving corresponds,

59. The definite article can be left out with a noun like ἄνθρωποι. Cf. L. Radermacher,
Neutestamentliche Grammatik (HNT 1; second ed., Tübingen, 1925), 113.

60. So correctly Schlatter, *Petrus und Paulus,* 153: "Peter does not compose an 'order
of salvation' for the dead, nor does he describe the effectiveness of Christ among the dead."

61. As in I Pet. 3:18d.

"condemned."[62] The condemnation is executed in their death.[63] This happens "humanly," i.e., as belongs to humans.[64]

In contrast life is communicated through the gospel[65] "according to God":[66] ζῶσι δὲ κατὰ θεόν. This surely means, not "according to God's kind," namely eternal and holy, but founded through God's will, which creates something new, as the anthesis is stated in 4:2. The dead live at the same time as Christ according to 3:18, πνεύματι, "in the Spirit," in that they are personal entities and belong to the Spirit of God encompassed by the gospel.[67]

Thus the author portrays the effective development of the gospel for the dead according to the analogy of the gospel's activity in history. The questions that arise from speculative attempts to conceptualize all this remain open: Can one imagine the hiddenness of salvation's disclosure through the gospel beyond the limits of death — such hiddenness being its characteristic mark in history — and thereby the possibility for a decision of faith by the dead? The faithful interpreter can

---

62. Here κρίνειν refers, not, as in v. 5, to the passing of judgment, but to judging that brings about the opposite of ζῆν (thus Jn. 5:21f., 24).

63. κρίνειν manifests itself, according to I Pet. 4:17, as in I Cor. 11:32 and similarly 5:5, in suffering and dying; cf. Gen. 2:17; 3:19; Isa. 26:16; Wis. 2:24. In the OT and Judaism death is not only, as in Hellenistic thought, a natural phenomenon (R. Bultmann, "θάνατος," *TDNT* III, 10f.), but also expulsion out of the life-relationship to the Creator as the judgment of God (Str.-Bill. III, 155-157, 228f.; correspondingly, Rom. 5:12; 6:23). See further, Bultmann, *TDNT* III, 15f. Death is for Christians, however, not, as it was for the Jews (II Macc. 6:20; *II Bar.* 13:10; 78:6 [*OT Pseudep.* I, 625, 648]), an atonement that blots out one's guilt for sin (see above, n.30).

64. The expression κατὰ ἀνθρώπους is found often in the singular in Paul to express what occurs "in a human way," not according to God's way: I Cor. 9:8 (λαλεῖν); Rom. 8:5; Gal. 3:15 (λέγειν); I Cor. 3:3 (περιπατεῖν). So also here: "according to the manner of humans," not: "in the opinion of people" or "in the eyes of people" (as in Selwyn, 215; Kelly, 175f.).

65. As in 2:4f., 24 (see the comments there).

66. The expression has the two meanings in Paul that are suggested for its occurrence here: 1) Rom. 8:27: κατὰ θεόν, "according to God's will" the Spirit intercedes for us; II Cor. 7:9-11: λύπη κατὰ θεόν, "sorrow in accord with God's will." This sense is applied here by Schlatter, *Petrus und Paulus*, 153. 2) Eph. 4:4: The new person is created "according to God," i.e., as in Col. 3:10, according to the image of the Creator. So here according to Knopf, 169f.; Selwyn, 215f.; Kelly, 176: in the same way as God lives, i.e., eternally. Cf. BAGD s.v. "κατά" II.5. Here we are reminded of IV Macc. 15:3: "Instead, he loved religion, which saves for eternal life according to God (κατὰ θεόν)."

67. Schweizer, "1. Petrus 4,6," refers to causal use of ἵνα in koine Greek and translates: "For this reason it was also preached to the dead: because although they were judged in a human way, yet in a divine way they should live in the Spirit" (somewhat differently in Schweizer's commentary, 83, 87f.). See also Cranfield, "I Peter 3,19 and 4,6."

neither regard such a conclusion as plain and obvious[68] nor assume that what is referred to is a proclamation of salvation to the righteous on the grounds that the statement is otherwise inconceivable.[69] Rather, one must take the statement as a kerygmatic confession without trying to objectify it as an order of salvation for the dead or as a portrayal of a Hades proclamation. As a kerygmatic confession it declares that the universal activity of salvation accomplished by Jesus' suffering unto death encompasses even the dead, indeed all (cf. Rom. 14:9). Moreover, it confirms thus the principle that applies to those who live in history that no life comes from the gospel unless the flesh dies (4:1).

4:7-11: The Inner Life of the Eschatological Community

7 *The end of all things has drawn near.*
   So be wise and sober for prayer.
8 *Above all, have persistent love for one another,*
   for love covers a multitude of sins.
9 *Be hospitable to one another without grumbling.*

10 *As each has received a gift of grace,*
   so serve one another with it
   as good stewards of God's manifold grace:
11 *If one speaks, (let him or her do so) as (speaking) God's words,*
   if one does acts of service, (let him or her do so) as from the
   strength God bestows,
   so that in all things God may be glorified through Jesus Christ,
   to whom the glory and the power belong forever.
   Amen.

Structure and Tradition

1. With the reference to the imminent end of all things in v. 7a, the new section is distinguished from what preceded, i.e., the conflict with society and

---

68. So Knopf, 169: "The prerequisite for reaching this goal is, of course, that the dead in Hades become believers in response to the proclamation. This prerequisite is a given and therefore does not need to be stated explicitly. And it is also assumed that not all the dead come to new life in the Spirit. . . ." Whoever does not consider the second thesis to be "assumed" must find here with Windisch, 75, a reference to the ἀποκατάστασις πάντων.

69. So Schelkle, 116f., and already in the early catholic understanding of the Hades proclamation in *Herm. Sim.* 9.16 (LCL AF II, 261-265; see the comments above on 3:19).

one's own old human existence, and seeks to activate the life that alone survives beyond this imminent end, i.e., the inner life of the Church. The Church is summoned to prayer (v. 7b), to the active experience of brotherly love, especially to the extension of hospitality (v. 8f.), and to mutual service with the *charismata* in proclamation and *diakonia* (vv. 10-11a). In conclusion, the author directs the readers' attention to the final goal, which is the glorification of the One to whom the Church is indebted for all positive expressions of its life (v. 11b).

2. The congregational parenesis in 4:7-11 has an instructive counterpart elsewhere in the letter, not the fundamental directive in 2:4-10, which says that faith is to be experienced in taking up one's own place in the congregation, but the practical rule for "elders" in 5:1-5, which says that elders are to function as "shepherds" of the congregation. 4:7-11 and 5:1-5 represent two early Christian conceptual frameworks for congregational organization.[1] Only here in the NT outside the Pauline corpus, in I Pet. 4:7-11, do we see the Pauline concept of the congregation as an organism living out gifts of service toward one another. 5:1-5 presupposes the presbyterial organization of the congregation, which stems from the Palestinian Church and which is mentioned nowhere in the genuine Pauline Epistles.

Do the two sections reflect then situations that were geographically and chronologically separated from one another? Should we assign these situations to different parts of the letter, written at different times? We already observed in 2:24f. that the letter placed Pauline and Palestinian traditions alongside one another. A similar linking of organizational elements is to be found in Acts: In Acts 6:2f., distinct service with respect to the word and "of tables" is recommended, as here in v. 11a; in Acts 2:28, 32-35, however, elders are obligated, as in I Pet. 5:1-5, to shepherd the flock of Christ. Acts 2 and Acts 6 address, to be sure, situations that differ chronologically and geographically, but they still belong together for the author of Acts through the continuity of the Church's emergence. In fact, the presbyterial organization of congregations was adopted in the second generation even by the Pauline communities (cf. the Pastoral Epistles). Therefore, in a document of the post-Pauline period, to which I Peter belongs, both organizational traditions could be combined in parenesis. They are not mutually exclusive in substance, even if age as such is not a *charisma*.[2] Even according to the Pauline Epistles congregational organization contains, moreover, a regulatory-institutional element.[3] Thus, the form of congregational leadership depicted in 5:1-5 does not preclude the view in 4:10f. of each member serving with his or her *charisma* and the functional poles of this service being proclamation and *diakonia*.

---

1. Cf. Goppelt, *Apostolic*, 183-189.

2. See E. Hatch, *The Organization of the Early Christian Churches* (Bampton Lectures 1880; Oxford, 1881), 63ff., 118ff.; Goppelt, *Apostolic*, 187 with n.22.

3. It was not, as often has been claimed, purely pneumatic-charismatic; cf. I Cor. 14:40; 16:16; see the comments on I Pet. 5:5.

3. The search for tradition-historical parallels to I Pet. 4:7-11 yields the following:

a. The classical Pauline passages on *charismata* are I Cor. 12:4-11, 28-31 and Rom. 12:6-8. Almost all the *topoi* of I Pet. 4:7-11 are repeated in Romans 12 and its context. Following an initial summons to σωφρονεῖν (Rom. 12:3; I Pet. 4:7b), the χαρίσματα are referred to. In the χαρίσματα, χάρις becomes concrete (Rom. 12:6; I Pet. 4:10). In Rom. 12:6b as in I Pet. 4:11a, διακονεῖν, in a specialized sense of the word, is named as an example alongside the word of prophets and teachers; the concentration of *charismata* on proclamation and *diakonia*, which is fundamental for I Pet. 4:7-11, has its closest correspondence in Acts 6:2f. Taking its place alongside the *charismata* without express connection is brotherly love (Rom. 12:9f.; I Pet. 4:8), which is to be demonstrated particularly in the extension of hospitality (Rom. 12:13; I Pet. 4:9). In I Pet. 4:7-11 the reference to the imminent end comes at the beginning; it follows Romans 12 in 13:11-14 as a conclusion. And the accommodation to the service of worship, which in I Pet. 4:11b concludes the section, stands at the beginning in Rom. 12:1f. So, of the *topoi* mentioned in I Pet. 4:7-11 only prayer (v. 7b) and doxology (v. 11b) are not in Romans 12–13. This is not by chance since Romans 12–13 accommodates itself more to the breadth of neighbor ethics, while I Pet. 4:7-11, like Acts 2:42, is oriented more to worship.

b. With this kind of accent, the parenesis in I Pet. 4:7-11 approaches that of I Thess. 5:1-10, which Selwyn and Kelly refer to as a parallel. But comparison of the two does not turn up nearly as many points of contact as the comparison with Romans 12–13. The congregational parenesis of I Thessalonians 5 begins — and this is actually the only real correspondence — with a reference to the imminent "day of the Lord" (5:1-5) and urges the reader to "be sober" (5:6f.; cf. I Pet. 4:7b). The subsequent directives to "admonish one another" (I Thess. 5:11) and to obey "those who are over you" (5:12f.) come only into loose proximity with what is said in I Peter 4 in vv. 8ff. And what emerges here as points of correspondence can be found more immediately in another text, namely, James 5.

c. In spite of the close points of contact with Romans 12, I Pet. 4:7-11 is not derived directly from Pauline tradition. The Pauline elements have been incorporated into a parenetic schema that is also found in the closing portion of James (5:7-20). This section begins in Jas. 5:7f.(9-11) with a reference to the imminent parousia (cf. I Pet. 4:7a) and goes on in 5:12, as in I Pet. 4:8, with πρὸ πάντων in an especially important directive, and then speaks in 5:13(14-18) about prayer (cf. I Pet. 4:7b). Finally, in 5:20, the one who concerns himself or herself with a brother committing sin is encouraged with the same phrase used in I Pet. 4:8: Thereby "a multitude of sins is covered." Following this structurally quite similar parenesis I Peter 4 goes on to address the *charismata* in vv. 10-11a, which, like the doxological conclusion in v. 11b, has no parallel in James 5.

d. It may be concluded then that in I Pet. 4:7-11 traditional schemata and *topoi* of parenesis have been appropriated for the shaping of life in the congregation. No immediate tradition-historical contexts are revealed. The particular accent through which this section is distinguished from similar parenetic sections is the idea of God's work of grace as that which sets things in motion (vv. 10-11a) and of God's honor as the goal (v. 11b). "The God of all grace" (5:10), who leads one through all affliction to the end, comes into view here.

4. Stylistically, it is striking in comparison to the related texts just how much the ideas in I Pet. 4:7-11 avoid all development and breadth, which are so characteristic, e.g., of Jas. 5:7-20, and formulations about current issues, such as we find in Romans 12 — all this in spite of the traditional material in I Pet. 4:7-11. It is also striking how the passage is shaped in brief catechistic directives, which can almost be read as following stichometric patterns.

Vv. 7-9: Prayer, Love, and Hospitality

7a The introductory reference to the imminent end of the world is prompted by a traditional parenetic schema,[4] but is also motivated for substantive reasons within the context. The concluding statements of the preceding section brought the final judgment into consideration (4:5f.); δέ, "but," which serves as a connector in 4:7, should not, however, be overemphasized.[5] What is decisive is the relationship to what now follows.

Elsewhere in the letter where the view is toward the future eschaton, the judgment (1:17; 4:5, 17-19) and especially the consummation, the coming of the Lord (1:4f., 8-12, 13; 4:13; 5:10), are always singled out for attention. But here the transience of the world existing until now is brought to mind: πάντων δὲ τὸ τέλος ἤγγικεν. τέλος, which has no fixed meaning, designates in 4:17 the "end result" of disobedience and in 1:9 the "goal" of faith, but here it designates the "end" in the sense of "cessation."[6] "All things" (πάντα), the entire present existence of the world, challenge and threaten Christians in manifold ways, as the earlier main part of the letter developed extensively; but for "all things" the end "has drawn near."[7] ἤγγικεν is an early Christian technical term

---

4. I Thess. 5:1; Phil. 4:4-6; Rom. 13:11-14; Heb. 10:23-31; Jas. 5:7-11; I Jn. 2:18f.; Rev. 22:12; cf. *Barn.* 4:9; 21:3; Ignatius, *Eph.* 11:1; *II Clem.* 12:1; 16:3 (LCL AF I, 351-353, 409, 185-187, 147, 155).

5. One can hardly translate it with such emphasis as Kelly, 176: "But the end of all things is at hand."

6. The three meanings elsewhere in the NT are "end result," "departure" in Rom. 6:21f.; Phil. 3:19; II Cor. 11:15; "goal" in I Cor. 10:11; "conclusion" in Mk. 13:7 par.; I Cor. 15:24 (II Cor. 3:13). Cf. G. Delling, "τέλος," *TDNT* VIII, 54-56.

7. Cf. *Did.* 10:6 (LCL AF I, 325): "Let grace come and let this world pass away." *Barn.* 21:3 (*ibid.*, 409): "The day is at hand when all things shall perish with the Evil one; 'The Lord and his reward is at hand.'"

coming from the Jesus tradition and indicating the chronological nearness of the eschaton.[8]

I Peter advocates the expectation of the imminent parousia in as emphatic a manner as Revelation (1:3; 22:20), though both belong to the second generation. This expectation was even articulated among the Apostolic Fathers, not only as a parenetic formula but also as the overall context for Christian existence.[9] Throughout the entire history of the Church this kind of expectation has come to the fore again and again, by no means only among apocalyptic fanatics.[10] Its essential content consists of more than just the concept of a brief time-frame, which was, at any rate, disproved in the first generation by the delay of the parousia. In the idea of nearness there speaks forth, rather, an assessment of the world situation that corresponds to God's approach, which overtakes space and time, or which more precisely corresponds to the "already" and "not yet" of the eschaton in history.[11]

The author draws the parenetic consequence from this orientation to expectation of an imminent parousia by turning to what remains when life "in the flesh," which I Peter does take very seriously, passes away:

---

8. As was already the case in deutero-Isaiah LXX, ἐγγίζειν (intransitive) and ἐγγύς became technical terms in the NT for the approach of God's promised salvation in history: in the Jesus tradition: Mk. 1:15 (par. Mt. 4:17; cf. 3:2; 10:7; Lk. 21:31); in Paul, rarely of course: Rom. 13:12; cf. Phil. 4:5; otherwise: Lk. 21:38; Jas. 5:8; Rev. 1:3; 22:10. See W. G. Kümmel, *Promise and Fulfillment: The Eschatological Message of Jesus* (tr. D. Barton, London, 1957), 19-25; *idem,* "Die Naherwartung in der Verkündigung Jesu" (1964), *idem, Heilsgeschehen und Geschichte* (Marburg, 1965), 457-470; H. Preisker, "ἐγγύς," *TDNT* II, 330-332; J. Becker, *Das Heil Gottes* (StUNT 3; Göttingen, 1964), 201.

9. Whereas the former may apply for some of the formulas mentioned above in n.4, the latter is the case in *Did.* 10:6 (LCL AF I, 325) and *Herm. Vis.* 3.8.9; *Sim.* 9.12.3; 10.4.4 (*ibid.*, 49, 249f., 305; cf. Goppelt, *Apostolic,* 135-139).

10. For example, Luther yearned in the affliction of the hidden Church for "the most happy last day" (cf. *D. Martin Luthers Werke. Kritische Gesamtausgabe. Briefwechsel* IX [Weimar, 1941], 175 = *Luther's Works* L: *Letters III* [ed. and tr. G. G. Krodel; Philadelphia, 1975], 220, and passim; P. Althaus, *The Theology of Martin Luther* [tr. R. Schultz; Philadelphia, 1966], 419ff.).

11. See P. Althaus, *Die letzten Dinge* (tenth ed., Gütersloh, 1970), 263-269; O. Cullmann, *Salvation in History* (tr. S. Sowers, et al.; New York, 1967), especially 179-183 (in debate with Bultmann, quoting p. 181):

The *abiding factor* in eschatology is not the detemporalized situation of decision, but the retention of the tension, temporally understood. The expectation of the imminent end rests upon a particularly intensive, "enthusiastic" experience of the tension between "already" and "not yet." Because the "already" is really present, and hence offers the firm guarantee for the early cessation of the "not yet," the tension first of all assumes the form of an anticipation of an imminent end.

turning to God in prayer (v. 7b), brotherly love (vv. 8f.), and service in the congregation (vv. 10-11a), i.e., a life for the honor of the One who gives this life (v. 11b).

7b σωφρονήσατε οὖν καὶ νήψατε εἰς προσευχάς, "So be wise and sober for prayer." σώφρων, "wise," appropriated by early Christian parenesis in accord with ancient Greek tradition, characterizes one who observes and follows whatever standard is established for such a person and his or her environment (Rom. 12:3).[12] Whoever observes the standard established by imminent expectation becomes "sober for prayer." The sober person does not lose himself or herself, as was already stated in 1:13, in worldly existence like one who is intoxicated,[13] but sees everything under the aspect of hope. For I Peter, in contrast to I Cor. 7:29-31, this does not demonstrate itself in the posture of "having as though one had not," but, according to 5:8 and as in I Thess. 5:1-10, in vigilance that keeps one from being outwitted by evil. Therefore, according to I Pet. 4:7-11, like Jas. 5:7-20, it demonstrates itself in prayer that breaks through that which is immanent and in congregational life that receives its shape from that which is transcendent.

προσευχή is the most comprehensive of the various designations (I Tim. 2:1) for prayer. Even in its most basic meaning it refers to calling on God.[14] The commonly used plural brings to mind the plurality of acts of prayer. The life of the early Christian community was surrounded by appeal, intercession, thanksgiving, and adoration from both individuals and groups, the content of which was oriented to the Lord's Prayer. The Church offered prayer "in the name of Jesus" (Jn. 14:13; 15:16b; 16:23; cf. Jas. 5:15), i.e., from the posture of faith, so that prayer was the characteristic mark of their eschatological existence.[15] The same is true of *agape*.

8 Both imperatives in v. 7b are linked to the additional directives in participial form in vv. 8 and 10 and the one with no verb form in

---

12. Cf. U. Luck, "σώφρων," *TDNT* VII, 1097-1100, 1102f.

13. νήφειν is always used figuratively in the NT: I Thess. 5:6, 8 (also in connection with the parousia); II Tim. 4:5; I Pet. 1:13; 4:7; 5:8. Here the admonition is directed, not, as in I Thess. 5:1ff.; II Thess. 2:1ff., against fanatical imminent expectation (contra Kelly, 177; Windisch, 75); such an expectation is to be documented nowhere in the letter as a possibility for the churches addressed. See Selwyn, "Eschatology."

14. H. Greeven, "εὔχομαι," *TDNT* II, 803-806.

15. A. Dietzel, *Die Gründe der Erhörungsgewißheit nach den Schriften des NT* (Dissertation, Mainz, 1955); W. Schmauch, "Gebet," *BHH* I, cols. 522f.

v. 9. The participles function as imperatives;[16] they do not express a logical subordination to the directive in v. 7b,[17] even if they do so grammatically. And on the other hand, πρὸ πάντων, "above all," which introduces v. 8, gives priority to brotherly love, not over the prayer just mentioned, but over all other communication among Church members. The parenetic "above all," which is found elsewhere in early Christian writings only in Jas. 5:12, i.e., within the schema that also underlies our passage, gives in both instances special catechetic emphasis to a directive, without giving it higher rank; this can also be seen in the explanation of the Jesus tradition of the commandments of the law (Mk. 12:30-33 par.).

πρὸ πάντων τὴν εἰς ἑαυτοὺς ἀγάπην ἐκτενῆ ἔχοντες. "Love for one another" is brotherly love, which was already named and given thorough foundation earlier in 1:22, along with hope and faith, as the foundation of Christian existence. As in 3:8, it is now moved to the fore in the framework of a practical parenesis for all communication within the congregation, since without it all other interaction is empty (I Cor. 13:1-3; Col. 3:14; Jas. 2:8; I John passim). Love should be ἐκτενής, "exerted," i.e., both zealous and persistent. This belongs to its essence and is for that reason, as in 1:2, emphasized.[18]

While love is at heart motivated in 1:22 by the new birth, here it is given support by an ambiguous maxim: ὅτι ἀγάπη καλύπτει πλῆθος ἁμαρτιῶν, "since love covers a multitude of sins." This statement circulated in early Christianity as a maxim; it is also to be found in Jas. 5:20 in the framework of the same schema, more distantly in *I Clem.* 49:5; *II Clem.* 16:4 (LCL AF I, 92f., 154f.).[19] I Peter has appropriated the statement as a circulating maxim, perhaps along with the parenetic schema, but not from the underlying OT text, Prov. 10:12, since the formulation does not follow the LXX text, which the letter quotes otherwise, but rather the Hebrew text.[20]

---

16. On imperatival use of the participle see above, p. 106, n.16.

17. Contra Knopf, 172; Schelkle, 118.

18. The adjective is used there as an adverb, here as a predicate adjective.

19. The Latin version of *Didascalia* 2.3.3 quotes the maxim as a saying of the Lord (the Greek text has Jn. 13:35; cf. R. Connolly, *Didascalia Apostolorum* [Oxford, 1929], 23).

20. Prov. 10:12: וְעַל כָּל־פְּשָׁעִים תְּכַסֶּה אַהֲבָה, LXX: πάντας δὲ τοὺς μὴ φιλονεικοῦντας καλύπτει φιλία. The expression πλῆθος ἁμαρτιῶν, which is not from either text, is perhaps from Ezek. 28:17f. or Sir. 5:6. The reading καλύψει (p72, א, Koine, a few others) is an accommodation to Jas. 5:20.

How does the author want this appropriated maxim to be understood in this context? To "cover" sins in OT usage meant to "forgive" them.[21] But whose love and whose sin is thought of here? (1) Perhaps the intention is to say that brotherly love should be practiced with persistence, since it always forgives anew the offenses of one's brother and is not exhausted by them (cf. I Cor. 13:7). In *I Clem.* 49:5 (LCL AF I, 92f.) the maxim is utilized in this way, and this usage also corresponds, certainly, to the Hebrew text of Prov. 10:12.[22]

(2) But "sin" in the NT is usually offense against God. For this reason many interpreters find here a statement that demonstrations of brotherly love cover one's own guilt for sin. This is how the maxim is understood in *II Clem.* 16:4 (LCL AF I, 154f.), by Tertullian and Clement of Alexandria while commenting on our passage, and by Origen while commenting on Jas. 5:20;[23] Origen quotes Lk. 7:47 in support of this exegesis.[24] But there is no place in I Peter's soteriology (cf. 1:18f.; 2:24f.)[25] for the idea that works of love are able to cancel out guilt for sin in the final judgment, which is supported in the rabbinic literature and often taken up among the Apostolic Fathers.[26]

(3) According to the clear declarations of I Peter about the matter, the maxim, whose wording, as with other OT quotations, should not be pressed, should be heard not as a soteriological dictum of instruction, but as a parenetic reference. It should be understood in the sense of the Jesus tradition, which the letter frequently takes up: To practice brotherly love with persistence is necessary, since love, both love of God and love of human beings, covers a multitude of offenses, among us (4:1-4) as well as among others. Heard ambivalently like this,[27] the

---

21. Ps. 32:1; LXX Ps. 84:3: "You forgave . . . ; you pardoned all their sin."

22. See among others, Bengel, ad loc.; with reservations Cranfield, 114; Beare, 184f.; cf. also *Test. Jos.* 17:2 (*OT Pseudep.* I, 823).

23. Tertullian, *Scorpiace* 6 (*ANF* III, 638f.); Clement of Alexandria, *Quis Dives Salvetur* 38 (*ibid.* II, 602); Origen, *Homiliae in Leviticum* 2.4.

24. Such exegetical results also in Schelkle, 118, who also quotes in support Dan. 4:24; Sir. 3:20, as well as the rabbinic interpretation of Prov. 10:12 (cf. Str.-Bill. III, 766). Following this with reservations are Knopf, 172f.; Kelly, 178; Spicq, 150.

25. Lk. 7:47 can not be given as suppport for the concept, since it is meant cognitively. Mt. 25:31-46, however, is not the description of an order of salvation, but a summons to repentance.

26. *I Clem.* 50:5; *Did.* 4:6; *Barn.* 19:10; Polycarp, *Phil.* 10:2 (LCL AF I, 95, 315f., 405, 295); cf. C. Spicq, *Agapé* II (Paris, 1959), 359-363.

27. That the maxim is ambivalent is emphasized, though with differing interpretations, by Windisch, 75; Selwyn, 217f.; Beare, 184f.; Cranfield, 114f.

maxim recalls the circular movement between the love we encounter and the love we pass on, which, according to the Jesus tradition, goes forth from God (Mk. 11:25; Mt. 6:14f.; 18:35). It thus portrays a correlation of personal relationships and not a settling of accounts. Heard in this way, the saying stimulates the practical exchange of brotherly love.

9 An important demonstration of brotherly love is the reception of fellow Christians as guests:[28] φιλόξενοι εἰς ἀλλήλους ἄνευ γογγυσμοῦ. There were hotels, inns, and rental quarters,[29] but hospitality was to a large extent a presupposition for Christian mission[30] and for the realization of Christian fellowship, especially when Christians gathered for worship,[31] which took place, of course, in private homes. This hospitality brought with it considerable burdens, even where it was not abused by religious frauds (about whom, e.g., *Didache* 11–13 warns).[32] Therefore, the realistic comment is added that hospitality should be offered "without grumbling" (Phil. 2:14), i.e., willingly out of love (II Cor. 9:7; cf. Prov. 15:17). In this hospitality the koinonia of those who live among the nations as "foreigners in the Diaspora" (1:1) is brought to expression in relation to fellow Christians. It is only a special application of preparedness to house strangers, which had already been named in the Jesus tradition as a demonstration of neighborly love and which repeatedly became an act of missionary witness.[33] Here, as in Heb. 13:1f., hospitality among Christians is emphasized within the framework of congregational parenesis and leads further to the matter of serving with one's *charismata*.

Vv. 10f.: Gifts of Grace and the Glorification of Christ

As with brotherly love in v. 8, so now in vv. 10-11a serving with *charismata* is referred to as a root of the activities through which the congregation lives. The

---

28. φιλοξενία, "hospitality" (Rom. 12:13; Heb. 13:2), characterizes the one who practices it as "hospitable," φιλόξενος (I Tim. 3:2; Tit. 1:8; I Pet. 4:9).

29. E.g., H. Schaal, *Ostia. Der Welthafen Roms* (Bremen, 1957), 95-100, 116-121. Inns and taverns are also mentioned in the NT; cf. G. Stählin, "ξένος," *TDNT* V, 18f.

30. Mt. 10:11; Acts 16:15; 21:7, 17; 28:14; Rom. 16:4, 23 (ὁ ξένος μου καὶ ὅλης τῆς ἐκκλησίας); III Jn. 3:7f.; *Did.* 11:2, 4 (LCL AF I, 325-327).

31. Rom. 16:5; I Cor. 16:19; Col. 4:15; it is expected especially of ecclesiastical office holders: I Tim. 3:2; Tit. 1:8; *Herm. Mand.* 8:10; *Sim.* 9.27.2 (LCL AF II, 106f., 285).

32. Cf. Lucian, *De Morte Peregrini* 11-13, 16 (LCL V, 13-15, 19).

33. Cf. Stählin, *TDNT* V, 17-25; C. Spicq, *Theologie morale du NT* II (Paris, 1965), 809ff.

two are brought together here, and are related in content, as in Rom. 12:4-8, 9f. and I Cor. 14:1, without being expressly connected. The word group based on διακονεῖν, "to serve," is absent from the LXX and does not have any precise meaning in Hellenistic language. It became, however, a technical term in early Christianity for all ecclesiastical discourse and action through which the gospel was passed on.[34] Probably this usage came from Jesus' introduction of the term as an image for the behavior of his disciples toward one another, which was to correspond to their belonging to the kingdom of God (cf. Lk. 22:24-27). Just as participation in earthly kingdoms shows itself in political power and legal position, so participation in God's kingdom shows itself in serving. To serve is, then, to pass on the demonstration of God's love that one has received while renouncing earthly advantages in the fullness of power, so that others will be embraced through such by God's dominion. It was in this way that Jesus himself established God's reign among people (Mt. 11:3-6 par.; 12:28 par.; Lk. 17:20). For this reason, all further work for the gospel can only be service. Therefore, service, as the passing on of God's demonstration of love with a view toward the establishment of his dominion, creates the presupposition for brotherly love and is also, on the other hand, one of its concrete expressions.

This concreteness of the expression of love comes from the *charismata*.[35]

10 This is the only early Christian passage outside the Pauline Epistles where the Pauline correlation between *charisma* and service appears. According to I Cor. 12:4f., a διακονία corresponds to the respective χάρισμα. Here it is said in just as fundamental a manner as in I Cor. 12:7, 11, that each Church member has received a *charisma:* ἕκαστος καθὼς ἔλαβεν χάρισμα.[36] From this principle comes the notion that the congregation, with respect to its structure, is an organism of serving members.

The concept of *charismata* as acts of service was, by all indications, developed by Paul and then, except here, disappeared very soon

---

34. See W. Brandt, *Dienst und Dienen im NT* (Gütersloh, 1931); H. W. Beyer, "διακονέω," *TDNT* II, 85-88; E. Schweizer, *Church Order in the NT* (SBT 32, tr. F. Clarke; Naperville, IL, 1961), 31ff., 173-187; see below, nn. 53f.

35. See F. Grau, *Der neutestamentliche Begriff χάρισμα, seine Geschichte und seine Theologie* (Dissertation, Tübingen, 1947); J. Brosch, *Charismen und Ämter in der Urkirche* (Bonn, 1951); J. Roloff, *Apostolat—Verkündigung—Kirche* (Gütersloh, 1965), 125-135; H. Conzelmann, "χαίρω, χάρισμα," *TDNT* IX, 403-406; K. Kertelge, *Gemeinde und Amt im NT* (Munich, 1972); U. Brockhaus, *Charisma und Amt. Die paulinische Charismenlehre auf dem Hintergrund der frühchristlichen Gemeindefunktionen* (Wuppertal, 1972).

36. ἕκαστος is the subject of the καθώς clause and does not introduce, therefore, an anacoluthon.

in post-Pauline early Christian literature: The Pastoral Epistles connect *charismata* only with church officials (I Tim. 4:14; II Tim. 1:6). In *I Clem.* 38:1 (LCL AF I, 72f.) natural gifts are called *charismata* and are used in a principle of mutual "subordination."[37] For Ignatius, however, *charismata* are Jesus Christ (*Eph.* 17:2 [*ibid.*, 190f.]) and more generally the blessings that come from him (*Smyr.* inscription; *Pol.* 2:2 [*ibid.*, 266-271]), which approaches Paul's more general use of the term in Rom. 1:11; 5:15f.; 6:23; 11:29; II Cor. 1:11.

Charismatic acts of service are derived in I Cor. 12:7f., 11 from the πνεῦμα, but here, as in Rom. 12:6 (cf. I Cor. 1:4, 7; Eph. 4:7), they are understood as individual expressions of χάρις, of the demonstration of God's love. The members of the Church are characterized as (καλοὶ) οἰκονόμοι ποικίλης χάριτος θεοῦ. χάρις is encountered, therefore, in "a variety of forms" (ποικίλη), but is always the demonstration of God's love. Genitive χάριτος approaches here an objective genitive and χάρις itself approaches the meaning "gift of grace"; one could, perhaps, understand it as a "showing of love."[38] The χάρισμα, the "gift of grace," is, then, the enablement that comes about from this showing of love, when it takes into service the natural capabilities of a person; according to I Cor. 12:6 χάρισμα is the activity of God in a person, and according to Rom. 11:29 it is its empowering summons. It is not, as the "pneumatics" in Corinth would have it, a supernatural energy that is infused into the natural person and expresses itself in ecstasy, but always the enabling for service given only by God's activity.

These capabilities were received (ἔλαβεν) with the summons to faith through baptism. For this reason, they do not become active automatically. Whoever receives them, has them, rather, as an οἰκονόμος; he or she is to make responsible use of them, as a "steward" makes use of financial resources, by "serving"[39] with them. The work of the steward became, through a parable of Jesus (Lk. 12:42-48 par. Mt.), an image for responsible use of what was given to the Church by its Lord.[40]

---

37. Cf. *I Clem.* 48:5f. (LCL AF I, 93), so also *Did.* 1:5 (*ibid.*, 311): "Give to everyone that asks thee . . . for the Father's will is that we give to all from the gifts we have received" (par. *Herm. Mand.* 2.4-6 [*ibid.*, II, 73], with ἐκ τῶν ἰδίων δωρημάτων instead).

38. Similarly I Cor. 1:4 (cf. v. 7); 3:10; Eph. 3:2.

39. διακονεῖν here as in 1:12 with the accusative of the thing (αὐτό) but not, as there, with the dative of person, but with εἰς.

40. Luke uses the parable in his interpretation of the apostolic office, as do the Pastoral Epistles in Tit. 1:7 (cf. Roloff, *Apostolat,* 267). In I Cor. 4:1f. οἰκονόμος is linked to Paul,

The Church lives in light of the reality that its members allow themselves to be taken into service by God's demonstrations of love and,
thus, faithfully make use of this ability for one another, i.e., from a
stance of stewardship.

11a This verse describes the two basic forms in which this service takes place: proclamation and *diakonia*.[41] To mention only these
two *charismata* looks like a reduction when compared to the colorful
abundance listed in I Cor. 12:8-11, 28-31 and Rom. 12:5-8.[42] But what
we have here is actually a concentration based on considerations of
substance. The two decisive functions necessary for congregational life
are singled out. They are the two sides of Jesus' ministry: the word and
help for physical need. They thus convey a whole coming into being
from God. The closest parallel to this verse is the differentiation between
διακονία τοῦ λόγου and διακονία τραπέζαις developed in Acts 6:1-4. But
here the differentiation is not aimed at an institutional division of labor,
as in Acts, but at a characterization of two functions.

εἴ τις λαλεῖ, ὡς λόγια θεοῦ, "if any one speaks, let that one speak
as God's words." In the NT λαλεῖν, "speak," is not fixed conceptually.[43]
Most NT occurrences refer to the passing on of the gospel, which I Pet.
1:12, 25 designates as the fundamental source of Christian existence.
This speaking was realized among early Christians in a number of
distinctive forms of speech, from unembellished basic missionary
preaching (Acts 10:44) to the various forms of reflective theological

---

in Tit. 1:7 to the bishops, and in Ignatius, *Pol.* 6:1 (LCL AF I, 273f.) to the Church; οἰκονομία
is used correspondingly in I Cor. 9:17; Col. 1:25; Eph. 1:10; 3:2, 9; I Tim. 1:4. In addition,
both are found in the normal sense: the former in Lk. 16:1, 3, 8; Gal. 4:2; Rom. 16:23, the
latter in Lk. 16:2ff. See O. Michel, "οἶκος οἰκονόμος," *TDNT* V, 149-151; J. Reumann,
" 'Stewards of God' — Pre-Christian Religious Application of OIKONOMOΣ in Greek,"
JBL 77 (1958), 339-349.

41. I Pet. 4:11 refers, like v. 10, to all Christians, not "office bearers in particular"
(contra Michel, *TDNT* V, 151). On the other hand, it is not impossible that these functions
were also realized by office bearers.

42. The list of gifts in Eph. 4:7, 11 could reflect, in relation to I Corinthians 12 and
Romans 12, a growing institutionalization. The list in *I Clem.* 38:1f. (LCL AF I, 73) could
for its part reflect a decline of spiritual gifts in favor of natural gifts.

43. In the word's other occurrence in I Peter (3:10) it certainly refers to everyday
speech. But here the specific usage is still more concentrated than with the more frequent
λέγειν, which does not appear in I Peter. In Acts, e.g., λαλεῖν is used throughout for the word
that comes from God (2:4, 6, 7, 11, 31; 3:21f., 24; 4:1, 17, 20, etc.), λέγειν also in this sense
(1:3; 2:17, 25, 34, 40; 3:25, etc.), in addition, however, often for ordinary human speech
(1:6; 2:7, 12f.; 4:16, 32, etc.).

teaching in the Pauline Epistles (Romans, passim), from ecstatic prophetic speech to "reasoned" speech appealing to believing thought
(I Cor. 14:2f., 19), from public proclamation to personal exhortation
(Gal. 6:11ff.). Paul reflected extensively about the structure of this
speaking, above all in view of his own words (cf. II Cor. 2:17; 4:13;
11:17; I Cor. 13:1f., etc.).

Here in I Peter only what is decisive receives attention — through
an easily remembered and brief formula: Speech by which the gospel
is passed on is meaningful only when it occurs ὡς λόγια θεοῦ, since
only then does it come to be effective, i.e., active as described in
1:23-25. τὸ λόγιον,[44] "saying," "utterance," had already come to refer
in extrabiblical Greek primarily to a saying from a deity, almost equivalent to "oracle." In the LXX τὸ λόγιον τοῦ θεοῦ is often synonymous
with ὁ λόγος τοῦ θεοῦ, the biblical revelation in word. Here in I Peter
the word comes closer to the original Greek sense than to LXX usage,
as in Acts 7:38, where Moses received at Sinai λόγια ζῶντα, "living
sayings (of God)." Here the speech that passes on the gospel should
become "as sayings of God." ὡς, "as," introduces here, as in the preceding verse and often in I Peter (1:14; 2:2, 5, 11; 3:7), a clarifying
qualification, which may imply at the same time a certain distancing
from the referent of the comparison.[45]

But in what sense are the words of those who pass on the gospel
"God's sayings," or do they become such? Certainly they are not the
word of God simply because the speaker repeats former words of God.
Reproduction of God's words in the entire NT shows that they become
so only by the fresh reformulation of the gospel for contemporary life.
Does the phrase say then that "in the word of the Church God's word
is delivered, indeed, the Church's word is God's word?"[46] What is said
here is not a theory for listeners that presupposes the teaching authority
of the Church; nor does it mention specific presuppositions that qualify
that turn human speech into God's word so that one could say, e.g., "if
you believe"[47] or that God's word is spoken by one to whom it is given
by the Spirit in accord with God's free choice.[48]

---

44. G. Kittel, "λέγω, λόγιον," *TDNT* IV, 137-139.

45. According to the other uses of ὡς in I Peter, however, it does not have such a
strongly distancing sense as Kittel, *TDNT* IV, 138f., assumes.

46. Schelkle, 120.

47. Kelly, 180.

48. Cranfield, 115f.

In light of the introduction in a conditional clause, as in Rom. 12:3-8, it would seem that this sentence is to be heard as parenesis for the speaker, especially one thought to be speaking in the context of *charismata*. But it does not say to such a person: You are to establish the authority of God for them and add nothing of your own to it,[49] or: You are to be aware that you are announcing revelations of God.[50] Such ideas identify human speech in an almost magical way with the word of God. As the history of interpretation has often perceived, the sentence contains for the parenetic context in the first instance this admonition: Whoever passes on the gospel should be intentional about speaking not from narrow individuality, but from a posture of having listened to God, i.e., as 1:12 puts it, in the Spirit and out of faith.[51] This admonition is, however, at the same time a promise: Human speech can and will become, even according to Jesus' promise, like his own words, speech that comes from God for those who listen, if it is actually determined by the gospel that seeks out each person in his or her situation.[52]

In the same sense, the διακονοῦντες, "those who perform deeds of service," are admonished to do so "out of the strength that God gives": εἴ τις διακονεῖ, ὡς ἐξ ἰσχύος ἧς χορηγεῖ ὁ θεός. διακονεῖν, "serve," is used absolutely here and has a more narrow meaning than in v. 10. It signifies all passing on of the "grace of God" that takes place, in contrast to preaching and teaching, through helping engagement, of course not without an accompanying word, i.e., *diakonia*. According to the context in Rom. 12:8b, which corresponds to the present passage in content, *diakonia* consists of "communicating" gifts, of "standing before," i.e., of shaping the gatherings of the congregation, and of "practicing compassion." According to I Cor. 12:26, 28b it consists of helping the sick, of comforting and sympathizing. The same follows from word usage: διακονεῖν designates, when used in the narrower sense, caritative work among the needy, sick, and imprisoned,[53] as well as organization of

---

49. Windisch, 76.

50. Knopf, 176.

51. Cf. Rom. 12:3; further II Cor. 2:17; 4:13 (of Paul) and Jn. 5:19 (of the Son of the Father).

52. Lk. 10:16 par. Mt. 10:40; I Thess. 2:13; II Cor. 5:20; Jn. 7:16-18; cf. K. H. Schelkle, *Discipleship and Priesthood* (tr. J. Disselhorst; London, 1966), 59-72.

53. Thus διακονεῖν in Mt. 25:44: "Lord, when did we see you hungry, thirsty, a stranger, naked, sick, or in prison and not minister (διηκονήσαμεν) to you?"; Acts 6:2: διακονεῖν τραπέζαις. In Rom. 15:25; II Cor. 8:19f. the word is used of gathering and delivering the collection for Jerusalem. The same is true of διακονία: so Acts 6:1; in Rom. 15:30f.;

congregational events.[54] Thus, the activity of the presbyters mentioned in I Pet. 5:1-4 can belong primarily but not exclusively to this *diakonia.*

To all this *diakonia,* as well as to proclamation, belong both admonition and promise: They should and can be done out of the power that God freely gives.[55] In the NT, as already in the LXX, ἰσχύς designates, like κράτος (alongside the frequently used δύναμις), primarily the power of God.[56] In contrast to v. 11b, this is not power that belongs only to God, but power that goes forth from God; it is not the active power that shapes history in hiddenness (Rom. 1:20), but the might that, concealed in weakness (II Cor. 12:9), creates a new existence out of faith through the gospel (Rom. 1:16; I Cor. 1:18, 24). It is, fundamentally, the Spirit of God (I Cor. 12:4, 6; cf. 2:4f.; Rom. 15:13, 19). To accomplish "worldly" helping and organizing in faith and prayer from this power does not withdraw ecclesiastical action from rationality, though it does withdraw it from a mechanized state and any need for satisfaction. Moreover, it makes such helping and organizing serve the goal of ecclesiastical existence, which is witness to and recognition of God as the Creator and Savior of all.

11b This purpose clause articulates, finally, the goal of the three previous statements, all of which end with θεός (vv. 10a, b, 11a) and, beyond that, of the entire section on congregational life (4:7-11). ἐν πᾶσιν, "in all things" (neuter, not masculine), that happen in service and in brotherly love, "God" should "be glorified": ἵνα . . . δοξάζηται ὁ θεός. God is glorified when his δόξα, his "glory," i.e., his essential being, predominates in speech and deed. This happens when, through the entire conduct of the congregation, God is confessed and praised as the One from whom all that is wholesome comes, i.e., as God (cf. I Cor.

II Cor. 8:1-6, and passim, again of the collection for Jerusalem; but in Rom. 12:7, between prophets and teachers, of a special service that is either like them in being a service of word or different from them in being a service of deed.

54. διακονία according to I Cor. 16:15 is the service that "the firstling of Achaia" practices by organizing gatherings of the church in his house; διακονεῖν designates in I Tim. 3:10, 13 the activity of the διάκονοι (v. 8); see above, n.35.

55. χορηγεῖν in the NT here and in II Cor. 9:10 (v.l.), originally: "to provide a chorus for the theater," "to cover the costs for something," "(liberally) to furnish"; here with ἧς by attraction for ἥν.

56. In I Peter all three terms are used: 1:5: δύναμις, which is preserved in faith; 4:11a: ἰσχύς, which makes service possible; and 4:11b; 5:11: κράτος, which belongs to God. Cf. already Isa. 40:26 LXX: ἐν κράτει ἰσχύος, *I En.* 1:4 (Greek; cf. *OT Pseudep.* I, 13): ἐν τῇ δυνάμει τῆς ἰσχύος αὐτοῦ (cf. W. Grundmann, "ἰσχύω," *TDNT* III, 397-402).

10:31; Acts 11:18; 21:20). Therefore what should happen in the congregation is that which at the beginning of this major part of the letter (2:12) was expected of other people as the final consequence of Christian behavior in society. As an existing liturgical phrase (Rom. 16:27; Jude 25) adds: This is made possible διὰ Ἰησοῦ Χριστοῦ, "through Jesus Christ," since through him God has disclosed himself as the One who is at work now in the Church.

This direct reference to God prompts the author to offer his confession to God in a doxology: ᾧ ἐστιν ἡ δόξα καὶ τὸ κράτος εἰς τοὺς αἰῶνας τῶν αἰώνων. There is no need that glory be given to God: God has it without beginning and without end. The antecedent of ᾧ is God, not Christ.[57] Whereas later ecclesiastical doxologies were usually formulated as wish, here the indicative is used expressly, as in Rom. 1:25; II Cor. 11:31 (Jude 25). No other NT doxologies are formulated as wish; even where the verb is missing, the indicative is to be supplied in each case.[58] In fact, glory and power without beginning or end have always belonged to God. δόξα is, according to the language of the LXX, God's essential being, often conceived of as his honor or as a divine radiant light.[59] While Pauline doxologies refer only to glory, here, as in I Tim. 6:16; Jude 25; Rev. 1:6; 5:13, κράτος, "power," "might," is added.[60] As Revelation proclaims (4:8 and passim; also II Cor. 6:18), God is the παντοκράτωρ, the "ruler of all" who carries through his plan for the world, though not by direct demonstrations of power, but by the exaltation of the crucified One (Rev. 5:13) and the resulting salvation and judgment.

---

57. With Windisch, 76; Kelly, 181f., and others; contra Selwyn, 219f. First, it is to be expected in terms of content that the δόξα belongs to the one of whom δοξάζεσθαι was spoken before. That the honor should be given both *to* Christ and *through* Christ would be artificial. Second, διὰ Ἰησοῦ Χριστοῦ directly preceding ᾧ is a fixed liturgical formula: It also stands before doxologies speaking of God in *I Clem.* 20:12; 50:7 (LCL AF I, 45, 97). On the other hand, ᾧ ἡ δόξα εἰς τοὺς αἰῶνας τῶν αἰώνων, ἀμήν was perhaps a closing formula in the worship service (Eph. 3:20; Heb. 13:20f.; Jude 24f.; Rev. 1:5f.), which was incorporated with others into the post-Pauline doxology in Rom. 16:25-27; so E. Kamlah, *Traditionsgeschichtliche Untersuchungen zur Schlußdoxologie des Römerbriefes* (Dissertation, Tübingen, 1955), according to *ThLZ* 81 (1956), col. 492.

58. So Lk. 2:14; Rom. 11:36; Eph. 3:21; Phil. 4:20; I Tim. 1:17; Jude 25; Rev. 1:6.

59. G. Kittel, "δοκέω, δόξα," *TDNT* II, 243f., 247f.

60. Rare in the NT; except in one instance, used only of God (or Christ); Eph. 1:19 (6:10); Col. 1:11; otherwise, in doxologies: I Tim. 6:16; I Pet. 4:11; 5:11; Jude 25; Rev. 1:6; 5:13; *I Clem.* (27:5) 64; 65:2; *Mart. Pol.* 20:2; *II Clem.* 17:5 (LCL AF I, 39, 119f., 121; II, 339f.; I, 157). Cf. W. Michaelis, "κράτος," *TDNT* III, 905-908.

The doxology is concluded with ἀμήν. That is, it stands as valid and confirmed.[61] With this "amen" doxologies receive acclamation in both the OT and the NT.[62]

At the end of 4:11 a caesura has undoubtedly been reached in the letter. But this is not indicated by the "amen" or by the doxology. "Amen" at the conclusion of a sermon or a letter was not customary at that time; rather, it confirmed a doxology as it does here. And of the many doxologies of the NT (sixteen have been identified) only two are at the end of a letter (Jude 25; II Pet. 3:18); Rom. 16:27 is a liturgical appendix. One cannot, therefore, conclude from the doxology that the thought developments of the letter originally ended here.[63]

---

61. Cf. II Cor. 1:20; H. Schlier, "ἀμήν," *TDNT* I, 335-338; A. Stuiber, "Amen," *JAC* 1 (1958), 153-159.

62. I Cor. 14:16; Rev. 5:14; Justin, *Apologia* 1.65.3 (*ANF* I, 185). Hence, both OT and NT doxologies often end with "amen": Neh. 8:6; Ps. 41:14; I Esdr. 9:47; Rom. 1:25; 9:5; 11:36; Gal. 1:5; Phil. 4:20; I Pet. 5:11; Jude 25; *I Clem.* 20:12, and passim (LCL AF I, 45).

63. So Selwyn, 32, n.2; Kelly, 182ff.; contra Beare, 25ff., 187, according to whom the doxology, which is similar to 5:11, concludes the material on baptism.

4:12–5:11: Third Major Part:
The Preservation of Christians in Society and in the Community of Faith (Closing Parenesis)

4:12-19: The Suffering of Those Who Believe as Grace and Judgment

12 *Beloved, do not be astonished by the purifying fire among you,*
which comes over you for testing, as though something strange
were happening to you;
13 *rather, since you are participating in Christ's sufferings,*
rejoice,
so that with jubilation you may also rejoice at the revelation of
his glory.

14 *If you are reviled for the sake of Christ's name, blessed are you,*
for the Spirit of glory and of God rests on you.

15 *Let none of you suffer, that is, as a murderer, thief, or evildoer,*
or as one who meddles in the affairs of others;
16 *but if one suffers as a Christian,*
then he or she should not be ashamed.
To the contrary, such a person glorifies God through this name
(of Christian).

17 *For the time has arrived that judgment should begin with*
God's household.
But if it (begins) first with us,

*what will be the end of those who do not obey the gospel of
God?*

18 *And "if the just one is barely delivered,
where will then the godless one and sinner appear?"* (Prov.
11:31)

19 *Therefore, those also who suffer according to the will of God
should commend their souls to the faithful Creator
—through just behavior.*

Structure and Tradition History

1. This section takes up again the "suffering" of Christians in society, which
was interpreted parenetically in 1:6f.; 2:18-25; 3:13–4:6. What does it add to what
has already been said? It is out of this question that the literary-critical problem
of I Peter grew.

a. Perdelwitz brought this question into sharp relief by taking the view that
the section offers no new perspectives on the interpretation of suffering, but in
fact presupposes a different situation. In his view, after 4:12 persecution came to
be actually experienced, while earlier, in 1:6; 3:13f., 17, persecution is only what
could possibly happen, "if God so wills it" (3:17).[1] This distinction requires,
Perdelwitz maintained, the literary-critical explanation that the letter "was put
together out of two fully independent and self-contained documents," a document
of comfort and warning contained in 1:1f.; 4:12–5:14 and a baptismal address
consisting of 1:3–4:11.[2]

This understanding of 4:12-19, including the broader literary-critical hypothesis, was appropriated with modifications by Windisch, Beare, Cranfield, and others.
Beare expressed it most sharply by stating that in 4:12ff. the letter concerned itself no
longer, as before, with the principles of Christian suffering in a non-Christian environment, but with the crisis and terror of a persecution in progress. V. 12, Beare claimed,
addressed a congregation over which had come an explosive and organized persecution
like a paralyzing shock wave. The image of πύρωσις, the "testing fire," could have a
familiar background from the Neronian persecution.[3]

---

1. Perdelwitz, *Mysterienreligion,* 13f.:

New perspectives are no longer advanced; πάσχειν διὰ δικαιοσύνην (III 14) corresponds to πάσχειν ὡς Χριστιανός (IV 15); the blessings in IV 14 and in III 14 are
the same; and in I 7 as in IV 13 the blessed glory at Christ's revelation is held out
as the final goal. One cannot understand, therefore, why all this has to be repeated
in the same letter. . . . [Surely, however, it shows] that the discussion of suffering in
I Peter presupposes two completely different situations. One looks hypothetically
toward suffering that the future could bring, while the other deals with suffering as
a present experience.

2. *Ibid.,* 16-26.
3. Beare, 188ff.

b. This explanation of 4:12-19 is, as we will see, exegetically indefensible. The difference in relation to what precedes reflects not a new situation but new aspects of the interpretation of suffering. V. 12 formulates by way of introduction the theme of the section: "Do not be astonished by the purifying fire among you . . . , as though something strange were happening to you." This statement points not to a change in the situation but to an enduring condition: The participles in which the situation is addressed (γινομένη, συμβαίνοντος) are present tense, not aorist, which would indicate the inception of change.

The only new contribution to the portrayal of the situation is in vv. 15f.: Christians may have to face arraignment before the courts and could be condemned there simply on the basis of belonging to the faith, i.e., on account of the name "Christian." But even this does not presuppose an organized persecution; it is, rather, always possible as a result of the social discrimination that has already been mentioned. A similar statement had already been made in the Gospel sayings about persecution (Mt. 5:11f. par.; 10:17f., 22 par.). Vv. 15f. are quite in keeping, therefore, with the portrayal of the situation up to this point in the letter; it offers at most greater concreteness of expression.

c. What is new is not the situation but the parenetic interpretation that is now given for this situation of permanent social discrimination and legal uncertainty (4:14: "if you are reviled"; 4:15f.). To this point the readers have been admonished to refute discrimination by just behavior in order to avoid conflicts and, yet, to be prepared at all times for "sufferings," which are both possible and also happening, indeed, again and again (3:13-17; 4:1f.). Here it is not the occurrence of suffering but the fundamental necessity of suffering that is addressed: "Do not be astonished . . . , as though something strange were happening to you." The "sufferings of persecution" do not contradict the essence of being a Christian; indeed, they belong to it fundamentallly.

This general idea is grounded in particular terms: According to vv. 12-16 such suffering is grace, and according to vv. 17-19 suffering anticipates the judgment to which all "flesh" will be subjected. Suffering has already been interpreted in these two directions (2:20; 3:14, 17f.: suffering is grace; 4:1f., 6: suffering anticipates judgment), but now both lines are thought through more fully within the new perspective of the salvation-historical necessity of suffering. This section thus introduces a new stage in the theology of suffering, one that nonetheless preserves continuity with what was said before.

2. How then should we understand the relationship of 4:12-19 to the letter as a whole? Without a doubt, a new major part of the letter begins with 4:12. This is indicated, as in 2:11, by direct address. This is not to be the concluding part of the letter. It not only adds new perspectives to what has already been said, but also alters the descriptive mode: Until now the author has laid out principles, but now the thought developments are connected to circumstances in a more concrete and direct way.[4] This distinction is to be observed not only here: In the same way in

---

4. Similar are the judgments of Lohse, "Parenesis and Kerygma," 50; Nauck, "Freude

which questions about the affliction of Christians at the hands of society are given renewed attention here, so also the next section, 5:1-5, does not introduce new concerns with regard to congregational structure, but gives attention very concretely to the *realization* of congregational order. In 5:6-11, finally, the author speaks again of suffering, now in brief concrete appeals, so that that section becomes the parenetic high point of the letter's conclusion.

3. In tradition-historical terms these sections do not adopt, like the preceding sections, an existing complex of tradition. Rather, they weave together various traditions and give them new accents.

In the process, the understanding of suffering as grace plays a decisive role. Three arguments are given for this understanding of suffering, each of which corresponds to traditions of its own: As was already stated in 1:6f. in terms of OT, Jewish, and early Christian tradition, suffering is fundamentally necessary testing that purifies faith (4:12). 4:13 develops, in conversation with a tradition characterized by Pauline terminology though not linked directly to him, the idea that suffering communicates κοινωνία with the sufferings of Christ and therefore becomes a reason for joy. According to v. 14, one who suffers is, moreover, on the basis of the Synoptic Jesus tradition, to be regarded as blessed because the Spirit of glory even now brings such a one into eschatological existence. In vv. 15f. the author adds a commentary on the first subsection (vv. 12f.). According to vv. 17f., suffering is anticipation of the judgment to which all flesh is subject. This statement, which is without parallel in the NT, is joined, as the quotation style indicates, to a tradition of OT prophecy that lived on in Judaism with modification. The statement was undoubtedly drawn up by the author of I Peter, or by a Christian source available to the author, through meditation on Scripture, in the context, of course, of Jewish interpretation of suffering. V. 19 is a parenetic conclusion, the content of which is typical for the author.

Like 2:11, 4:12-19 marks a new beginning with the address ἀγαπητοί, "beloved." After the two major parts of the letter dealing in fundamental terms with the essence of Christian existence and the conduct of Christians in society, now a short parenetic concluding part takes up the conflict with society in two sections (4:12-19 and 5:6-11); between the two sections it inserts a directly practical directive for the inner life of the congregation (5:1-5).

"Astonishment" at suffering is addressed from the beginning in 4:12 and is prohibited. What encounters Christians in their sufferings is precisely that to which they are called (2:21). As will be developed in subsections, one encounters eschatological grace in suffering (vv.

---

im Leiden," 79f.; van Unnik, "Christianity according to I Peter," 80; Schelkle, 123, n.1; Kelly, 183f.

12-16), which is always the experience of Christians while the old existence is being judged (vv. 17-19).

Vv. 12f.: Participation in the Sufferings of Christ as Grounds for Joy

12 The imperative, μὴ ξενίζεσθε ... ὡς ξένου ὑμῖν συμβαίνοντος, "Do not be astonished ..., as though something strange were happening to you," sets the theme of this new parenesis directed toward the "sufferings of persecution." This "astonishment" is more than the wonder that I Jn. 3:13 opposes in relation to the same issue. Just as in I Pet. 4:4 society is "estranged" over the conduct of Christians, so also these Christians can be "astonished" — the verb is ξενίζω in both cases — over that which encounters them from society. Both have the impression that something incongruous is happening. This impression may have been felt especially among Gentile Christians, who, unlike Jews from the Maccabaean period on, were not familiar with the hardships of a distinctive existence in society and its interpretation in a theology of martyrdom. But such estrangement is comprehensible on the part of all Christians, on the basis of their summons to eschatological salvation (1:3-9). Their summons into God's peace (1:2; 5:14) brings them into conflict with their entire social environment (cf. Mt. 10:34 par.); for the promise of salvation they reap suffering (1:5).

An initial foundation for the imperative is given already in v. 12 by the manner in which the situation of suffering is addressed. Reference is made here to τῇ ἐν ὑμῖν πυρώσει, "the purifying fire among you."[5]

---

5. πύρωσις is rare and means "burning," "destruction by fire" (so Rev. 18:9, 18). Here it refers to purifying fire, as in the LXX, where it occurs only in Amos 4:9; Prov. 27:21: δόκιμον ἀργύρῳ καὶ χρυσῷ πύρωσις (מַצְרֵף = "crucible"), "the crucible for silver and the furnace for gold"; so also in the Apostolic Fathers, *Did.* 16:5 (LCL AF I, 333): πύρωσις τῆς δοκιμασίας (F. Lang, "πῦρ, πύρωσις," *TDNT* VI, 950f.). This meaning is also suggested by the use of the verb πυροῦν for purification of metals in the LXX: Ps. 65:10 LXX (cf. Rev. 3:18); Judith 8:25-27: "Let us also give thanks to the Lord our God, who tries us just as he did our fathers. For he has not tried us in the fire, as he did them. . . . Nor has he taken vengeance on us" (cf. Wis. 3:4-6).

The Hebrew word represented by LXX usage of the noun is found in the OT only in Prov. 17:3; 27:21 and becomes a standard technical term in the Qumran writings for the necessary purification of the community through oppression by the dominion of Belial. 1QS 1:17f.: "They shall enter the covenant before God to obey all his commandments so that they do not abandon him during Satan's rule out of fear, terror, or affliction (מַצְרֵף)." 1QM 8:3f.: "Atone for sin by practicing justice and by suffering the sorrows of affliction." 1QM 17:8f.: "You, the sons of his covenant, be strong in the ordeal of God . . . , until he moves his hand for his trials to come to an end." 1QH 5:16: "You have placed him [= your servant] in the crucible [like gold] in the fire and like silver refined in the smelter's crucible to be purified seven times." This usage of the word comes the closest — when measured in terms

The letter again appropriates thereby the image with which its references to affliction began in 1:6f.: Affliction is like the purifying fire in which precious metals are refined. Here as there the image is interpreted as πειρασμός, as a "trial" that purifies faith under pain and strengthens it through preservation. This interpretation is brought up again here only in passing, however, through the visual description of the situation and a clarifying participle (ὑμῖν γινομένη). Two more significant clarifications follow as express reasons for the imperative.

13   Whoever must suffer at the hands of society for the sake of the faith has a share in Christ's sufferings. But how is this κοινωνεῖν, this "participation,"[6] to be understood? I Peter's theology of suffering is the perspective within which this question can be answered. To this point the letter has emphasized that "suffering for the sake of righteousness" (3:14) corresponds, or should correspond, in structure to Christ's suffering (2:21-23; 3:17f.) and that this happens not by means of *imitatio* but by means of his suffering for us, which leads the way to righteousness (2:21, 24; 3:18).

From this we can conclude with regard to 4:13 that if Christians suffer for the sake of their identity as Christians (4:4, 15f.), then they have a share in "Christ's sufferings" (παθήματα Χριστοῦ; cf. 5:1), i.e., in what Christ himself suffered (1:11), not, as in Paul's writings, in what those who belong to him experience for his sake.[7]

---

of the substantive context — to I Peter, but the word itself has a different meaning in the two contexts: While in Qumran it is a technical term for "purification," in I Peter, as in Prov. 27:21, it is a figure of speech that needs explanation as πειρασμός, which is never the case in the Essene texts. See E. T. Sanders, *ΠΥΡΩΣΙΣ;* Borchert, "Conduct"; D. E. Johnson, "Fire in God's House."

6. κοινωνεῖν, κοινωνός, and κοινωνία are found in the NT most often by far in Paul's letters. κοινωνεῖν occurs in I Pet. 4:13: "participate (in something)" (τινί, as in Rom. 15:27) and κοινωνός in 5:1: "one who participates (in something)" (with the genitive of the thing as in II Cor. 1:7; cf. BAGD s.v.). The only NT points of correspondence with the expression here are in Paul: II Cor. 1:7; Phil. 3:10: κοινωνίαν τῶν παθημάτων αὐτοῦ. See Filson, "Partakers."

7. τὰ παθήματα Χριστοῦ, "the sufferings of Christ," is found otherwise in the NT only in Paul. There it designates the sufferings that the apostle and the churches experience for Christ's sake (so II Cor. 1:5 and surely also Phil. 3:10; in II Cor. 4:10 in its place is νέκρωσις τοῦ Ἰησοῦ, "Jesus' suffering unto death"). Paul bears this suffering because, according to II Cor. 4:11, he is daily "handed over to death for Jesus' sake"; he "suffers with him" (Rom. 8:17); he bears the θλίψεις τοῦ Χριστοῦ (Col. 1:24).

In contrast, τοῦ Χριστοῦ παθήματα in I Pet. 4:13–5:1 refer, in accord with the statements about participation in the πάσχειν of Jesus (2:21-23) — statements not found in Paul — to the Passion, τὰ εἰς Χριστὸν παθήματα (1:11). The Pauline sense of the expression recurs

Participation in Christ's sufferings does not have merely a cogni-
tive significance: It is not just a sign but also the realization of a
solidarity with Christ that comes from him and is then brought to
realization by us: The idea of spiritual absorption into Jesus' suffering,
of a mysticism of the Passion, is far from what is thought of here. Paul
speaks of this solidarity with Christ with the term κοινωνία or in words
with the prefix συν-, while the Synoptic tradition speaks of this solidarity
with Christ in terms of discipleship.

Here, then, it is said that Christians participate in Christ's sufferings in two ways, the first named in v. 13, the second only implicitly
conveyed in v. 14. In v. 13 καθό[8] κοινωνεῖτε τοῖς τοῦ Χριστοῦ παθήμασιν
reflects the language of Pauline tradition,[9] but is not formulated in exact
Pauline terms. V. 14, on the other hand, is linked with the Synoptic
tradition. Once again, as in 2:24f., related statements are formulated
first in Pauline and then in Synoptic terminology.[10]

The motif of joy (χαίρετε) is now blended with that of participation: Because solidarity with Christ is represented in suffering, it is even
now a reason for joy — because of fellowship with Christ (1:8), above
all, because participation in Christ's glory follows from solidarity with
Christ in suffering, not as a reward but as the consequence of Christ's
faithfulness. This durability of relationship is anticipated in the Synoptic
Son of Man saying on confession (Lk. 12:8 par.); Paul is also certain
of the same on the basis of God's faithfulness (Rom. 8:17). But here
this outcome is not spoken of with the root κοινων- as participation,

---

in Ignatius, *Smyr.* 5:1 (LCL AF I, 257), the use found in I Peter in *I Clem.* 2:1 (*ibid.*, 11).
W. Michaelis, "πάσχω, πάθημα," *TDNT* V, 930-935, incorrectly assumes the former for I Peter
(934) and the latter for Phil. 3:10 (932; in contrast, J. Gnilka, *Der Philipperbrief* [HThK;
Freiburg, 1976], 196). Hebrews creates instead the expression "the humiliation (τὸ ὀνειδι-
σμόν) of Christ" (11:26; 13:13). On the discussion of the Pauline statements see E. Güttgemanns, *Der leidende Apostel und sein Herr* (FRLANT 90; Göttingen, 1966), especially
100-119; see below, n.16.

8. In this passage the causal component dominates in the καθό phrase; cf. BDF §456.4
(pp. 238f.).

9. Of the three key terms in the sentence — τὰ τοῦ Χριστοῦ παθήματα with κοινωνεῖν
and, in contrast, ἡ ἀποκάλυψις τῆς δόξης — the roots of all three recur in 5:1, and two (the
first and third) occur in 1:11. They are found together elsewhere in the NT only in Paul. The
first expression is found in the NT only in Paul (II Cor. 1:5; Phil. 3:10) and I Peter, as are
the linking of the root κοινων- with παθήματα (II Cor. 1:7; Phil. 3:10) and the contrast of
future δόξα and present sufferings (Rom. 5:2; 8:18: "The sufferings of the present are not
worth comparing with the glory to be revealed to us"; cf. II Cor. 4:17).

10. Nauck, "Freude im Leiden," 69-72, sees 4:13, incorrectly (as 4:14), exclusively
within the traditional context indicated by Mt. 5:11f.

which one would otherwise expect and which actually happens in 5:1, but as the consummation of joy over suffering: χαίρετε, ἵνα καὶ ἐν τῇ ἀποκαλύψει τῆς δόξης αὐτοῦ χαρῆτε ἀγαλλιώμενοι, "rejoice, so that with jubilation you may also rejoice at the revelation of his glory," i.e., because you will participate in his glory. The revelation of Christ's glory[11] is the effective emergence of glory from hiddenness. Jubilant joy is the joy of the consummation (cf. 1:5f.).

Even with this basis, the summons to rejoice because of suffering, not only in spite of it and in it, is paradoxical. "Blessed" (μακάριοι) in v. 14 corresponds to "rejoice" here. The basis for joy is like the basis for the pronouncement of blessing: It is that which provides meaning and fulfillment to existence and makes true life accessible. "Suffering," however, is the opposite, in this context, exclusion from the community life of society. As elsewhere in the biblical tradition, this characteristic of suffering is not overplayed dualistically or nihilistically, but is taken seriously, since God desires and gives historical and bodily life through all its vicissitudes. How then can suffering and joy be united?

Joy because of Suffering for Christ's Sake: The Origin of the Concept

1. I Peter speaks, first in 1:6, 8 and finally in 4:13b, of the joy or jubilation that in the future will replace the present distress when God's salvation dawns visibly.[12] This idea was well established in the OT and Jewish tradition, especially from deutero-Isaiah on: The future redemption of Israel, which abolishes judgment, brings joy. "How beautiful on the mountains are the feet of one who brings good news. . . . Break forth into song together, you ruins of Jerusalem, for Yahweh has comforted his people and has redeemed Jerusalem" (Isa. 52:7-12; cf. 40:1-11). In the apocalyptic literature this joy became joy over the future new life without death and after death: "Yahweh of hosts . . . will swallow up death forever. The Lord Yahweh will wipe the tears away from all faces. . . . Let us be glad and rejoice in

---

11. "The revelation of his glory" (4:13) corresponds to the ἀποκάλυψις Ἰησοῦ Χριστοῦ (1:7, 13). These christological expressions address the same event as the soteriological expressions in 5:1: τῆς μελλούσης ἀποκαλύπτεσθαι δόξης, and 1:5: εἰς σωτηρίαν ἑτοίμην ἀποκαλυφθῆναι ἐν καιρῷ ἐσχάτῳ.

12. On joy in the Bible, see R. Bultmann, "ἀγαλλιάομαι," *TDNT* I, 19-21; E. Gulin, *Die Freude im NT* I/II (Annales Academiae Scientiarum Fennicae, Series B 26/2, 37/3; Helsinki, 1932/37); J. Schniewind, "Die Freude im NT," *idem, Nachgelassene Reden und Aufsätze* (Berlin, 1952), 72-80 (= *idem, Die Freude der Buße* [Kleine Vandenhoeck-Reihe 32, Göttingen, 1956], 9-18); A. B. Du Toit, *Der Aspekt der Freude im urchristlichen Abendmahl* (Winterhur, 1965); H. Conzelmann, "χαίρω," *TDNT* IX, 359-372; W. M. Morrice, *Joy in the NT* (Grand Rapids, 1984).

his salvation" (Isa. 25:6-12); "Yahweh, in distress they sought you. They poured out a prayer when your chastisement[13] was on them. . . . Your dead will live, and their bodies will rise. Awake, you dwellers in the dust, and sing for joy" (Isa. 26:7-19; cf. 35:10; 51:11; 61:7). In the Psalms this collective-universal perspective is transferred to the destiny of the individual, e.g., Ps. 31:7: "I will rejoice and be glad because of your steadfast love, because you have seen my affliction . . ." (cf. 30:5f., etc.). This OT perspective is the framework for the modification of the theme of suffering and joy in Jewish and early Christian tradition. It is also directly appropriated, as with the passages used in I Peter.

2. Just as the accent in OT statements about joy is on future joy over eschatological salvation, so the emphasis in the NT is on the joy over the present dawning of salvation. This joy was already expressed in images and parables of Jesus (Mk. 2:19 par.; Lk. 10:20; 15:4ff. par. Mt.; 15:8ff., 32; Mt. 13:44). Paul articulated this early Christian tradition, using χαίρειν, "rejoice," and χαρά, "joy," as soteriological-eschatological technical terms (Rom. 14:17: "the kingdom of God is . . . joy in the Holy Spirit"; II Cor. 1:24: through his activity as apostle Paul wants to be the addressees' "coworker of your joy"; Phil. 4:4, and passim). Because soteriological-eschatological joy is already present, its relationship to πειρασμός, "inner struggle," to λύπη, "sorrow," and to suffering, which are characteristic for the present existence even of believers, is an issue.

a. The first response to this issue is dialectical conjunction. Paul characterizes himself as one of "those who experience sorrow, but rejoice at all times" (II Cor. 6:10) and the Thessalonian Christians as those who "imitate us and the Lord by receiving the word under affliction with joy" (I Thess. 1:6; cf. II Cor. 8:2).

b. But the suffering referred to here does not stand alongside present participation in salvation with no connection to it. Indeed, it encounters the believer on account of the gospel. Therefore, it can be related to participation in the gospel and as a result can be called a basis for joy. In I Pet. 3:14 and 4:14, the blessings pronounced on the persecuted are appropriated from the Jesus tradition (according to Mt. 5:10, 11f.). At their rudimentary level these blessings may very well go back to Jesus himself, since the beatitude for the persecuted also belongs to the four pronouncements passed on by Luke (Lk. 6:22f.) and has a comprehensive OT background (cf. Isa. 52:13–53:12; Psalms 22, 118, etc.). Jesus' pronouncement of blessing applies to the afflicted as well as to the poor because participation in God's reign is given to those who allow it to be given to them as a gift. It was the beatitude for the afflicted that was developed further for the post-Easter situation of the Church; the disciples were thereby placed permanently under the care of eschatological grace within the context of their ejection from solidarity with society. Therefore, it is not because suffering is to be rewarded as an achievement that they are pronounced blessed and admonished to rejoice in and over persecu-

---

13. The OT and Judaism have no single word for "suffering"; they speak of יִסּוּרִין, "chastisements," and צָרוֹת, "troubles." Cf. W. Michaelis, "πάσχω," *TDNT* V, 911.

tion. I Pet. 4:13 rightly adopts for itself the present tense χαίρετε of Mt. 5:12, not the future χάρητε ἐν ἐκείνῃ τῇ ἡμέρᾳ of the parallel passage in Lk. 6:23.

c. Paul portrays this situation in a substantively similar manner. In II Cor. 12:9b-10 he writes: "I would just as soon glory all the more in my weakness, so that Christ's power might remain on me. Therefore, I take pleasure in weakness, insults, crises, persecutions, and afflictions for Christ's sake . . ." (cf. Rom. 5:3-5). Although I Pet. 4:13 uses the language of Pauline tradition, the specifically Pauline καυχᾶσθαι, "to glory/boast," is not taken up there. In its place stands χαίρετε,[14] which was familiar from the beatitude tradition (Mt. 5:12); nowhere does Paul identify suffering directly as a reason for rejoicing.[15] Elsewhere in the NT, in Acts 5:41 and Heb. 10:34 one reads of joy over concrete suffering on account of faith, but this is motivated differently; in Jas. 1:2f.(12) the reader is admonished generally toward joy over inner struggles: The tradition used here is modified in I Pet. 1:6f. with a view to persecution.

3. The conceptual groundwork for these NT references to joy over suffering of persecution was laid not only by the OT background, but especially by further developments in extracanonical Judaism. The constant afflictions that confronted Jews from the Maccabean period on because of their obedience to the Torah provided the impetus for reflection on and explanation of this "suffering of persecution" in a theology of martyrdom. This reflective process came to be linked with reflection on the catastrophe that Israel experienced with the second destruction of Jerusalem in A.D. 70. Points of correspondence with NT statements about joy in suffering or at the prospect of suffering are seen in the following areas:[16]

a. In the course of thinking about Israel's catastrophe in A.D. 70, the author of II Esdras finds no explanatory formula, because the concept of a just person, one who can stand the test in judgment, became questionable in his penetrating reflection.[17] In contrast, a solution is developed in *II Baruch* (especially chs. 13–15 and 78:3-6 [OT

---

14. In I Peter only here. χαρά occurs in 1:8 and ἀγαλλιάομαι in 1:6, 8; 4:13. The rare word εὐφραίνειν does not appear in I Peter.

15. Even in II Cor. 8:2 suffering and rejoicing are not connected, though they appear next to each other: "In a severe test of affliction their abundance of joy and their extreme poverty have overflowed in a wealth of liberality on their part"; in Phil. 4:4-7 "rejoice in the Lord always" is joined only with the general "have no anxiety."

16. See Str.-Bill. III, 221f.; cf. 314; II, 193f., 274-282; W. Wichmann, *Die Leidenstheologie. Eine Form der Leidensdeutung im Spätjudentum* (BWANT 4/2; Stuttgart, 1930); H. Braun, "Vom Erbarmen Gottes über den Gerechten. Zur Theologie der Psalmen Salomos" (1950/51), *idem, Gesammelte Studien zum NT und seiner Umwelt* (Tübingen, 1962 [third ed., 1971]), 8-69; Michaelis, *TDNT* V, 905f., 909f.; E. Lohse, *Märtyrer und Gottesknecht* (FRLANT NF 46; Göttingen, 1963), especially 29-58; *idem, Colossians and Philemon* (Hermeneia, tr. W. R. Poehlmann and R. J. Karris; Philadelphia, 1971), 68ff.; J. A. Sanders, *Suffering as Divine Discipline in the OT and Post-Biblical Judaism* (Rochester, NY, 1955); E. F. Sutcliffe, *Providence and Suffering in the Old and New Testaments* (London, 1953); E. Kamlah, "Wie beurteilt Paulus sein Leiden?" *ZNW* 54 (1963), 217-232; Millauer, *Leiden als Gnade.*

17. Wichmann, *Leidenstheologie,* 43-51.

Pseudep. I, 625f., 648]), which stems perhaps from rabbinic Judaism and at least was generally advocated in rabbinic Judaism later. Formally, the statement in *II Bar.* 48:48-50; 52:5-7; 54:16-18 (*ibid.*, 637, 639f.), which certainly belong together,[18] comes closest to I Pet. 4:13. In 48:50 a "great light" in the other world is promised to those who have "endured much labor [i.e., hardship]" for a short time in this passing world; this is the path of the righteous one marked out in the OT.[19] Therefore, they are admonished to rejoice in their suffering: "And concerning the righteous ones, what will they do now? Rejoice [*OT Pseudep.:* "Enjoy yourselves"] in the suffering which you suffer now. . . . Prepare your souls for that which is kept for you, and make ready your souls for the reward which is preserved for you" (52:5-7). Why does suffering guarantee the eternal "reward" and become, therefore, the occasion for joy? "They were chastened that their sins might be removed" (13:9, translated differently in *OT Pseudep.;* cf. 78:5f.): Suffering anticipates atonement and is, therefore, the ground for joy.

This concept becomes familiar in the rabbinic literature, where it is applied to the individual. Thus Rabbi Akiba explains (ca. A.D. 135) that Israel should not behave like the Gentiles, who thank their deity for good and curse the same deity when punishment comes on them:

> But as to you, if I bring good upon you, give thanks, and should I bring suffering upon you, give thanks as well. . . . And furthermore, a person should rejoice in suffering more than in good times. For if someone lives in good times his entire life, he will not be forgiven for such sin as may be in his hand. And how shall he attain forgiveness? Through suffering.[20]

b. A positive view of suffering also emerged where it was understood as a test of the genuineness of one's loyalty to the covenant or as a learning experience for one's betterment. The former is seen in Judith 8:25-27: "Let us give thanks to the Lord our God, who tests (πειράζει) us as he did our fathers. . . . For he has not tested us in fire, as he tested them, to examine their hearts, nor has he taken vengeance on us (ἐπύρωσεν . . . οὐκ ἐξεδίκησεν)." Wis. 3:5-6 is similar: "When they have experienced a little chastening, they will receive great good, because God tested (ἐπείρασεν) them and found them worthy of himself. He proved (ἐδοκίμασεν) them like gold in the furnace. . . ."

The understanding of suffering as a learning experience that serves for one's betterment is certainly intended in *Pss. Sol.* 13:5-12 (*OT Pseudep.* II, 663):

> For he will admonish the righteous as a beloved son
> and his discipline is as for a firstborn.

---

18. Wichmann, *Leidenstheologie,* 41; cf. also Nauck, "Freude im Leiden," 73-76.
19. Cf. Str.-Bill. III, 244f.
20. Mekilta Ex. 56.1 (79b) on Ex. 20:23, cited in Str.-Bill. II, 277, cf. 274; III, 221f.; translation from J. Neusner, *Mekhilta according to Rabbi Ishmael: An Analytical Translation* II (Brown Judaic Studies 151; Atlanta, 1988), 95f.; cf. further, Wichmann, *Leidenstheologie,* 51-69; Lohse, *Märtyrer und Gottesknecht,* 29-32.

For the Lord will spare his devout,
and he will wipe away their mistakes with discipline (vv. 9f.).

This view, which comes into close contact with Hellenistic ideas,[21] is clearly developed in II Macc. 6:12-17, which was written in Greek: "Consider that our people were punished for chastening and not for destruction" (v. 12).

It is also in Greek terms that the martyr gives assurance that he bears bodily suffering joyfully in his soul: "The Lord, who has holy knowledge, understands . . . that I suffer harsh pains in my body from scourging and that I suffer this with gladness in my soul, because I fear him" (II Macc. 6:30). He bears it "gladly" (ἡδέως) also because he sets an example thereby and gives a "memorial of virtue" (v. 31). In IV Macc. 9:29-32 martyrdom becomes entirely the demonstration of the reasonable virtue that is superior to the world and, thereby, the basis for joy: "How sweet (ἡδύς) is any kind of death for the sake of our fathers' righteousness . . . seeing your tyranny's arrogant intention overcome by my endurance for righteousness' sake. . . . I am supported in my pain by the joys (ἡδοναῖς) that come from virtue, while you [the tyrant] are in torment, even while you glory in your godlessness" (cf. 7:22; 11:12). At the same time the Jewish concept of the atoning effect of death is developed further here, perhaps out of Greek thought as well, into an idea of vicarious atonement for the people (IV Macc. 6:27-29; 17:20-22).[22]

c. The Essenes interpreted their sufferings, especially those inflicted by their Jewish adversaries but also those brought on in other ways, in an entirely different manner, though they did associate suffering with joy. The conceptual developments in 1QH 9:9f. are typical: "I declare that your judgments are righteous. For I know your truth and I choose your judgment of me. I delight in having been scourged, because I hope for your kindness." So also 9:24f.: "Your chastisement will become my joy and gladness, and the scourges I have undergone will become eternal healing and endless peace. The scorn of my enemies will become a crown of glory, and my stumbling will become strength without end." Suffering becomes joy because healing, honor, strength, and thereby joy follow it.[23] The one who offers this prayer accepts suffering, knowing that the guilt that brought it on is deserved (9:15, 33) and, above all, that "the spirit of wickedness" must be purged from "the inner part of the flesh" (1QS 4:18ff.; cf. 1QH 11:8). Suffering is like a purifying fire (see above, pp. 313f., n.5). This

---

21. In the Greek world a watchword was πάθει μάθος, "learn through suffering" (Michaelis, *TDNT* V, 906). Later, however, in Hermetic Gnosis the desire is no longer to learn from suffering or, as in Stoicism, to distance oneself from πάθη through ἀπάθεια, but to be taken out of the way of πάσχειν through redemption and apotheosis (Michaelis, *TDNT* V, 907; cf. Lohse, *Märtyrer und Gottesknecht*, 66-69).

22. Lohse, *Märtyrer und Gottesknecht*, 60-72; H. Patsch, *Abendmahl und historischer Jesus* (Stuttgart, 1972), 155-158.

23. Therefore, it makes no essential difference whether one translates "became . . . for joy," so that a historical experience is spoken of (so E. Lohse, *Die Texte aus Qumran* [Darmstadt, 1964], 149) or "will [then] become my joy," i.e., at the consummation.

understanding of suffering as necessary to purify human nature, not only as a result of human failure, calls to mind I Pet. 4:1f., 6 and the mystery religions (see above, pp. 276-278). On the basis of this understanding, the righteous one agrees with the suffering that is experienced, but his joy is focused on God's mercy, which delivers him through it all and opens the door to joy after suffering is over (9:24f.); "infinite mercy accompanies your judgement of me" (9:34).

The Jewish interpretive currents thus developed further the OT interpretation of suffering, each in view of their situation and according to their understanding of the covenantal relationship between God and humankind. They did this in such a way that the solution for suffering includes not only removal of present suffering through future joy but also affirmation of that suffering. Thereby it becomes possible to speak of joy in spite of suffering, joy in the midst of suffering, and joy because of suffering.

It is within this background that the NT statements, which find a new interpretive content for suffering from the perspective of Jesus' beatitude for the persecuted and from his own suffering, came into being. This new content made possible the focal statement in I Pet. 4:13: "Since you take part in Christ's sufferings, rejoice." This admonition was prefigured in Judaism as a rational model. But here it is given an entirely different foundation.[24] Most of all, suffering no longer atones, though it is still judgment (cf. v. 17a).

Just as v. 13 pointed by means of the Pauline concept of "participation" to the partnership with Christ involved in suffering for the sake of faith — and it is the Christ hymns in I Peter that remind the reader of his path — so also the next verse takes up the words of promise from the Jesus tradition about suffering. Vv. 14-16 develop a third reason for seeing grace, the demonstration of God's love, in the midst of suffering: Whoever truly suffers for Christ's sake, the Spirit of glory already rests on that person.

V. 14: Blessing for Humiliation Suffered for Christ's Sake

14 For an understanding of this statement it is instructive to note beforehand the terminological connections between vv. 13 and 14, even though, of course, the verses are not synonymous. The presupposition

---

24. Nauck, "Freude im Leiden," 70-76, concludes on the basis of the relationships in content, arrangement, and terminology of Mt. 5:11f.; Jas. 1:2; I Pet. 1:6f.; 4:13f. that all these passages use the same early Christian tradition and that this tradition was based on a Jewish tradition, which appears only in *II Bar.* 48:49f.; 52:6f. (*OT Pseudep.* I, 637, 639). But one can only say that the interpretation of suffering in I Pet. 4:13f., as incidentally also in v. 17 (see the comments there), comes, within the realm of the Jewish theology of suffering, as close to *II Baruch* as that in I Pet. 4:1f. comes to the Qumran writings. In neither place are the points of contact sufficient to indicate a direct connection in tradition.

of consolation in v. 13 is participation in Christ's sufferings, while here the presupposition is abuse for the sake of the name of Christ. The consolation was represented by "rejoice" there, and by μακάριος, "blessed," "happy," here. The promise in v. 13 is "participation," not only in the suffering Christ, but also in his future; here it is the coming of the Spirit. These points of correspondence show how the same situation and the same experience of salvation are interpreted kerygmatically in different ways with the assistance of different terminology and, standing behind the terms, different forms of thought.

εἰ ὀνειδίζεσθε ἐν ὀνόματι Χριστοῦ, μακάριοι, "If you are reviled for the sake of Christ's name, blessed are you." In essence, this is the same portrayal of the situation as in 3:14, though there the possibility of such abuse is put more moderately in the optative mood: "If you should suffer for the sake of righteousness. . . ."[25] But 4:14 is not formulated with an eye to a specific situation, but was taken over as tradition. It is clearly linked to the last beatitude of Jesus, which as recorded in Mt. 5:11f. (par. Lk.) says: μακάριοί ἐστε ὅταν ὀνειδίσωσιν ὑμᾶς . . . ἕνεκεν ἐμοῦ. χαίρετε καὶ ἀγαλλιᾶσθε, κτλ.[26] ὀνειδίζειν, "abuse," is rare in the NT and is used in this way only in these two passages. Through abuse the perpetrator goes beyond καταλαλεῖν, "slander" (2:12; 3:16) and βλασφημεῖν, "blasphemy" (4:5) and deprives the other of respect and of the right to a place in society.[27]

This now happens to the members of the Church ἐν ὀνόματι Χριστοῦ. This expression, which elsewhere gives authority to the Church's actions, is used here as a foundation on the negative side. ἐν

---

25. In order to buttress his thesis about the altered situation, Beare, 191, understands εἰ here not as in 3:14 in a conditional sense, but as in 2:3: "seeing that." This is an unsubstantiated postulate that contradicts the formal parallelism of the two verses.

26. The final clause, Mt. 5:12, with its imperative χαίρετε is not appropriated here, but perhaps in the previous sentence, I Pet. 4:13; on the whole, however, it does not draw on the Synoptic tradition (see above, n.10).

27. In Rom. 15:3 ("The reproaches of those who reproached you fell on me") the term is used of the ostracism of Jesus on the basis of Ps. 69:10. According to Heb. 11:26; 13:13, one who shares "Christ's humiliation (ὀνειδισμός)" allows himself or herself to be cast out of society as Christ was. This word usage is shaped by the LXX: In Isa. 37:3 the day of misfortune is characterized by four genitives: ἡμέρα θλίψεως καὶ ὀνειδισμοῦ καὶ ἐλεγμοῦ καὶ ὀργῆς. The one who is abused becomes a stranger (Ps. 69:9) and is likened to a lonesome dove (Ps. 102:7f.). The abuse is refuted only through the demonstration of God's salvation, which mediates shalom (Ps. 119:42). But that one of these Psalms passages, namely, Ps. 89:51f., had a direct influence in the shaping of I Pet. 4:14 (so Windisch, 77) cannot be demonstrated.

ὀνόματι surely has the meaning of the rabbinic term לְשֵׁם, "in view of this" or "under the title that," so that it would be the same as saying ἐν ὀνόματι, ὅτι Χριστοῦ ἐστε (Mk. 9:37, 39, 41), i.e., "in view of this, that you belong to Christ."[28] It could be that the author was thinking of either substantive or nominal belonging. Christians are disqualified from society because their lives are oriented to Christ or because they belong nominally to this ill-reputed religion, i.e., according to 4:16, ὡς Χριστιανοί. In concrete situations the two overlap.

Whoever is thus deprived of membership in society is accorded "blessing": to such a person belong life and salvation. On this person "the Spirit of glory, even the Spirit of God"[29] comes to rest: ὅτι τὸ τῆς δόξης καὶ τὸ τοῦ θεοῦ πνεῦμα ἐφ᾽ ὑμᾶς ἀναπαύεται. The Spirit of God is a "Spirit of glory" because it goes forth from the essence of God, from God's glory, and grants participation in that glory to those it rests on. According to II Cor. 3:18, a transformation goes forth from "the Lord of the Spirit . . . from glory to glory." Thus "respect," "glory," and essential existence are given through the eschatological encounter of the Spirit from above to those from whom society's abuse has taken away respect and, thereby, the right to exist.[30] Through the Spirit they now already participate in the glory that they will receive visibly, according to 1:7; 5:4 (cf. II Cor. 4:17; Col. 3:4), at the consummation.[31]

---

28. Cf. BAGD s.v. "ὄνομα" II. In the ancient expression a preexisting traditional formula in the Jesus tradition could have been appropriated, while Mt. 5:11 represents an accommodation to the language of the Church. In the latter the motivation for persecuting those who belong to Jesus is expressed with ἕνεκεν τοῦ ὀνόματός μου (Lk. 21:12, and passim; cf. *Herm. Vis.* 3.1.9; 3.2.1 [LCL AF II, 29f.], and passim) or ἕνεκεν ἐμοῦ (Mt. 5:11).

29. Thus it should surely be translated (so Knopf, 180f.; Windisch, 76; Beare, 192; Schelkle, 124; Kelly, 186f.). The repetition of the article after καί makes the sentence difficult. Therefore, some minuscules have removed καὶ τό and the ancient translations have paraphrased in various ways. The original text has probably not been lost (contra Windisch, Kelly); the difficult formulation is rather the result of the author's augmentation of the familiar expression τὸ τοῦ θεοῦ πνεῦμα with τὸ τῆς δόξης for the sake of the antithesis to humiliation. The added phrase is not an independent substantival expression as, e.g., in Jas. 4:14 (cf. Mt. 21:21; I Cor. 10:24, and others), which would be translated "the presence of glory" and would refer to the Shekinah (contra Wohlenberg, 136f.; Selwyn, 222f.); δόξα has this meaning in the NT at best in Rom. 9:4.

30. The addition after δόξης of καὶ (τῆς) δυνάμεως (αὐτοῦ) has good manuscript support (א, other Alexandrian manuscripts, many others, Clement, Vulgate, syr^h). But this reading is secondary (so Knopf, 180; contra Beare, 192; Kelly, 188) because surely δόξα, "honor," not δύναμις, "power," would be the antithesis of humiliation; the phrase would have been added with formulaic interest in devotional application.

31. According to the account of Stephen's martyrdom, participation in the Spirit is

How did this foundation for the pronouncement of blessing come about? Like all substantive statements of the NT about the Spirit, it may indeed be based on promise and experience. The only promise of the Spirit in the Jesus tradition pledges that the Spirit will give the disciples the right word when they must give account of themselves (Mk. 13:11; Mt. 10:19f.; Lk. 12:11f.). Possibly, therefore, the second half of I Pet. 4:14, just like the first, grew out of a tradition coming from Jesus. It is formulated, nonetheless, in OT terms[32] so that it expresses at the same time the expectation that God will permit the Spirit to "rest" on his people in the eschaton as in primordial time. The accusative case in the phrase ἐφ' ὑμᾶς reflects OT passages, but indicates that ἀναπαύεται is middle voice: "to rest"; thus here a "resting upon" is promised, i.e., not an enduring condition, but a coming of the Spirit to the one assailed for each time at hand.

This kind of statement about the Spirit is harmonious with other statements about the Spirit in the letter, which refers to the Spirit far less frequently than Paul does. It does not speak of a constant presence of the Spirit in the believer or in the Church from which the *charismata* come (cf. 4:10). Except for the formulaic triadic reference to God's activity (1:2), the letter links the Spirit with OT prophecy and the preaching of the gospel, i.e., with the proclamation of the word (1:11f.). It is, therefore, consistent to say that the tradition of the promise of the Spirit is appropriated here with a view particularly to affliction and to Christians' need to give an account of themselves.[33]

It is out of this substantive context that the question posed by 4:14 is clarified: How are abuse and the resting of the Spirit related? Is it correct to say that "the abuses prove that Christians have the Spirit"?[34] If it were, this would mean that the Spirit, as in Paul, would be the constant correlative of faith. But according to I Peter's concept of the

---

shown by the pneumatic-visionary observation of the divine δόξα at the point of death (Acts 7:55f.). The Acts of the Martyrs also record corresponding material: *Mart. Pol.* 2:2 (LCL AF II, 315); *Passio Felicitatis et Perpetuae* 1.3ff. (*ANF* III, 700ff.); the account of the martyrs of Lyons in *HE* 5.1.1ff. (LCL I, 407ff.).

32. In terms of wording it makes use most closely of the messianic promise in Isa. 11:2, but calls to mind not this, but rather accounts from the wilderness wanderings, such as Num. 11:25f.: ἐπανεπαύσατο τὸ πνεῦμα ἐπ' αὐτούς (i.e., the seventy elders). At the same time "the glory" dwelled in Israel in the pillar of cloud during the wilderness period: Ex. 24:17; 29:43; cf. Ps. 89:17 LXX.

33. The statement is formulated with an eye toward Ps. 89:51f. and Isa. 11:2.

34. Windisch, 77.

Spirit and the structure of the pronouncements of blessing, the main part of the verse is a promise: When you are abused you are blessed, since *then* the Spirit comes as support to help you and gives you a share in God's glory.[35]

Vv. 15f.: Suffering as a Christian

15 The introductory μὴ γάρ characterizes vv. 15f. as a commentary that gives foundation to what was just said: "Let none of you suffer, that is (γάρ), as a murderer, etc.": μὴ γὰρ τις ὑμῶν πασχέτω ὡς φονεὺς, κτλ. The promise in v. 14 applies to one who is afflicted in society on account of being a Christian, not to everyone who suffers at the hands of society for other reasons. Like what is said in 2:20 of slaves, this is now explained for wider application in a drastic comparison of relationships. Just as the situation of the Christian slave is pressed to its limits in the experience of chastisement by the master, so too the situation of Christians in general in society finds its extreme in court proceedings against Christians. A "murderer or thief" is arrested on the appropriate charges, brought before the court, and most often, according to ancient law, punished by execution. Christians are not to provoke such action against them, as 3:17 has already made clear, since then they would actually be κακοποιοί, "evildoers" and lawbreakers.[36] They

---

35. Of course, what is referred to here is not future glory, which outweighs present sorrow (as in II Cor. 4:17; cf. Heb. 2:9). A surprisingly close parallel is in Sifre Dt. 6:5 §32 (cf. Str.-Bill. III, 243): "Favored before God are those who suffer, since God's glory rests on the one over whom suffering has come."

A group of manuscripts (P, Koine, many minuscules, Sahidic Coptic, Cyprian) add to v. 14: "among them he is blasphemed, among you glorified." The subject of this remark is the Spirit, not the name of Christ. The addition is a meditative reference to the saying about blasphemy against the Spirit (Mk. 3:28f. par.). See E. Fascher, *Textgeschichte als hermeneutisches Problem* (Halle, 1953), 87f.; P. R. Rodgers, "Longer Reading of 1 Peter 4:14."

36. Here κακοποιός is not alone, as in 2:12, 14, but follows individual transgressions; nevertheless, it surely has the same general meaning: "Let none of you suffer as a murderer, a thief, or [otherwise as] a wrongdoer." A special meaning seems to be supported when Tertullian, *Scorpiace* 12 (*ANF* III, 645f.), and Cyprian, *Ad Quirinum* 3.37 (*ANF* V, 529), translate it with "maleficus." This Latin word had on occasion the special meaning "magician" (Lactantius, *Divinae Institutiones* 2.16.4 [*ANF* VII, 64f.]; Jerome, *Commentariorum in Danielem* [Corpus Christianorum, Series Latina 75A; Turnhout, 1964] 2.2 [p. 784]; *Theodosian Code* 9.16.4 [*The Theodosian Code,* tr. C. Pharr (Princeton, 1952), 237]). Knopf, 181, and Windisch, 77, among others, posit this special meaning here for κακοποιός (cf. Bauer, "Aut maleficus"). It is probable, however, that Tertullian and Cyprian simply wanted to reproduce the Greek word verbatim with a Latin one. Nothing suggests that κακοποιός,

are also not to act as ἀλλοτρι(ο)επίσκοποι in a manner inappropriate to the social situation; they are not to pour new wine into old wineskins by fanaticism like that of Zealots, Pharisees, or Cynics. The sense of the word, which has not been located elsewhere independent of I Peter[37] — and of the whole sentence — depends entirely on this question: Is the sentence to be understood as a rhetorical antithesis, used to make clear two fundamentally different kinds of suffering under social circumstance,[38] or as a realistic warning not to bring shame on the name of Christ through criminal conduct?[39] It appears that while the beginning "murderers and thieves" is schematic-rhetorical, the warning not to become κακοποιοί is, in accord with 3:16, meant to be taken seriously, and this applies even more with regard to ἀλλοτριεπίσκοπος.

This perspective could be extended by our own observations and experiences. Does a given persecuted person suffer *only* for Christ's sake and not also for his or her own self-will and need to show off? Conduct is never free of second and third motives. But this verse does not intend primarily to provoke such probing of one's own behavior. It seeks to summon a person in a conflict situation to conduct that adheres not to its own possibilities, but to the promise of God.[40]

---

for which, moreover, the special meaning of the Latin word is not found anywhere else, should have a different meaning here than elsewhere in the letter.

37. The word was perhaps coined by the author; the root ἐπισκεπτ- is familiar to him (2:25; 5:2 v.l.). It is, in any case, one of the many compounds built with ἀλλοτριο- referring to conduct that in the face of hostility does not give the wrongdoer what is due. So H. W. Beyer, "ἐπισκέπτομαι, ἀλλοτριεπίσκοπος," *TDNT* II, 620-622; on the discussion, see BAGD s.v. (bibliography); Windisch, 77 (excursus on 4:15); S. Wibbing, *Die Tugend- und Lasterkataloge im NT* (BZNW 25; Berlin, 1959), 97. Even the Old Latin translators understood it in this sense: "aliene speculator" (Tertullian, *Scorpiace* 12 [*ANF* III, 645f.]); "curas alienas agens" (Cyprian, *Ad Quirinum* 3.37 [*ANF* V, 529]); "alienorum adpetitor" (Vulgate). What concepts the author connected with the word cannot be deciphered exactly. The commentaries offer conjectures from "secret police-agent," "informer," "missionary enthusiast" guilty of disturbing the peace (breaking and entering; Knopf, 181f.; Windisch, 77; Kelly, 188f.) to "proletarian revolutionary" (Knopf, 181f.; possibly also Beare, 193). Any attempt to make the word's meaning precise must take into account, in any case, that it is set in contrast by a further ὡς to the criminal examples listed before it; it is to be understood along the lines of other warnings against misguided leadership in society.

38. So Kelly, 191f., except for ὡς ἀλλοτριεπίσκοπος.

39. Holding to this possibility is Schelkle, 12, pointing to other warnings not reproduced in the catalogues of vices that were simply passed on: I Cor. 5:1-8; Eph. 4:28; cf. also I Cor. 5:9-13; 6:9-11; Eph. 5:3-12.

40. Already Basilides relativized the differentiation of bases emphasized by I Pet. 4:15 in his thesis that all evil has its basis in debt (apud Clement of Alexandria, *Stromata* 4.12, §217 [*ANF* II, 423-425]).

16 Therefore, even the positive statement in v. 16 is ambivalent for us, though not for the author: εἰ δὲ ὡς Χριστιανός (πάσχει), "But if one suffers as a Christian. . . ." Here a historical question arises directly from the text: Were Christians condemned for behaving as Christians or because they belonged to the Christian religious community? Χριστιανοί, "Christians," are, at least in the eyes of non-Christians, those who believe; the designation was coined and applied by outsiders, not by the Church.[41] Christians were, therefore, treated and condemned as criminals because they bore the name of Christian and because they lived as such — though the two things are surely not to be separated.

The fundamental conflict with the existing social situation, as the accounts in Acts and the references in the Pauline Epistles show, led repeatedly to intervention by the police and the courts. But the phrase ὡς Χριστιανός presupposes that Christians were known to the public as representatives of a strange and questionable religion; this was the case in the region between Rome and Asia Minor, the area addressed by I Peter, only after the police action of Nero in A.D. 64.[42] One ought not, on the other hand, press the statement so that it must presuppose Trajan's edict, according to which the *nomen ipsum* was worthy of punishment.[43] Even Nero's police action focused on the "name," and the sayings in the Gospels about persecution, formulated between 65 and 80, speak of Jesus' disciples being afflicted "for the sake of his name" (Mt. 5:11f.) and being brought before the courts (Mt. 10:17-22; Mk. 13:9-13 par. Lk. 21:12-17; Lk. 12:11f.). On the basis of these presuppositions it is possible to examine more exactly when in the history of early Christianity the situation reflected here existed.[44]

---

41. The designation Χριστιανοί is found first in Acts 11:26; 26:28; I Pet. 4:16; *Did.* 12:4 (LCL AF I, 329); Ignatius, *Eph.* 11:2; *Rom.* 3:2f.; *Pol.* 7:3 (*ibid.,* 187, 229, 275f.) and in Tacitus, *Annales* 15.44 (LCL IV, 283f.); Suetonius, *Nero* 16.2 (LCL I, 111); Pliny, *Epistulae* 10.96.1-3 (LCL II, 401f.); Lucian, *Alexander* 25.38 (LCL IV, 209, 223f.); *De Morte Peregrini* 11ff., 16 (LCL V, 13ff., 19). ‎א* reads Χρηστιανός here, reflecting the frequent confusion among non-Christians of "Christian" with a Latin name (Suetonius, *Claudius* 25 [LCL II, 53]: "impulsore Chresto").

42. Dibelius, "Rom und die Christen," especially 189ff.; J. Zeiller, "Institutum Neronianum — Hirngespinst oder Wirklichkeit?" *Das frühe Christentum im römischen Staat* (ed. R. Klein, WdF 267; Darmstadt, 1971), 236-243; Moreau, *Christenverfolgung,* 33ff.; Selwyn, "Persecutions"; Knox, "Pliny"; see also McCaughey, "Persecution Documents"; Losada, "Sufrir por el nombre."

43. Contra Beare, 193, according to whom 3:16 is concerned with debate over the content of being a Christian, but 4:16 with the public persecution of the name. This distinction is foreign to the text.

44. See the Introduction, pp. 41ff. above.

If a person is prosecuted and condemned in this way "as a Christian," "then he or she should not be ashamed,[45] but should glorify God through this name": μὴ αἰσχυνέσθω, δοξαζέτω δὲ τὸν θεὸν ἐν τῷ ὀνόματι τούτῳ. The condemnation is not shameful, not because the norms of society from which it arose are violated in each case, but because, in the opinion of the author, those norms were applied slanderously. But the opponents of the Christians see the situation more correctly than this: The Christians were certainly not lawbreakers like "murderers and thieves," but they did break with the social principle of life of the Hellenistic world, the fundamental principle of syncretism. The Christians arrested because of Nero's accusation were, to be sure, not convicted of arson, but of "hatred against humankind."[46]

With the concluding clause of the verse, the author himself surpasses his own comments regarding society. The parenetic consequence he draws is not that the Christian should regard condemnation as one's own glory, in the manner of a social-political revolutionary. Rather, one should "glorify God by means of this name."[47] The "name" is not "Christ," as in v. 14, but "Christian." One gives glory to God by acknowledging his or her identity of "Christian," by accepting the condemnation and bearing this name in that way. One's suffering, from accusation to execution of the sentence, like one's conduct in general according to 2:12, should be a witness — and has, indeed, been such.

For the author, the persecuted become witnesses, not as the blameless righteous do, who only have been misunderstood, but as people of faith, whose hope points to grace (1:13), who themselves have a share in the darkness and evil that lead to confrontation and suffering. This also becomes visible in the interpretation of suffering in the next verses: Christian suffering is not only grace, affirmation, and the strengthening of the bond with Christ, but is also judgment on the old person.

---

45. The reference is not connected tradition-historically with the saying about being ashamed (Mk. 8:38 par.; Lk. 12:9 par.; cf. II Tim. 1:8, 12), though it is related in content: Whoever is ashamed of condemnation for being a Christian must also be ashamed of Christ, i.e., must distance himself or herself from Christ.

46. See above, p. 43, n.114.

47. ἐν τῷ ὀνόματι is used instrumentally here, not, as in v. 14, "in this condition," i.e., as a Christian (Selwyn, 225f.), or "on account of," i.e., because this person was called to suffer as a Christian (Kelly 190f.). The weakly attested (P, Koine, many others) textual gloss ἐν τῷ μέρει τούτῳ, "in this respect," cannot be used to support the latter.

Vv. 17-19: The Beginning of Judgment with the Household of God

17a ὅτι ὁ καιρὸς (sc. ἐστιν) τοῦ ἄρξασθαι τὸ κρίμα ἀπὸ τοῦ οἴκου τοῦ θεοῦ. One should translate ὅτι here with "that is," since v. 17a gives the basis, not specifically for the preceding statement in v. 16, but as an additional argument for the theme of the entire section: The outlaw status given by society to Christians is not inappropriate, and, therefore, also no shame; it is, rather, an occasion to glorify God and not oneself (v. 16), to humble oneself, therefore, before God (cf. 5:6).

In I Peter whether ὁ καιρός, "the time,"[48] represents a point in time or a period of time is not definite. Therefore, the word is made more precise in 1:5 by an adjective (the coming "final time"), in 1:11 by a relative clause (the prophesied time of fulfillment), and here by an infinitive,[49] while it is used adverbially in 5:6. Here it is the time in which judgment — τὸ κρίμα used absolutely refers to final judgment[50] — "begins with the household of God." What the Church encounters now as affliction that obstructs and destroys life is seen in the larger picture of vv. 17-18 as a process that is continuous with the imminent, universal final judgment, to which the letter refers elsewhere with emphasis (1:17; 2:23; 4:5). In I Peter the judgment is not merely the forensic grand finale, but also the intervention into history that precedes, that puts things in order, and that brings about history's end.

This judgment "begins with the household of God." This graphic expression borrows from OT prophecy, though without a particular passage in mind.[51] οἶκος τοῦ θεοῦ represents the temple in the OT (Ezek. 9:6: "my sanctuary"). But in I Peter, e.g., the metaphorical usage in 2:5, it refers to the Church; in 4:17b "beginning with God's household" is echoed by "first among *us*" (πρῶτον ἀφ᾽ ἡμῶν).

---

48. The article before καιρός is to be preferred over anarthrous καιρός because of its attestation in 𝔭[72], B, Koine, etc. But this is not of importance for the meaning. Cf. Selwyn, 135, at 1:11.

49. So also Lk. 1:57 and elsewhere, e.g., *Ep. Arist.* 221 (*OT Pseudep.* II, 27).

50. κρίμα, "judgment," used only here in I Peter, has, like κρίνειν (see the comments on 1:17; 2:23; 4:5f.), the double meaning "juridical action" and "juridical decision (usually condemnation)." Here the thought is of God's final juridical action; his judgment is carried out initially in history, at the end of which the forensic act stands. This final juridical action is designated in other passages of the NT as the "eternal" (Heb. 6:2) or the "future" κρίμα.

51. In Ezek. 9:6 LXX it is said to those who are to carry out the judgment on Jerusalem: ἀπὸ τῶν ἁγίων μου ἄρξασθε. Cf. Jer. 25:29 (LXX 32:29): ἐν πόλει ἐν ᾗ ὠνομάσθη τὸ ὄνομά μου ἐπ᾽ αὐτὴν ἐγὼ ἄρχομαι κακῶσαι. Cf. also Mal. 3:1-6. The rabbinic parallel mentioned by Str.-Bill. III, 767, is merely verbal.

The καιρός is for I Peter, therefore, not the time of the woes that precedes the final judgment according to apocalyptic passages (Mk. 13:8-13 par.) and brings with it the persecution of the Church (Mk. 13:9 par.), but the "specific time" announced by prophecy, namely the end time, in which final judgment gets underway.[52] For the Church, this time is not one of the last stages of its path within the framework of an apocalyptic time plan, but something that, along with the Church's eschatological existence (1:11f.), has always been a reality, just as the "end" has always been "near" (4:7). Therefore, 4:17a explains the affliction that has come on the Church differently than early Christian apocalypticism; I Peter does not set the affliction into an apocalyptic picture of history, and division into periods, which might make calculation possible, is also rejected. The letter seeks, rather, to explain the affliction with the aid of meditation on OT prophecy and its view of history. How, then, did this interpretation come about?

Persecution of Christians as Judgment: Origin of the View[53]

1. I Pet. 4:17a is linked to the OT, but it has so little connection with the LXX (see n.51), which the author otherwise follows, that its formulation is certainly dependent on Christian tradition, not directly on Ezek. 9:6.

2. Only I Cor. 11:32 can be named in the NT as connected with I Pet. 4:17a. There noteworthy cases of sickness and sudden death in the Church are explained as the result of receiving the Lord's Supper to κρίμα (v. 29), and then it is added: "If we are judged by the Lord, then we will also be chastened, so that we are not condemned with the world." This passage expresses independently an OT and Jewish area of thought, just as does I Pet. 4:17.

3. OT prophecy taught that Israel's defeat and national collapse should be understood as the judgment of God, which happened precisely to the elect people of the covenant on account of its failure; it interpreted this judgment, moreover, as a sign that God judges all peoples.[54]

4. This OT concept was extended in various directions in Jewish writings:

a. First-century apocalyptic writings develop the idea that Israel's contem-

---

52. So Beare, 193f.; Kelly, 192f.; contra Schelkle, 125f., though Kelly obliterates the distinction by characterizing I Cor. 11:31f. as only a "variation" of the concept of the woes.

53. See above, n.16; see also F. Büchsel, "κρίνω, κρίμα," *TDNT* III, 942f.; W. Eichrodt, *Theology of the OT* I (tr. J. Baker; Philadelphia, 1961), 457-471; K. Koch, "Gibt es ein Vergeltungsdogma im AT?," *ZThK* 52 (1955), 1-42; *idem,* "Sühne und Sündenvergebung um die Wende von der exilischen zur nachexilischen Zeit," *EvTh* 26 (1966), 217-239.

54. Amos 1:3–2:16 is fundamental (cf. H. W. Wolff, *Joel and Amos* (tr. W. Janzen, S. McBride, Jr., and C. Muenchow, Hermeneia; Philadelphia, 1977]), 172 on 2:16; Ezek. 21:1-10.

porary misfortune is a suffering of punishment that atones for its transgressions; through this suffering the elect are to be preserved in the imminent, universal judgment of the nations. This concept comes to the fore in *II Baruch;* 13:1-12 (*OT Pseudep.* I, 625f.), e.g., says to the nations, for whom all goes well in the present: "Therefore, he did not spare his own sons first, but he afflicted them as his enemies because they sinned. Therefore they were once punished, that their sins might be removed [*OT Pseudep.:* "that they might be forgiven"]. But now, you nations and tribes, you are guilty, because you have trodden the earth all this time, and because you have used creation unrighteously" (vv. 9-11).[55]

b. The Qumran documents also divide judgment, but not between Israel and the nations, but between the repenting righteous ones and the "wicked ones." 1QS 4:18-21: "God has ordained an end for falsehood. At the time of visitation he will destroy it forever [cf. 5:10-13]. . . . (The world) has wallowed in wickedness during the reign of falsehood until the appointed time of judgment. . . . Then God will purify every human deed with his truth. He will refine humankind for himself by rooting out every spirit of falsehood from human flesh." 1QH 8:30f.: "Flames devour me for days on end, weakening me and destroying my flesh endlessly." 1QH 9:10: "I choose your judgment of me, and I delight in having been scourged, because I hope for your kindness." 1QH 11:8-10: "In your anger are all chastisements, but in your goodness is much forgiveness. . . . For the sake of your glory you have purified humankind from sin."

c. In the rabbinic literature everything is finally to be settled in a settling of accounts over good and evil deeds in the forensic judgment. Suffering receives, however, substantial consideration in the process as atonement for sins.[56]

5. This material indicates that what I Pet. 4:17 says about the final judgment first affecting the elect and then others is a well-known OT and Jewish concept. The statement of this concept in I Peter is related more to OT prophecy than to Jewish statements, since the focus of the latter on a final settling of accounts through atonement is absent from I Peter.

The interpretation of suffering as judgment is seen in the development of thought in I Pet. 4:1-6: According to v. 6, suffering should eliminate from the flesh the drive that lusts against the Creator (vv. 1f.). This anthropological interpretation has only minor points of correspondence in the Qumran writings, as became clear above (see 4b above and pp. 277f.). I Pet. 4:17 was formulated in conversation with

---

55. Cf. *II Bar.* 32:5 (*OT Pseudep.* I, 631), a word of comfort to Israel: "We should not, therefore, be so sad regarding the evil which has come now, but much more (distressed) regarding that which is in the future"; 78:6 (*ibid.,* 648): "Therefore, if you think about the things you have suffered now for your good so that you may not be condemned at the end and be tormented. . . ." This sequence of the judgment is also maintained according to *Test. Benj.* 10:8f. (*ibid.,* 828) at the final judgment after the resurrection: ". . . for the Lord first judges Israel for the wrong she has committed and then he shall do the same for all the nations."

56. Lohse, *Märtyrer und Gottesknecht,* especially 18-58; Str.-Bill. I, 417f.; see above, n.20.

the OT. But the statement is also, in keeping with the situation, focused on the individual: Those who confront the addressees are not the nations, but, like "the wicked" in the Essene documents, "those who are disobedient to the gospel." The focus in 4:17 is the intensification of the further realization of judgment. Therefore, the characterization of suffering as judgment is clearly not connected, as in Jewish texts, to joy arising from anticipation (pp. 316f.), but by implication to fear, in which nothing is left but to "entrust one's soul to the faithful Creator" (v. 19).

17b   "But if first with us" the judgment begins,[57] "what then will be the end of those who are disobedient to the gospel?" οἱ ἀπειθοῦντες τῷ τοῦ θεοῦ εὐαγγελίῳ are not non-Christians as such, but those who reject the gospel and express this rejection especially in aggression against Christians (cf. 2:7f.; 3:1). "What will their end be," i.e., the end of their path (τὶ τὸ τέλος)? It will be an incomparably more severe judgment than that which now affects Christians (cf. Lk. 23:31). The intensification of judgment toward the end is a fixed apocalyptic schema (cf. Revelation, passim). What are the readers to conclude from this reflection?

The statement has a counterpart in both theme and formulation in II Thess. 1:4-10 (which is post-Pauline), where an early Christian tradition is also seen. It is all the more instructive that there the connection between Christian suffering of persecution and future judgment of those who "do not know God and do not obey . . . the gospel" is portrayed in quite different terms: Christian suffering of persecution is "a sign of God's righteous judgment" over the persecutors (1:5) because it summons forth God's compensatory reward (1:6).

But I Peter does not point the readers to compensatory justice; it seeks, rather, to induce fear before God's exercise of judgment, which affects Christians along with the "disobedient." The Church is to weigh the terror of the imminent, universal judgment in terms of the suffering it has already experienced and to learn thereby fear of the One "who can destroy soul and body" (Mt. 10:28 par.). It would not be costly enough just for Christians to rejoice in the grace that visited them in the suffering to which they were called in 4:13f. What they are to do further — and what also belongs to the experience of suffering persecution — is to fear the One "who judges without respect of persons" (1:17). This fear excludes any kind of evasion in the face of conflict. Whoever evades the burden now can only expect a heavier one.

---

57. The clause is surely to be expanded: ἄρχεται τὸ κρίμα.

Whoever now, in order to avoid conflict, forfeits eschatological existence will become subject to the incomparably greater terror of the imminent eschaton.

18 What has just been said is now underscored in a Scripture quotation. Prov. 11:31 is reproduced almost verbatim according to the LXX:[58] καὶ εἰ ὁ δίκαιος μόλις σῴζεται, ὁ δὲ ἀσεβὴς καὶ ἁμαρτωλὸς ποῦ φανεῖται. This passage says for the author in different words what he himself has formulated in v. 17b. The parallelism between vv. 17b and 18 makes clear how the author intended that his OT quotations be understood. He views these OT expressions from the perspective of the gospel, but he wants, thereby, to let them express precisely their original intention. Therefore, "the just one" is, in accordance with the OT, one who does justice to his or her relationship to God. This happens in the OT through conduct in accord with the covenant of law, here through a life in accord with the gospel, i.e., speech and deed on the basis of faith (cf. 3:12). "Godless and a sinner" is now the one who is "disobedient to the gospel," who rejects the gospel and demonstrates this especially by estrangement toward a manner of life corresponding to the gospel (4:4). The "salvation" of the just and the "exposure" of the sinner was, for the OT, the turning point in existence; in I Peter it is the outcome of eschatological judgment.

In judgment even the "just one," the believer, is "barely saved" (μόλις σῴζεται). This OT accent is also important in I Peter. From a somewhat different perspective than Mk. 13:19f., the author may have been thinking about the possibility of failure (cf. 5:8f.) that accompanies the serious testing of faith that suffering under the pressure of society brings (1:6; 4:12). But in any case he believed that the universal judgment is even for the believer not a self-evident passageway, but a serious experience of being called into question, from which one is delivered only by boundless grace; on this grace one may place one's hope on account of God's faithfulness (1:17; 4:5; cf. Rom. 5:9f.; I Cor. 3:15).

If it is so difficult even for the believer to be delivered into life, then "where will the one be seen" (ποῦ φανεῖται) who rejects the gospel? Such a one will be cast out from the fellowship with God that means

---

58. Following εἰ ὁ the LXX's μέν is missing; on the other hand, δέ is inserted between ὁ and ἀσεβής in some manuscripts. The Hebrew text reads: "if the righteous is requited on earth [in the land], how much more the wicked and the sinner!" φανεῖται is "appear," "to be seen" (BAGD s.v.), as in Mt. 9:33.

life (cf. Mt. 25:41, 46; Rev. 20:15). Whoever sees the *de facto* available possibilities in this way will cling in this situation of history's final hour, in spite of all affliction, to the one thing that endures, namely, the word of the gospel (1:24f.).

19 Here the parenetic conclusion is drawn from vv. 17f. as well as from the entire section: ὥστε καί, "consequently," Christians should "also,"[59] especially in the affliction brought on them by society, entrust their "souls" to God. As the section has revealed, one experiences in this affliction not something strange or incongruous, but what is, in accord with God's plan of salvation, God's grace and God's judgment. Within the framework and meaning of this plan, even individual encounters do reflect not just human caprice but "the will of God." For this reason the author now refers to οἱ πάσχοντες κατὰ τὸ θέλημα τοῦ θεοῦ. As in 1:6 and 3:17, what is thought of here is God's providence, which shapes the individual encounter, not the general plan of salvation just developed but its application.[60] This special providence is neither blind fate nor care analogous to that of a human father, but judgment and grace in the sense of the gospel. Because God's grace and judgment encounter them in this way, even in the shaping of individual encounters through human caprice, the afflicted are to "entrust their souls to the faithful Creator": ὥστε . . . πιστῷ κτίστῃ παρατιθέσθωσαν τὰς ψυχὰς αὐτῶν.

The ψυχαί are, as in 1:9; 3:20, the personal entities that continue to exist as potentiality beyond bodily death. Christians are to "entrust" (παρατίθεσθαι) this their self to God as one hands over a valuable object to a reliable person for safekeeping (cf. παραθήκη in I Tim. 6:20).[61] This summons not only appropriates a conventional expression, but also aligns itself with the prayer in Ps. 31:6, which in the context of similar affliction also refers to God's faithfulness (though not directly with its application to Jesus in Lk. 23:46).[62]

---

59. καί is to be linked with the adjacent οἱ πάσχοντες, not with παρατιθέσθωσαν.

60. So Selwyn, 226f.; contra Cranfield, 122f.

61. παρατίθεμαι, middle voice, "hand over" something to someone (as a deposit), "entrust" (Lk. 12:48; I Tim. 1:18; II Tim. 2:2), "commit" someone to the protection or care of another (Acts 14:23; 20:32); between these two meanings: Lk. 23:46; I Pet. 4:19. Thus already in extrabiblical Greek (C. Maurer, "τίθημι, παρατίθημι," *TDNT* VIII, 162f.).

62. "To commit (someone) to God('s care)" was a standard expression (Acts 14:23; 20:32; cf. 7:59; *I Clem.* 27:1 [LCL AF I, 55]). It is expanded in Ps. 30:6 LXX: εἰς χεῖράς σου παραθήσομαι τὸ πνεῦμά μου ἐλυτρώσω με, κύριε ὁ θεὸς τῆς ἀληθείας; Lk. 23:46: εἰς χεῖράς σου παρατίθεμαι τὸ πνεῦμά μου.

Though this is the only place in the NT where God is designated as "Creator" (κτίστης),[63] creating is consistently spoken of, in various ways, as God's fundamental manifestation as God (Rom. 4:17; Rev. 4:11). In regard to preservation of human life, the sayings of Jesus against worrying, with which I Pet. 5:7 is aligned, already referred to God's governance as Creator. One can "entrust" his or her very self to the Creator because he is not only powerful in creation, but also "faithful" (πιστός); entrusting answers to faithfulness. The Creator has bound himself to his creatures through covenant promises and has shown himself to be faithful in relation to them (I Pet. 1:5; 5:10); this faithfulness is the foundation of all faith and hope.[64] The author of I Peter knows God because he made himself accessible as the "Father of Jesus Christ" (1:2f.), so that he can be called on in prayer as "Father" (1:17). Precisely because Christians "have been born anew" by him (1:3), they know God as the Creator,[65] who also gives and shapes historical life (2:13); they entrust their selves to God's power and faithfulness as Creator, therefore, in the suffering that threatens to extinguish and to

---

63. In the LXX: II Kgdms. 22:32; Sir. 24:8; II Macc. 1:24f.; 7:23; IV Macc. 5:25; 11:5; among the Apostolic Fathers: *I Clem.* 19:2 (LCL AF I, 43). Rom. 1:25; Col. 3:10 have instead ὁ κτίσας. For other circumlocutions see W. Foerster, "κτίζω," *TDNT* III, 1028f.

64. Pointing to it otherwise in the NT is above all Paul: Rom. 9:6; 11:29; II Cor. 1:18; cf. I Cor. 1:9; 10:13; I Thess. 5:24; also II Tim. 2:13; Heb. 10:23.

65. The basis given by Jesus for his saying against worrying (Mt. 6:25-34 par. Lk.) is in the final analysis God's eschatological dominion, which gives life ultimately in the sense of the requests of the Lord's Prayer (6:32f.). The Creator's care, to which reference is initially made, becomes comprehensible and certain by this One now establishing his eschatological dominion. Furthermore, after the saying about sparrows, which is directed against fear of persecution (Mt. 10:29-31 par. Lk.), Q places the eschatological promise for the one who confesses (Mt. 10:23f. par. Lk.).

This trust in the Creator's loyal care, which Jesus makes possible anew from the dimension of God's eschatological coming, has an extensive prehistory in the OT and Jewish tradition. For the OT, see Eichrodt, *Theology* II, 118-131. Among Jewish writings, *II Bar.* 21:3-25 (*OT Pseudep.* I, 628): ". . . I began to speak in the presence of the Mighty One, and said, 'O hear me, you who created the earth, . . . who causes the rain to fall on earth with a specific number of raindrops [and who knows] the end of times before it has arrived. Hear my prayer. For only you can sustain those who exist. . . . And now, show your glory soon and do not postpone that which was promised by you." II Esdr. 6:6: "They were created through me alone and no other, as the end will come through me alone and no other."

The rabbinic analogies mentioned by Str.-Bill. I, 435ff., 582ff., speak, unlike Jesus' sayings, of the preservation of the world in accord with a fixed plan. See A. Hamman, "La foi chrétienne au Dieu de la création," *NRTh* 86 (1964), 1049-1057; H. Bald, *Eschatologie und Schöpfung. Untersuchungen zum Problem des Gottesgedankens Jesu* (Dissertation, Munich, 1976), especially 183-218.

make meaningless their existence (cf. *I Clem.* 27:1 [LCL AF I, 54f.]). How God preserves them through to the conclusion of his judgment, faith leaves up to him.

This "handing over" of one's own "I" to the Creator, which liberates a person from fear, takes place, amid the danger of losing one's life, through prayer and through action arising from hopeful faith. Prayer is alluded to in the underlying Psalm passage (cf. Lk. 23:46); action is expressly mentioned in conclusion in what has become the keyword in I Peter: One hands over one's self ἐν ἀγαθοποιΐᾳ, "through just conduct." This word is defined by its usage earlier in I Peter (2:14, 15, 20; 3:6, 17; cf. 2:12; 3:13): what is intended here, too, is not general "doing good in love and service,"[66] but just conduct in society. Understood thus, the appeal has the specificity that corresponds to the letter's intention. "Just conduct" in society, even under "suffering," is required here for all, as it was urged on slaves, in their particular situation, in 2:20. "Suffering" (πάσχοντες) includes here, according to the context, the possibility of "suffering unto death," but, as the summons to just conduct shows, it is certainly not limited to it. The interpretation of suffering in I Peter is not intended just to "comfort," but to equip one for ἀγαθοποιΐα.

After this appeal for "just conduct" in society, even on the part of those who suffer, an appeal that is finally motivated by divine judgment, comes parenetic instruction about the life of the community similar to what is in 4:7-11.

5:1-5: Church Leaders[1]

1 *Now I admonish the elders among you*
  as a co-elder and witness of Christ's sufferings
  and as a participant in the glory soon to be revealed:
2 *Shepherd the flock of God among you and work as overseers,*
  not out of compulsion, but willingly — in conformity with God —
  not for shameful gain, but with dedication,

---

66. Contra Cranfield, 123; Spicq, 161f.

1. See Goppelt, *Apostolic,* 183f.; Nauck, "Probleme des frühchristlichen Amtsverständnisses"; E. Schweizer, *Church Order in the NT* (SBT 32, tr. F. Clarke; Naperville, IL, 1961), especially 110-112; J. Roloff, *Apostolat—Verkündigung—Kirche* (Gütersloh, 1965), 264-269; K. Kertelge, *Gemeinde und Amt im NT* (Munich, 1972), 144-148; Elliott, "Ministry and Church Order in the NT."

3 *not as those who rule over what is allotted,*
but as those who become examples for the flock.
4 *Then when the chief Shepherd appears*
you will receive the unfading garland of glory.

5 *Similarly, you who are younger,*
make yourselves subject to the elders.

All, in relation to one another,
put on humility.
For "God resists the proud,
but gives grace to the humble." (Prov. 3:34)

Form, Tradition, and Historical Situation

In this parenetic instruction to elders, to those who are "younger," and to all the members of the Church (vv. 1-4, 5a, 5b), the three segments are marked off by form, tradition, and content:

1. The words to the elders in vv. 1-4 recall, especially in vv. 2b-c and 3, the statements on the bishop and the deacon in the Pastoral Epistles (I Tim. 3:[1]2-7, 8-13; Tit. 1:[5f.]7-9). The section as a whole, however, is stylistically comparable neither to such texts in the Pastorals nor to later Church orders, but to the testamentary parenesis of Paul to the elders at Ephesus in Acts 20:17-36 and to Timothy in II Timothy. Indeed, it has so much in common with the substantive *topoi* with the farewell address in Acts 20 that one parenetic schema must have served as the traditional basis for both.

a. The intention of v. 1 is understandable against the backdrop of this tradition. Here alone in I Peter — opening and closing statements excluded — the author refers to himself. "Co-elder" and "witness" are not to be understood psychologically as a spontaneous solicitation for sympathy and authority among the Church leaders. Use of them emerges, rather, out of the givens of the parenetic schema and its intention in response to the Church situation as a whole. In Acts 20:18-22, 31 as well, the Apostle reminds the elders that he himself has carried out the service that is now given in commission to them. According to vv. 18, 21, 24 his service was a διαμαρτύρεσθαι under the suffering of persecution. Here also "Peter" is called μάρτυς τῶν τοῦ Χριστοῦ παθημάτων. Therefore, he addresses the elders as co-elder and witness in order to designate their commission as part of his own. They are to continue his service as shepherd to the individual congregation. They are able to do this only when they, as he, though to a different extent, become witnesses of Christ's sufferings.

I Peter appropriates here, just like the speech in Acts 20 and II Timothy, reflection on the relationship of the apostolic office, which is recognized in the Church as foundational, to the offices of service in local congregations, which emerged independently of the apostolic office. Such reflection became the key question for the understanding of ecclesiastical office in the second century. This *topos,* already provided by tradition, is formulated in I Pet. 5:1-5 in accord with the kerygma of the letter so that the involvement of elders and apostle in the congregation's situation (4:13) and in the path of Jesus (1:11) becomes clear: All travel the path through "suffering" to "glory" that Christ followed and to which he leads (3:18).

b. The commission of the elders is expressed, first of all, in v. 2a in the same language as in Acts 20:28: ποίμνιον, ποιμαίνειν, ἐπισκέπτεσθαι, and the promise with which the directive for the elders closes in v. 4 uses the same language as Acts 20:32, though "inheritance" is promised there, while here what is promised is "the garland of glory." Behind vv. 2a and 4 an Essene tradition using the same language becomes visible.

Between those verses, in vv. 2b-c and 3, proper conduct in office is expressed in three symmetrically arranged and formulated antitheses, which to this day are used formulaically in the Church. In content they recall the statements about bishops in the Pastorals more than they do Acts 20. αἰσχροκερδῶς in 5:2, e.g., returns verbatim in I Tim. 3:8; Tit. 1:7 and is seen only in terms of subject matter in Acts 20:33ff. The tradition behind these antitheses is not Jewish, but Hellenistic and early Christian.[2]

c. The same stage in the historical development of Church offices is reflected in Acts 20 and I Pet. 5:1-4. In both the elders (as in Jas. 5:14) are the only congregational office holders. The institution of elders, the presbyterate, came from the Palestinian Church (Acts 21:18), but assumes the function of the overseer that grew up in the Pauline realm (Phil. 1:1). In the Pastorals a further stage of development is already seen: Those among the elders who work actively as "administrative heads" and especially those involved in "preaching and teaching" are emphasized (I Tim. 5:17). A corresponding differentiation among elders can be observed in *I Clement* (54:2; 57:1 [LCL AF I, 100f., 106f.]). This differentiation led to the hierarchical gradation presupposed in the letters of Ignatius soon after A.D. 100 in the area addressed by I Peter: The elders and deacons stand beneath an overseer (*Magn.* 6:1; 13:1; *Trall.* 2 [*ibid.,* 200f., 208f., 212-215], and passim). In relation to these later developments, I Peter and Acts represent an earlier congregational administrative structure that was typical for the area from Rome to Asia Minor during the period A.D. 65-80. Any difference in this can hardly be discerned between I Peter and Acts 20; the congregational organization reflected in I Peter 5 is, in any case, not later, but probably earlier than that of Acts 20.[3]

---

2. See below, pp. 345-347.

3. G. Bornkamm makes the opposite conclusion ("πρέσβυς, πρεσβύτερος," *TDNT* VI, 666): The emphasis with which I Pet. 5:2f. refers to the temptations of the office of elder shows that "the office was more developed and fixed" than in Acts 20:17ff. Missing from this view, however, is a valid criterion. Such a criterion is the increasing involvement of

Further contributions to the development of organizational shape are to be drawn from v. 5.

2. The directive in v. 5a to those who are "younger" is distinguished from what precedes in style and content. The exegetical riddles that the verse poses are answered to a degree by recognition that the verse is in the stylistic form of the station codes. The transitional particle ὁμοίως, which cannot be explained by the logic of the context, is derived from that form, as πάντες δέ in v. 5b (cf. 3:1: ὁμοίως γυναῖκες . . . ; 3:7: οἱ ἄνδρες ὁμοίως . . . ; 3:8: τὸ δὲ τέλος πάντες . . .). As in the codes in ch. 3, so also here persons who are counterparts of each other (the νεώτεροι and the πρεσβύτεροι) are addressed in turn, and the subordinate parties are given the obligation of ὑποτάσσεσθαι. Certainly then, this "subjection," ὑποτάσσεσθαι, is to be, as consistently in the station codes, not simply to members of an age group, those who are older, but to those who carry out a particular function, i.e., to the "elders." Those who are "younger" are probably named, according to the same schema, primarily because they represent the formal counterpart to the πρεσβύτεροι.

The parenetic schema not only clarifies the formulation of the statement but also sharpens the problem of its meaning: Should the subjection that is constitutive for the stations of worldly life also apply in the eschatological community? How does this structural arrangement relate to the free shaping of congregational life on the basis of the *charismata* mentioned in 4:7-11? That this structure of subjection is not fundamental for the whole section, as it is in *I Clement,* is made quite clear by the concluding directive addressed to all.

3. The keyword of the concluding admonition to all in v. 5b, ταπεινο-φροσύνη, was, to be sure, familiar to the author not only from the presence of ταπεινόφρονες in the "catalogue of virtues" with which he closed the station code in 3:8. It was also passed on to him as the chief term of the tradition that stands behind the concluding parenesis in 5:6-10. It was suggested for v. 5b first of all by Jesus' saying about service (Mk. 10:42-44), which makes itself felt again and again as the background for this parenesis for congregational leadership; it is no mere coincidence, e.g., that this saying and v. 3 both use the keyword κατακυριεύειν.

Vv. 1-4: Admonition to the Elders

1 Though the preceding parenesis on suffering is not continued, this section on congregational leadership begins, loosely connected with it

---

elders in preaching and teaching (I Tim. 5:17; *Did.* 15:1 [LCL AF I, 331]). Defense against false teachers was made the elders' responsibility gradually, but in Acts 20 it is impressed upon them, while in I Pet. 5:2f. only the duties of leadership and administration that belonged to the elders from the beginning are addressed.

by οὖν, "now."[4] The πρεσβύτεροι, who are now addressed,[5] are not, as one might otherwise think because of the counterpart relationship to the νεώτεροι in v. 5a, simply "older ones," that group in the Church distinguished by age or length of membership. They are rather, according to all that is said to them in vv. 1-4, the "elders" or "presbyters," the bearers of Church office, who, to a large extent, were also among the older and more experienced members; indeed, they are, e.g., supposed to "tend" the congregation as shepherds (v. 2a). Technical use of πρεσβύτεροι for leaders of a community was customary in the OT and Jewish realm and comprehensible in the Hellenistic world.[6]

With Acts 14:23; 20:17; Jas. 5:14, this is one of the oldest statements that presuppose for the Hellenistic Church bodies of elders providing leadership for local congregations. This institution had developed in the Palestinian Church along the lines of the structural organization of the synagogue (Acts 21:18), while the Pauline Epistles never mention it. In the Pauline realm, congregational administrative and regulatory functions were carried out by those so gifted by the Spirit, those called "administrative heads" in I Cor. 12:28 and Rom. 12:18 (I Thess. 5:12) and later "overseers and deacons" (Phil. 1:1). In the post-Pauline period, this function was also taken over in the Church from Rome to Asia Minor by groups of men called "elders" in accord with their status and "overseers" in accord with their activity (Acts 20:17, 28; Tit. 1:5, 7; cf. I Pet. 5:1-2a [variant reading]). Thus there occurred a blending of the two forms of organizational structure. What position and function does I Peter assign to this institution?

In this section the author, who calls himself in 1:1 "Peter, an apostle of Jesus Christ," connects eldership with his own function. He turns to the elders as συμπρεσβύτερος, "co-elder." While Paul links himself to other missionaries through titles like συνεργός, "coworker," or σύνδουλος, "co-slave,"[7] the apostle here is related to the elders in

---

4. The particle οὖν, which connects this section as well as the next one in 5:6 to what precedes, does not indicate here a logical deduction: The parenesis addressed to the elders is not an application of the summons to ἀγαθοποιΐα in 4:19 (contra Beare, 197, and others). οὖν is merely a transitional particle: "now." For this reason it is replaced in a group of witnesses by τούς (L, P, Koine, Vulgate, Syriac), which resulted on occasion in οὖν τούς (ℵ).

5. The group addressed here is named, as in 3:1, without the definite article.

6. On this and what follows see Bornkamm, *TDNT* VI, 660-666, and the literature cited above in n.1.

7. συνεργός: Rom. 16:3, 9, 21; Phil. 2:25; 4:3; Phlm. 1:24; Col. 4:11; II Cor. 8:23. In Col. 1:7; 4:12 Paul characterizes one who participates in his commission as a σύνδουλος.

reverse fashion through a designation that was coined perhaps by the author himself.[8] This was done, not to solicit the elders' sympathy through "modesty,"[9] but to make the elders aware of their commission. They now carry out a function originally carried out by the apostle himself. As Paul bore "care for all congregations" (II Cor. 11:28), so too these elders are responsible for their own congregations. Thus we read: πρεσβυτέρους οὖν ἐν ὑμῖν παρακαλῶ ὁ συμπρεσβύτερος. They participate in the service of shepherding included in the apostolic office. The task of the elders is thereby given its proper legitimation and is defined as established with the apostolic office by Christ himself. This does not, however, give a legal guarantee to their personal authority, as happened later through the principle of succession.[10]

In contrast to the connectional term "co-elder," the self-designation "witness," which stands alongside it, appears to emphasize the unique foundational function of the apostle and, thereby, differentiation from the elders. μάρτυς is linked specifically with the content of the gospel in only two other NT writings, Luke-Acts and Revelation.[11] In Luke-Acts, with whose terminology I Peter often overlaps, the μάρτυς is the eyewitness, the one who gives witness confessionally to Jesus' earthly path, but above all to his resurrection, i.e., the apostle (Lk. 24:48; Acts 1:21f.; cf. 1:8; 22:15, etc.). In Revelation, however, witnesses are those who preach, those who give witness to the truth of the gospel (Rev. 11:3). In Revelation (2:13; 11:3; 17:6) and possibly in Acts (22:20) the witnessing activity is connected to suffering, without the term itself having to state this.

Here in I Pet. 5:1 μάρτυς corresponds to κοινωνός in the second half of the verse: Peter is μαρτύς τῶν τοῦ Χριστοῦ παθημάτων, "witness

---

This is appropriated by Ignatius with a different meaning in *Eph.* 2:1; *Magn.* 2:1; *Phld.* 4:1; *Smyr.* 12:2 (LCL AF I, 175, 199, 243, 265). In Phlm. 23 Paul refers to one who participates in his destiny as a συναιχμάλωτος.

8. συμπρεσβύτερος, used only here in early Christian literature; cognates are common, e.g., συμπρεσβευτής, one "sent along" (BAGD s.v.).

9. Knopf, 188; Windisch, 78f.

10. On discussion of the relationship between apostolic and ecclesiastical office see Kertelge, *Gemeinde und Amt,* 129-144 (bibliography on p. 140); L. Goppelt, "Kirchenleitung und Bischofsamt in den ersten drei Jahrhunderten," *Kirchenpräsident oder Bischof?* ed. I. Asheim and V. R. Gold (Göttingen, 1968), 9-35; Roloff, *Apostolat,* 227-235, 249-271.

11. In the Gospel of John and I John μαρτυρεῖν and μαρτυρία come to the fore; these words also play a role in Revelation (the verb also in Acts). Cf. J. Beutler, *Martyria. Traditionsgeschichtliche Untersuchungen zum Zeugnisthema bei Johannes* (FrThSt 10; Frankfurt, 1972).

of the sufferings of Christ," in such a way that, as in 4:13, he participates in those sufferings,[12] so that he may also participate in the coming glory of Christ. Witness to the sufferings of Christ was already given through the OT prophets, i.e., on the basis of the prophesying Spirit (1:11); now it is given on the basis of observation or of the tradition, which is understood in light of the prophetic word. I Peter thus takes up the special aspects of Christ's sufferings mentioned in 2:22f. Here the idea of personal observation could be included, but the emphasis is not on the position of eyewitness but on the testimony that leads to participation in the suffering and, therefore, in the glory.[13]

The last clause of the verse states, without fixing a time frame, that the apostle will be a "participant" in the glory soon to be revealed: ὁ καὶ τῆς μελλούσης ἀποκαλύπτεσθαι δόξης κοινωνός. To be sure, this will not come on him in a way different from that of all believers, according to 4:13, i.e., in the future at the parousia. The inserted comment that the glory of Christ, which is now, like his exaltation, still hidden (1:11, 21; 3:22), also defines the participation chronologically.[14]

If the reference to being a witness is to be understood in this manner, how then is μάρτυς to be related to συμπρεσβύτερος? The reference does not emphasize the office belonging to the apostle, but the central content of that which he shares, without detriment to any individuality, with the elders. If, according to 4:13, all members of the Church are charged with "participation in the sufferings of Christ," then witnessing to these sufferings is the commission given to each person who "serves" (4:10f.). The author has given unmistakable witness in

---

12. One should not import the Pauline expression "the sufferings of Christ" and explain (see the comments on 4:13) that the author is a witness because he has experienced "the sufferings of Christ," i.e., the sufferings of persecution, and, therefore, is able to talk about them (contra H. Strathmann, "μάρτυς," *TDNT* IV, 494f.; W. Michaelis, "πάσχω," *TDNT* V, 934).

13. So Beare, 198f.; Kelly, 198f.; contra Knopf, 188f.; Schelkle, 127f. In *I Clem.* 5:4 (LCL AF I, 17) the root μαρτυρ- goes beyond our passage and approaches the meaning of "suffering-witness": "Peter, who . . . suffered not one or two but many trials, and having thus given his testimony went to the glorious place which was his due. . . ." Cf. N. Brox, *Zeuge und Märtyrer* (StANT 5; Munich, 1961), 36-40, 224f.

14. That Peter, as *I Clem.* 5:4 (LCL AF I, 17) emphasizes, participates even now after his death in the glory, in the sense of an individual eschatology (Knopf, 189; Beare, 199), is no more intended here than that he became a participant in it at the transfiguration (so, in accord with II Pet. 1:16-18, Selwyn, 228f.; A. M. Ramsay, *The Glory of God and the Transfiguration of Christ* [London/New York, 1949], 101-147). On the construction of the expression, which corresponds to Rom. 8:18 in vocabulary, cf. BDF §474.7 (p. 250).

the whole letter up to now to Christ's suffering as the foundation from which and toward which Christian life acquires its shape; he has truly spoken to the churches as "a witness of Christ's sufferings." The "elders" are able to exercise their service in the congregations, especially in this situation, only if they take up this witness in their concrete circumstances. They for their part only become "co-elders" of the apostle when they, too, become "witnesses" in the sense that he is a witness. "Co-elder" and "witness" are not coincidentally connected under the same definite article just to form a simple hendiadys. This introductory verse is by no means a casual reference to solidarity and authority; it shows, rather, the substantive context of the elders' service together with that of the apostle, and thereby its foundational content.

2a This summons expresses the field of responsibilities within which this foundational content is to be applied: ποιμάνατε τὸ ἐν ὑμῖν ποίμνιον τοῦ θεοῦ ἐπισκοποῦντες, κτλ.," "shepherd the flock of God among you by carrying out your service as overseers. . . ." As in 1:3, 17, 22, the imperative is an ingressive aorist; it does not call for the elders to continue what they are already doing, but for constant new beginnings.

The image of "shepherding the flock" is applied to congregational leadership in only two passages in the NT, here and in Acts 20:28(f.),[15] which agree terminologically almost completely, so that a common tradition must lie behind them.[16] In both, the "shepherding" is explicated by ἐπισκοπεῖν, "be active as overseer."[17] They are to do

---

15. Cf. Jn. 21:15-17, addressing Peter: ποίμαινε τὰ πρόβατά μου (v. 16); Mt. 18:10-14, an application of the parable of the lost sheep to the Church's situation; Jude 12: The false teachers "look after themselves"; Polycarp, *Phil.* 6:1 (LCL AF I, 291): The elders are to restore those who have gone astray. The noun "shepherd" is used of Church leaders in the NT only in Eph. 4:11; further in *Herm. Sim.* 9.31.5f. (LCL AF II, 293) and thereafter for bishops: Ignatius, *Phld.* 2:1; *Rom.* 9:1 (LCL AF I, 239f., 237); Hippolytus, *Apostolic Tradition* 3.6 (*Hippolytus,* tr. G. Cuming [Grove Liturgical Study 8; Bramcote, England, 1976], 9); *Didascalia* 4 (R. H. Connolly, *Didascalia Apostolorum* [Oxford, 1929], 152-160). "Flock" is used of the Church in Lk. 12:32, differently formulated in Jn. 10:1ff.; in *I Clement* it is nearly a fixed designation: 44:3; 54:2; 57:2; cf. 16:1 (LCL AF I, 85, 101, 107, 35). Christ is called "shepherd" in Mt. 2:6; Jn. 10:16; Rev. 7:17, further, e.g., *Mart. Pol.* 19 (LCL AF II, 339): He is "the Shepherd of the Catholic Church throughout the world." The image of shepherd and flock has a comprehensive OT and Jewish background and an immediate point of departure in Jesus' imagery (Lk. 15:4-7 par. Mt. 18:12-14; cf. Mk. 6:34 par. Mt. 9:36; 14:27 par. Mt.; Mt. 10:6; 15:24; 25:32). Cf. J. Jeremias, "ποιμήν," *TDNT* VI, 487-490; H. Merklein, *Das kirchliche Amt im Epheserbrief* (StANT 23; Munich, 1973), 362ff.

16. Acts 20:28: . . . τῷ ποιμνίῳ, ἐν ᾧ . . . ἔθετο ἐπισκόπους, ποιμαίνειν τὴν ἐκκλησίαν τοῦ θεοῦ. . . . I Pet. 5:2a: ποιμάνατε τὸ ἐν ὑμῖν ποίμνιον τοῦ θεοῦ, ἐπισκοποῦντες. . . .

17. ἐπισκοποῦντες is read after τοῦ θεοῦ by 𝔭72, A, L, P, Koine, Old Latin, Syriac,

this in regard to the ποίμνιον, the "flock" that is ἐν ὑμῖν, "in your midst," at the time.[18]

The Origin of the Image of Shepherding the Flock

The image of shepherding the flock, like the term ἐπισκοπεῖν,[19] has a direct prior history among the Essenes. In CD 13:7-12 we read: "This is the rule for the overseer (מְבַקֵּר = ἐπίσκοπος) . . . : Like a shepherd his sheep, he shall loosen all the fetters. . . . He shall examine (פקד) everyone entering his congregation . . . and shall place each one in his place according to his rank in the lot (גּוֹרָל)." 1QS places directly parallel to *mebaqqēr* (6:12, 20) the technical term פָּקִיד (6:14), which is represented in the LXX by the root ἐπισκεπ-. In some of the many OT occurrences of this root, פקד represents the activity of the shepherd, who seeks and restores the lost and scattered sheep (Jer. 23:2; Ezek. 34:6; Zech. 10:3; 11:16). This Essene tradition thus aligns itself directly with the weighty theological meaning of the shepherd image in the OT. It is primarily according to the Psalms and exilic prophecy that Yahweh is the Shepherd by whom Israel is kept in safety (Psalm 23; Isa. 40:11; Ezek. 34:11-22, etc.); in contrast to the shepherds who have failed, the messianic ruler is promised as shepherd (Jer. 23:1-4; Ezek. 34:23f., etc.; *Pss. Sol.* 17:40 [*OT Pseudep.* II, 668]).

It is no coincidence that already in Paul Church leadership is designated with this root ἐπισκεπ- (Phil. 1:1). The high demands placed on the local congregation created the necessity, as among the Essenes, of a type of service that attended to the individual and restored those beset by inner conflict and those who had gone astray. In addition, the designation was also comprehensible among Hellenistic people, since administrative officials in cities and organizations were referred to as ἐπίσκοποι. In I Pet. 5:2 and Acts 20:28, the term is linked with the shepherd image, which does not appear — perhaps coincidentally — in Paul. I Peter also applies this image to Christ (2:25; 5:4) and suggests, thereby, an association with Jesus' self-understanding in the parable of the shepherd (Lk. 15:4-7 par. Mt.) and with the theological background of the image in the OT.

---

and Bohairic, while it is missing in ℵ, B, 33, and Sahidic. The evidence is thus equal in weight for both readings. The word could have been inserted because it belonged to the traditional field of expression or omitted because it had become objectionable from the second century on to speak of elders carrying out the duties of the bishop's office. Since, according to 2:25, connection of "shepherd and overseer" was familiar to the writer of I Peter, it is more probable that ἐπισκοποῦντες is original (so Selwyn, 230; Kelly, 189; contra Knopf, 189; Schelkle, 128, n.4; Spicq, 164).

18. The flock is the Church as represented in each local congregation. Cf. I Cor. 1:2: "to the Church of God *at Corinth*."

19. ποιμαιν- and ἐπισκεπ- occur together, beyond I Pet. 2:25; 5:2; Acts 20:28, also in *I Clem.* 44:3 (LCL AF I, 85); Ignatius, *Rom.* 9:1; *Phld.* 1:1–2:1 (*ibid.*, 237, 239-241); Hippolytus, *Apostolic Tradition* 3.6; *Didascalia* 4 (see above, n.15). See H. W. Beyer, "ἐπισκέπτομαι, κτλ.," *TDNT* II, 618f.; Schnackenburg, "Episkopus und Hirtenamt"; Nauck, "Probleme des frühchristlichen Amstverständnisses," 201-207; Goppelt, *Apostolic*, 183f.

What does the image of shepherding say about the elders' commission? Like the elders of the synagogue, their fundamental role is to organize congregational events, to manage its resources from donations, and to watch over congregational life. All this took place in a setting in which Christian churches could not organize themselves according to the laws governing associations; it was possible only through charismatic activity on behalf of individual members, through which they were won over from within for voluntary participation, though in this setting one had to fight constantly against contagious centrifugal tendencies (cf. 5:8). "Therefore, be alert, remembering that for three years I did not cease night or day to admonish everyone with tears" (Acts 20:31).

Therefore, even organizing, managing, and watching over a church for the sake of its social situation as well as its being founded on faith can only take place as a service of shepherding, which is rooted in the service of Jesus (2:25), i.e., which takes place in such a way that it becomes a "pasturing," an opening up of life-giving possibilities. To just what extent individual elders exercise the service of proclamation and *diakonia* (4:11) remains unspecified, beyond the tasks already assigned them personally. In the following subsection, with its three antithetical directives in vv. 2b-c, 3 the author develops, not what the elders are to do in particular, but how they are to carry out their work in regard to the managing and leading assigned to them as individuals.

2b μὴ ἀναγκαστῶς ἀλλὰ ἑκουσίως κατὰ θεόν, "not out of compulsion, but willingly, as is fitting in relation to God." The negated "out of compulsion/obligation" presupposes that the elders were chosen and appointed.[20] Their task in relation to the congregation was linked with many personal and substantive hardships and exposed them to special danger in the public domain. To take on the task and to exercise it over a period of time could be perceived as a burden borne only at the urging of supporters or for the sake of prestige in the Church. In accord with its essence, the task must be carried out "willingly," i.e., not only out of the joy connected with such work, but also because one has placed oneself willingly at the disposal of the God whose concerns are, after all, at stake here. According to the history of OT and Jewish usage[21] this is what is

---

20. Cf. Acts 14:23; Tit. 1:5; *I Clem.* 42:4; 44 (LCL AF I, 81, 83f.).

21. In the LXX ἑκούσιος and ἑκουσιάζεσθαι represent the hithpael of נדב, "place oneself at God's disposal" (Judg. 5:2, 9; Ps. 53:8 LXX; I Macc. 2:42ff.). In the Essene texts "to place oneself willingly at one's disposal" was a circumlocution for membership in the community: 1QS 5:8, 10; cf. 1:7, 11; 5:1, 6, 21f.; 6:13. Analogies in the NT are: Phlm. 14,

intended by ἐκουσίως, and this is given expression correctly by the κατὰ θεόν added for commentary: "as is in conformity with God's will," which breaks up the rhythm (cf. 4:6). Only this willingness transforms the work of an elder into διακονία (4:10f.), into a labor of love; otherwise, everything becomes "a noisy gong or a clanging cymbal" (I Cor. 13:1f.).

2c The second antithesis intensifies the positive side of ἐκουσίως in the direction of πρόθυμος, a willing dedication to passionate engagement.[22] It is intended to overcome the subconscious tendency to replace genuine motivation, which is lacking, with satisfaction arising from material advantages: μηδὲ αἰσχροκερδῶς ἀλλὰ προθύμως. Such compensation, even if it is not acquired illegally, becomes "shameful profit" by the very motivation itself.[23] The possibility of acquiring for oneself personal material advantages was in many cases a reality: Elders received from the Church an income or at least some kind of support (Mt. 10:10 par.; I Cor. 9:7-12). Furthermore they managed donations from the congregation (Acts 5:1-5; II Cor. 8:20; Polycarp, *Phil.* 11:1-4 [LCL AF I, 296f.]) and had, through their reputations, influence over the financial affairs of the congregation (cf. Mk. 12:40 par. Lk; Lk. 16:14; I Tim. 6:5). It is not important that this generally involved modest sums, but that thereby genuine engagement could be impaired. It is no coincidence that, in accord with Jesus' saying about mammon (Mt. 6:19-24 par.), one's relationship to money repeatedly becomes the test in early Christian parenesis for the stance of office holders.[24]

3 The final antithesis proscribes a third tendency that is in op-

---

generally of Christian conduct: μὴ ὡς κατὰ ἀγάγκην . . . ἀλλὰ κατὰ ἐκούσιον; Heb. 13:17 of the ἡγούμενοι: "Do this joyfully, and not sadly."

22. πρόθυμος, in Greek literature "willing," "eager," "passionate," rare in the LXX: twice for נָדִיב, once adverbial for יִשְׁרֵי לְבָב (II Chr. 29:34), in the NT: Mk. 14:38b par. Mt.: "The spirit is willing"; Rom. 1:15: "eager" (cf. K. H. Rengstorf, "πρόθυμος," *TDNT* VI, 694-697). In Hellenistic literature the adverb προθύμως is often used of the desired posture of office holders or of benefactors of a city (W. Dittenberger, ed., *Sylloge Inscriptionum Graecarum* [third ed., Leipzig, 1915-24], 10f.).

23. Already in Sophocles, *Antigone* 1055f. (LCL I, 395), the accusation was brought against the mantic-seers that they were a φιλάργυρον γένος and loved the "shameful gain" (αἰσχροκέρδειαν) coming from the tyrants. According to Aristotle, *Ethica Nicomachea* 4.1, 43 (LCL XIX, 203) an αἰσχροκερδής is one who draws profit from illegitimate sources; Theophrastus, *Characters* 30.1f. (LCL 121), defines: . . . ἔστι δὲ τοιοῦτος ὁ αἰσχροδερδής, οἷος ἐστιῶν ἄρτους ἱκανοὺς μὴ παραθεῖναι.

24. Office holders should not be αἰσχροκερδής (Tit. 1:7; I Tim. 3:8), as are the false teachers (Tit. 1:11), but ἀφιλάργυρος, "not avaricious" (I Tim. 3:3; *Did.* 15:1; Polycarp, *Phil.* 5:2 [LCL AF I, 331, 289]; cf. Acts 20:35: "It is more blessed to give than to receive").

position to the character of the office as service and is, in fact, its counterfeit in the exercise of control: μηδ' ὡς κατακυριεύοντες τῶν κλήρων ἀλλὰ τύποι γινόμενοι τοῦ ποιμνίου. This brings us to the starting point for all ecclesiastical ministry: The "domination"[25] customary in the political realm is, according to Jesus' saying in Mk. 10:42 par., the opposite of the principle of service that is to be in effect among the disciples, because God's saving dominion among people can only be, and through Jesus was, established along this path.

For this reason, the elders are prohibited from "ruling over what is allotted," although in a regulatory way they are to give instructions (cf. v. 5a). The exegetically controversial word κλῆρος, the "share" or the "participation" designated by a share, is used figuratively for the participation allotted one (by God) and stands in this context parallel to ποίμνιον. It is, therefore, the participation in the "flock" allotted variously to the elders, i.e., the particular congregation entrusted to each of them.[26] Wherever the elders serve in capacities of management and oversight, this is not to have the character, therefore, of domination (cf. Mt. 23:4).

The tendency to dominate is eliminated when elders become aware that ultimately in all their work they can only be a τύπος, an "example" that exercises a shaping influence because it is itself shaped by God. Paul uses this word for his own role in relation to the churches.[27] In II Thess.

---

25. On κατακυριεύειν see W. Foerster, "κύριος," *TDNT* III, 1098.

26. As in 5:1: τὸ ἐν ὑμῖν ποίμνιον, "the flock, as it is among you"; so Knopf, 190; Windisch, 79; BAGD s.v.; Beare, 199 (Kelly, 202f., regards this as possible). The word does not refer here either to payments and donations (so Wohlenberg) or the places of the believers in the eschatological kingdom, as in Wis. 5:5 (cf. Col. 1:12; Acts 26:18; so Selwyn, 231; W. Foerster, "κλῆρος," *TDNT* III, 764).

Nor does it refer to positions of rank or office in the Church. Nauck ("Probleme des frühchristlichen Amstverständnisses," 209-213) argues for this understanding, referring to Essene analogies: "Only Aaron's sons are to command in matters of justice and property, and every rule concerning community members shall be determined by their word" (1QS 9:7; cf. 5:20-24; 6:22; CD 13:12f.). The word does have this sense in later Church constitutions, e.g., in the dedicatory prayer for the bishop in Hippolytus, *Apostolic Tradition* 3.4f. (cf. 9.7): ". . . Father . . . bestow upon this your servant, whom you have chosen for the episcopate, to feed your holy flock . . . , to have the power to forgive sins according to your command, to confer orders according to your bidding, to loose every bond according to the power which you gave to the apostles" (*Hippolytus,* tr. G. Cuming [Grove Liturgical Study 8; Bramcote, 1976], 9, 13). Hippolytus himself used the word in the sense of "cleric" in distinction to lay person (9.3 [*ibid.,* 13]). But this sense, "position of rank," is quite remote from the structure of the Church in Acts (even according to 1:17 and 26:18) and I Pet. 5:3 (so H. Braun, *Qumran und das NT* I [Tübingen, 1966], 287).

27. τύπος in the sense of "shaping model" is found only in the Pauline writings and in I Peter (Phil. 3:17; I Thess. 1:7; II Thess. 3:9; I Tim. 4:12; Tit. 2:7). See L. Goppelt,

3:9, it receives substantively accurate commentary when it is placed in parallel relationship to tradition (3:6) and parenesis (3:10ff.). Like tradition and parenesis, an example functions only through faith, since it gives witness to the life lived out of faith, which is given by God and which can only be effected by faith. Hence, the instructions of elders in the daily life of the congregation function legitimately only when they are oriented to the gospel, which shapes one's own manner of life.

Leaders as Example

Such an obligation for leaders to set an example is rarely found in Jewish writings; like the other instructions of these antitheses, this obligation was familiar, though in a different sense, of course, in the Greek-Hellenistic world.[28] In early Christianity it arose out of the concept of discipleship; in the saying against domination among the disciples Jesus himself is named as the obligating example (Mk. 10:45 par. Mt.). In accord with this, Paul developed the concept with a christological foundation: "Be imitators of me, as I am of Christ" (I Cor. 11:1); "you became imitators of us and of the Lord . . ." (I Thess. 1:6). Similarly I Pet. 5:4, which strengthens the parenesis through promise, refers the elders as shepherds to Christ as the "chief shepherd," the One wo commissioned them and will repay them, but who is also the archetype of their calling, just as the apostle was the archetype in another way as their "co-elder."

4 The "appearing of the chief Shepherd"[29] is the parousia of Christ.[30] He comes for the shepherds as the ἀρχιποίμην. In the hour of

---

"τύπος," *TDNT* VIII, 249f.; on other NT references to human models see A. Schulz, *Nachfolgen und Nachahmen* (StANT 6; Munich, 1962), 318-331. For the content cf. Acts 20:35: "In all things I have shown you that . . ."; *Herm. Vis.* 3.9.10 (LCL AF II, 51f.): "How will you correct the chosen of the Lord if you yourselves suffer no correction?"

28. Rabbinic literature does, in fact, emphasize that the teacher should also hold to what is taught, but nothing is said of the teacher being a model (Str.-Bill. I, 910f.). The Greek concept of mimesis was adopted by some Hellenistic Jewish writers (e.g., IV Macc. 9:23; cf. *Test. Benj.* 3:1 [*OT Pseudep.* I, 825]). Greek and Hellenistic literature referred to the παράδειγμα (a word not used in the NT) or, more rarely, to the τύπος (W. Michaelis, "μιμέομαι," *TDNT* IV, 660f.; Goppelt, *TDNT* VIII, 247).

29. ἀρχιποίμην, "chief shepherd," has been documented as a vocational designation in *Test. Jud.* 8:1 (*OT Pseudep.* I, 797), in an Egyptian inscription (A. Deissmann, *Light from the Ancient East* [tr. L. Strachan; New York, [2]1927], 97-99), and in Papyrus Leipzig 97.11.4 (*ibid.*, 98, n.5). Similar constructions are familiar, e.g., ἀρχιβούκολος, "chief herdsman," which was used of the chief priest of Dionysius (Perdelwitz, *Mysterienreligion,* 100f.). But use of this designation for Christ in I Pet. 5:4 (cf. 2:25) was undoubtedly inspired not by Hellenistic usage, but by the OT and early Christian tradition (see above, n.15). In Heb. 13:20 Christ is called, in direct dependence on the OT promise (cf. Isa. 63:11 LXX), "the great shepherd of the sheep." See J. Jeremias, "ποιμήν," *TDNT* VI, 493f.; Jost, *ΠΟΙΜΗΝ* (all Christian evidence for ἀρχιποίμην on pp. 47f.); T. K. Kempf, *Christus der Hirt* (dissertation, Rome, 1942).

30. φανεροῦσθαι is used in 1:20 of Christ's first coming, the incarnation (I Tim. 3:16;

accounting he will recognize those who actually worked for him and not for themselves (cf. Lk. 12:8f. par.; Mt. 25:34ff.): καὶ φανερωθέντος τοῦ ἀρχιποίμενος κομιεῖσθε τὸν ἀμαράντινον τῆς δόξης στέφανον. These shepherds will "receive,"[31] like all Christians according to 1:8f., "the goal of faith," salvation. As for Peter himself (5:1) and all who suffer like him in the life of discipleship (4:13), this goal will be participation in "glory." The shepherds will receive this participation as a "garland," i.e., as recognition of their faithfulness.[32] All receive the same salvation, though it takes on a different shape according to the content of each person's calling, since it consists of fellowship with the One who calls (cf. Mt. 20:1-16; 25:24-30 par. Lk.). "The garland of glory" is "unfading";[33] the participation in the glory that it represents has, in contrast to all fading earthly recognitions, eternal permanence.

Heb. 9:26; *Barn.* 6:7 [LCL AF I, 359f.], and passim). Here and in I Jn. 2:28; 3:2; Col. 3:4 it is used of the parousia.

31. κομίζεσθαι is also used of reception of the eschatological reward in Eph. 6:8; Col. 3:25; Heb. 10:36; 11:13, 39.

32. The wreath was a widely known symbol in the ancient world. It was used primarily as a sign of honor and a protective talisman in cultic life, the military, and sports and to honor the deceased. Because of its mythic background it is referred to in the OT and Jewish realm only with reservation — in the OT primarily in later strata — usually just as a figure. Cf. W. Grundmann, "στέφανος," *TDNT* VII, 617-628.

In the NT the wreath became a standard image for eschatological approbation. Therefore, the statement in I Pet. 5:4 was not derived from a parallel in everyday life. The closest analogies to "wreath of glory" are II Tim. 4:8: "wreath of righteousness," and Jas. 1:12; Rev. 2:10: "wreath of life" (epexegetical genitive in both expressions). "Wreath of glory" also appears already in the OT: Isa. 28:5: "The Lord of hosts will be a crown of glory and a diadem of beauty [LXX: ὁ στέφανος τῆς ἐλπίδος ὁ πλακεὶς τῆς δόξης] to the remnant of his people"; cf. Jer. 13:18; Sir. 47:6.

The expression is used eschatologically in 1QS 4:6ff.: "The visitation of all who walk in the Spirit [of truth] will be healing, great peace in a long life, and fruitfulness, with every eternal blessing and joy in life without end, a crown of glory (כליל כבוד), and a garment of majesty in unending light" (in 1QH 9:25 of present fulfillment; so also *Test. Benj.* 4:1 (*OT Pseudep.* I, 826): "Be imitators of him because of his compassion in order that you may wear crowns of glory." Therefore, we find in I Pet. 5:4 the same conspicuously close contact with the Essene texts as in v. 2a (which is not present in the antitheses in vv. 2b-3). "Wreath of glory" is not otherwise found in Jewish texts in an eschatological sense (Grundmann, *TDNT* VII, 627f.; *Asc. Isa.* 9:9ff.; 11:40 [*OT Pseudep.* II, 170, 176] is surely a Christian interpolation). Since "wreath of glory" is, in accord with both this OT and Jewish prehistory and the NT analogies, an image for the conveying of glory, I Pet. 5:4 does not refer to crowning with a heavenly garland of radiance (contra Knopf, 191); "the golden crowns" in Rev. 4:4, 10; 12:1; 14:14 are visionary symbols. The participation of the whole person in glory is much more than a mythic halo-radiance.

33. ἀμαράντινος, "unfading," appears only here in early Christian literature. It does not refer to (a wreath of) amaranth, i.e., of unfading flowers (contra Knopf, 191). Cf. 1:4: ἀμάραντος, "unfading" (cf. Wis. 6:12); I Cor. 9:25: ἄφθαρτος στέφανος.

V. 5: Admonition to the Younger and to All Church Members

5a After these directives for the work of the elders in the congregations, one expects to hear a word about the relationship of the congregation to the elders. Surprisingly, however, it is now said: ὁμοίως,
νεώτεροι, ὑποτάγητε πρεσβυτέροις, "similarly, you who are younger,
subject yourselves to the elders." This exegetically controversial sentence is clarified to some extent by the observation that it follows what
is addressed to the elders in the form of the household code parenesis
in 3:1, 7.[34] ὁμοίως, "similarly," with which both begin, is here merely
a connective particle that indicates a general correspondence: Just as
the elders have their duties, so too do "those who are younger."

Who are the νεώτεροι? They are named in similar early Christian
texts in three different ways alongside the πρεσβύτεροι: (1) In Acts 2:17
(= Joel 3:1) the νεανίσκοι, the "youths" (synonymous in Acts 5:10 with
νεώτεροι in 5:6), represent together with the πρεσβύτεροι the entirety of
the Church with respect to age (I Jn. 2:13f. is similar). This usage was
appropriated with the OT quotation and is found elsewhere in the OT
too (II Chron. 15:13: ἀπὸ νεωτέρου ἕως πρεσβυτέρου; cf. Ps. 148:2).

(2) In the congregational parenesis in the Pastoral Epistles the
νεώτεροι are, alongside old men, old women, slaves, etc., a stratum of
the Church (Tit. 2:2-10; cf. I Tim. 5:1f.).

(3) In the Apostolic Fathers these strata of the Church are
enumerated together with their office holders: In Polycarp, *Phil.* 4:1–6:3
(LCL AF I, 286-291), men, women, widows, deacons, young men,
young women, and elders are addressed in succession, and the young
men are admonished to subject themselves to the elders and deacons
(cf. 1QS 1:2, 4). *I Clement* has similar lists (1:3; 21:6 [LCL AF I, 10f.,
46f.]), condemning therein the attempt to remove elders as an "insurrection" of "the foolish against the wise, of the νέοι against the
πρεσβύτεροι, of the young against the old, to which also the elders
belong" (3:3; cf. 57:1 [*ibid.*, 12f., 106f.]).[35]

---

34. This is seen by Kelly, 204f., correctly when he — though in too systematic a
fashion — considers the statement a displaced fragment of the regulation in 2:12–3:9.

35. No supporting texts from early Christian writings are to be found for the suggestion
of Spicq, "Place ou rôle des jeunes," who points to the fact that fraternities of young men
had been established in the cities of Asia Minor (see F. Poland, *Geschichte des griechischen
Vereinswesens* [Leipzig, 1909]). Spicq assumes that something similar existed in early Christian communities and refers to Acts 5:6, 10 to support this claim. But it cannot be concluded

Are the νεώτεροι of our passage addressed in this third way? Is subjection to elders urged here especially on "those who are younger" because they are particularly inclined to resist this institutionalization of congregational leadership, perhaps even for the sake of the freedom of the *charismata*?[36] This was presumably the situation with which *I Clement* is concerned. But here "those who are younger" are not addressed, as in the Apostolic Fathers, as a stratum alongside others, but as the only counterparts of the πρεσβύτεροι. The latter are not merely "those who are older," to whom veneration is due (*I Clem.* 1:3; 21:6); they are, rather, as in 5:1, the "elders," to whom subjection is due.[37] In this case, then, the νεώτεροι are surely named here as representing all Church members in relation to the elders,[38] since Paul has already obligated all members to subject themselves to the leaders (I Cor. 16:16; I Thess. 5:12).

Subjection to Elders

The problem implied by this directive to subject oneself to the elders comes into sharp relief in the debate of *I Clement* with the church in Corinth. Is subjection and established congregational leadership, as represented by the elders, at all appropriate in a community in which, according to I Pet. 4:10f., each person as "steward" is to utilize in a serving way the *charisma* given to him or her? Does not subjection, as it is constitutive for stations in the world, contradict the essence of the eschatological community?

In I Corinthians 14, Paul makes clear, in response to a pneumatic fanaticism, that even among people of the Spirit, as long as they live "in the flesh," i.e., in history, a τάξις is necessary (I Cor. 14:40). In Paul this takes the form of designated

---

from I Pet. 5:5 that "the young men" were an organized group. Even less likely is the association of this statement directed to "the young men" with the novices of CD 6:16-21; 12:17f., who, because of their lesser ritual holiness, could bury the dead (see Braun, *Qumran und das NT* I, 147). Thus, from the perspective of Acts 5:6, 10, these hypotheses that "the younger ones" represented organized groups (Spicq, 170f.) or even office holders, who had as it were the function of deacons (Beare, 201), cannot be supported; nor is this made more probable by Ex. 24:5; Ezek. 39:14 LXX.

36. So Knopf, 191f.; Schelkle, 130.

37. Contra Wohlenberg, 148f.; Selwyn, 233.

38. So Windisch, 79 (though more in the sense of identification); Kelly, 204f. That "the younger ones" represent, to an extent, the whole Church, is also probable because of the ancient division by age groups. Dio Chrysostom 57 (74; LCL V, 219) refers to παῖς, μειράκιον, νεανίσκος, and πρεσβύτης. Cf. Aristoxenus, fragment 18: (νήπιος), παῖς, νεανίσκος, ἀνήρ, and πρεσβύτης. The πρεσβύτης is, according to Hippocrates, a man of fifty to fifty-six years (BAGD s.v. πρεσβύτης).

leaders, to whom the others are to be subject (I Thess. 5:12; I Cor. 16:16; cf. I Cor. 12:28; Rom. 12:8), though, of course, they are not for him a constituted institution like the body of elders. But is it permissible to apply the legitimate principle of subjection *to such an institution?* This question does not yet enter the picture for I Peter because the congregational group of elders is only in the process of coming into existence. According to 5:2b, there appears to be no pressure to take over this task and to exercise it for any duration. The problem came some decades later for *I Clement* and is resolved there with the aid of a concept of "order," which then spawned a legal misunderstanding of the ecclesiastical system of government.[39] But I Peter does not support this development. In contrast, it emphasizes in the directive to the elders the service character even of congregational leadership (5:2b, 3) and retains alongside it the freedom of the *charismata* (4:10f.), so that "ordering" does not become the mark of the entire life of the congregation, but remains confined to a necessary and narrow sector.

5b   As in 3:8f., parenesis directed to specific groups ends with a word to all. This concluding statement removes the polarity between those who "shepherd" and those who "subject themselves" in the obligation to show mutual "humility": πάντες δὲ ἀλλήλοις τὴν ταπεινο-φροσύνην ἐγκομβώσασθε, "All put on humility in relation to one another."[40] The acquisition of moral qualities in such a way that they shape one's self-presentation is often expressed graphically in early Christian parenesis as the putting on of clothing.[41] This image is given a special profile here by use of the rare verb ἐγκομβόομαι: The act of dressing becomes a tight "binding around," and the garment becomes the ἐγκόμβωμα, the "work apron" of slaves and shepherds.[42] The image reminds one of the binding around of the linen cloth on the occasion

---

39. Cf. *I Clem.* 44:3-6 (LCL AF I, 85); Goppelt, *Apostolic,* 139f., 201f.

40. ἀλλήλοις is dative of mode or of relationship and is linked to both πάντες and the verb. It is, therefore, not so "strange" grammatically (G. Delling, "ἐγκομβόομαι," *TDNT* II, 339; so also Wohlenberg, 149) to link πάντες ἀλλήλοις to the preceding sentence: ". . . be subject to the elders, all of you toward one another." This understanding is reflected in the weakly supported addition of ὑποτασσόμενοι after ἀλλήλοις (P, Koine, Majority text, Harclean Syriac), which surely arose as an accommodation to Eph. 5:21.

41. Col. 3:12: ἐνδύσασθε . . . ταπεινοφροσύνην, as an sign that those addressed had already "put on" the "new person" (v. 10). Another figure is the putting on of spiritual armor (Rom. 13:12; I Thess. 5:8; Eph. 6:11, 14; further material in A. Oepke, "δύω," *TDNT* II, 319f.; E. Lohse, *Colossians and Philemon* [tr. W. R. Poehlmann and R. J. Karris, Hermeneia; Philadelphia, 1971], 141ff.).

42. ἐγκομβοῦσθαι, "wrap something around," "tie on" (BAGD s.v.), appears in the NT only here and is used of the ἐγκόμβωμα, "belt," with which one could, e.g., cinch up one's clothing and thus prepare to go. Pollux, *Onomasticon* 4.119, defines it thus: τῇ δὲ τῶν δούλων ἐξωμίδι καὶ ἱματίδιόν τι πρόσκειται λευκόν, ὃ ἐγκόμβωμα λέγεται ἢ ἐπίρρημα.

of washing feet (Jn. 13:4), but there is here no tradition-historical connection with that scene.[43] ταπεινοφροσύνη is to be put on in this way. While "humility" is named in 3:8, as in Eph. 4:2; Phil. 2:3; Col. 3:12, alongside other ways of conducting oneself as an expression of the will for fellowship among Christians, it is emphasized here alone. It is the basis of contact among Christians, particularly in the polarity between leaders and those subjecting themselves in an afflicted community (cf. Acts 20:19), since it is, as v. 6 goes on to say, one's posture in relation to God.[44]

Of what does this humility consist? In Greek-Hellenistic ethics the posture of ταπεινός is regarded negatively as a lowly slave mentality, which is unworthy of the one who is free.[45] In contrast, for OT and Jewish people and all the more for Christians it is the elementary recognition of their true situation, especially that of their dependence on God as their Creator and Savior. Jesus' proclamation started from the pronouncement of blessing over the "poor" (Mt. 5:3 par.), the deprived, who in the OT are identical with those who are "bent down," the *anawim,* and Jesus referred to himself as an *anaw* (Mt. 11:29). Paul then in the parenetic kerygma refers to the self-abasement of the Son as the directing motif also for the conduct of Christians among one another (Phil. 2:3-9). Beyond the OT, he was also familiar with a humility among the members of the people of God and refers to it as ταπεινοφροσύνη, as does the author of I Peter here. "Humility" among Christians is, therefore, what is carried out by one who places the other

---

43. Contra W. Grundmann, "ταπεινός," *TDNT* VIII, 23, n.75, no additional relationship of I Pet. 5:5b to the Johannine tradition about Peter cannot be seen.

44. ταπεινοφροσύνη, "humility," does not occur in the LXX. In the NT (Acts 20:19; Eph. 4:2; Phil. 2:3; Col. 3:12; I Pet. 5:5) it is used of the conduct of Christians among themselves (Col. 2:18, 23 of self-chosen "debasement" on the part of the false teachers). I Pet. 3:8 has the adjective ταπεινόφρων, "humble," which is also missing (Prov. 29:23 v.l. excepted) from the LXX. The two words, which in Greek literature appear only rarely and are used pejoratively in the sense of "downwardly disposed," "despondent," play no role in Jewish literature. In the meaning "humility/humble" they represent Christian linguistic coinage, developed in connection with the portrayal of Christ (Phil. 2:3-7). This was prepared for through the use of the root ταπειν- in the LXX (see the comments on 5:6), but these two words are not present there because the posture of humility envisaged is in relation to God, not in relation to one's neighbor. The latter becomes truly possible in the sense of the saying in Mk. 10:42-45 par. for the first time among Jesus' disciples. See A. Vögtle, *Die Tugend- und Lasterkataloge im NT* (NTA 16/4-5; Münster, 1936), 153f., 252 s.v.; A. Dihle, "Demut," *RAC* III, cols. 735-778 (bibliography); BAGD s.v.

45. Cf. W. Grundmann, *TDNT* VIII, 1-5, 11f.; BAGD s.v. 2b.

higher than himself or herself and "serves" the other (Phil. 2:3; Mk. 10:42ff. par.), one who knows in an elementary way that he or she is given to that person and, therefore, gives heed to that person (cf. Rom. 1:11f.).

The summons to humility is given a basis in an OT quotation. Even when seen historically, this is in accord with its content, since it is rooted there. As is consistently the case in I Peter, ὅτι introduces the theological foundation for a ethical directive (2:31; 3:18; 4:8). The quotation from Prov. 3:34 LXX is repeated in Jas. 4:6 with the same divergences from the LXX,[46] showing that it comes from a Christian tradition; it appears again in *I Clem.* 30:2; Ignatius, *Eph.* 5:3 (LCL AF I, 58f., 178f.). The quotation formulates as a rule of wisdom[47] what Israel experienced in its history[48] and what became certain conclusively through the abasement and exaltation of Christ (cf. Acts 8:33 = Isa. 53:8): ὁ θεὸς ὑπερηφάνοις ἀντιτάσσεται, ταπεινοῖς δὲ δίδωσιν χάριν.

The "proud"[49] whom the OT saying condemns are, in the language of the gospel tradition, those to whom Jesus' declarations of woe apply (Lk. 6:24-26; Matthew 23) and, in the language of Paul, those who live out of "self-glory," out of καύχησις (Rom. 3:27). "Pride" shows itself in disobedience against the gospel and passes away with acceptance of it. It always manifests itself both in relation to God and in relation to other people. One who is proud has God against him or her; this person falls prey to futility, quite apart from the question of historical success (4:17f.).

"But the humble receive grace." Humility is not rewarded as a virtue or as self-abasement; it receives God's gracious turning of himself in mercy because it stretches out its hands toward it: "Humility" is to

---

46. In both instances ὁ θεός stands in place of LXX κύριος.

47. Sir. 3:18; 10:15; Job 5:11; 12:21; Ps. 146:6 LXX.

48. The *anawim,* who accept their situation from God, acknowledge that he is right, and thereby do "justice" in their relationship to him, are elected and saved by him (Num. 12:3; Judg. 6:15; I Sam. 2:7; Pss. 17:28; 33:15 LXX; Ezek. 17:24; 21:31; Zeph. 2:3; cf. Lk. 1:51-53). See H.-J. Kraus, *Psalms 1-59: A Commentary* (tr. H. Oswald; Minneapolis, 1988), 92-95.

49. ὑπερήφανος, "proud," is used in the NT either as here in contrast to humility (Lk. 1:51; Jas. 4:6) or in catalogues of vices (Rom. 1:30; II Tim. 3:2; so also ὑπερηφανία in Mk. 7:21). In the LXX both ὑπερήφανος and ὑπερηφανία occur relatively frequently, especially in the Psalms and, above all, in proverbial wisdom. They are nearly synonymous, as already in Greek literature, with ὕβρις and those characterized by it (Isa. 13:11: ὕβρις ὑπερηφάνων; cf. Prov. 8:13, and elsewhere). See G. Bertram, "ὑπερήφανος," *TDNT* VIII, 525-529.

know oneself to be dependent on God's mercy. The quotation refers, then, to pride and humility in one's relationship to God; in the OT this is its only meaning. According to what precedes here, however, one's relationship to other people is included. One who is humble also seeks to be a "gracious neighbor." According to its basic meaning, however, the OT quotation directs one to the statement on humility that follows in v. 6, since ταπεινοῦσθαι means, quite in keeping with the OT sense, to bear affliction at the hands of human adversaries as abasement from God. The NT roots of the parenesis in 5:5b become visible, thereby, in 5:6f.

5:6-11: Accepting and Enduring the Test of Affliction

6 *So humble yourselves now under God's mighty hand,*
 so that he may exalt you in the (last) time.
7 *Cast all your care on him,*
 since he cares for you.

8 *Be sober, stay awake!*
 Your adversary, the devil, stalks about like a roaring lion
 and seeks whom he can devour.
9 *Resist him steadfastly in faith,*
 knowing that the same sufferings have come on your
 brotherhood in the (whole) world.

10 *But the God of all grace,*
 who has called you to his eternal glory in Christ —
 you who suffer for a short time —
 will himself restore, strengthen, empower, and establish you.
11 *His is the power forever. Amen.*

Structure and Tradition

1. This section concludes the parenesis of the letter with a final word about the struggle with society, a statement that in directness goes beyond everything that precedes it. What Christians encounter in the hostile acts of the surrounding society is ultimately both the God who "abases" in order to "exalt" (vv. 6f.) and the devil who wants to destroy their existence as believers (vv. 8f.). If the believer wants to stand the test of this struggle going on behind the scenes, he or she must both accept God's engagement through willing submission and resist the adversary through steadfast opposition. What is required of Christians in the situation of

conflict is finally, according to v. 10, accomplished by God's grace, which ultimately rescues those who are called. This verse constitutes, at the same time, the
closing word of the letter.

2. This section is arranged transparently and applies in vv. 6-9 and in v. 10
a parenetic schema of early Christian tradition to the thematic focus of the letter.
In v. 11, then, a doxology rounds off the thought developments.

a. The expressions that shape the structure of vv. (5)6-9 are also seen in Jas.
4:6-10: Like Jas. 4:6, v. 5 quotes Prov. 3:34 LXX with the same change as in
James. V. 6 (ταπεινώθητε οὖν ὑπὸ τήν . . . χεῖρα τοῦ θεοῦ, ἵνα ὑμᾶς ὑψώσῃ) corresponds to Jas. 4:10 (ταπεινώθητε ἐνώπιον κυρίου, καὶ ὑψώσει ὑμᾶς; cf. Jas. 4:7:
ὑποτάγητε οὖν τῷ θεῷ). Also the idea in vv. 8f. (διάβολος . . . , ᾧ ἀντίστητε) is
matched verbatim in Jas. 4:7 (ἀντίστητε δὲ τῷ διαβόλῳ). Both authors have, therefore, developed in accord with their own purposes a parenetic tradition that gave
schematic shape to the theme of submission under God and resistance to the devil.[1]

I Peter gives emphasis to this antithesis by use of the OT images of "the
hand of God" (v. 6) and "a roaring lion" (v. 8). In the honing of individual directives
he uses other formulaic and sayings material of early Christian parenesis, as in
v. 7 with its parenetic expansion of Jesus' saying against worrying and v. 8 with
its formula regarding staying awake, which similarly grew out of the Jesus tradition: "Be sober, stay awake," which is also found in I Thess. 5:6 (cf. nn. 7 and
10). Prior to Christian usage, the antithesis between God and the adversary is found
exclusively, both in terms of content and with respect to the two images, in the
Essene texts, but an Essene formulaic tradition corresponding to this passage in
I Peter cannot be confirmed (cf. nn. 3, 16, and 11).

b. V. 10, a promise that not only concludes the section, but also the entire
letter, summarizing its intention, follows in structure and key terminology a
parenetic schema of final words that also appears in I Thess. 5:23f.; Heb. 13:20f.;
II Thess. 2:16f., and which in I Thessalonians and Hebrews, as here in I Peter,
also comes before the epistolary conclusion. Even this traditional schema (cf. n.27)
is shaped independently by the author of I Peter in such a way that his intention
is thereby expressed.

Vv. 6f.: Accepting Affliction from God

6 The author now draws a consequence — directly in the sense of the
quotation — from the scriptural promise for the humble quoted in v. 5b,
which in the first instance was to give foundation to humility in one's
relations with fellow Christians (v. 5a): ταπεινώθητε οὖν ὑπὸ τὴν
κραταιὰν χεῖρα τοῦ θεοῦ, "Therefore humble yourselves under the
mighty hand of God." This imperative is not merely aimed at an ongoing

---

1. Boismard, *Quatre hymnes,* 135, conjectures that the two passages are based on a
baptismal hymn. This is more than improbable.

basic posture, but at submission[2] in concrete circumstances as the response to the pressures brought by society. "God's hand" is an OT image
for God's mighty activity, carried out, though hidden, by historical
events.[3] In the vexations and hurts inflicted on Christians on account
of their being Christian, what is at work is not only human delusion
and malice but also, as this image notes at the end, God in judgment
and grace (1:6; 2:20; 3:17; 4:17, 19). Therefore, one should accept these
obstacles to life in the sense of the third petition of the Lord's Prayer
in submission before God, and that without bitterness or thoughts of
retaliation (3:8f.; cf. Jn. 19:11).

Whoever accepts the pressures brought by society, concretely
demonstrating faith thereby, as "abasement" from God, may be certain
of his or her "exaltation" by God: ἵνα ὑμᾶς ὑψώσῃ. . . . Here the author
conveys in the language of the OT God's pledge, that which in 4:13
and 5:1 was promised by Christ to those who participate in his suffering.
God "exalts" by granting a share in the glory that Christ received by
his exaltation (1:11; 3:22), a share in a life free of evil and pain, not by
mediating a "future position of power" or a "triumph over the afflicting
ones."[4] This will take place ἐν καιρῷ, "at an appointed time," namely,
ἐν καιρῷ ἐσχάτῳ (1:5), in the end at the parousia.

That God exalts the one who bows before God, accepting his or
her destiny, is attested variously in "Scripture"; v. 5 reminds one of this.
It is brought home to Christians even more in v. 7 through a saying
from the Jesus tradition found in Matthew and Luke and in a parenetic
tradition of the Church growing out of the saying.[5] Ultimately, the future

---

2. ταπεινόω, "make lower" (Lk. 3:5), figuratively "humiliate," "humble," is often used
in a precise sense in the LXX for ענה, whose derivative עני is translated with ταπεινός (cf.
W. Grundmann, "ταπεινός," *TDNT* VIII, 4f., 6f.). In the NT the verb is found, as here, in
Jas. 4:10 in the antithesis "humiliate"-"exalt," in the Synoptic saying in Mt. 18:4 par. (four
occurrences; see below, n.5), and in the christological formula in Phil. 2:8. In Paul verb and
adjective are used differently; only ταπεινοφροσύνη (Phil. 2:3b) corresponds to the usage in
I Peter (see the comments on 5:5). I Pet. 5:5b-6 belongs, therefore, even in terms of the
history of word-usage, with the passages in the Synoptic Gospels and James.

3. For Israel, the deliverance from Egypt became the intervention "of God's hand" in the
interpretation of prophecy (Ex. 3:19; 6:1; 13:3, 9, 14, 16; Dt. 9:26, 29; 26:8; cf. Jer. 21:5; Ezek.
20:33f., and others). This OT image was given intensive attention among the Essenes, while both
Hellenistic and rabbinic Judaism were very hesitant to use it (E. Lohse, "χείρ," *TDNT* IX, 431f.).
In the NT it is found primarily in Acts: God's hand becomes active through adversaries (4:28),
and at the same time against them (13:11), all the more through missionaries (4:29; 11:21).

4. The former, Windisch, 79; the latter, Kelly, 207f., and others.

5. That the parenetic tradition takes this saying tradition as its point of departure is

exaltation becomes a certainty through Jesus' own exaltation. The believer can understand and accept this pledge on the basis of the interpretation of his or her situation of suffering as judgment and grace.

7   Believers may not only accept the oppressive encounters that occur in this sense from God and have hope regarding their future reception by God. They may at the same time hand over to God the fear for their existence, for its meaning and future, that presses in on them with society's discrimination; they are to "cast" as a burden "all worry" on him: πᾶσαν τὴν μέριμναν ὑμῶν ἐπιρίψαντες ἐπ' αὐτόν. To a degree this directive corresponds to the one in 4:19. It appropriates in parenetic formulation⁶ that which was intended by Jesus' saying against worry over what is necessary for life together with its foundation (Mt. 6:25-34 par. Lk.).⁷

---

to be shown both by the identical arrangement and by the differences: The divine passive, which is typical for the saying, is decoded, and out of the saying of proverbial wisdom, which spoke in circumlocution, comes the direct imperative:

I Pet. 5:6:   ταπεινώθητε . . . , ἵνα ὑμᾶς ὑψώσῃ.
Jas. 4:10:   ταπεινώθητε . . . , καὶ ὑψώσει ὑμᾶς.
Lk. 14:11:   . . . ὁ ταπεινῶν ἑαυτὸν ὑψωθήσεται.

6. The participle ἐπιρίψαντες is not a circumlocution for the imperative, but indicates the close connection with the preceding sentence.

7. The parenesis here is not based on OT and Jewish tradition in terms of the history of word usage. The Greek words for "worry"/"be anxious" do not have Hebrew equivalents. In the LXX μέριμνα represents a Hebrew word in only one of its twelve occurrences (Ps. 54:23 LXX: יְהָב, found only there and uncertain in meaning). μεριμνᾶν occurs nine times in the LXX and represents six different Hebrew words. The same is true in postcanonical Jewish literature (R. Bultmann, "μεριμνάω," *TDNT* IV, 590; Str.-Bill. I, 435). I Pet. 5:7a was formulated in accord with Ps. 54:23 LXX, which is unique in the OT: ἐπίρριψον ἐπὶ κύριον τὴν μέριμνάν σου. . . . This is the case even if v. 7b was shaped in accordance with Wis. 12:13 (οὔτε γὰρ θεός ἐστιν πλὴν σοῦ, ᾧ μέλει περὶ πάντων . . .), μέλει μοι περί . . . occurring only five times in the LXX and only in Wis. 12:13 in a formulation comparable to I Pet. 5:7b. μέλει μοι περί . . . is not used with the same sense as in I Pet. 5:7 elsewhere in the NT (cf. Jn. 10:13).

μεριμνᾶν and μέριμνα occur in the NT only here, in the Synoptics, and in Paul. The Synoptic saying suggests itself as the point of departure for NT sayings against anxiety, but there the term is not used absolutely, but as a circumlocution in accord with a Hebrew backgound: μὴ μεριμνᾶτε τῇ ψυχῇ ὑμῶν, τί φάγητε, κτλ. (Mt. 6:25, 27f., 31 (34) par. Lk.; Mt. 10:19; Lk. 10:41; in F. Delitzsch's Hebrew NT [Berlin, 1878] μεριμνᾶν is represented by דאג, "be troubled/apprehensive," "be afraid," which the LXX translates with μεριμνᾶν only in Ps. 38:19). It is first in Phil. 4:6 that we find the absolute formulation taken from Greek word usage (Bultmann, *TDNT* IV, 589f.): "Do not be anxious"; on other occasions Paul uses these words in a different direction. I Pet. 5:7 is not dependent on this Pauline parenesis, but on a tradition that appropriated Jesus' directive with the aid of the LXX. Jesus' words were already applied redactionally in the Synoptic tradition (Mk. 4:19 par.; Lk. 21:34). This

Worry, anxiety for oneself and striving to secure one's own life, which are marked by fear, is lifted from those who are called to faith, since God "cares" for them: ὅτι αὐτῷ μέλει περὶ ὑμῶν. This foundation is to be understood in terms of the one in Jesus' saying in Mt. 6:26-33 par.: God now opens up the life, which no person can create for himself or herself, by establishing his gracious dominion (Mt. 6:33). In light of this eschatological event, which is made known and realized through the word, the care of the Creator, hidden by so much, becomes manifest (Mt. 6:26-30). For this reason, under life-threatening circumstances Paul clings to the God who raises the dead and so is able to give thanks for preservation in the meantime (II Cor. 1:8-11).[8] This casting off of fear is just as necessary as submission: If a person does not succeed at separating himself or herself from fear, fear separates him or her from God. Affliction either drives one into the arms of God or severs one from God. Vv. 8f. make this alternative clear: During affliction not only "surrender" but also "resistance" is necessary.

Vv. 8f.: Resistance against the Aggression of Evil

In affliction it is not only God who is at work, but also "your adversary, the devil." This aspect of the situation, not yet mentioned up to this point, follows from its interpretation as πειρασμός (1:6; 4:12). As viewed by both OT and NT tradition, πειρασμός not only goes forth from God as examination (cf. the comments above), but also from Satan as temptation.[9] Jesus himself developed the idea that the eschatological drawing near of God

---

tradition then generalized Jesus' admonition, which had been formulated with illustrations, and summarized his foundational remarks in the consolation: "for he cares for you."

The saying against worry in I Pet. 5:7 is presupposed as established Christian parenesis in *Herm. Vis.* 3.11.3; 4.2.4 (LCL AF II, 55f., 65), and *Vis.* 4.2.5 repeats: ἐπιρίψατε τὰς μέριμνας ὑμῶν ἐπὶ τὸν κύριον . . . (μεριμνᾶν and μέριμνα do not occur elsewhere in the Apostolic Fathers).

8. Bultmann, *TDNT* IV, 590-593, interprets too much toward human self-understanding, too little toward God's activity.

9. The same blunder of David is traced back in II Sam. 24:1 to Yahweh's wrath and in I Chr. 21:1 to Satan (a similar development is seen from Gen. 22:1 to *Jub.* 17:16 [*OT Pseudep.* II, 90]). The two aspects represent in the OT differing explanations within the history of OT theology, and in the NT they belong together on a substantive level: Unlike I Peter (1:6; 4:12), the NT usually traces πειρασμός back to Satan (Mk. 1:13 par. Mt. 4:1[3] par. Lk. 4:2[13]; I Cor. 7:5; I Thess. 3:5), but then the same authors also, with emphasis, trace it to God (Mk. 6:13 par.; I Cor. 10:13; this is rejected only as an excuse in Jas. 1:13f., purely on parenetic grounds). Cf. H. Seesemann, "πεῖρα," *TDNT* VI, 28-32.

provokes, at the same time, the powers of evil and brings them into alliance under Satan for a unified counteraction (Mt. 12:25f., 28f. par.); evil thus also takes on an eschatological shape. This eschatological opposition between the work of God and the work of Satan is especially active in the tension between Christians and society (Lk. 22:31-36; Revelation 12).

8 This verse begins with the eschatological summons to wakefulness: νήψατε, γρηγορήσατε, "Be sober, stay awake."[10] No other NT letter admonishes the readers so vigorously to sobriety. Whoever becomes sober through faith sees the situation in society realistically, turns to God in hope and prayer (1:13; 4:7), and puts up resistance, as is added here, in a watchful way and, therefore, with vigilance against the threat: ὁ ἀντίδικος ὑμῶν διάβολος ὡς λέων ὠρυόμενος περιπατεῖ, "Your adversary, the devil, stalks about like a roaring lion." This image is not a freely constructed visualization of the threat. It is a traditional simile, appropriated here, as most often in the NT, in connection with the OT, which uses the image frequently.[11]

In the conflicts with surrounding society a strong predator is on the prowl everywhere, who, craving spoil and spreading terror — more is not to be derived from the expression "roaring"[12] — uses every

---

10. The closest parallel in NT parenesis is I Thess. 5:6, 8: "Let us keep awake and be sober . . . put on the breastplate of faith." This admonition applies to a situation that has been characterized as eschatological and has recourse to a parousia parable. In the Synoptic tradition the summons to "stay awake" is rooted in the parousia parables (Mk. 13:[33-]35 par. Mt. 24:42 = 25:13; Lk. 12:37; 21:34-36) and in the Gethsemane pericope (Mk. 14:[34, 37] 38 par. Mt.). The same imperative is found in parenesis that goes beyond I Thess. 5:6 in a generalizing way in I Cor. 16:13 (Rom. 13:11); Col. 4:2; Rev. 3:2; 16:15. See E. Lövestam, *Spiritual Wakefulness in the NT* (Lund, 1963), 60ff., 136ff.

11. Here I Peter follows Ps. 21:14 LXX: ἤνοιξαν ἐπ᾽ ἐμὲ τὸ στόμα αὐτῶν, ὡς λέων ὁ ἁρπάζων καὶ ὠρυόμενος. In Qumran as well the image of the lion is appropriated often and almost throughout in dependence on the OT (while it is absent from the rest of Jewish writings): 1QH 5:9, 13f. makes use of the situation of Daniel (Dan. 6:23), as does Heb. 11:33. 4QpNah 1:5 interprets this OT passage in terms of a prince afflicting the community (cf. 4QpHos 1). In Rev. 13:2, the anti-Christian world ruler who persecutes the Church as a tool of the devil bears motifs of the lion, which in Dan. 7:4-6 represents one of the last kingdoms of the world. This is the general background of the expression in I Pet. 5:8, the closest NT analogy to which is II Tim. 4:17 (cf. further *Herm. Vis.* 4.1f. [LCL AF II, 61f.]). I Pet. 5:8 does not borrow from the use of the lion as symbol of the Phrygian mother-god Cybele (contra Perdelwitz, *Mysterienreligion,* 101f.).

12. Schwank, "Diabolos tamquam leo," explains: The roaring is intended to stir a panic among the flock in the fold and cause it to break out. But such visual imagery does not lie within the purview of the traditional imagery represented here. In contrast, the "roaming about" of the lion can be compared, in accordance with Job 1:7, with Satan's roving about in the world.

opportunity to devour whomever he can: ζητῶν τίνα καταπιεῖν.[13] "Devoured," utterly destroyed, is the person who under the pressure of the situation surrenders faith (cf. v. 9a).[14] The "lion" is not, as often in the OT and the Essene writings, a human opponent of the community, but "your adversary" absolutely, namely, "the devil." ὁ διάβολος, in Greek usage "the slanderer," refers in the LXX, where it translates Hebrew שָׂטָן, to either "accuser" (Zech. 3:1; Job 1–2) or "tempter" (I Chr. 21:1), depending on context, i.e., always "adversary." It is in this sense of the word that it became the designation "devil."[15] In the NT, which goes beyond the OT and Jewish concepts, the σατανᾶς, or usually in later documents as here the διάβολος, becomes the adversary of God and his Church absolutely, the one who seeks to hinder the eschatological event of salvation and to wrest believers from the life with God through bodily harm and, above all, through temptation.[16]

Here, as nowhere else in the NT, the devil is called the "adversary" (ἀντίδικος). This corresponds to the technical meaning of διάβολος in the OT as well as to what the term signifies in the NT.[17] I Peter 5 does

---

13. The grammatically difficult but possible reading ζητῶν τίνα καταπιεῖν should be regarded as original (cf., e.g., *Test. Jos.* 7:1 [*OT Pseudep.* I, 821]: περιεβλέπετο ποίῳ τρόπῳ με παγιδεῦσαι). See BDF §368 [p. 186]; Windisch, 80; Selwyn, 237f.; Schelkle, 132, n.1; Kelly, 210. The textual variants presuppose unaccented τινα and try to smooth out the construction: B, 0206, and a few others remove τινα (this is not original, as Beare, 203, 205, supposes); 𝔭72, A, Koine, others, Vulgate, Syriac, and Origen smooth out the reading with καταπίη. Accented τινά would be, in terms of content, too weak.

14. καταπίνω, actually "drink down," was already in Greek literature usually more general: "swallow down," "devour," referring to total destruction (L. Goppelt, "πίνω," *TDNT* VI, 158f.). It is applied similarly in Jer. 28:34 LXX (= 51:34): κατέπιέν με ὡς δράκων, of Nebuchadnezzar, who is then called ἀντίδικος and compared with a lion (vv. 36, 38).

15. W. Foerster, "διάβολος," *TDNT* II, 73.

16. Judaism developed the figure of Satan beyond the OT, above all, in order to let evil originate from Satan rather than God. But it did not give that figure either a sharp profile or a ruling position among the powers of evil. Only among the Essenes is "Belial" or the "angel of darkness" the ruling power of evil, who leads the righteous astray and to whose rule is credited "all their chastisements and every season of their distress" (1QS 3:21-23). Independent of this, though equally conditioned by the eschatological situation of decision, the NT gives to Satan a similar position: From him comes hurt among people (Mk. 3:23-26 par.; Lk. 13:16; I Cor. 5:5; I Thess. 2:18, etc.) and, above all, temptation (see above, n.9).

17. ἀντίδικος originally meant "courtroom opponent" and has that meaning in Prov. 18:17 LXX and, except in I Pet. 5:8, throughout the NT, though in illustrative application (Mt. 5:25 par.; Lk. 18:3). Here, as is often the case in I Peter, it has a general sense: the "adversary" (so also Esth. 8:11 LXX). Satan is called "adversary" elsewhere only in *Life of Adam and Eve* 33 (*OT Pseudep.* II, 272): "Immediately the adversary, the devil, found opportunity. . . ." Among the five designations for Satan in Rev. 12:9f. κατήγωρ, "accuser," comes closest to the technical term ἀντίδικος.

not emphasize as much as Rev. 2:10; 12:17; 13:7 that the devil unleashes aggression against the Church, but more that he uses the pressures brought by society to intimidate believers into accommodating themselves to ordinary customs and, thereby, into abandoning their eschatological existence (cf. 4:4).[18]

Though I Peter thus sees the "adversary," the "devil," at work in social discrimination against Christians, it does not ultimately appropriate a traditional mythological explanation. It correctly states, rather — in a traditional form, to be sure — that behind the aggression against Christians stands not only individual deceit and malice, but also a supraindividual orientation in society, which is called into question by Christians and is, thereby, provoked (cf. Eph. 6:12).[19] It is precisely knowledge of this supraindividual background that liberates one to encounter the human opponent in accord with the commandment to love one's enemy, i.e., "not to resist" this one (3:9; Mt. 5:39), in order, however, all the more decisively to fight and to resist "evil." It is only a question of how the individual person is capable of overcoming this supraindividual principle of evil.

9 ᾧ ἀντίστητε στερεοὶ τὶ πίστει. Onc who resists[20] is one who remains "firm with respect to faith"[21] and in daily life conducts himself or herself in accord with faith, defying all pressures to conform and thus keeping faith amid God's testing (1:7). Only at the beginning (1:5, 7, 9, 21) and here at the conclusion does I Peter refer to "faith." But faith is for the letter the orientation of one's entire conduct toward God as it has become directed by the gospel (see the comments on 1:21). One who keeps faith is one who in daily life lives "in obedience to the truth" (1:22). Faith overcomes evil, but it does so not as a human stance,

---

18. Ignatius understood his path to martyrdom in this sense as a battle with Satan: *Trall.* 4:2 (LCL AF I, 217).

19. Beare, 204f., fails to recognize this supraindividual character of the conflict, when he, with respect to what is said about the "devil," wants to reduce the matter to the "unregenerate heart."

20. The command ἀντίστητε, "resist," is also found verbatim in Jas. 4:7 and similarly in Eph. 6:12, further in *Herm. Mand.* 12.5 (LCL AF II, 133f.). Kelly, 210, conjectures that this tradition belonged to pre-baptismal parenesis, but this cannot be made probable.

21. στερεός, "firm," "hard," of objects, but from Homer on also of human character: "solid"; cf. BAGD s.v. The closest NT verbal parallel is Acts 16:5: αἱ . . . ἐκκλησίαι ἐστερεοῦντο τῇ πίστει . . . , "the churches were strengthened in the faith." The closest parallel in content is Col. 1:23: "provided that you continue in the faith, stable and steadfast" (τεθεμελιωμένοι καὶ ἑδραῖοι).

but by the power of its content (cf. I Jn. 5:4f.; Rev. 12:10-12). Therefore, the letter's parenesis for the persecuted concludes not with this imperative, but with the promise in v. 10.

First, however, that which was just stated is underscored with a view to Christianity's worldwide common experience: εἰδότες τὰ αὐτὰ τῶν παθημάτων τῇ ἐν τῷ κόσμῳ ὑμῶν ἀδελφότητι ἐπιτελεῖσθαι, "knowing that the same sufferings have come on your brotherhood in the world."[22] Once again the author expresses the bond connecting Christians to one another with the collective term unique to him: ἀδελφότης, "brotherhood" (cf. 2:17). This worldwide fellowship — "world" is here the inhabited earth, not humanity hostile to God[23] — is bound together, not like the Jewish Diaspora by organization, but through the exchange of faith experience and parenesis (Rom. 1:8; Phil. 1:30; *I Clem.* 2:4 [LCL AF I, 10-13], etc.). From the mid-second century on churches have especially exchanged their accounts of martyrs.[24] "Peter," who is writing in "Babylon" (v. 13), can say to the Christians in Asia Minor that their brothers and sisters in the whole Empire are exposed to the same affliction.[25] But how could

---

22. V. 9b is very cumbersome grammatically: εἰδότες with the meaning "knowing" normally is followed by ὅτι, but the accusative with the infinitive is already possible in classical Greek (so also Lk. 4:41; *I Clem.* 62:3 [LCL AF I, 117]; cf. BDF §397.3 [pp. 204f.]). One does not have to assume here, therefore, εἰδέναι with the infinitive = "to understand how to do something, to be able to do something" (e.g., Mt. 7:11) and translate ἐπιτελεῖσθαι as middle (in analogy to Xenophon, *Memorabilia* 4.8.8 [LCL IV, 357]: τὰ τοῦ γήρως εἰτελεῖσθαι, "to pay the old man's forfeit . . ."): "show yourselves able to fulfill the same debt to suffering as your brotherhood in the world" (contra Beare, 206). The verb is, rather, passive, ἀδελφότητι is dative of disadvantage, and τὰ αὐτὰ τῶν παθημάτων is merely an emphasized circumlocution for τὰ αὐτὰ παθήματα, so that one should translate: "by knowing that the same suffering is being experienced by your brotherhood in the world" (so also G. Delling, "ἐπιτελέω," *TDNT* VIII, 61f.; Kelly, 211).

23. ὁ κόσμος here, as in II Macc. 3:12; Rom. 1:8; I Cor. 14:10; Mk. 14:9 par. Mt. (εἰς ὅλον τὸν κόσμον; in Mt. 24:14, ἐν ὅλῃ τῇ οἰκουμένῃ), does not have the special sense seen in Jn. 15:18f.: "Because you are not of the world, . . . the world hates you"; 16:33. So Selwyn, 238; Schelkle, 132, n.2; Kelly, 212; G. Johnston, "Οἰκουμένη and κόσμος in the NT," *NTS* 10 (1963/64), 354f.; contra Beare, 206.

24. The account of Polycarp's martyrdom was sent from Smyrna to Philomelium (prescript [LCL AF II, 313]), and the churches of Lyons and Vienna reported to the churches in Asia and Phrygia about the events of A.D. 177-178 (*HE* 5.1.1–2.8 [LCL I, 405-441]).

25. It is not to be derived from this reference regarding the historical situation that a state-organized wave of persecution was in progress throughout the Roman Empire, but only that the conflicts addressed in I Peter were to be found everywhere because a corresponding estimate of the Christian religion had spread about and Christians everywhere caused offense in society in the same way. This situation was a reality from the police action of Nero up into the time of Trajan. So Selwyn, 238; Kelly, 211ff.; contra Windisch, 80 ("One would almost like to assume a general edict").

knowing this help anyone? The barb of suffering is having it happen arbitrarily to oneself alone. Sharing a destiny, not standing alone in affliction, is even humanly speaking an important help.[26] But more than this, the general experience of all Christians confirms that one's own painful barriers to life, one's "sufferings," are not the personal misfortune of individuals, but belong to the essence of faith and are signs of its power against evil. Even more, they are signs that faith is sustained through grace.

Vv. 10f.: Promise as Conclusion

10 This final word is a promise, not, as in the tradition-historical parallels, an entreaty.[27] It summarizes the intention of the entire letter. Attention is focused on the "God of all grace." I Peter also knows God as the judge (4:5f., 17), but it expects from God, at first and at the last, grace, the demonstration of love (1:10, 13; 3:7; 5:5, 12) in everyday life both in society (2:19f.) and in the Church (4:10). God is ὁ θεὸς πάσης χάριτος because he surrounds each person and every situation with his demonstrations of grace.[28]

God's grace manifests itself in all that is said here about him, fundamentally in his summons, which becomes effective ultimately in baptism (cf. 1:15; 2:9, 21). The summons is given ἐν Χριστῷ, "in Christ," i.e., on the basis of the resurrection and the living presence of

---

26. Cf. Thucydides 7.75.6 (LCL IV, 155): . . . ἡ ἰσομοιρία τῶν κακῶν, ἔχουσά τινα ὅμως τὸ μετὰ πολλῶν κούφισιν. . . .

27. L, P, Koine, and many others have optative στηρίσαι, and 614 and a few others have the optative also in the other three verbs; as part of the Textus Receptus the optative was taken over in Luther's translation: "may you be . . ."

This alteration came about by accommodation to other NT closing statements that are similar to I Pet. 5:10 in beginning with "the God of peace" (I Thess. 5:23; Heb. 13:20; cf. "the God of all grace" in I Pet. 5:10), emphasized by αὐτός (I Thess. 5:23; II Thess. 2:16f.), by referring to God's calling (I Thess. 5:24; cf. "who loved" in II Thess. 2:16) and the eschatological goal ("the parousia" in I Thess. 2:16), and by focusing on God's protection (I Thess. 5:24: "he will do it"; Heb. 13:21: καταρτίσαι; II Thess. 2:17: στηρίξαι). In Heb. 13:21, as in I Pet. 5:11, a doxology is attached. In I Thess. 5:25-28 and Heb. 13:22-25, as in I Pet. 5:12-14, the epistolary conclusion follows. The three passages in I Thessalonians, Hebrews, and I Peter are clearly based on the same schema, which speaks of the protection of the called for the consummation. But this schema is shaped in each instance in accord with the intention of the particular letter.

28. The closest parallel is II Cor. 1:3: θεὸς πάσης παρακλήσεως. Cf. I Pet. 4:10: ποικίλης χάριτος; Jas. 1:17.

the crucified One (1:3; 4:13).[29] The goal of the summons, which spawns faith and hope, is eternal glory (cf. at 4:13; 5:1): ὁ καλέσας ὑμᾶς εἰς τὴν αἰώνιον αὐτοῦ δόξαν. The arch reaching from calling to participation in glory spans across and encompasses Christian existence in time. Its shape in history is characterized again, as at the beginning of the letter in 1:6, as ὀλίγον παθόντας, "suffering for a brief (time)," so that the "eternal" consummation comes after a period made brief by the nearness of the end (1:7; cf. Rom. 8:18; II Cor. 4:17).

How the journey through this valley of affliction can be maintained beneath the arch of one's calling to its conclusion is the vital question of Christian existence as I Peter sees it. The letter was written to help the "elect strangers in the Diaspora" (1:1) in this question by directive and encouragement. It closes with the promise that God will be true to his calling and will bring those who are called through the darkness to the goal, since everything flows from God's "grace," his free turning in love to humankind.

αὐτός, "he himself," will do it.[30] He is not the distant principle of origin for the world; he is near those who are called and becomes active in relationship to them, as is brought to expression now in four verbs: καταρτίσει, στηρίξει, σθενώσει, θεμελιώσει. These verbs do not say what will happen at the consummation after the "suffering," but now in the brief time of affliction.[31] καταρτίσει, "he will restore" those who have failed or have suffered losses: He will bring to wholeness what is fragmentary.[32] στηρίξει, he will "strengthen" those who have become weak and unsteady so that their faith remains "firm" (v. 9).[33] σθενώσει,

---

29. ἐν Χριστῷ, so also in 3:16 (see the comments there) and 5:14, belongs with καλέσας (Bengel, ad loc.; Kelly, 212f.), not with δόξα (so von Hofmann, 197f.) or with both (Selwyn, 240).

30. αὐτός, used here emphatically to emphasize God's personal engagement. αὐτός is used of God about nine times in the NT, five of those in I and II Thessalonians, including the tradition-historical "parallels" I Thess. 5:23 and II Thess. 2:16; cf. Rev. 21:3; different are I Pet. 2:24 and Rom. 8:16, 26: "the Spirit itself."

31. παθόντας has, like λυπηθέντες in 1:6, a present meaning; one ought not press the aorist to the extent that the promise extends to reinstatement of that which the persecution impaired (contra Selwyn, 239f.; Wohlenberg, 154).

32. καταρτίζω is based on ἄρτιος, "appropriate," and actually means "make complete," e.g., to set a limb (Herodotus 5.106 [LCL III, 128-131]) or outfit a ship (Polybius 1.21.4 [LCL I, 57f.]). Figuratively it means "correct," "make complete, ready"; thus often with various antecedents in parenesis: I Thess. 3:10 (faith); I Cor. 1:10 (the unity of a local church); Heb. 13:21 (in everything good); Lk. 6:40 (entirely). Cf. G. Delling, "καταρτίζω," *TDNT* I, 475f.

33. στηρίζω, "set up," "secure," "support," figuratively: "make firm," "make strong," "strengthen," "make steadfast"; often in parenesis: in Acts 14:22; I Thess. 3:2f., (13), as here, of the strengthening of faith in affliction for the consummation, similarly in the

he will empower, he will give power for the fulfillment of the calling and for defense against the adversary.[34] θεμελιώσει, "he will establish," he will give to the Church and to individuals a firm place on the foundation to which the gospel points (cf. 2:6).[35]

11 The promise of v. 10 enables the grace and faithfulness of God to shine in a direct and imposing way. Therefore, a doxology of adoration responds to the promise. The doxology in 4:11 mentioned both δόξα and κράτος, but this one leaves aside δόξα and concentrates on κράτος, "power": To God belongs the power/might.[36] The preceding assurance is strengthened thereby. Promise and doxology in vv. 10f. conclude in summary fashion the entire parenesis of the letter. There follows now the letter's closing.

---

tradition-historical "parallel" II Thess. 2:17; cf. Lk. 22:32; Acts 15:32; 18:23; Rom. 1:11; 16:25; II Thess. 3:3; Jas. 5:8; Rev. 3:2.

34. σθενόω occurs quite rarely in Greek literature, in the Greek Bible only here: "make strong," "impart strength" (BAGD s.v.); Greek literature normally has in its place σθένω, "be strong," which is absent from the NT (in the LXX only in III Macc. 3:8).

35. θεμελιώσει is to be read with 𝔓[72], ℵ, and others against A, B, Old Latin, and Vulgate (so Windisch, 80; Schelkle, 133, n.1; Beare, 207; Spicq, 176; Kelly, 213, and others; contra Selwyn, 241); it was not inserted under the influence of Col. 1:23 but omitted on the basis of homoioteleuton. θεμελιόω, "provide a foundation" (Mt. 7:25: the house on the rock), "furnish with a foundation," figuratively, "secure," "establish"; so Eph. 3:17: "being rooted and grounded in love"; Col. 1:23: "provided that you continue in the faith, stable and steadfast, not shifting from the hope . . ."; cf. *Herm. Vis.* 3.13.4; 4.1.4 (LCL AF II, 59, 61) and the figurative meaning of θεμέλιον, "ground," in I Cor. 3:10ff.; Eph. 2:20; II Tim. 2:19; Heb. 11:10; Rev. 21:14, 19.

36. One ought to supply, as in 4:11 (see the comments there), ἐστίν, not ἔστω; cf. 5:6: κραταιὰ χείρ.

5:12-14: The Letter's Closing

12 *Through Silvanus,*
a faithful brother in my judgment,
I have written to you briefly,
summoning
and giving witness that this is the true grace of God,
so that you may stand in it.

13 *Greetings to you from the co-elect (church) in Babylon*
and from Mark, my son.

14 *Greet one another with the kiss of love.*
Peace to all of you who are in Christ.

The Closing Formula and Its Setting

1. In his letters to churches Paul shaped a closing formula that is even more different than his letter opening from what was customarily used in letters of the time. The Greco-Roman letter usually closed briefly with ἔρρωσθε, "live well" (e.g., II Macc. 11:21, 33; Acts 15:29), or, in letters to those of higher social position, with εὐτύχε, "good luck" (e.g., Plato, *Epistulae* 4.321c [LCL VII, 446f.]), and the date.[1] In place of this brief closing Paul always inserts, written in his own hand, a liturgical wish for blessing, which communicates grace (see n.5 below). Before this wish he extends personal greetings. While greetings appear only rarely in pre-Christian Greek letters and somewhat more often in letters from an eastern context,[2] Paul developed this feature

---

1. O. Roller, *Das Formular der paulinischen Briefe* (BWANT 4/6; Stuttgart, 1933), 68-70, 114-116, 481-488 (bibliography 75, n.2); W. G. Doty, *Letters in Primitive Christianity* (Philadelphia, 1973), 39f.; S. K. Stowers, *Letter Writing in Greco-Roman Antiquity* (Philadelphia, 1986), 20f.; BAGD s.v. ῥώννυμι.
2. Roller, *Formular,* 67f.; H. Windisch, "ἀσπάζομαι," *TDNT* I, 494f., 500-502.

in order to strengthen the *koinonia* of the one *ekklesia* through expressions of personal contact. Before these greetings is often found an introduction of the letter carrier, as in other ancient letters,[3] and sometimes also a comment about the composition of the letter and its intention.[4] I Peter has a full letter ending consisting of the elements just mentioned, though it fashions them in a particular way, one that indicates that it is not directly dependent on the Pauline formula.

a. The reference to the mediation of the letter through Silvanus in v. 12a shows greater affinity in its formulation with Acts 15:22 than it does with the Pauline notations about the letter carrier. The comment about the intention of the author in v. 12b has its closest parallel in Heb. 13:22: In both cases, παρακαλεῖν is named as the intention and the brevity of the document are emphasized. The greetings in v. 13 are extended first from the entire church (as in II Cor. 13:12; Phil. 4:22; II Jn. 13) and then, as is often the case, from an individual. The concluding admonition in v. 14a for the addressees to greet one another with the liturgical kiss is found elsewhere in the NT only in Paul (Rom 16:16; I Cor. 16:20; II Cor. 13:12; I Thess. 5:26), who formulates it differently: Paul calls this kiss of the brotherhood the φίλημα ἅγιον, while I Peter calls it the φίλημα ἀγάπης.

b. In place of the final greeting v. 14b has a liturgical wish for blessing, which speaks of "grace,"[5] which Paul sometimes mentions in such contexts, but elsewhere in the NT (only III Jn. 15) is replaced by "peace." In Paul, wishes for peace are found, but more often earlier in the closing section of a letter.[6]

Thus, the letter ending of I Peter follows the early Christian formula as it was developed especially by Paul, but fashions it in keeping with the tradition and intention articulated in the entire letter.

2. In 5:12-14, more is said about the situation of composition than in most other NT letter endings: Peter writes through the mediation of Silvanus from "Babylon," i.e., from Rome, while (John) Mark is also in his company. Those named, especially Peter, could in fact have been, according to other reliable information, in Rome around the mid-60s.[7] But the content of the letter — and the

---

3. Rom. 16:1; I Cor. 16:17; II Cor. 8:17; Eph. 6:21; Phil. 2:25; Col. 4:7f.; Phlm. 11f. (Phlm. 21f.: announcement of his own visit). This notice about the bearer is often formulated otherwise with: "writing through": Ignatius, *Rom.* 10:1; *Phld.* 11:2; *Smyr.* 12:1 (LCL AF I, 237f., 251, 265): ". . . I am writing to you by Burrhus, whom you . . . sent with me, and he has in every way refreshed me"; Polycarp, *Phil.* 14 (*ibid.,* 301): "Haec vobis spripsi per Crescentem" ("I have written this to you by Crescens, whom I commended to you . . ."). So also in a non-Christian letter: ἔπεμψά σοι ἄλλας δύο ἐπιστολάς, διὰ Νηδύμου μίαν, διὰ Κρονίου . . . μίαν (*Ägyptische Urkunden aus den Staatlichen Museen zu Berlin: Griechische Urkunden* [1895-1970], no. 1079).

4. Gal. 6:11-17; I Tim. 6:20f.; Phlm. 21f.; Heb. 13:22.

5. Rom. 16:20; I Cor. 16:23; II Cor. 13:13; Gal. 6:18; Eph. 6:24; Phil. 4:23; Col. 4:18; I Thess. 5:28; II Thess. 3:18; Phlm. 25; so also I Tim. 6:20; II Tim. 4:22; Tit. 3:15; also Heb. 13:25.

6. Rom. 15:33; II Cor. 13:11; Gal. 6:16; Eph. 6:23; II Thess. 3:16.

7. See the Introduction above, p. 10.

designation of Rome as "Babylon" — suggests that it was written sometime after the Neronian persecution, that is to say, not directly by Peter. Consequently, one should ask whether what is said about these three men here reveals what could have been derived from generally available tradition, or if it represents the kind of circulated material corresponding to the tradition out of which the letter emerged. Put another way: Are these statements merely artful pseudepigraphic depiction or the signature of the tradition that found its repository in the letter?

In the first sentence of the letter closing Peter refers to the mediator of his letter (v. 12a) and to his intention (v. 12b) — or an unknown author has him say these things.

12a διὰ Σιλουανοῦ . . . δι' ὀλίγων ἔγραψα, "Through Silvanus . . . I have written to you briefly." The phrase characterizes Silvanus, who for the whole Church from Jerusalem to Rome was the representative of the primitive Church and Paul's coworker, as the mediator, in any case, of this letter. Of what did this mediation consist?

Very often the expression, "written through (someone)" refers to the person delivering the letter, who when required would attest to its authenticity and interpret it (see n.3). In the prescript of the apostolic decree the same Silvanus is named together with a second representative of the primitive Church in a similar formula as the carrier of the document: . . . πέμψαι . . . ἄνδρας ἡγουμένους ἐν τοῖς ἀδελφοῖς, γράψαντες διὰ χειρὸς αὐτῶν (Acts 15:22f.). But here in I Peter this figurative understanding of "have written" is excluded by the addition of δι' ὀλίγων ἔγραψα. Furthermore, with the addressees spread all over Asia Minor (1:1f.), a single carrier is hard to imagine.[8] Another sense in which the formula was used is seen when Dionysius of Corinth, writing toward the end of the second century to the church in Rome, refers to *I Clement* as: τὴν προτέραν ὑμῖν διὰ Κλήμεντος γραφεῖσαν, "the (letter) written earlier to us through Clement."[9] Clement was not the letter carrier or the scribe who wrote it out as it was dictated, as, e.g., Tertius wrote Romans.[10] Rather, he wrote it under the commission of and in keeping with the desires of the church in Rome, but very much as his

---

8. Contra Schlatter, *Petrus und Paulus,* 174f.; Selwyn, 241f., who see him as co-author and deliverer of the letter.

9. *HE* 4.23.11 (LCL I, 383).

10. Since the physical preparation of a letter through a scribe was an everyday occurrence, this person could be referred to, as is Tertius in Rom. 16:22, as a brother among brethren, but nowhere is a scribe referred to with the expression "writing through" (Roller, *Formular,* 14-18, 291-304).

own composition.[11] Something corresponding to this is said here of Silvanus; he is thus characterized with emphasis as a reliable coworker.

But who then referred here at the end of the letter to Silvanus in this manner? (1) Peter could have engaged Silvanus as a translator[12] and as cofounder of some of the churches being addressed to lay out the letter and could have named him as his coworker.

(2) But if the letter was first written, as various indicators suggest, sometime after Peter's death,[13] what, then, is intended by this addition to the pseudonym? Is it intended to make the authorship of Peter, whose death was known immediately in the entire Church, seem more probable?[14] The clearly pseudepigraphal letter called II Peter does not even begin to think of such ways of supporting Petrine authorship, but simply claims it.[15] The mention of Silvanus here, therefore, does not correspond to tactics of pseudepigraphy.

Did Silvanus himself encode his authorship in this way, having written the letter as the legacy of Peter (cf. 5:1) as an act of responsibility for churches familiar to him in Asia Minor? In this case, his characterization as "reliable" ($\pi\iota\sigma\tau\acute{o}\varsigma$) would be a guarantee of his loyalty, not inappropriate self-praise. This widely held view[16] is possible. Peter would certainly have named Silvanus along with himself, as Paul does in I Thess. 1:1; Silvanus himself, however, could have placed himself in relationship to Peter in this way on the basis of his function as mediator.

(3) At least as probable, however, is that representatives of the Roman church are passing along in the letter a tradition shaped by Peter and Silvanus.[17] The letter is not, after all, focused on a particular

---

11. This is comparable only in a very conditional sense with the ordinary work of a secretary, which often has been applied (Roller, *Formular,* 18-20, 334-341). It is not correct to say that "Silvanus drew up the letter, but also left traces in it that indicate that writing was his occupation" (Radermacher, "Erster Petrusbrief und Silvanus," 293).

12. So Knopf, 198, referring to *HE* 3.39.15 (LCL I, 297), however, as pseudepigraphal fiction.

13. Cf. the Introduction above, p. 51.

14. So, e.g., Knopf, 18; Beare, 208f.

15. II Pet. 1:1, 14-16; 3:1f., 15f.

16. So P. Feine and J. Behm, *Einleitung in das NT* (ninth ed., Heidelberg, 1950), 248f.; W. Michaelis, *Einleitung in das NT* (third ed., Bern, 1961), 287; with reservations: van Unnik, "Christianity according to I Peter," 79f.; Schelkle, 133f., 14f.; Kelly, 214f.

17. Similar is Kelly, 215f., who until now has been the only one to develop a similar way of posing the question.

situation, but, as we have seen section by section, uses well-defined tradition in regard to the situation of the entire Church, which had developed in directions of estrangement for the readers. The tradition that the letter conveys corresponds thoroughly in terms of origin and type to the course of Silvanus's life and work: It agrees with Paul without having originated from him, it contains elements from the Palestinian Church in larger quantity than does the Pauline tradition, and yet, at the same time, it is fashioned more to fit the thought and language of the Hellenistic world.

Silvanus

Silvanus is undoubtedly identical to Paul's coworker of the same name.[18] According to the certainly reliable data in Acts 15:22, 32f., he was a much appreciated and prophetically gifted representative of the primitive Church in Jerusalem and arose in this context as one of the persons to deliver the apostolic decree to Antioch (15:27). From there Paul took him along as coworker on the so-called second missionary journey to Asia Minor and Greece.[19] This tradition is confirmed by Paul's mention of him in II Cor. 1:19 as cofounder of the Corinthian church (cf. I Thess. 1:1; II Thess. 1:1). After this he disappears from the group of people around Paul. Later he could very well have belonged to a group of missionaries and teachers around Peter during the latter's last days in Rome, so that the situation presupposed here in I Pet. 5:12a could be historical.[20]

Silvanus is adjudged as "faithful" in regard to his mediation of this letter. This corresponds to Pauline tradition: πιστός, "faithful," "reliable," is what Paul calls his coworkers, not only because they are personally loyal to him, but because they represent the gospel reliably in the Church.[21] They are his "brothers" not only as fellow Christians, but also because they participate in the apostle's special form of service.[22] Finally, the passing remark ὡς λογίζομαι, "as I think" (or

18. The form Σιλουανός reflects "Silvanus," the Latinized form of the Aramaic name שִׁילָא, and is also used in the Pauline Epistles. Acts, on the other hand, uses Σίλας, which is shaped directly in Greek (BAGD s.v.; Radermacher, *Erster Petrusbrief und Silvanus,* 293-295).

19. Acts 15:40; cf. 16:19, 25, 29; 17:4, 10, 14f.; 18:5. According to Acts 16:37f. he might have been, like Paul, a Roman citizen.

20. O. Michel, "Silas," *BHH* III, col. 1793 (bibliography).

21. I Cor. 4:17 of Timothy; Eph. 6:21 and Col. 4:7 of Tychicus: ἀγαπητὸς ἀδελφὸς καὶ πιστὸς διάκονος . . . ἐν κυρίῳ. Cf. Col. 1:7; 4:9; Heb. 3:5 (of Moses).

22. The latter, e.g., in I Cor. 1:1; II Cor. 1:1; 2:13; Eph. 6:21; Col. 1:1; 4:7; Phlm. 1. ἀδελφός appears only here in I Peter, but its derivatives appear often (see the comments on 5:9).

"judge"), also uses Pauline vocabulary. The comment is not intended to diminish the statement to a personal opinion, but to characterize it as a specific judgment of the apostle.[23]

12b Following the reference to the mediator of the letter comes a brief resumé of what is intended by the letter. The way is prepared for this by a polite formula often encountered in letters: The author has written "in brief"; long letters were considered inappropriate.[24] "Brief" is also appropriate for I Peter in view of the difficulty and breadth of its thematic focus.

And now the author's intention is summarized in striking key terms: παρακαλῶν καὶ ἐπιμαρτυρῶν ταύτην εἶναι ἀληθῆ χάριν τοῦ θεοῦ, εἰς ἣν στῆτε. He has wanted first of all to "summon," "demand," "admonish," "encourage." The verb παρακαλεῖν is used absolutely here. It refers to the parenesis, which assumes in this letter a greater and different place than in Paul and which begins in 2:11 with this very verb. From this beginning on long series of imperatives weave their way through the document in order to point the way regarding the fundamental posture of the Church, and especially its conduct, in the institutions of society and under circumstances of conflict with society.

But unlike James, I Peter is not devoted to parenetic declaration alone. It gives the basis for parenesis again and again through witness to the grace that makes parenesis possible (while Paul offers this basis before he turns to parenesis). Its decisive concern is to "give witness[25] that this is the true grace of God, in which you may stand/are standing." From the beginning of their summons to faith the addressees were told that from then on they were able to live by the grace of God that appeared in Jesus (1:10; 4:10) and to go forth to meet it in the consummation (1:13; 3:7). The author has confirmed this word of summons through the witness to God's activity of salvation. He has made it clear

---

23. II Cor. 11:5; in Rom. 3:28 and 8:18 of theological judgments.

24. In the NT so also in Heb. 13:22, διὰ βραχέων of that much longer document; also Ignatius, *Rom.* 8:2; Polycarp, *Phil.* 3:1-3 (LCL AF I, 237, 287). According to Roller, *Formular,* 34-39, even Philemon exceeded the size regarded as appropriate for a private letter. Seneca, e.g., apologizes for the atypical length of a letter that approached the limits of the length appropriate for an essay (Roller, *Formular,* 226f.). Analogies are found in Isocrates, *Epistulae* 2.13; 8.10 (LCL III, 391, 467); Pliny, *Epistulae* 3.9.27 (LCL I, 225f.). ἔγραψα is epistolary aorist: "I write," "I have written (here)."

25. ἐπιμαρτυρέω occurs in the NT only here (cf. Heb. 2:4: συνεπιμαρτυρέω). ἐπι- intensifies: "witness (in a confirming way)." The following accusative with infinitive depends only on this verb, not on the preceding verb as well. The verbal analogy often cited, Lucian, *Alexander* 42 (LCL IV, 228f.: καὶ οἱ ἄνδρες ἀπεμαρτύρουν ὅτι ἀληθῆ λέγουσιν), speaks of deeds testified to, while here, as in 5:1, a giving of testimony is intended.

to his readers that in spite of all hardships they are surrounded by grace, by the demonstrations of God's love that lead to salvation (5:10), that even affliction leads to grace (5:5), indeed, that affliction itself is grace (2:19f.; cf. 4:14). It is not religious fanaticism that has brought them to this troubled path, but the ἀληθὴ[26] χάρις τοῦ θεοῦ, which leads to salvation. The closing relative clause, εἰς ἣν στῆτε, can be translated simply as (what would be expected): "in which you stand." But it is better translated as a wish that combines an indicative and an imperative: "in which you may stand."[27]

13a The type of greetings that are specific to NT letters, i.e., those that serve to enhance the contact between churches, have here, like what is in v. 12a, a fundamental significance and correspond once again to the tradition of the whole Church. ἀσπάζεται ὑμᾶς ἡ . . . συνεκλεκτή: Just as the recipients of the letter have been addressed in the opening as "the elect" (1:1), so too the church in whose midst the letter was composed is referred to as "co-elect."[28] In this way the bond of relationship is made clear beyond the communication already articulated in the greeting. Also in this way the concept of election (cf. 1:1) typical for the letter is echoed once again by way of conclusion. Βαβυλών (Greek for Hebrew בָּבֶל), "Babylon," the location of the church sending greetings, is without doubt a symbolic name for Rome.[29] The use of

---

26. ἀληθής in I Peter only here, of persons: "truthful," of things: "true," here: "real," "genuine" (BAGD s.v.).

27. After ταύτην one expects an indicative relative clause, as in Rom. 5:2; II Cor. 1:24. But the reading εἰς ἣν ἑστήκατε, "in which you stand" (L, P, Koine, and the majority of minuscules and versions [Vulgate, Peshitta]), is a smoothing over and accommodation to those passages. The original reading is undoubtedly εἰς ἣν στῆτε (p[72], B, ℵ, and others), which may be imperative "stand in it" or hortatory aorist subjunctive "so that you stand in it" (BDF §377 [p. 191]). If the circumlocution "in which you may stand" is to be rejected, then one must assume (with Kelly, 217; Spicq, 178) on the basis of content and sentence structure that the author inadvertently wrote στῆτε for ἑστήκατε. Grammatical irregularities have already been seen in the concluding statements of vv. 8 and 9. But surely here alone in the NT letters, as often in vernacular Hellenistic Greek, εἰς is used in place of ἐν (BDF §205 [pp. 110f.]).

28. συνεκλεκτός, "co-elect," appears only here in the NT and is substantival here. Some manuscripts (ℵ, a few others, Vulgate, Peshitta) enlarge the content with ἐκκλησία. Similarly, in II Jn. 13 ἐκλεκτῇ κυρίᾳ and ἀδελφῆς σου τῆς ἐκλεκτῆς refer to churches. It is therefore not the case (as Bengel, ad loc., posits) that Peter's wife (I Cor. 9:5; cf. Mt. 8:14) is being mentioned in this way (on the discussion see T. Zahn, *Introduction to the NT* II [tr. M. W. Jacobus, et al.; Edinburgh/New York, 1909], 157, n.11). Applegate, "Co-Elect Woman," 604, sees here a female missionary associate and co-sender of the letter, who was able by her involvement in this way "to help authorize the household code" in anticipation of resistance by women leaders in Asia Minor.

29. So already *HE* 2.15.2 (LCL I, 143f.), claiming the support of Clement of Alex-

this symbol characterizes the situation of the Church, which the letter addresses.

"Babylon" as a Symbolic Name

As early as the book of Daniel "Babylon" had become a symbolic name for the world power that placed into conflict situations those who belonged to the people of God scattered throughout its realm as part of its society.[30] Everyone who read this document in NT times as a Jew or as a Christian — and it was very popular among both groups — thought of Rome when it spoke of Babel, even though historically Daniel had the Seleucid Empire in mind.

"Babylon" came into use as an attention-claiming designation for Rome in Jewish and Christian literature at particular points in time: In Jewish literature it

---

andria and Papias, as also the minuscule 2138 (with the reading ʿΡώμη; see Zahn, *Introduction* II, 158ff.).

The two possibilities for understanding the name literally have no inherent probability (for bibliography see BAGD s.v.). (1) Babylon, the metropolis on the Euphrates River, lost its significance after the death of Alexander the Great, but was still inhabited in the first century A.D. and included a Jewish community (Josephus, *Antiquitates Judaicae* 2.15.1; 15.2.2 [LCL IV, 303; VIII, 9f.]). Its further demise took place so quickly, however, that Trajan came across little more than ruins there in A.D. 115 (Dio Cassius, *Historia* 68.30 [LCL VIII, 417f.]). The Jews there, whom one can imagine as the basis for a Christian community, especially in view of Peter (Gal. 2:9), had already emigrated to Seleucia by the middle of the first century (*Antiquitates* 18.9.8f. [LCL IX, 207f.]; see W. Baumstark, "Babylon," *RAC* II/2, col. 2682; E. Schürer, *The History of the Jewish People in the Age of Jesus Christ*, III/1 [rev. and ed. by G. Vermes, F. Millar, and M. Goodman; Edinburgh, 1986], 8f.). Thus, it is quite improbable that Peter would have come to Babylon during his missionary journeys (I Cor. 9:4; cf. Gal. 2:9) and would have written from a place in the remote Southeast to the Christian communities of Asia Minor (contra J. Munck, *Paul and the Salvation of Mankind* [tr. F. Clarke; Atlanta, 1959], 275; similarly A. Schlatter, *The Church in the NT Period* [tr. P. Levertoff; London, 1961], 253: Babylon was the name of "the whole area on the other side of the Euphrates"; cf., however, Schlatter, *Petrus und Paulus*, 177ff.). Even the tradition of the Syrian Church knows nothing of this; it was posited for the first time in Photius, *Bibliotheca* (ed. I. Bekker; Berlin, 1824-25), 273, surely on the basis of I Pet. 5:13 (cf. Zahn, *Introduction* II, 165ff., n.4). NT and other early Church traditions do not link Silvanus and Mark to the city on the Euphrates, but with Rome.

(2) In the first century there existed near what is now the old city of Cairo a Roman military base that was given the name "Babylon" by the legion headquartered there (Strabo, *Geographia* 17.1.30 [LCL VIII, 85f.]; Josephus, *Antiquitates* 2.15.1 [LCL IV, 303]). According to early Church tradition the Church in Egypt traced its apostolic origin — by all indications legendarily — to Mark (*HE* 2.16.24 [LCL I, 145, 179]), but not to Peter. The Coptic Church in Cairo claims Peter as its founder; this rests quite probably on hypotheses of historical research. This place of origin is proposed for I Peter by, among others, J. de Zwaan, *Inleiding tot het Nieuwe Testament* III (second ed., Haarlem, 1948), 38f.

30. E.g., Dan. 1:1-8; 3:8-12; 6:2-24. "Babel" acquired this symbolic meaning through its characterization in prophecy: Isaiah 13; 43:14; Jer. 50:29; 51:1-58.

was first used as a symbolic name for Rome after A.D. 70;[31] the reason was clearly the second destruction of Jerusalem. In Christian apocalyptic literature the name came into use for the first time in Rev. 14:8; 17:5, 18; 18:2. In the latter the occasion was not the destruction of Jerusalem but the Neronian persecution: Babylon is "drunk from the blood of the saints" (Rev. 17:5ff.). Furthermore, Christian apocalyptic use of the symbol came about, as far as we can tell, independently: It was not appropriated from Jewish apocalypticism, since in Revelation there are no echoes from any Jewish apocalypse known to us, except Daniel.[32]

I Peter was written, therefore, for Christians for whom Rome was not only the governmental authority in the sense of 2:13-17, but also, in accord with Daniel, the eschatological world power, from whose ideological representatives came the pressure to conform and which denied legal protection to Christians who called into question its moral and religious rules of conduct (4:15). But the point of the reference here to "Babylon" may very well be that it demonstrates at the end of the letter the situation of "foreigners in the Diaspora,"[33] which is the letter's point of departure (1:1). This may have been more important than suggesting that judgment of the world power was soon to take place, an inference drawn from this apocalyptic name from Daniel on (cf. I Pet. 4:17f.). "Babylon" is, however, not merely a symbol for exile, like "Damascus" is in the Essene documents,[34] i.e., a symbol for Christian existence in alienation,[35] and of course not merely a "code word,"[36] but a symbolic name for Rome that rounds off the letter's interpretation of the situation.

13b Together with the church in the capital city of the world, greetings are sent by Mark, whom "Peter" calls "my son" because he had won Mark over for discipleship and had thereby also gained him as a student and because he was loyal to Mark as teacher and "shepherd" in a spiritual father-son relationship.[37]

---

31. So ca. A.D. 80 in the Jewish *Sib. Or.* 4.143; 5.159 (*OT Pseudep.* I, 387, 397) and ca. A.D. 90 in *II Bar.* 11:1; 67:7 (*ibid.,* 625, 644) and II Esdr. 3:1, 28, 31; additional material in the rabbinic literature (Str.-Bill. III, 816).

32. Cf. K. G. Kuhn, "βαβυλών," *TDNT* I, 514f. Hunzinger, "Babylon," observes correctly that the symbolic name is used first in Jewish literature after A.D. 70 and presupposes incorrectly that early Christian apocalypticism was linked with Jewish usage, so that I Pet. 5:13 could only have been written after A.D. 70.

33. The name "Babylon" brought to mind also in the OT the situation of exile as foreigners in a foreign land (Psalm 137). Daniel develops, in terms of the situation in Babel, Israel's possibilities and destiny in the Diaspora. See Prete, "L'espressione he en Babyloni syneklekte."

34. CD 6:5, 19; 7:15, 19; 8:21, and passim.

35. Contra Heussi, *Römische Petrustradition,* 38: " 'Babylon' designates this earthly world, in which Christians see themselves as homeless." Similarly, Boismard, "Liturgie baptismale," 181.

36. Contra Schelkle, 135, and others; the name is not meant to conceal anything, but to open Christians' eyes regarding the situation. See further Thiede, "Babylon, der andere Ort."

37. The imagery of "father" and "child" (τέκνον) is used in the NT, in a development

For the apostle to send greetings both from Rome and from Mark corresponds to Church tradition back into the first century. For Ignatius in the East as well as for *I Clement* in the West, the course of Peter's life ended in Rome.[38] Furthermore, an Asian tradition, recorded by Papias ca. A.D. 120, indicates that Mark worked as Peter's student and interpreter in Rome, so that he was able after Peter's death to write there the Gospel of Mark.[39] The tradition of Peter's death is certainly historical, and the tradition of Mark as his coworker could also be historical in its essence, in accord with NT statements, even though it is cast in a legendary framework.

Mark, always the same person in all NT occurrences of the name, also known as John Mark, grew up in Jerusalem in a home that Peter visited (Acts 12:12-17). He became a coworker of Paul in Antioch (12:25; 13:5) and accompanied Paul and Barnabas, Mark's uncle (Col. 4:10), on part of the first missionary journey (Acts 13:5, 13). When Paul refused to take him on the second missionary journey, Mark went with Barnabas to Cyprus (15:36-41). After a temporary estrangement, he returned, as may be concluded from the reliable information in Phlm. 24 (cf. Col. 4:10), to the Pauline circle. This probably occurred during Paul's imprisonment in Rome (something like that is presupposed in II Tim. 4:11). Nothing speaks against the possibility that soon thereafter, after Paul's death, he was at work there among the Petrine circle.[40]

In view of this tradition, it must be asked whether the presence of Peter and Mark in Rome and the relationship between the two men, presupposed in v. 13, are taken there from these early Church traditions or rest on direct knowledge or special traditions possessed by the author. The early composition of the letter and the agreement of these precise data with the letter's fundamental connections speak for the latter. And the Markan tradition from Asia Minor recorded by Papias might have been influenced by I Pet. 5:13.

Quite apart from these questions, this verse represents an important contribution to early Church history: I Peter is the earliest known Christian document showing that there was contact between the churches in Rome and Asia Minor. It was this bridge that became the basis for the catholic

---

of Jewish imagery (Str.-Bill. III, 240f.), of the teacher-student relationship, which was concentrated into the concept of "begetting" through conversion (I Cor. 4:15; Gal. 4:19; Phlm. 10) and expanded into a circumlocution for pastoral care for the churches (I Thess. 2:11f.; cf. G. Schrenk, "πατήρ," *TDNT* V, 1005). Here υἱός, "son," which is used in Mt. 12:27; Acts 23:6 of the students of the Pharisees, appears in place of "child."

38. See above, pp. 10f.

39. *HE* 2.15; 3.39.15 (LCL I, 143, 297).

40. J. J. Vincent, "Markus," *BHH* II, cols. 1152f. Opting for direct involvement of Mark in the composition of the letter is Gamba, "L'Evangelista Marco."

Church in the second century.[41] Luke and Ignatius — and Romans before them — draw the line of development in the opposite direction, toward Rome, like many religions of the Near East. I Peter is the first Church document with an ecumenical horizon going forth in the name of Peter from Rome to other Christian communities. Of course, Rome is not, thereby, as Jerusalem was for the Jewish Diaspora, the capital city of Christianity, but that of the world empire, the empire in which Christians are only strangers. And the apostle Peter speaks not as one who "reigns" like the emperor, but as "co-elder and witness of Christ's sufferings" (5:1, 3).

14a The intention of the greetings becomes clear here, as in the Pauline Epistles, in the admonition to the addressees that concludes the greetings: "Greet one another with the kiss of love" — in Paul "the holy kiss"[42] (ἀσπάσασθε ἀλλήλους ἐν φιλήματι ἀγάπης). Just as brothers separated by geography greet one another by letter, so, too, do those who have gathered together in the worship service, after the letter has been read, with the "kiss of love." The extension of greetings is, therefore, not only an expression of friendship, but a turning to one another as brothers.

A kiss is, of course, even in the etymology of the Greek word φίλημα, a demonstration of love among those who belong together, those bound by the love designated by φιλεῖν. Kissing was done in the ancient Greek world, therefore, especially among relatives, while the erotic kiss first came about later.[43] What kissing meant in the Christian community is expressed in its characterization by genitive ἀγάπης here: The kiss expresses neither ἔρως, an exclusive love, nor φιλεῖν, love for relatives, but ἀγάπη, the supportive acceptance of the other out of a spontaneous turning to him or her. In view of 1:22, this turning of oneself corresponds to sanctification; therefore, this kiss is "holy," an expression of shared acceptance by "the God of all grace" (5:10).[44] Here again I Peter empha-

---

41. Goppelt, *Apostolic,* 125f.

42. The admonition of the "holy kiss" is found in the NT here and four times in Paul (Rom. 16:16; I Cor. 16:20; II Cor. 13:12; I Thess. 5:26). See G. Stählin, "φιλέω," *TDNT* IX, 139f., 142-145; C. Spicq, *Agape in the NT* II (tr. M. McNamara and M. Richter; St. Louis, 1965), 363-365; K. M. Hofmann, *Philema hagion* (BFChrTh 2/38; Gütersloh, 1938), especially 26ff.

43. Stählin, *TDNT* IX, 115, 119f.

44. The custom is genuinely of Christian origin; it was foreign to the synagogue (cf. Stählin, *TDNT* IX, 139, n.233) and is remote from the practice of kissing in extrabiblical cultic life, which served primarily the conveyence of power from images of the gods (*TDNT* IX, 123f.). The Christian practice is related to the OT practice of a kiss among relatives and on meeting someone, especially at a time of reconciliation (Gen. 33:4; 45:15; *TDNT* IX,

sizes the horizontal dimension where we find in Paul the vertical; the letter underscores the concrete, earthly shape of the realization of salvation.

The "holy kiss" was apparently already practiced liturgically during the Pauline period in Church worship.[45] Why then do Paul and the author of I Peter expressly admonish the addressees to do what was already customary? The admonition focuses the parenesis for brotherly love, for which I Peter has special concern (1:22), on an act in the context of worship. After the reading of the letter, the act is to demonstrate by a sign the brotherly bond, which is also articulated by the greetings from afar (v. 13).

14b   The concluding wish for blessing communicates to the readers not, as in Paul, "grace," but — emphasizing more strongly the horizontal aspect — εἰρήνη, "peace," the relationship of wholeness to God and to one's neighbors (cf. 1:2), which overcomes the conflict situation in hope, faith, and love (1:3-7; cf. Jn. 14:27). The consolation of peace applies πᾶσιν τοῖς ἐν Χριστῷ, "to all who are in Christ," those whose course is set by the crucified and resurrected One (cf. 3:16; Rom. 8:1). Peace is thus imparted to all who are baptized or, as it is put earlier, to all who are elect (1:1), those who listen to the letter's parenesis, which issues forth from their calling through baptism, a parenesis that has its foundation in the witness to God's grace (v. 12b).[46]

125f.) and was occasioned by the understanding of discipleship to Jesus as *familia Dei* (Mk. 3:35; 14:44 par.; cf. Lk. 15:20) and as brotherhood, which is shown by constantly new manifestations of mutual forgiving love. The kiss of Judas may indicate that the brotherly kiss was customary in the circle of Jesus' disciples (so Schlatter, *Petrus und Paulus,* 180f.; Selwyn, 244f.; see discussion in Stählin, *TDNT* IX, 140f.). While the custom is not mentioned in the Apostolic Fathers, it had a firm place and is referred to as the "kiss of peace" in eucharistic liturgy, in the East before the offertory (Justin, *Apologia* 1.65 [*ANF* I, 185]) and in the West after the canon before the communion (e.g., Augustine, *Sermon* 227 = *MPL* 38, 1101 = *St. Augustine: Sermons on the Liturgical Seasons* [tr. M. Muldowney; The Fathers of the Church; New York, 1959], 195-198; cf. *TDNT* IX, 142ff.). Further history-of-religion comparative data is in Klassen, "Sacred Kiss."

45. In I Corinthians 16 the liturgical formulas introducing the Lord's Supper (v. 22) follow the admonition regarding the holy kiss (v. 20b). The liturgical act of the kiss is intended to show that the participant is prepared for the *koinonia* into which the Lord's Supper brings one, so that the elements will not be received "to condemnation" (cf. 10:16f.; 11:20f., 27f.), not only (as with the "kiss of peace" in later liturgies) that one is prepared for reconciliation in the sense of Mt. 5:23f. Similarly, Stählin, *TDNT* IX, 139f.

46. Many manuscripts (ℵ, Koine, Majority text, Vulgate, Syriac) add here, as in the rest of the NT letters, the ἀμήν with which the church responds at the reading of the letter.

Appendix:
Leonhard Goppelt (1911-1973)[1]

John E. Alsup

Born November 6, 1911 and raised in Munich, Germany, Goppelt attended the Theresiengymnasium in preparation for university studies. He majored in philosophy and the natural sciences before turning to theology. His student days and early years of teaching were spent at the University of Erlangen, where he earned his doctorate with a dissertation on the NT use of the OT (1939)[2] and a habilitation on Christianity and Judaism in the first and second centuries (1942, 1954).[3] In 1947-48 he represented J. Jeremias in Göttingen during the latter's convalescence. In 1952 he became the professor of NT on the newly formed Protestant Theological Faculty of the University of Hamburg, having taught at Hamburg's Kirchliche Hochschule since 1948. He remained in Hamburg until he accepted the invitation to become professor of NT on Munich's newly formed Protestant Theological Faculty in 1967-68. There he taught until his sudden death on December 21, 1973.

An accurate appraisal of his life and work presupposes acquaintance with his context. He was a man both of the church and of the university, maintaining a critical posture toward both sides. He had experienced two world wars on German soil; the second interrupted the beginning of his professional career as scholar. The two decades of

---

1. From *The Dictionary of Biblical Interpretation,* edited by John H. Hayes (Nashville: Abingdon Press, forthcoming).

2. Translated by D. H. Madvig and published as *Typos: The Typological Interpretation of the Old Testament in the New* (1982).

3. The first half translated by E. Schroeder and published as *Jesus, Paul and Judaism: An Introduction to New Testament Theology* (1964).

development within the German church and university were the context-shaping developments for his life and thought. For the university these were the years of the Bultmann Schule. Though considered an outsider by this school he cultivated objective dialogue with it, especially with Bultmann's own publications. He never sought to join a school nor to acquire one around himself. In principle he opposed cartels, valued independence, challenged and expected to be challenged constructively by others — most of all by his students and friends. His posture was one of dialogue and critical debate with all positions represented in the spectrum of NT interpretation. Though commonly grouped together with Jeremias, Kümmel, and the conservative right, he really was much more in active conversation with Bultmannians, as the footnotes in his publications give ample evidence. These partners in conversation were posing the right questions, he maintained, but were, for the most part, giving the wrong answers.

He was exceedingly interested in the dawning new epoch in NT studies and gave considerable thought to the matter of charting a course for the future. The chief literary result was his NT theology.[4] He saw much promise in the works of *Heilsgeschichte* scholars like Zahn, Schlatter, Schniewind, Cullmann, von Rad, et al., but he did not view his conversation with them as a fence or a static hermeneutical decision, but as a door of opportunity through which to ponder and describe the reality of God at work in history. He sought a dialogue toward understanding that would honor the intention of the NT writers themselves using the principles of critique, analogy, and correlation (cf. Troeltsch). While this orientation obligated him to maintain dialogue with all the classical disciplines of theological education, he was most purposeful in his dialogue with OT studies. He was convinced that the on-going dialogue on the relationship between the testaments was crucial with implications extending beyond the discussion within the context of biblical studies, because of the manner in which this discussion forces the issue of God and history.

Both as scholar and churchman he was a critic of easy identification of the church and Christian mission with culture and "Zeitgeist." He could be equally determined, however, in his opposition to the empty

---

4. Translated by John Alsup and published as *Theology of the New Testament* (two volumes, 1981, 1982); a comprehensive bibliography of Goppelt's published works appears in the second volume of this work.

slogans of popular ecclesiastical conservatism; he was not at all pleased with the "anti-modern theology" voices of the 60s in Germany. His voice made regular contribution to the appeal for a course of balanced reason in critical debates. He never gave up trying to be helpful at all levels of ecclesiastical dialogue, working tirelessly at local and synodal conferences and internationally at ecumenical meetings. His last official act before his death was to participate in the EKD dialogue with the Russian Orthodox Church over the Eucharist in Sagorsk in the winter of 1973.

On Nov. 6, 1971 Goppelt became sixty years old; in honor of the occasion the volume *Die Predigt als Kommunikation* [Preaching as Communication], ed. J. Roloff, Stuttgart, 1972, was dedicated to him with the following words:

> When we greet Prof. Dr. Leonhard Goppelt with these articles on the occasion of his sixtieth birthday we do this so that our gratitude may be expressed to a theological teacher who has always understood his service to the Church and to preaching as the chief goal of his work. Every student who has sat in his company in the lecture hall or in a seminar and every academic coworker or colleague who has entered into his personal circle of contact has been impressed with the consistent, substantive quality of his thinking, which is always directed toward the central task of theology and resists the temptation to make scholarly details goals in themselves and to lose oneself in that which is merely interesting. That as coeditor of the Calwer Predigthilfen Leonhard Goppelt decisively shaped the New Testament series in its profile is certainly the most visible expression of his fundamental conviction that there cannot be a renewal of preaching without a better understanding of the New Testament.
>
> H. Breit, J. Roloff, Calwer Verlag Stuttgart

Index